Digital Citizenship and the Future of AI Engagement, Ethics, and Privacy

Mahmoud M. Kh. Hawamdeh
Al-Quds Open University, Palestine

IGI Global
Scientific Publishing
Publishing Tomorrow's Research Today

Published in the United States of America by
IGI Global Scientific Publishing
701 East Chocolate Avenue
Hershey, PA, 17033, USA
Tel: 717-533-8845
Fax: 717-533-8661
Website: https://www.igi-global.com E-mail: cust@igi-global.com

Library of Congress Cataloging-in-Publication Data

Names: Hawamdeh, Mahmoud, 1972- editor.
Title: Digital citizenship and the future of AI engagement, ethics, and privacy / edited by Mahmoud Hawamdeh.
Other titles: Digital citizenship and the future of artificial intelligence engagement, ethics, and privacy
Description: Hershey, PA : IGI Global Scientific Publishing, 2025. | Includes bibliographical references and index. | Summary: "The book aims to investigate the multidimensional relationship between digital citizenship and the influence of artificial intelligence (AI), with a focus on ethical behavior, privacy, and civic engagement"-- Provided by publisher.
Identifiers: LCCN 2024055578 (print) | LCCN 2024055579 (ebook) | ISBN 9798369390153 (hardcover) | ISBN 9798369390160 (paperback) | ISBN 9798369390177 (ebook)
Subjects: LCSH: Political participation--Technological innovations. | Artificial intelligence--Political aspects. | Artificial intelligence--Educational applications.
Classification: LCC JF799.5 .D54 2025 (print) | LCC JF799.5 (ebook) | DDC 323/.042028563--dc23/eng/20250208
LC record available at https://lccn.loc.gov/2024055578
LC ebook record available at https://lccn.loc.gov/2024055579

British Cataloguing in Publication Data
A Cataloguing in Publication record for this book is available from the British Library.

Editorial Advisory Board

Table of Contents

Detailed Table of Contents

The chapter aims at investigating the reality of academic integrity in the era of AI and the institutional responsibilities to be taken into account to guarantee solid and genuine academic work by university students. This chapter addresses the extent to which academic integrity and institutional responsibilities are enhanced in Palestinian higher educational institutions (HEIs) as perceived by the faculty members. The role played by these institutions and the challenges they face will also be highlighted. Moreover, some strategies and solutions that aim at fostering academic integrity and institutional obligations will be proposed by the author. This chapter is expected to make both students and faculty more aware of the reality, advantages, and disadvantages of AI utilization in HEIs and its relation to Academic integrity.

This chapter explores the transformative potential of digital technologies and artificial intelligence (AI) in bridging the gap between learner needs and innovative inclusion for individuals with disabilities. This provides a comprehensive analysis of how such advancements contribute to access and citizenship by examining socio-historical contexts, current practices, and future implications. Neither disability nor advanced technologies exist in a vacuum. Powerful historical, social, and economic forces have shaped the development of both. In understanding the inter-relationship, it is critical to engage with a range of associated issues. Over the past two centuries, disability has been at the forefront of technological innovation and adaptation. Digital emancipation provides digital technologies that empower individuals with disabilities by providing new opportunities for learning, communication, and participation. Digital tools and platforms offer unprecedented levels of accessibility and flexibility.

As the digital landscape evolves, the intersection of artificial intelligence (AI) and education is reshaping the way citizens interact with technology and information. This chapter addresses the critical need for digital literacy and the preparation of individuals to engage with AI in ethical and privacy-conscious ways. The chapter begins by examining the concept of digital citizenship and its relevance in an AI-driven society, emphasizing the importance of equipping citizens with the skills to navigate and contribute to the digital world responsibly. The core of the chapter explores the integration of AI in educational systems, highlighting both the opportunities and challenges it presents.

Artificial intelligence (AI) has become a transformative force in mental health and digital well-being, offering personalized wellness programs and AI-driven mental health applications. However, these advancements present significant ethical challenges, particularly regarding algorithmic bias and privacy. This chapter discusses the implications of algorithmic bias, where the underrepresentation of diverse demographics in AI models can lead to inequitable outcomes and privacy risks stemming from the misuse or mishandling of sensitive user data. Through real-world case studies, the chapter illustrates these challenges and their impact on equitable and trustworthy AI in mental health. It also proposes strategies to mitigate these risks, emphasizing fairness, transparency, and privacy in AI design. The chapter underscores the role of responsible digital citizenship, advocating for informed and ethical engagement with AI tools by users, developers, and policymakers for creating inclusive, ethical, and privacy-conscious AI systems to advance mental health and digital wellness.

We are in a landscape characterized by the rapid advancement of technology and education. This transformation's hub is the connection between digital literacy and artificial intelligence (AI). Within a short period, educators, policymakers, and our society have come to the realization that AI will play a central role in their lives. This chapter explores the critical imperatives of preparing citizens for a future where digital competencies and AI fluency are advantageous and could be central to survival. The authors examine the current global landscape and how nations integrate digital literacy and AI into their educational framework to foster more adaptive and innovative societies. This discussion will then focus on local initiatives, illustrating how these global trends can be tailored to meet individual communities' specific cultural, economic, and societal needs.

This chapter will first emphasize the critical need for active political and civic engagement in maintaining democracy's enduring vitality. The author analyzes the evolution of citizen participation over time, especially with the proliferation of the internet and the prevalence of social media, which have altered individual engagement in the digital era. This chapter will examine how artificial intelligence has expanded the opportunities for public participation and the possible advantages this entails. However, it will also address significant concerns about the potential use of AI by governments with authoritarian tendencies. The author examines how new technologies may jeopardize human liberties, distort election processes—even in stable democracies—and raise concerns over the future erosion of democratic systems.

This research explores the ethical implications of integrating AI into higher education, focusing on the responsibilities of faculty and institutions in ensuring adherence to ethical standards. The research highlights the urgent need for comprehensive ethical guidelines to regulate the use of AI in educational settings. The findings also underscore the critical role that faculty play in promoting digital citizenship and ethical practices among students. To address the ethical challenges associated with the integration of AI. The results did not show any statistical differences attributed to the gender variable, or the academic rank variable of the faculty member, while there were statistical differences in the variables of academic qualification and years of teaching experience. The results showed that the field of (the right to protection, security, and digital privacy) had the highest arithmetic mean (3.96). The research makes several recommendations, including establishing strong data governance policies.

Digital and AI literacy are vital as technology shapes the future, requiring skills beyond basic computer knowledge. Integrating AI in education personalizes learning by identifying students' needs, adapting content, and providing instant feedback, creating engaging, tailored experiences. Ethical issues, including data privacy, algorithmic bias, and tech access disparities, must be addressed to ensure AI's responsible use in education. Teachers play a key role in fostering AI literacy, helping students understand both the potential and ethical considerations of technology. Embedding these skills into curricula prepares students with critical thinking, creativity, and collaboration skills necessary for a digital world. This approach equips students to engage with technology responsibly, building a generation ready to navigate and shape a fair, inclusive digital landscape.

Citizenship fundamentally alters how individuals interact, communicate, and engage with the world around them. Digital citizenship encompasses the skills, knowledge, and ethical considerations necessary responsibly. It is not merely about technical proficiency but includes a deep understanding of the rights and responsibilities that come with digital engagement—ranging from social media platforms to online education and healthcare. Understanding the interplay between digital citizenship and AI is crucial for harnessing opportunities while addressing associated challenges. One of the core concepts of digital citizenship is the notion of which effectively in an environment. As AI systems are often involved in curating content, automating responses, and personalizing user experiences, digital citizens must develop critical skills to assess the reliability and bias of AI-driven information. This includes understanding how algorithms work, recognizing the limitations of AI, and discerning the ethical implications of AI decisions.

Combating misinformation has become a critical challenge in today's information-driven society, particularly with the proliferation of fake news, propaganda, and biased content across various domains. This study explores advanced natural language processing (NLP) techniques, including feature extraction and selection, to analyze and classify datasets such as Q-Prop, ISOT, GRAFN, and PubHealth. The relief algorithm is employed for feature selection to identify the most relevant attributes, enhancing the efficiency of machine learning models. XLNet, a powerful transformer-based model, is utilized for document representation and classification due to its ability to capture bidirectional and long-term contextual dependencies. The proposed methodology demonstrates how robust embeddings, combined with domain-specific datasets and optimized feature selection, can accurately classify content across news, politics, and public health domains.

As we delve into the transformative landscape of artificial intelligence (AI), we encounter a critical juncture where innovation meets the pressing need for digital privacy. Various sectors, including healthcare, finance, and education, offer unprecedented efficiencies and capabilities. The relationship between AI and digital privacy is multifaceted. On the other hand, the same capabilities that enable enhanced security can also be exploited to infringe upon individual privacy. However, enforcement remains a challenge, especially in the face of rapidly changing technologies and the global nature of data flows. This includes prioritizing fairness, accountability, and transparency, particularly when handling personal data. Organizations are encouraged to adopt principles such as data minimization—collecting only the information necessary for a specific purpose—and to implement privacy questions about the implications for marginalized communities.

With changed dynamics in the delivery of education in this generation, it can be affirmatively deduced that social networks will play a growing role. New technologies including artificial intelligence, blockchain, and IoT are possibilities for improving the learning process. But this progress brings in new privacy issues and that is why constant monitoring and constant change is the key here. This chapter strives to give a detailed analysis of the relationship between the educational advantages and privacy issues in social network-based learning. Thus, it tries to provide the reader with knowledge of its advantages and limitations as well as hints on how to avoid the pitfall in this rather sophisticated area. Finally, the goal is to create an educational environment that will enable innovation and preservation of privacy of students and educators in the modern era.

The rapid growth of artificial intelligence (AI) presents significant opportunities for innovation but also raises substantial privacy challenges. This chapter explores the

decisions about deploying adaptive learning tools and automated assessments while ensuring inclusive and meaningful learning experiences. By combining global perspectives with localized strategies, this chapter presents actionable insights to empower educators to harness AI's potential while maintaining the humanistic essence of teaching.

This chapter delves into the perceptions of artificial intelligence (AI) experts on the societal implications, governance, and ethical responsibilities associated with AI. Drawing on qualitative research, including interviews with six AI experts, the study investigates three key questions: experts' perceptions of AI's societal impacts, their visions for an AI-governed society, and their views on their responsibilities in addressing AI's consequences. The findings suggest that AI experts emphasize the importance of balancing innovation with education and regulation to ensure AI's responsible development and application, leaving out important questions to analyze further, such as their role in AI political governance, and the interest of wide public participation in the process of AI creation.

In an era where artificial intelligence and big data have become integral to corporate management, the ethical challenges associated with their deployment cannot be overlooked. As businesses increasingly rely on AI-driven insights and vast data streams for decision-making, the potential for misuse, bias, and violations of privacy grows. This chapter explores into the ethical considerations that corporations must address to harness AI and big data responsibly. It explores the implications of these technologies on corporate decision-making, highlighting the risks of algorithmic bias, data exploitation, and transparency issues. Through a comprehensive analysis, the chapter proposes a framework for ethical AI and big data utilization, emphasizing the need for corporate governance structures that prioritize ethical practices, data integrity, and accountability. The chapter aims to provide business leaders, managers, and policymakers with actionable insights to balance innovation with ethical responsibility.

Foreword

In an era where artificial intelligence (AI) is already reshaping human interactions, its influence extends beyond mere engagement—it has the potential to redefine governance, education, human development, and corporate decision-making. As AI becomes increasingly integrated into personal and professional spheres, it is imperative to understand its ethical, social, and civic implications. The intersection of AI and digital citizenship necessitates a paradigm shift from passive consumption to active participation in shaping AI's societal impact. This transition is essential to ensuring that digital environments serve as spaces of empowerment rather than mechanisms of control.

The study of digital citizenship within the context of AI is of paramount importance. AI-driven platforms now curate news, influence elections, recommend educational content, and shape hiring decisions. These capabilities raise questions: How can we ensure transparency while safeguarding privacy? How can individuals and organizations cultivate information literacy skills to engage critically with AI-driven systems? The fusion of technological power with human experience presents a unique opportunity to navigate global challenges and guide societal progress in the coming century.

Digital citizens must actively develop their information literacy to challenge unethical AI practices, while organizations are responsible for embedding fairness and accountability into AI models. The responsible deployment of AI requires collective vigilance and proactive governance to ensure that technological advancements enhance, rather than undermine, the democratic principles that define responsible global engagement.

In *Digital Citizenship and the Future of AI: Engagement, Ethics, and Privacy*, Dr. Mahmoud Hawamdeh presents a compelling synthesis of theoretical insights and practical solutions. This book identifies the inherent risks of AI integration and proposes robust frameworks for mitigating its unintended consequences. Structured into 19 insightful chapters, each offering a unique perspective on the intersection of AI and digital citizenship, the book begins by establishing a foundational understanding of AI's role in digital engagement. It then progresses into specialized discussions on ethics, privacy, education, misinformation, and governance. By grounding its analyses in real-world case studies and empirical research, this volume provides scholars and practitioners with a comprehensive roadmap for navigating the complexities of an AI-driven digital landscape.

The future of AI is not predetermined; rather, it must be human-led. It will be shaped by the ethical frameworks we establish, the policies we implement, and the human-centered awareness we cultivate. Today's choices will define AI's role in shaping tomorrow's society.

Digital Citizenship and the Future of AI: Engagement, Ethics, and Privacy is an essential resource for scholars, policymakers, and professionals invested in the ethical and responsible development of AI. It equips readers with the critical knowledge to navigate the challenges of an AI-driven world while inspiring them to contribute to a digital society prioritizing ethics, privacy, and responsible engagement.

Jeff Allen
College of Information, University of North Texas, USA

Preface

As technology continues to permeate every aspect of our personal, professional, and societal lives, the integration of artificial intelligence (AI) into digital systems raises complex questions that demand our attention. It is no longer enough to marvel at AI's capabilities; we must critically examine its implications on ethics, privacy, and our shared responsibilities as digital citizens. This book, *Digital Citizenship and the Future of AI: Engagement, Ethics, and Privacy*, was born from a desire to address these pressing issues and to offer a comprehensive examination of the role AI plays in shaping our digital future.

At its core, this volume explores the intersection of digital citizenship and artificial intelligence, focusing on ethical concerns, privacy challenges, and civic engagement in an AI-driven world. It seeks to bridge theoretical insights with practical applications, providing an interdisciplinary framework that equips readers to navigate the opportunities and challenges posed by emerging technologies. Through this lens, we delve into the importance of fostering ethical AI practices and enhancing digital literacy, both of which are essential for building a responsible, inclusive, and equitable society.

The chapters in this book bring together contributions from leading scholars, educators, policymakers, and technologists. They highlight diverse perspectives and present thought-provoking analyses of ethical dilemmas, privacy concerns, and the societal impact of AI. Together, these works provide a roadmap for understanding how AI can either reinforce or undermine the principles of digital citizenship, depending on how it is designed, implemented, and governed.

This book is more than a collection of academic discussions; it is a call to action. It challenges researchers and practitioners to consider the ethical deployment of AI technologies and to prioritize inclusivity, transparency, and accountability. It also underscores the critical need for digital literacy initiatives that prepare individuals to engage responsibly in digital spaces.

The audience for this work is as diverse as its contributors. Academic researchers, educators, graduate students, technology professionals, and anyone with an interest in the ethical, social, and educational dimensions of AI and digital citizenship will find valuable insights within these pages. Those working in the fields of educational technology, computer science, ethics, and civic engagement will particularly benefit from the book's interdisciplinary approach.

By expanding the conversation on the relationship between AI and digital citizenship, this book aims to inspire further research, inform policy development, and promote ethical AI practices. I hope it will serve as a vital resource for those striving to shape a future where technology enhances human potential while safeguarding the rights and responsibilities of all digital citizens.

ORGANIZATION OF THE BOOK

Chapter 1: The Global Impact of AI on Digital Citizenship

This chapter sets the stage by exploring the transformative role of artificial intelligence (AI) in shaping digital citizenship. It highlights the multifaceted nature of digital citizenship, extending beyond technical expertise to encompass ethical considerations, critical thinking, and an understanding of AI-driven processes. As AI systems increasingly curate content and influence decision-making, citizens must develop the skills to evaluate algorithmic reliability, identify biases, and navigate the ethical implications of AI. By delving into the interplay between AI and digital engagement, this chapter underscores the need to balance opportunities and challenges to foster responsible digital citizenship.

Chapter 2: Empowering Citizens: Preparing for the Future of Digital Literacy and AI in Education

This chapter examines the critical connection between digital literacy and AI in education, emphasizing the urgent need to prepare citizens for a technologically advanced future. It explores global and local efforts to integrate digital literacy and AI into educational frameworks, fostering adaptability and innovation. By analyzing how nations and communities tailor these initiatives to cultural, economic, and societal contexts, the chapter offers a comprehensive guide to equipping individuals with the competencies necessary for thriving in a rapidly evolving digital landscape.

Chapter 3: Empowering Digital Citizens: Navigating AI Ethics, Engagement, and Privacy in the Era of Advanced Education

This chapter explores the intersection of AI and education, focusing on the ethical, engagement, and privacy dimensions of digital citizenship. It stresses the importance of equipping individuals with the skills to engage responsibly in an AI-driven society. The discussion delves into the opportunities and challenges posed by integrating AI in educational systems, advocating for informed and ethical practices to ensure a balanced approach to innovation and responsibility.

Chapter 4: Digital Well-Being and AI: Navigating the Intersection Between Technology and Mental Health

Addressing the intersection of digital well-being and mental health, this chapter evaluates the impact of AI-driven technologies on personalized wellness and mental health care. It highlights ethical challenges such as algorithmic bias and privacy risks, offering real-world case studies to illustrate these concerns. The chapter emphasizes the need for fairness, transparency, and privacy in AI design, advocating for responsible digital citizenship to foster equitable and ethical AI systems for mental health and wellness.

Chapter 5: Access and Citizenship for Those With Disabilities: Digitally Enabled Education and AI as a Bridge to Innovative Inclusion

This chapter explores the transformative potential of digital technologies and AI in fostering inclusion for individuals with disabilities. By examining socio-historical contexts and current practices, it underscores the role of AI and innovative pedagogical design in bridging access gaps. The chapter advocates for inclusive educational frameworks that integrate historical, social, and economic perspectives to enhance digital citizenship and accessibility for all.

Chapter 6: Artificial Intelligence and the Advancement of Civic and Political Engagement: Opportunities and Challenges for Democracy

This chapter examines the transformative role of AI in enhancing civic and political engagement while addressing the challenges it poses to democratic systems. It explores how AI can expand public participation but also highlights concerns about misuse by authoritarian regimes and potential threats to human rights and electoral integrity. By balancing the opportunities and risks, this chapter provides insights into safeguarding democracy in an AI-driven era.

Chapter 7: Ethics of Digital Citizenship in the Age of Artificial Intelligence in Higher Education Institutions from the Perspective of Faculty Members

Focusing on higher education, this chapter investigates the ethical implications of integrating AI into academic environments. It emphasizes the role of faculty in fostering digital citizenship and ethical practices among students while addressing privacy, security, and governance challenges. The chapter proposes strategies for establishing robust ethical guidelines to navigate the evolving landscape of AI in education responsibly.

Chapter 8: Preparing Citizens for the Future: Digital Literacy and AI in Education

This chapter underscores the importance of digital and AI literacy in preparing future generations for a technology-driven world. It examines how AI personalizes learning experiences while addressing ethical considerations such as privacy and access disparities. By embedding critical thinking, creativity, and collaboration into curricula, this chapter advocates for an inclusive and responsible approach to digital education.

Chapter 9: Digital Citizenship in the Age of AI in Higher Education Institutions: Academic Integrity and Institutional Responsibilities

This chapter investigates the implications of AI on academic integrity and institutional responsibilities in higher education. Using the context of Palestinian institutions, it highlights the challenges and strategies for fostering ethical AI practices. The chapter emphasizes the importance of awareness and accountability among students and faculty in navigating AI's impact on academic work.

Chapter 10: Combating Misinformation in Social Media and News: A Deep Learning Approach

This chapter addresses the critical issue of misinformation in social media and news, leveraging advanced natural language processing (NLP) techniques to combat fake content. It demonstrates the effectiveness of deep learning models like XLNet in analyzing and classifying domain-specific datasets, offering a robust methodology for improving the accuracy and reliability of information dissemination.

Chapter 11: Balancing Innovation and Privacy: Understanding AI in the Digital World

Exploring the complex relationship between AI innovation and digital privacy, this chapter advocates for a balanced approach to technological progress. It discusses the transformative potential of AI across sectors while highlighting privacy challenges, such as data dependency and algorithmic bias. By promoting ethical principles and robust privacy frameworks, the chapter aims to ensure responsible AI adoption.

Chapter 12: Balancing Educational Benefits with Privacy Concerns in Social Network-Based Learning

This chapter examines the dual aspects of educational innovation and privacy concerns in social network-based learning. It provides a detailed analysis of the advantages and limitations of using AI, blockchain, and IoT in education while addressing privacy challenges. The chapter offers strategies for creating a secure and innovative educational environment that respects the privacy of students and educators.

Chapter 13: Balancing Innovation and Privacy in the Age of Artificial Intelligence

Focusing on the intricate balance between innovation and privacy, this chapter explores AI's potential for advancing efficiency and personalization alongside its privacy implications. It reviews regulatory frameworks and advocates for ethical AI practices to mitigate risks while fostering technological progress. The chapter emphasizes the importance of fairness, accountability, and transparency in navigating the challenges of AI in the digital age.

Chapter 14: Navigating the Future of Education in Critical Thinking and AI in Digital Citizenship

This chapter focuses on the intersection of AI, critical thinking, and academic integrity in education, offering strategies for integrating AI into assessment systems while preparing students for digital citizenship.

Chapter 15: Preparing Citizens for the Future of Digital Literacy and AI: With a Focus on Indonesian EFL Teachers

This chapter explores digital literacy and AI in education with a specific focus on Indonesian EFL teachers, emphasizing localized strategies and ethical concerns like accessibility and algorithmic bias.

Chapter 16: Exploring Experts' Positionings Towards AI

This chapter discusses experts' perspectives on AI's societal and governance implications, delving into their roles in shaping responsible AI practices and encouraging public participation in the AI development process.

Chapter 17: Ethical Considerations in the Use of AI and Big Data in Corporate Decision-Making

This chapter examines the ethical challenges of AI and Big Data in corporate decision-making, proposing a framework to ensure transparency, accountability, and ethical data practices.

Chapter 18: Data Cooperatives to Strengthen Digital Citizenship: Opportunities and Risks

This chapter introduces data cooperatives as a means of empowering digital citizens, reducing power imbalances, and promoting equitable data economies, while also addressing associated risks and implementation challenges.

Chapter 19: Educational Leadership and AI in the Post-COVID-19 Era: Ethical Challenges and Opportunities in Catalonia

The last chapter reflects on the integration of AI into education in Catalonia post-COVID-19, focusing on ethical challenges such as digital inclusion, data privacy, and fairness, with recommendations for equitable AI use.

CONCLUSION

As the world becomes increasingly interconnected and digital technologies permeate every aspect of our lives, the role of artificial intelligence and its ethical, social, and educational implications grows ever more critical. This volume explores the intersection of AI, digital literacy, and citizenship, offering diverse perspectives that reflect the challenges and opportunities of this transformative era. The chapters in this book provide not only theoretical insights but also actionable strategies to navigate the evolving landscape of AI integration across education, governance, and corporate environments.

From addressing ethical dilemmas in AI-powered decision-making to reimagining education for a digitally literate generation, this book underscores the importance of balancing innovation with responsibility. It highlights the need for inclusive frameworks that empower individuals, institutions, and societies to embrace AI while safeguarding equity, privacy, and integrity. The authors have enriched this discourse with global perspectives and localized case studies, ensuring that the findings and recommendations resonate across diverse contexts.

As editor, it is my hope that this book serves as a valuable resource for educators, policymakers, researchers, and industry leaders who are striving to harness the potential of AI for the greater good. Together, let us shape a future where technology serves as a catalyst for progress, equity, and shared prosperity.

Chapter 1
Digital Citizenship in the Age of AI in Higher Education Institutions:
Academic Integrity and Institutional Responsibilities

Mahmoud Itmeizeh
Palestine Ahliya University, Palestine

ABSTRACT

The chapter aims at investigating the reality of academic integrity in the era of AI and the institutional responsibilities to be taken into account to guarantee solid and genuine academic work by university students. This chapter addresses the extent to which academic integrity and institutional responsibilities are enhanced in Palestinian higher educational institutions (HEIs) as perceived by the faculty members. The role played by these institutions and the challenges they face will also be highlighted. Moreover, some strategies and solutions that aim at fostering academic integrity and institutional obligations will be proposed by the author. This chapter is expected to make both students and faculty more aware of the reality, advantages, and disadvantages of AI utilization in HEIs and its relation to Academic integrity.

INTRODUCTION

Each society evolves once behavioral and ethical mechanism becomes an integral part of its individuals' character and educational institutions' policies. In these societies, the highly appreciated values that are based on credibility, reliability honesty, and transparency become the main pillars that direct the mentality of both individuals

DOI: 10.4018/979-8-3693-9015-3.ch001

and institutions. In light of the evolution of generative AI apps, teachers and educational institutions encounter serious educational and behavioral challenges related to academic integrity. This dilemma requires all involved in the process of teaching and learning in HEIs to stand firm in the face of academic dishonesty whether it is practiced by faculty members or students. This does not mean that HEIs should refrain from benefiting from or using AI generative apps in teaching and learning. On the contrary, we must get the ultimate benefit from these generative apps but for constructive uses that enhance academic integrity not eradicating it. This also necessitates launching open discussion sessions that trigger a comprehensive understanding of the advantages and disadvantages of utilizing AI apps.

Due to the rapid evolution in the field of educational technology in general and AI apps in particular, a plethora of questions floated on the surface waiting for satisfactory and convincing answers. This chapter is supposed to respond to most of these questions posed by all those engaged in incorporating AI apps into the process of teaching and learning. Some of these questions include, but are not limited to, the following: How do researchers, instructors, and students manipulate academic integrity in light of the exaggerated use of AI apps that generate human-like information in the field of researching, teaching, and learning? Are we to consider AI apps an ally and supporter of academic integrity or a fatal enemy to it? If they are allies and supporters, what limitations should be enforced to lessen their negative impacts on academic integrity? If AI apps are counted as enemies of the higher education system, what policies and institutional measures should be adopted to eradicate any use of these apps? On the other hand, if it is an unavoidable evil, how we should successfully operate this issue to decrease its harm on HEIs and academic integrity to the minimum level? How can we prevent students from using AI apps to cheat? To logically and comprehensively respond to this question, all involved in the process of teaching and learning should take these concerns seriously by meeting their responsibilities. Each of the stakeholders should also know his/her role in enhancing citizenship, the culture of academic integrity, and enforcing institutional responsibility.

Nowadays, the world witnesses a drastic significant change in all aspects of our life. The rapid technological advancement is one of the aspects that showed countless digital and AI apps that obligate each individual to keep chasing these new apps trying to study them and then use these apps in the field of education. The plethora of AI apps in our lives, specifically in the process of teaching and learning, necessitates that each instructor and student behave in a way that meets the agreed-upon universal standards regarding the ethical utilization of AI apps. This sudden advancement in AI in general and generative AI in particular triggers to coining of new terminology to minimize the side effects of using generative AI tools in education. Therefore, the term digital citizenship has been coined with many sub-technical terms such as academic integrity and institutional responsibility. Hence, this chapter elaborates on digital citizenship, and academic integrity with institutional responsibilities in Palestinian higher educational institutions (HEIs) as perceived by the faculty members. This chapter is supposed to make both teachers and students more aware of the importance of enhancing digital citizenship to guarantee fruitful use of AI apps by adhering to the agreed-upon ethical criteria. The chapter will highlight the role of the educational institution in meeting its responsibilities and obligations to lessen the negative effects of using AI apps. It will also propose some recommendations regarding digital literacy, academic integrity, institutional obligations and responsibilities, and creating a culture of academic integrity. In addition to the theoretical framework, the author conducted a study on PAU faculty members to support literature with data collected from the educational field.

Digital citizenship in general and academic integrity in addition to institutional responsibility should address lifelong habits, practices, and learning. Once academic integrity and institutional obligations become part of the individual's personality and the higher education institution's mentality, the sustainability of academic integrity and lifelong learning will be guaranteed. Moreover, internalization of these positive values will always enhance academic integrity and institutional responsibilities. For example, when students become autonomous learners due to the use of digital apps, lifelong learning is greatly enhanced since they become independent without taking refuge from their teachers.

THEORETICAL FRAMEWORK

The theoretical background of this chapter will elaborate on digital citizenship, generative AI apps, academic integrity, and institutional responsibility in the age of AI.

Thanks to the rapid development of information and communication technology (ICT) worldwide, it becomes a must for each individual to be aware of at least the basics of the huge number of digital and artificial intelligence (AI) apps that are created or curated currently. Educational institutions, as an integral part of any country, do their best to ethically utilize these technological innovations in the process of teaching and learning. During the last three decades, Palestinian Higher Educational Institutions (HEIs) have tried varied digital and AI apps synchronously and asynchronously. In his study, Sari (2023) stated that the implementation of asynchronous and synchronous learning has facilitated students' learning and made them more motivated and productive.

The use of these technologies was significantly intensified during COVID-19 time and currently after the 7th October event. In such a revolutionary setting, all institutions of all countries perish themselves to meet the requirements of these newly created apps. These requirements are not only restricted to the abundance of the needed infrastructure to guarantee successful utilization of these apps but also need a human individual who is equipped with all needed morals, etiquettes, standards, linguistic and social intelligence, etc. In addition to these personal qualities, being a digital citizen necessitates many other qualities to be available such as academic integrity and the institutional responsibilities that each educational institution should assume to enhance digital citizenship. In its first part, this chapter will elaborate on the theoretical background concerning the definition of digital citizenship, academic integrity with its main components, and the institutional responsibilities that may create a digital citizen who is equipped with all needed qualities as a reflection of the crazy spread of digital apps. The second part of this chapter will answer some research questions based on data collected via a questionnaire that aimed at investigating the reality of academic integrity in HEIs, the challenges, the institutional policies, the suggested solutions, and some recommendations.

ARTIFICIAL INTELLIGENCE APPLICATIONS (AI APPS)

Artificial intelligence is a machine-displayed intelligence that can simulate human behaviors, products, and thoughts. It can also be trained to solve real-life questions. Deep learning and machine learning have constituted AI apps. Generative AI can create responses that are so close to or similar to human-made responses. By producing original text, graphics, and code in response to human input, generative AI develops artificial intelligence. It redefines how we work and innovate by emphasizing creativity and human-like interactions, in contrast to standard AI. This opens up new opportunities in fields like software development, art, education, and customer service.

There are several types of generative AI, each with its unique capabilities to handle inputs, whether text, image, or video, and its outputs in various forms of text, audio, image, and video. The following is a list of common types of generative models based on the type of their outputs:

1. **Text generation**: It is one of the most important applications of generative AI which produces new content in natural language. Generative models can be used to generate new creative text. For example, a language model such as Chat GPT can be trained on large amounts of text data and then used to generate new, coherent, and grammatically correct text in various languages.
2. **Image generation**: It is the process of using generative models such as generative networks and diffusion models to create a new image that visually resembles real-world images.

3. **Video generation**: In this process, one can use generative models to create new videos from a text description. An example of this is the Dreamix model, which edits the video using text, changing the video content according to the text entered by the user. Dreamix uses diffusion technology to reconstruct the video in a time-consistent manner, preserving the color, position, size of objects, and camera angle.
4. **Speech generation**: These are generative models that have been trained on converting various and huge audio recordings, and can convert text to speech. An example of this is the Voice box model from Meta, and the Play HT website for cloning and imitating voice.

Generative AI is a subset of technologies within the AI umbrella and includes a class of systems that can generate new content such as text, images, audio, and video. In higher education, this technology can make multiple contributions including (Aljumaily, 2024):

1. **Personalization of education**: AI can analyze student performance and provide personalized learning experiences, by adapting study materials and teaching methods to each student's needs based on their skills and personal characteristics.
2. **Generating educational content**: AI can create new educational content such as question models, interactive materials, and content tailored to the curriculum, saving academics time and effort, especially with the increasing number of students in most academic disciplines and the increasing time required to follow up on their assignments and exams, and to develop questions and model solutions, etc.
3. **Academic support**: AI systems can provide immediate support to students with queries related to academic subjects, enhancing the self-learning process and reducing reliance on human teachers for everything.

Aljumaily (2024) elaborated about the term 'University 4.0' and he defined it as the new generation of academic institutions that rely heavily on digital technology to deliver education and conduct research. According to Aljumaily (2024) university 4.0 is characterized by:

1. **Digital and interactive learning**: It is the use of digital platforms to provide interactive lessons, digital study materials, and direct communication with experts and lecturers.
2. **Collaboration and innovation**: This feature facilitates collaboration between students and academics across the world through online collaboration tools, and creating virtual environments for collaborative research.

3. **Data analytics**: It is the use of data analytics to understand student behavior, improve learning outcomes, and provide strategic advice for developing curricula and teaching methods.
4. **Inclusiveness and Sustainability**: It promotes open education and access to higher education through digital tools that transcend geographical and economic barriers so that students can obtain distinguished and affordable higher education anywhere and anytime.

To conclude, in the era of generative AI and university 4.0, the enhancement of digital citizenship is of paramount importance. An educational environment that is rich with a plethora of digital and AI apps is supposed to be a fertile soil of dishonest conduct and behaviors that minimize digital citizenship and maximize academic dishonesty. On the other hand, AI apps have many benefits just like any other tool or device. The harms or the benefits of AI apps depend on the user himself. Personalization and autonomy learning are greatly enhanced while using AI tools. These apps also meet learners' needs and enhance self-dependence since each learner can learn at his own pace.

DIGITAL CITIZENSHIP

There are several definitions for digital citizenship seen in varied resources, but generally speaking, most of these definitions emphasize that any digital citizen should use all internet products responsibly, respectfully, and safely. However, digital citizenship has emerged as one of the pivotal pre-requirements before delving into the bottom of the digital world. All users of the internet should own all skills needed to deal with at least the basics of successful utilization of all technologies needed in educational institutions. A digital citizen is defined as an individual who genuinely is adaptive to the needs of a digital city (Schuler, 2002). Mossberger, Tolbert & McNeal (2011) stated that those who regularly and effectively use the Internet, are digital citizens. Moreover, an American study (Robble, 2017) defined digital citizenship as the reliable and accountable utilization of technology by any person who uses computers, the internet, or digital apps in the context of education. Hummel (2024) stated that digital citizenship represents the responsible utilization of technology in all aspects of life. These definitions highlight the importance of digital citizenship in educational institutions since they are the producers of the future generation who will be the leaders of this world in the coming years. Taking the 21st century digital citizenship goals into account, Ribble & Baily (2007) stated digital citizenship touchpoints as seen in this figure.

Figure 1. Digital citizenship touchpoints

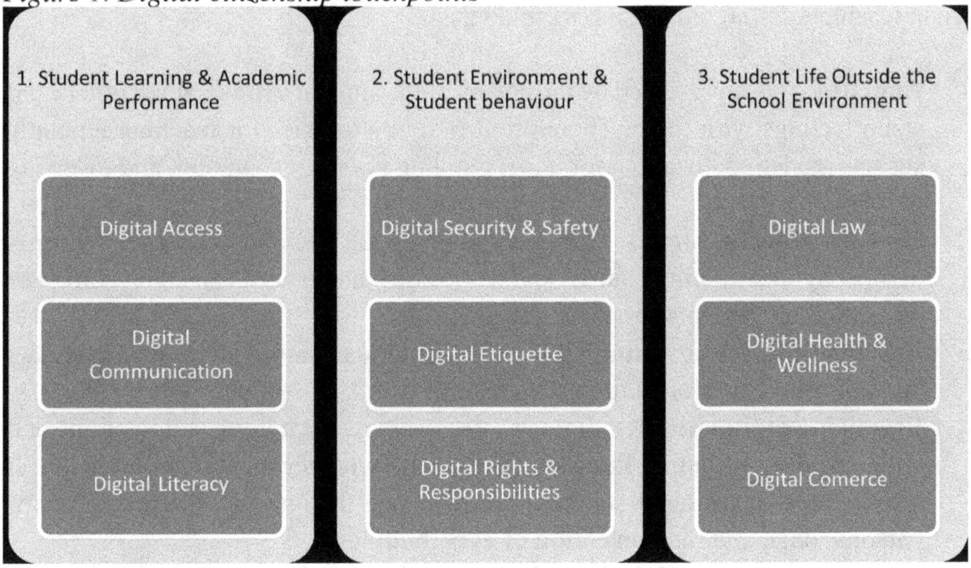

(Ribble & Baily, 2007)

As seen in Figure 1 above, the main three keys of digital citizenship were subdivided into nine areas of behaviors. Students in their learning and academic performance should show full electronic participation in society through communication and exchanging and/or sharing information which means that students are excellent users of technology in general and digital apps in particular. In internet environments, students' ultimate behavior must reflect a secure and safe use of internet apps with a high degree of netiquette that shows awareness of the user's duties and responsibilities, from one side and others' rights from the other side. The third key element focuses on the student's life outside the school environment that requires all users to conform to digital laws to enjoy digital healthy educational and commercial practices. Operationally, digital technology can be defined as a compound system that consists of knowledge and ethics. Knowledge requires each user to be competent in all areas of computers and the internet needed in his/her work; the ethical side is represented by the user's behavior that is accepted by society and in harmony with the social norms and the country's laws. This operational definition leads us to elaborate on academic integrity that should be available in all educational institutions.

Institutional responsibility in enhancing digital citizenship is not only restricted to creating policies and codes of behaviors that all partners must stick to but also knowing the main concepts of digital citizenship that should be taught to all students at HEIs. Hummel (2024) highlighted seven key concepts that HEIs should consider when teaching digital citizenship to students.

1. **Empathy**: It is represented by the ability of the student to understand others and share feelings with them. There are different strategies for teaching empathy such as modeling, listening for understanding not for responding, and investing in others.
2. **How the Internet work**s: HIEs should eradicate computer illiteracy by organizing ongoing training courses and workshops that focus on all about computer usage that all students should know.
3. **Understanding user data**: Each user should learn more about personal data and know how to protect himself/herself.
4. **Practicing digital literacy**: It means that users read the information online and understand its meaning, know its origin, and whether it is accurate or not. It also includes learning about the ethics of using the internet, the protection of personal data, and the prevention of cyberbullying.
5. **Acknowledging the digital divide:** It shows the gap between people who have access to contemporary digital technologies (such as computers and the internet) and those who do not. This is known as the "digital divide."
6. **Practice digital wellness:** The technique of avoiding excessive use of digital media and the internet for a fair period is known as digital wellness. It's the art of understanding when to "take a break" from screens, to put it another way. Because excessive screen time can negatively impact pupils, digital well-being is crucial.
7. **Securing digital devices:** Securing digital devices is the last component of being a good digital citizen. Because it integrates all that students have learned to real-life situations.

Poth (2023) mentioned three important digital citizenship skills:

1. **Privacy and security:** Knowing how to protect our privacy is essential. It is crucial to incorporate activities that will help children better understand how to protect themselves and respect the privacy of others, especially because more students are utilizing digital technologies at younger ages. For example, one of the most important things to do is to educate pupils on how to make their passwords.
2. **Communications:** HEIs must routinely concentrate on giving students the chance to practice appropriate posting because of the wide range of social media platforms accessible and the speed at which we may post and reply.

3. **Cyberbullying:** Because publishing online is so easy, cyberbullying is a major issue that should be covered in every university. By training students to be sympathetic online, all instructors may emphasize the need to identify and combat cyberbullying more. Guidelines should be established in universities so that students are aware of their rights and obligations regarding the usage of technology.

ACADEMIC INTEGRITY

Academic integrity is one of the main components of digital citizenship since it targets all those involved in the process of teaching and learning. Communities' growth is genuinely related to the morale system experienced by inhabitants in their daily lives. These behaviors should be based on the values of truth, commitment, reliability, transparency, accountability, justice, and respect. In this digital era, educational institutions encounter real challenges in assuring academic integrity by eradicating all the side effects that negatively impact the values and social norms of society. Macfarlane et al. (2014) defined academic integrity as "*the values, behavior, and conduct of academics in all aspects of their practice*". East and Donnelly (2012) added that "academic integrity means being honest in academic work and taking responsibility".

These definitions emphasize the fact that academic integrity should be reflected in users' behaviors during their work. The International Center for Academic Integrity (ICAI) defined academic integrity as a commitment to six fundamental values: honesty, fairness, courage, responsibility, trust, and respect. By adhering to these six essential values both teachers and students will create a culture of academic integrity that may lead to a drastic positive change in the process of teaching and learning in the era of digitalization and generative AI. Hence, institutional responsibility is one of the integral parts of academic integrity that automatically enhances the culture of digital citizenship. Therefore, institutional measures should be taken to lessen academic misconduct. Amid the concerning acceleration in the negative use of artificial intelligence applications, there is no disagreement, at least within our Palestinian community, that academic integrity within our educational institutions is at risk. For example, Schmidt (2016) reported that international students enrolled at American Universities are more likely to cheat than their American counterparts. She also added that American public universities reported five cheating cases out of every one hundred international students while only one American student cheated for every one hundred American students. Moreover, it has been stated that nearly 50.000 university students were caught cheating during the years 2012-2015. These results show that the challenges of academic integrity are a global issue that has been intensified in the era of AI. Moreover, Daily experiences across all our universities reveal the clear discontent among academics about the behaviors some students have resorted to, including cheating, plagiarism, impersonation, and forgery, relying on digital technology, particularly generative AI applications. For example, a survey study conducted by Donald McCabe (2020) on a sample of his students in America revealed that 25% of them used prohibited online sources to complete their academic work, and 28% completed assignments collaboratively when they were required to be done individually. The results also showed that 15% of the sample copied from internet sources without citation, 65% admitted to cheating on tests in one way or another, with 58% confessed to plagiarizing others' work without proper documentation. If this is the situation outside of Palestine, then what about our case? Worsening the matter, and in light of the development of internet services and their increasing accessibility, some institutions, centers, and individuals now provide cheating services to students for money. All these factors have led to a decline in students' performance, especially with the adoption of e-learning due to the harsh reality that the Palestinian people face. We are witnessing a notable increase in cheating, a lack of academic integrity, dishonesty, and a lack of responsibility among many students, particularly evident in their test-taking and academic assignments. This is further proof that academic integrity is not in an ideal state within higher education institutions, which necessitates a concerted effort by all concerned parties to enhance academic integrity and advance the educational process in Palestine.

In his paper, Rodrigues (2023) distinguishes two crucial thematical forms: academic integrity and negative predictors of academic integrity. This paper emphasizes a few contributions by stating that apps associated with AI could act as detectors of students with academic misconduct like plagiarism. That is, they can be useful in detecting learners with deceitful actions. Therefore, it will necessitate a joint effort of public, private academic, and educational institutions and the community with reasonable policies.

The vast challenges posed by internet applications in the educational field are significant and require collective effort, not only at the level of individuals and institutions but also across the state and among policymakers. One of the main challenges is providing the necessary technical infrastructure to benefit from digital applications in alignment with academic integrity. The second challenge relates to the content offered by these digital applications, especially regarding the accuracy or inaccuracy of the data, particularly when dealing with ethical issues related to the humanities, or religious, historical, or political content. The third challenge I would like to highlight is the availability of clear, applicable mechanisms to strengthen academic integrity and digital citizenship amid the spread of generative AI applications.

THE CULTURE OF ACADEMIC INTEGRITY

Creating a culture of academic integrity is not an easy job. In the era of technological advancement and the generative AI apps in particular, Palestinian HEIs still lack not only the infrastructure needed for promoting academic integrity but also score significant deficiencies in the culture of academic integrity. The absence of this culture from the minds of many students and some instructors complicates the scene and makes it nearly impossible for us to eradicate academic dishonesty. In any respectful higher education institution, the human values of credibility, trust, courage, responsibility, fairness, honesty, reliability, trustworthiness, self-respect, and accountability should be considered as core pillars on which all behaviors and decisions should spring. In these HEIs, the culture of academic integrity is to exist at the roots of the institution as an inevitable integral component of the mentality and psychology of this organization. Creating such a culture requires noticeable actions and a solid commitment at the bottom, the top, and throughout the educational institution. Reaching the optimal level of academic integrity should be in harmony with the institution's vision and mission to bring theory to practice.

Though the 'One-size-fits-all' formula is inapplicable in all institutional environments, ICAI (International Center for Academic Integrity) (2021) suggests twelve steps that institutions should consider to enhance the culture of academic integrity.

1. Institutions should frequently and clearly show how the culture of academic integrity enhances the institutions' mission and vision.
2. All institution employees need to be educated about the principles of academic integrity as an integral element of the organization's culture.
3. Stakeholders' perceptions of academic integrity should repeatedly be investigated.
4. Pedagogy that reinforces self-reflection on individuals' competencies, performances, and outcomes should be considered so that each can learn from his/her mistakes and learn from them which promotes the culture of academic integrity.
5. Adopting partnerships and collaborations in universities to assist instructors in building positive instructional environments and promote integrity in classes.
6. Adopting academic integrity policies that are fair, clear, procedurally sound, and effectively understood by all.
7. Advance the positive components of academic integrity among all elements of the campus community.
8. To ensure consistency, equitability, transparency, and effectiveness of aims, academic integrity policies should be regularly reviewed.
9. The HEIs should reward those who meet the academic integrity policies and required standards.

10. Regularly assess the institutions' pedagogical principles to decrease incentives for academic dishonesty.
11. Encourage creating curricular and extracurricular services to nurture students' success.
12. All available institutional resources should be recruited for the sake of the institutions' goals despite the scarcity of these resources sometimes.

INSTITUTIONAL RESPONSIBILITY

In any HEI, academic integrity is the backbone of a welcoming, inspiring, and healthy academic environment. The rise of new technologies and AI generative apps creates sound challenges for all educational institutions. These challenges spring from varied issues such as technology infrastructure, and stakeholders' behaviors that either promote or eradicate academic integrity in HEIs. Creating clear and transparent institutional strategies is of paramount importance for academic integrity enhancement. The policies adopted by HEIs should eliminate all types of academic dishonesty in universities in particular. In fact. In many educational institutions, most of the faculty members complain about the increase in dishonest practices such as:

1. **Plagiarism**: some students present others' work as their own. This generally happens when students are asked to conduct their BA graduation projects, MA theses, and PhD. Dissertations, reports, projects, etc.
2. **Collusion**: This occurs when students or researchers have illegal collaboration with unauthorized partners. For example, a student may conduct his graduation project for his MA thesis by secretly working in collusion with commercial educational centers.
3. **Falsification**: This dishonest phenomenon occurs when an individual exhibits manipulated or fabricated results, data, or references.
4. **Copying**: This happens when a person uses data that he has just copied and pasted without any reference to the original owner claiming that it is his.
5. **Deception**: Deception occurs when a student gets benefit from others using unethical ways.
6. **Identity Theft**: This happens when an individual pretends to be someone else so that they can gain some advantages through this dishonest behavior.

Establishing a culture of academic honesty necessitates consensus that honesty and integrity are desirable traits in every member of the university community. Furthermore, the idea that those who value education would never consider cheating to be a realistic option is inherent in all discussions about academic integrity.

Colleges use different approaches to cultivating academic integrity, but there are certain commonalities across several categories (McCabe, 2004):

1. Encourage and engaging students in conversations about maintaining and advancing an academic integrity-focused institutional atmosphere.
2. Creating and disseminating precise definitions and illustrations of academic dishonesty.
3. Creating lucid and reliable channels of communication on inappropriate conduct and its consequences.
4. Providing due process, explicit repercussions for inappropriate behavior, and clear procedures for recording violations.

Academic integrity entails consensus within the institution about attitudes and activities related to learning, achievement, and taking accountability for one's actions. Therefore, the promotion of institutional academic integrity requires trustworthiness measures and procedures from HEIs that should target all aspects of the process of teaching and learning. For instance, HEIs should create a clear code of conduct that elaborates on each partner's duties and responsibilities. This may start with the institution's responsibility, students' behaviors, teachers' and community's commitment to academic integrity pillars.

In the context of institutional responsibility in the era of technology, there are many technical, societal, legal, and ethical duties that all educational institutions should adopt to guarantee the appropriate use of technology in education. Students and teachers' academic integrity is of no significant value if educational institutions do not meet their responsibilities and obligations in this smart crazy world. Today, we are witnessing digital and AI apps that significantly impact the higher education system. Therefore, universities should do their best to transform the traditional system of teaching, learning, and assessment into a system that encounters all the negative effects of utilizing AI apps by teachers and students. This requires Palestinian HEIs to enforce rules and regulations to be obeyed by all involved in the educational system.

To learn more about academic integrity and institutional responsibility in reality, the author conducted a study that aimed at investigating how academic integrity and institutional responsibility are perceived and practiced within Palestinian higher education institutions (HEIs) as viewed by faculty members at Palestine Ahliya University (PAU). The next part of this chapter will elaborate on this study coming up with genuine conclusions and recommendations.

PRACTICAL FRAMEWORK

The practical part of this chapter will include a quantitative and qualitative tool to collect the needed data from a sample that constitutes instructors at Palestine Ahliya University (PAU). A questionnaire that includes both closed-ended and open-ended questions was distributed to the subjects of the study to collect needed data.

Statement of the Problem

Due to the rapid development of technology that impacted all aspects of life, many issues, problems, and concerns have emerged. One of the problems that emerged is the consequences that resulted from the vast use of digital and AI apps in HEIs. Based on experience, I noticed that some teachers and students exploited these apps inappropriately which negatively affects the output of universities in general. Some researchers and students plagiarized and/or cheated easily without being detected. Moreover, many of my colleagues complained about the increasing use of these apps for cheating and plagiarizing by students. Therefore, this study was conducted to investigate the reality of academic integrity and the university's responsibility that enhance digital citizenship in HEIS institutions.

Significance of the Study

The importance of this study is of two parts, the theoretical importance and the practical importance. Theoretically, this chapter enriches the literature on digital citizenship, academic integrity, and institutional responsibility. Teachers, students, and universities themselves will be more aware of the importance of enhancing digital citizenship in general and academic integrity and institutional responsibility in particular. The practical side benefits all parties by providing them with practical principles, guidelines, and measures that may put an end to the negative use of these technologies in the process of teaching and learning. Teachers, students, and universities will be equipped with the necessary recommendations and steps that positively enhance academic integrity.

Aims of the study

The study aims to address the following objectives:

1. Exploring the reality of academic integrity in the age of AI as perceived by instructors at Palestinian HEIs.

2. Investigating the impact of AI utilization on academic integrity at Palestinian HEIs.
3. Identifying challenges that Palestinian HEIs face in eliminating the side effects of the students' AI utilization in their academic work?
4. Proposing strategies and solutions to enhance academic integrity at Palestinian universities in the age of AI.

Questions of the Study

The study will address the following questions:

RQ1. What is the reality of academic integrity in the age of AI as perceived by instructors?
RQ2: What is the impact of AI utilization on academic integrity?
RQ3: What challenges do Palestinian HEIs face in eliminating the negative effects of the students' AI utilization in their academic work?
RQ4: What strategies and solutions can be proposed to enhance academic integrity in the age of AI?

METHODOLOGY

The researcher used the descriptive analytical method to analyze the data of the study. The data of the study was collected via a questionnaire that consisted of two sections. The first section was on the demographic information that included gender, faculty, and years of experience of the participants. The second section included the items of the questionnaire. There were 9 items, five of them were closed questions and four were open-ended questions which makes the tool a qualitative and quantitative one. The validity and reliability of the questionnaire were guaranteed via known scientific methods.

Data Collection

To gain a more comprehensive understanding of the reality of academic integrity and institutional responsibility in the context of AI, the questionnaire was distributed to a sample of university instructors. The questionnaire covers several ideas: the reality of academic integrity, the impact of AI on academic integrity, PAU policies on academic integrity, and the instructors' views on the effectiveness of these policies.

Sample

The study sample included full-time instructors from various faculties at PAU. Table 1 below shows the distribution of the subjects of the sample by gender, faculty, and years of experience showing their numbers and percentages.

Table 1. Distribution of subjects of sample

Demographic Variable	Categories	Number of Participants	Percentage
Gender	Male	13	61.9%
	Female	8	38.1%
Faculty	Humanities & Social Sciences	5	23.8%
	Engineering and IT	7	33.3%
	Medical Allied Sciences	6	28.6%
	Law	3	14.3%
Years of Teaching Experience	Less than 5 years	4	19.0%
	5-10 years	5	23.8%
	11-20 years	10	47.6%
	Over 20 years	2	9.5%

Table 1 above reveals that the majority of the participants were males (61.9%) while females constituted (38.1%) of the total number which reflected the gender distribution in PAU. Concerning faculty representation, most subjects were from the faculty of Engineering and IT with a percentage of (33.3%), followed by the faculty of Humanities and Social Sciences (23.8%). Faculty of Medical Allied and Law comprised (28.6%) and (14.3%) of the participants respectively. The largest group of participants was from those with 11-20 years of experience (47.6%), followed by (23.8%) from those with experience of 5-10 years. Participants with less than 5 years of experience got a percentage of (19.0%) and the lowest percentage (9.5%) goes to those with more than 20 years of experience.

Data Analysis

Since the instrument of the study includes closed-ended and open-ended questions, both quantitative and qualitative methods were used. Quantitatively, the researcher calculated the frequencies and the percentages of participants' responses to closed-ended questions. The thematic analysis was used to qualitatively analyze the responses of the participants to the open-ended questions.

Based on the aims and questions of the study, the discussion of the findings below will be thematically presented and discussed. Thematic analysis was mainly adopted to address the open-ended questions in the questionnaire used as an instrument of the study.

FINDINGS, DISCUSSION, AND RECOMMENDATIONS

1. The Reality of Academic Integrity in HEIs

Table 2 below shows the participant's responses to the questionnaire items on the reality of academic integrity in Palestinian HEIs. The first question was 'What AI tools do your students use in their academic work?' and the second question required students to say the extent to which their students use AI tools. Their answers range from the options 'frequently' to 'never'. Table (2) below shows the AI tools used and the frequency and percentage of their usage.

Table 2. Items, AI tools utilized, frequencies, and percentages

Question	AI Tools Utilized	Frequencies	Percentage
AI tools used by students	Chat GPT	12	57.1%
	Gemini	1	4.8%
	Translation apps	3	14.3%
	Writing apps	2	9.6%
	AI Apps on Mobile Phones	1	4.8%
Frequency of AI tool usage by students	Frequently	8	38.1%
	Occasionally	8	38.1%
	Rarely	4	19.0%
	Never	0	0%

As seen in Table 2 above, the most frequent AI application used by university students was Chat GPT with a percentage of 57.1% of the total sample responses followed by AI translation apps with a percentage of 14.3%. The students' use of AI writing apps scored 9.6% of the sample responses. Gemini app and AI apps on mobile phones got 4.8% of the participant's responses each. The findings of the above table showed that Chat GPT was the most famous AI app used by Palestinian university students. This result can be attributed to the fact that Chat GPT was the first generative AI app known to Palestinian students who were able to use it without complications. This wide use of Chat GPT can be also due to its ability to generate as accurate and reliable information as possible. AI apps used for translation scored second rank since most university students recourse to such apps due to their significant weakness in the English language. Moreover, students save much time when they use these apps for translating from English to Arabic and vice versa. Though Gemini is as effective as Chat GPT, it is not widely used by university students compared to Chat GPT. This may be attributed to the fact that students became accustomed to Chat GPT and they refrain from trying new ones.

2. Institutional Policies Addressing Academic Integrity

Thematic analysis was used to analyze question number 6 in the questionnaire which requires respondents to report the institutional policies adopted in addressing AI academic integrity issues. In response to this question, some participants reported a shortage of comprehensive, clear, and transparent policies concerning AI integrity. This shortage of clear policies was considered one of the main sources of students' academic dishonesty. For example, one of the respondents said that there is no clear policy to eliminate cheating through the use of AI tools in research and assignments. Moreover, two participants said that there is no policy used to address academic integrity. Five of the respondents asked the university administration to only adopt onsite exams and cancel electronic exams. Though, the university uses the Turnitin app to check the percentage of citations in MA theses, one of the respondents reported that the university administration should use varied effective AI apps to detect plagiarism specifically in writing graduation projects, assignments, and MA theses.

It is worth mentioning that although Palestine Ahliya University (PAU) adopts a specific policy to address academic integrity, many students still behave dishonestly, mainly in exams, using their mobile phones or electronic watches. The university does place some punishment measures that are nearly always limited to exams. With the lack of clear, comprehensive, and transparent policies regarding academic integrity, educational institutions will suffer from academic dishonesty like cheating and plagiarism.

3. Suggested Solutions and Policies

Participants, in this study, provided varied suggestions to enhance the university policies in addressing academic integrity. One of the participants proposed 'PAU should create a policy about AI ethics usage and academic integrity, this policy should be published for all'. HEIs including PAU should adopt clear and comprehensive policies to minimize the negative effects of AI apps on academic integrity. For example, the educational institution should hold training sessions for all academic staff to highlight the importance of academic integrity and propose some effective policies that may enhance academic integrity. Faculty should also be provided with different resources and apps that help them detect any dishonest behavior in students' academic work. Promoting faculty and students' awareness about all ethical issues connected to academic integrity and institutional responsibility fosters positive, right, and ethical utilization of AI apps in HEIs. One of the participants asked for 'promoting students' awareness on the use of AI tools and providing courses on how to use them ethically'. Three of the respondents emphasized the importance of raising awareness of all ethical issues related to academic issues and institutional responsibilities. They added that universities should adopt policies and guidelines on the legitimate use of AI tools in the process of teaching and learning. Some of the participants proposed the use of alternative assessments such as projects, and presentations to eliminate cheating via electronic devices. Four participants stated that 'each course syllabus should include a clear, strong statement about academic integrity and its types, commitments, regulations and penalties'. He also proposed 'orientation for new students about the importance of academic integrity'. One respondent suggested 'Using questions of higher levels in exams that make it difficult for students to cheat'.

4. Impact of AI Utilization on Academic Integrity

To answer this question, the questionnaire included two different questions. First, results showed that 95.2% of the participants assured that AI apps highly or moderately impact academic integrity negatively. This result shows that the academic staff is aware of the risks that the students' use of AI poses to academic integrity. Moreover, 66.7% of the respondents stated that they witnessed occasional incidents of academic dishonesty and 14.3 of them reported that students frequently practice dishonest behaviors while delivering their academic work. Such results suggest that HEIs should take responsibility and enforce preventive measures that may lessen academic dishonesty among students. In response to the question regarding the frequency of academic dishonesty issues, the majority (81.0%) of the participants reported that the students' utilization of AI apps significantly increases academic dishonesty. 76% of university students assured that the use of AI apps does highly or moderately contribute to the enhancement of academic dishonesty. When the participants were asked about the effectiveness of the current institutional policies adopted by the university administration, 61.9% of them responded by saying these policies are 'somewhat effective', while 14.3 stated that these policies were effective.

5. Challenges

In response to this question, most respondents indicated that the academic staff faces varied difficulties in distinguishing between human and AI-generated work due to the sophistication and complications of AI apps and the lack of academic experience in using or dealing with these AI apps. Moreover, some academics reported not only their weakness in knowing the basics of AI apps but also their illiteracy in this area. For example, a participant reported 'The presence of AI tools that transform writing into a human-like product makes it difficult to detect whether it is plagiarized or not'. Another participant added 'The presence of AI apps that paraphrase plagiarized texts makes us confused and undetermined'. Many participants added that unclear institutional policies regarding academic integrity are one of the challenges that we face'. Participants indicated students' indifferent behaviors since they intensively use AI apps for cheating and plagiarism. One respondent noted 'There is a lack of awareness among students about academic integrity and the ethical implications of using AI tools. These responses highlight the need for ongoing updates of AI apps for detection adopted by universities in addition to adhering to effective policies and practical measures that aim at minimizing the negative effects of AI tools on academic integrity. Moreover, some of the faculty suggested holding orientation sessions and workshops to increase teachers' and students' awareness of the importance of academic integrity and the institutional responsibilities towards this academic phenomenon. The rapid spread of AI apps makes it more difficult to firmly resist academic dishonesty which is mainly represented by cheating and plagiarism. One respondent said 'Once I learn much about a specific AI app, a new one emerges and this makes me confused and stressed'. Moreover, this rapid evolution of AI apps poses additional challenges to HEIs in addition to faculty members. For example, one of the participants stated that 'The rapid spread of new AI tools makes it hard for faculty to stay updated on what students might use'. This reality necessitates that HEIs invest in ongoing professional development for both faculty and students to keep up with technological trends.

6. Suggestions for Practical Solutions

To sum it up, all participants proposed varied solutions that focus on institutional responsibilities commitment to enforcing comprehensive AI ethics, academic integrity culture, and adopting solid measures and penalties that may bring about a drastic change in the students' and academics' academic integrity culture. Educational initiatives should also be activated such as workshops, symposiums, and forums. For example, most of the participants urged higher educational institutions to adopt firm and concise measures that eliminate academic dishonesty. They also universities to enforce clear and transparent rules and regulations that strengthen academic integrity among teachers and institutions. They also asked the university administration to construct and provide the needed infrastructure that facilitates the implementation of academic integrity.

Based on my experience in the field of education for more than 27 years, the theoretical framework stated above, and the results of the aforementioned study, I can provide the following proposed solutions, suggestions, and recommendations for all involved in the process of teaching and learning. Following are proposed solutions for creating an academic integrity culture and elaboration on academic integrity at the level of higher education institutions, teachers, and students.

PROPOSED SOLUTIONS FOR CREATING A CULTURE OF ACADEMIC INTEGRITY

1. Strengthening the Core Values of Academic Integrity, Which Are

A. **Honesty**: Researchers and students must be honest with themselves and others, crediting the source through proper citation, maintaining objectivity, and providing a realistic and logical justification for any idea they present.

B. **Trust**: To enhance this value, transparency must be ensured, and expectations should be clear, specific, and measurable for monitoring and evaluation. Additionally, credibility and trust in others, along with mutual understanding, are essential.

C. **Fairness**: To achieve this value, it is essential to excel in responsibility, maintain an open mindset, and treat others justly, ensuring that policies are applied consistently without bias or neglect.

D. **Respect**: To show respect for others, one must actively listen to them, accept their feedback, engage with them, and maintain open communication, even in the presence of disagreement. It is important to consider their ideas and opinions as having some validity and recognize that your ideas and opinions may contain some errors.

E. **Responsibility**: To activate this value, it is essential to take responsibility for our actions, follow up on our assigned tasks, engage others in dialogue and discussion, and respect them by general codes of conduct. F. Courage: What distinguishes those who embody this core value of academic integrity is their willingness to take risks to achieve their desired goals. It requires courage in situations that call for it, even when others may falter in defending integrity, truth, and what is right. Those who hold this value support the rightful positions of others, regardless of the harassment or challenges they may face.

2. Academic Integrity at the Institutional Level

Palestinian higher education institutions should promote a culture of academic integrity by implementing several measures and steps, the most important of which are:

A. **Formulating Policies that Support Academic Integrity:** These policies should align with the institution's vision and mission, providing a clear and unambiguous framework based on general codes of conduct that encompass the core values of academic integrity.
B. **Adopting Clear Mechanisms to Detect Academic Integrity:** This includes utilizing search engines, relevant internet applications, and e-learning platforms, including generative artificial intelligence applications.
C. **Institutionalizing the Concept of Digital Citizenship**: Higher education institutions should contribute to preparing students and academics who can effectively utilize digital technology and generative artificial intelligence in a manner consistent with codes of conduct and regulations. These codes should stem from our ethics, religion, and the laws applicable within the institution, including guidelines related to online etiquette (Netiquette).
D. **Initiating an Educational Awareness Campaign**: This campaign should target the university and the local community, focusing on the concept and standards of academic integrity and its importance in cultivating a creative, thoughtful, and entrepreneurial generation capable of taking responsibility.
E. **Evaluating and Reviewing Academic Integrity Policies and Concepts:** This includes reviewing teaching, assessment, and learning methods, as well as integrating digital technology and artificial intelligence applications in education to observe innovative methods of misconduct related to the use of artificial intelligence applications.
F. **Providing an Institutional Environment that Fosters Academic Integrity**: This involves equipping classrooms and laboratories with the necessary logistical and digital resources, enhancing partnerships between colleges, and assisting students in adopting a culture of academic integrity so that it becomes an integral part of their identity and personal traits.
G. **Organizing Study and Training Sessions:** The institution should organize study and training sessions and distribute periodic newsletters to create positive attitudes towards the concept of academic integrity and the ways to benefit from generative artificial intelligence. This aims to deepen understanding and assist

in organizing and coordinating academic work, without relying entirely on it or engaging in cheating, plagiarism, or other forms of misconduct.

H. **Adopting Authentic/Alternative Assessment Tools:** The university should generally adopt realistic alternative assessment tools, especially when transitioning to e-learning, aiming to increase the percentage of non-traditional assessments. This approach would help reduce cheating, even when utilizing generative artificial intelligence technologies.
I. **Eradicating Digital Illiteracy among Academics**: The institution should specifically focus on eliminating digital illiteracy among academics so that they can recognize mechanisms of cheating using digital technology and methods to detect it.

3. Academic Integrity at the Level of Faculty Members

For a faculty member to exemplify academic integrity, they need to assess whether they possess the following qualities or not:

A. **Honesty with Oneself:** One of the highest forms of respect is self-respect. This feeling stems from faculty member's commitment to fulfilling their duties to the best of their ability and their strong desire for change, growth, research, and exploration. Academic integrity requires a constant effort to update course syllabi, textbooks, teaching methods, assessment techniques, and the integration of digital technologies that keep pace with the latest advancements in educational technology, including generative artificial intelligence.
B. **Utilizing Generative Artificial Intelligence Applications**: Faculty members are expected to stay informed about technological advancements, particularly those that students might use for cheating and forgery. They should have the ability to employ generative artificial intelligence applications in the educational process to support students, organize their learning, and deepen their understanding of educational content— not just for copying and pasting without engaging in critical thinking and putting in the necessary effort.
C. **Supporting and Assisting Students**: Faculty members should remember that students are present in the classroom to learn effectively and to engage positively in their roles. This means that the instructor's role should be one of facilitation, support, guidance, and monitoring, rather than performing tasks that students are expected to complete themselves. Such an approach hinders students from experiencing genuine learning that prepares them for the future.

4. Academic Integrity at the Student Level

To promote academic integrity among students, they must adhere to the following:

A. **Self-Reliance**: It is essential for students to independently complete the tasks required of them, whether in the classroom or outside of it, using digital applications or not. This self-reliance is crucial for enhancing academic integrity.
B. **Values internalization**: Achieving this trait may be challenging and requires consistent and organized effort. Nonetheless, students must develop a self-motivated commitment to uphold the values of academic integrity, reflected in their real-world behavior. They should cultivate a strong belief that their interests lie in taking responsibility and adhering to academic codes of conduct, driven by intrinsic motivation and self-regulation rather than institutional oversight.
C. **Beneficial Utilization of Digital Technology**: Students should leverage digital technology, including generative artificial intelligence applications, to enhance and deepen their understanding, transforming themselves from passive recipients of knowledge into active producers. They should shift from being mere imitators to becoming critical thinkers.

Last, but not least, amidst this immense technological advancement, higher education institutions must recognize their role in benefiting from the innovations of the electronic revolution to mitigate the negative effects arising from internet applications, particularly generative artificial intelligence, on academic integrity. In this regard, higher education institutions are left with one of three options: either to completely prohibit the use of these applications, ignoring the negative consequences of such a ban; or to allow unrestricted use, ignoring the massive damage caused by the misuse of these applications on academic integrity; or to regulate this use and monitor it in a way that benefits students, academics, and researchers, within a general framework based on systems, laws, and restrictions that everyone adheres to. Believing in adopting the third option, I think that academic integrity is highly maintained if we apply it correctly and adhere to the agreed-upon laws, systems, and codes of conduct.

THE CONCLUSION

As mentioned earlier, at its core, academic integrity is represented by six basic values: honesty, trust, fairness, respect, responsibility, and courage. These six values should guide individuals' and institutions' behaviors to validate ethical practices and fruitful contributions to teaching, learning and researching. For instance, honesty means that both students, teachers and researchers should objectively recourse to original sources and provide scientific, rational, and logical justification for any single idea they present. To enhance trust, mutual understanding, logical expectations and transparency should be adopted by all. Effective and clear policies with open communication promote trust among all members of the educational institution. Fairness requires educational institutions to treat all equally and apply rules consistently in an open-minded manner. Respect means listening to others more than respectfully addressing them and acknowledging their values and ideas. Finally, I think all should be courageous to frankly defend truth and integrity when corrupted institutions or individuals behave dishonestly.

Palestinian higher education institutions may provide a basis for academic integrity at the institutional level. To provide a clear framework for moral academic behavior, institutions should create regulations that are consistent with their vision and goal. It is necessary to set up systems for identifying wrongdoing, such as generative AI tools and plagiarism detection software. To train teachers and students in moral technology usage while upholding cultural, moral, and religious principles, digital citizenship should be institutionalized. Campaigns to raise awareness among university communities and the general public may highlight how crucial academic integrity is to developing responsible, enterprising people. While tackling new issues, regular reviews of policies, instructional strategies, and evaluation instruments may guarantee alignment with technology developments. To encourage comprehension and adoption of ethical practices, institutions should also set up training sessions, cultivate multidisciplinary relationships, and furnish classrooms and labs with the tools they need. Preventing academic dishonesty also requires addressing faculty members' lack of digital literacy and implementing alternate evaluation methods.

Faculty members are essential in promoting academic integrity. Since it entails a dedication to ongoing development through the updating of course materials, the adoption of creative teaching strategies, and the responsible integration of technology, self-honesty is essential for professors. To improve learning, faculty should employ generative AI technologies that prioritize deeper comprehension and critical thinking over rote job fulfillment. Teachers also need to take on the role of mentors, encouraging students to actively participate in their education while offering them support, direction, and critical criticism. Internalizing the values of academic integrity by all students is vital since it enhances self-esteem and self-regulation. This will enable students to reflect on their values and morals in the

Students also should have their responsibilities in enhancing academic integrity. They should depend on themselves and accomplish their academic work and duties autonomously and independently. So, they should use technology constructively through deep learning that helps them widen their knowledge by using AI apps as tools to deepen and enrich their understanding.

To mitigate academic misconduct, preventive measures should be enforced on all involved in the process of teaching and learning. Students for example should be equipped with ethical issues needed for them to be honest instead of cheating. Updating academic integrity policies is of paramount importance from time to time. Teachers and students should be involved in regular training sessions that aim at promoting academic integrity.

It recommended that AI app designers take 21st-century skills and CEFR (Common European Framework of Reference for Languages) scale into account while creating/developing these apps.

In conclusion, enhancing a culture of academic integrity needs constant efforts by all stakeholders. By prioritizing basic values, applying institutional strategies and measures and raising individuals' accountability, a culture of academic integrity can be created in all educational institutions. For example, an educational institution can establish a foundation for academic integrity and institutional responsibility. This foundation can arrange varied training courses and workshops to enhance academic integrity. I think putting an end to academic misconduct should be internationally addressed by creating strategic plans in collaboration with international higher education institutions.

REFERENCES

Aljumaily, M. (2024). The future of higher education and scientific research in the age of generative AI, University 4.0, and the metaverse. Retrieved from https://ae.linkedin.com/pulse/aljumaily-i7qpe

Alto, V. (2023). *Modern generative AI with ChatGPT and OpenAI models*. Packt.

Bell, E. (2023). *Generative AI: How it works, history, and pros and cons*. Investopedia.

East, J., & Donnelly, L. (2012). Taking responsibility for academic integrity: A collaborative teaching and learning design. *Journal of University Teaching & Learning Practice*, 9(3), 2. DOI: 10.53761/1.9.3.2

Hammel, B. (2024). Digital citizenship: What is digital citizenship & how do you teach it? *iCEV.* Retrieved from https://www.icevonline.com/blog/what-is-digital-citizenship

International Center for Academic Integrity (ICAI). (2021). *The fundamental values of academic integrity* (3rd ed.). ISBN: 978-0-9914906-7-7 (pbk). Retrieved from https://academicintegrity.org/images/pdfs/20019_ICAI-Fundamental-Values_R12.pdf

Macfarlane, B., Zhang, J., & Pun, A. (2014). Academic integrity: A review of the literature. *Studies in Higher Education*, 39(2), 339–358. DOI: 10.1080/03075079.2012.709495

McCabe, D. L. (2004). *Ten principles of academic integrity: How faculty can foster student honesty*. Heldref Publications.

Mossberger, K., Tolbert, C. J., & McNeal, R. S. (2011). *Digital citizenship: The Internet, society, and participation*. The MIT Press.

Poth, R. D. (2023). Developing students' digital citizenship skills. *Edutopia*. Retrieved from https://www.edutopia.org/article/teaching-digital-citizenship-skills/

Ribble, M., & Bailey, G. (2007). *Digital citizenship in schools*. ISTE.

Robble, M. (2017). *Digital citizenship in schools: Nine elements all students should know*. International Society for Technology in Education.

Rodrigues, M. M. M., Silva, R., Borges, A., & Oliveira, C. (2023). Artificial intelligence: Threat or asset to academic integrity? A bibliometric analysis. *Kybernetes*. Advance online publication. DOI: 10.1108/K-09-2023-1666

Sari, I. N. (2023). Effectiveness of Implementing Synchronous and Asynchronous Blended E-Learning in Stunting Prevention and Treatment Training Programs. Jurnal Teknologi Pendidikan, April 2023, 25 (1), 101-106 DOI: http://dx.doi.org/ p-ISSN: 1411-2744 e-ISSN: 2620-3081DOI: 10.21009/JTP2001.6

Schmidt, E. D. (2016). The global challenge of academic integrity. *International Higher Education*, 87(87), 4–6. Advance online publication. DOI: 10.6017/ihe.2016.87.9494

Schuler, D. (2002). Digital cities and digital citizens. In *Digital Cities II: Computational and sociological approaches. Lecture Notes in Computer Science, 2362*, 71–85. DOI: 10.1007/3-540-45636-8_6

APPENDIX

The Questionnaire: English Version

Dear Professor,

I would be grateful if you participate in completing the attached questionnaire, which serves as one of the key instruments for gathering data for a chapter titled "**Digital Citizenship in the Age of AI in Higher Education Institutions: Academic Integrity & Institutional Responsibilities.**" This chapter will be part of the forthcoming book "***Digital Citizenship and the Future of AI: Engagement, Ethics, and Privacy***". The book aims to explore the multifaceted relationship between digital citizenship and the impact of artificial intelligence (AI), focusing on ethical behavior, privacy, and civic engagement. It seeks to provide an interdisciplinary framework grounded on both theoretical perspectives and real-world applications, emphasizing the need for ethical AI practices and enhanced digital literacy for fostering a responsible and inclusive future society. In particular, this chapter will investigate how academic integrity and institutional responsibility are perceived and practiced within Palestinian higher education institutions (HEIs) as viewed by faculty members at Palestine Ahliya University (PAU). Your responses will be invaluable, and the information provided will be used exclusively for scientific research purposes.

Thank you in advance for your time and invaluable assistance.

Author: Dr. Mahmoud Itmeizeh.

Demographic Information

1. Gender: a. Male b. Female
2. Faculty: ....
3. Years of Teaching Experience:
   a. Less than 5 years b. 5-10 years c. 11-20 years d. Over 20 years

1. What AI tools do your students use in their academic work?
2. How often do your students use AI tools?
   a. Frequently b. Occasionally c. Rarely d. Never
3. To what extent do you believe AI tools impact academic integrity negatively?
   a. High b. Medium c. Low
4. How often do you encounter issues related to academic dishonesty in your classes?
   a. Frequently b. Occasionally c. Rarely d. Never

5. Have you observed an increase in academic dishonesty linked to the use of AI tools by students?

   a. Yes b. No

   If yes, to what extent do you believe AI tools contribute to these issues?

   a. Very high b. High c. Medium d. Low e. Very low

4. What policies does the PAU administration currently use in addressing AI-related academic integrity issues?
5. How effective are the current policies at PAU in addressing AI-related academic integrity issues?

   a. Effective b. Somehow effective c. Ineffective

6. What additional policies, strategies or solutions do you suggest to enhance academic integrity at PAU in the context of AI?
7. What challenges do you face with enforcing academic integrity in the context of AI?
8. Do you have any additional comments or suggestions regarding AI and academic integrity at PAU?

Chapter 2
Access and Citizenship for Those With Disabilities:
Digitally Enabled Education and AI as a Bridge to Innovative Inclusion

Alan Bruce
https://orcid.org/0000-0002-3051-1528
Universal Learning Systems, Ireland

Lee Ann Williams
https://orcid.org/0009-0006-6884-0120
University of North Dakota, USA

ABSTRACT

This chapter explores the transformative potential of digital technologies and artificial intelligence (AI) in bridging the gap between learner needs and innovative inclusion for individuals with disabilities. This provides a comprehensive analysis of how such advancements contribute to access and citizenship by examining socio-historical contexts, current practices, and future implications. Neither disability nor advanced technologies exist in a vacuum. Powerful historical, social, and economic forces have shaped the development of both. In understanding the inter-relationship, it is critical to engage with a range of associated issues. Over the past two centuries, disability has been at the forefront of technological innovation and adaptation. Digital emancipation provides digital technologies that empower individuals with disabilities by providing new opportunities for learning, communication, and participation. Digital tools and platforms offer unprecedented levels of accessibility and flexibility.

DOI: 10.4018/979-8-3693-9015-3.ch002

1. THEMATIC INTRODUCTION AND OVERVIEW

This thematic introduction examines the historical exclusion and marginalization experienced by individuals with disabilities. It provides a detailed account of how these histories have shaped contemporary understanding of access, revealing the multifaceted nature of inclusion. By examining the impact of exclusion on various populations, the stage is set for understanding trajectories of inclusion and such progress as has been made in recent years. This background underpins discussion on how digital technologies and AI are poised to further enhance access and citizenship.

Histories of Exclusion and Marginalization

The long and complex histories of exclusion and marginalization faced by individuals with disabilities form the thematic basis of this chapter. Historically, societies have often relegated people with disabilities to the margins, reflecting broader societal attitudes and prejudices (Mackelprang & Salsgiver, 1996; Braddock & Parish, 2001; Lester & O'Reilly, 2021). While perspectives on human rights and individual dignity have had a profound influence on movements for redress and inclusion regarding ethnic difference, gender, sexual orientation, religious belief, and cultural difference, they have not been as prominent in the discourse regarding disability until recent years (Degener, 2016; Quinn & Degener, 2002; Kayness & French, 2008; Stein & Stein, 2022). Partly this is explained by the extraordinary levels of fear, ignorance, and medicalization which attended consideration of disability, a "place apart" in the pantheon of human exclusion (Lieffers, 2024; Stiker, 2019). However, it has also been due to deep levels of institutionalization, charity, quasi-religious appropriation, and the parallel models of care and dependence which arose from these contexts (Oliver,1996; Amponsah, 2013; Marini, et al, 2023; Smart, 2019). Such mindsets made the central policy drive of rehabilitative endeavor (if it even existed) center around normalization or mainstreaming rather than adapting the external environment to the needs, expectations, and rights of those labelled as different.

In many societies, disabilities were often perceived through a lens of pity or fear rather than understanding (Breen, et al, 2024; Smart, 2019). Individuals with disabilities were sometimes deemed incapable or less valuable, leading to systemic discrimination (Breen & Forwell, 2023). Institutions such as asylums, which were designed to isolate and control rather than support and integrate, became symbols of this exclusionary approach (Burns, 2018; Houston, 2020). In many cases, marginalization was compounded by inadequate or non-existent legal protections and societal supports (Bartlett & Wright, 1999; Kaliski, 2017; Malathouni, 2020; Rotoli, et al., 2023).

Understanding Access in All Its Dimensions

Social exclusion implies both a *structure* and a *process* in the ordering of human relations (DeWilde, 2003). As a structure, social exclusion relates to unequal levels of ownership of resources, unequal levels of opportunity and unequal levels of privilege and status in accessing goods, services or information (Room, 2006; Sen, 2000). As a process, social exclusion is concerned with categories that historically may vary but are, in whatever form, denied full participation and equality (Silver, 2007). As a process, it is also further concerned with the forces and groups that, for whatever reason, implement and maintain exclusion.

Social exclusion concerns itself with:

- Groups that can be defined as excluded
- The nature of the exclusion experienced
- The attitudes of those who maintain exclusionary practices
- The knowledge, skills and attitudes of officials in developing policies in these areas
- The body of knowledge and practice regarding equality legislation and practice.

Two issues emerge strongly from this. One is the question of *equality of opportunity*. Embedded firmly in the thinking and values of the French Revolution, equality as a concept has been a highly contentious issue in Europe ever since (Censer, 2019). From Napoleon to Thatcher, equality has been often derided and demeaned as a concept. From securing the franchise to ensuring a documented Bill of Rights in Northern Ireland, equality has been at the coalface of resistance and opposition from vested social interests. In the United States there is a richer tradition of acceptance and assertion of rights but a corresponding marginalization of the need to accept any underlying a priori equal status between human beings, except in the context of the obligations of citizenship. Equality should not be seen therefore as axiomatic and widely accepted in all western societies (Wolff, 2014).

Second is the question of the *norm* against which exclusion is judged. In charting poor levels of access for those experiencing social exclusion, European Union policy, for example, refers constantly to 'average' persons. In a context where the average is never defined or the normal spelled out, it is difficult to see social exclusion as anything other than that which is variably defined at any one time by individuals and structures which envisage themselves as average or normal (The Social Norms Learning Collaborative, 2021). Clearly this value-ridden concept is less than useful. The norm clearly does not refer to a statistical average (Fuentes, 2014). Nor does it refer to a historical constant. Its very use excludes. Its very use contains the bias against which equality approaches must engage.

It can be assumed that average refers to white, male, urban, able-bodied, young and educated people. However, this is only an assumption. What is important is that conceptual clarity needs to be employed from the outset in approaching issues around social exclusion (Jehoel-Gijbers & Vrooman, 2007). A rigorous analysis of the existing conditions and characteristics of the presenting society is required to make sense of any discrimination in practice and the attitudes underlying this that undoubtedly exists.

This new open and competitive environment means that the emphasis on quality and transparency becomes more important than ever. It is incumbent on professionals and agencies to understand the structures, objectives and terminology. It is also important to have a strategic sense of the wider environment of social exclusion. Individual sectors experiencing exclusion will more and more have to engage with other sectors and groups marginalized by the attitudes and prejudices of "mainstream" society to develop networks and generic models of practice (Mitchell, et al., 2021).

In a profoundly altered global learning environment there will be a need for educational policy makers to be alert and responsive (Scheunpflug, 2021). This does not apply merely to securing additional funding. It applies even more so to the opportunities for innovative educational project developments and linkages that can maximize the benefit and learning of social inclusion related activities within a community development model (Ainscow, 1999). Social exclusion is now central to the debate about the direction of social policy. It is clear from what has been reviewed that it does not have a distinct definition – or rather that its definitions can vary from setting to setting. As a result, there is often confusion about the exact meaning of social exclusion (Silver, 2007).

Some are dismissive, suggesting that it is simply old-fashioned concern about the poor dressed up in fancy garb (Redmond, et al., 2024). In one sense, they are right: social exclusion is tied to the past. To suggest otherwise would be to devalue the commitment of previous generations to reducing poverty and inequality as well as expanding democracy. At the same time, it would be misleading to view it as simply a new veneer on old problems. 'Social exclusion' is also contemporary, even forward-looking, as it is used to emphasise that changes in economic and social life have rendered old remedies to social problems less effective, if not obsolete (Alemanji, et al., 2022; Wesselmann, et al., 2016). New times have brought different forms of poverty and inequality, requiring modern solutions. It places equal emphasis – as we have seen – on the dynamic or rationale of the 'excluder' as much as the conditions of the 'excluded'.

By social exclusion we mean not just a static snapshot of inequality. What is also meant and implied is a set of *processes,* within both the labour market and national welfare systems, by which individuals, households, communities or even whole social groups are pushed towards or kept within the margins of society. It encompasses not only material deprivation but, more broadly, the denial of opportunities to participate fully in social and educational life. It is associated with stigmatisation and stereotyping (Cedeno, 2023). At first sight, paradoxically, some of those who experience exclusion even develop survival strategies which are premised upon its continuance. Finally, it highlights the primary responsibility of the wider society for the condition of its marginal members, of the need for all to share equally in the fruits of citizenship.

In this section we have seen that, whatever definition is employed, the process of social inclusion is intimately linked to three themes:

- Equality
- Lifelong learning
- Democracy.

To address and remedy exclusion, it is crucial to understand access in its multifaceted dimensions. Access encompasses more than just physical entry to spaces (Fitzsimons, 2017; Sterkenburg, et al., 2022; UND Today, 2024). It also includes cognitive, social, technological, and economic dimensions. Physical access refers to the ability to enter and use buildings, transport, and public spaces (United Nations, 2006; United Nations, 2015; U.N. *Disability Inclusion Strategy*, 2021). Cognitive access ensuring that information and communications are available in formats understandable to everyone (CDC, 2024; Federal Communication Commission, 2016). Social access pertains to the inclusion of individuals in community, social and educational activities, both in objective and subjective dimensions (not perceiving discrimination for example) (Bruce, 2024; Wilson, et al, 2016; Perrin, 2019; Stancliffe & Hall, 2023). Economic access involves opportunities for adequate financial resources, stability and independence.

Understanding these dimensions highlights that access is not a one-size-fits-all concept but requires tailored approaches to meet diverse needs (Marme & Bruce, 2014; Bruce, 2021). For example, a ramp or elevator may address physical access, but accessible digital content and support services are necessary for cognitive and social inclusion. Addressing access in all dimensions creates environments where people with disabilities have the potential to participate and engage fully (Badawy, et al., 2020; Department for International Development, 2018; Fleming, et al, 2024).

The changes that have swept the world of disability and professional rehabilitation in recent decades have also drawn explicitly on models of civil rights and legal redress for dealing with any discrimination experienced (Bruce, 2021; Perachoriti, 2002; United Nations, 2006; Welch & Palames, 2015). This process, by no means completed, has re-appropriate work and employment as a measure of inclusion rather than as a mere mechanism to secure recovery. In this dynamic, disability has reasserted its right to redefine work in terms of what benefits it can bring to those with disabilities rather than as an externally determined construct into which people must be obliged to fit (Aksnes & Ulstein, 2024; International Labour Organization, 2019).

Social Justice and Impact on Disability

Social justice conceptually emerges from the struggles of countess individuals and groups for recognition, respect, and equitable distribution of resources (Khechen, 2013). It links powerfully to two other dimensions, that of human rights and that of advocating remedial measures to contain and reverse injustice (Miller, 1999). Classically we can define four principles of social justice:

- Equity
- Access
- Participation
- Rights.

Linking to social justice means a new emphasis on histories of oppression and containment that have shaped the contours of the experience of disability (Mladenov, 2016). It means forging links internally within the disability sector, such as those between intellectual disabilities and physical ones, or psychiatric disability and sensory (Cross & McWay, 2023; Ee, et al., 2020; World Health Organization, 2022). This is not to conflate or minimize the specific impairment categories. Rather it is to recognize the common experiences endured by those labelled disabled in their efforts to be accepted, integrated, valued, and responded to as autonomous human beings with equal rights (United Nations, 2006; United Nations 2016).

The Impact of Exclusion on Specific Populations

The impact of exclusion on individuals with disabilities is profound and multifaceted (Berkman & Glass, 2000; Horne-Shuttleworth, et al., 2024; Liamputtong & Rice, 2024). Exclusion can lead to reduced quality of life, limited opportunities for education and employment, and diminished social participation (Davey & Gordon, 2023; Freedman, et al., 2016; Hall, et al., 2019). For specific populations within the disability community (like those with sensory impairments, cognitive disabilities, or chronic health conditions) the impact of exclusion can be even more severe due to compounded barriers and social stigmas (Huang, et al., 2024; Timpe, 2022). These challenges are not uniform but are shaped by intersecting factors that amplify inequities, revealing the urgent need for targeted and inclusive strategies.

The intersectionality of disability with factors such as gender, ethnicity, age, and socioeconomic status magnifies the barriers to inclusion, creating complex layers of disadvantage across different global contexts (Bixby, 2024; Brown et al, 2022; Pettinicchio, et al., 2022) . Women with disabilities, for instance, face compounded discrimination in many parts of the world, where cultural norms and systemic gender inequalities limit their access to education, healthcare, and employment opportunities (Matin, et al., 2021). In lower-income countries, this intersection often leaves women with disabilities disproportionately affected by poverty and excluded from development initiatives (Chan & Hutchings, 2023) Similarly, ethnic minorities with disabilities frequently encounter structural inequities, such as limited access to culturally appropriate services or heightened exposure to discrimination, perpetuating cycles of exclusion and economic vulnerability (Greaux, et al., 2023; Hoagland & Kipping, 2024; Mezzina, et al., 2022).

Globally, age and socioeconomic status further deepen the disparities. Older adults with disabilities in both developed and developing nations often experience systemic neglect, lacking access to age-appropriate care, assistive technologies, or social safety nets, which leaves them particularly vulnerable to poverty and isolation (Tabin, et al., 2024; The Lancet Public Health, 2021; World Health Organization, n.d.). Children with disabilities, particularly in low- and middle-income countries, face significant barriers to education due to inadequate resources, stigma, and inaccessible infrastructure, which severely limits their potential to escape cycles of marginalization (Kamiya, 2021; Thota et al., 2023) These challenges are further exacerbated in humanitarian crises, where individuals with disabilities, especially those from marginalized backgrounds, are often excluded from disaster relief and recovery efforts (Mendis, et al., 2023).Economic consequences are serious, as exclusion often results in reduced employment opportunities and significant income disparities (Bonaccio, et al., 2020; Praslova, 2023; Qiu, et al., 2023). Educational exclusion prevents individuals from acquiring necessary skills, knowledge and attitudes thus perpetuating vicious circles of disadvantage (Tarabini, et al, 2017; White & Cooper, 2013, UNESCO, 2003). By understanding such impacts, the need for comprehensive strategies to promote inclusion and address specific barriers faced by different groups with disability is more clearly demonstrated. Recognizing the global dimensions of these intersecting challenges underscores the need for comprehensive, culturally informed strategies to dismantle barriers and promote inclusion. Efforts must prioritize equitable resource distribution, strengthen international frameworks for disability rights, and address the systemic biases that amplify disadvantages, ensuring that all individuals, regardless of intersecting identities, can fully participate and thrive in society.

Trajectories of Inclusion for Those With Disabilities

Trajectories of inclusion concern historical and ongoing efforts to integrate individuals with disabilities into all dimensions of society with a view to full social, educational, vocational and economic participation (Saran et al., 2023; United Nations, 2006). These illustrate progress and developments over time, from the early days of institutionalization and segregation to more recent advancements in rights, access and independent living (Fox & Marini, 2024; Marini et al., 2024). Historically, the dominant model was institutional care, with little or no emphasis on community integration or human rights (Livneh, 2012; Marini, 2024). The mid-20th century saw the emergence of disability rights movements that advocated for civil rights and improved public awareness. Landmark legislation, such as the *Americans with Disabilities Act* (ADA – 1990) in the United States and the *Equality Act* (1990) in Ireland, marked significant milestones, establishing legal frameworks for non-discrimination, redress and inclusion.

In recent decades, the focus has shifted towards promoting universal design, inclusive education, and digital accessibility (International Disability Alliance, 2021). Efforts are increasingly centered on removing barriers to participation and ensuring that technology and educational practices are inclusive (Deroncele-Acosta & Ellis, 2024). The inclusion trajectory continues to evolve with advances in technology, social attitudes, and policy frameworks, reflecting ongoing efforts to achieve a fully inclusive society where individuals with disabilities can participate on equal terms (Haug, 2017, Mackelprang, et al., 2021; UN News, 2024).

2. THE VOYAGE TO CITIZENSHIP

Struggle and Empowerment Within Disability Communities

The voyage to citizenship for individuals with disabilities is marked by profound struggles for recognition, rights, and empowerment (Degener & Begg, 2017). Historically, disability communities have faced significant barriers to full participation in society: social stigma, prejudice, systemic discrimination, and limited access to resources (Balcazar, et al., 2023; Mitchell, et al, 2021; Mulcahy, et al., 2022). Despite these challenges, disability advocacy and grassroots activism have played a key role in challenging injustices and advocating for change (Evans, 2022; Griffiths,

2024; Pineda & Catalano, 2023; Sachs, 2003). Through grassroots efforts, people with disabilities have organized protests, formed advocacy groups, and engaged in political lobbying to address inequities and promote their rights. Activists and advocates have worked tirelessly to raise awareness, shift public perceptions, and demand policy changes (Mustaniemi-Laakso, et al., 2022).

The fact remains that in the special environment of segregated education, significant innovation occurred (Disabled But Not Really, 2024). This resulted from an open attitude of curiosity on how potential could be reached rather than a condemnatory approach of how difference could be contained. Communicative innovation was developed, particularly in and for the deaf community. Use of Sign, enhanced technologies and the growing acceptance of deaf culture were hallmarks of a changed environment (Constantinou, et al, 2020). In the world of visual impairment, the process of integration has been profound with major impacts on mainstream education through development of speech activated software and other advanced digital technologies (McNicholl, et al., 2019). Product design and modification have been driven by the experience of physical disability and the need to make adaptations to meet human needs, not the other way around (Aniyamuzaala, 2023). Closely associated have been the extraordinary advances occasioned by military dimensions and rehabilitation especially since World War II (Pasquina & Shero, 2016). A key outcome has been the development of Universal Design approaches and, since 1985, the evolution of UDL – Universal Design for Learning.

A number of observations and some preliminary conclusions can be made from this cursory overview of the history of specialized education. The struggle against segregation mirrored, and in some cases imitated, other struggles against racist segregation and discrimination against minorities, women and migrants (Elder, et al., 2021). Specialized schooling was not simply a uniform desert of abuse. It was also a laboratory of hope and raised expectations in the midst of a profoundly discriminatory external environment. Extraordinary insights and techniques were developed rooted in a sense of scientific observation and open and accepting humanity. Specialist perspectives were frequently a hotbed of innovation as seen, for example, in the pedagogy, technology, independent living, vocational rehabilitation services pioneered in the University of Illinois (Shreve, 2011). Linkage between civil rights struggles for citizens with disabilities and other groups demonstrates that inclusion cuts both ways: access for one requires total change on the part of the other.

Demonization of past practices is in many cases understandable because of the egregious abuses experienced and witnessed. But past inadequacies must be related to the contexts of the time. History is neither neat nor linear. Experiments in special education explicitly referenced the need to find emancipatory approaches and to challenge the low expectations prevalent in existing society (Galloway, 2012). Processes and procedures were experimental, limited by available technologies and surrounded by values and assumptions which are no longer dominant. There is a rich tradition of options and alternatives but remaining a critical need to probe contexts related to the socio-economic milieu. That milieu determined dependency and subjugation - its contours remain powerfully present.

The real discourse in education for marginalized groups and populations remains located between Access and Citizenship (Slee & Tait, 2022). Access denied is the same as rights denied. Opening access is the first step in an emancipatory process (Richmond, 2022). The essential issue is, however, a clear assertion of the importance of equal citizenship. Citizenship takes access from being present to active participation (Council of Europe, 2012). This remains the critical determinant today in the rights of people with disabilities. In a similar sector it is also evident – among migrants and refugees. And many of our educational interventions for migrants today echo those patronizing approaches of the nineteenth century – a profound rejection masked by a token sense of educating them to be "like us", assimilated, tame and powerless. Invisible echoes of a past denied (Fejes, et al., 2022).

Specialized education and specialized interventions are things that act as a bridge – not just transmitting information and knowledge to learners but enabling learners to contribute and influence the world and society of which they are part. That is the emancipatory dialectic that lies at the heart of special education pioneers from the eighteenth century on.

Legislation and Policy: Securing Rights

Legislation and policy have advanced rights of citizens with disabilities in their journey towards full citizenship (The White House, 2021). Key legislative milestones have established legal protections and frameworks for inclusion. One of the most significant legislative achievements in this regard is the *Americans with Disabilities Act (ADA),* enacted in 1990. The ADA represents a landmark shift in the legal landscape, prohibiting discrimination on the basis of disability and mandating equal access to public services, employment, and education (Americans with Disabilities Act, 1990). The ADA has been a crucial tool in promoting accessibility and providing individuals with disabilities the legal recourse to challenge discrimination (Nguyen-Finn, 2024).

In addition to the ADA, other important legislative measures have contributed to this journey. For example, the *Individuals with Disabilities Education Act* (IDEA) in the United States mandates that children with disabilities receive free and appropriate public education tailored to their needs (U.S. Department of Education, 2004). Powerful equality rights legislation in Ireland and EU initiatives on equal participation have contributed to global initiatives on disability rights and inclusion (European Commission, 2020).

Professional interventions and advocacy efforts play a critical role in supporting individuals with disabilities and facilitating their journey to citizenship (Mitus & Levine, 2021). These interventions often involve a range of services designed to address the diverse needs of individuals with disabilities, including legal support, educational and vocational guidance, and social services (Rawlins-Williams & Oswald, 2025). Advocacy organizations and professionals work to ensure that individuals with disabilities have access to necessary resources and support (National Institute for Health and Care Excellence (NICE), 2022). This includes legal advocacy to protect rights, career counseling to assist with employment, and social services to address various aspects of daily living (Herbert, 2016). These efforts are essential in helping individuals navigate complex systems and overcome barriers to full participation.

Role of Vocational Rehabilitation

Vocational rehabilitation programs are also a key component (Pruett, et al., 2008). These programs offer a range of services, including job training, career counseling, and placement assistance, tailored to the specific needs of individuals with disabilities (Bolton & Akridge, 1995; Bolton, et al., 2000; Lustig, et al., 2002). Successful vocational rehabilitation programs not only assist individuals in securing employment but also contribute to their overall empowerment and self-sufficiency. By providing the tools and support needed to navigate the job market, these programs play a crucial role in facilitating the broader goals of inclusion and equality (Blessing, et al., 2012).

Issues around disability are universal. However, professional responses are conditioned by national laws, traditions, and structures. For many decades, the U.S. tradition (based on vocational integration, accommodation, and robust advocacy and supported by a wealth of academic, research, and educational resources) led the world. This tradition has in recent decades been undermined by an excessive structural complexity, increasingly isolationist outlook, fragmentation of service and educational provision, and an inability or unwillingness (or both) to engage with significant international emerging trends. The professional crisis of identity could not come at a worse time for those with disabilities who are living through an unprecedented assault on services, resources, and values (Patterson, 2008; Mak, et al., 2022). In a cultural environment where entitlements are replaced by allocated perks, where charity re-emerges in place of social guarantees, it is deeply disturbing that rehabilitation professionals remain shackled by a sense of uncertainty about their identity and core value system.

The emerging community-based model for rehabilitation counselling (Millington, 2016; Millington & Marini, 2015) aligns the profession with the social justice paradigm of the UN *Convention on the Rights of Persons with Disabilities,* the vision of the WHO *Global Disability Action Plan*, the principles of *Community-Based Rehabilitation* (CBR), and the epistemology of the *International Classification of Function* (ICF). This shift away from the traditional U.S. model opens the door for an evidence-based and culturally responsive international identity for rehabilitation counselling with a legitimate role among community-based care providers worldwide.

Best practice for Rehabilitation Counsellor (RC) education is founded upon an ethos of social justice (Levine, et al., 2023). This is framed by community, disciplined by rigorous social science and experiential learning, legitimated by a growing body of evidence and advanced by innovations inspired by the fundamental mission of full community inclusion for people with disabilities. If community inclusion is the fundamental mission of the profession, then the community must be included in the design of the system that produces the professional (Salzer, 2021).

The Rehabilitation Counselling Discipline at the University of Sydney has developed a strategy for fundamental curriculum change that is realigning professional student education. The process has been designed to:

(a) capture the universal standards that define the profession of rehabilitation counselling (as they should be rather than as they presently are)
(b) facilitate culturally responsive expression of those standards within the curriculum
(c) encourage culturally appropriate specializations beyond the standards
(d) install a system for continuously improving and innovating experiential learning and curriculum in pursuit of best local practice and evidence.

In the training, professional development and deployment of people working within rehabilitation and disability, a new matrix of active social justice is needed (Marmé & Bruce, 2014; Perrin, 2019). This means developing an informed and critical understanding regarding structures of inequality. It also means developing competence in learning how to respond to inequity and to develop associated professional skills to support and implement change. Revisiting conceptual and academic frameworks helps to understand discrimination in equipping professionals to provide meaningful interventions to support rights-based trajectories.

Illustrating Ongoing Efforts

The voyage to citizenship for people with disabilities is characterized by ongoing efforts to secure equal rights and opportunities. While significant progress has been made, challenges remain. Continued advocacy is essential to address emerging issues and evolving needs (Suarez-Balcazar, et al., 2023). This journey involves a dynamic interplay between legislation, advocacy, and personal empowerment. Each element contributes to the broader goal of achieving full inclusion and participation for individuals with disabilities. Through legislative advancements, professional support, and advocacy, the journey towards citizenship continues to evolve.

3. ADDRESSING EDUCATIONAL INCLUSION

Legacies of Segregated Special Education Systems

Educational inclusion has evolved significantly, moving from institutionalized segregated special education systems to more integrated and inclusive ones (Boroson, 2017; Smith, 2022; Tomasello, et al, 2024). Historically, students with disabilities were often placed in separate institutions, isolated from their mainstream peers (Dudley-Marling & Burns, 2014). These segregated settings based their justification on the belief that students with disabilities were inferior, incapable of learning and defective (Winzer, 1993). Initially intended to provide asylum or specialized support, segregated systems evolved into rigid systems of control, disempowerment and even medical experimentation and control (Jaffee, 2022). Students with disabilities missed out on opportunities for peer interaction, exposure to diverse perspectives, and participation in general education curricula (Fisher & Meyer, 2002; Burstein, et al., 2004; Salend & Duhaney, 1999). Such separation perpetuated stigmatization and reinforced notions that disability was inherently incompatible with mainstream education emphasizing separation rather than integration.

Special education emerged in the 19th century as a response to the recognition that certain students required tailored instruction to meet their unique needs (Smith, 1998) . This period saw the establishment of specialized schools and programs designed to provide education to students with disabilities who had been previously excluded from any form of mainstream education (Winzer, 2009). Key figures in this movement included Édouard Séguin, who advocated for individualized education plans, and Samuel Gridley Howe, who founded the Perkins School for the Blind. These early efforts were driven by a humanitarian impulse to provide access to education for all children, regardless of their abilities (Gargiulo & Bouck, 2021).

At its inception in the early nineteenth century, leaders of social change set out to cure many ills of society. Physicians and clergy, including Jean-Marc-Gaspard Itard (1775–1838), Edouard O. Seguin (1812–1880), Samuel Gridley Howe (1801–1876), and Thomas Hopkins Gallaudet (1787–1851), wanted to ameliorate the neglectful, often abusive and exploitive treatment of individuals with disabilities. A rich literature describes the treatment provided to individuals with disabilities at this time who were often confined in prisons and almshouses, lacking decent food, clothing, personal hygiene, and exercise (Nelson, 2021; Roth, 2018; Rothman, 2017). During much of the nineteenth century, and early in the twentieth, professionals believed individuals with disabilities were best treated in residential facilities in rural environments. Advocates of these institutions argued that environmental conditions such as urban poverty and associated vices induced behavioral problems (Friend, 2022).

Reformers such as Dorothea Dix (1802–1887) prevailed upon state governments to provide funds for bigger and more specialized institutions (Fox & Marini, 2024). These facilities focused more on a particular disability, such as intellectual disability (known at the time as “feeble-mindedness”, “retardation” or “idiocy”), mental illness (labeled “insanity” or “madness”), sensory impairment (deafness or blindness), and behavioral disorders such as criminality and juvenile delinquency. Children who were judged delinquent or aggressive, but not insane, were sent to *houses of refuge* or *reform schools.* Children and adults judged to be “mad” were consigned to psychiatric hospitals (Dix, 1843). Dix and her followers believed that institutionalization of individuals with disabilities would provide asylum and end the abuse endured (confinement without treatment in jails or poorhouses). Such institutions could also provide some form of care or treatment (Gollaher, 1995). ‘Moral treatment’ was the dominant approach of the early nineteenth century in psychiatric hospitals, the aim being eventual cure. Moral treatment employed methods analogous to today's occupational therapy, systematic instruction, and positive reinforcement (Evers, 2021). Evidence suggests this approach was often humane and effective, but the treatment was generally abandoned by the late nineteenth century, due largely to the failure of moral therapists to train others in their techniques and the belief that mental illness was largely a result of brain disease and had to be contained, controlled or medicated (Jutras, 2017).

Although State mandated special education is relatively new in the western world, modern special education practices can be traced to Itard, and his work marks the beginning of widespread attempts to instruct students with disabilities. In 1817 the first special education school in the United States, the *American Asylum for the Education and Instruction of the Deaf and Dumb* (now called the American School for the Deaf), was established in Hartford, Connecticut, by Gallaudet (Valentine, 1993). That school is still there and is one of the leading schools internationally for students with auditory disabilities and a pioneer in innovative research and development in technological applications to enhance communicative competence. However, the lasting success of the American School for the Deaf was the exception and not the rule. Rich traditions of research and amelioration were evidenced in Europe with the work of advanced educators from Rousseau in France, Edgeworth in Ireland and Louis Braille in France.

But translating good theories into practice in Europe was at best uneven and at worst profoundly discriminatory. Despite moves towards inclusive education, there have been ironies in application of innovation within traditional segregated frameworks (Blake, 2023). For example, while technology has advanced significantly and offers numerous tools designed to support diverse learning needs, these tools have sometimes been introduced within separate, special education settings rather than integrated into mainstream classrooms (Satterfield, 2016). This approach can create a dichotomy where technological advancements meant to enhance learning are confined to segregated environments, limiting their potential to benefit all students. Innovations such as assistive technologies, while providing valuable support, may inadvertently reinforce divides between students with disabilities and their peers (Ahmed, 2018). This paradox highlights the need for a more integrated approach where innovative practices are embedded within general education settings to ensure equitable access and benefits for all students.

Adaptive technologies play a crucial role in transforming learning environments for students with disabilities (Adeline, 2024). These technologies, ranging from text-to-speech software and screen readers to specialized communication devices and ergonomic tools, are designed to address specific needs and enhance accessibility (Kandati, et al., 2024). The impact of adaptive technologies extends beyond merely providing accommodations (Fernández-Batanero, et al., 2022). They enable students with disabilities to participate more fully in classroom activities, access educational materials, and demonstrate knowledge in ways that align with their strengths. By facilitating personalized learning experiences, adaptive technologies bridge gaps in access and support diverse learning needs. Teachers must be trained to effectively implement and support these technologies to maximize their benefits (Ahmed, 2020; Atanga, et al., 2020; Coleman et al., 2015)

Digital Emancipation

Digital emancipation provides an idea that digital technologies can empower individuals with disabilities by providing new opportunities for learning, communication, and participation. Digital tools and platforms offer unprecedented levels of accessibility and flexibility, allowing students with disabilities to engage with educational content and peers in ways previously unattainable (Polyviou, et al., 2021).

The interaction between technology and globalization creates new challenges but also new opportunities (Weisblat, 2019). Digitalization connects people, cities, countries and continents in ways that vastly increase both individual and collective potential. At its core, digitalization is a democratizing force. It is now possible to connect and collaborate with anyone (Manyika et al., 2016). But digitalization also has the ability to concentrate extraordinary power. Digitalization can make the smallest voice heard everywhere but can also quash individuality and cultural uniqueness. Digitalization can be incredibly empowering: the most influential companies over the past decade all started out with an idea, and they had the product before they had the financial resources and physical infrastructure for delivering that product.

(Council of Europe, 2024) But digitalization can also be disempowering, when people abandon their freedom for individual responsibility and critical thought in exchange for convenience and become reliant on the advice and decisions of computers.

Whatever about particular technologies or new methods, the characteristics of human learning remain driven by issues around motivation, skill acquisition, improved understanding and tangible benefit (Oudeyer, 2016). They also relate critically to power and ability to control one's own environment, needs, expectations, relationships and rewards (Cherry, 2023).

Digital emancipation is particularly significant in an era where technology plays an increasingly central role in education. The ability to access digital resources, participate in online learning, and engage with digital communities can transform the educational experience for students with disabilities.

Introduction of Universal Design for Learning (UDL)

Universal Design for Learning (UDL) represents a significant advancement in creating inclusive educational practices (Sewell, et al., 2022). UDL is an educational framework that emphasizes the design of flexible learning environments and materials that accommodate the diverse needs of all students (Bruckner & Nunn, 2023). By incorporating multiple means of representation, expression, and engagement, UDL aims to provide equitable access to learning opportunities and support diverse learning styles. From its origins in the built environment and enhanced accessibility for those with disabilities, Universal Design has extended as an operational philosophy into other areas and, most particularly, learning (Story, et al., 1998). While there is evidence that some UDL principles are being applied in policy and practice to a varying extent in some countries, it is still significantly undeveloped in Europe and, at a minimum, more implicit rather than explicit. The implementation of UDL involves creating curricula and teaching strategies adaptable to various needs and preferences (Cairns, et al., 2023).

The struggle against segregation mirrored, and in some cases imitated, other struggles against racist segregation and discrimination against minorities, women and migrants (Winzer, 2009). Specialist perspectives were frequently a hotbed of innovation as seen, for example, in the pedagogy, technology, independent living, and vocational rehabilitation services pioneered in the University of Illinois in Urbana-Champaign.

Recently critical voices have been raised about the reliability of UDL when applied to the entire population, largely because its contours bear strong resemblance to discredited theories of learning styles. As Gary Boysen wrote in 2021, human learning occurs according to standard principles, and both learning-style theories and UDL indicate that these principles are subject to individual differences. Educators can choose how much to emphasize shared human principles of learning and how much to emphasize learning differences. However, the assertion that education is more effective if it emphasizes diversity over universality is a hypothesis that can be empirically tested. In the case of learning styles, the hypothesized benefits of emphasizing diversity in learning style was not supported by research. The same may be true of UDL (Boysen, 2021). The key aspect is to recognize that UDL has its roots in the experience of disability and the strategy of the movement for inclusion for those with disabilities. As such, UDL is a powerful tool for this sector. But it may not be feasible or appropriate to extend this to other sectors of the population.

Considering UDL and higher education, Anthony Moss builds on this to advocate for a reconceptualization of UDL as a technique linked to more dynamic concepts such as trust, empathy and connection. Provided we do not see it as a wholesale solution, frameworks such as UDL can provide a key resource. 'Alongside efforts to decolonise courses and institutions, we can create learning environments where everyone feels included by design, not as an afterthought. This provides a foundation for students to feel connected, and for us to connect.' (Moss, 2022).

All this underlines the key shift in thinking and learning design that UDL can facilitate, when linked to disability but also to community, utility and applicability to the needs of learners everywhere. This creates a powerful basis for continuing efforts to promote inclusion and emancipatory learning. In our era of change and increasing risk, that is no small achievement.

4. INTEGRATING ADAPTIVE TECHNOLOGIES AND AI

Successful implementation of adaptive technologies and UDL requires ongoing training and professional development for educators (Theodorio, 2024). Teachers must be equipped with the knowledge, skills and attitudes to effectively integrate these tools and strategies into their teaching practices. This includes understanding the range of adaptive technologies available, learning how to incorporate UDL principles into lesson planning, and developing strategies for supporting diverse learners.

Professional development programs function best when they focus on practical, hands-on training to enable educators to apply new technologies and approaches in real-world classroom settings. Additionally, providing support and resources for educators to continuously refine their skills and stay updated on emerging technologies is essential for maintaining effective and inclusive teaching practices (James, 2024; OCED, 2020).

Evolving Educational Practices for Inclusion

The purpose of educational inclusion is to create learning environments that accommodate and support all students, regardless of their abilities. This involves moving away from segregated systems towards more integrated approaches that leverage innovations such as adaptive technologies, artificial intelligence, flexible assessment and UDL. By challenging legacies of segregation, questioning assumptions of accepted norms, asserting rights and embracing digital emancipation, educational inclusion creates the opportunities for systemic transformation. This can be achieved by investing in educator training, flexible educational practices, and promoting a more inclusive and equitable learning experience for hitherto excluded learners. This analysis highlights the importance of ongoing efforts to advance educational inclusion, ensuring that all students have opportunities to succeed and thrive in diverse, integrated and supportive learning environments (Akbar, et al., 2023).

Digital Citizenship and Disability: The Role of AI

Artificial Intelligence (AI) has the potential to significantly influence digital citizenship and inclusion for individuals with disabilities. The impact of AI can be viewed through two contrasting lenses: as a powerful tool for enhancing inclusion and accessibility, or as a mechanism that could perpetuate existing exclusions and inequalities (Krishnan & Kumar, 2024).

On one hand, AI can be a powerful ally in promoting digital inclusion. AI technologies, such as speech recognition, predictive text, and image recognition, can enhance accessibility by providing tailored support that meets the diverse needs of individuals with disabilities (Chalkiadakis, et al., 2024). For example, AI-powered tools can assist individuals with visual impairments by providing real-time audio descriptions of visual content or enabling voice commands for interaction. Similarly, AI-driven communication aids can help individuals with speech impairments by converting text to speech or facilitating alternative forms of communication.

However, there are concerns that AI might also reinforce existing power dynamics and inequalities. If AI systems are not designed with inclusive in mind, they may inadvertently perpetuate exclusion. For example, AI algorithms that are trained on biased data can produce outcomes that disadvantage individuals with disabilities or fail to accommodate their specific needs (Min, 2023). Additionally, the deployment of AI in ways that prioritize efficiency over accessibility can exacerbate digital divides and reinforce existing barriers.

Generative AI-based systems can support people with disabilities by fueling existing assistive technology ecosystems and robotics, learning, accommodation and accessibility solutions. Ultimately, Generative AI can empower broader health and assistive solutions (Zhang & Boulos, 2023). However, Generative AI also poses unique risks associated with transparency, understanding systems outcomes, cognitive silos, potential misinformation and manipulation, privacy and ownership. These rights and categories are underlined by AI-specific laws, such as the European AI Act, and digital frameworks, such as the EU Digital Market and Services Act, Accessibility Act and the Convention on the Rights of Persons with Disabilities.

Since the introduction of the EU AI Act and mirrored frameworks, policies and acts worldwide aim to categorize AI systems based on risks and related compliance frameworks. Generative AI systems became the most discussable category, not being related to the high-risk category, but still posing increased risks and breaches, especially for groups with disabilities and impairments (Stanford - Vienna Transatlantic Technology Law Forum, 2021)

Since then, governments and multilateral agencies, such as the Organisation for Economic Co-Operation and Development (OECD), the WHO and Unesco, with its Generative AI in education and research, worked on dedicated reports and sets of recommendations and guidelines to reflect the use of Generative AI in specific areas, such as education, healthcare, the workplace, related professional and user literacy and capacities to further improve the process of adoption. (Welker, 2023)

Concerns About Ownership and Autonomy

Ownership and autonomy are critical concerns in the context of AI and digital citizenship (Tariq & Sergio, 2025). The development and use of AI technologies can impact how individuals with disabilities engage with digital platforms and services, raising questions about control and self-determination.AI systems often require users to share personal data, which raises concerns about privacy and data security. For individuals with disabilities, the balance between benefiting from AI-driven support and maintaining control over their personal information is crucial. There is a risk that AI systems could exploit or misuse personal data, leading to concerns about surveillance, consent, and autonomy (Adeyeye, et al., 2024).

Design and implementation of AI systems can influence how much control individuals with disabilities have over their interactions with technology. AI tools designed without user input or lacking customization options may limit users' ability to tailor technology to their specific needs. Ensuring that individuals with disabilities have meaningful control over how AI technologies are used and how their data is managed is essential for promoting autonomy and protecting rights.

AI and Independent Living

One of the key promises of AI is its potential to support independent living for individuals with disabilities. AI technologies have the potential to enhance autonomy by providing assistance with daily activities, facilitating communication, and enabling greater participation in various aspects of life (Prunkl, 2024). Smart home technologies powered by AI can assist individuals with mobility impairments by enabling voice-activated controls for lighting, heating, and appliances. AI-driven personal assistants can help manage schedules, provide reminders, and facilitate access to information. These technologies empower individuals with disabilities to live more independently and socially participate more fully. However, the effectiveness of these technologies in supporting independent living depends on their design and implementation. AI tools must be accessible, user-friendly, and adaptable to individual needs to truly enhance independence. Additionally, there must be ongoing support and maintenance to ensure that these technologies remain effective and relevant as users' needs evolve.

Emancipatory Creativity Versus Subordination

AI can foster emancipatory creativity as it has the potential to enable individuals with disabilities to engage in creative expression and innovation in ways previously unimagined. AI tools can facilitate artistic creation, writing, and other forms of expression by providing adaptive interfaces and assisting with tasks that are difficult due to physical or cognitive limitations. Yet, there is a concern that AI could also reinforce subordination if used in ways that limit or control creative expression. If AI systems are designed with restrictive parameters or lack flexibility, they may constrain users' ability to explore and express their creativity freely. Ensuring that AI support does not limit creative potential requires thoughtful design prioritizing user agency and adaptability (Matias, 2024).

Designing AI to Address Specific Needs

The latest data from WHO shows that about 1.3 billion people worldwide live with some form of disability. In addressing challenges related to the inclusion of individuals with disabilities through the use of AI, it is important to examine potential concerns and identify specific areas of focus. An essential inquiry involves the manner in which society will harness AI to establish economic and social systems that are inclusive (Odun. As indicated by the International Labour Organization (ILO), individuals with disabilities encounter reduced involvement in the labor force, lack of access to vocational training, and biases in recruitment and career advancement.

A recent UNDP report found that only 5.8% of people with disabilities living in rural areas are employed. These challenges do originate from inherent restrictions but from intricate societal, legal, and economic settings.

Individuals with disabilities encounter barriers in both the private sector and education, such as inadequate school infrastructure and learning materials that do not meet their needs. In higher education, they face challenges like inaccessible campuses and unsupportive academic arrangements (Li, et al., 2024). Similarly, the healthcare sector and labor market present obstacles due to inaccessible physical infrastructures, reluctance to provide reasonable accommodations, and unconscious biases that hinder the full participation and inclusion of people with disabilities, ultimately limiting their opportunities (Blanck, et al., 2023).

In contributing to digital inclusion, AI systems must meet individual needs. This involves adopting inclusive design principles to ensure AI technologies are accessible, adaptable, and responsive to diverse requirements (Goodman, 2024). Inclusive design means developing AI systems that consider the full range of user needs from the outset, rather than as an afterthought. This includes involving individuals with disabilities in the design and testing processes to ensure that their perspectives and experiences inform the development of AI tools (Eziamaka, et al., 2024). It also means creating AI technologies that can be customized to meet individual preferences and needs, allowing users to tailor interactions and functionalities to their specific contexts.

To avoid pitfalls of increased subordination, AI developments need a commitment to equity and justice. This involves addressing biases in AI algorithms, ensuring transparency in how AI systems operate, and providing users with control. Developers and policymakers must work together to create frameworks that promote ethical AI practices and safeguard rights of individuals with disabilities (Khan, 2024). Effective AI applications for people with disabilities include using robotic process automation to assist neurodiverse individuals, utilizing exoskeletons for paraplegics, and implementing AI-powered recruitment and decision-making tools. These practical instances showcase AI's capability to improve accessibility and productivity. Despite the significant opportunities presented by AI, it is crucial to address challenges such as concerns about replacing human services and the implementation of poorly designed systems (Hafizov, 2023). By prioritizing ethical development and user-centered design, AI can significantly improve lives and promote accessibility.

One example of AI usage creating barriers for people with disabilities is in the area of voice recognition technology. Many AI systems rely on voice commands for operation, which can be challenging for individuals with speech disabilities or accents that are not easily understood by the technology (Esquivel, et al, 2024). Another example is in the realm of accessible websites and apps, where AI-powered content and features may not be designed with the needs of individuals with visual or motor impairments in mind, creating accessibility barriers (Silva, 2023). Additionally, AI-powered automated decision-making systems may unintentionally discriminate against people with disabilities by not accounting for their unique needs and circumstances.

The growing use of AI in the workplace requires reconsideration of the government's responsibility to guarantee fundamental welfare for everyone. Research has indicated significant job reductions in manufacturing as a result of automation, and AI is being utilized in recruitment across different sectors (Gordon, 2024). Safeguarding the inclusion and safety of individuals with disabilities in the AI era involves addressing societal prejudice and putting in place comprehensive ethical and regulatory protocols.

The impact of AI, especially machine learning-based AI, on people with disabilities is substantial (White, 2022). AI has the potential to address barriers and promote inclusivity but also poses risks of excluding individuals with disabilities from advancements. It is essential to engange persons with disabilities in designing AI solutions to maximize benefits and minimize risks, ensuring that AI's evolution supports inclusivity and accessibility.

5. CONCLUSIONS AND IMPLICATIONS

The role of Artificial Intelligence (AI) in digital citizenship and inclusion is both transformative and complex. AI offers significant potential to enhance accessibility and support independent living for individuals with disabilities through innovations like adaptive communication tools, intelligent personal assistants, and smart home systems. These technologies can empower users by addressing specific needs and promoting greater autonomy. However, this potential is accompanied by considerable challenges, including concerns about reinforcing existing inequalities, biases in algorithms, and issues related to data privacy and user control. To realize fully AI benefits, it is crucial to prioritize inclusive design, user autonomy, and ethical practices. Ensuring that AI technologies are developed with these principles in mind will help create more equitable digital environments and prevent the perpetuation of exclusion and discrimination. AI can be a powerful tool for promoting digital inclusion and empowering individuals with disabilities.

Lingering Questions and Power Dynamics

As AI continues to evolve, several key questions remain regarding its role in digital citizenship. One critical issue is whether AI functions as a lever for greater inclusion or as a means of control. The inherent power dynamics in AI systems can significantly impact how individuals with disabilities interact with technology. Unequal access to power and control further impacts how learners experience realities of inclusion or exclusion. Addressing these power dynamics is essential to ensure that AI promotes empowerment rather than reinforcing or increasing existing barriers.

The intersectionality of disability with other sectors (gender, ethnic origin, sexual orientation, age, cultural identity or class) develops a more dynamic understanding of the impact of AI on digital inclusion. AI systems need to be designed to account for intersecting identities and to avoid stereotypical and biased assumptions in their applied algorithms. Otherwise, existing inequalities can even be exacerbated. Inclusive design must consider cultural and linguistic diversity to ensure that AI technologies serve all users equitably. Recognizing and addressing intersectional issues is critical for developing more diverse, inclusive and impactful digital landscapes.

The need for continuous innovation and thoughtful implementation of AI technologies is paramount. Ongoing research, user feedback, and adaptive practices are necessary to address evolving needs to ensure that AI deployment is effective and inclusive. A commitment to inclusive design, user autonomy, and enforced ethical practices will help in developing AI systems with potential to foster genuine digital inclusion. By maintaining a proactive approach to innovation and implementation, the potential for AI to drive meaningful progress for individuals with disabilities can be fully realized.

This highlights the importance of a nuanced and comprehensive approach to digital citizenship and inclusion in the context of AI. It underscores both the potential of AI to effect positive change and the challenges to achieve true equality.

REFERENCES

Adeline, W. D. (2024). Adaptive learning technologies: Customizing education to individual needs. *Research Output Journal of Arts and Management*, 3(3), 1–6.

Adeyeye, O. J., Akanbi, I., Emeteveke, I., & Emehin, O. (2024). Leveraging secured AI-driven data analytics for cybersecurity: Safeguarding information and enhancing threat detection. *International Journal of Research and Publication and Reviews*, 5(10), 3208–3223. DOI: 10.55248/gengpi.5.1024.2911

Ahmed, A. (2018). Perceptions of using assistive technology for students with disabilities in the classroom. *International Journal of Special Education*, 33(1), 129–139.

Ahmed, A. (2020). Perceptions of Using Assistive Technology for Students with Disabilities in the Classroom. *International Journal of Special Education*, 33(1), 129–139.

Ainscow, M. (1999). *Understanding the development of inclusive schools*. Falmer Press.

Akbar, K., Syahmahita, H., Damanik, J., Akib, F., & Setyo, I. (2023). Inclusive Education Practices: Fostering an Accessible Learning Environment for Diverse Learners. *Global International Journal of Innovative Research*, 1(3), 227–232. DOI: 10.59613/global.v1i3.35

Aksnes, S. Y., & Ulstein, J. (2024). Sustainable employment for people with disabilities: A scoping review on workplace practices and positive employment outcomes. *Scandinavian Journal of Disability Research*, 26(1), 189–210. DOI: 10.16993/sjdr.1089

Alemanji, A. A., Meijer, C. M., Kwazema, M., & Benyah, F. E. K. (2023). *Contemporary discourses in social exclusion*. Palgrave Macmillan.

Americans with Disabilities Act of 1990, Public Law 101-336. 108th Congress, 2nd session (July 26, 1990).

Amponsah-Bediako, K. (2013). Relevance of disability models from the perspective of a developing country: An analysis. *Developing Country Studies, 3*(11), 121. Retrieved from https://core.ac.uk/download/pdf/234681343.pdf

Aniyamuzaala, J. R. (2023). Inclusion of Persons with Disabilities by Design: From Product Centered to Justice and Person-Centered Inclusive Co-Design. In Rioux, M. H., Viera, J., Buettgen, A., & Zubrow, E. (Eds.), *Handbook of Disability*. Springer. DOI: 10.1007/978-981-16-1278-7_51-1

Atanga, C., Jones, B. A., Krueger, L. E., & Lu, S. L. (2020). Teachers of Students w ith Learning Disabilities: Assistive Technology Knowledge, Perceptions, Interests, and Barriers. *Journal of Special Education Technology*, 35(4), 236–248. DOI: 10.1177/0162643419864858

Badawy, U. I., Jawabrah, M. Q., & Jaeada, D. E. A. (2020). Adaptation of accessibility for people with disabilities in private and public buildings using appropriate design checklist. *International Journal for Modern Trends in Science and Technology*, 6(6), 125–137. DOI: 10.46501/IJMTST060627

Bartlett, P., & Wright, D. (1999). *Outside the walls of the asylum: The history of care in the community 1750-2000*. Athlone Press.

Berkman, L., & Glass, T. (2000). Social integration, social networks, social support, and health. In Berkman, L., & Kawachi, I. (Eds.), *Social epidemiology* (pp. 137–173). Oxford University Press. DOI: 10.1093/oso/9780195083316.003.0007

Bixby, L. E. (2024). Interscetional inequalities: How socioeconomic well-being varies at the intersection of disability, gender, race, ethnicity and age. *Research in Social Stratification and Mobility*, 91(1), 100938. DOI: 10.1016/j.rssm.2024.100938

Blake, E. (2023). (Re)Imagining Inclusive Education: How Boundaries can Come to Matter More than Children Within Public Schools. *Interchange*, 54(4), 425–438. DOI: 10.1007/s10780-023-09503-w

Blanck, P., Hyseni, F., & Goodman, N. (2023). Economic inclusion and empowerment of people with disabilities. In Rioux, M. H., Viera, J., Buettgen, A., & Zubrow, E. (Eds.), *Handbook of Disability*. Springer Publishing., DOI: 10.1007/978-981-16-1278-7_81-1

Blessing, C. (2012). Vocational rehabilitation, inclusion, and social integration. In Kennedy, P. (Ed.), *The Oxford Handbook of Rehabilitation Psychology* (pp. 453–473). Oxford University Press. DOI: 10.1093/oxfordhb/9780199733989.013.0025

Bolton, B., & Akridge, R. L. (1995). A meta-analysis of skills training programs for rehabilitation clients. *Rehabilitation Counseling Bulletin*, 38, 262–273.

Bolton, B. F., Bellini, J. L., & Brookings, J. B. (2000). Predicting client employment outcomes from personal history, functional limitations, and rehabilitation services. *Rehabilitation Counseling Bulletin*, 44(1), 10–21. DOI: 10.1177/003435520004400103

Bonaccio, S., Connelly, C. E., Gellatly, I. R., Jetha, A., & Martin Ginis, K. A. (2020). The participation of people with disabilities in the workplace across the employment cycle: Employer concerns and research evidence. *Journal of Business and Psychology*, 35(2), 135–158. DOI: 10.1007/s10869-018-9602-5 PMID: 32269418

Boroson, B. (2017). Inclusive education: Lessons from history. *Educational Leadership*, 74(7), 18–23.

Braddock, D., & Parish, S. (2001). An institutional history of disability. In Albrecht, G. L., Seelman, K. D., & Bury, M. (Eds.), *Handbook of Disability Studies* (pp. 11–68). Sage Publications., DOI: 10.4135/9781412976251.n2

Breen, J. S., & Forwell, S. J. (2023). Models, theory and assumptions. In Breen, J. S., & Forwell, S. J. (Eds.), *Disability in the workplace: The politics of difference* (pp. 30–54). Routledge. DOI: 10.4324/9781003220695-4

Breen, J. S., Shiffman, V. J., & Forwell, S. J. (2024). Disability, pity, and the workplace. *Journal of Occupational Rehabilitation*. Advance online publication. DOI: 10.1007/s10926-024-10247-2 PMID: 39487909

Brown, R. L., Maroto, M. & Pettinicchio, D. (Eds.). (2022). The Oxford handbook of the sociology of disability. Oxford University Press. DOI: 10.1093/oxfordhb/9780190093167.013.49

Bruce, A. (2021). Disability at the crossroads: Asserting rights and empowerment in an unequal world. *Journal of Applied Rehabilitation Counseling*, 52(1), 5–17. Advance online publication. DOI: 10.1891/JARC-D-20-00028

Bruce, A. (2024a). Creativity, innovation and inclusion mythology: Voices from special education ghetto. In *Proceedings of theInternational Conference on the Future of Education* (pp. 1-8). Bologna, Italy: Filidiretto.

Bruce, A. (2024b). *From awareness to action: International best practice social justice and the evolving disability rights struggle*. Presentation for the University of North Dakota, Inaugural Disability Awareness Day. DOI: DOI: 10.13140/RG.2.2.16296.79367

Bruckner, S., & Nunn, N. (2023, April 27). Universal design for learning: Meeting the needs of diverse learners. *Education Development Center*. Retrieved from https://www.edc.org/universal-design-learning-meeting-needs-diverse-learners

Burns, T. (2018). Asylums and the origins of psychiatry. In *Psychiatry: A very short introduction* (2nd ed.). Oxford University Press. DOI: 10.1093/actrade/9780198826200.003.0002

Burstein, N., Sears, S., Wilcoxen, A., Cabello, B., & Spagna, M. (2004). Moving toward inclusive practices. *Remedial and Special Education*, 25(2), 104–116. DOI: 10.1177/07419325040250020501

Cairns, M., Kelly, S., Nelson, L. L., & Recabarren, C. (2023). Incorporating principles of UDL into education activities guidance note. *USAID.* Retrieved from https://www.usaid.gov/sites/default/files/documents/Incorporating_Principles_of_UDL_into_Education_Activities_Guidance_Note.pdf

Cedeño, D. (2023). Social Exclusion and Inclusion: A Social Work Perspective. *Families in Society*, 104(3), 332–343. DOI: 10.1177/10443894221147576

Censer, J. R. (2019). Intellectual history and the causes of the French Revolution. *Journal of Social History*, 52(3), 545–554. DOI: 10.1093/jsh/shy082

Centers for Disease Control and Prevention, National Center on Birth Defects and Developmental Disabilities. (2024, July 10). *Disability and health inclusion strategies.* https://www.cdc.gov/ncbddd/disabilityandhealth/disability-strategies.html

Chalkiadakis, A., Seremetaki, A., Kanellou, A., Kallishi, M., Morfopoulou, A., Moraitaki, M., & Mastrokoukou, S. (2024). Impact of Artificial Intelligence and Virtual Reality on Educational Inclusion: A Systematic Review of Technologies Supporting Students with Disabilities. *Education Sciences*, 14(11), 1223. DOI: 10.3390/educsci14111223

Chan, X. W., & Hutchings, K. (2023). Inequalities, barriers, intersectionality, and facilitators of careers of women with disabilities: Themes and future research agenda from a scoping review. *Frontiers in Psychology*, 14, 1104784. DOI: 10.3389/fpsyg.2023.1104784 PMID: 37954186

Cherry, K. (2023, May 23). Autonomy in psychology—What it means and how to be more autonomous. *Verywell Mind.* Retrieved from https://www.verywellmind.com/autonomy-in-psychology-4173959

Coleman, M. B., Cramer, E. S., Park, Y., & Bell, S. M. (2015). Art Educators' Use of Adaptations, Assitive Technology, and Special Education Supports for Students with Physical, Visual, Severe and Multiple Disabilities. *Journal of Developmental and Physical Disabilities*, 27(5), 637–660. DOI: 10.1007/s10882-015-9440-6

Constantinou, V., Ioannou, A., Klironomos, I., Antona, M., & Stephanidis, C. (2020). Technology support for the inclusion of deaf students in mainstream schools: A summary of research from 2007 to 2017. *Universal Access in the Information Society*, 19(1), 195–200. DOI: 10.1007/s10209-018-0630-8

Council of Europe. (2012). *Compass: Manual for Human Rights Education with Young People*. Citizenship and Participation.

Council of Europe. (2024). Understanding the impact of digitisation on culture. *Council of Europe*. Retrieved from https://www.coe.int/en/web/culture-and-heritage/culture-and-digitisation

Davey, S., & Gordon, S. (2023). Concepts of social inclusion and social exclusion: Perspective of individuals with mental distress. In Liamputtong, P. (Ed.), *Handbook of social inclusion: Research and practices in health and social sciences*. Springer publishing.

Degener, T. (2016). Disability in a human rights context. *Laws*, 5(3), 35. DOI: 10.3390/laws5030035

Degener, T., & Begg, A. (2017). From invisible citizens to agents of change: A short history of the struggle for the recognition of the rights of persons with disabilities at the United Nations. In Della Fina, V., Cera, R., & Palmisano, G. (Eds.), *The United Nations Convention on the Rights of Persons with Disabilities* (pp. 1–39). Springer. DOI: 10.1007/978-3-319-43790-3_1

Department for International Development. (2018). *Education and child disability: A guide for practitioners*. UK Government. https://assets.publishing.service.gov.uk/media/5a789f7ced915d04220640dd/edu-chi-disabil-guid-note.pdf

Deroncele-Acosta, A., & Ellis, A. (2024). Overcoming challenges and promoting positive education in inclusive schools: A multi-country study. *Education Sciences*, 14(11), 1169. DOI: 10.3390/educsci14111169

DeWilde, C. (2003). A life-course perspective on social exclusion and poverty. *The British Journal of Sociology*, 54(1), 109–128. DOI: 10.1080/0007131032000045923 PMID: 12745821

Disabled But Not Really. (2024). *The future of disability innovation in accessibility and inclusion*. Disabled But Not Really. https://disabledbutnotreally.org/awareness/blog/the-future-of-disability-innovation-in-accessibility-and-inclusion/

Dix, D. (1843). I tell what I have seen—The reports of asylum reformer Dorothea Dix. *American Journal of Public Health*, 96(4), 622–624. DOI: 10.2105/AJPH.96.4.622 PMID: 16551962

Dudley-Marling, C., & Burns, M. B. (2014). Two perspectives on inclusion in the United States. *Global Education Review*, 1(1), 14–31.

Ee, C., Lake, J., Firth, J., Hargraves, F., de Manincor, M., Meade, T., Marx, W., & Sarris, J. (2020). An integrative collaborative care model for people with mental illness and physical comorbidities. *International Journal of Mental Health Systems*, 14(83), 83. Advance online publication. DOI: 10.1186/s13033-020-00410-6 PMID: 33292354

Elder, T., Figlio, D., Imberman, S., & Persico, C. (2021). Segregation and racial gaps in special education. *Education Next*, 21(2), 62–68.

Esquivel, P., Gill, K., Goldberg, M., Sundaram, S. A., Morris, L., & Ding, D. (2024). Voice Assistant Utilization among the Disability Community for Independent Living: A Rapid Review of Recent Evidence. *Human Behavior and Emerging Technologies*, 2024, 1–39. Advance online publication. DOI: 10.1155/2024/6494944

European Commission. (2020). *Building a Union of Equality*. Retrieved from https://commission.europa.eu/strategy-and-policy/priorities-2019-2024/new-push-european-democracy/equality-and-inclusion_en

Evans, E. (2022). Political intersectionality and disability activism: Approaching and understanding difference and unity. *The Sociological Review*, 70(5), 986–1004. DOI: 10.1177/00380261221111231

Evers, D. (2021). Nineteenth Century Moral Treatment of Mental Illness Wore Many Hats: Moral Therapy in Practice. *Medical History*, 5(2), e2021016. https://www.mattioli1885journals.com/index.php/MedHistor/article/view/10693

Eziamaka, N., Odonkor, T., & Akinsulire, A. (2024). AI-Driven accessibility: Transformative software solutions for empowering individuals with disabilities. *International Journal of Applied Research in Social Sciences*, 6(8), 1612–1641. DOI: 10.51594/ijarss.v6i8.1373

Federal Communications Commission. (2016, October 6). *Individuals with cognitive disabilities: Barriers to and solutions for accessible information and communication technologies* (Consumer and Governmental Affairs Bureau, White Paper). Federal Communications Commission. Retrieved from https://docs.fcc.gov/public/attachments/DOC-341628A1.pdf

Fejes, A., Chamberland, M., & Sultana, R. G. (2022). Migration, educational and career guidance and social inclusion. *International Journal for Educational and Vocational Guidance*, 22(1), 347–361. DOI: 10.1007/s10775-021-09493-0

Fernández-Batanero, J. M., Montenegro-Rueda, M., Fernández-Cerero, J., & García-Martínez, I. (2022). Assistive technology for the inclusion of students with disabilities: A systematic review. *Educational Technology Research and Development*, 70(5), 1911–1930. DOI: 10.1007/s11423-022-10127-7

Fisher, M., & Meyer, L. H. (2002). Development and social competence after two years for students in inclusive and self-contained educational programs. *Research and Practice for Persons with Severe Disabilities : the Journal of TASH*, 27(1), 165–174. DOI: 10.2511/rpsd.27.3.165

Fitzsimons, J. K. (2017). *More than access: Overcoming limits in architectural and disability discourse*. Routledge publishing.

Fleming, A. R., Umucu, E., & Phillips, B. (2024). Interventions to improve the well-being of people with disaiblities and chronic illness. In I. Marini, A.R. Fleming & M. Bishop (Eds.), *The psychological and social impact of chronic illness and disability* (8th ed., pp. 401-416). Springer Publishing. DOI: 10.1891/9780826151117

Fox, D. D., & Marini, I. (2024). History of treatment toward persons with disabilities in American and abroad. In *The psychological and social impact of chronic illness and disability*, (8th ed., pp. 5-16). Springer Publications.

Freedman, G., Williams, K. D., & Beer, J. S. (2016). Softening the blow of social exclusion: The responsive theory of social exclusion. *Frontiers in Psychology*, 7, 1570. DOI: 10.3389/fpsyg.2016.01570 PMID: 27777566

Friend, M. (2022). *Special education: Contemporary perspectives for school professionals* (6th ed.). Pearson.

Fuentes, A. (2014, March). Why normal is a myth. *Psychology Today*. https://www.psychologytoday.com/intl/blog/busting-myths-about-human-nature/201403/why-normal-is-myth

Galloway, S. (2012). Reconsidering emancipatory education: Staging a conversation between Paulo Freire and Jacuques Ranciere. *Educational Theory*, 62(2), 163–184. DOI: 10.1111/j.1741-5446.2012.00441.x

Gargiulo, R. M., & Bouck, E. C. (2019). *Gar* (7th ed.). SAGE Publications.

Gollaher, D. L. (1995). *Voice for the Mad: The Life of Dorothea Dix*. Free Press.

Goodman, C. (2024, March 27). AI For Accessibility Means AI For All—No Magic Needed. *Forbes*. Retrieved from Forbes website https://www.forbes.com/councils/forbescommunicationscouncil/2024/03/27/ai-for-accessibility-means-ai-for-all-no-magic-needed/

Gordon, R. (2024, January 22). Rethinking AI's Impact: MIT CSAIL Study Reveals Economic Limits to Job Automation. MIT CSAIL. Retrieved from MIT CSAIL https://www.csail.mit.edu/news/rethinking-ais-impact-mit-csail-study-reveals-economic-limits-job-automation

Gréaux, M., Moro, M. F., Kamenov, K., Russell, A., Barrett, D., & Cieza, A. (2023). Health equity for persons with disabilities: A global scoping review on barriers and interventions in healthcare services. *International Journal for Equity in Health*, 22(1), 236. Advance online publication. DOI: 10.1186/s12939-023-02035-w PMID: 37957602

Griffiths, M. (2024). Disabled youth participation within activism and social movement bases: An empirical investigation of the UK Disabled People's Movement. *Current Sociology, 72*(1), 83-gollaher100. DOI: 10.1177/00113921221100579

Hafizov, H. (2023, December 8). The AI Revolution: Is it a Game Changer for Disability Inclusion? *United Nations Development Programme*. Retrieved from UNDP website https://www.undp.org/uzbekistan/blog/ai-revolution-it-game-changer-disability-inclusion

Hall, T., Kakuma, R., Palmer, L., Minas, H., Martin, J., & Kermode, M. (2019). Social inclusion and exclusion of people with mental illness in Timor-Leste: A qualitative investigation with multiple stakeholders. *BMC Public Health*, 19(1), 702. DOI: 10.1186/s12889-019-7042-4 PMID: 31174504

Haug, P. (2017). Understanding inclusive education: Ideals and reality. *Scandinavian Journal of Disability Research*, 19(3), 206–217. DOI: 10.1080/15017419.2016.1224778

Herbert, J. T. (2016). Counseling persons with disabilities. *American Counseling Association Practice Briefs*. The Center for Counseling, Practice, Policy, and Research, 1-5.

Hoagland, A., & Kipping, S. (2024). Challenges in promoting health equity and reducing disparities in access across new and established technologies. *The Canadian Journal of Cardiology*, 40(6), 1154–1167. DOI: 10.1016/j.cjca.2024.02.014 PMID: 38417572

Horne-Shuttleworth, M., Somma, M., & Wlodarczyk, K. A. (2024). Intersectionality, diversity, identity, and disability. In M. Horne-Shuttleworth, M. Somma, & K.A. Wlodarczyk (Eds.) *Teaching Inclusive Education through Life Story Inquiry*, (pp. 33-47). Palgrave Macmillan. DOI: 10.1007/978-3-031-59983-5_3

Houston, R. A. (2020). Asylums: The historical perspective before, during and after. *The Lancet. Psychiatry*, 7(4), 354–362. DOI: 10.1016/S2215-0366(19)30395-5 PMID: 31862356

Huang, A. R., Cudjoe, T. K. M., Rebok, G. W., Swenor, B. K., & Deal, J. A. (2024). Hearing and vision impairment and social isolation over 8 years in community-dwelling older adults. *BMC Public Health*, 24(1), 779. DOI: 10.1186/s12889-024-17730-8 PMID: 38475742

International Disability Alliance. (2021). *Universal design for learning and its role in ensuring access to inclusive education for all.* International Disability Alliance. Retrieved from https://www.internationaldisabilityalliance.org/sites/default/files/universal_design_for_learning_final_8.09.2021.pdf

International Labour Organization. (2019). *Making the future of work inclusive of people with disabilities.* Fundación ONCE and the ILO Global Business and Disability Network. https://www.ilo.org/publications/making-future-work-inclusive-people-disabilities

Jaffee, L. J. (2022). Disabling learning conditions. In Cole, M. (Ed.), *Equality, education and human rights in the United States: Issues of gender, race, sexuality, disability and social class* (pp. 190–216). Routledge Publishing. DOI: 10.4324/9781003150671-8

James, S. (2024, December 10). Professional development for teachers: Tips, resources & more. *Education Walkthrough.* https://educationwalkthrough.com/professional-development-for-teachers/

Jehoel-Gijsbers, G., & Vrooman, C. (2007). *Explaining social exclusion: A theoretical model tested in the Netherlands.* The Netherlands Institute for Social Research.

Jutras, M. (2017). Historical perspectives on the theories, diagnosis, and treatment of mental illness. *British Columbia Medical Journal*, 59(2), 86–88.

Kaliski, S. Z. (2017). Institutions: Prisons and asylums and the deinstitutionalization. In Okkels, N., Kristiansen, C., & Munk-Jørgensen, P. (Eds.), *Mental Health and Illness in the City* (pp. 155–168). Springer Publications. DOI: 10.1007/978-981-10-2327-9_17

Kamiya Y. (2021). Current situation of children with disabilities in low- and middle-income countries. *Pediatrics International: Official Journal of the Japan Pediatric Society, 63*(11), 1277–1281. DOI: 10.1111/ped.14904

Kandati, D. R., Sirasanambeti, A., & Hussain, A. B. (2024). Technologies to Assist Students with Specific Learning Disabilities in Higher Education: Concepts, Challenges and Future Directions. In Kaluri, R., Mahmud, M., Gadekallu, T. R., Rajput, D. S., & Lakshmanna, K. (Eds.), *Applied Assistive Technologies and Informatics for Students with Disabilities: Applied Intelligence and Informatics*. Springer. DOI: 10.1007/978-981-97-0914-4_14

Kayess, R., & French, P. (2008). Out of darkness into light? Introducing the Convention on the Rights of Persons with Disabilities. *Human Rights Law Review*, 8(1), 1–34. DOI: 10.1093/hrlr/ngm044

Khan, M. R. (2024). Role of AI in Enhancing Accessibility for People with Disabilities *Journal of Artificial Intelligence General Science, 3*(1), 125-142. DOI: 10.60087/jaigs.vol03.issue01.p142

Khechen, M. (2013). *Social justice: Concepts, principles, tools and challenges.* Economic and Social Commission for Western Asia (ESCWA). https://www.unescwa.org/sites/default/files/pubs/pdf/social-justice-concepts-principles-tools-challenges-english.pdf

Krishnan, R., & Kumar, M. (2024). Enhancing Accessibility: Exploring the Impact of AI in Assistive Technologies for Disabled Persons. *Nafath*, 9(25). Advance online publication. DOI: 10.54455/MCN2505

Lester, J. N., & O'Reilly, M. (2021). Historical and social constructions of disability. In Lester, J. N., & O'Reilly, M. (Eds.), *The Social, Cultural, and Political Discourses of Autism* (pp. 17–36). Springer. DOI: 10.1007/978-94-024-2134-7_2

Levine, A., Harley, D. A., & Fleming, A. (2023). The Use of Social Justice Concepts in Rehabilitation Counselor Education: Results of an Exploratory Study. *Rehabilitation Counseling Bulletin*, 67(1), 34–45. DOI: 10.1177/00343552221080416

Li, Y.-F., Zhang, D., Dulas, H. M., & Whirley, M. L. (2024). Academic learning experiences and challenges of students with disabilities in higher education. *Journal of Postsecondary Student Success*, 3(4), 257–284. DOI: 10.33009/fsop_jpss134617

Liamputtong, P., & Rice, Z. S. (2024). Social Inclusion, social exclusion and health promotion. In Liamputtong, P., & Rice, Z. S. (Eds.), *Handbook of Concepts in Health, Health Behavior and Environmental Health* (pp. 1–18). Springer. DOI: 10.1007/978-981-97-0821-5_14-1

Lieffers, C. (2024). Disability in US History. In Rioux, M. H., Buettgen, A., Zubrow, E., & Viera, J. (Eds.), *Handbook of Disability*. Springer. DOI: 10.1007/978-981-19-6056-7_4

Livneh, H. (2012). On the origins of negative attitudes toward people with disabilities. In Marini, I., & Stebnicki, M. A. (Eds.), *The psychological and social impact of illness and disability* (6th ed., pp. 13–25). Springer Publications.

Lustig, D. C., Strauser, D. R., Rice, N. D., & Rucker, T. F. (2002). The relationship between working alliance and rehabilitation outcomes. *Rehabilitation Counseling Bulletin*, 46(1), 24–32. DOI: 10.1177/00343552020460010201

Mackelprang, R. W., & Salsgiver, R. O. (1996). People with disabilities and social work: Historical and contemporary issues. *Social Work*, 41(1), 7–14. DOI: 10.1093/sw/41.1.7 PMID: 8560321

Mackelprang, R. W., Salsgiver, R. O., & Parrey, R. C. (2021). *Disability: A diversity model approach in human service practice*. Oxford University Press.

Mak, S., Hunt, M., Boruff, J., Zaccagnini, M., & Thomas, A. (2022). Exploring professional identity in rehabilitation professions: A scoping review. *Advances in Health Sciences Education : Theory and Practice*, 27(3), 793–815. DOI: 10.1007/s10459-022-10103-z PMID: 35467304

Malathouni, C. (2020). Beyond the asylum and before the 'care in the community' model: Exploring an overlooked early NHS mental health facility. *History of Psychiatry*, 31(4), 455–469. DOI: 10.1177/0957154X20945974 PMID: 32748672

Manyika, J., Lund, S., Bughin, J., Woetzel, J., Stamenov, K., & Dhingra, D. (2016). Digital globalization: The new era of global flows. *McKinsey Global Institute*. https://www.mckinsey.com/~/media/McKinsey/Business%20Functions/McKinsey%20Digital/Our%20Insights/Digital%20globalization%20The%20new%20era%20of%20global%20flows/MGI%20Digital%20globalization%20Executive%20summary.ashx

Marini, I. (2024). Societal attitudes and myths about disability: Improving the social consciousness. In *The psychological and social impact of chronic illness and disability*, (8th ed., pp. 17-35). Springer Publications.

Marini, I., Fleming, A. R., & Bishop, M. (2024). *The psychological and social impact of chronic illness and disability* (8th ed.). Springer publications.

Marmé, M., & Bruce, A. (2014). Creating a global community: All hands on deck! *National Council on Rehabilitation Education Spring Conference*.

Matias, C. F. (2024). Generative AI, Copyright and Emancipation: The Case of Digital Art. *Law. Technology and Humans*, 6(3), 123–138. DOI: 10.5204/lthj.3567

Matin, B. K., Williamson, H. J., Karyani, A. K., Rezaei, S., Soofi, M., & Soltani, S. (2021). Barriers in access to healthcare for women with disabilities: A systematic review in qualitative studies. *BMC Women's Health*, 21(1), 44. DOI: 10.1186/s12905-021-01189-5 PMID: 33516225

McNicholl, A., Casey, H., Desmond, D., & Gallagher, P. (2019). The impact of assistive technology use for students with disabilities in higher education: A systematic review. *Disability and Rehabilitation. Assistive Technology*, 16(2), 130–143. DOI: 10.1080/17483107.2019.1642395 PMID: 31335220

Mendis, K., Thayapara, M., Kaluarachchi, Y., & Pathirage, C. (2023). Challenges faced by marginalized communities in a post-disaster context: A systematic review of literature. *Sustainability (Basel)*, 15(14), 10754. DOI: 10.3390/su151410754

Mezzina, R., Gopikumar, V., Jenkins, J., Saraceno, B., & Sashidharan, S. P. (2022). Social Vulnerability and Mental Health Inequalities in the "Syndemic": Call for Action. *Frontiers in Psychiatry*, 13, 894370. DOI: 10.3389/fpsyt.2022.894370 PMID: 35747101

Miller, D. (1999). *Principles of social justice*. Harvard University Press. DOI: 10.2307/j.ctv1pdrq04

Min, A. (2023). Artifical Intelligence and Bias: Challenges, Implications, and Remedies. *Journal of Social Research*, 2(11), 3808–3817. DOI: 10.55324/josr.v2i11.1477

Mitchell, U. A., Nishida, A., Fletcher, F. E., & Molina, Y. (2021). The Long Arm of Oppression: How Structural Stigma Against Marginalized Communities Perpetuates Within-Group Health Disparities. *Health Education & Behavior*, 48(3), 342–351. DOI: 10.1177/10901981211011927 PMID: 34080480

Mitus, J., & Levine, A. (2021). Putting Advocacy Back Into Rehabilitation: A Discourse on Needs Identified in the Field. *Rehabilitation Counselors and Educators Journal*, 10(1). Advance online publication. DOI: 10.52017/001c.25413

Mulcahy, A., Streed, C. G.Jr, Wallisch, A. M., Batza, K., Kurth, N., Hall, J. P., & McMaughan, D. J. (2022). Gender Identity, Disability, and Unmet Healthcare Needs among Disabled People Living in the Community in the United States. *International Journal of Environmental Research and Public Health*, 19(5), 2588. DOI: 10.3390/ijerph19052588 PMID: 35270279

Mustaniemi-Laakso, M., Katsui, H., & Heikkilä, M. (2022). Vulnerability, Disability, and Agency: Exploring Structures for Inclusive Decision-Making and Participation in a Responsive State. *International journal for the semiotics of law = Revue internationale de semiotique juridique*, 1–29. Advance online publication. DOI: 10.1007/s11196-022-09946-x

National Institute for Health and Care Excellence (NICE). (2022, November 9). *Advocacy services for adults with health and social care needs* (NICE Guideline No. 227). London: NICE. Retrieved from https://www.ncbi.nlm.nih.gov/books/NBK588853/

Nelson, E. A. (2021). Dorothea Dix's liberation movement and why it matters today. *The American Journal of Psychiatry Residents' Journal*, 16(2), 14–18. DOI: 10.1176/appi.ajp-rj.2021.170203

News, U. N. (2024, December 2). *Disability rights: UN chief calls for amplified leadership roles to shape more inclusive future*. UN News-Global Perspective Human Stories. Retrieved from https://news.un.org/en/story/2024/12/1157691

Nguyen-Finn, K. L. (2024) History of treatment toward persons with psychiatric disabilities. In Marini, I., Fleming, A.R., & Bishop, M. (Eds.), *The psychological and social impact of chronic illness and disability* (8th ed., pp. 37-54). Springer Publications

OECD. (2020). *Professional growth in times of change: Supporting teachers' continuing professional learning and collaboration*. OECD Publishing. DOI: 10.1787/753eaa89-

Oliver, M. (1996). The social model in context. In *Understanding disability: From theory to practice* (pp. 30–42). St. Martin's Press. DOI: 10.1007/978-1-349-24269-6_4

Oudeyer, P.-Y., Gottlieb, J., & Lopes, M. (2016). *Intrinsic motivation, curiosity, and learning: Theory and applications in educational technologies* (Vol. 229). Elsevier. DOI: 10.1016/bs.pbr.2016.05.005

Pasquina, P. F., & Shero, J. C. (2016). Rehabilitation of the Combat Casualty: Lessons Learned from Past and Current Conflicts. *U.S. Army Medical Department Journal, 2*(16), 77–86.

Patterson, J. B. (2008). Professional identity and the future of rehabilitation counseling. *Journal of Applied Rehabilitation Counseling*, 39(4), 60–63. DOI: 10.1891/0047-2220.39.4.60

Perachoriti, M. (2002). Globalization and education: A relationship of interaction. *Proceedings of the 2nd International Conference, Education in the dawn of 21st century, Historical and Comparative Approaches*. University of Patras.

Perrin, P. B. (2019). Diversity and social justice in disability: The heart and soul of rehabilitation psychology. *Rehabilitation Psychology*, 64(2), 105–110. DOI: 10.1037/rep0000278 PMID: 30985180

Pettinicchio, D., Maroto, M., & Brooks, J. D. (2022). The sociology of disability-based economic inequality. *Contemporary Sociology*, 51(4), 249–270. DOI: 10.1177/00943061221103313

Pineda, V. S., & Catalano, S. L. (2023). Introduction: Disability activism and advocacy. In Rioux, M. H., Viera, J., Buettgen, A., & Zubrow, E. (Eds.), *Handbook of Disability*. Springer. DOI: 10.1007/978-981-16-1278-7_88-1

Polyviou, A., Pouloudi, N., Pramatari, K., & Dhillon, G. (2021). Digital Emancipation: Are We Becoming Prisoners of Our Own Device? In *Digital Transformation and Human Behavior*. Lecture Notes in Information Systems and Organisation, vol.37. Springer Publishing. DOI: 10.1007/978-3-030-47539-0_12

Praslova, L. (2023). Disability inclusion in the workplace: Special issue introduction. *Consulting Psychology Journal*, 75(3), 197–201. DOI: 10.1037/cpb0000264

Pruett, S. R., Swett, E. A., Chan, F., Rosenthal, D. A., & Lee, G. K. (2008). Empirical Evidence Supporting the Effectiveness of Vocational Rehabilitation. *Journal of Rehabilitation*, 74(2).

Prunkl, C. (2024). Human Autonomy at Risk? An Analysis of the Challenges from AI. [prue]. *Minds and Machines*, 34(26), 26. Advance online publication. DOI: 10.1007/s11023-024-09665-1

Qiu, N., Jiang, Y., Sun, Z., & Du, M. (2023). The impact of disability-related deprivation on employment opportunity at the neighborhood level: Does family socioeconomic status matter? *Frontiers in Public Health*, 11, 1232829. DOI: 10.3389/fpubh.2023.1232829 PMID: 37621604

Quinn, G., & Degener, T. (2002). Human rights and disability: The current use and future potential of United Nations human rights instruments in the context of disability. United Nations. https://www.un.org/esa/socdev/enable/dispaperdes0.htm

Rawlins-Williams, L. A., & Oswald, G. (2025). *Fundamentals of case and caseload management: Skills for rehabilitation practice*. Springer Publishing Company.

Redmond, G., Main, G., O'Donnell, A. W., Skattebol, J., Woodman, R., Mooney, A., Wang, J., Turkmani, S., Thomson, C., & Brooks, F. (2024). Who excludes? Young people's experience of social exclusion. *Journal of Social Policy*, 53(1), 236–259. DOI: 10.1017/S0047279422000046

Richmond, O. P. (2022). What is an emancipatory peace? *Journal of International Political Theory*, 18(2), 124–147. DOI: 10.1177/17550882211036560

Room, G. (2006). The dynamics of social exclusion. *International Journal of Social Welfare*, 15(1), 1–10.

Roth, A. (2018). *Insane: America's criminal treatment of mental illness*. Basic Books.

Rothman, D. J. (2017). *The discovery of the asylum: Social order and disorder in the new republic*. Routledge.

Rotoli, J., Poffenberger, C., Backster, A., Sapp, R., Modi, P., Stehman, C. R., Mirus, C.IV, Johnson, L., Siegelman, J. N., & Coates, W. C. (2023). From inequity to access: Evidence-based institutional practices to enhance care for individuals with disabilities. *AEM Education and Training*, 7(S1, Suppl 1), S5–S14. DOI: 10.1002/aet2.10871 PMID: 37383833

Sachs, J. (2003). *The activist professional*. Oxford University Press.

Salend, S. J., & Duhaney, L. M. G. (1999). The impact of inclusion on students with and without disabilities and their educators. *Remedial and Special Education*, 20(2), 114–126. DOI: 10.1177/074193259902000209

Salzar, M. S. (2021). Community inclusion and social determinants: From opportunity to health. *Psychiatric Services (Washington, D.C.)*, 72(7), 836–839. DOI: 10.1176/appi.ps.202000394 PMID: 33730879

Saran, A., Hunt, X., White, H., & Kuper, H. (2023). Effectiveness of interventions for improving social inclusion outcomes for people with disabilities in low-and middle-income countries: A systematic review. *Campbell Systematic Reviews*, 19(1), e1316. Advance online publication. DOI: 10.1002/cl2.1316 PMID: 37132016

Satterfield, B. (2016). History of assistive technology outcomes in education. *Assistive Technology Outcomes and Benefits*, 10(1), 1–11.

Scheunpflug, A. (2021). Global learning: Educational research in an emerging field. *European Educational Research Journal*, 20(1), 3–13. DOI: 10.1177/1474904120951743

Sen, A. (2000). *Social exclusion: concept, application and scrutiny. Social Development Paper no. 1*. Asian Development Bank.

Sewell, A., Kennett, A., & Pugh, V. (2022). Universal Design for Learning as a theory of inclusive practice for use by educational psychologists. *Educational Psychology in Practice*, 38(4), 364–378. DOI: 10.1080/02667363.2022.2111677

Shreve, M. (2011). *The Independent Living Movement: History and Philosophy to Implementation and Practice*. IL NET: How IL History and Philosophy Shape Our Future Training Manual. https://www.ilru.org/sites/default/files/resources/il_history/IL_Movement.pdf

Silva, D. (2023, July 31). Breaking Barriers: How AI Transforms Website Accessibility for Users with Disabilities. UX Planet. Retrieved from UX Planet website https://uxplanet.org/breaking-barriers-how-ai-transforms-website-accessibility-for-users-with-disabilities-62cfac1b0165

Silver, H. (2007). The process of social exclusion: The dynamics of an evolving concept (CPRC Working Paper No. 95). Chronic Poverty Research Centre.

Slee, R., & Tait, G. (2022). *Ethics and Inclusive Education: Disability, Schooling and Justice*. Springer Nature Switzerland AG. DOI: 10.1007/978-3-030-97435-0

Smart, J. (2019). *Disability across the developmental lifespan: An introduction for the helping professions*. Springer Publications. DOI: 10.1891/9780826139238

Smith, J. D. (1998). Histories of Special Education: Stories From Our Past, Insights for Our Future. *Remedial and Special Education*, 19(4), 196–200. DOI: 10.1177/074193259801900402

Smith, L. (2022). History of inclusive education timeline: Journey towards. *National Association of Special Education Teachers*. https://naasln.org/history-of-inclusive-education-timeline/

Stancliffe, R. J., & Hall, S. A. (2023). Social inclusion of adults with intellectual and developmental disabilities: Toward belonging. *International Review of Research in Developmental Disabilities*, 64, 253–306. DOI: 10.1016/bs.irrdd.2023.06.002

Stanford - Vienna Transatlantic Technology Law Forum. (2021). Transatlantic Antitrust and IPR Developments (Issue No. 2). Stanford University. https://law.stanford.edu/publications/eu-artificial-intelligence-act-the-european-approach-to-ai/

Stein, P. J., & Stein, M. A. (2022). Disability, human rights and climate justice. *Human Rights Quarterly*, 44(1), 81–110. DOI: 10.1353/hrq.2022.0003

Sterkenburg, P. S., Ilic, M., Flachsmeyer, M., & Sappok, T. (2022). More than a physical problem: The effects of physical and sensory impairments on the emotional development of adults with intellectual disabilities. *International Journal of Environmental Research and Public Health*, 19(24), 17080. DOI: 10.3390/ijerph192417080 PMID: 36554959

Stiker, H. J. (2019). *A history of disability*. University of Michigan Press. DOI: 10.3998/mpub.11575987

Story, M., Mace, R., & Mueller, J. (1998). A brief history of universal design. *Ronald L. Mace Universal Design Institute*. Retrieved from https://udinstitute.org/history-of-universal-design

Suarez-Balcazar, Y., Balcazar, F., Labbe, D., McDonald, K. E., Keys, C., Taylor-Ritzler, T., Anderson, S. M., & Agner, J. (2023). Disability rights and empowerment: Reflections on AJCP research and a call to action. *American Journal of Community Psychology*, 72(3-4), 317–327. DOI: 10.1002/ajcp.12710 PMID: 37853910

Tabin, M., Khemka, I., & Hickson, L. (2024). Reducing the risks of maltreatment of older adults with intellectual and developmental disabilities: Development of a research-based intervention. *Journal of Intellectual & Developmental Disability*, 49(4), 462–474. DOI: 10.3109/13668250.2024.2366283 PMID: 39815943

Tarabini, A., Jacovkis, J., & Montes, A. (2017). Factors in educational exclusion: Including the voice of the youth. *Journal of Youth Studies*, 21(6), 836–851. DOI: 10.1080/13676261.2017.1420765

Tariq, M. U., & Sergio, R. P. (2025). Nurturing Digital Citizenship in Society 5.0 Through AI and Computational Intelligence Education. In Pandey, R., Srivastava, N., Prasad, R., Prasad, J., & Garcia, M. (Eds.), *Open AI and Computational Intelligence for Society 5.0* (pp. 59–84). IGI Global Scientific Publishing. DOI: 10.4018/979-8-3693-4326-5.ch003

The Lancet Public Health. (2021). Disability—a neglected issue in public health. *The Lancet Public Health, 6*(6), e346. DOI: 10.1016/S2468-2667(21)00123-4

The Social Norms Learning Collaborative. (2021) Social Norms Atlas: Understanding global social norms and related concepts, Institute for Reproductive Health, Georgetown University, Washington, DC. Retrieved https://www.unicef.org/media/111061/file/Social-norms-definitions-2021.pdf

The White House. (2021, December 3). *Advancing Disability Inclusive Democracy in the US and Globally*. Briefing Room Statements and Releases.

Theodorio, A. O. (2024). Examining the support required by educators for successful technology integration in teacher professional development program. *Cogent Education*, 11(1), 2298607. Advance online publication. DOI: 10.1080/2331186X.2023.2298607

Thota, A. B., Mogo, E. R. I., Igbelina, D. C., Sheaf, G. S., Mustafa, R., Bakrania, S., Vásquez Encalada, A., & Wood, G. A. (2023). *Effectiveness of inclusive interventions for children with disabilities in low- and middle-income countries: Protocol for an evidence and gap map*. UNICEF Office of Research – Innocenti. https://files.eric.ed.gov/fulltext/ED627821.pdf

Timpe, K. (2022). Cognitive disabilities, forms of exclusion, and the ethics of social interactions. *The Journal of Philosophy of Disability*. .DOI: 10.5840/jpd20226714

Today, U. N. D. (2024, October 29). Building an inclusive campus and culture. *UND Today*. Retrieved from https://www.und.edu/today/building-inclusive-campus

Tomasello, L., Trunfio, A., Ranno, M., & Zitelli, G. (2024). The evolution of the concept of disability: Social and educational inclusion. *American Journal of Clinical and Medical Research*, 4(11), 2835–9496.

UNESCO. (2003). *Overcoming exclusion through inclusive approaches in education: A challenge & a vision*. Section for Early Childhood and Inclusive Education, Basic Education Division. Retrieved December 8, 2024 from https://unesdoc.unesco.org/ark:/48223/pf0000134785

United Nations. (2006, December 13). *Convention on the Rights of Persons with Disabilities*. 61st session of the General Assembly, Resolution A/RES/61/106. Retrieved from https://www.un.org/disabilities/documents/convention/convoptprot-e.pdf

United Nations. (2015, September 26). Global issues: Persons with disabilities. Author. https://www.un.org/en/globalissues/disabilities/index.shtml

United Nations. (2016). *10th anniversary of the adoption of Convention on the Rights of Persons with Disabilities (CRPD)*. https://www.un.org/development/desa/disabilities/convention-on-the-rights-of-persons-with-disabilities/the-10th-anniversary-of-the-adoption-of-convention-on-the-rights-of-persons-with-disabilities-crpd-crpd-10.html

United Nations Development Coordination Office Disability Inclusion Strategy. (2021, January). *Practice notes: Physical accessibility. Making UN premises & facilities accessible through the Business Operations Strategy (BOS) 2.0*. Working Draft. Retrieved from https://unsdg.un.org/sites/default/files/2021-04/Physical%20Accessibility-BOS-Disability%20Inclusion-Practice%20Note-20210303.pdf

United Nations. (2006). Convention on the rights of persons with disabilities. Author.

U.S. Department of Education. (2004). Individuals with Disabilities Education Act (IDEA). Retrieved from https://sites.ed.gov/idea/

Valentine, P. K. (1993). *American Asylum for the Deaf: A first experiment in education*, 1817-1880 (Doctoral dissertation). University of Connecticut. ProQuest Dissertations & Theses Global. (9423797).

Weisblat, I. A. (2019). Technology and Globalization: The Evolution of Human Interactions, Values, and Management Practices. In Gordon, P. A., & Overbey, J. A. (Eds.), *Advances in the Technology of Managing People: Contemporary Issues in Business (The Changing Context of Managing People)* (pp. 1–12). Emerald Publishing Limited. DOI: 10.1108/978-1-78973-073-920191001

Welch, P., & Palames, C. (2015, August 16). A brief history of disability rights legislation in the United States. Global Universal Design Education Network: http://www.udeducation.org/resources/ 61.html

Wesselmann, E. D., Grzybowski, M. R., Steakley-Freeman, D. M., DeSouza, E. R., Nezlek, J. B., & Williams, K. D. (2016). Social Exclusion in Everyday Life. In *Social Exclusion*. Springer. DOI: 10.1007/978-3-319-33033-4_1

White, J. J. G. (2022). Artificial Intelligence and People with Disabilities: a Reflection on Human–AI Partnerships. In Chen, F., & Zhou, J. (Eds.), *Humanity Driven AI*. Springer Publishing. DOI: 10.1007/978-3-030-72188-6_14

White, R., & Cooper, K. (2013). Towards an understanding of social justice in our schools: Globalization, inclusive leadership and the transformation of schooling. In Bogotch, I., & Shields, C. (Eds.), *International handbook of educational leadership and social (In) justice* (pp. 1063–1079). Springer Publishing Company.

Wilson, N. J., Jaques, H., Johnson, A., & Brotherton, M. L. (2016). From social exclusion to supported inclusion: Adults with intellectual disability discuss their lived experiences of a structured social group. *Journal of Applied Research in Intellectual Disabilities*, 30(5), 847–858. DOI: 10.1111/jar.12275 PMID: 27554436

Winzer, M. A. (1993). *The history of special education: From isolation to integration*. Gallaudet University Press.

Wolff, J. (2014). Social equality and social inequality. In Fourie, C., Schuppert, F., & Walliman-Helmer, I. (Eds.), *Social equality: On what it means to be equals* (pp. 209–225). Oxford Publications., DOI: 10.1093/acprof:oso/9780199331109.001.0001

World Health Organization. (2022). Global competency framework for universal health coverage. https://www.who.int/news/item/19-07-2022-global-competency-framework

World Health Organization. (n.d.). *Abuse of older people*. World Health Organization. Retrieved January 24, 2025, from https://www.who.int/news-room/fact-sheets/detail/abuse-of-older-people

Zhang, P., & Kamel Boulos, M. N. (2023). Generative AI in Medicine and Healthcare: Promises, Opportunities and Challenges. *Future Internet*, 15(9), 286. DOI: 10.3390/fi15090286

APPENDIX I

Case Study 1: The Intersectionality of Disability and the Role of Universal Design for Learning (UDL)

Maria's Story

Maria is a 42-year-old Latina woman with cerebral palsy. As a single mother living in a low-income neighborhood, she faces multiple layers of marginalization. Her disability impacts her mobility and access to education, while her gender, ethnicity, age, and socioeconomic status create additional challenges. In her pursuit of higher education, Maria encounters significant barriers, such as inaccessible physical environments, cultural biases, and financial limitations.

Maria's experience in the classroom is shaped by assumptions about her abilities, both as a woman with a disability and as a Latina. She struggles to find accessible learning materials, and the lack of cultural competence among instructors further complicates her educational journey. Her disability is often misunderstood, and her needs go unaddressed, leaving her feeling excluded and unsupported.

Despite these challenges, Maria has shown resilience and a strong desire to continue her education. However, the traditional educational system, designed for an "average" student, does not meet her needs. Maria's story illustrates how intersectionality—where disability intersects with factors like gender, ethnicity, age, and socioeconomic status—creates compounded barriers to inclusion and accessibility.

Universal Design for Learning (UDL) Solutions

UDL offers a flexible approach to learning that can help break down these barriers. The principles of UDL—providing multiple means of engagement, representation, and action/expression—can be used to support Maria's academic success:

1. **Multiple Means of Engagement**: Offering choices in learning activities and engagement methods, including culturally relevant materials that reflect Maria's Latina heritage, would help her connect with the content and stay motivated.
2. **Multiple Means of Representation**: Using multimedia, adaptive technologies, and bilingual materials would ensure that Maria can access content in formats that work best for her, addressing both her disability and language barriers.

3. **Multiple Means of Action and Expression**: Allowing Maria to express her learning through alternative assessments, such as projects or oral presentations, rather than traditional exams, would accommodate her unique strengths and needs.

By adopting UDL principles, educational environments can become more inclusive, meeting the diverse needs of students like Maria, who face multiple forms of disadvantage due to their intersecting identities.

Case Study 2: Generative AI in Education: A Global Perspective on Accessibility and Inclusion

Background

Emerging technologies like generative AI are rapidly transforming the landscape of education worldwide. These technologies hold the promise of enhancing accessibility, personalizing learning, and making education more inclusive for a diverse range of students, including those with disabilities or from marginalized groups. However, the implementation of these tools varies significantly across regions, shaped by factors such as technological infrastructure, cultural contexts, and access to resources.

Generative AI encompasses a range of technologies that can create content or offer personalized learning experiences, such as AI-driven tutoring systems, adaptive learning platforms, and real-time content generation. These innovations have the potential to address longstanding barriers to education, such as lack of personalized support, language differences, and accessibility challenges. However, the widespread adoption of these technologies raises important questions about equity, bias, and cultural relevance, especially in low-resource or underserved regions.

Global Case Studies

1. **United States – AI-Powered Accessibility Tools**

In the United States, the integration of generative AI in educational settings has seen significant advancements, especially in supporting students with disabilities. AI-driven technologies such as real-time captioning, speech-to-text applications, and personalized learning platforms are helping students with visual, auditory, and learning impairments. For example, platforms like Microsoft's Immersive Reader use AI to offer reading assistance to students with dyslexia, providing text-to-speech options, customizable fonts, and background colors. However, there are challenges related to the accessibility of these technologies across different school districts. Wealthier districts tend to have greater access to these technologies, while schools in lower-income areas may lack the necessary infrastructure, limiting the reach and impact of AI tools.

2. **India – AI-Based Learning in Rural Schools**

In India, where educational disparities are marked by geography, socioeconomic status, and infrastructure, AI has shown promise in bridging educational gaps. AI-driven platforms like *Vedantu* and *BYJU's* provide personalized tutoring and learning assistance for students across the country, with a focus on rural and underserved communities. These platforms use AI to assess individual student needs and provide targeted lessons, adapting content to the student's pace and learning style. However, while these AI-based solutions are providing educational support, challenges remain around the availability of stable internet access and affordable devices. Rural students often face issues of connectivity, making it difficult for them to fully benefit from AI-powered learning tools.

3. **Brazil – Language Barriers and AI-Powered Translation Tools**

In Brazil, where there is a large population of students who speak indigenous languages or non-Portuguese dialects, AI is being used to break down language barriers. AI translation tools such as *Google Translate,* and custom AI solutions developed by local tech companies are being integrated into schools to support non-Portuguese-speaking students. These tools allow students to access the same learning materials as their Portuguese-speaking peers, fostering greater inclusion and participation in classrooms.

Despite the potential for AI to support language inclusion, the technology's success heavily depends on the quality of the AI models and their ability to accurately translate diverse dialects and regional languages. Furthermore, students in remote areas often lack access to the internet, limiting the reach of these tools.

4. **South Africa – AI in Resource-Constrained Environments**

In South Africa, where educational inequality remains a significant issue, AI technologies are being implemented to improve literacy and numeracy rates, particularly in low-income communities. AI tools such as *Dr. Maths* offer personalized learning experiences for students struggling with basic math skills, providing them with real-time feedback and adaptive learning pathways. However, the success of these tools is contingent upon factors like stable internet access and digital literacy. In areas with poor infrastructure, even AI tools designed for educational enhancement can fail to make a meaningful impact. The digital divide continues to be a major barrier to the equitable use of emerging technologies.

5. **China – AI in Urban and Rural Educational Disparities**

In China, AI has been integrated into both urban and rural educational settings, although with varying degrees of success. Urban schools, with better access to technology, have introduced AI tools to assist teachers in grading, personalized student assessments, and enhancing classroom engagement. These tools help reduce teacher workload while providing personalized content to meet the needs of individual students. In contrast, rural schools in China face significant challenges in accessing these technologies due to inadequate infrastructure, a lack of trained personnel, and limited resources. While China's government is investing heavily in AI-powered educational solutions, the disparity between urban and rural access to these tools highlights the importance of addressing digital inequality.

Challenges and Opportunities

The global implementation of generative AI in education comes with both significant opportunities and challenges:

1. **Access to Technology:**

In many countries, the digital divide continues to be a major barrier to the equitable implementation of AI tools. While students in wealthier regions may have easy access to AI-powered educational platforms, those in low-income or rural areas often lack the necessary infrastructure, such as reliable internet or access to devices. Governments and institutions must address these disparities to ensure that AI benefits are distributed equitably.

2. **Bias and Fairness:**

AI algorithms are often trained on data that may reflect cultural, racial, or socioeconomic biases. For example, if AI systems are designed primarily for English-speaking students or those from cultural backgrounds, they may not serve the needs of students from different linguistic or cultural contexts. To avoid perpetuating inequalities, AI solutions must be designed with inclusivity in mind, ensuring that they account for diverse student needs and experiences.

3. **Cultural Adaptation:**

Educational systems and cultural contexts vary greatly around the world. AI tools must be adaptable to local contexts, considering language differences, cultural norms, and educational structures. For instance, AI translation tools may work well in global languages like Spanish and French but struggle with indigenous languages or dialects. Tailoring AI solutions to the cultural and educational contexts of different countries is crucial to their effectiveness.

4. **Teacher Training and Integration:**

To ensure that AI technologies are used effectively in classrooms, teachers must be adequately trained on how to incorporate these tools into their teaching practices. In many regions, educators may lack the skills or resources to effectively integrate AI into their classrooms. Providing teachers with professional development opportunities is key to maximizing the impact of AI technologies.

Chapter 3
Empowering Digital Citizens:
Navigating AI Ethics, Engagement, and Privacy in the Era of Advanced Education

Goh Ying Yingsoon
https://orcid.org/0000-0002-6654-2887
Universiti Teknologi MARA, Malaysia

Nurul Ain Chua
https://orcid.org/0000-0003-2915-1577
University Terengganu Malaysia, Malaysia

Zhang Suyan
https://orcid.org/0009-0003-4518-1650
Shandong Jianzhu University, China

Chen Yiming
https://orcid.org/0009-0002-8906-2736
Shenzhen University, China

Zhang Haiyan
https://orcid.org/0009-0007-3245-9552
Jining Normal University, China

Tie Xiaoyao
Qilu Institute of Technology, China

ABSTRACT

As the digital landscape evolves, the intersection of artificial intelligence (AI) and education is reshaping the way citizens interact with technology and information. This chapter addresses the critical need for digital literacy and the preparation of individuals to engage with AI in ethical and privacy-conscious ways. The chapter begins by examining the concept of digital citizenship and its relevance in an AI-driven society, emphasizing the importance of equipping citizens with the skills to navigate and contribute to the digital world responsibly. The core of the chapter explores the integration of AI in educational systems, highlighting both the opportunities and challenges it presents.

DOI: 10.4018/979-8-3693-9015-3.ch003

INTRODUCTION

A. The Evolving Digital Landscape

The digital landscape is in a constant state of flux, with technological advancements reshaping the way we live, work, and interact. The proliferation of smartphones, the internet of things, and cloud computing has created a hyper-connected world where information flows at an unprecedented rate. This dynamic environment has given rise to new platforms, tools, and applications that continue to push the boundaries of what is possible, making the digital space more complex and multifaceted than ever before. As a result, individuals and societies must adapt to these changes, learning to navigate and harness the power of digital technology to enhance their daily lives and future prospects (Wider, et al, 2024).

In the realm of education, the evolving digital landscape has introduced a paradigm shift, transforming traditional learning environments into more flexible, personalized, and accessible spaces. The integration of artificial intelligence, virtual reality, and other cutting-edge technologies has opened up new avenues for teaching and learning, enabling educators to cater to the diverse needs of students. However, this digital evolution also brings challenges, such as ensuring equitable access to technology, addressing the digital divide, and preparing students for an uncertain job market that will be heavily influenced by automation and AI. As the digital landscape continues to evolve, so too must our strategies for educating and empowering the next generation of digital citizens (Camacho, 2024).

A comprehensive historical overview of AI's progress in education, from the pioneering intelligent tutoring systems to the sophisticated machine learning models of today, is vital for us to comprehend the profound influence AI has on contemporary educational practices. By understanding this trajectory, readers can better appreciate how AI has transformed the learning environment and the potential it holds for the future of education. This comprehensive review delves into the transformative power of AI in education, illustrating how it is revolutionizing the learning landscape by personalizing experiences and amplifying student engagement. By examining the multifaceted ways AI is being integrated into teaching methods, the review highlights the potential for enhanced educational outcomes and a more inclusive approach to learning. (Onesi-Ozigagun et al., 2024).

B. The Intersection of AI and Education

The intersection of AI and education represents a paradigm shift in how knowledge is imparted, processed, and applied. AI's integration into the educational ecosystem has the potential to personalize learning experiences, adapting to the individual pace and style of each student. Through intelligent tutoring systems, machine learning algorithms can identify learning gaps and tailor educational content, accordingly, thus optimizing the learning process. This customization not only enhances student engagement but also empowers educators with actionable insights into student performance, enabling them to provide targeted support where it is most needed (Gašević, et al, 2023).

Furthermore, AI's role in education extends beyond the classroom, revolutionizing administrative tasks and educational research. By automating routine processes such as grading and data analysis, AI frees up valuable time for educators to focus on curriculum development and student interaction. Moreover, AI-driven predictive analytics can forecast educational trends and outcomes, guiding policy decisions and resource allocation to improve overall educational quality and accessibility. This symbiotic relationship between AI and education is poised to democratize learning, making it more efficient and effective for a diverse range of learners across the globe (Davies, et al, 2021).

The evolution of AI In education has transitioned from basic automated systems for rote learning to sophisticated adaptive learning platforms that personalize instruction and facilitate more nuanced, interactive educational experiences. This progression has been marked by increased sophistication in AI algorithms, which now enable the customization of educational content, support for diverse learning styles, and real-time feedback to both students and educators. (Lestari, 2024).

C. The Importance of Digital Citizenship in an AI-Driven Society

The concept of digital citizenship assumes paramount importance in an AI-driven society, where the lines between the physical and digital worlds are increasingly blurred. As AI systems become more integrated into daily life, individuals must be equipped with the skills to navigate this complex environment responsibly. Digital citizenship encompasses a range of competencies, including critical thinking, ethical decision-making, and privacy protection, which are essential for individuals to engage with AI technologies in a manner that upholds societal values and personal integrity (Calzada, 2023).

In an era where AI can influence public opinion, job markets, and even governance, the role of digital citizens cannot be overstated. Active and informed digital citizens are necessary to ensure that AI development and deployment are aligned with the common good. They can advocate transparency, fairness, and accountability in AI systems, and they are crucial in holding both developers and policymakers accountable for the societal impacts of AI. By fostering a culture of digital citizenship, we can create a society that leverages AI for positive change while mitigating potential risks and biases, thereby ensuring that the benefits of AI are broadly shared and that the rights of all are respected in the digital realm (Henry, et al, 2022).

The Integration of AI in education raises significant issues, such as the potential for automated systems to perpetuate biases and the displacement of educators by machines, which could undermine the relational and nuanced aspects of teaching. Additionally, there is a concern about the unequal access to AI-enhanced educational tools, which may exacerbate disparities in learning outcomes between privileged and under-resourced institutions. These have to be handled seeing the importance of developing digital citizenship in this AI-driven society. (Dayal et al., 2024).

UNDERSTANDING DIGITAL CITIZENSHIP

A. Definition and Relevance of Digital Citizenship

Digital citizenship refers to the rights and responsibilities of individuals in the digital realm, encompassing the ethical, legal, and social aspects of engaging with technology. It involves the ability to access, analyze, evaluate, create, and communicate information safely and responsibly. Digital citizenship encompasses a range of skills and knowledge, including digital literacy, online etiquette, privacy protection, critical thinking, and responsible use of digital tools and platforms. It is not merely about being adept at using technology but also about being aware of the impact of one's actions in the digital world and contributing positively to online communities (Fernández-Prados, et al, 2021).

The relevance of digital citizenship in the era of advanced education cannot be overstated. As technology continues to evolve and play an increasingly integral role in our daily lives, the ability to navigate the digital landscape is crucial for personal, social, and professional success. Digital citizenship equips individuals with the skills needed to engage safely and effectively with online content, fostering informed and responsible participation in digital society. Moreover, it empowers learners to critically assess the credibility and ethical implications of information, protecting themselves from potential risks such as cyberbullying, identity theft, and misinformation. By promoting digital citizenship, educators can help shape a generation of responsible, ethical, and engaged digital citizens, better prepared to thrive in an increasingly connected and technology-driven world (Chen, et al, 2021).

B. Skills Required for Responsible Digital Citizenship

Responsible digital citizenship requires a multifaceted set of skills that enable individuals to engage with digital technology in a manner that is ethical, secure, and beneficial to themselves and society (Lauricella, et al, 2020; Pangrazio, & Sefton-Green, 2021). Here are some of the key skills required (refer table 1).

Table 1. Skills required for responsible digital citizenship

Number	Skill	Elaboration
1	Digital Literacy	Understanding how to use digital tools and platforms effectively, including the ability to navigate the internet, use productivity software, and manage digital content.
2	Information Literacy	The ability to locate, evaluate, and use information from digital sources critically. This includes discerning between credible and unreliable information and understanding copyright and intellectual property rights.
3	Cybersecurity Awareness	Knowledge of how to protect personal information and digital assets from online threats, including phishing scams, malware, and hacking attempts.
4	Privacy Management	Understanding privacy settings and practices to control personal information shared online, as well as the implications of data collection and usage by third parties.
5	Online Etiquette	Knowing how to communicate respectfully and appropriately in digital environments, including social media, forums, and email exchanges.
6	Critical Thinking	The capacity to analyze and evaluate digital content, discerning bias, propaganda, and the potential manipulation of information.
7	Problem-Solving	The ability to troubleshoot technical issues and find solutions to digital challenges independently or through collaborative efforts.
8	Collaboration and Communication	Proficiency in using digital tools to work effectively with others, whether in educational, professional, or social contexts.
9	Digital Footprint Management	Awareness of one's digital presence and the ability to manage it in a way that reflects positively on personal and professional identity.
10	Legal and Ethical Understanding	Knowledge of the legal and ethical implications of digital actions, including copyright laws, digital rights, and the social impact of technology use.
11	Digital Creativity	The skill to create and share digital content responsibly, contributing to the cultural and informational wealth of the online community.
12	Adaptability	Adaptability

By developing and honing these skills, individuals can become responsible digital citizens who contribute positively to the digital world and mitigate the risks associated with technology use.

C. The Role of Digital Citizenship in Engaging With AI

The role of digital citizenship in engaging with AI is multifaceted, encompassing both the active participation in the development of AI and the ethical considerations of its deployment. As AI becomes increasingly integrated into everyday life, digital citizens must be equipped to understand the underlying algorithms and data processes that drive AI systems. This knowledge allows individuals to critically assess the potential biases, limitations, and societal impacts of AI applications. By engaging with AI in an informed manner, digital citizens can contribute to the shaping of AI that aligns with societal values and promotes equitable outcomes, ensuring that technology serves the broader public interest rather than just select groups (Gonzalez-Mohino, et al, 2023).

Moreover, digital citizenship plays a crucial role in fostering a culture of accountability and transparency around AI. As users of AI-powered tools and services, responsible digital citizens demand transparency in how AI systems make decisions that affect them. They advocate for the right to understand and challenge AI-generated outcomes, and they support initiatives that promote open-source AI models and data sharing. By doing so, digital citizens help to create a framework for AI governance that respects privacy, protects against discrimination, and upholds human rights, thereby ensuring that AI engagement is both ethical and beneficial to the broader community (Choi, & Cristol, 202).

AI IN EDUCATIONAL SYSTEMS: OPPORTUNITIES AND CHALLENGES

A. Personalizing Learning Experiences With AI

Personalizing learning experiences with AI represents a transformative opportunity within educational systems. AI-powered tools can analyze individual students' learning patterns, strengths, and weaknesses to tailor educational content and delivery methods accordingly. This customization allows for a more dynamic and responsive learning environment, where students can progress at their own pace, receive targeted support in areas where they struggle, and be challenged with material that matches their abilities and interests. The result is a more engaging and effective educational journey that can lead to improved outcomes and a deeper understanding of the subject matter (Murtaza, et al, 2022).

However, the integration of AI in personalizing learning experiences also presents challenges. There is a risk that over-reliance on AI could diminish the human element of education, potentially reducing the interaction between teachers and students.

Additionally, concerns about data privacy and the potential for AI algorithms to perpetuate or amplify biases must be addressed. Ensuring that AI systems are designed with inclusivity and fairness in mind is essential to prevent the marginalization of certain student populations and to uphold the principle that education should be accessible and equitable for all (Klašnja-Milićević, & Ivanović, 202).

B. Enhancing Educational Outcomes Through AI

Enhancing educational outcomes through AI has the potential to revolutionize the way students learn and teachers instruct. AI can provide real-time feedback, adaptive learning paths, and predictive analytics that help educators understand where students may need additional support. By identifying knowledge gaps and tailoring interventions, AI can significantly improve the efficiency of teaching and learning processes. This technology can also offer interactive simulations and virtual reality experiences that make complex concepts more accessible and engaging, thereby increasing student motivation and retention rates. Ultimately, AI's role in education can lead to a more profound comprehension of subjects and better preparation for the challenges of the modern workforce (Harry, & Sayudin, 2023).

Despite these benefits, there are challenges to consider in the pursuit of enhancing educational outcomes through AI. The initial investment in AI technology can be substantial, and not all educational institutions may have the resources to implement it effectively. Moreover, there is a need for ongoing professional development for educators to integrate AI tools into their teaching practices. There is also the question of how to measure the effectiveness of AI in education, as traditional assessment methods may not fully capture the nuanced impact of personalized learning experiences. Ensuring that AI is used to complement rather than replace the critical thinking and creativity that are central to a well-rounded education is another key consideration for educators and policymakers (Adıgüzel, et al, 2023).

How can AI be effectively utilized to enhance educational outcomes? The integration of AI in education can be approached through several key strategies (refer table 2) as discussed by Baidoo-Anu, & Ansah, (2023).

Table 2. Key strategies in the integration of AI in education

Number	Strategy	Elaboration
1	AI can be used to personalize learning experiences.	By analyzing data on students' learning patterns, AI systems can tailor educational content to individual needs, ensuring that each student progresses at a pace that suits them best. This personalization can extend to providing additional resources, such as videos or interactive exercises, that cater to different learning styles and help students grasp difficult concepts more effectively.
2	AI-powered tools can offer immediate and constructive feedback to students, which is crucial for their development.	Through the use of AI in grading assignments and tests, educators can save time and focus on providing more in-depth feedback and one-on-one support. Additionally, AI can identify at-risk students early on by detecting patterns that suggest potential dropouts or learning challenges, allowing for timely interventions.

By adopting these strategies, educators can harness the power of AI to create a more dynamic, responsive, and student-centered learning environment that ultimately leads to improved educational outcomes.

C. Democratizing Access to Knowledge With AI

Democratizing access to knowledge with AI has the potential to revolutionize the educational landscape by breaking down barriers that traditionally limit who can learn and how much they can learn. AI-driven platforms and applications can make high-quality educational resources accessible to students regardless of their geographical location or socioeconomic status. By offering free or low-cost online courses, AI can ensure that learners from diverse backgrounds can access the same level of education as those in more privileged settings, thereby reducing the educational gap and fostering a more equitable society (Murphy, & Taylor, 2023).

Moreover, AI can democratize access to specialized knowledge that was once reserved for a select few. Through advanced learning management systems, AI can provide personalized learning paths for students interested in niche subjects, enabling them to delve into areas of study that might not be available in their local schools or universities. This democratization not only empowers individuals to pursue their interests and expand their horizons but also nurtures a more informed and skilled workforce capable of addressing the complex challenges of the modern world (Himmelreich, 2023).

D. Ethical Dilemmas and Privacy Concerns in AI Education

1. Data Security

Data security is a paramount ethical dilemma and privacy concern in the realm of AI education. As educational systems increasingly rely on AI to personalize learning experiences, a vast amount of sensitive student data is collected, stored, and analyzed. This data includes not only academic performance metrics but also personal information that could potentially be misused if not properly secured. The risk of data breaches poses a significant threat, as it could lead to the exposure of students' personal information, compromising their privacy and potentially leading to identity theft or other forms of exploitation (Dhirani, et al, 2023).

To address these concerns, educational institutions must implement robust data security measures. This includes ensuring that all data is encrypted, that access to sensitive information is strictly controlled and monitored, and that there are clear policies in place for data retention and deletion. Additionally, transparency about what data is being collected and how it is being used is crucial. Students and parents should have a clear understanding of the data practices and the rights they have over their information. By prioritizing data security, educational institutions can help maintain the trust of their communities and fulfill their ethical obligation to protect the privacy of their students (Akgun, & Greenhow, 2022).

2. Algorithmic Bias

Algorithmic bias is a significant ethical dilemma within AI education, posing a threat to fairness and equality in learning environments. AI systems that inform educational decisions, such as admissions, grading, and personalized learning, are often trained on datasets that reflect historical biases. If these biases are not identified and corrected, they can perpetuate unfairness, leading to discriminatory outcomes where certain groups of students are systematically disadvantaged. For example, if an AI system used for college admissions is biased against applicants from certain socioeconomic backgrounds, it could unfairly limit their educational opportunities (Li, 2024).

Addressing algorithmic bias requires a proactive and multifaceted approach. Developers must ensure that AI systems are trained on diverse and representative datasets to prevent the amplification of existing biases. Additionally, regular audits and transparency in AI algorithms are essential to detect and mitigate bias. Educators and policymakers must also be vigilant in monitoring the impact of AI on students, ensuring that no group is unfairly penalized or marginalized by technology. By prioritizing ethical AI development and implementation, educational institutions can work towards creating a more equitable and just learning environments for all students (Slimi, & Carballido, 2023).

3. Impact on Employment

The impact of AI on employment within the educational sector raises significant ethical dilemmas and concerns. As AI technologies advance, there is a growing possibility that they could replace certain educational roles, such as administrative staff, librarians, and even teaching positions. This shift could lead to job displacement for educators and staff, potentially disrupting careers and the economic stability of those employed in the field. The ethical question arises about the responsibility of educational institutions to balance the benefits of AI with the livelihoods of their employees (Borenstein, & Howard, 2021).

Moreover, the integration of AI in education may also alter the skill requirements for educators, necessitating a shift in professional development and training. While AI can enhance teaching by handling repetitive tasks and data analysis, educators will need to adapt by developing new skills in AI literacy, data interpretation, and technology integration. This transition poses a challenge for educators who may struggle to keep up with the pace of technological change, highlighting the need for ethical frameworks that support continuous learning and professional growth. Balancing the potential benefits of AI with the impact on employment and the need for ongoing education is crucial for maintaining a sustainable and equitable educational workforce (Du, & Xie, 2021).

A COMPREHENSIVE FRAMEWORK FOR ADDRESSING AI ETHICS, ENGAGEMENT, AND PRIVACY

A. Fostering Digital Literacy

1. Technical Skills

Fostering digital literacy with a focus on technical skills is a critical component of a comprehensive framework for addressing AI ethics, engagement, and privacy in education. Educators must be equipped with the ability to understand and navigate the technologies that are becoming integral to their teaching practices. This includes proficiency in using AI tools and platforms, as well as the knowledge to interpret and act on the data these systems provide (Chiu, et al, 2024).

To achieve this, educational institutions should offer ongoing professional development programs that are designed to enhance teachers' technical skills. These programs should cover a range of topics, from the basics of AI and machine learning to more advanced concepts such as algorithmic transparency and data privacy. By empowering educators with these technical skills, they can effectively integrate AI into their curriculum, guide students in using AI responsibly, and address potential ethical issues that may arise. This approach not only prepares teachers to use AI as a tool for personalized learning but also ensures that they can educate students on how to be informed and responsible digital citizens in an AI-driven world (Ng, et al, 2021).

2. Ethical Judgment

A comprehensive framework for addressing AI ethics, engagement, and privacy in the era of advanced education must begin with fostering digital literacy. In an increasingly digital world, it is crucial for individuals to develop the skills necessary to navigate and critically evaluate the vast amount of information available. Digital literacy encompasses not only the technical skills to use AI and other digital tools but also the ability to understand the ethical implications of these technologies. By promoting digital literacy, educators can empower students to make informed decisions, discern between reliable and biased sources, and engage with AI in a responsible and ethical manner (Abulibdeh, et al, 2024).

Ethical judgment is a cornerstone of digital literacy and a vital component in the framework for AI ethics, engagement, and privacy. As AI becomes more integrated into various aspects of our lives, individuals must be equipped to assess the moral dimensions of AI applications. Ethical judgment involves considering the potential consequences of AI use, ensuring fairness and inclusivity, and respecting the privacy of individuals. By instilling strong ethical judgment in students, we can cultivate a generation of digital citizens who are prepared to navigate the complexities of AI and contribute to a more equitable and ethical digital society (Peters, et al, 2020).

3. Privacy Awareness

A comprehensive framework for addressing AI ethics, engagement, and privacy must prioritize fostering digital literacy. In an era where artificial intelligence permeates every aspect of society, from healthcare to social media, it is crucial that individuals possess the knowledge and skills necessary to navigate and understand these technologies. Digital literacy encompasses not only the technical know-how to use AI systems but also the critical thinking skills to assess their ethical implications. By promoting digital literacy, we empower individuals to make informed decisions about their engagement with AI, ensuring that they can fully participate in and benefit from the digital economy while mitigating potential risks (Kong, et al, 2023).

Privacy awareness is a vital component of this framework, as it addresses the increasing concern over the collection, use, and protection of personal data by AI systems. As AI becomes more integrated into daily life, the potential for data breaches and misuse grows. Therefore, it is essential to educate individuals about their privacy rights and the importance of safeguarding their personal information. Privacy awareness initiatives should focus on teaching people how to manage their online presence, understand privacy policies, and use privacy settings effectively. By fostering a culture of privacy consciousness, we can encourage responsible AI development and ensure that individuals' rights are respected in the digital realm (Wilton, et al, 2022).

B. Multi-Faceted Approach to AI Education

1. Curriculum Development

A multi-faceted approach to AI education is pivotal within a comprehensive framework for addressing AI ethics, engagement, and privacy. Central to this approach is the development of a robust curriculum that equips learners with a nuanced understanding of AI systems. Curriculum development should begin by identifying the core competencies required for individuals to engage with AI responsibly. This includes foundational knowledge of AI principles, algorithms, and their societal impacts, as well as advanced skills for those pursuing careers in AI development and implementation. The curriculum should be adaptable and continuously updated to reflect the evolving nature of AI technologies and the ethical challenges they present (Saxena, et al, 2023).

To ensure effectiveness, curriculum development for AI education must be a collaborative effort involving educators, industry experts, policymakers, and ethicists. This collaborative approach ensures that the curriculum remains relevant and addresses the multifaceted aspects of AI, including technical, ethical, and social dimensions. It should integrate hands-on learning experiences, case studies, and ethical reasoning exercises to foster critical thinking and practical application. Additionally, the curriculum should be designed to be inclusive, catering to diverse learning styles and backgrounds, and should emphasize the global implications of AI, preparing students to navigate the complexities of an AI-integrated world (Al-kfairy, et al, 2024).

2. Teacher Training

An essential component of a multi-faceted approach to AI education is the training of teachers who will impart this knowledge to students. Teacher training programs must be designed to ensure that educators are not only proficient in the technical aspects of AI but also equipped to address the ethical, social, and privacy implications of AI systems. These programs should provide comprehensive instruction on AI fundamentals, including machine learning, data analytics, and the potential biases inherent in AI algorithms. By doing so, teachers can effectively guide students through the complexities of AI and its impact on society, fostering a generation that is both AI-literate and ethically conscious (Kamalov, et al, 2023).

Furthermore, teacher training should focus on innovative pedagogical methods that encourage critical thinking and problem-solving skills. Educators need to be trained in how to create inclusive learning environments that accommodate various levels of AI knowledge and how to facilitate discussions around the ethical use of AI. This includes training on how to incorporate project-based learning, ethical debates, and real-world scenarios into their teaching practices. By investing in teacher training, educational institutions can build a workforce capable of preparing students for a future where AI plays an increasingly significant role, ensuring that the next generation is ready to engage with AI in an informed, responsible, and privacy-conscious manner (Ouyang, & Jiao, 2021).

3. Policy Initiatives

To effectively implement a multi-faceted approach to AI education, policy initiatives at the governmental and institutional levels are crucial. These initiatives should aim to create an environment that supports the integration of AI education across all educational sectors. Policies could include the establishment of national standards for AI education, funding for AI-related programs and resources in schools, and the promotion of partnerships between educational institutions and the tech industry. By setting clear guidelines and providing the necessary support, policymakers can ensure that AI education is not only accessible but also aligned with the rapidly evolving demands of the digital economy (Chan, 2023).

Moreover, policy initiatives should address the need for continuous professional development for educators and the updating of educational frameworks to include AI. This could involve the creation of incentives for teachers to engage in AI-related training, the development of certification programs for AI education, and the incorporation of AI into the core curriculum from primary to tertiary levels. Such policies not only facilitate the widespread dissemination of AI knowledge but also help in nurturing a workforce that is adept at leveraging AI technologies while maintaining a strong ethical compass and a commitment to privacy and social responsibility (Judijanto, et al, 2022).

CASE STUDIES AND EXAMPLES

A. Successful Implementations of AI in Education

Table 3 shows the Successful Implementations of AI in Education. Carnegie Learning's Cognitive Tutor has demonstrated significant educational impact, with students experiencing a notable boost in their standardized test scores by leveraging AI to tailor the learning experience. The integration of cognitive science and machine learning in the program's design is crucial to its effectiveness in personalizing education for diverse learners. Knewton's adaptive learning platform has proven its efficacy at Arizona State University, where it significantly enhanced pass rates and final grades by dynamically personalizing educational content. The platform's sophisticated algorithm, which fine-tunes instruction based on real-time analysis of student interactions, is central to its educational benefits. Duolingo has achieved widespread success with over 300 million users, leveraging AI to offer personalized language learning experiences that are both engaging and effective, thanks to its gamified approach and adaptive exercises. The app's innovative use of AI to tailor the learning process has earned it recognition as one of the top language learning tools in the educational and tech communities. Gradescope has revolutionized the grading process for educators at over 1,000 institutions, significantly reducing grading time by up to 90% with its AI-powered platform that adeptly handles a range of assignment types. The platform's efficiency and accuracy in providing quick feedback to students have made it an invaluable tool in the educational sector. AltSchool's AI-driven personalized learning environments have garnered praise across the board for fostering a student-centered approach that enhances engagement and learning outcomes. The platform's AI capabilities in tracking and tailoring education to each student's unique needs are fundamental to its effectiveness in modern education. Lastly, Georgia Tech's online Master's degree program, supported by AI-driven virtual teaching assistants like Jill Watson, has successfully scaled enrollment by 60% without overburdening faculty, showcasing the potential of AI to enhance classroom support and student engagement. The accuracy and efficiency of Jill Watson in managing online forums have been instrumental in lightening the workload for human teaching assistants and maintaining a high level of student support.

Table 3. Successful implementations of AI in education

Number	Successful Implementations	
1	Intelligent Tutoring Systems (ITS)	
	Case Study: Carnegie Learning's Cognitive Tutor	D'Mello, & Graesser, 2023
	Implementation	Carnegie Learning developed the Cognitive Tutor, an AI-based tutoring program designed to assist students in mathematics. The program adapts to the individual learning pace and style of each student, providing personalized feedback and guidance.
	Success Metrics	Studies have shown that students using the Cognitive Tutor improved their performance on standardized tests by an average of 20 percentile points compared to students who did not use the program.
	Key Factors	The success of the Cognitive Tutor can be attributed to its use of cognitive science principles and machine learning algorithms to provide a highly individualized learning experience.
2	Adaptive Learning Platforms	
	Case Study: Knewton	Dutta, et al, 2024
	Implementation	Knewton is an adaptive learning technology provider that partners with educational institutions and publishers. The platform personalizes educational content for students based on their learning needs and performance.
	Success Metrics	In a pilot program at Arizona State University, students using Knewton's adaptive learning platform had higher pass rates and final grades compared to those who did not use the platform.
	Key Factors	Knewton's success is due to its sophisticated algorithm that continuously analyzes student interactions and adjusts the content and sequence of instruction accordingly.
3	Language Learning Applications	
	Case Study: Duolingo	Portnoff, et al, 2021
	Implementation	Duolingo is a popular language learning app that uses AI to teach users new languages. The app provides personalized learning experiences, including exercises that adapt to the user's progress and needs.
	Success Metrics	Duolingo boasts over 300 million users worldwide and has been named one of the best language learning apps by various educational institutions and tech reviews.
	Key Factors	The gamification aspect, combined with AI-driven adaptive learning, makes Duolingo engaging and effective for language acquisition.
4	Automated Grading Systems	
	Case Study: Gradescope	Mäkelä, 2021

continued on following page

Table 3. Continued

Number	Successful Implementations	
	Implementation	Gradescope is an AI-powered grading platform that streamlines the grading process for educators. It uses machine learning algorithms to automatically grade assignments, saving teachers time and providing students with quick feedback.
	Success Metrics	Gradescope has been adopted by over 1,000 institutions, including many top universities, and has reduced the time spent on grading by up to 90% in some cases.
	Key Factors	The platform's ability to handle various question types, including multiple-choice, free response, and programming assignments, has made it versatile and effective for educators.
5	Personalized Learning Environments	
	Case Study: AltSchool	Selvarani, & Ganeshan, 2024
	Implementation	AltSchool is a network of schools that uses AI to create personalized learning experiences for students. The platform tracks student progress and tailors educational content and activities to individual learning goals.
	Success Metrics	AltSchool has received positive feedback from educators, parents, and students for its innovative approach to education. Students have shown improved engagement and learning outcomes.
	Key Factors	The use of AI to create a student-centered learning environment that focuses on individual strengths and areas for improvement is a key aspect of AltSchool's success.
6	AI-Enhanced Classrooms	
	Case Study: Georgia Tech's Online Master's Degree Program	Kadel, 2024
	Implementation	Georgia Tech partnered with AT&T and Udacity to offer an online Master's degree in Computer Science. The program includes AI-driven virtual teaching assistants named Jill Watson, which help answer students' questions in online forums.
	Success Metrics	The program has seen a 60% increase in enrollment without a corresponding increase in faculty, demonstrating the efficiency of AI in supporting large-scale educational initiatives.
	Key Factors	The development of Jill Watson, which can answer questions with a high degree of accuracy, has significantly reduced the workload for teaching assistants and improved student support.

In each of these cases, the successful implementation of AI in education relies on a combination of factors, including the personalization of learning experiences, the efficiency gains for educators, and the overall improvement in student outcomes. These examples illustrate the potential for AI to transform and enhance the educational landscape.

B. Lessons Learned From Challenges and Setbacks

Table 4 shows the Lessons Learned from Challenges and Setbacks in AI Implementations in Education. For Intelligent Tutoring Systems like Carnegie Learning's Cognitive Tutor, the lesson learned is that seamless integration into the curriculum, along with ongoing support and training, is key to user acceptance and effective data collection. Additionally, for scalability, a modular and flexible system design is essential to cater to diverse educational needs. In general, the implementation of AI in education necessitates a collaborative approach with educators to align with educational goals and balance personalization with generalization. Moreover, ethical considerations, continuous improvement, and a feedback-driven evaluation process are imperative for the optimal and responsible use of AI in learning environments.

Table 4. Lessons learned from challenges and setbacks in AI implementations in education

Number	Lesson learned	Elaboration
Specific cases		
1	Intelligent Tutoring Systems (ITS)	
	Lessons from Carnegie Learning's Cognitive Tutor	D'Mello, & Graesser, 2023
	User Acceptance	The initial challenge was to ensure that students and educators accepted and were willing to use the AI tutoring system.
	Lesson Learned	It's crucial to integrate the AI system into the curriculum in a way that complements existing teaching methods and addresses the concerns of educators and students through training and support.
	Data Quality	Ensuring the quality and relevance of the data collected from students is vital for the effectiveness of the system.
	Lesson Learned	Continuous monitoring and improvement of data collection methods can help in refining the AI's understanding of students' needs and learning styles.
	Scalability	Scaling the Cognitive Tutor to different subjects and levels of education posed a challenge.
	Lesson Learned	Modular design and flexible architecture are necessary for adapting AI tutoring systems to various educational contexts.
2	Adaptive Learning Platforms	
	Lessons from Knewton	Dutta, et al, 2024

continued on following page

Table 4. Continued

Number	Lesson learned	Elaboration
	Integration with Curriculum	The challenge was to seamlessly integrate the adaptive learning platform with the existing curriculum and teaching methods.
	Lesson Learned	Close collaboration with educators and curriculum developers is essential to ensure that the adaptive learning platform is aligned with educational goals and standards.
	Privacy and Data Security	Handling sensitive student data requires strict adherence to privacy laws and regulations.
	Lesson Learned	Clear policies on data privacy and security must be in place to build trust with educational institutions and students.
	Feedback Loop	Creating a robust feedback loop that allows for real-time updates to the learning content based on student performance is complex.
	Lesson Learned	Regular updates and continuous iteration of the algorithms are needed to maintain the platform's effectiveness.
3	Language Learning Applications	
	Lessons from Duolingo	Portnoff, et al, 2021
	Engagement Over Accuracy	Duolingo faced criticism for focusing more on engagement than on the accuracy of language learning.
	Lesson Learned	Balancing fun and engagement with educational rigor is important for long-term user retention and learning outcomes.
	Cultural Relevance	The app had to adapt to different cultural contexts and language nuances.
	Lesson Learned	Incorporating diverse content and considering cultural differences is essential for global reach and relevance.
	Monetization	Finding a sustainable business model that doesn't compromise the user experience can be challenging.
	Lesson Learned	Transparent and user-friendly monetization strategies can maintain user trust and loyalty.
General Lessons Learned from AI Implementations in Education (Goh, & Nurul Ajleaa, 2024)		
1	Collaboration with Educators	AI in education should be developed in close partnership with educators to ensure it meets educational needs and standards.
2	Personalization vs. Generalization	Striking the right balance between personalization and generalization to cater to a wide range of students while maintaining individualized learning experiences.
3	Continuous Improvement	AI systems require ongoing refinement and updates to adapt to changing educational landscapes and student needs.
4	Ethical Considerations	Ensuring that AI in education is ethically implemented, with a focus on fairness, transparency, and accountability.
5	Evaluation and Feedback	Regular evaluation of AI systems and incorporating feedback from users can lead to significant improvements in the effectiveness of AI in education.

COLLABORATIVE EFFORTS FOR A SUPPORTIVE AND INCLUSIVE DIGITAL ENVIRONMENT

A. The Role of Educators

Educators play a pivotal role in fostering a supportive and inclusive digital environment. By integrating digital literacy and responsible online behavior into their curriculum, they equip students with the necessary skills to navigate the digital world safely and respectfully. Teachers can encourage open dialogue about the challenges and opportunities of the online realm, promoting empathy and understanding among students. Through project-based learning and collaborative assignments, educators can model the importance of teamwork and mutual respect, which are essential components of a positive digital culture (Ní Bhroin, & King, 2020).

Furthermore, educators must serve as advocates for digital equity and accessibility. By addressing the needs of all students, including those with disabilities and those from diverse backgrounds, teachers can ensure that everyone has equal opportunities to participate in the digital environment. This involves not only providing the right tools and resources but also adapting teaching methods to accommodate different learning styles and abilities. By doing so, educators contribute to building a more inclusive digital space where every student feels valued and supported (Haleem, et al, 2022).

B. The Role of Policymakers

Policymakers are instrumental in shaping the legal and regulatory frameworks that underpin a supportive and inclusive digital environment. They have the responsibility to enact and enforce laws that protect users from cyber threats, such as bullying, harassment, and privacy violations. By establishing clear guidelines and standards for digital platforms, policymakers can ensure that online spaces are safe and accessible to all individuals, regardless of their background or identity. This involves collaboration with educators, industry experts, and advocacy groups to develop policies that reflect the evolving digital landscape and the needs of its users (Hoogerwerf, & Mavrou, 2020).

Moreover, policymakers must prioritize digital literacy and inclusion in their legislative agenda. This includes funding initiatives that provide equal access to technology and internet connectivity, particularly in underserved communities. By promoting digital skills training and supporting programs that bridge the digital divide, policymakers can empower individuals to fully participate in the digital economy and society. Their role also extends to fostering international cooperation to address global digital challenges, such as cross-border data protection and cybersecurity, thereby contributing to a more cohesive and supportive digital environment on a worldwide scale (Simonofski, et al, 2021).

C. The Role of Technology Professionals

Technology professionals are at the forefront of creating and maintaining a supportive and inclusive digital environment. They design, develop, and implement technologies that shape our online experiences, and thus have a profound impact on accessibility and user interaction. By prioritizing universal design principles, these professionals can ensure that digital products and services are usable by people with a wide range of abilities, including those with disabilities. This involves incorporating features like screen reader compatibility, adjustable text sizes, and intuitive navigation, which not only benefit individuals with specific needs but enhance the overall user experience for everyone (Smith, et al, 2020).

Additionally, technology professionals have a crucial role in safeguarding the integrity and security of digital platforms. They work to protect user data and privacy, develop algorithms that mitigate bias, and implement measures to prevent the spread of misinformation and harmful content. By adhering to ethical standards and promoting transparency in their work, these professionals contribute to building trust within the digital community. Their ongoing efforts to innovate and improve technology also help in addressing emerging challenges, thereby ensuring that the digital environment remains an inclusive and empowering space for all users (Sterrett, & Richardson, 2020).

D. The Role of Government

The role of government in society is multifaceted, encompassing the creation and enforcement of laws, the provision of public services, and the protection of citizens' rights and well-being. Governments are responsible for establishing a legal framework that maintains order, protects property rights, and ensures justice. This involves the drafting and passage of legislation, as well as the operation of courts and law enforcement agencies. By upholding the rule of law, governments provide a stable environment that fosters economic growth, social cohesion, and individual freedom, while also addressing societal issues such as poverty, inequality, and discrimination (Chen, et al, 2021).

Furthermore, governments play a pivotal role in providing essential public services and infrastructure that are critical to the functioning of a modern society. This includes healthcare, education, transportation, and utilities like water and electricity. Through taxation and public spending, governments redistribute resources to support the most vulnerable members of society and to invest in the collective future. They also have a duty to promote general welfare by creating policies that enhance economic stability, support environmental sustainability, and protect citizens from internal and external threats. Through diplomacy and defense, governments engage with the international community to maintain peace and security, advance national interests, and contribute to global cooperation and development (Chohan, & Hu, 2022).

CONCLUSION

A. Summary of Key Points

In conclusion, this chapter has underscored the pivotal role of digital citizenship in the era of advanced education, highlighting the intersection of AI and learning as a transformative force. We have explored the importance of ethical AI integration, the need for active engagement from all stakeholders, and the critical issue of privacy in digital spaces. The chapter has emphasized the necessity for a collaborative approach among educators, technology experts, and policymakers to foster a supportive and inclusive digital environment that equips citizens with the skills and knowledge to navigate the evolving digital landscape responsibly and effectively.

B. The Importance of Preparing Future Generations for a Digital Future With AI

Preparing future generations for a digital future with AI is of paramount importance as artificial intelligence becomes an integral part of our daily lives and the workforce. As AI continues to evolve and automate tasks, it is essential that young people are equipped with the skills to navigate and thrive in this new landscape. This includes not only technical skills, such as programming and data analysis, but also soft skills like critical thinking, problem-solving, and creativity, which will be crucial for working alongside AI and for jobs that AI cannot replicate. By integrating AI education into the curriculum, we can ensure that students are not just consumers of technology but creators and innovators who can harness AI to solve complex problems and drive societal progress (Gill, et al, 2022).

Moreover, preparing for a digital future with AI also involves instilling an ethical and societal understanding of technology. As AI systems make decisions that can have far-reaching consequences, it is essential that future generations understand the implications of AI, including its potential biases and the ethical considerations surrounding its use. Educating students about the social, economic, and philosophical aspects of AI will empower them to shape a future where technology serves the common good, respects human rights, and enhances the quality of life for all. This comprehensive approach to AI education will not only prepare students for careers but also for the broader role they will play as informed citizens in a society increasingly influenced by artificial intelligence (Cazzaniga, et al, 2024).

The critical analysis of AI's impact on digital citizenship and education underscores the need to examine both the potential for personalized learning and the risks of algorithmic bias and privacy violations, advocating for a balanced discourse that considers the ethical dimensions and societal implications of AI integration in educational systems. This approach ensures that the discussion around AI in education is not merely celebratory but also addresses the potential for discrimination and the erosion of privacy rights, which are fundamental to fostering an inclusive and equitable digital citizenship. (Filgueiras, 2024).

C. Call to Action for Stakeholders in Education, Technology, and Government

We call on all stakeholders in education, technology, and government to unite in a collaborative effort to prepare our society for the digital future with AI. Educators must prioritize the integration of AI and digital literacy into the curriculum, ensuring that students from all backgrounds have access to the necessary resources and support to develop a strong foundation in these areas. Technology professionals must commit to developing inclusive technologies and to sharing their expertise with educational institutions, while also advocating for ethical AI practices within their industries. Policymakers must enact legislation that supports digital education and fosters an environment where AI can be developed and used responsibly, with a focus on equity and accessibility (Ifenthaler, et al, 2021).

Now is the time for action. We urge government bodies to invest in educational programs that promote digital skills and to create partnerships with the private sector and academia to advance AI research and education. Technology companies should actively engage in mentorship programs and internships to provide real-world experiences for students. Educators must continue to evolve their teaching methods to meet the dynamic needs of a tech-driven world. Together, we can ensure that our future generations are not just ready for the digital future with AI but are also at the forefront of shaping it in a way that is beneficial, inclusive, and sustainable for all (Brunetti, et al, 2020).

To effectively use AI for diverse educational and cultural backgrounds, the technology should be adapted to include culturally relevant content and pedagogies, while also being designed to accommodate varying levels of access to resources and infrastructure. Additionally, AI systems should be regularly evaluated for biases and adjusted to ensure equitable outcomes across different cultural and educational contexts. (Lin et al., 2024).

To balance the benefits and risks of using AI in education, it is crucial to implement comprehensive ethical guidelines that ensure the technology enhances learning while protecting student privacy and mitigating biases. Moreover, educators should engage in ongoing evaluation to weigh the advantages of personalized learning against the potential for over-reliance on AI and the displacement of critical thinking skills. (Iu Zaman, 2024).

To enhance the depth of analysis regarding AI in education, future studies should delve into the nuanced ways in which AI algorithms impact learning outcomes, addressing both the adaptive learning capabilities and the potential for reinforcing educational inequalities. Additionally, a thorough examination of AI's role in personalizing education could shed light on the long-term cognitive and social effects on students. (Samala et al., 2024).

REFERENCES

Abulibdeh, A., Zaidan, E., & Abulibdeh, R. (2024). Navigating the confluence of artificial intelligence and education for sustainable development in the era of industry 4.0: Challenges, opportunities, and ethical dimensions. *Journal of Cleaner Production*, 437, 140527. DOI: 10.1016/j.jclepro.2023.140527

Adıgüzel, T., Kaya, M. H., & Cansu, F. K. (2023). Revolutionizing education with AI: Exploring the transformative potential of ChatGPT. *Contemporary Educational Technology*, 15(3), ep429. DOI: 10.30935/cedtech/13152

Akgun, S., & Greenhow, C. (2022). Artificial intelligence in education: Addressing ethical challenges in K-12 settings. *AI and Ethics*, 2(3), 431–440. DOI: 10.1007/s43681-021-00096-7 PMID: 34790956

Al-kfairy, M., Mustafa, D., Kshetri, N., Insiew, M., & Alfandi, O. (2024, August). Ethical Challenges and Solutions of Generative AI: An Interdisciplinary Perspective. In Informatics (Vol. 11, No. 3, p. 58). MDPI.

Baidoo-Anu, D., & Ansah, L. O. (2023). Education in the era of generative artificial intelligence (AI): Understanding the potential benefits of ChatGPT in promoting teaching and learning. *Journal of AI*, 7(1), 52–62. DOI: 10.61969/jai.1337500

Borenstein, J., & Howard, A. (2021). Emerging challenges in AI and the need for AI ethics education. *AI and Ethics*, 1(1), 61–65. DOI: 10.1007/s43681-020-00002-7 PMID: 38624388

Brunetti, F., Matt, D. T., Bonfanti, A., De Longhi, A., Pedrini, G., & Orzes, G. (2020). Digital transformation challenges: Strategies emerging from a multi-stakeholder approach. *The TQM Journal*, 32(4), 697–724. DOI: 10.1108/TQM-12-2019-0309

Calzada, I. (2023). Emerging digital citizenship regimes: Pandemic, algorithmic, liquid, metropolitan, and stateless citizenships. *Citizenship Studies*, 27(2), 160–188. DOI: 10.1080/13621025.2021.2012312

Camacho, N. G. (2024). The Role of AI in Cybersecurity: Addressing Threats in the Digital Age. Journal of Artificial Intelligence General Science (JAIGS), 3(1), 143-154.

Cazzaniga, M., Jaumotte, M. F., Li, L., Melina, M. G., Panton, A. J., Pizzinelli, C., & Tavares, M. M. M. (2024). *Gen-AI: Artificial intelligence and the future of work.* International Monetary Fund. DOI: 10.5089/9798400262548.006

Chan, C. K. Y. (2023). A comprehensive AI policy education framework for university teaching and learning. *International Journal of Educational Technology in Higher Education*, 20(1), 38. DOI: 10.1186/s41239-023-00408-3

Chen, C. L., Lin, Y. C., Chen, W. H., Chao, C. F., & Pandia, H. (2021). Role of government to enhance digital transformation in small service business. *Sustainability (Basel)*, 13(3), 1028. DOI: 10.3390/su13031028

Chen, L. L., Mirpuri, S., Rao, N., & Law, N. (2021). Conceptualization and measurement of digital citizenship across disciplines. *Educational Research Review*, 33, 100379. DOI: 10.1016/j.edurev.2021.100379

Chiu, T. K., Ahmad, Z., Ismailov, M., & Sanusi, I. T. (2024). What are artificial intelligence literacy and competency? A comprehensive framework to support them. *Computers and Education Open*, 6, 100171. DOI: 10.1016/j.caeo.2024.100171

Chohan, S. R., & Hu, G. (2022). Strengthening digital inclusion through e-government: Cohesive ICT training programs to intensify digital competency. *Information Technology for Development*, 28(1), 16–38. DOI: 10.1080/02681102.2020.1841713

Choi, M., & Cristol, D. (2021). Digital citizenship with intersectionality lens: Towards participatory democracy driven digital citizenship education. *Theory into Practice*, 60(4), 361–370. DOI: 10.1080/00405841.2021.1987094

D'Mello, S. K., & Graesser, A. (2023). Intelligent tutoring systems: How computers achieve learning gains that rival human tutors. In *Handbook of educational psychology* (pp. 603–629). Routledge. DOI: 10.4324/9780429433726-31

Davies, H. C., Eynon, R., & Salveson, C. (2021). The mobilisation of AI in education: A Bourdieusean field analysis. *Sociology*, 55(3), 539–560. DOI: 10.1177/0038038520967888

Dayal, G., Verma, P., & Sehgal, S. (2024). A Comprehensive Review on the Integration of Artificial Intelligence in the Field of Education. Leveraging AI and Emotional Intelligence in Contemporary Business Organizations, 331-349.

Dhirani, L. L., Mukhtiar, N., Chowdhry, B. S., & Newe, T. (2023). Ethical dilemmas and privacy issues in emerging technologies: A review. *Sensors (Basel)*, 23(3), 1151. DOI: 10.3390/s23031151 PMID: 36772190

Du, S., & Xie, C. (2021). Paradoxes of artificial intelligence in consumer markets: Ethical challenges and opportunities. *Journal of Business Research*, 129, 961–974. DOI: 10.1016/j.jbusres.2020.08.024

Dutta, S., Ranjan, S., Mishra, S., Sharma, V., Hewage, P., & Iwendi, C. (2024, February). Enhancing Educational Adaptability: A Review and Analysis of AI-Driven Adaptive Learning Platforms. In 2024 4th International Conference on Innovative Practices in Technology and Management (ICIPTM) (pp. 1-5). IEEE.

Fernández-Prados, J. S., Lozano-Díaz, A., & Ainz-Galende, A. (2021, March). Measuring digital citizenship: A comparative analysis. In Informatics (Vol. 8, No. 1, p. 18). MDPI. DOI: 10.3390/informatics8010018

Filgueiras, F. (2024). Artificial intelligence and education governance. *Education, Citizenship and Social Justice*, 19(3), 349–361. DOI: 10.1177/17461979231160674

Gašević, D., Siemens, G., & Sadiq, S. (2023). Empowering learners for the age of artificial intelligence. *Computers and Education: Artificial Intelligence*, 4, 100130.

Gill, S. S., Xu, M., Ottaviani, C., Patros, P., Bahsoon, R., Shaghaghi, A., Golec, M., Stankovski, V., Wu, H., Abraham, A., Singh, M., Mehta, H., Ghosh, S. K., Baker, T., Parlikad, A. K., Lutfiyya, H., Kanhere, S. S., Sakellariou, R., Dustdar, S., & Uhlig, S. (2022). AI for next generation computing: Emerging trends and future directions. *Internet of Things : Engineering Cyber Physical Human Systems*, 19, 100514. DOI: 10.1016/j.iot.2022.100514

Goh, Y. S. & Nurul Ajleaa (2024). Chapter 14 Personalized Language Learning with AI for Pedagogical and Andragogical Approaches. In Integrating AI Into Pedagogical and Andragogical Education. https://www.igi-global.com/book/integrating-into-pedagogical-andragogical-education/343053DOI: 10.4018/979-8-3693-6130-6

Gonzalez-Mohino, M., Rodriguez-Domenech, M., Callejas-Albiñana, A. I., & Castillo-Canalejo, A. (2023). Empowering critical thinking: The role of digital tools in citizen participation. *Journal of New Approaches in Educational Research*, 12(2), 258–275. DOI: 10.7821/naer.2023.7.1385

Haleem, A., Javaid, M., Qadri, M. A., & Suman, R. (2022). Understanding the role of digital technologies in education: A review. Sustainable Operations and Computers, 3, 275-285.

Harry, A., & Sayudin, S. (2023). Role of AI in Education. *Interdiciplinary Journal and Hummanity*, 2(3), 260–268.

Henry, N., Vasil, S., & Witt, A. (2022). Digital citizenship in a global society: A feminist approach. *Feminist Media Studies*, 22(8), 1972–1989. DOI: 10.1080/14680777.2021.1937269

Himmelreich, J. (2023). Against "democratizing AI". *AI & Society*, 38(4), 1333–1346. DOI: 10.1007/s00146-021-01357-z

Hoogerwerf, E. J., & Mavrou, K. (2020). Inclusive education and digital empowerment as part of wider societal challenges. In *The Role of Assistive Technology in Fostering Inclusive Education* (pp. 131–143). Routledge. DOI: 10.4324/9780429428241-6

Ifenthaler, D., Gibson, D., Prasse, D., Shimada, A., & Yamada, M. (2021). Putting learning back into learning analytics: Actions for policy makers, researchers, and practitioners. *Educational Technology Research and Development*, 69(4), 2131–2150. DOI: 10.1007/s11423-020-09909-8

Iu Zaman, B. U. (2024). Transforming education through AI benefits risks and ethical considerations.

Judijanto, L., Aini, M. A., Asfahani, A., Sain, Z. H., & Vandika, A. Y. (2022). Utilization AI for Socially Responsive Education as a Path to Inclusive Development. *Journal of Artificial Intelligence and Development*, 1(2), 69–78.

Kadel, R. S. (2024). Georgia Tech's Center for 21st Century Universities. His research emphases.

Kamalov, F., Santandreu Calonge, D., & Gurrib, I. (2023). New era of artificial intelligence in education: Towards a sustainable multifaceted revolution. *Sustainability (Basel)*, 15(16), 12451. DOI: 10.3390/su151612451

Klašnja-Milićević, A., & Ivanović, M. (2021). E-learning personalization systems and sustainable education. *Sustainability (Basel)*, 13(12), 6713. DOI: 10.3390/su13126713

Kong, S. C., Cheung, W. M. Y., & Zhang, G. (2023). Evaluating an artificial intelligence literacy programme for developing university students' conceptual understanding, literacy, empowerment and ethical awareness. *Journal of Educational Technology & Society*, 26(1), 16–30.

Lauricella, A. R., Herdzina, J., & Robb, M. (2020). Early childhood educators' teaching of digital citizenship competencies. *Computers & Education*, 158, 103989. DOI: 10.1016/j.compedu.2020.103989

Lestari, V. L. (2024). Transformative Impact: The Evolution of Learning through AI in Education. *Education Studies and Teaching Journal*, 1(1), 93–112.

Li, Z. (2024). Ethical frontiers in artificial intelligence: Navigating the complexities of bias, privacy, and accountability. *International Journal of Engineering and Management Research*, 14(3), 109–116.

Lin, M. P. C., Liu, A. L., Poitras, E., Chang, M., & Chang, D. H. (2024). An Exploratory Study on the Efficacy and Inclusivity of AI Technologies in Diverse Learning Environments. *Sustainability (Basel)*, 16(20), 8992. DOI: 10.3390/su16208992

Mäkelä, P. (2021). Selection process of an automated assessment system at LUT University.

Murphy, J. W., & Taylor, R. R. (2023). To democratize or not to democratize AI? That is the question. *AI and Ethics*, 1–7.

Murtaza, M., Ahmed, Y., Shamsi, J. A., Sherwani, F., & Usman, M. (2022). AI-based personalized e-learning systems: Issues, challenges, and solutions. *IEEE Access : Practical Innovations, Open Solutions*, 10, 81323–81342. DOI: 10.1109/ACCESS.2022.3193938

Ng, D. T. K., Leung, J. K. L., Chu, K. W. S., & Qiao, M. S. (2021). AI literacy: Definition, teaching, evaluation and ethical issues. *Proceedings of the Association for Information Science and Technology*, 58(1), 504–509. DOI: 10.1002/pra2.487

Ní Bhroin, Ó., & King, F. (2020). Teacher education for inclusive education: A framework for developing collaboration for the inclusion of students with support plans. *European Journal of Teacher Education*, 43(1), 38–63. DOI: 10.1080/02619768.2019.1691993

Onesi-Ozigagun, O., Ololade, Y. J., Eyo-Udo, N. L., & Ogundipe, D. O. (2024). Revolutionizing education through AI: A comprehensive review of enhancing learning experiences. *International Journal of Applied Research in Social Sciences*, 6(4), 589–607. DOI: 10.51594/ijarss.v6i4.1011

Ouyang, F., & Jiao, P. (2021). Artificial intelligence in education: The three paradigms. *Computers and Education: Artificial Intelligence*, 2, 100020. DOI: 10.1016/j.caeai.2021.100020

Pangrazio, L., & Sefton-Green, J. (2021). Digital rights, digital citizenship and digital literacy: What's the difference? Journal of New Approaches in Educational Research, 10(1), 15-27.

Peters, D., Vold, K., Robinson, D., & Calvo, R. A. (2020). Responsible AI—Two frameworks for ethical design practice. *IEEE Transactions on Technology and Society*, 1(1), 34–47. DOI: 10.1109/TTS.2020.2974991

Portnoff, L., Gustafson, E., Rollinson, J., & Bicknell, K. (2021). *Methods for Language Learning Assessment at Scale: Duolingo Case Study*. International Educational Data Mining Society.

Samala, A. D., Zhai, X., Aoki, K., Bojić, L., & Zikic, S. (2024). An in-depth review of ChatGPT's pros and cons for learning and teaching in education. *International Journal of Interactive Mobile Technologies*, 18(2), 96–117. DOI: 10.3991/ijim.v18i02.46509

Saxena, A. K., García, V., Amin, M. R., Salazar, J. M. R., & Dey, S. (2023). Structure, Objectives, and Operational Framework for Ethical Integration of Artificial Intelligence in Educational. *Sage Science Review of Educational Technology*, 6(1), 88–100.

Selvarani, S., & Ganeshan, M. K. (2024). Blending Pedagogy and Technology: Case Studies of Success in Higher Education.

Simonofski, A., Fink, J., & Burnay, C. (2021). Supporting policy-making with social media and e-participation platforms data: A policy analytics framework. *Government Information Quarterly*, 38(3), 101590. DOI: 10.1016/j.giq.2021.101590

Slimi, Z., & Carballido, B. V. (2023). Navigating the Ethical Challenges of Artificial Intelligence in Higher Education: An Analysis of Seven Global AI Ethics Policies. TEM Journal, 12(2).

Smith, E. E., Kahlke, R., & Judd, T. (2020). Not just digital natives: Integrating technologies in professional education contexts. *Australasian Journal of Educational Technology*, 36(3), 1–14. DOI: 10.14742/ajet.5689

Sterrett, W., & Richardson, J. W. (2020). Supporting professional development through digital principal leadership. *Journal of Organizational and Educational Leadership*, 5(2), 4.

Wider, W., Jiang, L., Lin, J., Fauzi, M. A., Li, J., & Chan, C. K. (2024). Metaverse chronicles: A bibliometric analysis of its evolving landscape. *International Journal of Human-Computer Interaction*, 40(17), 4873–4886. DOI: 10.1080/10447318.2023.2227825

Wilton, L., Ip, S., Sharma, M., & Fan, F. (2022, July). Where is the ai? Ai literacy for educators. In *International Conference on Artificial Intelligence in Education* (pp. 180-188). Cham: Springer International Publishing. DOI: 10.1007/978-3-031-11647-6_31

ADDITIONAL READING

Abulibdeh, A., Zaidan, E., & Abulibdeh, R. (2024). Navigating the confluence of artificial intelligence and education for sustainable development in the era of industry 4.0: Challenges, opportunities, and ethical dimensions. *Journal of Cleaner Production*, 437, 140527. DOI: 10.1016/j.jclepro.2023.140527

Balbaa, M. E., Abdurashidova, M., Khalikov, U., & Ismailova, N. (2023, November). Educational ethics in the digital age: addressing contemporary challenges. In *Proceedings of international conference on academic studies in technology and education* (pp. 84-96).

Brossi, L., Castillo, A. M., & Cortesi, S. (2022). Student-centred requirements for the ethics of ai in education. In *The Ethics of Artificial Intelligence in Education* (pp. 91–112). Routledge. DOI: 10.4324/9780429329067-6

Chandralingam, R. (2024). Role of AI in Enhancing Citizen Engagement in Finnish Municipal Services: Ethical Considerations in UX Design.

Kayyali, M. (2024). Future possibilities and challenges of AI in education. In *Transforming education with generative AI: Prompt engineering and synthetic content creation* (pp. 118–137). IGI Global. DOI: 10.4018/979-8-3693-1351-0.ch006

Kumar, S., Verma, A. K., & Mirza, A. (2024). Digital Revolution, Artificial Intelligence, and Ethical Challenges. In *Digital Transformation, Artificial Intelligence and Society: Opportunities and Challenges* (pp. 161–177). Springer Nature Singapore. DOI: 10.1007/978-981-97-5656-8_11

Mattson, K. (2021). *Ethics in a Digital World: Guiding Students Through Society's Biggest Questions*. International Society for Technology in Education.

Schmarzo, B. (2023). *AI & Data Literacy: Empowering Citizens of Data Science*. Packt Publishing Ltd.

KEY TERMS AND DEFINITIONS

AI in Education: Artificial Intelligence (AI) in education refers to the integration of AI technologies in teaching and learning processes. This includes the use of AI-powered tools and platforms to personalize education, automate administrative tasks, and provide adaptive learning experiences for students.

Curriculum Development: Curriculum development is the process of designing, reviewing, and implementing educational programs and courses. It involves setting learning objectives, selecting appropriate content, organizing course materials, and determining the best methods for teaching and assessment to meet the educational needs of students.

Digital Citizenship: Digital citizenship refers to the rights and responsibilities of individuals in the digital world. It encompasses the norms of appropriate, responsible behavior when using technology, as well as the knowledge and skills necessary to engage safely, respectfully, and effectively in the online environment.

Digital Literacy: Digital literacy is the ability to find, evaluate, use, and create digital information effectively. It encompasses a range of skills, from basic computer functions to advanced digital skills, and the critical thinking necessary to navigate and participate in the digital world.

Ethics in AI: Ethics in AI pertains to the moral principles and guidelines that govern the development, deployment, and use of artificial intelligence systems. It involves ensuring that AI is fair, transparent, accountable, and respects the rights and well-being of individuals and society.

Privacy Concerns: Privacy concerns in the context of digital technology and AI refer to the protection of personal data and the preservation of individuals' right to privacy. It involves addressing issues related to data collection, storage, sharing, and usage, as well as the potential for unauthorized access and surveillance.

Chapter 4
Digital Well-Being and AI:
Navigating the Intersection Between Technology and Mental Health

Sanchita Mandal
https://orcid.org/0009-0001-7213-6092
Tata Institute of Social Sciences, India

Mahmoud M. Kh. Hawamdeh
https://orcid.org/0000-0001-5321-2400
Al-Quds Open University, Palestine

ABSTRACT

Artificial intelligence (AI) has become a transformative force in mental health and digital well-being, offering personalized wellness programs and AI-driven mental health applications. However, these advancements present significant ethical challenges, particularly regarding algorithmic bias and privacy. This chapter discusses the implications of algorithmic bias, where the underrepresentation of diverse demographics in AI models can lead to inequitable outcomes and privacy risks stemming from the misuse or mishandling of sensitive user data. Through real-world case studies, the chapter illustrates these challenges and their impact on equitable and trustworthy AI in mental health. It also proposes strategies to mitigate these risks, emphasizing fairness, transparency, and privacy in AI design. The chapter underscores the role of responsible digital citizenship, advocating for informed and ethical engagement with AI tools by users, developers, and policymakers for creating inclusive, ethical, and privacy-conscious AI systems to advance mental health and digital wellness.

DOI: 10.4018/979-8-3693-9015-3.ch004

INTRODUCTION

The rapid integration of artificial intelligence (AI) into various aspects of modern life has revolutionized how individuals interact with technology and manage their mental health. As societies increasingly depend on digital tools, AI has emerged as a powerful enabler of opportunities and challenges for digital well-being. Digital well-being refers to mindful and responsible engagement with technology to promote mental, emotional, and social health (Vanden Abeele, 2020). In this context, AI-powered systems, ranging from chatbots to predictive analytics platforms, have demonstrated the potential to transform mental healthcare by making it more accessible, personalized, and proactive (Smith et al., 2023). However, deploying these technologies raises profound ethical and practical concerns, including algorithmic bias, privacy violations, and unintended social consequences. AI's role of AI in mental healthcare has diverse applications. This includes providing 24/7 mental health support through intelligent chatbots, detecting early signs of psychological distress using advanced analytics, and delivering personalized interventions through wellness platforms (Nguyen et al., 2020; Brown et al., 2021). For instance, machine learning models are increasingly being used to predict depressive episodes or suicidal ideation, enabling timely intervention (Jones & Patel, 2022). Similarly, digital therapeutics, such as Calm and Headspace, integrate AI algorithms to adapt their recommendations to individual users' preferences and behaviors, enhancing the efficacy of mindfulness practices (Thompson et al., 2022). These innovations underscore the transformative potential of AI in reshaping the conceptualization and delivery of mental healthcare.

Despite these promising developments, the deployment of AI in digital well-being is fraught with several challenges. An algorithmic bias is a significant concern, wherein AI systems may perpetuate or exacerbate existing inequalities owing to imbalances in training data or flawed model designs (Mehrabi et al., 2021). For example, studies have shown that mental health apps often perform poorly when applied to data from underrepresented demographic groups, leading to inequitable outcomes (Zhao et al., 2022). Furthermore, using sensitive user data in AI systems raises critical privacy issues because inadequate safeguards can result in unauthorized data sharing, breaches, or exploitation for commercial purposes (Huckvale et al., 2019). These ethical challenges necessitate robust governance frameworks and interdisciplinary collaboration to ensure that AI technologies are responsibly developed and deployed.

Another dimension of this discourse is the evolving concept of responsible digital citizenship. As users increasingly engage with AI-powered tools, there is a growing need for digital literacy initiatives that equip individuals with the skills to critically evaluate these technologies and advocate their ethical use (Livingstone &

Helsper,2007). Policymakers, developers, and educators also play crucial roles in fostering a culture of accountability and inclusivity within the AI ecosystem (Floridi et al.,2018). This chapter explores these interrelated themes, comprehensively analyzing AI's potential to enhance digital well-being while addressing the ethical challenges accompanying its adoption.

The Conceptual Framework of Digital Well-Being

Digital well-being encompasses the strategies and practices individuals and communities adopt to maintain healthy technological relationships. It involves balancing leveraging digital tools for productivity and leisure while minimizing their potential adverse effects on mental and emotional health (Vanden Abeele, 2020). AI technologies play a pivotal role in this framework by offering innovative solutions for stress management, mental health support, and behavioral change. For instance, AI-based interventions can provide real-time feedback and personalized recommendations, empowering users to make informed decisions regarding their digital habits (Nguyen et al.,2020).

However, the conceptualization of digital well-being extends beyond individual behaviors to include systemic factors such as the design and governance of AI systems. Ethical principles, including fairness, transparency, and accountability, ensure that AI technologies positively contribute to digital well-being (Binns, 2018). This requires a multidisciplinary approach integrating psychology, computer science, ethics, and public policy insights.

Historical Context and Evolution of AI in Mental Health

The application of AI in mental healthcare is not a recent phenomenon. Early efforts in this domain focused on developing expert systems that could simulate human reasoning to assist clinicians in diagnosing psychological disorders (Shortliffe,1976). Over time, advancements in machine learning and natural language processing (NLP) have expanded the capabilities of AI systems, enabling them to analyze complex datasets and generate actionable insights (Brown et al., 2021).

The proliferation of smartphones and wearable devices has accelerated the adoption of AI-driven mental health tools. These devices generate vast amounts of user data that AI algorithms can process to identify patterns and correlations associated with mental health outcomes (Jones & Patel, 2022). For example, sentiment analysis techniques have been used to detect signs of depression in social media posts, offering new avenues for early intervention (Thompson et al., 2022). However, these developments also raise important questions regarding data ethics, consent, and potential misuse.

The Dual Role of AI: Opportunities and Challenges

The dualistic nature characterizes AI's impact of AI on digital well-being. On the one hand, it offers unparalleled opportunities to enhance mental health care by addressing critical gaps in access, affordability, and personalization. For instance, AI-powered chatbots, such as Woebot and Wysa, provide scalable solutions for delivering mental health support to underserved populations, reducing the stigma associated with seeking help (Brown et al.,2021). Additionally, predictive analytics tools enable healthcare providers to allocate resources more effectively and improve outcomes in high-risk individuals (Nguyen et al.,2020).

However, the widespread adoption of AI technologies has revealed significant challenges, particularly in ethics and governance. Algorithmic bias, privacy violations, and the potential for unintended harm are among the most pressing concerns (Mehrabi et al., 2021). For example, relying on historical data to train AI models can perpetuate systemic inequalities, whereas inadequate regulatory frameworks may fail to address emerging risks (Zhao et al., 2022). These challenges underscore the need for a balanced approach that leverages the strengths of AI while mitigating its limitations.

Ethical Considerations in AI-Driven Digital Well-Being

Ethical considerations are integral to discourse on AI and digital well-being. Key issues include:

- Algorithmic bias: AI models are trained on diverse and representative datasets to avoid discriminatory outcomes (Mehrabi et al., 2021).
- Privacy and Data Security: Implementing robust safeguards to protect sensitive user information from unauthorized access or misuse (Huckvale et al., 2019).
- Transparency and Accountability: Promoting explainable AI (XAI) methodologies that enhance users' understanding of how decisions are made (Doshi-Velez and Kim 2017).

Addressing these ethical challenges requires a collaborative approach involving stakeholders from multiple sectors, including technology, healthcare, and civil society. For example, initiatives like the European Union's General Data Protection Regulation (GDPR) have set important precedents for balancing innovation with user rights (GDPR, 2018).

Objectives and Structure of the Chapter

This chapter aims to comprehensively analyse AI's role in digital well-being, focusing on its potential to transform mental health care while addressing the ethical challenges that arise. The discussion explores the transformative applications of AI in digital well-being, highlighting real-world examples and case studies, the issue of algorithmic bias, its implications for mental health outcomes, and strategies for mitigating privacy concerns associated with AI-driven mental health tools. It outlines ethical and regulatory frameworks for data protection, discusses the role of responsible digital citizenship in promoting ethical AI adoption and fostering digital literacy, and considers future perspectives and recommendations for ethical AI development in mental health care. By integrating insights from the academic literature, case studies, and moral frameworks, this chapter seeks to contribute to the ongoing discourse on AI and digital well-being, offering practical guidance for stakeholders navigating this complex landscape.

THE PROMISE OF AI IN DIGITAL WELL-BEING

Transformative Applications

AI has introduced a range of applications to enhance digital well-being and mental health. AI technologies such as machine learning and deep learning have been integrated into systems to enhance diagnostics, treatment planning, and personalized medicine to improve patient outcomes and promote healthier lifestyles. These applications range from conversational AI-driven fitness bots to comprehensive AI platforms for personal well-being. Below are some notable examples of AI's successful application of AI in wellness. Popular tools include as following:

- Mental Health Chatbots: Through conversational interfaces, AI-powered chatbots such as Woebot and Wysa offer round-the-clock mental health help (Brown et al., 2021). These tools provide evidence-based coping strategies and engage with users in an empathic manner through natural language processing (NLP).
- Predictive Analytics and Diagnostic and Treatment: AI methods have been used in healthcare to improve treatment planning and diagnosis. For example, AI models examine vast datasets, including electronic health records and medical imaging, to increase the precision of diagnosis and support the creation of individualized treatment plans. These models minimize side effects by optimizing medication regimes and forecasting therapeutic responses.

Machine learning algorithms analyze large datasets to find trends that predict mental health problems, allowing for early intervention (Jones & Patel, 2022).

- Personalized Wellness Platforms: Applications like Calm and Headspace leverage AI to deliver customized meditation and mindfulness programs based on user behavior and preferences (Nguyen et al., 2020).

Personalized Fitness Platforms: A healthcare bot powered by conversational AI has been created to offer customized fitness advice. This bot provides personalized workout recommendations based on user preferences and health profiles using machine learning and natural language processing. The solution addresses scalability and algorithmic biases while guaranteeing strong user data protection and adhering to privacy regulations such as HIPAA (Thakur et al.,2023). An AI-powered app helps those who lead unhealthy lives, especially those who struggle with obesity and overweight. This software offers customizable workout plans, image-based component recognition, and indirect BMR computation by combining AI technologies like MoveNet and Mediapipe. Combining many AI models, including Multiple Linear Regression and Inception-ResNet-v2, the program seeks to lower disease risks and direct users toward better living (Karunarathne et al.,2023).

Case Studies of Success

The successful application of AI to digital wellness has been demonstrated through various case studies, highlighting its transformative potential in healthcare and personal well-being.

- Ellie, a virtual therapist driven by artificial intelligence, has shown impressive accuracy in identifying signs of post-traumatic stress disorder (PTSD). Ellie, created by researchers at the University of Southern California, uses linguistic patterns, facial expressions, and voice modulation to detect emotional distress (Ramos et al., 2020). According to a study, Ellie could identify 90% of the symptoms of post-traumatic stress disorder (PTSD) (Golubovic et al., 2024), significantly increasing the likelihood of early diagnosis and directing specialized treatments.
- The AI-Driven Suicide Prevention Initiative: The Crisis Text Line in Canada leverages advanced technologies to enhance response times and prioritize high-risk individuals effectively. The integration of AI has demonstrated significant improvements in crisis interventions with reported life-saving outcomes. Techniques such as deep learning and Particle Markov Chain Monte Carlo (PMCMC) enhance predictive accuracy by modeling complex interac-

tions among risk factors, and the Crisis Text Line reported a 40% decrease in response times, allowing counsellors to engage with high-risk texters more promptly (Zahan et al.,2024). In 2021, the program credited AI with saving over 5,000 lives through its prioritization system (Zahan et al.,2024).

Woebot: A randomized controlled study revealed that Woebot, an AI chatbot that uses cognitive-behavioral therapy (CBT) techniques, significantly improved mental health in 20 nations. Within two weeks, the AI chatbot reduced depressed symptoms by 38% (Siddals et al., 2024). make mental health care more accessible to a variety of populations, especially overseas students who face particular difficulties, by offering real-time responses and individualized therapy sessions. (Fu and Liu, 2024).

- MindStrong: An AI-driven mobile application that effectively addresses the early detection of mood disorders in India by analyzing behavioral data from smartphone usage. This innovative approach is particularly beneficial in rural areas, where access to mental health services is limited. By analyzing smartphone usage patterns and keyboard dynamics, the app identified potential risks among users in rural areas and bridged gaps in mental health access (Gupta et al., 2023).
- AI-Assisted Recovery Application: AI-assisted recovery applications, such as Australia's "Recovery Record," leverage artificial intelligence to enhance the treatment of eating disorders by providing personalized recovery plans based on user inputs and clinician insights. A longitudinal study showed that 72% of users experienced significant improvement in their recovery journeys (Smith et al., 2023).
- Kiosk: Kenya's introduction of AI-powered mental health kiosks represents a significant advancement in accessible mental health care. These kiosks utilize chatbots for screening and basic counseling, demonstrating promising user engagement and follow-up care outcomes. The initial trials in Nairobi revealed that 68% of users reported improved mental health awareness, while 43% sought further assistance at local clinics (Pawar et al.,2024)
- Teletherapy: Teletherapy platforms in Brazil utilize AI to match patients with therapists based on compatibility. This approach has improved therapy adherence by 30%, particularly in underserved regions (da Silva et al., 2021).
- AI and Substance Abuse Recovery: In Russia, AI applications have facilitated substance abuse recovery by predicting relapse triggers using biometric data analysis. Programs integrating AI into rehabilitation centers have reported a 25% reduction in relapse rates over three years (Ivanov et al., 2022).
- AI-powered Stress Management: Japanese corporations use AI-driven platforms to monitor employee stress levels through wearable devices. These

platforms provide personalized relaxation techniques, resulting in a 15% decrease in workplace burnout (Tanaka et al., 2021).

- Resilience Training: AI-enabled resilience training programs in the UK use gamification to teach stress management. Companies adopting these programs have observed a 20% improvement in employee productivity (Clark et al., 2022).

ETHICAL CONSIDERATIONS: CHALLENGES AND OPPORTUNITIES IN AI-DRIVEN DIGITAL WELLNESS

Integrating artificial intelligence (AI) in digital wellness presents many opportunities but raises significant ethical challenges that must be addressed to ensure equitable and effective implementation. These considerations span data privacy, cultural sensitivity, resource allocation, and the inherent limitations of AI systems. This section thoroughly explores these issues and emphasizes the balance between innovation and responsibility.

Data Privacy Concerns

Safeguarding user data is one of the foremost ethical challenges in AI-driven digital wellness. To provide personalized care, AI systems often require access to highly sensitive personal information, including emotional states, behavioural patterns, and medical histories. However, users usually hesitate to share such data due to concerns over misuse, breaches, or unauthorized sharing. This reluctance can limit AI's effectiveness in achieving optimal outcomes. Users often hesitate to share sensitive data, limiting AI's effectiveness. To mitigate these concerns, robust data governance frameworks, including encryption, anonymization, and strict consent protocols, must be implemented (Zhang & Wang, 2024).

- Algorithmic bias: Despite its potential, AI in digital wellness faces limitations that necessitate human oversight. One primary concern is the risk of misinterpreting emotional cues, leading to inappropriate interventions. For instance, an AI system might misjudge a user's tone or fail to identify critical mental health crises because it relies on predefined algorithms. Algorithmic bias remains a significant hurdle. AI systems trained on non-representative data can reinforce existing inequalities, offering suboptimal support to underrepresented populations (Al Makinah et al., 2024). Such biases undermine the equity of mental healthcare and can even perpetuate harm. Similarly, although AI's capacity for data analysis is unparalleled, it cannot replicate the nuanced understanding and empathy inherent in human therapists. This emotional depth is particularly crucial for individuals dealing with complex mental health issues such as trauma or grief (Andrade-Arenas & Yactayo-Arias, 2024).

- Cultural Sensitivity: AI systems operate globally and interact with diverse populations. However, tools designed using a one-size-fits-all approach may fail to resonate with users from varied cultural and socioeconomic backgrounds. For example, mental health terminology and treatment preferences differ significantly across cultures. An AI tool effective in one region may be irrelevant or even harmful if it does not account for cultural nuances. Adapting AI systems to reflect cultural contexts such as language preferences, social norms, and localized mental health practices is crucial for fostering user trust and engagement (Singh et al., 2024).
- Resource Allocation: Developing AI solutions for mental health and digital wellness requires significant financial and technological investment. Low-resource settings often lack the infrastructure to support these advancements, exacerbating disparities in mental healthcare access. While AI promises to bridge gaps in underserved communities, achieving this requires collaborative initiatives involving governments, private organizations, and non-profits. Such efforts must create cost-effective, scalable, and inclusive solutions (Andrade-Arenas & Yactayo-Arias, 2024).
- AI Strengths: A Non-Judgmental Approach: AI systems have demonstrated the ability to foster a non-judgmental environment, encouraging users to disclose sensitive information more openly. This can lead to better therapeutic outcomes by enabling individuals to communicate their concerns without fear of stigma or judgment (Zhang & Wang, 2024). For example, virtual agents and mental health chatbots can provide users with a safe space to discuss issues they might hesitate to share with human therapists. Additionally, continuous monitoring and real-time support can help maintain patient engagement and adherence to therapy plans.
- Data Quality and Bias Mitigation: Ensuring the integrity of the data used in AI systems is another critical ethical consideration. Poor quality data or datasets riddled with biases can significantly impair the effectiveness of AI models. Efforts to standardize data collection practices, validate datasets, and diversify data sources are essential for reducing these risks (Singh et al., 2024). Transparency in AI decision-making processes can foster greater trust between users and stakeholders.

ALGORITHMIC BIAS IN AI SYSTEMS

Understanding Algorithmic Bias

Algorithmic bias in AI refers to unfair, inscrutable, or harmful outcomes that result from flawed algorithms. This occurs when data used for training reflect societal biases, leading to skewed predictions or decisions that disproportionately affect certain groups or individuals (Dwivedi,2023). Algorithmic bias in AI occurs due to insufficient data variation or flawed learning policies, leading to the unjust treatment of specific groups based on attributes such as race or gender. It manifests in real-world applications, exacerbating discrimination and social inequality (Jain & Menon, 2023). This bias can manifest in various forms, including selection, confirmation, and measurement biases, and is primarily rooted in the data used to train AI systems, which may reflect existing societal prejudice. Understanding when and how algorithmic bias occurs is crucial in developing ethical AI systems. The sources of algorithmic bias happen when insufficient data variation or flawed data collection methods can lead to biased outcomes, Choices made during the algorithm's design phase can inadvertently embed biases, AI systems often replicate biases present in human-generated data, perpetuating existing social inequalities (Jain & Menon, 2023). Such biases can have profound implications for digital wellness and mental health applications.

- Misdiagnoses for underrepresented groups: AI models trained on predominantly Western datasets may fail to account for cultural variations in symptom expression, leading to inaccurate diagnoses in individuals from different cultural or ethnic backgrounds (O'Neil, 2016).
- Reduced accessibility for marginalized populations: Populations with limited access to digital technology are often underrepresented in training data, exacerbating existing health disparities (Mehrabi et al., 2021). Algorithmic bias also reflects broader societal inequalities embedded within datasets, perpetuating stereotypes and systemic inequities.

Consequences of Bias

Algorithmic bias undermines the reliability, fairness, and trustworthiness of mental health. For examples:

- Racial and Ethnic Bias: An analysis of mental health applications demonstrated that models often underperform when analyzing data from racial minorities. This misalignment can lead to improper interventions and a lack of efficacy in therapeutic processes (Zhao et al., 2022).

- Gender Disparities: Mental health apps have exhibited biased symptom analysis, often overlooking unique symptom patterns in women, thereby providing recommendations that do not align with their experiences (Smith et al., 2023).
- Socioeconomic Bias: Data derived from predominantly affluent populations can reduce accuracy for lower-income groups, as observed in AI systems trained on data lacking socioeconomic diversity (Chen et al., 2021).
- Ethical Concern: The ethical implications of biased AI systems raise questions about fairness and accountability in decision-making processes (Dwivedi,2023).
- Social Inequality: Algorithmic bias can exacerbate discrimination, leading to unequal treatment in critical areas, such as healthcare and employment(Jain & Menon, 2023).

These consequences diminish the overall value of AI in mental health, especially when equitable outcomes are not prioritized.

Mitigation Strategies

Addressing algorithmic bias requires proactive measures at every AI development and deployment stage. Effective strategies include the following.

- Diverse and Inclusive Datasets: Using datasets that reflect the diversity of the target population helps reduce representational bias (Mehrabi et al., 2021). For instance, mental health tools should include data from various racial, cultural, gender, and socioeconomic groups to improve diagnostic accuracy.
- Fairness-aware machine learning: Techniques such as re-weighting or resampling datasets ensure that minority groups are adequately represented (Hardt et al., 2016). Developing fairness metrics during model evaluation helps to detect and address biases before deployment.
- Explainable AI (XAI): Explainable AI methodologies enable users to understand the rationale behind AI decisions, thereby fostering transparency and accountability (Doshi-Velez & Kim, 2017).
- Interdisciplinary Collaboration: Engaging experts from diverse fields, such as ethics, psychology, and sociology, ensures that potential biases are identified and mitigated during design and implementation (Binns, 2018).

- Continuous Monitoring and Feedback: Periodic audits and user feedback loops can help identify new biases that arise after deployment and adapt AI models accordingly (Raji et al., 2020).

PRIVACY VIOLATIONS IN AI TOOLS

Nature of Privacy Risks

AI-driven mental health tools collect sensitive and personal information, including emotional states, behavioral patterns, and private communication. Mismanagement or misuse of these data can result in various serious risks, as elaborated below.

- Unauthorized Data Sharing: One of the most significant privacy concerns arises when user data are shared with third parties without explicit consent. For example, many apps share data with advertisers to target users with personalized advertisements, bypassing ethical standards for obtaining informed consent (Solove, 2020). This lack of transparency compromises user trust and creates vulnerability.
- Data Breaches and Identity Theft: Insufficiently robust security frameworks make these tools vulnerable to hacking, resulting in large-scale data breaches. For instance, studies have shown that inadequate encryption or reliance on weak authentication protocols in mental health apps leaves sensitive information, such as mental health records and private communications, susceptible to exploitation. Such incidents expose users to identity theft and fraud, directly impacting their personal and financial security (GDPR 2018).
- Secondary Data Use: User data are often repurposed for secondary objectives, including commercial research, marketing analytics, or even sale to third-party data brokers. This usage is typically conducted without notifying users or seeking consent, which raises significant ethical concerns and breaches the trust in the system's integrity. For instance, a 2021 study on mobile health apps revealed that over 30% of the analyzed apps engaged in non-consensual secondary data usage, undermining user privacy and autonomy (Huckvale et al., 2019).

Case Studies of Privacy Breaches

- FTC vs. Mental Health App (2021): Despite claiming confidentiality, a leading mental health app faced legal action for sharing user data with advertisers. This incident highlights the urgent need for stringent data protection policies (FTC, 2021).

- Encryption Issues in Mental Health Apps: Huckvale et al. (2019) revealed that nearly 29% of mental health apps lack robust encryption, exposing sensitive data to potential breaches.
- Cambridge Analytica Scandal: Although not directly related to mental health, the Cambridge Analytica case underscores the broader implications of unauthorized data exploitation in AI systems (Isaak & Hanna, 2018).

Ethical and Regulatory Frameworks

Adequate privacy protection is required.

- Adherence to Regulations: Following frameworks like GDPR (General Data Protection Regulation) and HIPAA (Health Insurance Portability and Accountability Act) ensures user rights and data security (Cavoukian, 2010).
- Privacy-by-Design Principles: Incorporating privacy measures into the AI development process, such as data minimization and consent mechanisms, reduces privacy risks (Cavoukian, 2010).
- User-Centered Data Governance: Empowering users with control over their data through tools that allow data access, modification, and deletion enhances trust.
- Federated Learning Systems: These systems process data locally on user devices, thereby minimizing the need for centralized data storage and reducing privacy risks (Yang et al., 2019).

THE ROLE OF RESPONSIBLE DIGITAL CITIZENSHIP

Responsible digital citizenship involves informed and ethical engagement with AI tools. Key components include digital literacy to understand AI's capabilities and limitations of AI (Livingstone & Helsper, 2007), advocacy for transparency and fairness in AI systems (Floridi et al., 2018), and active participation in discussions on AI ethics and governance (Schiff et al., 2021).

Strategies for Ethical Engagement With AI Tools

- Understanding Privacy Policies and Data Usage: Users should familiarize themselves with the privacy policies of AI-driven platforms to understand how their data are collected, stored, and used. This knowledge empowers individuals to make informed decisions regarding sharing personal information. For instance, the European Union's General Data Protection Regulation (GDPR) requires companies to disclose their data practices clearly, setting a precedent for global standards (European Commission, 2018).

- Advocating for Transparency and Fairness: Advocacy for transparency involves demanding clear communication from AI developers regarding how algorithms function and make decisions. Users can also support initiatives, such as open-source AI projects, which promote fairness by allowing public scrutiny and collaborative improvement (Binns, 2020).
- Balancing Technology Use with Offline Wellness Practices: Maintaining a healthy balance between digital and offline activities is vital to mental health. Strategies include:

Digital Detox: Designating tech-free times to focus on personal relationships and self-care.

Mindfulness Practices: Engaging in activities like meditation to counteract the stress induced by constant digital connectivity (Kabat-Zinn, 2013).

- Fostering Digital Literacy and User Awareness Education: Promoting digital literacy equips individuals with the responsibility to navigate AI tools. Educational programs should focus on the following:
    1)Understanding the basics of AI and machine learning, identifying misinformation, and combating algorithmic bias.

    2) Developing skills to assess the credibility of digital content (Livingstone & Sefton-Green, 2016).

User awareness is fundamental for mitigating the risks associated with AI tools. Awareness campaigns can highlight the potential dangers of unregulated AI applications, such as misuse of personal data. Educate users on their digital rights, including data protection and algorithmic transparency. Participating in digital literacy programs enhances awareness of potential AI risks (Ribble 2011). Global initiatives like UNESCO's Media and Information Literacy program provide a model for improving digital citizenship education (UNESCO, 2022).

Mitigating AI-Related Risks Through Responsible Citizenship

Responsible digital citizenship serves as a buffer against the risks posed by AI to digital wellness.

- Privacy Protection: Encouraging the use of privacy-preserving technologies such as encryption.
- Ethical Advocacy: Supporting regulations and standards that promote responsible AI development.
- Collaborative Solutions: Engaging communities in discussions about the ethical implications of AI-driven tools.
- Reading and understanding privacy policies before using AI tools.
- Advocating for open-source AI models to enhance transparency.
- Limiting data sharing to essential use cases.

FUTURE PERSPECTIVES FOR ETHICAL AI IN DIGITAL WELL-BEING

Future Perspectives for Ethical AI in Mental Health

Integrating AI into digital well-being, especially in mental health care, has transformative potential, but realizing this promise requires a forward-looking, ethical framework. Several trends highlight the evolving role of AI in mental health:

- Personalization and Precision: AI systems are increasingly designed to offer highly personalized interventions. For instance, adaptive learning algorithms adjust therapy content based on user responses, improving engagement and outcomes (Holland et al., 2021).
- Integration with Wearable Technology: Wearable devices combined with AI provide real-time insights into mental health. For example, Apple's Health app uses AI to monitor stress through heart rate variability, enabling early interventions (Apple, 2023).
- Global Accessibility Initiatives: Efforts to expand AI-driven mental health care to underserved populations are gaining traction. Projects like Friendship Bench in Zimbabwe combine AI with community support to address mental health gaps (Chibanda et al., 2020).
- Human oversight and Explainability: Use of explainable AI (XAI) to improve transparency and trust (Doshi-Velez & Kim, 2017). While XAI methods can provide valuable insights, the complete interpretability of complex AI models might not always be achievable. Human oversight remains essential to ensure responsible AI development and deployment.
- Development of federated learning systems to enhance data privacy (Yang et al., 2019) and Increasing integration of interdisciplinary approaches that combine technical expertise with ethical frameworks (Binns, 2018).

- There is a growing emphasis on the role of AI in mental health equity, particularly in underserved regions (Smith et al., 2023).

Recommendations

- Collaborative Efforts for Ethical AI: Addressing these barriers requires collaborative efforts among developers, healthcare providers, and policymakers. Developers must prioritize fairness and inclusivity during design, incorporating mechanisms to detect and rectify biases. Policymakers should establish clear regulations governing data use, AI deployment, and accountability for failures. Healthcare providers, on the other hand, play a vital role in ensuring that AI tools are used as complementary aids rather than replacements for human intervention. Interdisciplinary collaboration between technologists, ethicists, and mental health professionals to ensure ethical AI development (Floridi et al., 2018). By fostering partnerships across sectors, it is possible to unlock AI's full potential in digital wellness while maintaining ethical and equitable standards. Innovations like AI-driven mental health platforms should aim to complement, rather than replace, traditional care models.
- Human -AI Collaboration: While AI tools enhance counselor efficiency, human expertise is essential for nuanced decision-making (Salmi,2024). Human oversight complements AI-based bias detection capabilities and addresses complex bias scenarios that might be challenging for automated methods.
- Feature Attribution Perturbation: During bias analysis, we perturb feature attributions to prevent the direct identification of individual records. This approach strikes a balance between accurate bias detection and privacy preservation.
- Regulatory Compliance: Ensuring compliance with existing privacy regulations and standards, such as GDPR in Europe or HIPAA in healthcare. Adhering to regulatory requirements provides a legal framework for protecting individuals' privacy rights while holding AI developers and organizations accountable for bias mitigation efforts.
- Context-Aware Bias Detection: Developing techniques that can account for the contextual factors influencing bias is crucial. For instance, the definition of fairness might differ depending on the specific application of the AI model. Context-aware bias detection methods can help identify and address these nuanced aspects of bias.
- Mitigating Bias in Complex Models: State-of-the-art AI models are often highly complex, making it challenging to pinpoint the root causes of bias. New bias detection and mitigation methods tailored to complex models are needed.

- Cultural Sensitivity: AI tools must adapt to cultural and linguistic contexts to resonate with diverse populations.
- Standardization of AI tool Practices: There is a lack of standardized use of practices for AI systems. This inconsistency can make it difficult to compare results across different results and hinder the development of robust analytical methodologies. It is essential to consider the potential limitations of AI in digital well-being, such as the need for human oversight and the risk of misinterpretation of emotional cues, which could lead to inappropriate interventions.
- Balancing Fairness and Privacy: Striking a balance between achieving fairness through effective practices and protecting individual privacy remains an ongoing challenge. Privacy-preserving techniques like federated learning enable AI systems to operate without compromising user data (Kairouz et al., 2021).

CONCLUSION

AI holds immense potential to transform mental health care and digital well-being. AI platforms can operate continuously, providing support to users regardless of geographical constraints, thus increasing accessibility to mental health resources (Zhang & Wang,2024). Users often feel more comfortable sharing sensitive information with AI, leading to more honest interactions and improved engagement in their recovery process (Pawar et al.,2024). However, its ethical challenges—algorithmic bias and privacy violations—must be addressed through inclusive design, robust regulatory frameworks, and responsible digital citizenship. By prioritizing ethical considerations, stakeholders can harness AI's transformative power to create a more equitable and secure mental health landscape. Addressing these barriers is critical to unlocking AI's full potential in digital wellness. Collaborative efforts among developers, governments, and healthcare providers can drive innovation while ensuring ethical and equitable implementation.

REFERENCES

AlMakinah, R., Norcini-Pala, A., Disney, L., & Canbaz, M. A. (2024). Enhancing mental health support through human-AI collaboration: Toward secure and empathetic AI-enabled chatbots. *arXiv*. /arxiv.2410.02783DOI: 10.48550

Andrade-Arenas, L., & Yactayo-Arias, C. (2024). Chatbot with ChatGPT technology for mental well-being and emotional management. *IAES International Journal of Artificial Intelligence*, 13(3), 2635–2635. DOI: 10.11591/ijai.v13.i3.pp2635-2644

Ankit, S., Faryaz, A., Sumit, K., & Sunita, J. (2024). Driven Predictive Models for Suicide Risk Assessment: Challenges and Opportunities. DOI: 10.1109/ICAIT61638.2024.10690713

Apple. (2023). *Health app and heart rate variability*. Apple Inc. Retrieved from https://www.apple.com

Binns, R. (2018). Fairness in machine learning: Lessons from political philosophy. *Proceedings of the 2018 Conference on Fairness, Accountability, and Transparency*, 149–159. DOI: 10.1145/3287560.3287600

Brown, A., Smith, L., & Johnson, P. (2021). The role of AI in enhancing mental health services: A review of applications and challenges. *Journal of Digital Health and AI*, 10(3), 200–215. DOI: 10.1016/j.digai.2021.03.002

Brown, M., Wilson, A., & Thompson, K. (2021). Chatbots in mental health: An exploration of AI-driven conversational agents for emotional support. *Journal of Mental Health Technology*, 34(2), 123–137.

Chen, X., Zhang, Y., & Liu, J. (2021). Socioeconomic disparities in AI-driven health care. *Journal of Digital Health Equity*, 5(2), 112–127.

Chibanda, D., Weiss, H. A., Verhey, R., Simms, V., Munjoma, R., Rusakaniko, S., Chingono, A., Munetsi, E., Bere, T., Manda, E., Abas, M., & Araya, R. (2020). Effect of a primary care–based psychological intervention on symptoms of common mental disorders in Zimbabwe: A randomized clinical trial. *Journal of the American Medical Association*, 316(24), 2618–2626. DOI: 10.1001/jama.2016.19102 PMID: 28027368

Clark, P., Matthews, J., & Hall, T. (2022). Enhancing workplace resilience through gamified AI training programs: A UK case study. *Workplace Wellness Quarterly*, 28(3), 98–112.

Da Silva, L. M., & Campos, P. R. (2021). AI in teletherapy: Addressing mental health disparities in underserved regions of Brazil. *Brazilian Journal of Telemedicine*, 15(1), 42–58.

Divya, Dwivedi. (2023). Algorithmic Bias: A Challenge for Ethical Artificial Intelligence (AI). DOI: 10.1007/978-981-99-8834-1_5

Doshi-Velez, F., & Kim, B. (2017). Towards a rigorous science of interpretable machine learning. *arXiv preprint arXiv:1702.08608*.

Doshi-Velez, F., & Kim, B. (2017). Towards a rigorous science of interpretable machine learning. *arXiv preprint arXiv:1702.08608*.

European Commission. (2018). General Data Protection Regulation (GDPR). Retrieved from https://ec.europa.eu

Floridi, L., Cowls, J., Beltrametti, M., Chatila, R., Chazerand, P., Dignum, V., Luetge, C., Madelin, R., Pagallo, U., Rossi, F., Schafer, B., Valcke, P., & Vayena, E. (2018). AI4People—An ethical framework for a good AI society: Opportunities, risks, principles, and recommendations. *Minds and Machines*, 28(4), 689–707. DOI: 10.1007/s11023-018-9482-5 PMID: 30930541

Floridi, L., Cowls, J., King, T., & Taddeo, M. (2018). How to design AI for social good: Seven essential factors. *Science and Engineering Ethics*, 24(3), 723–743. PMID: 32246245

Fu, X., & Liu, Y. (2024). A review of chatbots application on supporting international students' mental health. *Arts, Culture, and Language*, 1(9). Advance online publication. DOI: 10.61173/g27kbp22

GDPR (2018). General Data Protection Regulation.

General Data Protection Regulation (GDPR). (2018). Regulation (EU) 2016/679 of the European Parliament and of the Council. Official Journal of the European Union. https://gdpr-info.eu

Golubović, G., Đurđević, S., Kerac, J., Juretić, I., & Cvetojević, S. (2024). Use of AI in mHealth mobile applications: The influence of virtual therapists' visual characteristics on user perception. *Proceedings of the GRID 2024 Conference*. DOI: 10.24867/GRID-2024-p35

Gupta, R., Sharma, M., & Verma, A. (2023). Leveraging AI for mental health accessibility in rural India: The MindStrong initiative. *Indian Journal of Digital Health*, 17(4), 301–319.

Hardt, M., Price, E., & Srebro, N. (2016). Equality of opportunity in supervised learning. *Advances in Neural Information Processing Systems*, 29, 3315–3323.

Holland, J., Kensinger, E. A., & Krendl, A. C. (2021). Cognitive behavioral therapy enhanced by artificial intelligence: The future of mental health care. *Current Psychiatry Reports*, 23(12), 38–47.

Huckvale, K., Torous, J., & Larsen, M. E. (2019). Assessment of the data sharing and privacy practices of smartphone apps for depression and smoking cessation. *JAMA Network Open*, 2(4), e192542–e192542. DOI: 10.1001/jamanetworkopen.2019.2542 PMID: 31002321

Ivanov, A., & Petrova, L. (2022). Biometric data and AI in substance abuse rehabilitation: Successes and challenges in Russia. *Eastern European Medical Journal*, 29(3), 112–130.

Jones, B. A., & Patel, S. (2022). Predictive analytics for mental health: Opportunities and challenges. *AI in Psychiatry Review*, 11(2), 88–99.

Jones, S., & Patel, V. (2022). AI in early detection of mental health disorders: Opportunities and challenges. *Journal of Psychological Science*, 15(1), 45–62.

Kairouz, P., McMahan, H. B., Avent, B., Bellet, A., Bennis, M., Bhagoji, A. N., & Zhao, S. (2021). Advances and open problems in federated learning. *Foundations and Trends in Machine Learning*, 14(1), 1–210. DOI: 10.1561/2200000083

Karunarathne, P. G. D. R. V., Somarathna, H. K. H. N., Liyanage, N. D. H., Vithanage, M. R., Bandara, P. S., & Wijesiri, P. (2023). AI-integrated single platform to enhance personal well-being. *2023 5th International Conference on Advancements in Computing (ICAC)*, 508–513. DOI: 10.1109/ICAC60630.2023.10417473

Lakshitha, R., & Vineetha, M. (2023). AI Algorithmic Bias: Understanding its Causes, Ethical and Social Implications. DOI: 10.1109/ICTAI59109.2023.00073

Livingstone, S., & Helsper, E. J. (2007). Gradations in digital inclusion: Children, young people, and the digital divide. *New Media & Society*, 9(4), 671–696. DOI: 10.1177/1461444807080335

McCarthy, J., & Wright, P. (2004). *Technology as experience*. MIT Press. DOI: 10.7551/mitpress/6687.001.0001

Mehrabi, N., Morstatter, F., Saxena, N., Lerman, K., & Galstyan, A. (2021). A survey on bias and fairness in machine learning. *ACM Computing Surveys*, 54(6), 1–35. DOI: 10.1145/3457607

Mwangi, J., & Njoroge, P. (2022). AI kiosks for mental health in Kenya: Bridging the gap in low-resource settings. *African Journal of Community Health*, 19(1), 56–73.

Nguyen, T., Walker, R., & Baxter, R. (2020). AI-enabled mental health support: Bridging gaps in care. *Digital Therapeutics Journal*, 8(2), 100–115.

Nguyen, T. Q., Lee, H., & Wang, J. (2020). AI in personalized wellness: An evaluation of Calm and Headspace. *Digital Health Review*, 9(4), 405–419.

O'Neil, C. (2016). *Weapons of math destruction: How big data increases inequality and threatens democracy*. Crown.

Pawar, A. (2024). Study of Web-Based Mental Health Applications. *Deleted Journal*, 2(11), 2586–2592. DOI: 10.47392/IRJAEH.2024.0356

Raji, I. D., & Buolamwini, J. (2020). Actionable auditing: Investigating the impact of public scrutiny of AI systems. *Proceedings of the AAAI Conference on AI Ethics and Society, 2*(1), 109-120.

Ramos, G., Nguyen, D., & Watson, L. (2020). Ellie: Enhancing PTSD diagnosis with AI-powered virtual therapists. *American Journal of Virtual Care*, 27(6), 554–573.

Rifat, Z., Mikuliak, J., & Osgood, N. (2024). Developing a tool to assess the impact of simulated intervention strategies on suicide and suicidal behaviors in Canada: A dynamic modeling and machine learning approach. *Preprints*. https://doi.org/DOI: 10.20944/preprints202405.0813.v1

Salmi, S. (2024). From words to actions. *Thesis*. DOI: 10.5463/thesis.912

Siddals, S., Torous, J., & Coxon, A. (2024). "It happened to be the perfect thing": Experiences of generative AI chatbots for mental health. *NPJ Mental Health Research, 3*(1). DOI: 10.1038/s44184-024-00097-4

Singh, A., Ansari, F., Kumar, S., & Joshi, S. (2024). Driven predictive models for suicide risk assessment: Challenges and opportunities. *2024 International Conference on Artificial Intelligence and Information Technology (ICAIT)*, 1–6. DOI: 10.1109/ICAIT61638.2024.10690713

Smith, J. P., Chen, Y., & Gupta, D. (2023). The impact of AI on recovery from eating disorders: Evidence from Australia. *Journal of Behavioral Health Innovations*, 16(2), 215–233.

Smith, L., Johnson, P., & Taylor, K. (2023). The integration of AI in healthcare: Innovations and ethical dilemmas. *Global Health Innovation*, 15(4), 112–135.

Tanaka, H., Yamamoto, K., & Kuroda, S. (2021). Stress management through AI-driven wearable devices in Japanese corporations. *Asia-Pacific Journal of Occupational Health*, 33(1), 45–60.

Thakur, S. N., Sinha, A., Singh, M. K., Bagaria, M. K., Grover, R., & Shrivastava, K. (2023). Optimizing wellness: A comprehensive examination of a conversational AI-driven healthcare bot for personalized fitness guidance. *2023 International Conference on AI in Healthcare and Industry (ICAIHI)*. https://doi.org/DOI: 10.1109/ICAIIHI57871.2023.10489319

Thompson, R., Williams, S., & Harper, M. (2022). AI and mindfulness: A review of emerging technologies in stress management. *Journal of Mental Health Technologies*, 6(1), 25–40. DOI: 10.1016/j.mhte.2022.01.005

UNESCO. (2022). *Media and information literacy: Key initiatives*. United Nations Educational, Scientific and Cultural Organization.

Vanden Abeele, M. M. (2020). Digital well-being as a dynamic construct. *Social Media + Society*, 6(3), 205630512094288. DOI: 10.1177/2056305120942884

Whittaker, M., Alper, M., Bennett, C. L., Hendren, S., Kaziunas, E., Mills, M., & Wong, V. (2021). Disability, bias, and AI. *AI Now Institute*. Retrieved from https://www.ainowinstitute.org

Zhao, J., Wang, J., & Tan, C. (2022). Bias in AI mental health diagnostics: A case study. *Digital Psychology*, 10(3), 24–37.

Zhao, Y., Adibi, S., & Sharif, H. (2022). Examining equity in mental health apps: Algorithmic performance across diverse populations. *Health Technology Assessment Journal*, 18(3), 150–165.

Zhihui, Z. (2024). Can AI replace psychotherapists? Exploring the future of mental health care. *Frontiers in Psychiatry*, 15, 1444382. Advance online publication. DOI: 10.3389/fpsyt.2024.1444382 PMID: 39544371

Chapter 5
Empowering Citizens:
Preparing for the Future of Digital Literacy and AI in Education

Grace Kaletski-Maisel
https://orcid.org/0009-0004-4220-7402
University of Central Florida, USA

Rohan Jowallah
University of Central Florida, USA

ABSTRACT

We are in a landscape characterized by the rapid advancement of technology and education. This transformation's hub is the connection between digital literacy and artificial intelligence (AI). Within a short period, educators, policymakers, and our society have come to the realization that AI will play a central role in their lives. This chapter explores the critical imperatives of preparing citizens for a future where digital competencies and AI fluency are advantageous and could be central to survival. The authors examine the current global landscape and how nations integrate digital literacy and AI into their educational framework to foster more adaptive and innovative societies. This discussion will then focus on local initiatives, illustrating how these global trends can be tailored to meet individual communities' specific cultural, economic, and societal needs.

INTRODUCTION

In 2022, a significant global movement responded to the rise of artificial intelligence. This wave of digital transformation will affect education, work, and daily life. Central to this shift is the rapid integration of AI into systems that make de-

DOI: 10.4018/979-8-3693-9015-3.ch005

cisions or solve problems (Wang et al. 2024). Although it may boost productivity, AI's infiltration into various sectors may challenge education. As AI becomes more widespread, substantial digital literacy skills will be essential for citizens to navigate a complex, tech-driven world (Nu et al. 2021). Historically, digital literacy has been connected to basic computer skills. However, "New Literacy Studies" extends these boundaries by emphasizing the skills and strategies needed for new technologies and media forms (Pahl & Rowsell, 2005). "Critical Literacy" further underscores the importance of questioning media origins and content producers (Jowallah, 2015). While these literacy areas are valuable, the authors argue that unique digital literacy is essential for digital transformation. This literacy should encompass understanding algorithms, data privacy, health, and safety in AI, which are critical for global educational reform. Ensuring people can engage with innovation is part of this mission.

This chapter will address the crucial need to prepare citizens for a future requiring an updated digital literacy framework. As nations adapt, learners must possess skills to navigate this evolving landscape. The chapter will start with key definitions and an overview of current digital literacy and AI in education. It will propose a robust framework to enhance existing digital literacy models within the context of AI literacy. Additionally, it will highlight strategies and explore future trends to strengthen global digital citizenship.

Definitions

Before progressing future in this chapter, it is essential to define and operationalize a few key terms. Gardenier et al. (2024) suggest that digital citizenship has three dominant components: private, social, and public spheres. In the private sphere, citizens navigate autonomy and privacy; in the social sphere, they foster community engagement and collective identity; and in the public sphere, they participate in governance and advocate for the public good. This framework highlights how citizens balance the opportunities and risks of digitization, shaping society through empowerment and resilience in a digitally mediated world. Therefore, based on their work, they have put out a framework which will be discussed later in this chapter in relation to the connection to the digital citizenship needed for future productive AI engagement.

However, for this engagement to occur, AI literacy is essential. While there is no universally accepted definition of AI literacy, several common themes underpin the term. These include awareness of AI functionality, critical evaluation of AI technology, responsible use, ethical awareness, critical thinking, and global and cultural understanding (Jowallah 2024; Long & Margerko 2020; Bashir 2021; Cox 2024). AI literacy extends beyond media literacy by empowering users to question developers' motives, critically assess intended audiences, and evaluate the authenticity of media forms. It aims to help users understand how AI is developed, deployed, and utilized across social, economic, health, and financial domains (Jowallah 2024).

Frameworks and definitions for digital literacy were once adequate for articulating the needs of all digital systems. In the past, digital literacy served to ensure that citizens were able to navigate the world of technology and use these technologies to improve their lives. This also ensured citizens understood how technology could include or exclude them (Audrin et al., 2022). Today, the landscape of digital literacy has evolved significantly. The rapid advancement of technology has introduced new challenges and opportunities that require a deeper understanding and more sophisticated skills (Seung 2024). Therefore, citizens must be adept at using digital tools and critically evaluating information, protecting their privacy, and participating in the digital economy.

Moreover, digital literacy encompasses many competencies, from basic technical skills to advanced problem-solving abilities. Individuals must develop these skills to stay competitive in the job market and fully engage in social and civic life. Therefore, educational institutions, governments, and organizations are crucial in providing access to digital literacy training and resources (HogoNext 2024). As we look to the future, it is clear that digital literacy will continue to be a fundamental component of a well-rounded education. We can ensure everyone can thrive in an increasingly digital world by fostering a continuous learning and adaptation culture. However, this framework may need to be revised to address the current emergence of AI within the landscape (Jowallah 2024).

According to the United Nations (2023), no form of technology has emerged that can change every aspect of our society as profoundly as AI. In the same article, the United Nations also suggested that previous forms of training on digital literacy are inadequate and that there needs to be a new form of literacy connected to AI. The UN's position is that since AI mimics human behavior, this needs to be addressed urgently. Therefore, it is the authors' position that for AI technologies to be effectively integrated into learning, AI literacy must be taught, which will be crucial in molding future digital citizens. However, the future of the digital citizen will depend on the effective interaction of artificial intelligence in education and the wider society. According to Jowallah (2023), the way we consider teaching and learning should change and globally, governments must ensure that they view AI as an opportunity while addressing possible ethical issues.

THE CURRENT GLOBAL LANDSCAPE OF DIGITAL LITERACY AND AI IN EDUCATION

In education, the landscape of digital technology, particularly artificial intelligence (AI), has seen significant growth globally. In the United States, AI in the education market was valued at $1.7 billion in 2023, with projections indicating substantial growth in the coming years. This expansion reflects the increasing integration of AI tools in educational settings (Benson, 2024). Internationally, investment in AI-related to education is also significant, with worldwide investments expected to exceed previous estimates. This growth underscores the importance of developing systems and strategies to ensure adequate literacy skills for global citizens (UNESCO, 2022). As AI continues to transform education, it is crucial to create effective frameworks that support learners and educators alike.

Moreover, the potential of AI in personalizing learning experiences, automating administrative tasks, and providing data-driven insights is immense. These advancements can lead to more efficient and effective teaching methods, ultimately enhancing student outcomes. As we progress, the collaboration between technology developers, educators, and policymakers will be crucial in harnessing the full potential of AI in education. However, a framework is needed. UNESCO's AI literacy position could be applied within the context of digital citizenship (2023). It expands the traditional concept of digital literacy to include a focus on AI. UNESCO aims to empower individuals worldwide to understand and engage with artificial intelligence through comprehensive education. This initiative focuses on making AI learning accessible to all by integrating AI concepts into school curricula, promoting ethical and inclusive AI usage by raising awareness about data privacy and bias, and encouraging critical understanding of AI's societal impact.

By achieving these goals, UNESCO intends to create an informed and empowered society capable of actively participating in the governance of AI. This ensures that AI is used ethically and inclusively, serving the public good and respecting human rights. Emphasizing ethical considerations and inclusivity will help mitigate potential biases and privacy issues, fostering a more equitable technological landscape. In doing so, we can ensure that AI technology benefits everyone, paving the way for a future where AI enhances human capabilities and contributes to a just society. Further on in this chapter a revised framework will be suggested that will also make connection to the guidelines provided by UNESCO.

While UNESCO has deployed its AI guidance, it should be noted that many countries, such as Finland, are pioneers in promoting AI literacy among their citizens. By championing this cause, Finland equips its population with the knowledge and skills necessary for thriving in an AI-driven world (Hautla & Heino, 2023). The Finnish government has made significant efforts to integrate AI literacy into the national curriculum through practical activities and collaborative design projects involving AI applications. The leaders in Finland regard AI as essential for their society and have demonstrated this commitment by comprehensively incorporating AI education.

Moreover, Finland's approach to AI literacy is holistic, encompassing various age groups and educational levels. This method ensures that even young students develop a foundational understanding of AI technologies, preparing them for advanced studies and future careers. The Finnish model emphasizes the importance of hands-on experiences, encouraging students to experiment with AI tools and technologies and fostering creativity and problem-solving skills. In addition to educational initiatives, Finland actively involves industry partners and research institutions in its AI literacy programs. This collaboration bridges the gap between academic knowledge and practical application, providing students real-world insights and opportunities to work on cutting-edge AI projects. Such partnerships also ensure the AI curriculum remains relevant and aligned with technological advancements and industry demands. Finland's proactive stance on AI literacy is an inspiring example for other nations aiming to prepare their citizens for the future. By prioritizing AI education, Finland not only enhances its workforce's capabilities but also strengthens its position as a leader in technological innovation and digital transformation (Jowallah, 2024).

AI, DIGITAL CITIZENSHIP, AND THE GLOBAL DIGITAL DIVIDE

Luis et al. (2024) argue that social inequalities mirror the digital divide, and the need to address this in the emergence of AI is more relevant than ever. However, the need for digital citizenship, according to the authors, is fundamental to democracy. Digital citizenship is about having the rights, responsibilities, and opportunities to engage in a digitally connected society effectively. When considering AI deployment, one key question is how digital citizens navigate these "fake" media forms. If citizens are not equipped with literacy "fit for purpose" in this advanced digital age, they will be at risk. For example, Luis et al. (2024) postulate that AI's potential risk exceeds other technology based on its ability to mimic human interaction. Furthermore, not knowing to know about the possibilities associated with AI is another issue.

The reality is that unequal access to AI technologies and digital resources will create a landscape in which certain groups are disenfranchised and left behind, unable to participate meaningfully. This will lead to socioeconomic factors such as income disparities, lack of infrastructure, and unequal access to quality education (Carter et al. 2020). These barriers hinder many people from accessing AI tools and understanding their implications. Without AI literacy, individuals cannot effectively navigate, contribute, or benefit within digital spaces. Furthermore, marginalized voices will not be heard, ultimately leading to a future diminishing of what it means to be a digital citizen. However, if there are engagement and proactive pathways for AI literacy to be integrated into digital citizenship, the outcomes will be different in relation to engagement, ethics, and privacy.

Addressing the Digital Divide

According to McGrath et al. the digital divide is concerning and will impact people significantly (2024). To bridge this gap, there must be a concerted effort to provide equal access to AI technologies and education. Governments, educational institutions, and private sectors should collaborate to create inclusive policies and programs that ensure all citizens have the opportunity to become digitally literate. This includes investing in infrastructure, providing affordable internet access, and developing educational curricula that incorporate AI literacy from an early age (United Nations, 2023)

Empowering Digital Citizens

Empowering digital citizens involves fostering critical thinking and ethical understanding. Educational programs should emphasize the importance of discerning credible information from misinformation and understanding the ethical implications of AI. Citizens should be encouraged to engage in discussions about AI and its impact on society, promoting a culture of informed and active participation.

Ensuring Ethical AI Use

Ethical AI use is paramount to maintaining trust and integrity in digital spaces. There should be transparent guidelines and regulations governing the development and deployment of AI technologies. These regulations should ensure that AI systems are designed and used in ways that respect human rights, promote fairness, and prevent biases (DelAguila, 2024). By addressing these issues and fostering a culture of digital literacy and ethical engagement, we can ensure that all citizens are prepared to navigate the complexities of the digital age and contribute meaningfully to society.

The Local Context: Digital Literacy and AI

China has generally been seen as a leader in implementing AI in education (Yuan, 2024), and research on this topic has proliferated in recent years. These factors position the country as a compelling case study. Given the reliance on internet connectivity to access many AI tools, examining data on internet access in China offers insight into the nation's potential for advancing digital literacy and AI adoption. 2023 data from the World Bank indicates that 77.5% of the population in China is using the internet, which is higher than the global rate of 67.4% and slightly lower than the 79% of the population using it in the East Asia and Pacific region. Within the country, a disparity in internet access persists between rural and urban populations. About 80% of the population in cities like Beijing and Shanghai use the internet, compared to 63.8% percent in rural China (Statista, 2024). However, state initiatives have helped decrease this inequity in recent years. In 2014, fewer than 30% of rural China had internet access, so this gap has narrowed significantly over the past decade. Income level, generation, and education level also have an impact on internet use, with higher incomes, higher education levels, and younger generations being more likely to be online (Ma, 2024).

Digital literacy around AI begins early in China. A 2024 study of children between the ages of three and six in central China found digital literacy skills develop early: 38.1% could use a TV without adult assistance, 23.3% could use a touchscreen device on their own, and 19.5% could use AI independently. Only 33.8% knew nothing about AI use (Cao et al., 2024).

In 2017, the government of China issued the *New Generation Artificial Intelligence Plan*, a document that charts out its approach to developing AI and aiming to "mak[e] China the world's primary AI innovation center" by 2030 (Stanford, 2017). Additionally, China has made intentional strides towards incorporating AI into its K-12 and higher education systems. Its centralized authority has allowed China to mandate AI curriculum at the K-12 level, with AI companies partnering with schools to provide training (Ng et al, 2023, CSET, 2021). An AI textbook, introduced by China's Education Ministry and supported by SenseTime, teaches students AI basics such as image, sound, and text recognition, and deep learning was piloted in 40 schools in 2018 (Ng et al, 2023). Since 2018, the Chinese government has approved 345 universities to offer an AI major, and 34 have launched AI institutes (CSET, 2021).

The AI technology being used in Chinese classrooms comes with some ethical concerns. AI tools incorporate video cameras, facial recognition technology, drones, and "brain headsets" to collect biometric data, which is used to assess students' attention levels and then communicated to teachers and parents. The collection and use of this data are unregulated, and schools may not ask for student or parent consent. The benefits of using the technology this way, if any, are unclear (Yuan, 2024).

PREPARING CITIZENS FOR THE FUTURE

Preparing the citizens for the future will require the emergence of various frameworks. As mentioned earlier in the chapter, the framework by Gardenier et al. had three main components (2024). The framework of technological citizenship explores how citizens engage with digitization across three interconnected spheres: private, social, and public. In the private sphere, grounded in liberalism, the focus is on individual autonomy, privacy, and rights. Digitization provides tools to enhance personal freedom and access to resources but poses risks such as surveillance, manipulation, and privacy violations. Citizens can empower themselves by leveraging digital tools for self-expression and development while building resilience through digital literacy and cybersecurity to protect their autonomy and privacy.

The social sphere emphasizes individuals' responsibilities towards their communities and the fostering of collective identity. Digitization enables new forms of community engagement and collaborative action but can fragment traditional social bonds or create echo chambers. Citizens in this sphere empower themselves by using technology to build and sustain online and offline communities, contributing to shared values and goals. Resilience in the social sphere involves promoting safe and equitable digital spaces while addressing risks such as misinformation or harmful online behavior.

In the public sphere, emphasis is on civic participation, governance, and the collective pursuit of the public good. While digitization offers opportunities for enhanced democratic engagement and activism, it also risks undermining free discourse and democratic norms through misinformation and domination by private tech entities. Citizens empower themselves by advocating for policies that uphold digital rights and enable inclusive participation, such as net neutrality. Resilience in this context involves addressing threats to democratic integrity, such as surveillance or discriminatory policies, through protests, lobbying, and legal action. Together, these spheres illustrate the dynamic roles citizens play in shaping a resilient and inclusive digital society.

Earlier in this chapter, we also defined AI literacy. Therefore, it is now fitting to combine both AI literacy and the Gardenier et al. framework (2024). The framework of technological citizenship and critical AI literacy are closely connected but differ in scope and focus. Technological citizenship encompasses the broader role of citizens in navigating and shaping the digital landscape across private, social, and public spheres, addressing issues like privacy, community engagement, and democratic governance. AI literacy, as outlined earlier is a more focused subset on equipping citizens with the knowledge and skills to understand, analyze, and engage with AI technologies, emphasizing their ethical, societal, and operational impacts. While technological citizenship emphasizes active participation in governing and shaping all forms of digital technology, critical AI literacy delves specifically into understanding and addressing the challenges posed by AI systems. Together, they empower citizens to critically evaluate and influence the digital world, with technological citizenship providing a structural lens for action and AI literacy, offering a deeper understanding of AI's specific implications (Bashir 2021 & Cox 2024 and Jowallah 2024a).

By combining a framework that makes connections to Gardenier et al. (2024) and AI literacy we should be able to develop a rigid framework that will develop a pathway for the inclusion of key tenets for the future digital citizen who is ready to engage in AI within an ethical framework. The combined framework is articulated in Table 1 below.

Table 1. Framework for preparing citizens for inclusive and ethical engagement with AI

Sphere	Focus	Opportunities	Challenges	Key Actions
Private	Individual autonomy, privacy, and rights	● AI tools for self-improvement, personalized learning, and empowerment. ● Privacy-enhancing technologies to safeguard personal data.	● Risks of surveillance and manipulation. ● Bias in AI algorithms.	● Promote critical AI literacy to understand AI operations. ● Encourage cybersecurity practices. ● Advocate for explainable AI for transparency.
Social	Community engagement and collective identity	● Collaborative innovation through AI platforms. ● Amplifying marginalized voices and reducing digital exclusion.	● Fragmentation of social bonds. ● Polarization through echo chambers and biased algorithms.	● Use AI for inclusive community-building. ● Regulate harmful content and misinformation with AI. ● Foster trust-building through digital literacy.
Public	Civic participation and governance	● Enhanced policymaking and digital activism using AI. ● Improved access to government services through AI-driven platforms.	● Threats to democratic norms from biased or opaque AI. ● Concentration of power in tech entities controlling discourse.	● Advocate for transparent AI governance. ● Educate on AI policy frameworks(e.g., net neutrality). ● Monitor and mitigate biases in public AI platforms.
Interconnection	Unified engagement through AI literacy	● Equips citizens with foundational AI knowledge. ● Enables critical analysis of AI's societal impact. ● Empowers advocacy for ethical AI usage.	● Lack of understanding of AI's broader implications.	● Integrate critical AI literacy across spheres. ● Build tools to connect AI education to ethical, societal, and operational impacts.

The above figure offers a structured view of how various components interact and contribute to preparing citizens for a digital and AI-driven future. The spheres delineate critical components necessary for fostering digital citizenship and areas requiring focused attention. In the "Opportunities" section of the table, possibilities for enhancing digital citizenship are outlined. For example, in the public domain, there is a need to emphasize civic participation and governance. This can be achieved by enhancing policymaking processes and promoting digital activism through AI. The table also identifies potential threats and challenges that must be addressed. One significant threat is the risk to democratic norms posed by biased or opaque AI systems. To mitigate these threats, the table highlights the required action points, including promoting AI literacy across all spheres. These measures aim to ensure informed and equitable engagement with AI technologies, thereby fostering a robust digital citizenship framework.

Educational Reforms and Curriculum Development

For the framework mentioned above to be effective within a digital citizenship structure, the outlined tenets must be purposeful and included in national curricula (Figure 1). Policymakers should address the course spheres, identifying opportunities to include AI literacy while remaining aware of the potential risks associated with AI. However, the curriculum goes beyond being a written document; therefore, teacher training and professional development will be essential to equip stakeholders with the skills needed to teach and deploy the focus areas mentioned in the table (Pahl & Rowsell, 2005). For instance, teachers should be able to articulate what it means to engage within an AI community and how to foster collective or individual identities within a global digital citizenship framework.

A critical element of the framework's success is ensuring opportunities for lifelong learning, as AI currently impacts everyone in society. This may necessitate adult learning opportunities to equip adults with the necessary skills to contribute meaningfully. In this context, community centers and libraries could play a significant role in this development.

Strategies for Effective Implementation

While the educational policy issue was addressed in the paragraph above, it represents a long-term solution. However, the authors believe there will also be a need for comprehensive national strategies encompassing all sectors to guide them in acquiring the necessary skills for the digital age. For these strategies to succeed, governments must prioritize funding to engage their populations on the importance of AI engagement within digital spaces. A national strategy must also ensure population involvement (Jowallah 2023). For Instance, incorporating parents' perspectives could provide insights into their children's digital practices at home, ensuring that any initiative is fit for purpose and relevant to the household's context and culture. Additionally, the implemented strategies should be evaluated and adjusted continuously to align with AI advancements. Any strategy must remain flexible enough to adapt to the evolving technological landscape.

BALANCING GLOBAL INNOVATIONS WITH LOCAL NEEDS

The issue of addressing digital citizenship and the need for engagement with AI should be a priority for all global organizations, including the United Nations. Regardless of the model selected, it is essential to adopt one that emphasizes the deployment of digital citizenship skills. A key imperative for developing these skills lies in the potentially destructive nature of AI when used without ethical oversight. Similarly, in the 1950s, atomic regulations were introduced to mitigate the destructive potential of nuclear technology for humanity (Mazuzan & Walker 1997). According to the United Nations, the danger with AI is that it mimics humans (2023). If left unchecked, this could lead to catastrophic consequences. With this in mind, it is essential to establish global regulations that align with digital citizenship principles.

Through global collaboration, we can ensure customized best practices that fit within local contexts and benefit everyone from AI. Addressing marginalized and underserved populations and ensuring accessibility is key to seamlessly adopting digital citizenship tenets globally. Achieving this will require the global allocation of resources and active citizen participation in educational spaces, enabling them to become lifelong learners (United Nations, 2023, Floridi & Cowls, 2019).

FUTURE TRENDS AND PREDICTIONS

Emerging Technologies in Education

Artificial intelligence is evolving in tandem with other emerging technologies that have potential to transform education. Among these, Virtual Reality (VR) and Augmented Reality (AR) stand out as innovative tools that promote active learning. VR immerses students in realistic, interactive environments where they can explore concepts and develop skills in a hands-on way Through VR headsets, learners can experience immersive simulations such as traveling to historical landmarks, exploring the ocean, or practicing medical procedures (Gorski et al, 2016). Likewise, AR enhances the real world by overlaying digital objects, enabling students to interact with virtual elements in their physical surroundings (Billinghurst et al, 2015). These technologies become even more impactful when combined with AI, as generative AI can enhance the creation of custom simulations and learning scenarios tailored to individual or group needs (Kaviyaraj & Uma, 2021). As VR and AR increasingly blur the boundaries between the physical and digital worlds, the need for robust digital literacy skills is critical. These skills empower learners to navigate, interpret, and critically engage with these technologies, ensuring they can effectively utilize immersive experiences for educational growth. Furthermore, digital literacy fosters an understanding of the ethical, social, and technical implications of using such tools, preparing students to be thoughtful and informed participants in a technologically integrated society. By cultivating these competencies, educators can help learners maximize the potential of VR and AR while mitigating challenges related to misinformation and over-reliance on technology.

AI itself is reshaping education by providing personalized and adaptive learning experiences. AI-driven tutoring systems can identify each student's strengths and areas for improvement, tailoring content to their unique learning style and pace. Automated performance assessment tools reduce the administrative workload for educators by streamlining tasks like grading, freeing them to focus on teaching and mentoring. Additionally, AI-powered predictive analytics can help identify at-risk students early, enabling educators to intervene with targeted support to promote success (Dimitriadou & Lanitis, 2023). Professional development is crucial for educators integrating these technologies into their teaching, with maintaining strong AI literacy skills and awareness of ethical implications being especially essential.

The Evolving Job Market

The impact of artificial intelligence on the future job market is still unfolding, making its full implications on students' career trajectories difficult to predict. AI is poised to significantly reshape job responsibilities across industries while simultaneously generating entirely new roles that have yet to be imagined. Educators face the critical challenge of equipping students for careers in this uncertain landscape. By prioritizing digital literacy, critical thinking, and problem-solving, they can help students develop adaptable, transferable skill sets, empowering them to learn and thrive as technology continues to evolve (Jumaev, 2024).

However, this shift risks exacerbating the digital divide and economic disparities between countries with advanced AI infrastructure and those with limited access. Nations with less digital access may struggle to compete in AI-driven industries, leading to a growing equity gap (Bozic, 2023). To address this, global efforts must prioritize equitable technology access, workforce reskilling, and policies that foster inclusion, ensuring that the benefits of AI are shared across diverse economies.

Ethical Considerations

A crucial aspect of AI literacy is understanding the ethical challenges that accompany the use of this technology. In educational contexts, four major categories of ethical and social risks warrant particular attention: privacy, bias and discrimination, surveillance, and autonomy (Akgun & Greenhow, 2021). Developing critical literacy in AI empowers users to identify and navigate these risks, fostering a more informed and responsible approach to integrating AI in learning environments.

Protecting privacy is a critical concern in the use of AI applications, which often collect user data, including personal information. Students may be required to accept user agreements that authorize the release of their data, often without fully understanding the implications of these terms. This can create a significant dilemma for students who wish to protect their privacy but need to use these tools to participate in class. Educators should exercise caution when requiring tools with such agreements and proactively educate students about the associated risks. Empowering students with this knowledge enables them to make informed choices about sharing their personal information.

Surveillance is another critical concern when using AI tools in education. As these tools collect data on students, including their demographics, behaviors, and preferences, this information could be used to predict or influence future actions, often without the students' knowledge or consent. This creates an environment where students might feel insecure or even unsafe and potentially limiting their participation in the course. The perception of being constantly tracked can undermine trust and stifle authentic engagement. Educators should carefully evaluate how such tools collect and utilize data, prioritize transparency, and help students build critical digital literacy skills that help them understand the risks involved.

The use of predictive AI systems in education also raises concerns about autonomy, a person's ability to act in alignment with their own interests and values. These systems, by analyzing and predicting behaviors or outcomes, can inadvertently undermine self-governance and limit students' ability to make decisions for themselves. For instance, if students are steered toward certain actions based on algorithmic predictions, their potential to explore diverse paths or challenge assumptions may be restricted. Moreover, these systems often perpetuate existing biases embedded in the data they analyze, reinforcing stereotypes and inequities. To preserve autonomy, educators should critically assess how predictive tools influence decision-making and strive to empower students to remain active agents in their own educational journeys.

AI algorithms often inherit the biases of their creators, reflecting the perspectives and worldviews of predominantly white, male developers from developed countries. As a result, these algorithms are prone to reinforcing systemic discrimination based on race, gender, ethnicity, nationality, and other identity factors. In a global context, this can amplify harmful stereotypes and marginalize individuals from less developed regions, perpetuating inequities on a broad scale. Recognizing these patterns is essential for fostering equity in education. Students who cultivate critical digital literacy skills can learn to identify and challenge these biases in AI systems, helping to disrupt cycles of discrimination and avoid perpetuating them in their own work or decisions.

CONCLUSION

In this chapter, we have explored the importance of preparing students for an AI-powered future, emphasizing the significance of AI literacy skills. The rapid advancement of AI technologies necessitates a comprehensive understanding of digital tools and ethical considerations. We highlighted the global landscape of AI in education and discussed the need for a robust framework that includes AI literacy to empower individuals to navigate and contribute to an increasingly AI-infused world.

Stakeholders, including educators, policymakers, and community leaders, must prioritize digital literacy skills. By incorporating AI literacy into curricula and providing continuous professional development for educators, we can ensure that learners of all ages are equipped with the necessary skills to thrive. Governments and organizations must collaborate to create inclusive policies and programs that bridge the digital divide, ensuring equitable access to AI technologies and education for all citizens.

Looking ahead, we hope that digital literacy skills will contribute to building a society where individuals are not only proficient in using AI tools but also possess the critical thinking skills to engage with AI ethically and responsibly. This future society will be characterized by informed and active citizens who can utilize AI to enhance their lives while advocating for ethical standards and inclusiveness. By fostering a culture of lifelong learning and adaptation, we can build a community that is ready to meet the challenges and opportunities of the AI age.

REFERENCES

Akgun, S., & Greenhow, C. (2022). Artificial intelligence in education: Addressing ethical challenges in K-12 settings. *AI and Ethics*, 2(3), 431–440. DOI: 10.1007/s43681-021-00096-7 PMID: 34790956

Audrin, C., & Audrin, B. (2022). Key factors in digital literacy in learning and education: A systematic literature review using text mining. *Education and Information Technologies*, 27(6), 7395–7419. DOI: 10.1007/s10639-021-10832-5

Bashir, D. (2021). *Ai literacy : understanding shifts in our digital ecosystem* (1st ed.). New Degree Press.

Benson, T. (2024). *Education: Growth, Adoption & Impact Statistics*. Retrieved: https://aistatistics.ai/education/?utm_source=chatgpt.com

Billinghurst, M., Clark, A., & Lee, G. (2015). A survey of augmented reality. *Foundations and Trends® in Human–Computer Interaction, 8*(2-3), 73-272.

Božić, V. (2023). Artifical intelligence as the reason and the solution of digital divide. *Language Education and Technology, 3*(2).

Cao, S., Dong, C., & Li, H. (2024). Emergent digital literacy in Chinese preschoolers: Developmental patterns and associated predicators. *Early Child Development and Care*, 194(2), 281–295. DOI: 10.1080/03004430.2024.2303480

Carter, L., Liu, D., & Cantrell, C. (2020). Exploring the Intersection of the Digital Divide and Artificial Intelligence: A Hermeneutic Literature Review. *AIS Transactions on Human-Computer Interaction, 12*(4), 253-275. DOI: 10.17705/1thci.00138

Cox, A. (2024). Algorithmic Literacy, AI Literacy and Responsible Generative AI Literacy. *Journal of Web Librarianship*, 18(3), 1–18. DOI: 10.1080/19322909.2024.2395341

CSET. (2021). AI education in China and the United States. CSET.

DelAguila, A. T. (2024, August 12). *6 strategies for teaching digital citizenship and balance in the era of AI*. Share My Lesson. Retrieved from https://sharemylesson.com/blog/6-strategies-teaching-digital-citizenship-ai

Dimitriadou, E., & Lanitis, A. (2023). A critical evaluation, challenges, and future perspectives of using artificial intelligence and emerging technologies in smart classrooms. *Smart Learning Environments*, 10(1), 12. DOI: 10.1186/s40561-023-00231-3

Floridi, L., & Cowls, J. (2019). *A Unified Framework of Five Principles for AI in Society. Harvard Data Science Review.* Retrieved:https://hdsr.mitpress.mit.edu/pub/l0jsh9d1/release/8

Gardenier, A. M., van Est, R., & Royakkers, L. (2024). Technological citizenship in times of digitization: An integrative framework. *Digital Society : Ethics, Socio-Legal and Governance of Digital Technology*, 3(21), 21. Advance online publication. DOI: 10.1007/s44206-024-00106-1

Górski, F., Buń, P., Wichniarek, R., Zawadzki, P., & Hamrol, A. (2016). Effective design of educational virtual reality applications for medicine using knowledge-engineering techniques. *Eurasia Journal of Mathematics, Science and Technology Education*, 13(2), 395–416. DOI: 10.12973/eurasia.2017.00623a

Hautala, J., & Heino, H. (2023). Spectrum of AI futures imaginaries by AI practitioners in Finland and Singapore: The unimagined speed of AI progress. *Futures : The Journal of Policy, Planning and Futures Studies, 153*, 103247. DOI: 10.1016/j.futures.2023.103247

HogoNext. (2024). How to Address the Digital Divide and Ensure Equitable Access to E-Learning for All Learners. Retrieved on November 22 from https://hogonext.com/how-to-address-the-digital-divide-and-ensure-equitable-access-to-e-learning-for-all-learners/#google_vignette

Jowallah, R. (2015). Awakening Students through Critical Literacy: Implications for Teaching and Learning within Contemporary Education. *The International Journal of Literacies*, 21(3-4), 17–27. DOI: 10.18848/2327-0136/CGP/v21i3-4/48837

Jowallah, R. (2023). Integrating Artificial Intelligence (AI) Into the Curriculum: Empowering the Next Generation Through Proactive AI Education. In *Generative AI in Teaching and Learning*. IGI Publishers. DOI: 10.4018/979-8-3693-0074-9.ch015

Jowallah, R. (2023). Empowering Education: Designing and Implementing a Sustainable Digital Change Framework. YouTube. https://youtu.be/ovSoAma-WGg?si=-dSSqIRv5jo7XPTa

Jowallah, R. (2024). How Finland is Leading the Fight Against Misinformation. YouTube. https://youtu.be/-8pAXKoKEKU?si=aw32j6rh9Tw1QrTN

Jowallah, R. (2024a). The Evolution of Content: AI for Enhanced Creativity and Personalization. YouTube. https://youtu.be/-8pAXKoKEKU?si=aw32j6rh9Tw1QrTN

Jumaev, G. (2024). The Impact of AI on Job Market: Adapting to the Future of Work. *Modern Science and Research, 3*(1).

Kaviyaraj, R., & Uma, M. (2021, March). A survey on future of augmented reality with AI in education. In *2021 International Conference on Artificial Intelligence and Smart Systems (ICAIS)* (pp. 47-52). IEEE. DOI: 10.1109/ICAIS50930.2021.9395838

Long, D., & Magerko, B. (2020). What is AI Literacy? Competencies and Design Considerations. *Proceedings of the 2020 CHI Conference on Human Factors in Computing Systems*, 598–598. https://doi.org/DOI: 10.1145/3313831.3376727

Ma, X. (2024). Internet use and income gaps between rural and urban residents in China. *Journal of the Asia Pacific Economy*, 29(2), 789–809. DOI: 10.1080/13547860.2022.2054133

Mazuzan, G., & Walker, S. (1997). Controlling the Atom: The Beginnings of Neclear Regulations 1946 to 1962. Retrieved December 5, 2024 from https://www.nrc.gov/reading-rm/doc-collections/nuregs/staff/sr1610/index.html

McGrath, D., Irons, J., & Cooper, S. (2024). The digital divide in the age of AI: Implications for equity and inclusion. *Journal of Digital Equity*, 14(2), 123–136. DOI: 10.1007/s43681-024-00452-3

Ng, D. T. K., Leung, J. K. L., Su, M. J., Yim, I. H. Y., Qiao, M. S., & Chu, S. K. W. (2023). *AI literacy in K-16 classrooms*. Springer International Publishing AG.

Pahl, K., & Rowsell, J. (2005). *Literacy and education: Understanding the new literacy studies in the classroom*. SAGE Publications.

Santana, I., Trauthin, I., & Woodley, S. (2024). We Can Harness Digital Citizenship to Confront AI Risk. Retrieved December 2, 2024, from https://www.cigionline.org/articles/we-can-harness-digital-citizenship-to-confront-ai-risks/

Seung, Y. (2024). Conceptuaizing AI Literacy: A Critical Skill for the 21st Century. Retrieved November 22, 2024, from https://ciddl.org/conceptualizing-ai-literacy-a-critical-skill-for-the-21st-century/?utm_source=chatgpt.com

Stanford University. (2017). *Full translation: China's New Generation Artificial Intelligence Development Plan (2017)*. DigiChina. Retrieved November 21, 2024, from https://digichina.stanford.edu/work/full-translation-chinas-new-generation-artificial-intelligence-development-plan-2017/

Statista. (n.d.-a). *Internet penetration rate in rural areas in China from 2014 to 2024*. Retrieved November 21, 2024, from https://www.statista.com/statistics/1062706/china-internet-penetration-rate-rural-areas/

Statista. (n.d.-b). *Internet usage in China - statistics & facts*. Retrieved November 21, 2024, from https://www.statista.com/topics/1179/internet-usage-in-china/#topicOverview

UNESCO. (2022). The Ethics of Artificial Intelligence. Retrieved: https://unesdoc.unesco.org/ark:/48223/pf0000381137

UNESCO. (2024). AI Competency Framework for students. https://unesdoc.unesco.org/ark:/48223/pf0000391105?posInSet=6&queryId=466caf26-326a-46f3-88ac-27bbc16ce6a9

United Nations. (2023). *Digital inclusion and artificial intelligence: Bridging the divide for equitable access*. Retrieved from https://www.un.org

Wang, S., Wang, F., Zhu, Z., Wang, J., Tran, T., & Zhao, D. Artificial intelligence in education: A systematic literature review, Expert Systems with Applications, Volume 252, Part A. Retrieved December 4th. 2024 from https://www.sciencedirect.com/science/article/pii/S0957417424010339

World Bank. (n.d.). *Individuals using the Internet (% of population)* [Data set]. Retrieved November 20, 2024, from https://databank.worldbank.org/reports.aspx?dsid=2&series=IT.NET.USER.ZS#

Yuan, L. (2024). Where does AI-driven Education, in the Chinese Context and Beyond, go next? *International Journal of Artificial Intelligence in Education*, 34(1), 31–41. DOI: 10.1007/s40593-023-00341-6

Chapter 6
Artificial Intelligence and the Advancement of Civic and Political Engagement:
Opportunities and Challenges for Democracy

Zafer Kuş
Ahi Evran University, Turkey

ABSTRACT

This chapter will first emphasize the critical need for active political and civic engagement in maintaining democracy's enduring vitality. The author analyzes the evolution of citizen participation over time, especially with the proliferation of the internet and the prevalence of social media, which have altered individual engagement in the digital era. This chapter will examine how artificial intelligence has expanded the opportunities for public participation and the possible advantages this entails. However, it will also address significant concerns about the potential use of AI by governments with authoritarian tendencies. The author examines how new technologies may jeopardize human liberties, distort election processes—even in stable democracies—and raise concerns over the future erosion of democratic systems.

INTRODUCTION

Despite decades of heated debate, no commonly accepted accurate definition of artificial intelligence (AI) exists. Overall, the developed definitions are either too wide or too narrow. While some feel AI has the ability to save lives, others believe

DOI: 10.4018/979-8-3693-9015-3.ch006

it is a forerunner to disaster. Both extreme ways fail to take into account the varied and intricate nature of these ideas, preventing a fair and accurate appraisal. In reality, many of the other concepts I'll examine in this section, such as political involvement, digital citizenship, and democracy, lack clear and unequivocal bounds. When examining the always changing social, cultural, and technological contexts, it is critical to have a good understanding of the dynamic nature of these concepts. Different cultures and groups use and interpret these principles in various ways, reflecting the breadth of their applications and interpretations. The meaning and function of these concepts are constantly evolving as a result of technological advancements. On the one hand, this ambiguity encourages an unduly positive perspective of technology, portraying it as a savior, but on the other, it constitutes a threat, potentially leading to terrible outcomes.

Nevertheless, in spite of all these uncertainties, AI is having an increasingly significant impact on society today, and it is abundantly obvious that it is bringing about transformation in a variety of domains. It is becoming increasingly widespread in a variety of domains, including agriculture, education, health, and the economy, with the goal of optimizing processes and outcomes in these areas. AI, in particular, has the potential to improve economic decision-making processes by accelerating financial assessments. Similarly, it has the potential to improve student success in the field of education by providing individualized learning experiences. AI is improving the quality of healthcare services by facilitating early diagnosis and treatment procedures. It improves farmers' planning chances in agriculture by evaluating data pertaining to crops and weather. However, AI's influence extends beyond these specific fields and significantly influences ongoing political processes. The participation of individuals in a variety of governance processes, the structure of democratic representation, and the mechanisms for shaping public opinion have all begun to undergo transformations as a result of the introduction of AI. It is possible that AI applications could promote democracy by increasing citizens' political and civic participation. Particularly, there is a growing anticipation that AI will enhance democratic involvement, ensure social equity, and aid individuals in voicing their opinions. On the other hand, AI also presents new dangers that have the potential to disrupt democratic processes. AI poses a risk of becoming a weapon that supports authoritarian inclinations, particularly in developing democracies where democratic principles are not completely ingrained and authoritarian impulses are strong. This risk is especially prevalent in countries where authoritarian tendencies are strong.

In this section, I will attempt to examine the potential opportunities and hazards that are associated with the discussion of subjects such as AI, political participation, digital citizenship, and digital democracy. I will do this by analyzing the impact that AI has on citizens' social and political engagement. In this section, I will concentrate on the criticisms that bring to light particularly unfavorable scenarios, such as the possibility that technologies based on AI could endanger individual liberties, result in the manipulation of information, and undermine democratic procedures.

CITIZEN PARTICIPATION

Contemporary democracy is founded on representative democracy implemented throughout extensive regions, as opposed to the direct democracy exercised in the limited confines of Ancient Greece, where democracy originated. The essence of representative democracy is the execution of the populace's will in the administration of extensive communities via elected officials. This system, despite its diverse implementations across global locations, inherently depends on public engagement and representation. Lincoln's assertion, "*Democracy is the government of the people, by the people, for the people*" delineates a governance model executed by representatives chosen by the populace, emphasizing the primacy of public interests. This definition posits that the populace constitutes both the origin of governmental authority and the fundamental principle that the government must cater to the interests of the people. The essential tenets of democracy are crucial for comprehending the role of citizens within this framework. In representative democracy, where the desires and interests of the populace are articulated through representatives, citizens occupy a pivotal role as individuals endowed with rights and as members accountable for the obligations inherent in this system. In this context, citizenship is defined as a legal and political status that permits individuals to engage in democratic processes. The notion of contemporary citizenship denotes a constitutional position that articulates the rights and responsibilities an individual possesses in respect to the state. This position allows citizens to engage actively in the operation of the democratic system. Citizenship, in a political context, beyond mere legal status; it encompasses an individual's active engagement in the community's public life, political processes, and institutions. This involvement affords individuals a sense of social belonging and identity, allowing them to contribute to the democratic framework of society (Kymlicka & Norman 2000). Citizenship is a vital component of democracy, encompassing the safeguarding of individual rights and the acceptance of community obligations through active participation.

The phrase "*citizen participation*" has been employed in various settings across different regimes and as previously noted, lacks a definitive interpretation. Citizen participation, in its most fundamental essence, refers to the active engagement of individuals in governance or societal matters through several means. In democratic societies, participation can manifest in several ways, including voting in elections, attending public meetings, sitting on boards or commissions, or remaining informed about community affairs. The engagement of citizens in decision-making processes, including voting and public discourse, fortifies democratic systems. Citizen engagement is a vital component that sustains the operation and legitimacy of democratic processes. The level of citizen participation in the political process is the primary indication of the prevalence of democracy (Briggs, 2017). Civic engagement denotes the involvement of citizens in social and political activities aimed at enhancing societal welfare, improving the living situations of others, or influencing the future of the community (Richard and Gogg, 2005). Civic involvement seeks to improve the quality of life in a democratic society through political and non-political avenues. Civic engagement is characterized as a component that enhances representative democracy by broadening the domains in which citizens can exert influence (Salinas et al., 2018; Michels, 2011). Genuine democracy is present only when citizens are well educated, possess accessible avenues for involvement and advocacy, and have influence over decisions that impact them (Innerarity, 2024).

Risse (2022) highlights two essential risks to contemporary democracy: The initial issue is the erosion of trust stemming from the sense of state and society as abstract and remote entities. The second concern is the potential for the executive power to evolve into a repressive apparatus. In contemporary democracies, bureaucracy may evolve their own dynamics, resulting in citizens feeling alienated from government processes. Historically, the predominant method for citizen engagement is via elections (Verba &Nie 1987). While elections are regarded as the principal and most prevalent method of citizen engagement in democratic administration, options for civil and political participation have notably broadened in modern times, extending beyond electoral periods, to foster a robust and sustainable democracy. Citizen engagement beyond electoral processes is crucial in averting potential totalitarianism. This involvement fosters candid dialogues and cultivates resilience against repressive policies. In a nation such as Turkey, where the head of the Executive branch is directly elected, there exists a risk that excessive executive power may devolve into personal authority. Engaged citizens enhance transparency by scrutinizing the conduct of political leaders and ensuring that public authorities serve the public interest.

Political engagement is fundamental to a democratic state and serves as a significant measure of political modernization. Individuals engaging in elections, affiliating with political parties, or endorsing social movements exemplify diverse modalities of political participation. This engagement extends beyond voting; it also augments the transparency of democratic processes, fortifies awareness of social issues, and advances social justice. Civic engagement pertains to people actively engaging in social, economic, and political matters within society. This involvement transpires via volunteer activities, community events, and collaboration with non-governmental groups. The correlation between political and civic engagement is essential for the effective operation of a democratic society; robust civic participation motivates citizens to partake in political processes, whilst political participation heightens awareness of social issues. Simultaneously, citizen engagement unites diverse social groupings, fostering a collective feeling of accountability and strengthening democratic culture. Engagement cultivates critical thinking and political consciousness among citizens, so facilitating the questioning of authority, the pursuit of reform, and the advocacy for social justice.

TRANSITIONING FROM CONVENTIONAL PARTICIPATION TO DIGITAL PARTICIPATION

Despite the fact that citizen participation is a crucial tenet of democracy, research has revealed that less people are getting involved in politics, particularly younger generations (Euyoupart, 2005; Shultz et al., 2010; Theocharis & Quintelier, 2014) In particular, many nations' preferences have shifted away from more conventional forms of participation. Everyday life for the general public has changed drastically and irrevocably as a result of the fast evolution of traditional media tools and the broad use of the internet. An age of network democracy with tremendous participation options was born with the advent of Web 2.0 in the early 2000s, following the broad adoption of the internet in the early 1990s. During this time, social media also began to gain popularity. The democratic public sphere is feeling the consequences of a major shift in the sites where users create and consume materia (Berg and Hofmann). People are now more educated about global events in real time, information is more readily available, and the media significantly influences people's views on social, cultural, and political issues. While television and newspapers dominated for a long time, the proliferation of internet usage has transformed the way people communicate and diversified the sources of information. There have been major shifts in how people participate in society and politics as a result of the proliferation of digital tools.

Berg and Hofmann (2021) delineate the three phases of digital democracy to exemplify the transformation of political engagement through technology. The preliminary stage, referred to as e-democracy, occurred in the 1980s and facilitated the creation of direct participation platforms through cable television and bulletin board systems. Cyber democracy (1990s) denotes the period during which techno-libertarian ideals and transnational internet communities thrived. Digital platforms played an ambiguous role in democratic processes throughout the network democracy era of the 2000s, when participation surged due to the influence of Web 2.0 and social media.

From its inception in the early 1990s in Western European and North American nations including the US, Canada, and Singapore, the notion of electronic governance has now expanded to every country on Earth. When it comes to e-government, for instance, Turkey has invested much and achieved great strides. The e-government development index number is increasing at a faster rate than in many other countries, including Turkey (2020 United Nations E-Government Survey). A lot of money and effort has gone into e-government in Turkey. Since its inception in the early 2000s, the e-Government Gateway has grown into a framework that integrates hundreds of governmental organizations and provides access to thousands of public services. This platform, which currently has 66 million users (URL, 1), is crucial in modern times because it facilitates public engagement, streamlines bureaucratic processes, and makes government services easily accessible to citizens.

Citizens' engagement in politics and civic life has entered a new age with the broad use of Web 2.0 tools, particularly social media. People now have more ways than ever before to become involved, join campaigns, and lend their support to social movements all thanks to the proliferation of online platforms. Digital tools and online platforms have transformed traditional modes of involvement into more dynamic and expansive means of engagement. A new public arena has emerged thanks to the proliferation of online platforms, where the 'fourth estate' can no longer control the flow of information or censor viewpoints. Thanks to the accessibility and personalization offered by social media, new tools for public engagement have emerged (Boulianne, 2015; Fyfe, 2009). There are a lot of ways in which people's interactions online affect their voting behavior, their involvement in political movements, and the reasons for various types of participation. As stated by Koc-Michalska & Lilleker in 2017. Taking into account the levels of political participation described by Milbrath (1965), it is observed that younger generations are increasingly participating in politics through open or covert digital platforms, as opposed to more conventional means of engagement like party membership, badge wearing, donation-making, or campaign support (Kuş et al., 2024). New entry points made possible by social media platforms allow for the use of several modes of communication, opening up new avenues for political discourse, information collecting, and engagement (Vitak et al., 2011). Direct contacts between people and organizations are now feasible because to platforms such as YouTube, Facebook, and Twitter. Through data mining and trend prediction, social media has opened up new avenues for networking while also producing massive volumes of data. With the proliferation of digital media, the public sphere has grown in both size and importance. There is evidence that social media can boost democratic accountability on a global scale by reviving political engagement, increasing voting in legislative elections, and so on (Castells, 2013). Many see social media as a fresh and exciting way for young people to get involved in their communities, and their heavy usage of these sites lends credence to this idea

(Christensen, 2011). Several empirical research (Dzisah, 2018; Jennings, Suzuki, and Hubbard, 2021) have shown that social media can give people more agency by making it easier for them to get information, voice their opinions, and create groups to address certain problems. Numerous studies show that as digital environments have evolved, alternative methods of political participation have multiplied and informal participation has grown, all because of the potential these technologies bring (Vitak et al., 2011; Boulianne, 2015; Fyfe, 2009; Elchardus & Siongers, 2016; Boulianne, 2009).

HOW AI AFFECTS CIVIC AND POLITICAL PARTICIPATION

Within the framework of interactive governance, AI has revolutionized the way governments engage with their constituents, make decisions, and address societal issues. The use of AI has far-reaching effects on decision-making in many fields, including people's political leanings. Thanks to big data's ability to aggregate vast amounts of information on individual preferences and actions, novel strategies for guiding citizens in the digital realm can be more easily developed. Because of this situation, societal and political processes, as well as human decision-making, have undergone a metamorphosis. Thanks to the internet and AI-powered platforms, people are now more than just data consumers; they are active participants in the data creation process. Novel approaches and tactics have emerged in many fields as a consequence of these advancements, which have affected people's information-driven decisions and given rise to new forms of advertising and political campaigns.

Democracy is based on participation in society and collective intelligence that represents many points of view, not on individualism and uniformity. By making this method easier to implement, AI successfully includes numerous viewpoints and guarantees more involvement (Olariu & Onufreiciuc, 2020). For example, going beyond electoral voting might pave the way for more comprehensive and long-lasting forms of political participation. By increasing openness, AI can give new options for people who don't want to use traditional ways of getting involved. People in many countries, especially those with underdeveloped or emerging democracies, have a hard time interacting with government agencies. Regular participation from the populace is essential for democracies to run well. People rarely participate in civic engagement and avoid dealing with governmental institutions unless absolutely necessary because of the complex hierarchical systems and tedious bureaucratic processes (Onufreıcıuc, 2024 According to Lahdili, Önder, and Nyadera (2024), AI has the potential to improve citizen participation, but its implementation in governance and civic engagement must consider its strengths, flaws, possibilities, and risks. They emphasize AI's ability to collect and digitize massive amounts of correct data, assist predictive analytics, improve decision-making, and streamline difficult processes, resulting in a fast-evolving digital governance structure. They do, however, highlight important obstacles such as insufficient infrastructure, limited resources, a lack of strong legal frameworks, privacy concerns, algorithmic biases, and discriminatory behaviors.

Despite these obstacles, the authors see significant prospects for AI to encourage civic involvement by raising political awareness, strengthening government transparency and accountability, and improving public services. AI can also promote diversity, transparency, and capacity-building in data literacy, hence improving communication between citizens and government entities. Lahdili, Önder, & Nyadera (2024) warn that cybersecurity concerns, unethical activities, algorithmic biases, and the digital divide might undermine trust and equitable access. They advocate for inclusive, ethical, and transparent approaches to aligning AI capabilities with democratic principles, assuring responsible use in government and public participation.

AI-powered platforms have the potential to enhance citizen engagement by facilitating communication between people and their elected officials and providing an avenue for them to voice relevant concerns. Public services can be made more accessible and user-friendly with the use of AI-enhanced solutions. Citizens can access public services more quickly and efficiently thanks to AI's ability to streamline bureaucratic processes. In order to improve connections with public institutions, it is possible to streamline complex processes, use digital assistants to guide citizens, and develop technology that can autonomously handle requests. In addition, by analyzing individual remarks, it can help formulate better public policy.

AI capabilities also provide new ways for citizens to weigh in on how well government services are working. By providing a more direct and efficient means for residents to express their wants and needs, these platforms help governments improve services and formulate policies based on accurate information. With the help of AI, this complex feedback loop promotes a citizen-centric governance model that is quick to respond to and meets the requirements of its constituents. So, people have more say over services as public management becomes more open, participatory, and data-driven. Numerous research conducted in the past five years indicate that AI-based solutions can enhance public involvement (Engin & Treleaven, 2019; Harrison, & Luna-Reyes, 2020; Horvath et al., 2023; Onufreiciuc, 2024; Vereş-Cătău, 2019; Zuiderwijk, Chen, & Salem, 2021).

In order to protect human rights, democracy, and the rule of law within a democratic framework, it is vital that the intermediate function of AI adhere to humanist ideals such as inclusion, diversity, and equality. Assuring that AI technologies improve democratic processes and that all people's viewpoints are recognized should be the goal of this instrument. This approach allows for more active participation in political processes and gives people more agency in decision-making. When it comes to making decisions, AI can greatly improve the way citizens' voices are heard. Governments may make better use of modern technologies to incorporate citizen feedback into active decision-making, which will lead to more responsiveness and fair outcomes. This can help bring the needs and wants of the people into harmony with those of the government, leading to a more harmonious society.

AI has been employed in electoral procedures for an extended period. It facilitates more accurate audience targeting, which is crucial in political campaigns, and offers politicians graphics and adverts at no expense or sometimes at no charge. Chatbots and discussion forums on social media platforms prompt users to comment and yield significant insights regarding the sentiments of your target audience. AI can gather and evaluate this data instantaneously, enabling campaign strategists to modify their strategies according to public sentiment (Innerarity, 2024). Furthermore, AI can enhance certain inefficiencies by forecasting individual preferences, categorizing information, and influencing information flows.

A notable yet often overlooked benefit of AI in the public sector is its capacity to enhance the accessibility of government websites, papers, and official communications for citizens. This is highly significant in nations with numerous languages and varied dialects. AI, through its automated translation and language processing abilities, can eradicate language barriers by facilitating citizens' access to information in their native languages. This enhances access to public services and promotes citizen engagement, hence fostering the development of a more inclusive and efficient public administration framework. AI-driven solutions can promptly translate official documents into several languages, simplify intricate bureaucratic procedures, and enhance communication between the government and its citizens. Social integration is facilitated by promoting the active involvement of populations marginalized by linguistic obstacles.

Governments are progressively employing AI to promote citizen engagement and improve participation in policy-making processes. Estonia, recognized as the 'digital republic,' has revolutionized various governmental services through AI-centric initiatives such as e-Estonia. An exemplary instance is e-Residency, a government-issued digital identity enabling anybody worldwide to form and administer a global enterprise inside Estonia's jurisdiction. This illustrates the capacity of AI to enhance civic engagement effectively and inclusively. (URL, 2). Estonian individuals are connected with governmental officials through AI-supported applications, utilizing chatbot services to access information. Consequently, citizens can obtain information and data without encountering substantial barriers.

Turkey possesses one of the highest ratios of youth population among European Union nations. The internet usage rate for individuals aged 16-24 is approximately 99% (TÜİK, 2023). The extensive access of youth to digital tools and their proficiency in utilizing these means can enhance their engagement in political involvement and democratic processes. Digital platforms enhance young individuals' access to political knowledge, empower them to articulate their views, and enable more efficient organization on social concerns. Young individuals might utilize AI tools to examine facts pertaining to societal concerns and formulate strategic decisions. AI enhances democratic engagement, empowering youth to participate more actively in voter registration, electoral processes, and interactions with political candidates. Mobile applications and digital platforms can enhance youth engagement in these processes while aiding in the identification and prevention of misinformation and disinformation. This enables youth to obtain precise and trustworthy information, facilitating educated decision-making based on such data.

THREATS POSED BY AI TO DEMOCRATIC SYSTEMS

Despite the fact that technologies based on AI present opportunities for citizen participation, they also present substantial hazards to democratic institutions. These kinds of disputes are not new; conversations of a similar nature have been on the agenda ever since the introduction of radio and television, which was then followed by the advent of the internet and social media. This possibility of manipulation by AI is equally applicable to other regulated media, such as newspapers, television, and social media, according to an objective perspective. In a number of nations that are moving toward autocracy, we frequently observe that traditional mass media, which constitute a monopoly under the control of the government, are not transparent and manipulate in favor of the government. Hence, both channels, whether digital platforms or traditional media tools, pose the potential of manipulation. Because of this, it is essential to take into consideration the manner in which such technological advancements are being utilized, the actors that are driving these processes, and the goals that they are pursuing. As a result of the fact that technological technologies can either strengthen or hinder democracy, the ethical application of these tools and transparent government are of the utmost importance. It has been stated by Brandusescu and Reia (2022) that machines do not possess any feelings. The actual issue is the attempt by one group to exert control over another group. AI is a product of human ingenuity and does not represent any threat to our existence; it is highly unlikely that this technology would destroy us. As a result of the fact that algorithms have the potential to generate inequality, public scrutiny and transparency are very necessary, particularly in "black box" algorithms, the laws of which are unknown.

In point of fact, the transparency of all governing procedures is consistently regarded as one of the most essential characteristics of democracy. One of the most significant objections leveled against AI as a threat to democracy is the fact that the businesses that create applications for AI have a management approach that is more closed. Kasy (2024) brings attention to the challenges that arise when attempting to maximize the use of AI for the betterment of society. He argues that the self-interested actions of businesses make it difficult for AI to be compatible with societal welfare. The question of who will be the supervisory players in the process of developing, deploying, and regulating AI in a manner that is advantageous to society is another one that he brings up. When it comes to the premise that the private sector is primarily concerned with maximizing profits, Kasy believes that the dependence on the voluntary ethical behavior of firms is in direct opposition to this notion. The governance of AI for the purpose of social good will therefore be based on profit-oriented approaches rather than corporate voluntarism, and ethical concerns will continue to be either superficial or instrumental. In a similar vein, Susskind (2022) contends that the major objective of technology corporations is to generate profits, and that their primary responsibility is to their stakeholders, rather than to the residents of the country. As a result, the wants of consumers are likely to be prioritized above civic values, and efficiency is likely to be prioritized over justice. The authors Cupać et al. (2024) contend that the emergence of data-driven plutocrats is in direct opposition to the fundamental ideals that underpin democracy. As a result of this class's focus on profit, they believe that civic principles are replaced with consumer demands and efficiency, that they exert influence over political discourse without democratic scrutiny, and that they put democratic autonomy in jeopardy by influencing individuals' access to information.

There is just one danger that AI poses to democracy, and it is not limited to businesses that are not transparent and may violate democratic values. The argument put up by Filgueiras (2022) is that AI is altering the dynamic power between autocracies and democracies. According to Yuval Noah Harari (2018), AI has the potential to provide authoritarian regimes with an advantage over democracies via boosting efficiency. According to Harari, the reason democracies were successful in the 20th century was because they were better able to digest information. However, AI has the potential to tilt the scales and damage democratic circumstances. In point of fact, our previous experiences have repeatedly demonstrated how technology may increase tyranny, and democratic leaders ought to be aware of autocratic inclinations that originate from inside their own ranks. However, despite the fact that technology is essential to the operation of modern democracies, it is not a natural ally of democracy (Risse, 2022). All of these factors highlight the importance of democratic control and debate over the objectives of decision-making systems that are based on AI through the use of automated computer systems. mainly due to the fact that the safeguarding of democracy necessitates robust procedures to ensure the rights and liberties of individuals, rather than merely having good intentions.

In an authoritarian state, potent digital instruments like AI facilitate critical components of governmental repression and social control initiatives (Wright, 2020). Countries such as China, which exhibit no interest in democratic options, can effectively transform technological advancements into instruments of repression. The Chinese government has facilitated the economic advancement of local technology behemoths like Alibaba, Baidu, and Tencent, enabling them to achieve global competitiveness. Nonetheless, this economic strength has not been converted into social, political, and cultural impact as observed in the West. The Chinese Communist Party has rigorously regulated the operations of technological enterprises, mandating their alignment with the state's political aims. This indicates that the development of technology firms in China has been directed towards reinforcing governmental power rather than enhancing individual liberties (Cupać et al., 2024). Consequently, these technical advancements in China do not bolster democratic norms; instead, they augment official monitoring capabilities and further entrench the authoritarian framework.

China is the most pronounced case, and several developed and emerging democracies encounter analogous threats. Election periods are when governments are established and voters exhibit heightened political engagement. During these intervals, AI engages individually with voters, supplying campaign strategists with essential insights regarding voter behavior. Nonetheless, similar mechanisms may also be employed for manipulation. Targeted communications derived from psychographic and behavioral data can facilitate the manipulation of propaganda and political choices. Although digital platforms seem impartial, recommendation algorithms and content regulations can compromise democratic principles. Risk of swaying voters using tailored messaging derived on their psychological profiles. Such techniques can distort voter choices and compromise the transparency of democratic processes. Evidence indicates the utilization of bots—autonomous accounts designed to propagate messages and fabricate the appearance of public endorsement—in advanced democracies, including the United States, United Kingdom, and Germany (Cadwalladr, 2017; Neudert, Kollanyi, & Howard, 2017; Woolley & Guilbeault, 2017). The 2024 French elections exemplified the application of AI for such objectives. Far-right parties attempted to sway voters using visuals and videos generated by AI systems like MidJourney. The content focused on contentious topics including immigration, Muslims, the European Union, and President Emmanuel Macron. Notwithstanding the implementation of watermarking techniques, deepfakes remain a significant threat to information security initiatives (Malanowska et al. 2024). Innerarity (2024) highlights that misinformation, fake news, and hate speech proliferate more readily in digital media than in analog media, posing a threat to the public sphere essential for democracy. Although algorithms do not directly generate "echo chambers," they have substantially facilitated the dissemination of hate speech and misinformation (Stark et al., 2020).

In light of the myriad risks associated with AI, it is imperative to deliver extensive training to empower informed persons to utilize these technologies wisely, prioritizing societal benefit. Essential components of digital competency encompass AI literacy, critical engagement with digital technologies, and media literacy. These competencies are essential for addressing challenges such as information warfare, political manipulation threats, and disparities in digital and AI access (Calvo et al., 2020). Education in citizenship and digital citizenship should focus on instructing individuals on the efficient utilization of AI as a tool for civic and political engagement. This method requires consideration of both technological skills and the ethics of AI. Ethical concepts about AI utilization must be incorporated into the school curriculum to safeguard the interests of individuals and society. Moreover, AI ethics ought to be associated with educational ethics to foster the responsible, just, and equitable utilization of technology (Holmes et al., 2022). This enables individuals to identify risks to democracy and engage more actively and deliberately in addressing social issues.

In this process, both technological skills and political awareness of involvement are essential. It is essential for individuals to possess political literacy to mitigate the detrimental impacts of traditional media, social media, and the growing prevalence of AI tools on democracy. Political literacy fosters civic engagement, informed decision-making, and the safeguarding of individual rights and social welfare as essential components of a democratic society. This encompasses the abilities of analysis, critical assessment, decision-making, and active engagement. Political literacy integrates several fields, hence including diverse knowledge, skills, beliefs, and attitudes (Kuş, 2019). The initial dimension is the cognitive dimension, which refers to individuals' acquisition of essential political knowledge; this is crucial for comprehending political processes and making informed judgments. The second component encompasses the skills necessary for active engagement in social and political processes; this involves people not just obtaining knowledge but also possessing the capability to apply it effectively. The third factor encompasses the acquisition of universal values essential for democratic processes. Individuals who uphold democratic norms, including respect, fairness, equality, and transparency, will exhibit greater resilience against the adverse impacts of media and AI tools, thereby acting more deliberately to safeguard democracy. Politically literate people possess the capacity to comprehend the viewpoints of others, acknowledge the influence of these viewpoints on themselves, and respond ethically to them (Fyfe, 2007).

CONCLUDING REMARKS

The safety net for democracies is the active engagement of their citizens. Traditional modalities of civic and political participation are evolving at a rapid pace. Thanks to the rise of social media, web 2.0 tools, and the Internet, more people than ever before are able to voice their political opinions, join campaigns, and rally behind social movements. These changes may pave the way for more democratic processes that are receptive to all voices, but they also bring up valid concerns. New forms of artificial intelligence (AI) in politics are changing the way governments engage with their constituents, but they also bring up issues of transparency, inequality, and manipulation. Therefore, it is essential to weigh the benefits of increased engagement against the dangers posed by artificial intelligence and the digital landscape as societies experience digital transition. Citizens may only participate meaningfully in digital platforms if there is trust and transparency between all parties. Within this framework, we should establish and enforce guidelines for the responsible application of AI. In addition, legislation should be evaluated by continuously assessing the implications of digital engagement, and frameworks should be set up to encourage public participation. While communities harness the power of digital engagement and AI to strengthen democracy, they may also safeguard themselves against the dangers that come with these technological advancements.

REFERENCES

Berg, S., & Hofmann, J. (2021). Digital democracy. Internet Policy Review. *Journal on Internet Regulation*, 10(4), 1–23.

Boulianne, S. (2009). Does internet use affect engagement? A meta-analysis of research. *Political Communication*, 26(2), 193–211. DOI: 10.1080/10584600902854363

Boulianne, S. (2015). Social media use and participation: A meta-analysis of current research. *Information Communication and Society*, 18(5), 524–538. DOI: 10.1080/1369118X.2015.1008542

Brandusescu, A., & Reia, J. (Eds.). (2022). Artificial intelligence in the city: Building civic engagement and public trust. Centre for Interdisciplinary Research on Montréal, McGill University.

Briggs, J. (2017). *Young People and Political Participation*. Palgrave Macmillan. DOI: 10.1057/978-1-137-31385-0

Castells, M. (2013). *Communication power* (2nd ed.). Oxford University Press. (Original work published 2009)

Christensen, H. S. (2011). Political activities on the Internet: Slacktivism or political participation by other means? *First Monday*, 16(2). Advance online publication. DOI: 10.5210/fm.v16i2.3336

Cupać, J., Schopmans, H., & Tuncer-Ebetürk, İ. (2024). Democratization in the age of artificial intelligence: Introduction to the special issue. *Democratization*, 31(5), 899–921. DOI: 10.1080/13510347.2024.2338852

Engin, Z., & Treleaven, P. (2019). Algorithmic government: Automating public services and supporting civil servants in using data science technologies. *The Computer Journal*, 62(3), 448–460. DOI: 10.1093/comjnl/bxy082

EUYOUPART. (2005). Political participation of young people in Europe. *SORA*. Accessed March 8, 2010. https://www.sora.at/en/topics/political-culture/euyoupart-2003-2005/enreports

Filgueiras, F. (2022). The politics of AI: Democracy and authoritarianism in developing countries. *Journal of Information Technology & Politics*, 19(4), 449–464. DOI: 10.1080/19331681.2021.2016543

Fyfe, I. (2007). Hidden in the curriculum: Political Literacy and Education for Citizenship in Australia. *Melbourne Journal of Politics*, 32, 110–134.

Fyfe, I. (2009). Researching youth political participation in Australia: Arguments for an expanded focus. *Journal of Youth Studies Australia*, 28(1), 37–45.

Harari, Y. N. (2018). Why technology favors tyranny. The Atlantic. https://www.theatlantic.com/magazine/archive/2018/10/yuval-noah-harari-technology-tyranny/568330/

Harrison, T. M., & Luna-Reyes, L. F. (2020). Cultivating trustworthy artificial intelligence in digital government. *Social Science Computer Review*.

Horvath, L., James, O., Banducci, S., & Beduschi, A. (2023). Citizens' acceptance of artificial intelligence in public services: Evidence from a conjoint experiment about processing permit applications. *Government Information Quarterly*, 40(4), 101876. Advance online publication. DOI: 10.1016/j.giq.2023.101876

Innerarity, D. (2024). *Artificial intelligence and democracy*. UNESCO Office.

Kasy, M. (2023). The political economy of AI: Towards democratic control of the means of prediction. IZA Discussion Paper No. 16948. DOI: 10.2139/ssrn.4811763

Koc-Michalska, K., & Lilleker, D. (2017). Digital politics: Mobilization, engagement, and participation. *Political Communication*, 34(1), 1–5. DOI: 10.1080/10584609.2016.1243178

Kuş, Z. (2019). Politik Okuryazarlık (Ed. Bülent Aksoy ve Bülent Akbaba) Sosyal Bilgilerde Beceri Eğitimi. Ankara: Pegem Yayıncılık

Kuş, Z., Elvan, Ö., & Ozan, H. (2024). Digital and traditional political participation of high school students just before the 2023 presidential election in Turkey. *Citizenship Teaching & Learning, 19*(1).

Kymlicka, W., & Norman, W. (2000). *Citizenship in Diverse Societies*. Academic. DOI: 10.1093/019829770X.001.0001

Lahdili, H., Önder, E., & Nyadera, I. (2024). Artificial intelligence and citizen participation in governance: Opportunities and threats. *Journal of Amme İdaresi*, 57(3).

Michels, A. (2011). Innovations in democratic governance: How does citizen participation contribute to a better democracy? *International Review of Administrative Sciences*, 77(2), 275–293. DOI: 10.1177/0020852311399851

Milbrath, L. (1965). *Political participation: How and why do people get involved in politics?* Rand McNally College Publishing Company.

Onufreiciuc, R. (2024). Citizen participation in and through AI-enabled innovation. Logos Universality Mentality Education Novelty. *Law*, 12(1), 62–74. DOI: 10.18662/lumenlaw/12.1/91

Onufreiciuc, R., & Olariu, O. (2020). Collaborative legislation: With or without citizens? A technological and entrepreneurial approach. EuroMed Academy of Business Conference Book of Proceedings 2020. https://emrbi.org/wp-content/uploads/2020/09/euromed2020-book-of-proceedings-2020-09-07.pdf

Richard, P., & Gogg, A. (2005). What do we mean by "civic engagement"? *Journal of Transformative Education*, 3(3), 236–253. DOI: 10.1177/1541344605276792

Risse, M. (2022). Artificial intelligence and the past, present, and future of democracy. In The Cambridge handbook of responsible artificial intelligence: Interdisciplinary perspectives (pp. 85–103). Cambridge University Press. DOI: 10.1017/9781009207898.009

Salinas, L., Thorpe, A., Prendiville, A., & Rhodes, S. (2018). *Civic engagement as participation in designing for services*. London College of Communication.

Shultz, W., Ainley, J., Fraillon, J., Kerr, D., & Losito, B. (2010). *ICCS International report: Civic knowledge, attitudes, and engagement among lower secondary school students in 38 countries*. International Association for the Evaluation of Educational Achievement (IEA).

Theocharis, Y., & Quintelier, E. (2014). Stimulating citizenship or expanding entertainment? The effect of Facebook on adolescent participation. *New Media & Society*.

United Nations e-Government Survey. (2020). https://publicadministration.un.org/egovkb/en-us/Reports/UN-E-Government-Survey-2020

Verba, S., & Nie, N. H. (1987). Participation in America: Political democracy and social equality. University of Chicago Press. https://press.uchicago.edu/ucp/books/book/chicago/P/bo3637096.html

Vereş-Cătău, D. (2019). Contemporary forms and strategies of discursive manipulation: Storytelling or the art of telling stories on the public stage. *European Journal of Law and Public Administration*, 6(2), 203–212. DOI: 10.18662/eljpa/97

Vitak, J., Zube, P., Smock, A., Carr, C. T., Ellison, N., & Lampe, C. (2011). It's complicated: Facebook users' political participation in the 2008 election. *Cyberpsychology, Behavior, and Social Networking*, 14(3), 107–114. DOI: 10.1089/cyber.2009.0226 PMID: 20649449

Wright, N. D. (2020). Artificial intelligence and democratic norms meeting the authoritarian challenge. In Sharp power and democratic resilience series. International Forum for Democratic Studies.

Zuiderwijk, A., Chen, Y. C., & Salem, F. (2021). Implications of the use of artificial intelligence in public governance: A systematic literature review and a research agenda. *Government Information Quarterly*, 38(3), 1–19. DOI: 10.1016/j.giq.2021.101577

Chapter 7
Ethics of Digital Citizenship in the Age of AI in Higher Education From the Viewpoint of Faculty Members

Samar Shtawi
Alrawdah University College, Palestine

Aysha Mohammad Abd-Rabo
https://orcid.org/0000-0002-8817-6443
Alrawdah University College, Palestine

ABSTRACT

This research explores the ethical implications of integrating AI into higher education, focusing on the responsibilities of faculty and institutions in ensuring adherence to ethical standards. The research highlights the urgent need for comprehensive ethical guidelines to regulate the use of AI in educational settings. The findings also underscore the critical role that faculty play in promoting digital citizenship and ethical practices among students. To address the ethical challenges associated with the integration of AI. The results did not show any statistical differences attributed to the gender variable, or the academic rank variable of the faculty member, while there were statistical differences in the variables of academic qualification and years of teaching experience. The results showed that the field of (the right to protection, security, and digital privacy) had the highest arithmetic mean (3.96). The research makes several recommendations, including establishing strong data governance policies.

DOI: 10.4018/979-8-3693-9015-3.ch007

INTRODUCTION

The integration of artificial intelligence (AI) in higher education is rapidly transforming the landscape of teaching, learning, and administration. While these technologies offer numerous benefits—such as enhanced educational outcomes and increased efficiency—they also present ethical challenges that must be addressed to ensure their responsible use. Faculty members play a crucial role in implementing AI in a manner consistent with ethical principles, including fairness, accountability, and privacy protection.

To navigate these challenges, it is essential to establish comprehensive ethical frameworks to guide the integration of AI in higher education. Theoretical approaches such as utilitarianism, deontological ethics, and social contract theory provide valuable insights for addressing issues like algorithmic bias, privacy concerns, and lack of transparency (Abu Mukh, et al, 2024). These frameworks can serve as a foundation for creating guidelines that ensure the ethical use of AI technologies in educational settings (Boddington, 2017).

In this context, the concept of digital citizenship has become increasingly relevant, digital citizenship is defined as "the ability to use digital technology and the Internet responsibly and ethically, while respecting the rights of others and protecting them from risks in the digital world" (Ribble, 2011). Another definition states that it "refers to the skills and knowledge needed to participate effectively and responsibly in digital societies, while taking into account the ethical, social, and legal aspects of technology" (Ohler, 2010), It was also defined by (Arafat and Hamdan, 2023) as the ethical rules, legal controls, behavioral standards, and preventive measures aimed at protecting users from the dangers of digital technology, helping them to make the most of its advantages, enjoy their rights, and perform their duties safely.

As a modern and evolving concept, digital citizenship emphasizes key principles such as respect, education, and protection. These pillars enable individuals to navigate digital spaces safely and effectively (Iman Sharif, 2023). However, the rise of internet connectivity has also amplified challenges, including the spread of misinformation, hate speech, and harmful content. Teaching digital citizenship is therefore critical in fostering a balanced and informed digital society (UNESCO, 2024).

Given the ethical challenges posed by AI, higher education institutions must take the lead in developing targeted ethical frameworks- as one of the most important institutions concerned with using and benefiting from AI technology in developing and improving society and contributing to its comprehensive growth (Smith & Jones, 2022).addressing the ethical issues associated with AI in higher education requires collaboration among educators, administrators, and policymakers. By establishing clear ethical frameworks and mechanisms to monitor AI use, institutions can ensure fairness, accountability, and integrity in the application of AI technologies, as emphasized by studies such as Jones (2020) and Rogers (2021).

AI systems should be built to provide services and information, not to deceive and manipulate. Higher education institutions should cooperate to enhance safety standards in the use of this technology, and fund research that ensures the beneficial use of AI, so that this technology contributes to human prosperity. The long-term risks of AI must also be identified and prepared for in all fields, to ensure that students and teachers alike benefit from this advanced technology.

Locally, despite the decision to privatize the communications and technology sector in Palestine, which led to a significant development in this sector, this development is not enough. This sector is still characterized by overlap and the absence of policies and strategies that clarify its main features. There is no plan to spread information technology and artificial intelligence. Palestine also still lacks an organizational and legal structure. There is no law to protect intellectual property and copyrights, and there is no general regulatory framework based on issuing laws that regulate and control the technology environment, the uses of artificial intelligence, and related topics such as data security and privacy (Subaih et al., 2021 (. All these obstacles have led to an increase in the burdens placed on Palestinian universities as one of the institutions responsible for developing society.

STATEMENT OF THE PROBLEM

The introduction of artificial intelligence (AI) technology has brought about considerable changes to teaching, learning, and administrative operations in the quickly changing field of higher education. While AI has many advantages, such more individualized instruction and improved productivity, it also brings up serious privacy and ethical issues that affect digital citizenship. Higher education institutions are depending more and more on AI; thus, it is important to look closely at how these technologies affect people's rights and obligations online.

Despite AI's increasing use, little is known about how instructors' and students' perceptions of digital citizenship are impacted by these technologies. In particular, it's important to comprehend how AI affects digital citizenship ethics, such as privacy, data security, and algorithmic bias concerns. As important participants in the educational process, faculty members are essential in addressing these issues and assisting students in using technology responsibly. Their viewpoints and experiences with the ethical ramifications of AI, however, are still little known.

Finding and analyzing the ways that AI technologies affect digital citizenship in higher education institutions is the current challenge. This entails being aware of the moral conundrums that educators encounter, such as algorithmic prejudice and privacy infringement, and comprehending the ways in which these problems impact both educators and learners. Additionally, it's important to evaluate how present laws handle these issues and create suggestions for enhancing AI-related ethics.

By examining the moral dilemmas raised by AI in higher education, offering information on how AI affects digital citizenship, and suggesting methods to promote responsible AI usage in academic contexts, this research seeks to close this gap.

OBJECTIVES

This study aims to explore the concept of ethics of digital citizenship in the era of artificial intelligence (AI), the objectives include:

1. The study contributes to revealing the degree of availability of digital citizenship ethics in the era of artificial intelligence from the perspective of faculty members in Palestinian universities.
2. This study reveals the difference in the degree of availability of digital citizenship ethics attributed to the variables of gender, years of teaching experience, academic Rank, academic qualification

SIGNIFICANCE

There are several important ways in which this study on "Digital Citizenship Ethics in the Age of Artificial Intelligence" is valuable.

1. Contribution to Academic Discourse: As artificial intelligence (AI) is incorporated more and more into higher education; it is critical to comprehend its ethical ramifications. By examining the perspectives of higher education faculty and offering fresh perspectives on how AI affects digital citizenship and ethical issues in academia, this study will add to the expanding corpus of information on AI ethics.
2. Encouraging Ethical Mindset in high Education: The study will offer a greater understanding of the difficulties and worries involved in encouraging ethical behavior in the digital era by addressing the viewpoints of faculty members. This can assist educational institutions in creating policies and initiatives that promote the ethical and responsible usage of AI technology by educators and learners alike.

3. Institutional Policies and Decisions that Direct at particular, the conclusions about privacy, data protection, and individual rights might assist decision-makers at educational institutions in understanding the ethical challenges brought by AI. With this information in hand, institutions may create policies that uphold these rights and promote the ethical and scientific applications of AI.
4. The Preparing Digital Citizens of the Future research is to equip educators with the information and resources they need to better prepare students for the ethical dilemmas they may encounter in a society increasingly controlled by artificial intelligence. It is crucial to know how to impart digital citizenship values in order to raise a generation of tech-savvy, ethical, and responsible individuals.

In the end, our research will deepen our understanding of how AI affects digital citizenship from an ethical standpoint, assisting organizations, educators, and legislators in navigating AI's intricacies in a way that upholds human rights and encourages moral behavior online.

RESEARCH QUESTIONS

The study includes the following main question:

What are the ethics of digital citizenship in the era of artificial intelligence from the perspective of faculty members in Palestinian universities?

A number of sub-questions emerge from this question:

1- What is the degree of availability of digital citizenship ethics in the era of artificial intelligence from the perspective of faculty members in Palestinian universities?

2- Are there statistically significant differences in the degree of availability of digital citizenship ethics attributed to the variables of gender, years of teaching experience, academic Rank, academic qualification?

LITERATURE REVIEW

AI and the Future of Higher Education

Higher education is entering a new phase, which is primarily related to the uses of modern technology and its applications in various fields and specializations. The education process has become interactive and has clearly moved from the traditional method to a modern method based on the teacher directing students using artificial intelligence tools to various sources of knowledge (Boddington, 2017). This has necessarily led to reducing the time and effort associated with preparing the course content, in addition to reducing the costs associated with educational materials. It has become possible for the teacher and the student to communicate in person, electronically or integrated at times that suit them, without the need to absolutely adhere to lecture times (Smith & Jones, 2022). Artificial intelligence applications also help in preparing course plans by the teacher in a way that contributes greatly to saving time and increasing the knowledge presented by the teacher using various references and sources. Technologies such as Chat GPT and Chat PDF can also contribute to preparing the content of these courses in an interactive manner. Many educational platforms have emerged, such as Teams, Blackboard, and others, and there is a possibility to employ various artificial intelligence technologies in them, which contributes to making the learning process more attractive, in addition to facilitating the process of preparing courses electronically and making them available to the largest number of users (Subaih et al., 2021 (. By programming these technologies to help evaluate students' assignments, set their exam dates, and contribute to preparing them automatically, as well as the process of correcting them and analyzing their results later. Artificial intelligence tools also help improve the quality of the outcomes of the educational process, in addition to increasing the knowledge of graduates and improving their capabilities and thus developing programs to suit the personality and needs of each of them, as it has become possible to study the behavior of students, and then develop educational content in a manner that suits their abilities, orientations and personal interests, and this has contributed to increasing their interaction and then improving their capabilities to keep pace with the new labor market (Livingstone, 2018).

Ethical Frameworks for Integrating AI Into Higher Education

The integration of artificial intelligence (AI) in education has been guided by various ethical frameworks, each offering distinct perspectives on ensuring its responsible use. One such approach is utilitarian ethics, which emphasizes maximizing benefits while minimizing harm. In higher education, this principle supports using AI to enhance learning outcomes, improve efficiency, and foster student success. However, it also necessitates addressing risks, such as breaches of privacy or algorithmic biases that could disproportionately affect certain groups of students (Floridi, 2020; Vallor, 2016).

In contrast, deontological ethics focuses on the adherence to moral principles and duties, underscoring the ethical obligation of educators to uphold fairness, protect privacy, and ensure transparency in AI applications. This framework prioritizes respecting student rights and maintaining the integrity of education, even if these principles sometimes conflict with the immediate advantages of AI implementation (Boddington, 2017).

Another critical perspective is social contract theory, which examines the implicit agreements between educators, students, and institutions. Under this framework, institutions and educators are morally obligated to uphold ethical standards when deploying AI, while students place their trust in these systems to enhance their learning experiences responsibly and equitably (Rawls, 1999).

Complementing these ethical perspectives is the concept of digital citizenship, which entails the responsible participation in digital environments. Digital citizenship encompasses values such as respect, safeguarding personal data, and ethical online behavior. It is vital in educational contexts where AI-driven tools shape learning experiences. Educators play a pivotal role in instilling these values in students, enabling them to navigate the complexities of AI technologies responsibly (Ribble, 2015; Selwyn, 2019).

In addition to ethical considerations, the legal and institutional dimensions of AI use in education must be addressed. Digital law and governance frameworks ensure AI applications comply with regulations such as the General Data Protection Regulation (GDPR), safeguarding student and faculty data. Coupled with these legal safeguards, digital accountability emphasizes the need for transparency in AI deployment, requiring institutions to monitor and address ethical issues like data misuse or algorithmic bias (Floridi, 2019).

Equity is another critical pillar in the ethical integration of AI. Digital equality seeks to bridge the digital divide, ensuring all students, regardless of socioeconomic background, have access to AI-enhanced educational tools. Institutions must prioritize inclusivity, providing resources and support to create a fair and accessible learning environment (Selwyn, 2021).

Similarly, digital access rights underscore the importance of universal accessibility to AI tools and resources. These rights ensure that digital platforms accommodate individuals with disabilities and meet established accessibility standards (Floridi, 2019). Alongside access, institutions must consider digital health and safety, promoting safe and supportive interactions with AI technologies. This includes fostering healthy digital habits and preventing exposure to harmful content or excessive screen time, which can impact students' mental and physical well-being (Livingstone, 2018).

Finally, as AI increasingly interacts with content creation, digital intellectual property rights have become a significant concern. Institutions must implement clear policies to protect the intellectual property of students and faculty, ensuring fair use and ethical AI practices in educational settings (Selwyn, 2021; Ribble, 2015). These interconnected frameworks collectively guide the ethical, equitable, and responsible use of AI in higher education, fostering a balanced approach to innovation and ethical accountability.

The body of research on AI integration in higher education highlights a multi-faceted environment where ethics, faculty involvement, and digital citizenship are central to successful implementation. Ethical concerns, such as bias, fairness, transparency, and data privacy, are consistently noted as critical issues, pointing to the need for strong governance mechanisms to protect student privacy and uphold the integrity of educational processes (Floridi, 2020; Selwyn, 2019). Faculty members play a crucial role as "ethical gatekeepers," ensuring that AI technologies are used in ways that respect student rights while fostering inclusive learning experiences (Sharif, 2023). Their engagement in developing and overseeing AI systems is vital to aligning these tools with the educational values and goals of their institutions (Smith & Jones, 2022).

Additionally, the importance of digital citizenship has grown as students increasingly interact with AI-driven tools. Developing digital literacy and encouraging ethical online behavior are essential in helping students responsibly engage with AI technologies while understanding their risks and limitations (Ribble, 2015; UNESCO, 2024). Issues such as digital law, governance, equity, and accountability further reinforce the need for ethical practices, as institutions must address legal and social challenges to foster fair and transparent digital learning environments (Abbott & Wright, 2021; Watson, 2021).

In conclusion, the literature underscores the necessity for a comprehensive approach to AI in education, integrating ethical frameworks, faculty involvement, and responsible digital practices. Future research should focus on creating adaptable frameworks that evolve with AI advancements, ensuring that AI applications in higher education remain fair, transparent, and inclusive while adhering to the principles of equity and justice.

Digital Citizenship in the Palestinian Context

Encouraging responsible engagement in digital spaces is a key component of digital citizenship, a crucial idea in AI-driven education. Fostering digital citizenship in Palestine entails balancing ethical and cultural principles while tackling issues like traditional social norms and technical illiteracy. In order for students to use AI tools ethically and successfully, educators are essential in fostering values like respect, privacy, and ethical conduct (Ribble, 2015; Selwyn, 2019). In addition to local legal and institutional issues, the Palestinian context necessitates addressing international norms such as the GDPR. Geopolitical restrictions exacerbate data security and digital sovereignty issues, It also requires providing a technological infrastructure that enhances the use of artificial intelligence in all fields, especially higher education (Subaih et al., 2021). The occupation's practices of imposing restrictions on digital technological development in Palestine, and preventing higher education institutions from possessing the necessary infrastructure requirements to employ this technology, have exacerbated issues of digital sovereignty and data security. This requires the establishment of strong digital governance regulations by institutions. AI systems must be transparent and accountable, particularly in situations where societal and political factors may restrict supervision procedures (Floridi, 2019). As for equity is still a major issue in Palestine, as socioeconomic inequalities make the digital gap worse. Regardless of geography or financial situation, it is imperative to guarantee that all students have access to AI technologies. Institutions must create plans to offer inclusive learning opportunities, such as assistance for students in impoverished communities and those with impairments (Selwyn,2021).

In addition to what has been discussed, regarding the issues of digital health, safety, and intellectual property; then Promoting healthy interactions with AI technologies is crucial to safeguarding students' mental and physical well-being. Additionally, issues related to intellectual property rights are particularly pertinent in a context where resources are limited, emphasizing the importance of protecting faculty and student contributions (Livingstone, 2018; Ribble, 2015).

Studies have indicated the weakness of Palestinian universities in facing the challenges of scientific and technological progress (Arafat and Hamdan, 2023) and the weakness of the activities provided by universities to promote the use of artificial intelligence for their students (Sharif, 2023). In addition, studies have confirmed that artificial intelligence has affected the concept of digital citizenship among Palestinian youth, as a result of the defect represented in the lack of awareness among youth intellectually, culturally and legally about the dimensions of this citizenship (Selwyn,2021), which led to ambiguity in concepts and practices by youth, and this in turn was reflected in digital rights and duties (Al-Shamali, 2021). A study (Subaih et al., 2021) showed that the overall degree of need for education on the principles of digital citizenship among Palestinian university students was (82%), this requires developing a clear plan that regulates the use of artificial intelligence in Palestinian higher education institutions.

RESEARCH METHODOLOGY

The descriptive approach used in this study to describe the study as it is in reality, and to gain a comprehensive understanding of the ethical challenges and the impact of artificial intelligence (AI) on digital citizenship in higher education. The study conducted in several phases, targeting faculty members at number of higher education institutions to explore their perspectives on AI's ethical implications and its influence on digital citizenship

The Community of the Study

The study community include all faculty members in higher education institutions, in the following higher education institutions: Arab American University, Palestine Technical University (Kadoorie), Palestine Polytechnic University, Alrawdah University College.

The number of faculty members in the aforementioned universities reached (1572) who utilize or are familiar with AI technologies in their teaching or administrative roles.

The Sample of the Study

The study sample was selected in a simple random way, and the sample size was (144) faculty members.

Study Tool

The researchers used the questionnaire as a tool to collect data related to this study, with the aim of identifying the perceptions of faculty members in Palestinian universities and colleges about the ethics of digital citizenship in the era of artificial intelligence, The questionnaire included closed-ended questions using a Likert scale, and the validity and reliability of the study tool verified using scientific methods. The questionnaire was distributed online to faculty members through email invitations and institutional networks.

Score Determination Criteria

When coding the data, a five-point Likert scale was adopted to measure responses. To determine the length of the five-point Likert scale period, the range was calculated (5-1=4), then divided by the number of scale paragraphs to obtain the length of the period (5/4=0.8) (see Figure 1 below).

Figure 1. Intervals related to the effectiveness scores of any item

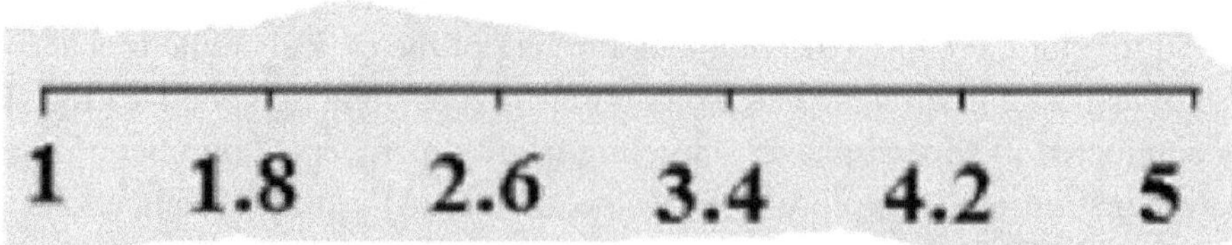

(Daher, 2019)

Validity of the Tool

The validity of the questionnaire was verified by presenting the questionnaire in its initial form to a group of specialized experts with a doctorate degree, including experts in Palestinian universities. who are experts in the domain of Psychological and educational sciences. The number of experts was (5). Based on their opinions and recommendations, the questionnaire was modified by deleting, adding, or rephrasing until it reached its final form.

Reliability of the Tool

The reliability coefficient of the questionnaire was extracted using Cronbach's alpha coefficient, and Table 1 shows the reliability coefficients of the study tool and its domains.

Table 1. Reliability coefficients (Cronbach's Alpha) of the study tool and its domains

The domains	Number of items	Cronbach's Alpha coefficient
Digital Law, Governance and Accountability	11	0.875
Digital Equity and Digital Access for Faculty and Students	12	0.893
Right to Digital Protection, Security and Privacy	20	0.792
Digital Health and Safety	11	0.751
Intellectual Property Rights in the Digital Environment	11	0.872
Total Domain	65	0.857

It is clear from Table 1 that the reliability coefficients of the questionnaire domains and its total score ranged between (0.751 - 0.893), which are good reliability coefficients that meet the purposes of scientific research (Hair, et al,2017).

Data Analysis

Quantitative Analysis: Descriptive and inferential statistics used to analyze the survey data. Measures of central tendency (mean, standard deviations, relative importance (ordinal), t-test for two independent samples, and one-way analysis of variance (One-way ANOVA) provided an overview of faculty members' perceptions, SPSS or a similar statistical software package used for data analysis.

THE RESULT

A number of sub-questions emerge from the main question: what are the ethics of digital citizenship in the era of artificial intelligence from the perspective of faculty members in Palestinian universities?

First Sub-Question Results

1- What is the degree of availability of digital citizenship ethics in the era of artificial intelligence from the perspective of faculty members in Palestinian universities?

To answer the question, means, standard deviations, and availability levels were extracted for each domain of the study tool.

Table 2. Means, standard deviations, and availability levels for each domain of the study tool

	The domains	Means	SD	Rank	Availability
1	Digital Law, Governance and Accountability	3.88	.61	4	often
2	Digital Equity and Digital Access for Faculty and Students	3.94	.58	3	often
3	Right to Digital Protection, Security and Privacy	3.96	.38	1	often
4	Digital Health and Safety	3.37	.55	5	sometimes
5	Intellectual Property Rights in the Digital Environment	3.95	.59	2	often
Total Domain		3.84	.38		often

The previous table shows that the domain of (the right to digital protection, security and privacy) had the highest arithmetic mean (3.96), while the domain of (digital health and safety) had the lowest mean (3.37), while the mean for the domain as a whole was (3.84).

As for the paragraphs of each domain, the results were as follows:

First domain: Digital law, governance and digital accountability. The means and standard deviations were calculated, and the rank and degree were determined for each paragraph of this domain, and Table 3 shows this.

Table 3. Means, standard deviations and relative importance of the domain of digital law, governance and digital accountability

	items	means	SD	rank	Availability
1	The Code of Conduct governing electronic ethical standards is applied in the institution where I work	3.79	.89	7	Often
2	The institution where I work provides responsible bodies that follow up on electronic violations and threats that I may be exposed to.	3.47	1.05	11	Often
3	The institution where I work provides open and powerful educational platforms capable of providing reliable educational resources.	3.67	1.13	9	Often
4	The faculty member at my institution complies with the laws regulating electronic ethical behavior.	4.05	.84	3	Often
5	The faculty member is subject to academic and administrative accountability when violating the e-learning ethics rules.	3.92	.83	5	Often
6	The faculty member is subject to judicial accountability when violating the e-learning ethics rules.	3.48	1.03	10	Often
7	The Academic Discipline Committee has the right to take appropriate action against violators of ethical behavior through educational platforms.	3.87	.84	6	Often
8	I comply with the ethical guidelines for electronic devices, programs or applications.	4.33	.72	2	Very often
9	I avoid the illegal use of modern technologies (such as hacking devices, unlicensed programs)	4.44	.69	1	Very often
10	The laws and policies within the institution in which I work guarantee the right to access reliable information through electronic websites.	3.96	.88	4	Often
11	The institution in which I work publishes policies for the use of electronic platforms on its official pages and websites.	3.73	1.12	8	Often
The domain as a whole		3.88	.61		Often

It is noted from Table 3 that the degree of availability of digital citizenship ethics in the era of artificial intelligence in higher education institutions from the point of view of faculty members for the paragraphs of the domain of digital law, governance and digital accountability ranged between (3.47-4.44). The paragraph (Stay away from the illegal use of modern technologies (such as hacking devices and unlicensed programs) came in first place with an availability degree of (very often). The paragraph (The institution in which I work has responsible bodies that follow up on electronic violations and threats that I may be exposed to) is considered the least phrase in terms of averages, as it came with an availability degree of (often).

The Second Domain: Digital Equality and the Right to Digital Access for Faculty Members and Students

The means and standard deviations were calculated, and the rank and degree were determined for each paragraph of this domain. Table 4 shows this.

Table 4. Means, standard deviations, and relative importance of the domain of digital equality and the right to digital access for faculty members and students

	items	means	SD	rank	Availability
1	I design e-learning content that suits all levels of students and takes into account individual differences.	3.91	.94	7	Often
2	I provide technical support and exchange information with colleagues.	4.01	.81	4	Often
3	The institution I work for provides technicians and consultants specialized in e-support	4.05	.86	3	Often
4	The institution I work for provides equal opportunities for all students to access digital platforms and educational content.	4.10	.77	2	Often
5	I take into account the needs of people with physical disabilities when preparing digital educational content to suit them.	3.74	.98	12	Often
6	I provide students with performance evaluation criteria for electronic activities to ensure fair evaluation for all.	3.94	.79	6	Often
7	Digital educational content is flexible to adapt to any new developments.	4.00	.74	5	Often
8	I accept other opinions and respect different points of view in forums and social media.	4.16	.75	1	Often
9	The institution I work for works to take into account low-income students in areas where internet service is not available.	3.90	.96	8	Often
10	The institution I work for is constantly working on developing the digital competencies of faculty members	3.84	.87	10	Often
11	The institution I work for is working on removing all challenges that prevent the optimal use of electronic services.	3.81	.88	11	Often
12	I have all the necessary means and technologies to access digital services	3.85	.76	9	Often
The domain as a whole		3.94	.58		

It is noted from Table 4 that the degree of availability of digital citizenship ethics in the era of artificial intelligence in higher education institutions from the point of view of faculty members for the paragraphs in the domain of digital equality and the right of digital access for faculty members and students ranged between (3.74 - 4.16). The paragraph (I accept other opinions and respect different points of view in forums and social networking sites) came in first place with an availability degree of (often). The paragraph (I take into account the needs of people with physical disabilities when preparing digital educational content to suit them) is considered the least phrase in terms of averages, as it came with an availability degree of (often).

The Third Domain: The Right to Protection, Security, and Digital Privacy

The means and standard deviations were calculated, and the rank and degree were determined for each paragraph of this domain, and Table 5 shows that.

Table 5. Means, standard deviations and relative importance of the domain of the right to protection, security and digital privacy

	items	means	SD	rank	Availability
1	I verify the source of data and links exchanged between students before running them.	3.93	.73	14	Often
2	I protect online class links and student data with strong passwords.	3.88	.90	15	Often
3	I respect the privacy of others on websites and social media sites.	4.31	.71	11	Very often
4	I know how to block suspicious websites or unsafe software.	3.42	1.06	17	Often
5	I work to protect students' and colleagues' data on educational electronic platforms from being violated	3.75	.93	16	Often
6	I use students' personal data for purposes other than those intended.	1.90	1.38	19	rarely
7	I ensure that e-learning platforms are free of any content that violates moral, religious and cultural aspects.	4.27	.96	12	Very often
8	I publish links to e-classes on public pages.	2.59	1.44	18	rarely
9	I avoid verbal and moral blackmail in electronic forums.	4.47	.80	7	Very often
10	Avoid creating and dealing with fake accounts.	4.59	.83	4	Very often
11	I urge students not to practice cyberbullying.	4.41	.86	9	Very often

continued on following page

Table 5. Continued

	items	means	SD	rank	Availability
12	The institution I work for prohibits the publication of any inappropriate content that does not fit the culture and beliefs of colleagues or students	4.54	.61	6	Very often
13	The organization I work for prohibits racist, hate speech, defamation, incitement to violence and mockery in any electronic content on educational platforms.	4.45	.75	8	Very often
14	I avoid posting harmful information or viruses	4.60	.58	3	Very often
15	I am careful not to spread rumors and misleading news on forums or social media sites.	4.61	.56	2	Very often
16	I respect religious, political and social beliefs in discussions on forums and social media.	4.56	.70	5	Very often
17	I give my passwords to academic and personal websites to others.	1.59	1.20	20	never
18	I exercise caution when forming new relationships through digital applications.	4.37	.87	10	Very often
19	I maintain the confidentiality of my organization's data and electronic information.	4.66	.62	1	Very often
20	My organization provides secure internet with protection software for e-learning users.	4.23	.92	13	Very often
The domain as a whole		3.96	.38		often

It is noted from Table 5 that the degree of availability of digital citizenship ethics in the era of artificial intelligence in higher education institutions from the point of view of faculty members for the paragraphs in the domain of the right to protection, security and digital privacy ranged between (1.59-4.66). The paragraph (I maintain the confidentiality of the data and electronic information of the institution I work for) came in first place with an availability degree of (very often). The paragraph (I give my passwords for academic and personal websites to others) is considered the lowest phrase in terms of averages, as it came in at a degree of (never).

Fourth Domain: Digital Health and Safety

means and standard deviations were calculated, and the rank and degree were determined for each paragraph of this domain, and Table 6 shows that.

Table 6. Means, standard deviations, and relative importance of the domain of digital health and safety

	items	means	SD	Rank	Availability
1	I have difficulty concentrating due to prolonged use of technology.	3.10	.95	11	sometimes
2	I suffer from symptoms of fatigue after using technology.	3.18	1.04	9	sometimes
3	I must sit correctly while using electronic devices.	3.50	.94	5	Often
4	Make sure to follow the rules of safe internet browsing.	4.10	.91	1	Often
5	Make sure not to sit for long hours on the internet.	3.47	1.01	6	Often
6	Allocate a specific time to use technology.	3.33	.97	7	sometimes
7	I make sure to use technology in a well-lit room.	3.75	.88	2	Often
8	I suffer from vision problems due to prolonged use of technology.	3.19	1.23	8	sometimes
9	I suffer from pain in the neck, back and shoulder muscles due to prolonged sitting when using technology.	3.55	1.14	4	Often
10	I feel isolated and lonely due to prolonged use of technology.	2.73	1.18	3	sometimes
11	I feel mentally exhausted due to prolonged use of technology.	3.17	1.08	10	sometimes
The domain as a whole		3.37	.55		sometimes

It is noted from Table 6 that the degree of availability of digital citizenship ethics in the era of artificial intelligence in higher education institutions from the point of view of faculty members for the paragraphs in the domain of digital health and safety ranged between (3.10-4.10). The paragraph (Be sure to follow the rules of safe browsing of the Internet) came in first place with an availability degree of (often). The paragraph (I feel difficulty in concentrating due to the long use of technological techniques) is considered the least phrase in terms of averages, as it came in at a degree of (sometimes).

Fifth Domain: Intellectual Property Rights in the Digital Environment

means and standard deviations were calculated, and the rank and degree were determined for each paragraph of this domain, and Table 7 shows that.

Table 7. Means, standard deviations, and relative importance of the domain of intellectual property rights in the digital environment

	items	means	SD	rank	Availability
1	I maintain the intellectual property of scientific and administrative content on websites.	4.05	.89	6	Often
2	I respect the right of others to publish their intellectual and scientific output in accordance with the electronic publishing policies adopted by the institution in which I work.	4.29	.73	3	Very often
3	I seek scientific integrity in documenting, transferring and using the scientific works of others.	4.31	.76	2	Very often
4	I commit not to download any electronic materials illegally.	4.21	.90	4	Very often
5	There are clear policies to protect the intellectual property of software, databases and open educational resources in my institution.	3.75	.99	7	Often
6	I cite the original source of the information I use.	4.17	.80	5	Often
7	My organization works to raise awareness of intellectual property rights, publishing and licensing.	3.73	1.05	8	Often
8	My organization has clear policies regarding ownership of digital content or educational materials.	3.70	.98	9	Often
9	My organization has systems for digital tracking of protected works and legal prosecution of infringers	3.43	.92	10	Often
10	The institution I work for provides a system for reporting legal violations of intellectual property rights.	3.34	.99	11	sometimes
11	I am careful not to violate the intellectual and personal freedom of fellow faculty members.	4.47	.69	1	Very often
The domain as a whole		. 3.95	.59		Often

It is noted from Table 7 that the degree of availability of digital citizenship ethics in the era of artificial intelligence in higher education institutions from the point of view of faculty members for the paragraphs in the domain of intellectual property rights in the digital environment ranged between (3.34-4.47). The paragraph (I am keen not to violate the intellectual and personal freedom of fellow faculty members) came in first place with an availability degree of (very often). The paragraph (The institution I work for provides a system for reporting legal violations of intellectual property rights) is considered the least phrase in terms of averages, as it came in at a degree of (sometimes).

Second Sub-Question Results

1- Are there statistically significant differences in the degree of availability of digital citizenship ethics attributed to the variables of gender, years of teaching experience, academic Rank, academic qualification?

To answer the question related to the gender variable, the means and standard deviations were calculated for all questionnaire domains for each level of the variable and the results as follows:

Table 8. Means, standard deviations, and a t-test for two independent samples to examine the significance of differences in the degree of availability of digital citizenship ethics in the era of artificial intelligence in higher education institutions from the point of view of faculty members according to the gender variable

The domains	males		females		T value	sig
	means	SD	means	SD		
Digital Law, Governance and Accountability	3.93	.58	3.80	.65	1.02	.47
Digital Equity and Digital Access for Faculty and Students	3.96	.60	3.92	.54	0.07	.38
Right to Digital Protection, Security and Privacy	3.98	.40	3.93	.36	1.85	.37
Digital Health and Safety	3.38	.55	3.35	.56	0.37	.65
Intellectual Property Rights in the Digital Environment	3.96	.56	3.93	.63	0.39	.58
Total Domain	3.86	.38	3.81	.38	0.82	.94

In general, Table 8 shows that the males' means were higher than the females' means in all study dimensions, and no statistically significant differences appeared in all study domains and the overall domain, as the statistical significance value for the overall domain reached (.94), which is a statistically insignificant value.

2- Question Related to Academic Qualification

To answer this question, means and standard deviations were calculated for all the questionnaire domains, and the results were as shown in Table 9.

Table 9. Means and standard deviations of the questionnaire dimensions according to the educational qualification variable

The domains	Academic qualification	N	means	SD
Digital Law, Governance and Accountability	Bachelor	29	3.83	.49
	Master	61	3.89	.61
	PhD	54	3.89	.68
Digital Equity and Digital Access for Faculty and Students	Bachelor	29	3.81	.51
	Master	61	4.00	.62
	PhD	54	3.94	.58
Right to Digital Protection, Security and Privacy	Bachelor	29	3.95	.35
	Master	61	3.99	.42
	PhD	54	3.93	.37
Digital Health and Safety	Bachelor	29	3.25	.63
	Master	61	3.38	.60
	PhD	54	3.49	.44
Intellectual Property Rights in the Digital Environment	Bachelor	29	3.76	.57
	Master	61	3.93	.64
	PhD	54	4.06	.53
Total Domain	Bachelor	29	3.77	.34
	Master	61	3.84	.41
	PhD	54	3.87	.37

Table 9 shows that the highest mean was in the domain of (Intellectual Property Rights in the Digital Environment) where the mean was (4.06) and was for faculty members with a PhD degree, while the lowest mean was in the domain of (Digital Health and Safety) where the mean was (3.25) and was for faculty members with a bachelor's degree.

To determine the degree of applicability of these results to the study community, one-way ANOVA was used. Table 10 shows these results.

Table 10. Results of one-way ANOVA to examine differences according to the academic qualification variable

The domains		Sum of Squares	df	Mean Square	F	Sig.
Digital Law, Governance and Accountability	Between Groups	.177	3	.059	.154	.927
	Within Groups	53.707	140	.384		
	Total	53.884	143			
Digital Equity and Digital Access for Faculty and Students	Between Groups	.822	3	.274	.803	.494
	Within Groups	47.758	140	.341		
	Total	48.580	143			
Right to Digital Protection, Security and Privacy	Between Groups	.090	3	.030	.195	.009
	Within Groups	21.600	140	.154		
	Total	21.690	143			
Digital Health and Safety	Between Groups	1.635	3	.545	1.771	.155
	Within Groups	43.084	140	.308		
	Total	44.719	143			
Intellectual Property Rights in the Digital Environment	Between Groups	1.592	3	.531	1.533	.209
	Within Groups	48.457	140	.346		
	Total	50.050	143			
Total Domain	Between Groups	.192	3	.064	.435	.728
	Within Groups	20.550	140	.147		
	Total	20.741	143			

Table 10 showed that there were no statistically significant differences between the averages of the sample responses in all domains and the overall domain, except for the domain (the right to protection, security and digital privacy), which showed a statistical significance of (0.009). To identify the source of the differences, the Scheffe test for post-hoc comparisons was used, which showed statistically significant differences at the significance level ($\alpha = 0.05$) between the responses of the study sample with an academic qualification (Master's) on the one hand, and the responses of the study sample with an academic qualification (PhD) in favor of those with an academic qualification (Master's).

3- Question Related to Years of Teaching Experience

To answer this question, means and standard deviations were calculated for all domain of the questionnaire and the results were as follows:

Table 11. Means and standard deviations of the questionnaire dimensions according to the variable of years of teaching experience

The domains	Years of teaching experience	N	Means	SD
Digital Law, Governance and Accountability	Less than 5 years	38	3.85	.55
	From 5-10 years	25	3.99	.61
	More than 10 years	81	3.86	.64
Digital Equity and Digital Access for Faculty and Students	Less than 5 years	38	3.98	.59
	From 5-10 years	25	4.02	.49
	More than 10 years	81	3.90	.60
Right to Digital Protection, Security and Privacy	Less than 5 years	38	3.93	.42
	From 5-10 years	25	3.97	.39
	More than 10 years	81	3.97	.37
Digital Health and Safety	Less than 5 years	38	3.29	.73
	From 5-10 years	25	3.35	.56
	More than 10 years	81	3.41	.45
Intellectual Property Rights in the Digital Environment	Less than 5 years	38	3.92	.56
	From 5-10 years	25	3.91	.71
	More than 10 years	81	3.98	.57
Total factor	Less than 5 years	38	3.81	.06
	From 5-10 years	25	3.87	.07
	More than 10 years	81	3.84	.04

Table 11 shows that the highest mean was in the domain of (Digital Equity and Digital Access for Faculty and Students) where mean was (4.02) and was for the level of faculty members with teaching experience (5-10 years), while the lowest mean was in the domain of (Digital Health and Safety) where the mean was (3.29) and was for the level of faculty members with experience (less than 5 years).

To determine the degree of applicability of these results to the study community, one-way ANOVA was used. Table 12 shows these results.

Table 12. Results of one-way ANOVA to examine differences according to the variable of years of teaching experience

The domains		Sum of Squares	df	Mean Square	F	Sig.
Digital Law, Governance and Accountability	Between Groups	.362	2	.181	.476	.622
	Within Groups	53.523	141	.380		
	Total	53.884	143			
Digital Equity and Digital Access for Faculty and Students	Between Groups	.333	2	.167	.487	.007
	Within Groups	48.247	141	.342		
	Total	48.580	143			
Right to Digital Protection, Security and Privacy	Between Groups	.040	2	.020	.130	.031
	Within Groups	21.650	141	.154		
	Total	21.690	143			
Digital Health and Safety	Between Groups	.403	2	.201	.641	.528
	Within Groups	44.316	141	.314		
	Total	44.719	143			
Intellectual Property Rights in the Digital Environment	Between Groups	.129	2	.064	.182	.834
	Within Groups	49.921	141	.354		
	Total	50.050	143			
Total factor	Between Groups	.046	2	.023	.158	.854
	Within Groups	20.695	141	.147		
	Total	20.741	143			

Table 12 showed that there were no statistically significant differences between the sample response averages in all domains and the overall domain, except for the domain (Digital Equity and Digital Access for Faculty and Students), which showed a statistical significance of (.007). To identify the source of the differences, the Scheffe test for post-hoc comparisons was used, which showed statistically significant differences at the significance level ($\alpha = 0.05$) between the responses of the study sample with teaching experience (5-10 years) on the one hand, and the responses of the study sample with teaching experience (more than 10 years) in favor of those with teaching experience (more than 10 years). There are also statistically significant differences in the domain of (the right to protection, security and digital privacy), which showed a statistical significance of (0.031). To identify the source of the differences, the Scheffe test for post-hoc comparisons was used, which showed statistically significant differences at the significance level ($\alpha = 0.05$) between the responses of the study sample with teaching experience (5-10 years) on the one hand, and the responses of the study sample with teaching experience (more than 10 years) in favor of those with teaching experience (5-10 years).

4- Question Related to the Academic Rank of the Faculty Member

To answer this question, the arithmetic means and standard deviations were calculated for all domains of the questionnaire, and the results were as follows:

Table 13. Means and standard deviations of the questionnaire dimensions according to the variable of academic rank

The domains	Academic Rank	N	means	SD
Digital Law, Governance and Accountability	Lecturer	83	3.84	.59
	Assistant Professor	39	3.88	.61
	Associate Professor	12	3.89	.69
	Professor	10	4.11	.66
Digital Equity and Digital Access for Faculty and Students	Lecturer	83	3.93	.57
	Assistant Professor	39	3.98	.58
	Associate Professor	12	4.02	.65
	Professor	10	3.86	.63
Right to Digital Protection, Security and Privacy	Lecturer	83	3.97	.38
	Assistant Professor	39	3.90	.40
	Associate Professor	12	4.07	.47
	Professor	10	3.96	.22
Digital Health and Safety	Lecturer	83	3.31	.62
	Assistant Professor	39	3.43	.47
	Associate Professor	12	3.63	.36
	Professor	10	3.34	.33
Intellectual Property Rights in the Digital Environment	Lecturer	83	3.89	.61
	Assistant Professor	39	4.04	.57
	Associate Professor	12	3.88	.57
	Professor	10	4.15	.45
Total Domain	Lecturer	83	3.81	.37
	Assistant Professor	39	3.86	.40
	Associate Professor	12	3.94	.40
	Professor	10	3.90	

Table 13 shows that the highest mean was in the domain of (Intellectual Property Rights in the Digital Environment) where the mean was (4.15) and was for faculty members with the rank of Professor, while the lowest mean was in the domain of

(Digital Health and Safety) where the mean was (3.31) and was for faculty members with the rank of (Lecturer).

To determine the degree of applicability of these results to the study community, one-way ANOVA was used. Table 14 shows these results.

Table 14. Results of one-way ANOVA to examine differences according to the variable of years of teaching experience

The domains		Sum of Squares	df	Mean Square	F	Sig.
Digital Law, Governance and Accountability	Between Groups	.792	3	.264	.696	.556
	Within Groups	53.092	140	.379		
	Total	53.884	143			
Digital Equity and Digital Access for Faculty and Students	Between Groups	.196	3	.065	.189	.903
	Within Groups	48.383	140	.346		
	Total	48.580	143			
Digital Health and Safety	Between Groups	.298	3	.099	.650	.584
	Within Groups	21.392	140	.153		
	Total	21.690	143			
Intellectual Property Rights in the Digital Environment	Between Groups	1.335	3	.445	1.436	.235
	Within Groups	43.384	140	.310		
	Total	44.719	143			
Total Domain	Between Groups	1.034	3	.345	.984	.402
	Within Groups	49.016	140	.350		
	Total	50.050	143			

Table 14 showed that there were no statistically significant differences between the averages of the sample responses to all domains and the total domain.

RESULTS AND DISCUSSION

Ethical Challenges in AI Usage in Education: The Palestinian Context

The findings of this study align with previous research conducted in Palestine, highlighting the unique challenges posed by the region's sociopolitical and technological landscape. According to AbuShanab and Al-Azzam (2021), the integration of AI in Palestinian higher education is still in its early stages, hindered by inadequate infrastructure and the absence of comprehensive policy frameworks. These limitations exacerbate the ethical concerns raised in this study, including privacy risks, algorithmic bias, and a lack of transparency.

- **Privacy Issues:** In the Palestinian context, concerns over privacy are intensified by the absence of strong data protection regulations and the reliance on external platforms for educational purposes. Participants emphasized the need for region-specific data governance policies, which reflect global calls for more stringent regulatory frameworks (Darwish & Hassan, 2020).
- **Algorithmic Bias:** Palestinian faculty members expressed concerns that AI systems, which are often designed in global contexts, may inadvertently reinforce local social and economic disparities when implemented in Palestinian institutions. As noted by Darwish and Hassan (2020), many AI tools fail to address the unique needs of Palestinian students, particularly in marginalized communities.
- **Transparency and Accountability:** Similar to global trends, Palestinian respondents underscored the lack of transparency regarding the selection and implementation of AI systems. The limited involvement of faculty in decision-making processes related to AI adoption often raises concerns about accountability and fairness in educational outcomes (Arafat & Hamdan, 2023).

Faculty's Role in AI Governance: Insights From Palestine

Faculty members in Palestine face additional challenges in governing the ethical use of AI due to resource limitations, inadequate training, and insufficient institutional support.

- **Faculty Awareness and Training:** As highlighted by Qasem and Said (2022), many Palestinian faculty members lack a deep understanding of the ethical implications of AI, despite being aware of its technological potential. This study confirms the need for professional development initiatives aimed at equipping faculty with the necessary skills to address AI's ethical challenges. Collaboration with international organizations could help bridge this gap.
- **Faculty Involvement in AI Design and Implementation:** Participants noted a significant gap in faculty participation in the design and implementation of AI systems in educational institutions, a concern consistent with findings from Arafat and Hamdan (2023). The lack of faculty involvement in these processes often leads to a disconnect between AI tools and institutional values. Greater faculty engagement is essential to ensure that AI tools are both pedagogically effective and ethically sound.

- **Ethical Stewardship:** Even though Palestinian faculty members are not directly involved in the development of AI systems, they see themselves as ethical stewards. They are committed to ensuring that AI technologies are used in a way that promotes fairness, transparency, and inclusivity, while also protecting students' rights.

Fostering Digital Citizenship Through AI Integration: A Regional Perspective

Promoting digital citizenship in Palestine is closely linked to efforts to enhance digital literacy and foster ethical awareness, particularly given the challenges of limited technological access and digital divides.

- **Digital Literacy in Education:** Participants emphasized the need to integrate digital literacy into the curriculum, especially given AI's increasing role in education. Previous studies, such as those by Al-Khalidi and Salem (2021), have demonstrated the positive impact of digital literacy programs in Palestinian schools, equipping students with the critical thinking skills necessary to navigate AI-driven environments. However, these programs need to be expanded to keep up with the growing influence of AI in education.
- **Digital Institutional Initiatives:** While some Palestinian universities have begun initiatives to promote responsible digital behavior, these efforts remain inconsistent. Respondents highlighted the need for a national strategy to foster digital citizenship and ethical AI usage, combining global best practices with local context

CONCLUSION

In summary, while the integration of AI in higher education offers numerous benefits, it also presents various challenges that require careful consideration. AI can improve learning outcomes and streamline administrative tasks, but its ethical deployment is essential to mitigate risks associated with student privacy, algorithmic bias, and lack of transparency. The theoretical frameworks of utilitarianism, deontology, and social contract theory provide valuable insights into the ethical aspects of AI integration in educational settings. Ultimately, the effective and responsible use of AI in education depends on the collaborative efforts of faculty, institutional leaders, and policymakers in establishing robust ethical guidelines and practices.

Recommendations

Drawing from the study's findings, several recommendations are proposed to promote the ethical integration of AI in higher education:

1 - Developing an integrated plan to teach and disseminate the principles of digital citizenship in Palestinian universities.
2 Including the subject of digital citizenship in the curriculum as one of the university courses taught to students in universities, Incorporating digital citizenship into academic curricula is essential for equipping students to responsibly navigate AI technologies..
3 Forming committees at the national level consisting of a group of experts and people with scientific competence who are responsible for developing a comprehensive plan to enhance the proper application of digital citizenship concepts at all levels.
4 Faculty members should undergo specialized training regarding the ethical implications of AI and its applications in education. Professional development initiatives can help educators develop the skills needed to critically evaluate AI tools, champion ethical practices, and integrate AI effectively into their teaching.

Future Research Suggestions

1- Investigate the particular difficulties Palestinian colleges encounter while attempting to include AI into their curricula.
2- Examine the ways in which economic and political limitations affect the moral use of AI technologies in Palestine.
3-Emphasis on Students: Compile information about Palestinian students' experiences with AI technologies, including their requirements, worries, and recommendations.

Ethical Considerations

Informed Consent

All participants will be informed about the purpose of the study, their rights as participants, and the confidentiality of their responses. Informed consent will be obtained from each participant before data collection begins.

Confidentiality

Personal information and responses will be kept confidential, and participants will be given the option to withdraw from the study at any time.

Bias Mitigation

Efforts will be made to ensure that the researcher's biases do not influence the data collection or analysis process. Multiple researchers may be involved in analyzing the qualitative data to cross-check the coding process.

LIMITATIONS OF THE STUDY

Sample Representation

While efforts will be made to include faculty from diverse disciplines, the results may not be generalizable to all higher education institutions, especially those in different cultural or technological contexts.

Self-Reported Data

The study relies on self-reported data, which may be subject to bias or inaccuracies in how participants perceive their experiences with AI and digital citizenship.

REFERENCES

Abbott, T., & Wright, C. (2021). *Digital Governance and Law in the Age of AI.* Educational Leadership Journal.

Abu Mukh, Y. N., Abd-Rabo, A. M., & Tarteer, S. (2024). Computer Competencies Needed for Implementing Artificial Intelligence in Special Education Schools from the Perspective of Pre-Service Teachers. *Trends in Higher Education*, 3(3), 602–622. DOI: 10.3390/higheredu3030035

AbuShanab, E., & Al-Azzam, A. (2021). Artificial Intelligence in Palestinian Higher Education: Challenges and Opportunities. *International Journal of Educational Technology and Learning*, 10(3), 45–57.

Al-Khalidi, R., & Salem, K. (2021). Digital Literacy as a Pillar of Digital Citizenship in Palestine: Challenges and Prospects. *Journal of Digital Learning*, 9(4), 15–28.

Al-Shamali. (2021). Awareness of digital citizenship values among upper primary school students in Palestine. The Seventh Virtual International Scientific Conference entitled: Information and Communication Technologies in Education and Training, December 18, 2021.

Arafat, S., & Hamdan, T. (2023). Faculty Involvement in Ethical AI Governance in Palestine. *Journal of Educational Technology Research*, 18(2), 102–119.

Binns, R. (2021). *Fairness in Machine Learning Systems*. Cambridge University Press.

Boddington, P. (2017). *Towards a Code of Ethics for Artificial Intelligence*. Springer.

Daher, W. (2019). Assessing students' perceptions of democratic practices in the mathematics classroom. Paper presented at the Eleventh Congress of the European Society for Research in Mathematics Education. Utrecht, The Netherlands.

Darwish, M., & Hassan, R. (2020). Algorithmic Bias and Cultural Contexts in AI: Case Studies from Palestinian Education. *Journal of AI Ethics*, 5(1), 85–100.

Diaz, R. (2020). Intellectual Property Rights in the Digital Age: The Impact of AI in Education. *Educational Technology Research and Development.*

Floridi, L. (2019a). *The Ethics of Artificial Intelligence*. Oxford University Press.

Floridi, L. (2019b). *The Logic of Information: A Theory of Philosophy as Conceptual Design.* Oxford University Press.

Floridi, L. (2020a). *The Ethics of Artificial Intelligence*. Oxford University Press.

Floridi, L. (2020b). *The Ethics of Artificial Intelligence: Human Self-Understanding in the Age of AI*. Springer.

Glover, M. (2022). Transparency and Accountability in AI-Driven Education Systems. *Learning, Media and Technology*.

Hair, J.F., Hult, G.T.M., Ringle, C.M., & Sarstedt, M. (2017). *A Primer on Partial Least Squares Structural Equation Modeling (PLS-SEM)* (2nd ed.). Sage Publications Inc.

Johnson, H., & Webb, D. (2023). Digital Health and Safety in the AI Classroom. *Journal of Educational Psychology*.

Livingstone, S. (2018). *Digital Literacy: What is it and How Can We Develop It?* SAGE Publications.

Qasem, A., & Said, N. (2022). Building Faculty Capacity for AI in Education: A Palestinian Perspective. *Journal of Higher Education Studies*, 15(4), 65–79.

Rawls, J. (1999). *A Theory of Justice*. Harvard University Press.

Ribble, M. (2015). *Digital Citizenship in Schools: Nine Elements All Students Should Know*. International Society for Technology in Education.

Sabih, L.,, Alian, H., &, & Abu Houli, M. (2021). Digital technology and its implications for the values of citizenship among Palestinian youth. *Journal of the Palestinian Educators Association for Literature.Educational and Psychological Studies*, 2(1), 187–209.

Selwyn, N. (2019a). AI in Education: Exploring the Ethical Issues. *Learning, Media and Technology*.

Selwyn, N. (2019b). *Should Robots Replace Teachers? AI and the Future of Education*. Polity Press.

Selwyn, N. (2021). AI for Education: Why Artificial Intelligence is not a Silver Bullet. *Policy Futures in Education*.

Sharif, I. (2023). *Ethical AI Integration in Higher Education*. Journal of Educational Technology.

Sharif, M. (2023). Ethical Challenges and Faculty Training in AI Adoption: Insights from Developing Nations. *Technology and Society Review*, 12(3), 45–60.

Smith, A., & Jones, B. (2022). Aligning AI Implementation with Institutional Values in Higher Education. *AI in Education Quarterly*, 14(2), 23–40.

Smith, J., & Jones, P. (2022). The Role of Faculty in AI Integration: Ethical and Practical Considerations. *The Journal of Educational Research*.

Smith, T., & Jones, R. (2022). Frameworks for Ethical AI in Higher Education. *AI & Society*.

UNESCO. (2024). *AI and Digital Citizenship: A Global Perspective*. UNESCO Publishing.

Vallor, S. (2016). *Technology and the Virtues: A Philosophical Guide to a Future Worth Wanting*. Oxford University Press.

Watson, D. (2021a). *Addressing Digital Equity in Higher Education: A Critical Framework*. International Journal of Educational Technology.

Watson, D. (2021b). *Digital Learning and the Future of Education*. Routledge.

Williamson, B., & Eynon, R. (2020). Datafication and Automation in Education: Critical Perspectives on AI and Learning. *Educational Researcher*.

Chapter 8
Preparing Citizens for the Future Digital Literacy and AI in Education

S. Bhavana
https://orcid.org/0009-0005-6134-1081
Jawaharlal Nehru Technological University, Hyderabad, India

Momin Sana Tabassum
Jawaharlal Nehru Technological University, Hyderabad, India

Thota Venkat Narayana Rao
https://orcid.org/0000-0002-1996-1819
Jawaharlal Nehru Technological University, Hyderabad, India

Chenchu Swetha
Jawaharlal Nehru Technological University, Hyderabad, India

ABSTRACT

Digital and AI literacy are vital as technology shapes the future, requiring skills beyond basic computer knowledge. Integrating AI in education personalizes learning by identifying students' needs, adapting content, and providing instant feedback, creating engaging, tailored experiences. Ethical issues, including data privacy, algorithmic bias, and tech access disparities, must be addressed to ensure AI's responsible use in education. Teachers play a key role in fostering AI literacy, helping students understand both the potential and ethical considerations of technology. Embedding these skills into curricula prepares students with critical thinking, creativity, and collaboration skills necessary for a digital world. This approach equips students to engage with technology responsibly, building a generation ready to navigate and

DOI: 10.4018/979-8-3693-9015-3.ch008

shape a fair, inclusive digital landscape.

1. INTRODUCTION

It is as true today, especially in light of modern world where technology is advancing at a much faster rate and place a much more emphasized value on preparing citizens for the future. The competency of Digital literacy has therefore gained immense prominence, besides being an asset for the people; it is also crucial for development. In moving through this brave new world of learning, the application of Information and Communications Technology more particularly Artificial Intelligence in teaching and learning is a promise of transforming learning and preparing the learners for the society of tomorrow.

The definition of digital skills is very general and it ranges from the appreciation of the internet search engines to evaluation of sources of information and use of technology in conveying information and in carrying out group activities. To live in today's society which is swimming in data and information, the development of skills and abilities to critically think through information and data is extremely crucial for learners. By attaining this ability, it allows an individual to effectively interact with the current happening around them, to be able to discuss it with the people and to make decision with right information and not with wrong information that is incline with bias. (Stolpe et.al,2024)

While people get used to having various types of digital tools in their work and personal lives, they are in a way better equipped to sort out through all the information sources in front of them. This skill set does not only improve the individual decision-making process but also develops the responsibility of the decision-makers in the online world. This makes it important for educators to ensure that they equip students with a knack on what is safe or otherwise to read when it is on the internet, hence ensure that students being produced are of those kind that can manage the current generation.

The AI tools can help determine students' approach to learning, choice of content, and rate and provide a personalized learning approach to accommodate the learners' differences. This particular approach does do more than just increase the attractiveness of content for learners but also allows them develop a better understanding of conceptual knowledge and consequently, learning becomes more effective and profound.

Furthermore, the adoption of AI into education can improve bureaucratic effectiveness such that more time is devoted to knowledge and guiding. The use of technology for grading, time- table, and resource allocation frees teachers from time consuming tasks therefore spend more time with the students. Such a change in trend from administrative work to actual content means better results for schools and more satisfaction for teachers. Ideally when a teacher can focus on the main task of teaching they are able to foster the development of the student's intellect and emotion.

However, there are challenges associated with the use of AI in learning environment. The concerns that come for disclosure are ethical in regard to data privacy, algorithmic fairness, and extending the digital divide. Reducing gaps in the provision of tools and technologies then becomes critical in order to avoid disparities in learning. Such learning environments can also widen inequality since learners from impoverished homes meet great challenges in accessing the technologies that make for digital learning. Hence, the stakeholders and policymakers and educators should have productive conversations about the proper and fair usage of AI in education.

In addition, to equip the citizens for future, this means much more than acquiring some technical abilities. It includes promoting social-emotional learning, USE and employability skills. Technology dependency as an aspect of human life advances, the people need to be taught not only how to operate the machines but also, how to overcome various issues related to technology. Such education systems have a challenge of bringing up a culture that is improvement oriented with the student being sensitive to change and see it as a positive thing.

Based on student's need for social-emotional learning in addition to information technology knowledge, educational institutions can develop knowledgeable as well as socially and emotionally well-developed individuals. Soft skills like the ability to communicate and understand others, and how to work with people that one might never physically meet is quite important. (Kong et.al,2024)

In future, educational institution, authorities and societies must aim to form an environment for learning where diverse people and learners can learn in an environment that is welcoming, suitable and sufficient developed to meet present day challenge and opportunities of the information society. Accepting this role shall guarantee that the society coming after us is fitted to cope with the problems of the future as well as to be socially responsible and responsible citizens equipped with adequate knowledge.

2. EDUCATIONAL BENEFITS OF ARTIFICIAL INTELLIGENCE (AI)

Figure 1. Educational benefits of artificial intelligence

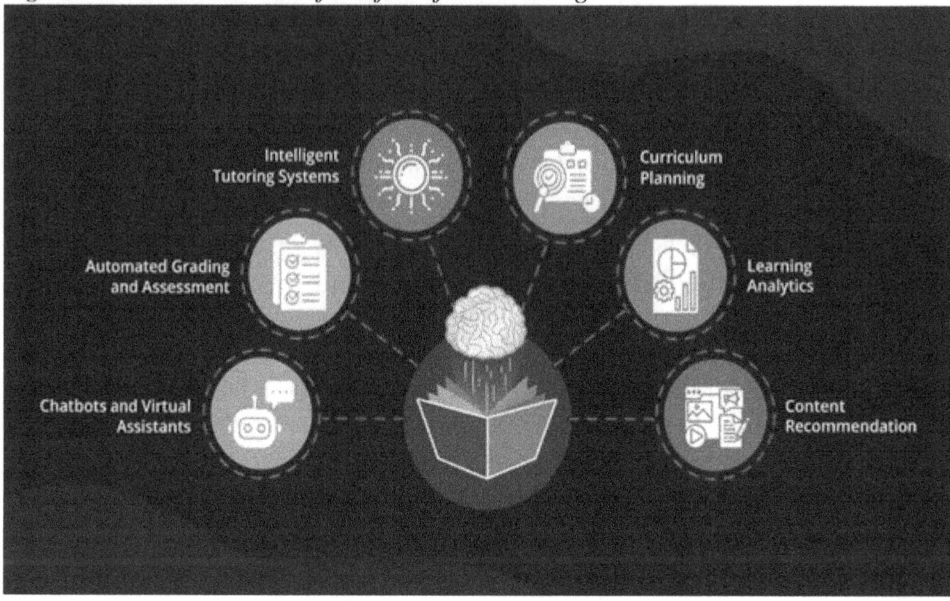

The technology commonly referred to as Artificial Intelligence (AI) is revolutionalizing education in a very big way by providing an array of features that are transforming the academic world, for teachers as well as learners. AI has the potential to develop greater levels of individualisation, effectiveness and enjoyment as an education system develops. From learning that is specific to a learner to increased access and improved teachers' efficiency, these are all valuable lessons that make AI a necessity in today's learning system. These components are; Personalization of Learning, Administration, Accessibility, Simulation and Experience, and Skills for the Future Workforce, and will be discussed elaborately in this essay.

Personalization is probably one of the most effective ways through which AI has impacted the education sector. Proficient traditional classroom learning approaches entail standard procedures that are not efficient for children who grasp materials at various speeds or use distinct methods. AI plays it by filling this gap by analyzing the data of the students, and providing the learning opportunity that best suits the student. Compenses for these approaches are the ability of the AI- powered system to navigate in real time, provide feedback, change level of difficulty of assignments, as well as to recommend extra material according to the pupil's progress. This particular learner-centered approach ensures that those learners who may require extra time to understand some certain concepts will not be kept awaiting their mates to complete their learning while those who complete their learning vastly can proceed faster thus enhancing learning and understanding. (CetindamarKozanoglu et.al,2021)

Moreover, AI results in enhancement of personalized learning as well as improvement in the administrative functioning. In most cases, teachers devote much of their working timeline to non-instructional tasks, administrative, and general flow responding to students' constant queries. Most of these tasks can be handled by AI in order to reduce the workload of the educators so that they can be more on the lesson delivery and students. Computer aided test can grade multiple choice questions, essays and especially some forms of written tasks and it is able to offer feedback to the students or even do the grading of a number of assignments on its own. Chatbots can be artificially intelligent to answer student's administrative inquiries, for instance, on deadlines, handouts, and class times. In freeing up time for these tasks AI, allows a teacher to spend more quality time with the learners improving the learning process.

AI is also incredibly helpful in increasing accessibility of education. Students with disabilities or learners that deal with language barriers are some of the people that find it difficult to get normal learning materials. Translations by AI, speech to text, text to speech, and real time translations help to make classroom education more accessible to such students. First let me describe some rather global examples; for example, multimedia enabled learners with visual impairments can access written information through screen readers based on artificial intelligence algorithms while multimedia enabled learners with hearing impairments alumni can benefit from real time captioning in classes. Besides, AI can help the remote and less-served education population get the actual quality education resources in the online educational programs. Since the methods deployed in these platforms offer customized learning approaches, the restricted or developing students in rural or disadvantaged areas will receive the same study Chances as the rest. (Pedro et.al,2019)

Another advantage that AI brings in learning is the establishment of realistic and innovative learning process designs. They include VR, AR, and simulations – are just examples of the applications of the AI technologies that help students enhance their understanding and move beyond reading books. For instance, in physics or chemistry, a simulation may be done in order to enable the student to perform an experiment, a method that is safe and also free from the financial constraints. It also helps the student dive into historical events or science, instead of using abstract concepts as a passive set of information. School-produced simulations aid in understanding content knowledge and compel the learners to find solutions to problems they face.

Furthermore, AI assist to build students readiness towards the future workforce since it assists in the development of key skills. Based on the importance of applying AI in industries day by day, the need for workers with competencies in applying AI, including data analysis, machine learning, and programming, has risen considerably. Learning tools, which use AI can offer students tailored models of how best to develop skills for the given career. Furthermore, AI helps in providing for continual education since education for working adults who wish to change or expand their careers is flexible. The adaptable learning solutions AI provide means learners of all ages can acquire the tools and support they need in today's global job landscape.

Aside from the pedagogical and content expertise, the use of Artificial Intelligence in education fosters ethical understanding and more importantly, responsible incorporation of AI. Since many years AI becomes broader in society and students need not only to know the mechanisms and functioning in the process of AI but also the ethical consequences of its work. It is possible to introduce AI ethic into learning, so students acquire skills in data protection and other effects of AI. AI literacy, thus, enable educational systems to prepare learners not only for the context where they will be using the AI technologies but also enable them have the competencies to engage in debates about the potential merits and demerits or rights and wrongs of applying AI in different areas. This model of teaching assist students to be responsible members of society with adequate knowledge of an AI controlled future.

All in all, the role of AI for education is immense, and it ranges from enhancing the administrative process and interactivity to learning process itself and student access to the classes. AI to improve the effectiveness of the teacher is because frees up the teacher from all the administrative work and gives him feedback on student progress. It also enables youngsters equip themselves with requisite knowledge and skills that future workforce will have to face while carrying out their duties in a world dominated by AI. AI is still redefining education, and it should be noted that ethical issues should also be incorporated into users' concerns so that students not only know how to work with and recognize AI's presence, but they also should have awareness of its consequences. Lastly, AI gives the probability to develop available, accountable and compellling educational conditions in which people-centered specialists and learners could thrive.

3. ETHICAL IMPLICATIONS

Ethical concerns form a core discussion when people discuss the usability of technology in society today. Progress in technology means that there raise many ethical issues that impact on people, business, and governments. These are so because technology has invariably broken the dials of privacy, security, fairness, and autonomy. Technology is not a villain that causes harm, but how it is designed and implemented, as well as what regulations surround it can prop up social benefit and integrate society or make social inequality worse.

One of the most significant ethical issues is probably privacy as the society becomes more connected through using electronic technologies. Writing encrypted messages on social media, or using online services, sharing personal data becomes quite easy. Business establishments and state agencies are in a position to gather a huge of information about a person or group and even their private life. Such information is employed in some uses as advertising or monitoring, its legal and ethical implications of concerns regarding consent. Currently, people provide their data freely in a manner that lacks clear understanding of how the data is going to be used or by whom, then complains of data exploitation. Lack of transparency and inadequate consent to the collection and use of personal information is a denial of privacy to persons and erodes the public's trust in innovations. (Kong et.al.2023)

Security is very much interconnected with the concept of privacy. Today due to advancement in technology the rates of cyber-attacks and data breaches have continued to rise. These risks are manifested in instances where an organization does not adequately safeguard its information or indeed where it neglects to report a breach in information security in good time. These are some of the risks that result from a neglect of security measures, which may equal financial loss, identity theft amongst other losses to persons. Furthermore, modern computer hacking tools have emerged to cause fear relating to the safety of things like health facilities, transport systems, and power sectors. He pointed out that governments and companies have obligation to protect these systems and that, in fact, many are open to attacks. Why should the organization suffer from scandals if its representatives are capable of defending it from external threats such as hackers and infiltrators?

The next big ethical question is justice, and the ability of technology, including AI and machine learning in particular, to be unbiased. Most of these systems are trained on a big data with biases and hence can result to biased solutions such as in employment, policing and treatment of diseases. For instance, when AI recruitment tools are trained on a sample of candidates, their results will always be skewed towards chosen preference of the sample. Likewise, historical experiences of facial recognition technology have demonstrated that this technology performs worse when it is is given samples of people of color due to the real possibility of discriminating against individuals who deserve justice. Ethical issues occur where such systems provide results that entrench the existing societal disparities of the minority leading to unfair treatment. Several measures to guarantee the equality in AI development and using: It is necessary to create full transparency, provide accountability as well as introducing passes to check the bias.

Consequently, the concept of digital citizenship relates to the measure of how artificial intelligence influences related rights and duties of individuals in the immediate virtual space. This encompasses matters to do with data protection, AI fairness, proper usage and understandability about the social implications of engaging with AI technologies.

The societal effects of AI concentrate on the organisational consequences of this technology on communities and systems although its potential to either diminish or amplify inequalities. These areas include equity issues, diverse practices, and mainstreaming practices, and sustaining the development of technology advances in conjunction with social welfare. The problem of accountability also concerns larger social effects that might include, for example, job losses caused by artificial intelligence. Although technology has its ways of creating ways of enhancing efficiency and productivity it has been noted that it sometimes has a way of causing unemployment especially to lager companies who lay off workers in order to adopt to the use of technology.

The use of technology also gives rise to ethical consideration(s) in the area of environmentalism. Hazards arising from the manufacturing, application and disposal of electronics include pollution, resource depletion and climatic change. For example, extracting the metals used in gadgets such as smart phones lead to adverse effects on the ecological structure and exploitation of labour in an economic system in the third world regions. Also, rising energy demands in data centers, which host the internet and artificial intelligence, cause carbon emission. There are questions about how to justify the push for technology given the ever-increasing concern for environmental conservation and sustainability.

Also, one can provide the examples of ethical issues which are connected with the application of the technology in monitoring and supervision. Frequently governments and corporations employ surveillance technologies to track people's behavior and actions and that results in the degeneration of human civil rights and freedom. For example, some surveillance measures might be launched with reference to terrorism prevention goals, while violating citizens' rights for personal privacy and freedom of speech. Sometimes the technologies of surveillance have been employed to stifle opposition and persecute minorities. Practical questions arise as to how effectiveness of such technologies could be guaranteed without triggering abuses or infringement of human rights. (Hristovska et.al,2023)

The effects of new technologies are also ethics issues and some of them are Unforeseen Consequences. In many instances, unquestionable technologies are created, which turn out to have outside negative impacts. For instance, application that were intended to be used to share posts and pictures have same been associated with the spread of fake news, bullying and other health related problems among the users. Likewise, the pro efficiency AI systems when implemented in fields, they have a secret agenda of rendering people jobless and thereby increasing unemployment ratio and showing high economic disparity. Ethical issues cannot be overemphasized in considering such unintended demotivating effects and in towards promoting an ethical use of technology.

4. BUILDING AI LITERACY

Figure 2. Establishment of AI literacy

It is well understood that developing AI literacy has become more important in today's world of education and services. AI literacy therefore combines aspects of technical knowledge and understanding of the implications of Artificial Intelligence both ethically, socially, economically and all other manners imaginable entail. Because artificial intelligence is now influencing decisions being made and alive, developing AI competence helps people adopt a critical lens and ability to make right decisions in a world system that is being influenced by intelligent systems.

The first and fundamental barrier to the general public when it comes to AI is – what it actually means? To the public, AI is associated with robots or other sophisticated systems which do not form the part of their community. But to some extent, AI is already present in the everyday use, virtual assistants, such as Siri, Alexa, algorithms in the domains of recommendation on such services as Netflix, YouTube and so on. If people always relate AI to robots this usually makes them think of it as irrelevant, but when they know it involves systems that can identify patterns, make forecasts and even help in automating processes, they start to see it in their own lives. Dispelling these misunderstandings is part of AI literacy because it turns AI from something that is beyond everyone's reach to something that affects everyone directly.

There is a possibility of delving in more detail in the content of AI in higher learning institutions. It has become clear that Universities and colleges need to groom AI specialists; to cater the growing need of the digital market and they have started to offer dedicated courses and degrees in AI. In these environments, students are informed about the latest advanced AI technologies and uses including, deep learning, vision systems, robotics and autonomous vehicles. All told, many degree programs also stress practical experience allowing students to undertake AI projects based on practical applications to such areas as health, finance, or the environment. This approach allows students to understand the applicability of AI and future workplace characteristics of the automated world. Also, ethics, social and other impacts of AI are also taught during AI education at this level, and these concepts enable learners to understand some of the challenges as bias in algorithms and possible job losses, the need for regulation of the use of AI for responsible development among other. (Yi et.al,2021)

But it is important to understand that incorporation of AI in the learning process has not been an easy task. Many teachers fortunately do not have adequate awareness and knowledge of AI systems and therefore may not be in a position to help students develop human-like intelligent systems. Many teachers may lack the experience or even the knowledge on computer science let alone data science to impart the information effectively. To this end, it becomes incumbent on the part of education-based institutions to train their teachers and organise relevant sessions to familiarise the educators with AI systems. Moreover, if the schools are to teach AI, there is a lack of proper technological tools and platforms they can use at times these can be expensive. It remains important for students from all different socioeconomic statuses to have an opportunity to study AI and not to be excluded from the technology and education advancements this creates even more inequality.

Another problem is a swift development and advancement of AI technology. Consequently, the program has to be sensitive to new developments in the field and therefore requiring constant update as well as changes. This is especially important for education, as what is considered innovative today may become outdated in several years, while AI should be able to accommodate any potentials, as long as students are taught basic principles of the technology. Secondly, there are evident needs for AI education while it is also a high time not to oversell AI education at the cost of downplaying other subjects. The targeted approach should be the incorporation of AI education in a balanced manner in order to improve particular aspects of students' learning environment.

Therefore, we suggest that efforts be made to ensure that AI finds its way into the curriculum in order to equip the students for the world that is swiftly being developed around Artificial Intelligence. At every level – from basic education to university – student needs to learn the rules and features of AI and its usage for actual cases together with critical thinking skills to use it properly. As much as there are some difficulties, arising, it is considerable important that so much could be achieved from the education of AI. That prepares students for the world that is rapidly becoming a defined entity in the job market; additionally, it includes acknowledgment of students into defining the technology that is going to transform the society in an ethical perspective.

5. INTEGRATING AI INTO THE CURRICULUM

Adding AI into the curriculum is becoming paramount each time as AI advances in almost all sectors of society. AI is no longer a concept of only highly technologically developed laboratories or technology companies, but participants in everyday life, starting with voice assistants such as Siri and concluding with recommenders on streaming platforms. Making sure that students have at least basic principles of AI is important to help them embrace the future with technology now being an inseparable part of our lives even more so in the future. It will therefore be important to introduce the use of AI in different levels of schooling so that students not only have mastery skills on using AI but also develop some level of consciousness on some of the effects it has in the society.

The first usage of Artificial Intelligence in educational systems is to foster the students' critical thinking and problem-solving skills. AI teaching also helps the students to learn and appreciate systems and learn how to try and demystify them into simpler components which is so relevant in any endeavor. Students acquire skills in the analysis of problems, using data to make certain decisions and constructing models to address problems for the resolution of existing and emerging challenges. The skills in the interaction with problems, which involve data and the ability to understand how the AI works is going to be instrumental even for those who will not have a technical career. AI literacy enables students to go beyond using technology as consumers and transforms them to be producers, problem solvers and thinkers who create and meet new future needs and address the ethical issues arising from the use of AI.

Education exposure is not all about coding or even understanding algorithms but it also encompasses the understanding of the social, economic and ethical impacts of the AI. As AI develops and takes control over the jobs, decisions, and policies' formation, students need to know what can lead to. This involves questions like privacy, ethnic preconceptions in the AI solutions and the society impacts of automation. An integrated curriculum assists learners to grasp the virtues and vices in these technologies because the latter's incorporation in our lives is pervasive and persistent. In this respect, it was important that education played its part to make sure that future generation adopt the technology within an ethical way that is fair to all.

While enrolling in the primary and secondary school levels, the impact of AI can still be incorporated in the systems without the have to complex it make it so complicated. Incorporating AI concepts into fun and curiosity temptations for the younger students is much easier given the current state of technology. Children like using different platforms such as Scratch in coding since it looks more like playing than doing computations. These early experiences begin to de-sensitise them on AI and coding and give confidence that building technologies is possible with their hands. Towards middle and high school other concepts such as machine learning, pattern recognition, or even simple algorithms can be introduced. These lessons can be correlated with other subjects such as mathematics, science as well as social studies. For instance, a teacher applies data analysis in a math lesson or mention its use of advances in an AI lesson plan in history or social studies.

More technical knowledge and skills are taught concerning artificial intelligence at the university level than at other levels of learning. While AI is penetrating each and every industry at the moment, starting from the healthcare and finishing with finance, a growing number of universities provide courses and programs for students to get degrees in AI-based industries. These programmes tend to be very applied and for instance they may propose students develop their own AI models or solve real-world problems. From these experiences, the students are able to relate and implement the AI techniques learnt in tackling such real-life problems, enabling them to acquire the practice necessary in the job industry. Also, liberal studies that to attain, higher level involve allowing for an exploration of the ethical considerations of AI and these discussions are focused on how best to eliminate biases in AI, prevent hacks to user data and tackle other issues related to the use of AI in automation. This is the balance that the program strikes to get the students AI Practitioners: An Insight and show that you can be technical and professional while being moral and conscious.

Yet, despite the apparent need for introducing more and more AI-related content into the curriculum, AI implementation has its issues. Perhaps the greatest challenge is fulfilling the criterion which states that teachers themselves must know how to impart these kinds of difficult subjects. AI teaching is an entirely different ball game, and many teachers may not have the background of computer science or data science. To meet this, schools need to strategically enhance ways of professional development for training teachers to enable them deliver on AI education. Also, when it comes to access to the appropriate technology is another challenge.

AI education involves the use of computers and software in addition to particular AI platforms that mean that some schools especially in the developing countries or those facing poor funding may not be able to provide for such a course. These differences could strengthen the division between those students who have access to expensive innovations ad those who do not have it at all. (Southworth et.al,2023)

The first difficulty becoming an expert in AI is that AI technology is constantly evolving with new and improved technology being released frequently. This is a fast-growing field, and it implies that targets must be fluid, so that curriculums can be updated fairly frequently. Many schools should bring academics to AI basics like algorithms, data handling, and neural networks while guaranteeing that learners engage with the most sophisticated tools and approaches. Maintaining this balance between core concepts and emerging trends guarantees that students are ready for present day employment, as well as tomorrow's unknowns as far as AI is concerned.

To appeal to computer scientists and those involved in the practical application of AI, the following AI tools and technologies currently used in education.

1. AI-Powered Learning Management Systems (LMS)
2. Intelligent Tutoring Systems (ITS)
3. Natural Language Processing (NLP) for Language Learning

Thus, it is not a question of how AI will be delivered to the students so that they will be ready for the jobs which will be related to AI in the near and distant future, but rather about how students can be prepared to live in the world which is to be filled with AI at every level. Not only does the implementation an AI-integrated curriculum prepare and challenge learners in thinking critically and solving problems, but it also presents principles in light of the ethics of Artificial Intelligence.

Figure 3. Integration of AI into curriculum

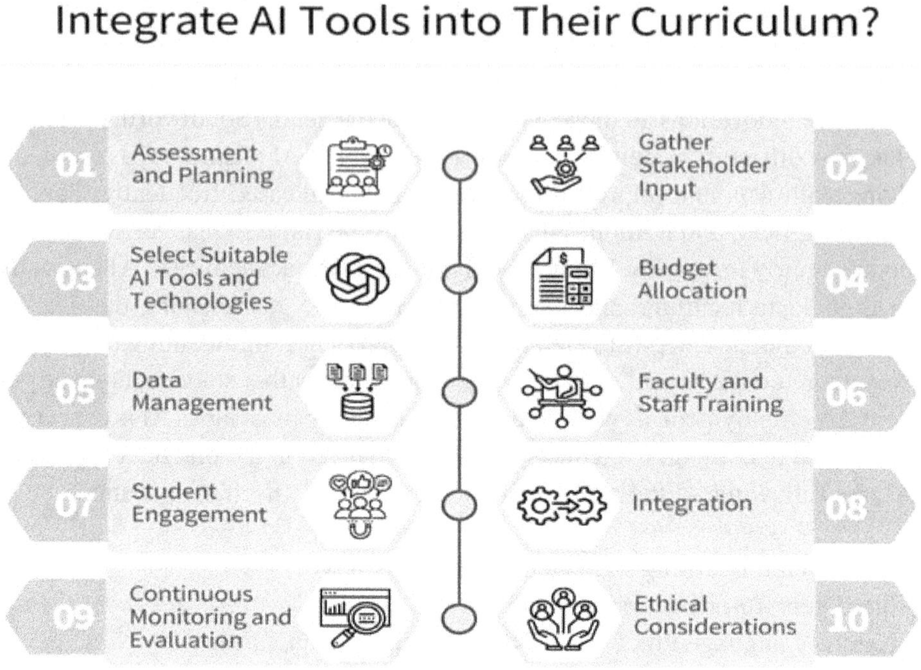

6. TRAINING TEACHERS

In the context of the contemporary society the enhancement of the usage of artificial intelligence and digital literacy in education is of great importance for the subject of education and in general the formation of the skills which are necessary for future citizens in the world based on technology. Given the increasing role of AI in different realms fairly closely touching all aspects of life, starting from the way people work and communicate and ending with the decision-making process, it is crucial to prepare students for interacting with AI. But in this pursuit, the teachers have a very significant position. For AI and digital literacy to be rolled out successfully in education, there is the need to train teachers. Therefore, when our students never get the kind of educators who have a grasp of these technologies, they will not be well prepared to have the skills required by a future AI-defined future. (Levitt et.al,2024)

Educating teachers in the area of artificial intelligence is a complex process that focus on digital competencies. Some educators practicing in school systems today may have prerequisite knowledge in computer science, coding AI technologies. Students may be used to technology enhanced learning environment but have no prior knowledge of the new frameworks such as Artificial Intelligence (AI), machine learning or data science which are new frontiers in education. To close this gap, there is the need for rigorous professional development programs. These programs should have the capacity to teach not only the content, or, more specifically, the mechanics of how AI works but also what it is, why it is important in the classroom as well as developing a willingness to continue learning. AI has to be remodeled continually and therefore teachers have to be in a position to update their knowledge all the time to ensure their students are equipped with the latest knowledge as it is produced.

Another method of using AI and delivering content aligned with its principles can be held through workshops and certification of teachers. These can be presented online, as well as face-to-face and this makes it easier for the teachers to work at their own convenient time. A diploma, for instance, could consist of fundamental areas like machine learning or data processing, the corresponding AI ethics. Some of the workshops may be more focused on actual use of AI technologies in teaching with directions to use various social media or other forms of platforms for teaching purposes. Basically, 16 programs include resources, tools and expert faculties, helping the teachers to gain the confidence and competency needed to integrate AI into classrooms.

For this reason, there is a need to ensure that the teachers that are being provided with this knowledge also understand the social impact of AI. It therefore means that teacher should be ready and capable of educating students on the ethics, social, and economic concerns that Artificial intelligence presents. This include learning of bias in AI, effects of use of AI in automation on employment and issues of privacy when data is collected and processed in AI. A well- informed teacher can therefore facilitate a group of students, and through critical debate on the societal impacts of AI develop active and responsible citizens of the society with both technical and moral values. This broader understanding will enable the students to make necessary decisions about use of AI in their life. (Shah et.al,2023)

But mere provision of training opportunities does not suffice. Obviously, there should be some policy support in order to guarantee that teachers can and will be willing and able to engage in these professional development activities. Educational and school administrators have to incorporate AI and digital literacy education into the course delivery plan. This could entail including within the school year time for teachers to attend workshops, offering finical incentives for teachers to undergo certification and including AI literacy as part of the preparation for prospective teachers. Finally, cooperation with schools and tech companies or universities could offer resources that may help in teacher training: the latest AI instruments and studies.

Teacher's contribution to increasing the perception of digital literacy and AI is not limited to The Classroom. Innovation and digital curiosity are the foundation that teachers establish in their student groups. When used in lesson plans and when the applications are explained to learners on the effectiveness of the technologies, then the learners will be encouraged to pursue careers in the applications' fields. Moreover, teachers can also explain how AI, as other digital tools, can be applied to address real-world issues, including climate change, medicine and etc through the presentation of interdisciplinary projects where students use their AI knowledge to address global challenges. Such practical teachings give much more than just an improvement in students' practical skills: it fosters problem-solving and creative thinking as well.

However, the main challenges persist whenever the aim is to train teachers in AI and digital literacy. One major obstacle is the fact that there may be very few resources available in school, especially in richer countries. The absence of technology may act as a barrier to making teachers available and equipped in the teaching of AI in schools with little technology. Moreover, there can be reluctance from the teachers as they may be overpowered by embracing new technologies or they may not see how AI can help them teach their subjects through all those technologies. Addressing these aspects calls for collective efforts from the leaders in education and policy together with the information technology industry to enable equal opportunities for schools to embrace the technology facilitated change in their operations.

Therefore, for FA and digital technologies to prepare citizens for the future, there is the need to train teachers. Teachers are the main way through which learners are educated on the appropriate use and understanding of the digital platform and AI. Overall, the government could provide necessary institutional support, invest more in teacher and trainer practices, and ensure the availability of textual and other resources that can help the stream of education to develop students with adequate tolerance and preparedness, to be able to withstand and deal with AI the way technologies pose social ethical questions and dilemmas to human civilisation. One will need to have a teacher with capacity to teach AI and digital skills among the future generations, hence the need to have capacity to teach AI.

7. CHALLENGES TO INCLUSIVE AI EDUCATION AND THEIR SOLUTIONS:

7.1 Resource-Constrained Areas

One of the primary reasons why the introduction of AI education in such areas is challenging is due to poor physical structures, and meager financial resources as well as poor access to current technological tools. These difficulties hinder students and teacher from having access to AI tools and materials as they ought to. Solving these problems calls for creativity such as, use of low-cost-AI tools, collaborations, and online learning systems ideal for contexts of scarcity. (Šumak, B et.al2024)

To overcome this challenge these techniques must be implemented:

Improving Infrastructure: Use strategies like inexpensive gadgets charged by solar energy, and paper-based instead of focusing solely on the ones connected to the internet.

Partnerships and Funding: Explain public partnerships with governmental, non-governmental organizations, and technology companies to support funding, resources, and technologies in needy schools.

Adapted Curriculum: Create AI curricula, which allows learners to learn in a way that is closer to their context and languages through the use of locally relevant problems as well as open-source tools.

7.2 Digital Divide

The digital divide reveals unfettered access to the digital world, in which disadvantaged rural areas and those in the economically challenged zones are left in the cold. Such a distribution is rather discouraging equal participation in AI education, hence aggravating existing gaps. Closing the gap depends on the adoption of special measures aimed at bridging the physical and digital connections and ensuring the access to the necessary devices in the regions with poor coverage, as well as education of people in the sphere of proper use of the Internet. To overcome this challenge these techniques must be implemented:

Expanding Connectivity: They should carry out nationwide broadband networks, and fund community-scale Internet projects so that all the remote and less inhabited regions can be connected to the world wide web.

Affordable Access: For the class to make good use of the tools and note progresses then it has to have the devices as follows: Subsidized or low cost.

7.3 Digital Literacy Programs

Develop awareness campaigns for fundamental computer literacy programmes which will facilitate efficient use of technologies in the learning system.

The awful truth regarding minorities is they cannot afford to get an AI education because they are victims of ai-based economic conditions as well as cultural prejudice and discrimination. These barriers affect the promotion and availability of the aforementioned disciplines and subsequently impaired growth in fields associated with AI. For these groups, integration of minority and disability friendly policies, relevant examples and materials by tutors and in teaching aids can promote equal participation. To overcome this challenge these techniques must be implemented:

Inclusive Policies: Fight for policies supporting equality in access to education and demand government policies involve funds to cater for reformative injustices.

Culturally Relevant Education: The common priority recommendation drawn from the two studies is as follows: Develop AI curricula that are relevant to the experience and context of marginalized communities.

Mentorship and Outreach: Develop partnership with schools to establish mentorship programs and promotions of students at the lower end of the socioeconomic scale, as a way of ensuring that they make it into the related fields of AI.

7.4 Job Displacement

As AI and automation technologies will become more developed some industries and professions are going to be at risk of being down staffed. Such occupation related to production, services delivery, and transportation are some of the most at risk occupations. These concerns need to be addressed in educating AI where learning outcomes should focus on areas that will support the AI system and prepare students for the new job market as well as how to retrain and adapt to AI systems. To overcome this challenge these techniques must be implemented:

Focus on Reskilling and Upskilling: Suggest courses which should educate students on how to interact with AI technologies; this includes knowledge in AI tools, programming, data analysis. This will ready them for other jobs which AI cannot handle fully for one reason or another.

Develop Complementary Skills: Cultivate typically non-technical skills as creativity, ability to work with emotions and resistance and critical thinking which are difficult to be adopted by a machine. These skills can be useful for people to succeed in new working environment in which AI plays crucial role.

Partnerships with Industry: Cooperate with industries to develop programs for skill enhancement in workforce that are relevant to the industries expecting to be impacted by AI in the future such as; AI policies, computer security, artificial intelligence and data analytics. This will make students to be trained to fit to be in the job market that is available.

Promote Lifelong Learning: Promote lifelong learning with vivid examples and models for workers to take refreshed skill enhancement by participating in railway activities and acquiring qualification awards from various institutions and the internet.

7.5 Privacy Concerns

Due to the aforementioned reasons, majority of the AI systems are based on the huge amounts of data that can also contain the personal data, hence, making data privacy and security issues at risk. These descriptions falls under the rights category of AI education that should focus on the ethical consequences of compiling, storing, and using such data. Students should receive information about the potential threats related to the usage of the gathered data, the significance of the privacy issue, and the purpose of mega regulations like GDPR to protect people's rights. To overcome this challenge these techniques must be implemented:

Incorporate Privacy into AI Curriculum: Make sure that issues concerning the use of AI for ethical purposed especially concerning data privacy is taught in the various institutions. Explain to students' rules regarding personal data, like GDPR, as well as general ethical rules concerning personal data collection, storage, and usage.

Data Security Education: Teach low-interest participants about best practices, encryption, and the use of technologies that protect user privacy such as differential privacy. This must enable the students to appreciate how user data can be protected from hacks and such unfavorable misplaced uses.

Promote Transparency: Champion practices that will enable the developers of AI to provide users with insights on the way their data is being used. Main learning: Education must extend the understanding of students regarding the importance of constructing transparent AI systems, signifying proper data practices.

Develop Ethical Guidelines: Extend ethics courses into programs of Artificial Intelligence to pass information about data privacy in the society. In this way, understanding how to strike the right balance between creativity and free development of artificial intelligence on the one hand, and human rights protection, on the other, students can play the significant role in the construction of the AI systems.

8. CASE STUDY

8.1 Finland's National AI Curriculum (Elements of AI)

In 2018, to respond to this need, Finland created the Elements of AI, an online course to teach its citizens the basics of AI. The initiative was an academic project developed by the University of Helsinki in cooperation with a tech company Reaktor, which provided free learning materials equally open to the public and mostly devoid of technical language. Finns have been trained in AI through the program and the goal set is to train at least 1% of the Finnish population. This case study will show how a government can introduce a national AI strategy for creating the digital civil society, and others can follow. (Neittaanmäki et.al,2024)

8.2 China's AI Textbooks for K-12 Students

In 2018 China officially included AI into the curriculum as a compulsory subject in some schools and as an option in other schools. Some Chinese major technology firms including iFlytek joined efforts with the Ministry of Education to develop AI laugh books for K-12 learners. These books touch on the basics of AI, machine learning, data science and computer vision, with the student being exposed to new technologies. The present case indicates that a nation can incorporate the acquisition of AI literacy into its foundational curricula to equip future citizens for a digital environment for the attainment of sustainable leadership in AI. (Wu et.al,2021)

8.3 Dubai's AI and Robotics in Schools Initiative

The United Arab Emirates' has come up with several programs that seek to implement AI in the education system. An example is an initiative known as the artificial intelligence and robotics in schools in Dubai which was meant to equip students for future jobs. It prepares AI and robotics as a set of subjects that should be taught in primary and secondary schools. It also encompasses AI professional development programs to guarantee teachers are capable of teaching students AI knowledge effectively. This paper also discusses the significance of the early introduction of AI and how countries should prepare and introduce changes in the method of training the generation that is expected to work in an AI environment. (Basheer et.al,2023)

8.4 Promoting Diversity in AI Education (AI4ALL)

AI4ALL is a young non-profit aimed at promoting greater use of AI by minority students. It offers summer programs as well as online courses aimed at high school students especially those interested in STEM but from low representation backgrounds. In effect, for AI4ALL, the key objectives are to ensure young learners are equipped with effective knowledge of and correctly applied skills in the future of Artificial Intelligence. From this case study it is evident that different groups of learners need to be targeted early enough in their learning so that a large cross section of future citizens are well prepared for participation in the digital economy (Daugherty et.al,2020).

8.5 Google's CS First Program

CS First is a program run by Google for students in grades from 4 to 8 with the aim to offer free simple materials for computer science and coding. By incorporating programming and AI learning within school and after school programs, CS First familiarises students with Digital literacy and beginning concepts of Artificial intelligence. The program aims at making the coding and AI interface easier to use especially from the part of the world that has limited access to technology education. This case study is indicative of how corporate leadership can play a critical in reaching out to the lowest level and transforming the perception of people towards technology. (Ashenfelter et.al,2017)

9. CONCLUSION

In the dawn of a digital frontier, technology, especially in the form of Artificial Intelligence (AI) and the promotion of that of digital citizenship is vital towards charting the citizen for the future. Technology continues to move the world forward to the center by altering the very fabric of how we interact and conduct business as well as responding to the modern day's most pressing issues. Therefore, there is need for the education systems in the different nations to embrace the above changes and popularize the use of computers and other artificial intelligent gadgets in creating the much-needed awareness among the learners on how to survive and succeed in the society enhanced by artificial intelligence.

Web literacy or the knowledge and skills required to use a browser, information, and tools proficiently have emerged as core competencies characterizing the contemporary population. At present, knowledge is relatively easy to find while at the same time, not all of it is accurate, hence it has become equally important to teach students how to search for accurate knowledge or information as it is to teach them how to read. Adult learning environments such as schools, colleges, and universities must strive to do more than just educate students about how to handle gadgets or application; they need to ensure students develop positive attitudes, determine appropriate use of technology, learn from it, and solve problems creatively and ethically. This will enable upcoming generations not only to be a reception of information from the new media but also producers of information and be innovative in their society.

In addition, the application of AI in learning cannot be underestimated. Machine learning approaches, ranging from individualized learning environments to automated assessment solution all hold promises of dramatically redefining the process of education. However, the use of these tools deems necessary the comprehension concerning the possibilities, strengths and weaknesses of AI applications, and its consequences. Including AI education in college curricula will ensure that students gain the knowledge in the development of AI to be enabled to critique the emerging technologies that dictate their existence. Apart from subject knowledge, the students will also have to know how AI relates to social, economic and political topics. This will afford them an opportunity to plan concretely for its application in their daily lives, private as well as in their professions and also be able to have a stake in it and take part in contributing positively to its advancement in an ethical manner.

Preparing citizens for the future also include bridging the digital divide and providing equal chance of using technologies and opportunities for learning. There are still many problems in using ICT in education that prevail in numerous regions and communities, including poor infrastructures, limited resources, or, for example, low levels of digital competencies among teachers and learners. Efforts to cultivating appropriate top-skill education and training for e-learning should be initiated by governments and can also be fostered by educational institutions and private sector organizations in order to close the existing gaps and improve an equitable digital learning environment. Only then can we guarantee parity of library usage between group A and group B with a view to accessing the benefits relating to computer illiteracy and AI.

Thus, there are the concluding remarks: The future of the educational process should be built on the emergence of digital literacy and artificial intelligence. By the help of the use of IT and education courses offered to the students, we create knowledgeable, responsible and creative society. It in turn promotes individual control, economic development, social change, and cooperation throughout the world. At the same time, it is important not to let children be prepared for the future but rather, prepared for creating it.

REFERENCES

Ashenfelter, E. (2017). From the Classroom: A guide to teaching coding using Google's CS First. *Gifted Child Today*, 40(4), 220–225. DOI: 10.1177/1076217517722578

Basheer, H. (2023). *Artificial Intelligence and Robotics: towards the evolution of sustainable graduate employability ecosystem: a contemporary perspective for higher education stakeholders in the UAE* (Doctoral dissertation, University of Bath).

Cetindamar Kozanoglu, D., & Abedin, B. (2021). Understanding the role of employees in digital transformation: Conceptualization of digital literacy of employees as a multi-dimensional organizational affordance. *Journal of Enterprise Information Management*, 34(6), 1649–1672. DOI: 10.1108/JEIM-01-2020-0010

Daugherty, P. R., Wilson, H. J., & Chowdhury, R. (2020). Using artificial intelligence to promote diversity.

Hristovska, A. (2023). Fostering media literacy in the age of ai: examining the impact on digital citizenship and ethical decision-making. *КАИРОС: Журналзамедиуми и комуникации, 2*(2), 39-59.

Kong, S. C., Cheung, M. Y. W., & Tsang, O. (2024). Developing an artificial intelligence literacy framework: Evaluation of a literacy course for senior secondary students using a project-based learning approach. *Computers and Education: Artificial Intelligence*, 6, 100214. DOI: 10.1016/j.caeai.2024.100214

Kong, S. C., Cheung, W. M. Y., & Tsang, O. (2023). Evaluating an artificial intelligence literacy programme for empowering and developing concepts, literacy and ethical awareness in senior secondary students. *Education and Information Technologies*, 28(4), 4703–4724. DOI: 10.1007/s10639-022-11408-7

Levitt, G., & Grubaugh, S. (2024). Why Do I Have to Learn this Stuff? Using AI to Assist Secondary Teachers in Teaching Future-Ready Practical Life Skills with any Social Studies Lesson. *Technium Soc. Sci. J.*, 59, 327.

Neittaanmäki, P., & Lehto, M. (2024). Finland's AI-supported Digital Social Welfare and Healthcare and School System 2030. *Informaatioteknologiantiedekunnanjulkaisuja*, (104/2024).

Pedro, F., Subosa, M., Rivas, A., & Valverde, P. (2019). Artificial intelligence in education: Challenges and opportunities for sustainable development.

Shah, P. (2023). *AI and the Future of Education: Teaching in the Age of Artificial Intelligence*. John Wiley & Sons.

Southworth, J., Migliaccio, K., Glover, J., Reed, D., McCarty, C., Brendemuhl, J., & Thomas, A. (2023). Developing a model for AI Across the curriculum: Transforming the higher education landscape via innovation in AI literacy. *Computers and Education: Artificial Intelligence*, 4, 100127. DOI: 10.1016/j.caeai.2023.100127

Stolpe, K., & Hallström, J. (2024). Artificial intelligence literacy for technology education. *Computers and Education Open*, 6, 100159. DOI: 10.1016/j.caeo.2024.100159

Šumak, B., López-de-Ipiña, D., Dziabenko, O., Correia, S. D., de Carvalho, L. M. S., Lopes, S., . . . Pušnik, M. (2024, May). AI-Based Education Tools for Enabling Inclusive Education: Challenges and Benefits. In *2024 47th MIPRO ICT and Electronics Convention (MIPRO)* (pp. 472-477). IEEE.

Wu, C., Li, Y., Li, J., Zhang, Q., & Wu, F. (2021, May). Web-based platform for K-12 AI education in China. *Proceedings of the AAAI Conference on Artificial Intelligence*, 35(17), 15687–15694. DOI: 10.1609/aaai.v35i17.17848

Yi, Y. (2021). Establishing the concept of AI literacy. *Jahr–European Journal of Bioethics*, 12(2), 353–368.

Chapter 9
The Global Impact of AI on Digital Citizenship

P. Selvakumar
https://orcid.org/0000-0002-3650-4548
Department of Science and Humanities, Nehru Institute of Technology, India

P. Sudheer
https://orcid.org/0009-0005-1912-6636
CVR College of Engineering, India

Nandini Kannan
https://orcid.org/0009-0000-8068-1747
HKBK College of Engineering, India

ABSTRACT

Citizenship fundamentally alters how individuals interact, communicate, and engage with the world around them. Digital citizenship encompasses the skills, knowledge, and ethical considerations necessary responsibly. It is not merely about technical proficiency but includes a deep understanding of the rights and responsibilities that come with digital engagement—ranging from social media platforms to online education and healthcare. Understanding the interplay between digital citizenship and AI is crucial for harnessing opportunities while addressing associated challenges. One of the core concepts of digital citizenship is the notion of which effectively in an environment. As AI systems are often involved in curating content, automating responses, and personalizing user experiences, digital citizens must develop critical skills to assess the reliability and bias of AI-driven information. This includes understanding how algorithms work, recognizing the limitations of AI, and discerning the ethical implications of AI decisions.

DOI: 10.4018/979-8-3693-9015-3.ch009

INTRODUCTION TO DIGITAL CITIZENSHIP AND AI: CONCEPTS, OPPORTUNITIES, AND CHALLENGES

Citizenship, fundamentally alters how individuals interact, communicate, and engage with the world around them. Digital citizenship encompasses the skills, knowledge, and ethical considerations necessary responsibly. It is not merely about technical proficiency but includes a deep understanding of the rights and responsibilities that come with digital engagement. One of the core concepts of digital citizenship is the notion of which effectively in an environment. As AI systems are often involved in curating content, automating responses, and personalizing user experiences, digital citizens must develop critical skills to assess the reliability and bias of AI-driven information. This includes understanding how algorithms work, recognizing the limitations of AI, and discerning the ethical implications of AI decisions., individuals can become more informed consumers and creators of digital content, empowering them to make sound decisions and participate meaningfully in online communities. The opportunities presented by the intersection of digital citizenship and AI are vast. AI can enhance digital citizenship education by providing personalized learning experiences, enabling individuals to develop essential skills at their own pace. For instance, AI-driven educational platforms can assess learners' progress, identify knowledge gaps, and suggest targeted resources, thereby fostering a more tailored approach to digital literacy. Additionally, AI can help bridge individuals from linguistic more fully digital spaces. Through natural language processing and translation technologies, AI can facilitate cross-cultural communication, promoting global dialogue and understanding. Moreover, enhancing civic engagement participation. Digital platforms powered by AI can analyze public sentiment, identify community needs, and facilitate connections between citizens and local government. By harnessing data analytics, AI can empower individuals to engage in advocacy community institutions This potential for enhanced civic engagement aligns with the core principles of digital citizenship, as individuals become more informed and active participants in their communities.

However, the realm of digital citizenship also significant challenges issue of privacy and data security. As increasingly, the use of AI to collect and analyze this data raises ethical questions regarding consent and ownership. The algorithms that power without transparent policies and robust protections, individuals risk losing control over their information. This highlights the necessity for digital citizens to be aware of their rights and to advocate for policies that safeguard privacy and ensure responsible data usage. Another pressing challenge is the potential for algorithmic bias, which. And if data results those in can have profound implications for various areas, such as hiring practices, law enforcement, and access to services. Consequently, fostering a nuanced understanding of how AI can impact equity and fairness is crucial for promoting responsible digital citizenship. Education around these issues should equip individuals with the skills to critically assess AI systems and advocate for ethical practices that mitigate bias. The digital divide is another critical challenge that intersects with digital citizenship and AI. Resources. This disparity can exacerbate existing inequalities, leaving marginalized communities at a disadvantage in a technology-driven world. Life is vital to these disparities by promoting equitable access to technology and education. Initiatives aimed at closing the digital divide can empower all individuals to engage fully in the digital landscape, thereby fostering a more inclusive society. In conclusion, the interplay between digital citizenship and AI presents a complex landscape of, individuals who must cultivate the skills and knowledge necessary to navigate the digital realm responsibly, recognizing inherent.

THE EVOLUTION OF DIGITAL CITIZENSHIP: FROM DIGITAL LITERACY TO AI-DRIVEN ENGAGEMENT

The evolution of digital citizenship is a dynamic journey that reflects the rapid, particularly the rise of the internet and, more recently, artificial intelligence (AI). Initially, digital citizenship centered primarily on digital literacy, which encompassed the skills necessary for individuals to navigate online spaces effectively and responsibly. As technology evolved, the concept expanded to include not just the ability to use digital tools but also a deeper understanding of the ethical implications and societal impacts of digital engagement (Hristovska A., 2023). Today, digital citizenship encompasses a broader framework that integrates critical thinking, ethical considerations, and active participation in the digital landscape, especially as AI increasingly shapes interactions and experiences. Digital literacy is defined as the ability to access and understand information online. This realization led to a growing emphasis on ethical behavior, critical thinking, and the need to engage thoughtfully with digital content. Educational initiatives began to incorporate these elements, teaching individuals to critically analyze information and consider the broader societal impacts of their digital interactions. The emergence of social media further transformed the landscape of digital citizenship. As platforms like Facebook, Twitter, and Instagram gained popularity, they reshaped how individuals communicated, shared information, and formed communities. Social media brought new dimensions to digital citizenship, as users navigated issues related to identity, privacy, and the complexities of online interactions. The power of social media to amplify voices and mobilize movements highlighted the potential for digital citizenship to drive social change. Individuals recognized that they could leverage their online presence to advocate for causes, engage in civic discourse, and participate in democratic processes (Sugumaran K. M., et al, 2024). This shift marked a significant evolution in the concept of digital citizenship, as it embraced active engagement and participation in broader societal issues.

AI-driven engagement presents both opportunities and challenges for digital citizenship. Personalized digital citizenship accessible powered by AI education meets the specific of learners, fostering skills and ethics., AI can facilitate connections between individuals and resources, helping them access information and support networks more efficiently. Policymakers must also address the regulations and frameworks in place to protect individuals' rights and promote equitable access to technology. In conclusion, the evolution of digital citizenship from a focus on digital literacy to AI-driven engagement reflects the changing landscape of technology and society. As individuals navigate an increasingly complex digital environment, the need for a comprehensive understanding of digital citizenship is more critical than ever (Sharma S., et al, 2022). This involves not only acquiring technical skills but also developing ethical reasoning, critical thinking, and active participation in digital spaces. While the associated foster a new generation of informed, responsible and engaged digital citizens. As we look to the future, continued dialogue and collaboration among educators, policymakers, and technology developers will be essential in shaping a digital landscape that values inclusivity, ethical engagement, and active citizenship in the age of AI.

AI FOUNDATIONS: MACHINE LEARNING, NATURAL LANGUAGE PROCESSING, AND COMPUTER VISION

Foundations (AI) are built on several core technologies, with standing out as pivotal components. Each of these areas contributes uniquely to the overall functionality and applications of AI, enabling learning, and ways to mimic. This exploration of AI foundations highlights how these technologies work individually and collectively, their interconnections, and their transformative impact across various industries. Another critical pillar, focusing on This technology encompasses, all of which require a deep understanding of grammar, semantics, and context. The development of NLP has been propelled by advancements in deep learning, particularly through the use of textual (Torfi A., et al, 2020). Notable models, such as OpenAI's GPT series, exemplify the capabilities of NLP by generating coherent and contextually appropriate text, demonstrating the potential for machines to be informative. As NLP continues to evolve, its applications in chatbots, virtual assistants, and automated customer service are transforming how businesses interact with customers. Computer Vision represents the third foundational technology in AI, enabling information from the world. By mimicking the human ability to see and understand images, computer vision allows AI systems to. The field has experienced significant growth due to advancements in data. Applications of computer vision are extensive, ranging from autonomous vehicles that rely on real-time image analysis to identify obstacles, to healthcare systems that utilize medical imaging for diagnostics (Ekman M., 2021). The integration of computer vision into various industries enhances operational efficiency, improves safety, and opens new avenues for innovation.

Moreover, the ethical implications of these foundational technologies cannot be overlooked. Pervasive, regarding bias, accountability in machine learning algorithms, NLP applications, and computer vision systems have emerged. For instance, biased training data can lead to discriminatory outcomes in machine learning models, while NLP systems may inadvertently propagate stereotypes or misinformation. Additionally, computer vision technologies, particularly facial recognition, raise questions about privacy and surveillance. Addressing these ethical challenges requires ongoing research, transparency, and the development of guidelines designed and deployed. Is also profoundly felt across various sectors, driving innovation and efficiency (Ling Y., et al, 2023). In healthcare, these technologies facilitate early disease detection through image analysis, enhance patient care through predictive analytics, and improve accessibility via NLP-powered tools for patients with communication barriers. -driven, assesses credit risk, and enhances fraud detection by processing vast amounts of transactional data. Furthermore, in the retail sector, personalized shopping experiences are created using analysis of customer preferences, while NLP-powered chatbots improve customer service by providing instant support. In conclusion, the foundations of AI, encapsulated in, represent the convergence of technologies that are transforming the way we interact with the world. Each component contributes uniquely to the broader AI landscape, enabling learning, and perceiving ways to enhance capabilities. As these technologies continue to advance, their applications will expand, driving innovation across industries and reshaping societal interactions. However, alongside these opportunities, ethical considerations must be prioritized for deployment, equitable, and beneficial for all. Harmonious these foundational technologies, ultimately lead to intelligent systems that not only augment human potential but also address the pressing challenges of our time.

AI-POWERED DIGITAL IDENTITY: AUTHENTICATION, VERIFICATION, AND PRIVACY

The emergence of AI-powered digital identity systems marks a significant evolution in how individuals and organizations manage authentication, verification, and privacy in an increasingly digital world. As technology continues to advance, the reliance on traditional identity verification methods—such as passwords, physical documents, and personal identification—has become increasingly inadequate in the face of sophisticated cyber threats and the demand for seamless user experiences. AI technologies offer innovative solutions to enhance digital identity management by improving security, streamlining authentication processes, and addressing privacy concerns. Powered identity is the capability to utilize advanced assess verify identities with greater accuracy and efficiency (Awad A.I., et al, 2024). Traditional authentication methods often rely on static information, which can be vulnerable to breaches or identity theft. In contrast, AI systems can analyze dynamic behavioral data, such as biometric information (fingerprints, facial recognition, and voice patterns) and user interactions (typing patterns and navigation habits), to create a more robust and multifaceted identity profile. This multifactor approach significantly enhances security by making it more difficult for unauthorized users to gain access, as they would need to replicate multiple aspects of a person's identity. Facial recognition technology, for instance, has gained traction as a primary means of AI-driven authentication. By capturing and analyzing facial features through sophisticated algorithms, these systems can match an individual's face against stored identity data in real-time. AI can streamline these processes by automating verification tasks and enhancing the speed and efficiency of identity checks (Mohammed I.A., 2021). For example, when opening a bank account online, AI systems can rapidly analyze submitted documents, cross-reference them with government databases, and authenticate users based on biometric verification—all within seconds. Allows organizations to minimize the risk of fraud and comply with regulatory requirements effectively. Furthermore, identity management fosters the concept of self-sovereign identity (SSI), where individuals maintain control over their personal data and identity credentials. SSI empowers users to manage their digital identities independently, deciding what information to share and with whom. AI technologies can facilitate this by creating verifiable credentials that are cryptographically secured and can be shared selectively. This shift towards user-centric identity management aligns with growing concerns about data privacy and ownership, enabling regain a landscape often characterized by data commodification.

However, while the potential of AI-powered digital identity systems is immense, they are not without challenges. Privacy concerns remain paramount and are integral to these technologies. Handling user consent. Such regulations require robust data governance frameworks and transparent practices that prioritize user privacy. Additionally, for training validation, the potential for data breaches and misuse poses significant risks that must be addressed through stringent security measures. Also poses a significant challenge in the context of digital identity. Machine learning models datasets, leading to discriminatory outcomes in identity verification processes. For instance, technologies there, particularly people of color. Addressing these biases requires a concerted effort to develop fair and inclusive AI systems, emphasizing the importance of diversity in training data and algorithmic transparency. As organizations adopt AI-powered digital identity solutions, the importance of user education cannot be overstated. Individuals must be informed about how their data is used, the benefits of these systems, and the implications for their privacy (Olabanji S O., et al, 2024). Empowering users with knowledge fosters trust and encourages responsible engagement with digital identity technologies. Moreover, organizations should prioritize building transparent relationships with users and providing clear information about data handling practices and security measures.

AI-DRIVEN DIGITAL PARTICIPATION: SOCIAL MEDIA, ONLINE ENGAGEMENT, AND CIVIC ACTIVISM

Significantly transformed the landscape of digital participation, particularly through social media platforms, online engagement, and civic activism., they reshape how individuals communicate, mobilize, and advocate for social change, creating new opportunities and challenges for civic involvement. This intersection of AI and digital participation reflects a profound shift in how citizens interact with one another and with the institutions that govern their lives, enabling a more dynamic and interconnected form of engagement that has the potential to drive social progress. Heart participation is the ability of AI algorithms (Paramasivam Selvakumar., et al, 2024). These algorithms can identify trends, sentiments, and emerging issues in real-time, providing insights that can inform both individual and collective actions. For instance, AI can help activists gauge public sentiment around specific topics, allowing them to tailor their messaging and strategies to resonate with broader audiences. This data-driven approach empowers citizens to be more effective in their advocacy efforts, as they can leverage insights gleaned from social media analytics to mobilize support and raise awareness about pressing social issues. Moreover, AI technologies enhance dissemination that foster engagement. Machine learning algorithms enable platforms to personalize users' feeds, promoting interests. While personalization is more meaningful interactions, it also raises concerns about polarizing public discourse and creating divisions among different social groups. Therefore, the challenge lies in balancing personalization and digital participation to foster constructive dialogue rather than exacerbating societal divides. AI-driven tools facilitating civic activism streamlining organization mobilization efforts. For instance, chatbots and automated messaging systems can efficiently disseminate information to supporters, provide updates on events, and encourage participation in campaigns. These technologies enable grassroots organizations to scale their outreach efforts without overwhelming their human resources. Identification of potential allies and collaborators, enabling activists to build coalitions across different communities and causes (Matveieva O., 2024).

Digital participation is also a significant ethical must. One major concern is the potential for misinformation and manipulation of public opinion. AI algorithms can be exploited to spread false narratives or disinformation, undermining the integrity of public discourse. This challenge is exacerbated by the speed at which information spreads on social media, making it difficult for users to discern fact from fiction. To combat this issue, digital literacy and critical thinking skills must be prioritized in educational initiatives, empowering individuals to navigate the complexities of online information and engage in informed discussions. Additionally, monitoring analyzing online activity privacy (Tyagi A K., et al, 2024). The collection of data on individuals' behaviors and preferences, while beneficial for understanding public sentiment, can also infringe upon personal privacy rights. As organizations harness AI technologies to track engagement and activism, transparency in data handling practices is crucial. Users should be informed about how their data is used, ensuring that they have agency over their digital footprints. Building trust in AI-driven systems will be essential for encouraging ongoing participation and mitigating concerns about surveillance and data misuse. The role of AI in digital participation also raises questions about inclusivity and accessibility. While AI technologies can enhance engagement, disparities in access to technology can limit participation for marginalized communities. Or geographic location can leverage AI-driven tools for civic engagement is vital for fostering equitable participation. Efforts to literacy underrepresented groups will landscape, empowering all citizens to engage meaningfully in civic life. Looking to the future, the potential for AI-driven digital participation is vast, but it requires a collaborative effort among stakeholders to maximize its benefits while mitigating risks. Policymakers, technologists, educators, and activists must work together to establish frameworks that prioritize ethical considerations, inclusivity, and user empowerment design fostering, society technology civic engagement social activism, ultimately leading to a more vibrant and participatory democracy (Kozinets R V., et al, 2024). In conclusion, AI-driven digital participation is reshaping the landscape of social media, online engagement, and civic activism, presenting both opportunities and challenges for individuals and communities.

AI-ENHANCED DIGITAL LITERACY: CRITICAL THINKING, MEDIA LITERACY, AND ONLINE SAFETY

The integration of digital literacy introduced a transformative approach to enhancing critical thinking, media literacy, and online safety. As technology evolves, the digital environment becomes increasingly complex, necessitating a robust framework for individuals to navigate information, discern truth from misinformation, and protect themselves in an online world. AI technologies offer innovative solutions that can bolster digital literacy, equipping users with the skills needed to engage responsibly and effectively in digital spaces. At the foundation of AI-enhanced digital literacy is the need for critical thinking skills (Ramakrishnan T.,et al, 2022). In an age where information is abundant and often overwhelming, the ability to evaluate sources, assess credibility, and synthesize diverse viewpoints is paramount. Providing tools that analyze information sources, flagging potential biases or misinformation. By fostering a deeper understanding of media dynamics, individuals can become more responsible content creators and consumers, contributing to healthier online ecosystems. Significant online by identifying digital engagement. As cyber threats continue to evolve, AI technologies can monitor online interactions for signs of harassment, bullying, or predatory behavior. Platforms increasingly algorithms detect pond to harmful content, enabling timely intervention and support for affected users (Danry V M., 2023).

However, while AI offers promising advancements in digital literacy, must. The reliance on AI tools for information processing can inadvertently lead to an overreliance on technology, potentially diminishing users' critical thinking skills. To counteract this risk, educational initiatives must emphasize the importance of human judgment in conjunction with AI-driven insights. Encouraging users to question AI-generated content and engage in active analysis fosters a balanced approach that leverages technology while cultivating independent thinking. The challenge of misinformation and disinformation underscores the need for comprehensive technologies vital combat these issues by providing tools that help users identify misleading content (Georgopoulou M S., et al, 2024). For example, AI algorithms can analyze the language, sentiment, and source credibility of information, offering users insights into potential biases or inaccuracies. Individuals' skills and identify misinformation, AI can help create a more informed and discerning public. Furthermore, as digital literacy becomes increasingly integrated into formal education, the role of educators in guiding AI-enhanced learning experiences is crucial. Teachers can leverage AI technologies to create engaging and interactive curricula that promote critical thinking and media literacy. Professional development programs should also focus on equipping skills needed tools, ensuring that they can foster a culture of digital literacy in their classrooms. Looking ahead, digital literacy is vast, but it varies. Policymakers, educators, developers, and civil society organizations must work together to establish frameworks that prioritize ethical considerations, inclusivity, and user empowerment in digital literacy initiatives. By fostering a culture of responsible AI use, society can harness the power of technology to promote critical thinking, media literacy, and online safety, ultimately leading to a more informed and engaged citizenry (Singh E., et al, 2024).

DIGITAL CITIZENSHIP IN THE GLOBAL SOUTH: CHALLENGES, OPPORTUNITIES, AND AI-DRIVEN SOLUTIONS

Presents a multifaceted landscape characterized by distinct challenges and opportunities, especially in the context of rapidly advancing technologies like artificial intelligence (AI). As nations in this region navigate the complexities of digital inclusion, socio-economic disparities, and cultural dynamics, the role of digital citizenship becomes increasingly pivotal. It encompasses not only the rights and responsibilities of individuals in the digital realm but also the broader societal implications of digital engagement. AI-driven solutions hold the promise of addressing some of these challenges, yet they also introduce new complexities that must be carefully managed (Calzada I., 2020). Digital citizenship in South digital divide. Access to reliable internet and digital technologies remains uneven, often skewed by socio-economic status, geographic location, and infrastructural limitations. In rural areas, where connectivity is often scarce, individuals may lack the means to engage fully in digital platforms, hindering their ability to participate in civic life, access educational resources, or engage in economic opportunities. Transformative bridging divide enabling more efficient resource allocation and fostering innovative connectivity solutions. For example, AI can analyze learners' engagement and comprehension levels, tailoring educational content to improve digital literacy. This approach not only enhances individual capabilities but also promotes critical thinking and responsible digital citizenship (Vijayakumar G., et al, 2024).

However, the integration of AI solutions in promoting digital citizenship also raises ethical concerns. For instance, the use of AI in monitoring and controlling online activities can lead to increased surveillance and potential abuses of power. Governments and corporations may misuse AI technologies or, undermine the very essence of democratic engagement. To counter these risks, ethical policies prioritize human rights and protect individual freedoms. Stakeholders, including civil society organizations and policymakers, must work together to enhance, rather than hinder, digital citizenship. The opportunities presented by AI in the Global South are also significant. As countries embrace digital transformation, AI can drive economic growth, innovation, and social development (Medrado A., et al, 2024). For instance,

AI-powered platforms can facilitate access to markets for local entrepreneurs, enabling them to connect with customers globally and expand their businesses. In sectors such as agriculture, AI can enhance productivity through precision farming techniques that optimize resource use and improve yields. By harnessing AI for economic empowerment, individuals can better their livelihoods and contribute to the overall development of their communities. Despite the benefits, ensuring that AI-driven solutions are inclusive and equitable is crucial. The implementation of AI technologies inequalities if marginalized groups are not adequately considered in the design and deployment processes. To address this, inclusive design practices that involve must be prioritized. Engaging local communities in co-creating technologies ensures that the tools developed are relevant and responsive to their needs, ultimately enhancing digital citizenship for all. As digital citizenship evolves, imperative digital engagement emphasizes ethical considerations, respect for diversity, and collaborative problem-solving. Initiatives aimed at promoting digital citizenship should prioritize education, encouraging individuals to become active participants in shaping their digital environments. This includes fostering critical awareness of the implications of their online actions, promoting civic responsibilities, and encouraging engagement in democratic processes. In conclusion, digital citizenship in the Global South presents challenges and opportunities, in the context of AI-driven solutions (Ben Dhaou S., et al, 2024). While significant barriers such as the digital divide, limited digital literacy, and socio-political constraints persist, AI technologies offer innovative pathways for empowerment, engagement, and development

AI and Digital Citizenship in Europe: GDPR, Data Protection, and Human Rights

(AI) digital citizenship in Europe is profoundly shaped by frameworks such as, which human rights. Prevalent life, implications for individual privacy, data sovereignty, and ethical governance are increasingly critical. Digital citizenship in this context refers not only to the rights and responsibilities of individuals in the digital space but also to how these rights are protected in the face of rapidly evolving technologies. The GDPR serves as a foundational pillar, providing a comprehensive legal framework designed to safeguard personal data and ensure that individuals maintain control over their information in an increasingly data-driven world. The GDPR, enacted in May 2018, was a landmark regulation that significantly altered across Europe (Calzada I., et al, 2020). It establishes strict guidelines for data handling, reinforcing the principles of transparency, accountability, and user consent. By promoting fairness and accountability in AI applications, the GDPR supports a vision of digital citizenship that is inclusive and equitable, safeguarding the rights of all individuals (Van Dijk N., et al, 2021). The enforcement of the GDPR has significant implications for how businesses and public institutions approach AI development and deployment. Organizations must prioritize compliance, which often involves reevaluating and investing. This necessity not only protects individual rights but also fosters a competitive advantage for organizations that prioritize ethical data practices. By adopting a proactive approach to data protection, businesses, enhance their reputations by fostering loyalty. This dynamic illustrates how adherence to the GDPR can catalyze innovation, encouraging organizations to develop AI solutions that respect user rights while driving growth.

The evolving discourse around digital citizenship in Europe also highlights the need for continuous education and awareness regarding data rights and AI technologies. As citizens increasingly engage with digital platforms, understanding the implications of data sharing and AI decision-making becomes paramount. Educational initiatives must focus on empowering individuals with knowledge about their rights under the GDPR, and the ethical considerations surrounding data usage. By fostering a culture of informed digital citizenship, European societies can cultivate critical thinkers who actively engage with technology and advocate for their rights in the digital realm. Furthermore, as Europe strives to position itself as a global leader in data protection and digital rights, the regulatory landscape may serve as a model for other regions grappling with similar challenges. The principles enshrined in the GDPR resonate with global human rights frameworks, emphasizing the importance of individual agency, transparency, and accountability. As other jurisdictions explore their own data protection regulations, the lessons learned from the GDPR can inform discussions on how to balance innovation with ethical considerations. This potential for cross-regional influence highlights the significance of Europe's approach to AI and digital citizenship on the global stage. However, the implementation of the GDPR is not without its challenges (Rughini R., et al, 2021). Organizations, especially smaller businesses and startups, may struggle with the complexities of compliance, potentially stifling innovation.

Digital Citizenship in Asia-Pacific: Cultural, Social, and Economic Implications of AI

Digital citizenship in the Asia-Pacific region is increasingly influenced by the rise of artificial intelligence (AI), shaping cultural, social, and economic landscapes in profound ways. As countries in this diverse region embrace digital transformation, the concept of digital citizenship expands to encompass not only the rights and responsibilities of individuals in the digital realm but also the broader societal implications of AI technologies. Daily life has unique opportunities and varies significantly across different cultural and socio-economic contexts, making the discourse around digital citizenship both complex and critical. Culturally, the Asia-

Pacific region is characterized by a rich tapestry of languages, traditions, and values that influence how digital citizenship is perceived and enacted. In many countries, traditional norms surrounding community, family, and authority significantly impact individuals' engagement with digital technologies (Yue A., 2022). For instance, in collectivist cultures, the emphasis on community well-being can shape how citizens utilize social media and other online platforms for civic engagement. Initiatives aimed at improving digital literacy and access to technology are essential in empowering all citizens to engage meaningfully in the digital landscape (Chen Y C., et al, 2024). Economically, AI presents both opportunities and challenges that influence digital citizenship across the Asia-Pacific region. The potential for AI to drive economic growth is significant, with many countries investing in AI research and development to enhance competitiveness and innovation. In sectors such as agriculture, healthcare, and finance, AI applications can improve efficiency and productivity, creating new job opportunities and economic pathways. However, also raises the future of work. As automation becomes more prevalent, individuals must adapt to changing job markets, necessitating a focus on reskilling and upskilling initiatives. Digital citizenship in this context includes advocating for equitable access to training and education that prepares citizens for the evolving economy.

Moreover, the intersection of AI and digital citizenship in the Asia-Pacific region is critical. Issues data, and surveillance, are paramount as governments and corporations increasingly rely on AI for decision-making. Citizens must navigate a landscape where their data is continuously collected, analyzed, and utilized, often without full awareness or consent. The implications of this dynamic are profound, as it challenges individuals' autonomy and agency in the digital realm. Digital citizenship is essential to the use of technology. Establishing robust legal frameworks that protect individual rights and promote ethical AI practices will be crucial in ensuring technological advancements. In the context of civic engagement, technologies can facilitate greater participation in democratic processes. For instance, AI-driven tools can enhance voter engagement by providing personalized information about candidates and policies, helping citizens make informed decisions. Social media platforms powered by AI algorithms can amplify marginalized voices, enabling grassroots movements to gain traction (Hara M., 2024). International cooperation and knowledge-sharing can facilitate the exchange of best practices and innovative solutions to common challenges, ultimately contributing to a more equitable and inclusive digital landscape (Mahadev Madgule., et al, 2023). In conclusion, digital citizenship is profoundly shaped cultural, social, economic implications of AI. As individuals navigate the complexities of digital engagement, the interplay between technology and citizenship becomes increasingly critical. While AI presents significant opportunities for enhancing connectivity, economic growth, and civic participation, addressed. By prioritizing inclusivity, transparency, and responsible use of technology, stakeholders can work together to foster a vibrant digital citizenship culture that empowers individuals and strengthens communities across the region. Ultimately, the integration of AI into the fabric of digital citizenship societal promotes human rights and contributes to the collective well-being of the Asia-Pacific community in an increasingly interconnected world.

AI AND DIGITAL RIGHTS: FREEDOM OF EXPRESSION, INFORMATION, AND ASSEMBLY

The relationship between artificial intelligence (AI) and digital rights is increasingly critical in the context of freedom of expression, information, and assembly. As AI technologies permeate various aspects of daily life, they have exercised their rights digital sphere. The rapid evolution of AI applications, including social media algorithms, content moderation systems, and surveillance technologies, presents both opportunities and challenges for protecting fundamental freedoms. Understanding this interplay is vital for ensuring that technological advancements do not undermine democratic values but instead promote a more inclusive and open society. At the heart of digital rights is the principle of In an era dominated by digital communication, AI plays a dual role (Dias Oliva T., 2020). On one hand, AI-powered platforms facilitate the dissemination of information and share and engage discourse on a global scale. The right to information is another critical dimension of digital rights affected by AI technologies. Access to accurate and timely information is essential for informed citizenship, enabling individuals to participate meaningfully in democratic processes (Benedek W., et al, 2020). However, the algorithms that govern content delivery can create echo chambers and filter bubbles, predominantly distort public discourse, and limit access to diverse perspectives. To promote a more informed citizenry, stakeholders must prioritize algorithmic transparency and accountability, individuals' broad information sources. Initiatives aimed at promoting media literacy can also empower users to critically evaluate information and recognize biases in AI-driven content delivery.

Design technologies can help mitigate biases and ensure that digital rights are upheld for all individuals. The global nature of the internet complicates the landscape of digital rights, as differing national laws and regulations can lead to tensions around freedom of expression, information, and assembly. While some countries prioritize protecting these rights, others impose stringent restrictions on digital discourse (Singh B., 2024). The extraterritorial reach of AI technologies raises questions about how to navigate these discrepancies and uphold universal human rights standards. International cooperation and dialogue among governments, civil society, and technology companies are essential in establishing shared principles that protect digital rights across borders. Collaborative efforts can promote best practices and frameworks that respect individual freedoms while posing. In conclusion, the intersection AI and digital rights, particularly concerning freedom of expression, information, and assembly, presents both significant opportunities and formidable challenges. AI technologies enhance democratic participation and empower individuals to engage in public discourse. However, the risks associated with content moderation, surveillance, and algorithmic bias must be addressed to safeguard these fundamental rights. By prioritizing inclusivity, stakeholders can work together to create a digital landscape that respects and upholds the rights of all individuals. Ultimately, fostering a culture of responsible digital engagement is crucial for ensuring empowerment and oppression, contributing to a more open and equitable society.

AI-DRIVEN DIGITAL RESPONSIBILITIES: ONLINE HARASSMENT, CYBERBULLYING, AND HATE SPEECH

The advent of artificial intelligence (AI) in digital spaces has transformed how individuals interact online, presenting both unprecedented opportunities and significant challenges, particularly regarding digital responsibilities. As digital communication platforms become central to personal, social, and professional lives, issues such as online harassment, cyberbullying, and hate speech have emerged as critical concerns. These phenomena not only affect individual well-being but also impact community cohesion and societal values. Understanding the role of AI in addressing these issues is essential for fostering a safer and more responsible digital environment, where the rights and dignity of all users are upheld. Demean individuals in digital spaces. It can manifest through targeted attacks, doxing, and the dissemination of personal information without consent, often exacerbated by the anonymity that the internet provides (Aggarwal A., et al, 2024). AI dual in this context: while they harass, they can also inadvertently facilitate harmful behaviors. For instance, AI algorithms employed in social media platforms can be programmed to identify and flag abusive content. However, the effectiveness of these systems is contingent upon their training data and algorithms. Includes biases or fails to account for context, it may lead to misclassifications or inadequate responses to harassment, leaving victims without the support they need. The nuances of language, context, and intent are difficult for AI systems to navigate, often leading to controversial decisions regarding what constitutes hate speech. Platforms must therefore that in moderating the systems are transparent and accountable (Louis F., et al, 2024). Central AI and responsibilities challenge systems effectively on which skewed and unrepresentative, resulting in reinforcing existing biases and inequalities. For instance, studies have shown that certain AI models may disproportionately flag content from specific demographic groups as harmful while failing to adequately address hate speech directed toward them. To combat this, developers must prioritize diversity in data collection and continuously audit their algorithms to identify and rectify biases. Engaging with affected communities in the design process tools more equitable and reflective of the diverse realities of digital users.

Moreover, the responsibility of combating online harassment, cyberbullying, and hate speech extends beyond technology companies to include individual users, educators, and policymakers. Digital citizenship education fosters responsible online. The international dimension of online harassment, cyberbullying, and hate speech also complicates the discourse around digital responsibilities (Rathod S B., et al, 2024). The internet transcends geographical boundaries, and the diverse cultural norms and legal frameworks across countries can lead to conflicting approaches to content moderation. While some nations may impose strict regulations to combat hate speech, others may prioritize free speech, leading to tensions in global digital interactions. Establishing international norms and cooperative frameworks that respect human rights while addressing the challenges posed by AI and online behavior is essential for fostering a more cohesive digital ecosystem. In conclusion, the intersection of AI and digital responsibilities surrounding online harassment, cyberbullying, and hate speech presents a complex landscape requiring collaborative efforts from technology companies, users, educators, and policymakers. While AI has the potential to enhance our ability to identify and address harmful behavior, it is not a panacea.

AI AND DIGITAL GOVERNANCE: POLICY, REGULATION, AND ETHICS

Various sectors prompted a re-evaluation of digital governance, focusing on the critical dimensions of policy, regulation, and ethics. As AI technologies become increasingly embedded in everyday life, their impact extends beyond mere technological advancement to fundamentally influence societal structures, economic models, and individual rights. The need for robust digital governance frameworks is more urgent than ever, as governments, corporations, and civil society grapple with the complexities and implications of AI deployment in areas such as public service delivery, data management, and ethical considerations (De Almeida P G R., et al, 2021). Effective digital governance must begin with the establishment of comprehensive policies multifaceted. Policymakers are tasked with creating frameworks that not only promote innovation and economic growth but also safeguard fundamental human rights. These policies should prioritize transparency, accountability, and inclusivity, ensuring systems dignity and public trust. For instance, guidelines should be developed to algorithms interpretable, enabling users and stakeholders to foster public AI technologies and mitigate concerns about opaque decision-making processes. Regulation governance, as it provides the legal framework necessary to manage the deployment of AI in society. Current regulatory approaches vary widely across regions, reflecting differing cultural, political, and economic contexts. Some countries have moved quickly to enact AI-specific legislation, while others rely on existing laws governing data protection and privacy. Landmark, establishing stringent guidelines for data handling and privacy that directly impact AI applications. This regulatory framework not only enhances individual rights but also encourages organizations to adopt ethical AI practices, promoting responsible innovation. However, effective regulation must be safe (Larsson S., 2020). Overregulation can stifle technological advancement, while underregulation can lead to misuse and harm.

The ethical considerations surrounding AI are paramount in discussions of digital governance. Criminal justice, employment, and ethical frameworks must be established their frameworks address fairness and transparency, and emphasize decision-making processes. For example, predictive policing is concerned about discrimination, as historical data can perpetuate systemic inequalities. Addressing these ethical dilemmas requires a commitment to diversity in AI development teams and an inclusive approach that considers the perspectives of marginalized communities. Furthermore, as AI technologies continue to evolve, the concept of ethical governance must also adapt. The rapid pace of technological change can outstrip regulatory frameworks, leading to gaps in oversight and accountability. Agile governance mechanisms that can quickly respond to emerging challenges will be essential in maintaining the balance between innovation and ethical considerations. This may involve in an environment, for iterative learning adaptation is widespread (Schiff D., et al, 2020).

AI-DRIVEN DIGITAL INCLUSION: ACCESSIBILITY, DISABILITY, AND SOCIAL JUSTICE

(AI) digital platforms advancing digital inclusion, particularly concerning accessibility for individuals with disabilities and broader social justice goals. As technology continues to permeate every aspect of life, ensuring that AI-driven innovations are accessible to all becomes a paramount concern. Digital inclusion is not merely about access to technology; it encompasses the ability to effectively engage with digital content and services, participate in online communities, and benefit from the opportunities that technology affords. This is particularly critical for people with disabilities, who often face systemic barriers that hinder their ability to navigate the digital landscape. AI technologies hold transformative potential for enhancing accessibility (Almufareh M F., et al, 2024). For instance, machine learning algorithms can analyze user interactions to tailor experiences for individuals with diverse needs, creating customized interfaces that simplify navigation. AI-driven solutions should therefore be designed with an intersectional lens that considers how different factors intersect to affect access and participation (Chemnad K., et al, 2024). For example, while AI can facilitate access to information and services, it is vital to ensure that these technologies are available in multiple languages and culturally relevant contexts, thereby addressing the needs of diverse populations. Digital literacy is another critical component of AI-driven inclusion. Access to technology does not equate to the ability to use it effectively. Therefore, initiatives that focus on enhancing digital literacy among underrepresented groups are essential. Individuals needed to navigate AI-driven tools, enabling them to engage meaningfully with digital platforms. This empowerment is particularly important for people with disabilities, who may require tailored educational resources to understand and utilize AI technologies effectively. By investing in digital literacy initiatives, stakeholders can foster greater participation and ensure that marginalized communities are not left behind in the digital revolution. These organizations can amplify the voices of marginalized communities, highlighting their experiences and needs in the digital space. By fostering partnerships between tech companies, governments, and advocacy groups, stakeholders can collaboratively address systemic barriers and create inclusive policies that promote equity also the importance of accessibility in context thereby fostering a culture of inclusivity and support for marginalized populations (Muhammad F., et al, 2024). Finally, as AI technologies continue to evolve, it is essential to maintain a commitment to continuous improvement and adaptation.

AI-POWERED DIGITAL EDUCATION: PERSONALIZED LEARNING, ACCESSIBILITY, AND EQUITY

Digital transforms traditional learning paradigms by enhancing personalized learning, improving accessibility, and promoting equity among diverse student populations. As educational institutions increasingly adopt AI-driven technologies, they can create more for each student. This individualized approach not only fosters a deeper engagement with educational content but educational journeys, paving the educational landscape. Educational tools provide immediate feedback, a critical element in the learning process (Goel A., 2020). Traditional assessment methods often delay feedback, hindering students' ability to identify areas for improvement. In contrast, AI systems can deliver instant evaluations of student work, allowing learners to reflect on their performance and make necessary adjustments almost immediately. This timely feedback loop enhances the learning experience, promoting a growth mindset and encouraging students to embrace challenges as opportunities for development. Accessibility is another key difference in education. For students with disabilities, traditional educational settings often pose challenges that can hinder their learning experiences. AI technologies can offer innovative solutions to enhance accessibility. For example, speech recognition software can assist students with physical disabilities in navigating educational platforms, while AI-driven tools can provide real-time captioning. By incorporating these technologies into the educational ecosystem, institutions can create more inclusive environments where all students have equal opportunities to succeed (Ayeni O O., et al, 2024). However, accessibility that these technologies are designed with a focus on equity. Remains marginalized communities, where access to technology and reliable internet connectivity can be limited. AI-driven educational tools must be accessible not only in terms of usability but also in their availability to diverse student populations. This means that initiatives aimed at integrating AI in education must prioritize resources for underfunded schools and communities, ensuring that all students can benefit from personalized learning experiences. This approach not only enriches the learning experience but also promotes a more comprehensive understanding of the world among students. Collaboration among various stakeholders is also critical for advancing AI-powered digital education. Partnerships between technology companies, educational institutions, policymakers, and community organizations implementation effective (Pawar P., 2023).

AI-DRIVEN DIGITAL HEALTH: TELEMEDICINE, HEALTH INFORMATICS, AND PATIENT EMPOWERMENT

In digital health the landscape of healthcare delivery, enhancing telemedicine, health informatics, and patient empowerment. As healthcare systems increasingly adopt AI-driven technologies, they are not only improving the efficiency of services but also transforming the patient experience. By leveraging AI's capabilities, healthcare providers can offer more personalized health management. Telemedicine has become a cornerstone of modern healthcare, particularly highlighted by the global health challenges posed by AI playing a pivotal in facilitating remote consultations, assess management from the comfort of their homes. Through AI-enhanced visits minimizing exposure to infectious diseases (Ahmadi A., 2024). As a result, patients benefit from a more comprehensive approach to care that prioritizes their individual health needs. Health informatics, the intersection of information science and healthcare, is another area significantly impacted by AI. The ability to collect, analyze, and leverage health data is crucial for improving clinical outcomes and operational efficiency. AI can process health studies and genomic information to support clinical decision-making (Bhambri P., et al, 2024). By providing healthcare professionals with evidence-based recommendations tailored to individual patients, AI enhances diagnostic accuracy and treatment efficacy. Moreover, disparities in access to digital health technologies is essential for promoting equity in healthcare (Ramachander A., et al, 2025). While AI has the potential to enhance care delivery, marginalized communities may face barriers to accessing these innovations.

THE GLOBAL IMPACT OF AI ON DIGITAL CITIZENSHIP - CHALLENGES, OPPORTUNITIES, AND FUTURE DIRECTIONS

The global impact of artificial intelligence (AI) on digital citizenship is multi-faceted, encompassing a range of challenges and opportunities that are reshaping how individuals interact with technology, engage in civic activities, and digital. As societies increasingly rely on life, education, and healthcare for governance and social interaction, understanding the implications of these technologies for digital citizenship becomes crucial. Digital citizenship refers to the ability to effectively and ethically engage with digital technologies, and AI is poised to both facilitate and complicate this engagement in profound ways. One of the primary opportunities presented by AI in the realm of digital citizenship is the enhancement of access to information and services (Sreenivasulu A., et al, 2022). This reality raises important questions about consent, autonomy, and the power dynamics inherent in digital interactions. Ensuring the implications of data collection is essential for fostering responsible digital citizenship (Yaqoob I., et al, 2023). Education initiatives must focus on empowering individuals to understand how their data is used and to advocate for greater transparency and accountability from technology companies. The global nature of AI technologies further complicates the landscape of digital citizenship. Different countries have varying approaches to regulating AI and protecting citizens' rights, leading to a patchwork of standards and practices. Requirements, while other regions may lack comprehensive frameworks to safeguard citizens' rights in the digital space. This disparity can create challenges for individuals who engage with cross-border digital services, as they may be subject to different rules and protections depending on where they are located. Collaborative international efforts are essential to establish shared norms and standards used to protect the rights of digital citizens globally.

Another impact of digital citizenship is the potential for enhancing civic engagement through technology. AI-powered platforms can facilitate citizen participation in governance by providing tools for feedback, collaboration, and advocacy. For example, AI can analyze public sentiment on various issues, helping governments understand the concerns and priorities of their constituents. Additionally, AI-driven platforms can enable citizens to engage in participatory budgeting, policy development, and community decision-making processes. By leveraging AI to amplify the voices of citizens, governments can foster more inclusive and responsive governance, which is considered in decision-making processes (Eom S J., et al, 2022). Additionally, educational institutions should prioritize curricula that promote digital literacy, critical thinking, and ethical considerations related to AI use (Chen L L., et al, 2021). In conclusion, the global impact of AI on digital citizenship presents both significant challenges and promising opportunities. The digital landscape is essential to prioritize considerations, and digital literacy, and ensure equitable access for all individuals. Through informed engagement, collaboration, and advocacy, societies' potential digital citizenship is empowered. Ultimately, the goal should be to create a digital ecosystem that upholds democratic values, promotes inclusivity, and empowers citizens to thrive in an increasingly interconnected world. Through collective efforts, we can shape a future where digital citizenship is characterized by active participation, informed decision-making, and a commitment to social justice in the face of rapid technological advancement.

FUTURE RESEARCH AGENDA: EMERGING THEMES, TRENDS, AND PRIORITIES IN AI-DRIVEN DIGITAL CITIZENSHIP

Is significantly reshaping the concept of digital citizenship, prompting a need for a comprehensive future research agenda that addresses emerging themes, trends, and priorities. As societies grapple with the profound implications of AI technologies, it is crucial to identify and prioritize research areas that will facilitate a deeper understanding of how AI can enhance or hinder the practice of digital citizenship. This agenda should encompass various dimensions, including ethical considerations, civic engagement, the divide, and the role of education in promoting responsible digital behavior. One of the most pressing themes for future research in digital citizenship. Increasingly integrated into everyday life, concerns about bias, privacy, and accountability are paramount (Matusevych T., et al, 2023). This includes examining the infrastructural, socioeconomic, and educational factors that contribute to the digital divide. Future studies could explore successful interventions that have bridged gaps in digital access and how these models can be scaled opportunity a fully digital world (Paramasivam Selvakumar., et al, 2024). Education is pivotal to responsible citizens, making it another vital theme for future research. As AI technologies become more prevalent, there is an urgent need to develop educational frameworks that equip individuals with the skills necessary to navigate the digital landscape effectively. Research should focus on curriculum development that emphasizes digital literacy, critical thinking, and ethical considerations related to AI use. This includes investigating pedagogical approaches that engage students on society their rights as digital citizens. Additionally, exploring the role of informal education and community-based initiatives in fostering digital citizenship skills can provide valuable insights into effective strategies for outreach and engagement.

Furthermore, understanding the role of policy and governance in shaping AI-driven digital citizenship is crucial for future research. As governments seek to regulate AI technologies, it is essential to analyze how policies can promote responsible AI use while safeguarding citizens' rights. Research should examine existing regulatory frameworks and their effectiveness in addressing issues related to privacy, data protection, and algorithmic accountability. Investigating the role of international cooperation in establishing shared norms and standards for AI governance will also be important, given the cross-border nature of digital technologies (Phuangthuean P., et al, 2024). This includes investigating how these technologies can be harnessed to enhance accessibility for individuals with disabilities, as well as examining their potential to empower underrepresented voices in the digital space. As new AI tools and applications emerge, continuous research will be necessary to evaluate their effects on citizenship practices technology inclusivity, and social justice. In the future research agenda on AI-driven digital citizenship should encompass a broad array of themes and priorities (Wolniak R., et al, 2024).

CONCLUSION

The global impact of artificial intelligence (AI) on digital citizenship presents a transformative paradigm that reshapes technology, engages in civic life, and exercises their rights in the digital realm. Social media and governance to education and healthcare—they carry the potential to empower citizens and enhance democratic processes. However, this evolution navigated including ethical considerations, issues of equity and access, and the preservation of individual rights in an age of surveillance and data commodification. To promote positive digital citizenship, it is crucial to prioritize algorithmic personnel and actively work to eliminate biases that may perpetuate existing social inequalities. Stakeholders must advocate for responsible AI practices that prioritize the well-being of citizens, fostering an environment in which individuals can engage with digital platforms confidently and equitably. Moreover, addressing the digital divide remains a critical component of enhancing digital citizenship in the context of AI. Disparities in access to technology and digital literacy threaten to marginalize certain populations, undermining their ability to participate fully in digital life. As AI technologies proliferate, initiatives aimed at improving access to digital tools, internet connectivity, and educational resources must be scaled up, can engage with the digital world. This commitment to inclusivity will help foster a more equitable society, where every citizen has the opportunity to be an informed and active participant in civic life. In conclusion, global digital citizenship presents both significant opportunities and formidable challenges. By embracing a holistic approach that emphasizes ethical considerations, equitable access, educational empowerment, and collaborative governance, societies can work towards cultivating a form of digital citizenship that is inclusive, informed, and resilient. An driven world, the collective responsibility lies with all stakeholders to ensure that digital citizenship evolves in a manner that enhances civic engagement, promotes social justice, and safeguards individual rights. Ultimately, the goal should be to create a digital ecosystem where all citizens are empowered to engage meaningfully with technology and participate actively in democratic processes, this vision requires sustained commitment, innovative thinking, and a proactive approach transformative for benefit.

REFERENCES

Aggarwal, A., & Gaur, S. (2024). *"Applying Artificial Intelligence to Explore Online Harassment and Cyberbullying Prevention." Impact of AI on Advancing Women's Safety*. IGI Global.

Ahmadi A, (2024). Digital Health Transformation: Leveraging AI for Monitoring and Disease Management. International Journal of BioLife Sciences.

Almufareh M F, Kausar S, & Humayun M, (2024). A Conceptual Model for Inclusive Technology: Advancing Disability Inclusion through Artificial Intelligence. Journal of Disability and Rehabilitation.

Awad A I, Babu A, Barka E, & Shuaib K, (2024). AI-Powered Biometrics for Internet of Things Security: A Review and Future Vision. Journal of Information Security and Applications.

Ayeni, O. O., Al Hamad, N. M., & Chisom, O. N. (2024). *AI in Education: A Review of Personalized Learning and Educational Technology*. GSC Advanced Research Journal.

Ben Dhaou, S., Isagah, T., Distor, C., & Ruas, I. (2024). *Global Assessment of Responsible Artificial Intelligence in Cities: Research and Recommendations to Leverage AI for People-Centred Smart Cities*. United Nations University.

Benedek, W., & Kettemann, M. C. (2020). *Freedom of Expression and the Internet: Updated and Revised 2nd Edition.*

Bhambri, P., & Khang, A. (2024). *Machine Learning Advancements in E-Health: Transforming Digital Healthcare. Diagnostics for a High-Tech Healthcare*. IGI Global. DOI: 10.4018/979-8-3693-2105-8.ch012

Calzada, I. (2020). Pandemic Citizenship Amidst Stateless Algorithmic Nations: Digital Rights and Technological Sovereignty at Stake. *SSRN*.

Calzada, I., & Almirall, E. (2020). *Data Ecosystems for Protecting European Citizens' Digital Rights. Transforming Government: People*. Process, Technology, Emerald.

Chemnad, K., & Othman, A. (2024). Digital Accessibility in the Era of Artificial Intelligence—Bibliometric Analysis and Systematic Review. *Frontiers in Artificial Intelligence*, 7, 1349668. DOI: 10.3389/frai.2024.1349668 PMID: 38435800

Chen, L. L., Mirpuri, S., Rao, N., & Law, N. (2021). Conceptualization and Measurement of Digital Citizenship Across Disciplines. Educational Research Review. DOI: 10.1016/j.edurev.2021.100379

Chen, Y. C., & Kim, S. (2024). *Introduction to the Special Issue: Digital Transformation of Government and the Asia Pacific Region*. Asia Pacific Journal of Public Administration, Taylor & Francis.

Danry V M. (2023). AI Enhanced Reasoning: Augmenting Human Critical Thinking with AI Systems.

De Almeida, P. G. R., Dos Santos, C. D., & Farias, J. S. (2021). Artificial Intelligence Regulation: A Framework for Governance. Ethics and Information Technology, Springer.

Dias Oliva, T. (2020). Content Moderation Technologies: Applying Human Rights Standards to Protect Freedom of Expression. Human Rights Law Review, Oxford University Press.

Ekman, M. (2021). *Learning Deep Learning: Theory and Practice of Neural Networks*. Computer Vision, Natural Language Processing, and Transformers Using TensorFlow.

Eom, S. J., & Lee, J. (2022). Digital Government Transformation in Turbulent Times: Responses, Challenges, and Future Direction. Government Information Quarterly, Elsevier.

Georgopoulou, M. S., & Krouska, A. (2024). *Redefining the Concept of Literacy: A DigCompEdu Extension for Critical Engagement with AI Tools. Computer*. IEEE Explore.

Goel A. (2020). AI-Powered Learning: Making Education Accessible, Affordable, and Achievable. arXiv preprint arXiv.

Hara M. (2024). Roles of Artificial Intelligence in Education for Sustainable Development in Asia-Pacific Contexts. Global Journal of Business and Integral Security.

Hristovska A. (2023). Fostering Media Literacy in the Age of AI: Examining the Impact on Digital Citizenship and Ethical Decision-Making. КАИРОС: Журнал за медиуми и комуникации.

Kozinets R V, & Seraj-Aksit M. (2024). Everyday Activism: An AI-Assisted Netnography of a Digital Consumer Movement. Journal of Marketing Management.

Larsson, S. (2020). On the Governance of Artificial Intelligence through Ethics Guidelines. Asian Journal of Law and Society. DOI: 10.1017/als.2020.19

Lee, S. (2023). *Discourses of Digital Citizenship in K-12 Education in South Korea*. The Citizenship Education of The Digital Era.

Ling, Y., Wu, F., Dong, S., Feng, Y., & Karypis, G. (2023). International Workshop on Multimodal Learning-2023 Theme: Multimodal Learning with Foundation Models. *Proceedings of the 29*th. DOI: 10.1145/3580305.3599208

Louis, F., & Mohamed, S. (2024). *Cyberbullying and Online Harassment: A Multifaceted Examination of Digital Platform Violence*. ResearchGate.

Mahadev Madgule, N. (2023). Mechanical properties and microstructure of activated TIG welded similar joints of Inconel alloys by desirability approaches. *Materials Today: Proceedings*, 77, 528–533. DOI: 10.1016/j.matpr.2022.12.250

Matusevych, T., & Zadorozhna, O. (2023). *Innovative Approaches in Citizenship Education Research: Conceptual Perspectives and Ethical Cautions*. Studia Warmińskie.

Matveieva O. (2024). A Gender Perspective on the Role of Technology in Democratic Development through Wartime Civic Engagement. Journal of Gender Studies.

Medrado, A., & Verdegem, P. (2024). *Participatory Action Research in Critical Data Studies: Interrogating AI from a South-North Approach. Big Data & Society*. SAGE Publications.

Mohammed, I. A. (2021). *Identity Management Capability Powered by Artificial Intelligence to Transform the Way User Access Privileges Are Managed, Monitored and Controlled. Journal of Creative Research Thoughts*.

Muhammad F, & Orji C M. (2024). Revolutionizing Education in the Digital Era: The Role of AI in Promoting Inclusivity, Equality, and Ethical Innovation. The American Journal of Social Science and Education.

Olabanji, S. O., Olaniyi, O. O., & Adigwe, C. S. (2024). AI for Identity and Access Management (IAM) in the Cloud: Exploring the Potential of Artificial Intelligence to Improve User Authentication, Authorization, and Access Control. *SSRN*. DOI: 10.2139/ssrn.4706726

Pawar, P. (2023). *AI-Enhanced Education: Personalized Learning and Educational Technology*. Global Academic Press.

Phuangthuean, P., & Nuansang, J. (2024). The Transforming Public Administration: The Role of AI in Shaping the Future. *Journal of Multidisciplinary Research*.

Ramachander, A., & Gowri, D. P. (2025). The Future of Digital Health in Transforming Healthcare. Digital Technology in Public Health and Healthcare, Elsevier. DOI: 10.1016/B978-0-443-22270-2.00021-6

Ramakrishnan, T., Mohan Gift, M. D., Chitradevi, S., Jegan, R., & Subha Hency Jose, P. (2022). Study of Numerous Resins Used in Polymer Matrix Composite Materials. Advances in Materials Science and Engineering. DOI: 10.1155/2022/1088926

Rathod, S. B., & Khandizod, A. G. (2024). *Cybersecurity Beyond the Screen: Tackling Online Harassment and Cyberbullying. AI Tools and Applications in Healthcare, Education, and Cybersecurity.* IGI Global. DOI: 10.4018/979-8-3693-1435-7.ch004

Rughini , R., Rughini , C., & Vulpe, S. N. (2021). From Social Netizens to Data Citizens: Variations of GDPR Awareness in 28 European Countries. Computer Law & Security Review.

Schiff, D., Biddle, J., Borenstein, J., & Laas, K. (2020). What's Next for AI Ethics, Policy, and Governance? A Global Overview. ACM Conference on AI, Ethics, and Society. DOI: 10.1145/3375627.3375804

Selvakumar, P., Mariappan, P., Shunmugam, S., Paul, R., & Jabez, S. (2024). Removal of chemicals from effluent using photobioreactor technology to improve environmental and health impacts. *Zeitschrift für Physikalische Chemie*, 2024(7), 1295–1302. Advance online publication. DOI: 10.1515/zpch-2023-0450

Selvakumar, P., Palanisamy, S. K., Cinthaikinian, S., Palanisamy, V., Mariappan, R., & Selvakumar, P. K. (2024). Biosensors and its diverse applications in healthcare systems. *Zeitschrift für Physikalische Chemie*, 2024. Advance online publication. DOI: 10.1515/zpch-2023-0406

Sharma S, Kar AK, Gupta MP, & Dwivedi YK, (2022). Digital Citizen Empowerment: A Systematic Literature Review of Theories and Development Models. Journal for Development.

Singh, B. (2024). *Cherish Data Privacy and Human Rights in the Digital Age: Harmonizing Innovation and Individual Autonomy. Human Rights, Social Responsibility, and Digital Ethics.* IGI Global. DOI: 10.4018/979-8-3693-3334-1.ch007

Singh, E., Vasishta, P., & Singla, A. (2024). *AI-Enhanced Education: Exploring the Impact of AI Literacy on Generation Z's Academic Performance in Northern India.* Quality Assurance in Education, Emerald.

Sreenivasulu, A., & Manimozhi, T. (2022). The Model of Smart Sensing Device For Sensitive Nanoclusters Modification in Sensing Properties. 2022 2nd International Conference on Advance Computing and Innovative Technologies in Engineering (ICACITE), 1043-1047. DOI: 10.1109/ICACITE53722.2022.9823846

Sugumaran, K. M. D., Pandiyarajan V., Y. B S, Selvakumar P., & M. S. (2024). Analysis of Electromyography Signals for Control of Mechanical Prosthesis using Machine Learning Techniques. 2024 2nd International Conference on Intelligent Data Communication Technologies and Internet of Things (IDCIoT), 1059-1067. DOI: 10.1109/IDCIoT59759.2024.10467707

Torfi A, Shirvani R A, Keneshloo Y, & Tavaf N. (2020). Natural Language Processing Advancements by Deep Learning: A Survey. arXiv preprint arXiv.

Tyagi, A. K., & Lakkshmanan, A. (2024). The Future of Artificial Intelligence and Machine Learning in Online Social Networking. Online Social Networks. DOI: 10.1002/9781394231126.ch9

Van Dijk, N., Casiraghi, S., & Gutwirth, S. (2021). The 'Ethification' of ICT Governance: Artificial Intelligence and Data Protection in the European Union. Computer Law & Security Review.

Vijayakumar, G., Rajkumar, M., Rajiv Chandar, N., Selvakumar, P., & Duraisamy, R. (2024). Environmentally friendly TDS removal from waste water by electrochemical ion exchange batch-type recirculation (EIR) technique. *Environmental Science. Water Research & Technology*, 10(4), 826–835. DOI: 10.1039/D3EW00793F

Wolniak, R., & Stecuła, K. (2024). *Artificial Intelligence in Smart Cities—Applications, Barriers, and Future Directions: A Review. Smart Cities*. MDPI. DOI: 10.3390/smartcities7030057

Yaqoob, I., Salah, K., Jayaraman, R., & Omar, M. (2023). *Metaverse Applications in Smart Cities: Enabling Technologies, Opportunities, Challenges, and Future Directions. Internet of Things*. Elsevier.

Yue, A. (2022). *From Digital Literacy to Digital Citizenship: Policies, Assessment Frameworks and Programs for Young People in the Asia Pacific*. Media in Asia. DOI: 10.4324/9781003130628-14

Chapter 10
Combating Misinformation in Social Media and News:
A Deep Learning Approach

Usharani Bhimavarapu
https://orcid.org/0000-0002-0246-1420
Department of Computer Science and Engineering, Koneru Lakshmaiah Education Foundation, Vaddeswaram, India

ABSTRACT

Combating misinformation has become a critical challenge in today's information-driven society, particularly with the proliferation of fake news, propaganda, and biased content across various domains. This study explores advanced natural language processing (NLP) techniques, including feature extraction and selection, to analyze and classify datasets such as Q-Prop, ISOT, GRAFN, and PubHealth. The relief algorithm is employed for feature selection to identify the most relevant attributes, enhancing the efficiency of machine learning models. XLNet, a powerful transformer-based model, is utilized for document representation and classification due to its ability to capture bidirectional and long-term contextual dependencies. The proposed methodology demonstrates how robust embeddings, combined with domain-specific datasets and optimized feature selection, can accurately classify content across news, politics, and public health domains.

DOI: 10.4018/979-8-3693-9015-3.ch010

INTRODUCTION

Social media has transformed the way people consume and engage with news, reshaping the global media landscape. Platforms like Twitter, Facebook, Instagram, and YouTube have become primary sources of news dissemination, allowing real-time updates and instant access to information. The interactive nature of social media enables users to share, comment, and discuss news, fostering a participatory approach to information consumption. This shift has democratized news creation and distribution, empowering individuals and smaller organizations to share their perspectives alongside traditional media outlets.

One of the defining characteristics of social media and news is the speed at which information spreads. Breaking news stories can go viral within minutes, reaching millions of users worldwide. This immediacy, however, comes with challenges, such as the difficulty of verifying information, leading to the proliferation of misinformation and fake news. The algorithms that drive social media platforms often prioritize engagement over accuracy, amplifying sensational or polarizing content that may not always align with journalistic integrity.

Social media has also played a pivotal role in citizen journalism, where individuals on the ground document events as they unfold. This has proven invaluable during crises, protests, and natural disasters, offering firsthand accounts and visual evidence. Yet, the lack of editorial oversight raises concerns about biases, incomplete narratives, and ethical considerations in reporting.

Additionally, social media's ability to personalize content through algorithms creates echo chambers, where users are exposed primarily to information that aligns with their views. This can deepen societal polarization, as individuals become less likely to encounter diverse perspectives. Despite these challenges, social media has also been a tool for raising awareness about critical issues, mobilizing social movements, and giving voice to marginalized communities.

The relationship between social media and news is dynamic and multifaceted. While it has expanded access to information and fostered global connectivity, it has also necessitated greater efforts to ensure accuracy, combat misinformation, and promote media literacy. As the boundaries between traditional journalism and social media blur, finding a balance between speed, engagement, and reliability remains a critical goal in the evolving digital age.

Naive Bayes Classifier assumes feature independence, which is unrealistic in natural language contexts, leading to reduced accuracy (Afchar et al., 2018). Support Vector Machines (SVM) struggle with large datasets and non-linear decision boundaries unless kernel methods are used, which increase computational complexity (Ahmed et al., 2018). Random Forest often overfits when the dataset is noisy or imbalanced and lacks interpretability for real-time decision-making (Barrón-Cedeño et al., 2019). Logistic Regression exhibits limited performance on complex datasets with non-linear relationships between features (Bazmi et al., 2023). K-Nearest Neighbors (KNN) is computationally expensive for large datasets due to the need to compute distances for every query (Blakley et al., 1986). Latent Dirichlet Allocation (LDA) focuses on topic modeling rather than misinformation detection and struggles with short or noisy social media texts (Bogonikolos et al., 1999).

Word2Vec ignores word order and out-of-vocabulary words, leading to loss of contextual information (Boneh & Shaw, 1998). TF-IDF (Term Frequency-Inverse Document Frequency) fails to capture semantic relationships and contextual dependencies in text data (Bradford & Marshall, 1999). Long Short-Term Memory (LSTM) requires large, labeled datasets and struggles with very long dependencies, leading to vanishing gradients (Braşoveanu & Andonie, 2019). Convolutional Neural Networks (CNN) are inefficient for capturing long-range dependencies in text and context-heavy inputs (Chen et al., 2022). Recurrent Neural Networks (RNN) face issues with long-term dependency retention and computational inefficiency (Diouf et al., 2019). BERT (Bidirectional Encoder Representations from Transformers) is computationally expensive and resource-intensive, making it less suitable for real-time applications (Dolhansky et al., 2019).

XLNet exhibits complex training and inference pipelines, leading to increased latency in deployment for real-time social media analysis (Goldani et al., 2021). GPT (Generative Pretrained Transformer) tends to hallucinate facts, generating plausible-sounding but incorrect information (Guo et al., 2020). RoBERTa (Robustly Optimized BERT) is similar to BERT in being computationally expensive and requiring fine-tuning for domain-specific tasks (Huh et al., 2018). DistilBERT sacrifices some accuracy and contextual depth compared to full-sized BERT due to its reduced model size (Jing et al., 2023). ALBERT (A Lite BERT) is lightweight but may not capture nuanced misinformation patterns in small datasets (Khan et al., 2021). OpenAI's DALL-E, primarily designed for image-related tasks, has limited application to misinformation in text-heavy datasets (Korshunov & Marcel, 2018).

Deep Belief Networks (DBN) are susceptible to overfitting and require extensive tuning of hyperparameters for effective performance (Korus & Memon, 2019). Transformer-XL is highly resource-intensive, limiting its feasibility for real-time social media monitoring (Kotonya & Toni, 2020). Bidirectional LSTM (BiLSTM), while improving upon LSTM, still struggles with high-dimensional and noisy data prevalent on social media (Li et al., 2023). Graph Neural Networks (GNNs) require graph-based representations, which can be computationally demanding and challenging to construct for textual data (Li et al., 2018). HAN (Hierarchical Attention Networks) performs well for document-level tasks but struggles with noisy, short social media posts (Luvembe et al., 2023). Hybrid approaches, such as CNN-LSTM, involve complex architectures, increasing training time and making them harder to interpret compared to simpler models (Megías et al., 2020).

Multimodal models, which combine text and images, are highly complex in data integration and model tuning, particularly when modalities are imbalanced or sparse (Megías et al., 2022). These limitations highlight the challenges and trade-offs in applying various machine learning and deep learning models to misinformation detection tasks.

To address the limitations of existing models for combating misinformation on social media, a combined approach leveraging feature extraction with GloVe, feature selection with ReliefF, and classification using XLNet provides a robust and comprehensive solution. Feature extraction with GloVe (Global Vectors for Word Representation) mitigates the shortcomings of models like Word2Vec and TF-IDF by embedding words into a high-dimensional vector space while preserving semantic relationships and word order. Unlike Word2Vec, which focuses on local contexts, GloVe captures global co-occurrence statistics, ensuring a more holistic representation of word meanings. This approach also overcomes TF-IDF's inability to capture semantic relationships, enabling the effective representation of social media texts with rich contextual nuances.

Feature selection using ReliefF further refines the input data by identifying the most relevant features, addressing the challenge of noisy, high-dimensional datasets prevalent in social media. Models like Random Forest and KNN often struggle with overfitting and computational inefficiency in such scenarios, but ReliefF reduces redundancy and noise, leading to improved generalization. By selecting features that are most predictive of the target class, it ensures that the classifier focuses on the most informative data, enhancing its performance.

Finally, classification with XLNet overcomes the challenges faced by traditional machine learning models like SVM and neural network architecture such as LSTM and CNN. XLNet, a transformer-based model, effectively captures bidirectional and long-range dependencies in text, addressing issues like vanishing gradients and context-heavy inputs. Its permutation-based training strategy ensures a better understanding of word dependencies, making it highly effective for misinformation detection. While computationally intensive, the combination with ReliefF reduces data complexity, making XLNet's deployment more feasible.

This integrated approach provides scalability, improved semantic understanding, and adaptability, making it well-suited to address the dynamic and noisy nature of misinformation on social media platforms.

MATERIALS AND METHODOLOGY

The methodology focuses on combating misinformation through advanced Natural Language Processing (NLP) techniques. Initially, the data undergoes preprocessing, including text cleaning, tokenization, and lemmatization. Feature extraction is performed using GROOVE techniques, generating robust word embeddings for document representation. The Relief algorithm is employed for feature selection, optimizing the model by identifying the most relevant features. XLNet, a transformer-based model, is used for classifying documents based on contextualized embeddings. Finally, the model's performance is evaluated on datasets from news, politics, and public health domains, showcasing its effectiveness in misinformation detection.

Materials

The dataset collection includes several datasets tailored for diverse domains. The Q-Prop dataset comprises 50,000 news articles labeled as either "legitimate" or "propaganda," making it valuable for analyzing and distinguishing credible news from propaganda. The ISOT dataset contains 44,898 documents, with 23,481 classified as fake and 21,417 as real, along with additional metadata. This dataset is ideal for studying trustworthy versus fake news. The GRAFN dataset consists of 13,000 posts on global political topics, featuring text and metadata sourced from 244 websites, enabling research on political discourse and content analysis. Lastly, the PubHealth dataset focuses on public health and biomedical topics, offering documents with labels and detailed explanations related to public health issues, which can be instrumental in health communication and misinformation studies (Barrón-Cedeño et al.,2019, Ahmed et al.,2018, Risdal et al.,2016, Kotonya et al.,2020).

Preprocessing

The preprocessing of the collected datasets involves several NLP techniques to prepare the text data for analysis and model training. Initially, text cleaning is performed, which includes converting all text to lowercase for uniformity, removing punctuation marks and special characters, and eliminating numbers that do not add meaningful context to the content. Following this, stopwords such as "is," "the," and "and" are removed to reduce noise and focus on the core semantics of the text. Tokenization is then applied to split the text into individual words or subwords, which are essential for further analysis. Lemmatization or stemming is used to reduce words to their base or root forms, ensuring consistency in representation.

To handle metadata, relevant information like timestamps, authorship, or source URLs is extracted and normalized if necessary. For datasets with multiple languages, language detection is performed, and non-English texts are either translated or excluded, depending on the study's focus. For context-aware tasks, sentence segmentation is applied to divide paragraphs into coherent sentences. Additionally, text vectorization techniques, such as TF-IDF or word embeddings like Word2Vec or BERT, are utilized to represent textual data in numerical form for machine learning models. These preprocessing steps collectively ensure the datasets are clean, structured, and ready for effective analysis and model development.

Feature Extraction

Feature extraction from the collected datasets can be enhanced using advanced NLP techniques such as GROOVE (Generalized Robust Optimal Orthonormal Vector Embeddings). GROOVE provides a robust method to transform textual data into meaningful vector representations that capture semantic relationships and contextual nuances. Initially, preprocessed text is tokenized, and embeddings are generated using pretrained models like Word2Vec, GloVe, or BERT, which GROOVE builds upon to refine the representation. GROOVE focuses on creating orthonormal embeddings, ensuring minimal redundancy and maximizing the distinctiveness of features extracted from the text.

The method identifies high-dimensional patterns and relationships, which are projected into lower dimensions while preserving critical information, making the embeddings highly efficient for downstream tasks. This is particularly useful for datasets like Q-Prop and ISOT, where distinguishing between fake and legitimate news requires capturing subtle differences in language patterns. GROOVE also incorporates techniques to handle outliers and noise, making it resilient to variations in text quality. By leveraging GROOVE, robust feature vectors are generated, enabling the datasets to be effectively used for machine learning tasks such as classification, clustering, and sentiment analysis. This approach ensures the extracted features are both meaningful and computationally efficient.

Feature Selection

Feature selection using the Relief algorithm is an effective method for identifying the most relevant features from the datasets, ensuring improved model performance by focusing on the most informative attributes. The Relief algorithm evaluates the relevance of each feature by estimating its ability to distinguish between similar instances of different classes. It operates by randomly selecting instances from the dataset and comparing them with their nearest neighbors (one from the same class and one from a different class) to compute feature weights.

For the collected datasets, the Relief algorithm is applied to the feature vectors generated during preprocessing. Each feature's weight is updated based on its contribution to classifying instances correctly. Features that vary significantly between instances of different classes but remain consistent within the same class are assigned to higher weights. This is particularly valuable for datasets like Q-Prop and ISOT, where distinguishing features such as word usage patterns or metadata attributes can help differentiate between legitimate and fake content.

The Relief algorithm is robust to noisy data and can handle both discrete and continuous features, making it well-suited for diverse datasets like GRAFN and PubHealth, where textual and metadata features may coexist. After applying the algorithm, features with low weights are removed, reducing dimensionality and enhancing model efficiency without compromising accuracy. This selection process ensures that the retained features are the most relevant for subsequent machine learning tasks.

XLNET

XLNet, a generalized autoregressive pretraining method, offers a powerful approach for document representation and classification, especially for datasets like Q-Prop, ISOT, GRAFN, and PubHealth. Unlike BERT, which uses a masked language modeling objective, XLNet employs a permutation-based language modeling approach, allowing it to capture bidirectional context more effectively while preserving the advantages of autoregressive models. This feature is particularly valuable for tasks requiring nuanced understanding and contextual relationships in textual data.

For document representation, XLNet tokenizes the text into subword units and generates contextualized embeddings for each token by considering all possible permutations of token order. This ensures that the model captures dependencies between words in diverse contexts, leading to richer representations. For datasets like Q-Prop and ISOT, where subtle differences in language usage distinguish legitimately from fake or propaganda content, XLNet's ability to model long-term dependencies and nuanced patterns in text makes it highly effective.

Once the document representations are generated, these embeddings are pooled using methods such as mean pooling, max pooling, or CLS-token embeddings to obtain fixed-length vectors. These vectors serve as input features for downstream classification tasks. For example, in the PubHealth dataset, XLNet can leverage its contextual understanding to identify patterns in health-related misinformation, while in the GRAFN dataset, it can differentiate political discourse across multiple contexts.

For classification, the pooled embeddings are passed through a fully connected neural network with a softmax layer to output class probabilities. XLNet's robust handling of out-of-distribution tokens and its ability to learn from large-scale pre-training datasets make it resilient to noisy or incomplete data, a common issue in real-world datasets. Furthermore, when combined with the Relief algorithm for feature selection, XLNet ensures that only the most relevant features contribute to the classification process, enhancing both efficiency and accuracy.

This combination of sophisticated document representation and context-aware classification makes XLNet a powerful tool for analyzing complex textual datasets and achieving high-performance results in classification tasks.

EXPERIMENTAL RESULTS

The experiments were conducted on a system configured with Windows 11, utilizing a robust computational environment to ensure optimal performance during model training and evaluation. The system was equipped with an Intel Core i7 processor, 16GB of RAM, and a dedicated NVIDIA GPU, enabling efficient handling of large datasets and complex NLP models. The software environment included Python 3.8, along with essential libraries such as TensorFlow, PyTorch, and scikit-learn for model implementation and training. This setup ensured seamless execution of the XLNet model, feature extraction processes, and subsequent classification tasks.

Table 1 provides a comparative analysis of feature importance performance across various models for the Q-Prop dataset, which consists of 50,000 news articles. The models were evaluated based on their effectiveness in capturing six key feature categories: Source URL, Sentiment Score, Text Length, Engagement Metrics, Author Information, and Publication Date/Time. Each feature's performance is represented as a normalized score, indicating the model's ability to utilize the feature effectively in misinformation detection.

The Proposed Model (XLNet) demonstrates a balanced performance across all features, with particularly strong scores in Source URL (0.86) and Sentiment Score (0.80), reflecting its capability to extract and leverage nuanced contextual information. It also achieves competitive results for Text Length (0.75) and Engagement Metrics (0.78), showcasing its adaptability to a wide range of data characteristics.

Among the baseline models, GPT-3 excels in overall performance, with the highest scores for Source URL (0.89), Sentiment Score (0.82), and Text Length (0.80). However, its slightly lower performance in features like Author Information (0.74) and Publication Date/Time (0.72) indicates room for improvement in metadata utilization.

RoBERTa also performs well, achieving scores comparable to the proposed model, particularly in Source URL (0.87) and Sentiment Score (0.80). However, it shows a slight drop in features such as Author Information (0.69) and Publication Date/Time (0.66), suggesting limitations in handling certain feature types.

In contrast, models such as DistilBERT, T5, and ELECTRA exhibit relatively lower scores across all features. DistilBERT, for example, achieves moderate performance in Source URL (0.83) and Sentiment Score (0.75) but lags behind in features like Engagement Metrics (0.72) and Publication Date/Time (0.62). Similarly, T5 and ELECTRA score lower across the board, particularly in Author Information (0.63 and 0.61, respectively) and Publication Date/Time (0.60 and 0.58, respectively), indicating less effective feature utilization.

Table 1. Feature importance for Q-prop dataset

Model	Source URL	Sentiment Score	Text Length	Engagement Metrics	Author Information	Publication Date/Time
Proposed Model	0.86	0.80	0.75	0.78	0.72	0.68
BERT	0.85	0.78	0.72	0.75	0.68	0.65
RoBERTa	0.87	0.80	0.73	0.77	0.69	0.66
DistilBERT	0.83	0.75	0.70	0.72	0.65	0.62
GPT-3	0.89	0.82	0.80	0.79	0.74	0.72
ALBERT	0.84	0.77	0.69	0.74	0.66	0.64
T5	0.82	0.74	0.68	0.71	0.63	0.60
ELECTRA	0.81	0.73	0.66	0.70	0.61	0.58
BART	0.84	0.76	0.71	0.73	0.65	0.63

Table 2 compares the performance of various models in terms of feature importance on the ISOT dataset, which comprises 44,898 documents. The models were evaluated based on six key features: Source URL, Sentiment Score, Topic Tags, Language Detection, Text Length, and Engagement Metrics. Performance is represented as a normalized score, reflecting each model's effectiveness in leveraging the respective features for detection of misinformation.

The Proposed Model (XLNet) achieves consistently strong results across all features, with top scores in Source URL (0.86), Sentiment Score (0.80), and Engagement Metrics (0.76). These scores highlight XLNet's robust ability to process diverse textual and metadata features, particularly those critical for assessing content reliability and user engagement.

Among the other models, GPT-3 stands out with the highest performance in several features, such as Source URL (0.87), Sentiment Score (0.84), and Topic Tags (0.82), showcasing its advanced natural language understanding. It also achieves excellent results for Language Detection (0.78) and Engagement Metrics (0.80). However, its slightly lower performance in Text Length (0.77) indicates some limitations in handling variability in content size.

RoBERTa also performs competitively, particularly excelling in Sentiment Score (0.81), Topic Tags (0.77), and Engagement Metrics (0.76), which align closely with the proposed model. However, it lags slightly in Language Detection (0.73) and Text Length (0.74), suggesting some challenges with metadata-driven features.

Other models, such as BERT and DistilBERT, deliver moderate performance. BERT, for instance, achieves respectable scores for Source URL (0.83) and Sentiment Score (0.79) but demonstrates weaker results in Language Detection (0.71) and Engagement Metrics (0.74). DistilBERT scores lower overall, with reduced performance across features like Language Detection (0.69) and Engagement Metrics (0.71), reflecting limitations in its lightweight architecture.

Lower-performing models like T5 and ELECTRA show significant limitations in handling the dataset's feature diversity. For example, T5 achieves its highest score in Source URL (0.81) but performs poorly in Language Detection (0.66) and Engagement Metrics (0.71). Similarly, ELECTRA struggles with Topic Tags (0.68) and Language Detection (0.65), indicating challenges in addressing more nuanced features.

Table 2. Feature importance for ISOT dataset

Model	Source URL	Sentiment Score	Topic Tags	Language Detection	Text Length	Engagement Metrics
Proposed Model	0.86	0.80	0.75	0.72	0.74	0.76
BERT	0.83	0.79	0.75	0.71	0.72	0.74
RoBERTa	0.85	0.81	0.77	0.73	0.74	0.76
DistilBERT	0.80	0.76	0.72	0.69	0.70	0.71
GPT-3	0.87	0.84	0.82	0.78	0.77	0.80
ALBERT	0.82	0.78	0.73	0.69	0.71	0.72
T5	0.81	0.74	0.70	0.66	0.69	0.71
ELECTRA	0.80	0.73	0.68	0.65	0.68	0.69
BART	0.82	0.75	0.71	0.70	0.72	0.73

Table 3 presents a feature importance performance comparison for various models applied to the GRAFN dataset, consisting of 13,000 posts on global politics. The models were evaluated based on six key features: Political Keywords, Sentiment Score, Source URL, Engagement Metrics, Text Length, and Topic Tags. The performance is represented as a normalized score, which demonstrates how well each model incorporates and processes these features for effective analysis.

The Proposed Model (XLNet) delivers impressive results, particularly in Political Keywords (0.87) and Sentiment Score (0.82), reflecting its ability to capture political context and sentiment effectively. It also performs well in Source URL (0.80) and Engagement Metrics (0.78), which are crucial for understanding the credibility and user engagement of the posts. However, it has slightly lower performance in Text Length (0.75) and Topic Tags (0.74) compared to other models, indicating that while XLNet handles many features well, it faces some challenges with more granular aspects like text size and topic identification.

GPT-3 demonstrates the highest scores across multiple features, including Political Keywords (0.90), Sentiment Score (0.85), and Source URL (0.84), showcasing its strong capability in political context analysis and sentiment extraction. Additionally, it performs excellently in Engagement Metrics (0.82) and Text Length (0.80), suggesting it effectively processes both the length and interactive elements of posts. Despite this, its performance in Topic Tags (0.78), while strong, is slightly lower than other top models, highlighting some limitations in categorizing complex topics.

RoBERTa also excels in several key features, with Political Keywords (0.88) and Sentiment Score (0.83) being their highest-performing attributes. It shows strong performance across Source URL (0.81) and Engagement Metrics (0.77) but has somewhat lower scores in Text Length (0.75) and Topic Tags (0.76) compared to XLNetand GPT-3. This suggests that while RoBERTa is robust in political and sentiment analysis, it may not handle textual data length and topic complexity as effectively.

Other models like BERT and ALBERT perform comparably, with BERT achieving solid results in Political Keywords (0.86) and Sentiment Score (0.81) but trailing behind the top performers in Engagement Metrics (0.75) and Text Length (0.72). ALBERT similarly shows strong performance in Political Keywords (0.85) and Sentiment Score (0.79), though its scores in Engagement Metrics (0.73) and Topic Tags (0.72) are lower, indicating room for improvement in capturing these features effectively.

DistilBERT, T5, ELECTRA, and BART show varying performance levels across the features. For example, DistilBERT has the lowest scores, particularly in Political Keywords (0.84) and Sentiment Score (0.78), reflecting its limitations in capturing political context and sentiment nuances. T5 and ELECTRA exhibit moderate performance across the features, with particularly low scores in Engagement Metrics (0.70 and 0.69), indicating their challenges in handling social media interaction data. BART, while competitive, particularly in Political Keywords (0.84) and Sentiment Score (0.79), still face limitations in Engagement Metrics (0.74) and Text Length (0.72).

Table 3. Feature importance for GRAFN dataset

Model	Political Keywords	Sentiment Score	Source URL	Engagement Metrics	Text Length	Topic Tags
Proposed Model (XLNet)	0.87	0.82	0.80	0.78	0.75	0.74
BERT	0.86	0.81	0.79	0.75	0.72	0.74
RoBERTa	0.88	0.83	0.81	0.77	0.75	0.76
DistilBERT	0.84	0.78	0.74	0.70	0.68	0.71
GPT-3	0.90	0.85	0.84	0.82	0.80	0.78
ALBERT	0.85	0.79	0.77	0.73	0.71	0.72
T5	0.83	0.77	0.73	0.70	0.68	0.69
ELECTRA	0.82	0.75	0.72	0.69	0.67	0.68
BART	0.84	0.79	0.76	0.74	0.72	0.73

Table 4 presents a feature of importance performance comparison for various models applied to the PubHealth Dataset, which contains public health documents. The models were evaluated based on six critical features: Medical Terms, Sentiment Score, Source URL, Engagement Metrics, Text Length, and Health Labels. The scores indicate how well each model processes and analyzes these features, which are essential for understanding and categorizing public health-related documents.

The Proposed Model (XLNet) demonstrates strong performance across all features, with particularly high scores in Medical Terms (0.86) and Sentiment Score (0.80). This suggests that XLNet is adept at identifying medical terminology and sentiment within public health documents. It also performs well in Source URL (0.78) and Engagement Metrics (0.75), which are important for evaluating the credibility of the sources and user interaction. However, it has slightly lower performance in Text Length (0.73) and Health Labels (0.74), indicating a challenge in effectively managing document length and health-related categorization.

GPT-3 achieves impressive results, particularly in Medical Terms (0.88) and Sentiment Score (0.84), reflecting its strength in processing and analyzing medical language and emotional content. It also performs well in Source URL (0.82) and Engagement Metrics (0.80), indicating its ability to evaluate source credibility and user engagement. Despite these strengths, its performance in Health Labels (0.79) is slightly lower than some other models, indicating room for improvement in classifying health-related topics.

RoBERTa follows closely behind, with high scores in Medical Terms (0.87) and Sentiment Score (0.83). It also performs well in Source URL (0.80) and Engagement Metrics (0.76), suggesting it is effective at processing medical and sentiment data, as well as evaluating source credibility and user interaction. However, its performance in Health Labels (0.77) is not as strong as GPT-3 and XLNet, showing some limitations in health topic classification.

BERT performs solidly, with a strong Sentiment Score (0.81) and Source URL (0.78). Its performance in Medical Terms (0.85) is also commendable, reflecting its ability to identify medical terminology. However, it has slightly lower scores in Engagement Metrics (0.74) and Text Length (0.72), which suggests it may struggle more with user engagement and document size analysis compared to the top-performing models.

Other models, such as DistilBERT, ALBERT, T5, ELECTRA, and BART, show more mixed results. DistilBERT has the lowest scores across most features, particularly in Engagement Metrics (0.67) and Text Length (0.69), suggesting it has limitations in handling user interaction and document length. T5 and ELECTRA also exhibit relatively low performance, especially in Engagement Metrics (0.68 and 0.66), indicating challenges in social media or interactive data processing. ALBERT shows solid results in Medical Terms (0.83) and Sentiment Score (0.79), but its performance in Text Length (0.70) and Health Labels (0.73) is not as competitive as the top models.

Table 4. Feature importance for PubHealth dataset

Model	Medical Terms	Sentiment Score	Source URL	Engagement Metrics	Text Length	Health Labels
Proposed Model (XLNet)	0.86	0.80	0.78	0.75	0.73	0.74
BERT	0.85	0.81	0.78	0.74	0.72	0.75
RoBERTa	0.87	0.83	0.80	0.76	0.74	0.77
DistilBERT	0.82	0.76	0.73	0.69	0.67	0.70
GPT-3	0.88	0.84	0.82	0.80	0.78	0.79
ALBERT	0.83	0.79	0.76	0.72	0.70	0.73
T5	0.81	0.75	0.72	0.68	0.66	0.69
ELECTRA	0.80	0.73	0.70	0.68	0.66	0.67
BART	0.82	0.76	0.73	0.70	0.69	0.71

Table 5 presents a comparison of feature extraction techniques using GROOVE for the Q-Prop Dataset, focusing on the effectiveness of different embedding methods: Word2Vec, GloVe, Table 6 compares the effectiveness of different feature extraction techniques using GROOVE for the ISOT Dataset, evaluating Word2Vec, GloVe, BERT, and GROOVE Enhanced Embeddings across five features: Sentiment Score, Topic Tags, Language Detection, Text Length, and Engagement Metrics.

For Sentiment Score, GROOVE Enhanced Embeddings perform the best, achieving a score of 0.86, outperforming BERT (0.80) and GloVe (0.76), indicating its superior ability to capture sentiment information in the dataset. A similar trend is observed for Topic Tags, where GROOVE leads with a score of 0.80, significantly surpassing Word2Vec (0.68) and GloVe (0.71), showcasing its high effectiveness in this feature.

In Language Detection, GROOVE achieves a score of 0.80, slightly ahead of BERT (0.75) and GloVe (0.72), though it is categorized as having medium effectiveness in this feature compared to its high performance in Sentiment Score and Topic Tags. Text Length also benefits from GROOVE, with a score of 0.81, higher than Word2Vec (0.72) and GloVe (0.75), suggesting a moderate improvement in this feature, though it remains medium in effectiveness. Finally, for Engagement Metrics, GROOVE achieves a score of 0.79, outperforming Word2Vec (0.69) and GloVe (0.71), reflecting its medium effectiveness in this feature as well.

Table 5. Feature extraction for Q-prop dataset

Feature	Word2Vec Embeddings	GloVe Embeddings	BERT Embeddings	GROOVE Enhanced Embeddings	Effectiveness
Sentiment Score	0.75	0.78	0.80	0.86	High
Source URL	0.70	0.72	0.75	0.80	Medium
Text Length	0.68	0.70	0.74	0.78	Medium
Engagement Metrics	0.72	0.75	0.78	0.84	High
Author Information	0.67	0.71	0.74	0.76	Medium

Table 6 compares the effectiveness of different feature extraction techniques using GROOVE for the ISOT Dataset, evaluating Word2Vec, GloVe, BERT, and GROOVE Enhanced Embeddings across five features: Sentiment Score, Topic Tags, Language Detection, Text Length, and Engagement Metrics.

For Sentiment Score, GROOVE Enhanced Embeddings perform the best, achieving a score of 0.86, outperforming BERT (0.80) and GloVe (0.76), indicating its superior ability to capture sentiment information in the dataset. A similar trend is observed for Topic Tags, where GROOVE leads with a score of 0.80, significantly surpassing Word2Vec (0.68) and GloVe (0.71), showcasing its high effectiveness in this feature.

In Language Detection, GROOVE achieves a score of 0.80, slightly ahead of BERT (0.75) and GloVe (0.72), though it is categorized as having medium effectiveness in this feature compared to its high performance in Sentiment Score and Topic Tags. Text Length also benefits from GROOVE, with a score of 0.81, higher than Word2Vec (0.72) and GloVe (0.75), suggesting a moderate improvement in this feature, though it remains medium in effectiveness.

Finally, for Engagement Metrics, GROOVE achieves a score of 0.79, outperforming Word2Vec (0.69) and GloVe (0.71), reflecting its medium effectiveness in this feature as well.

Table 6. Feature extraction for ISOT dataset

Feature	Word2Vec Embeddings	GloVe Embeddings	BERT Embeddings	GROOVE Enhanced Embeddings	Effectiveness
Sentiment Score	0.74	0.76	0.80	0.86	High
Topic Tags	0.68	0.71	0.74	0.80	High
Language Detection	0.70	0.72	0.75	0.80	Medium
Text Length	0.72	0.75	0.77	0.81	Medium
Engagement Metrics	0.69	0.71	0.74	0.79	Medium

Table 7 presents a comparison of different feature extraction techniques using GROOVE for the GRAFN Dataset, evaluating Word2Vec, GloVe, BERT, and GROOVE Enhanced Embeddings across five features: Political Keywords, Sentiment Score, Source URL, Text Length, and Engagement Metrics.

For Political Keywords, GROOVE Enhanced Embeddings achieve the highest score of 0.88, outperforming BERT (0.83) and GloVe (0.79), indicating its strong ability to capture political context in the dataset, which is classified as having high effectiveness. A similar pattern emerges with Sentiment Score, where GROOVE leads with a score of 0.84, surpassing BERT (0.79) and GloVe (0.75), again demonstrating high effectiveness.

In the case of Source URL, GROOVE Enhanced Embeddings score 0.78, slightly ahead of BERT (0.74) and GloVe (0.71), reflecting medium effectiveness in extracting relevant information from the URL feature. Similarly, for Text Length, GROOVE achieves a score of 0.80, outperforming Word2Vec (0.70) and GloVe (0.73), indicating moderate effectiveness in this feature as well.

Finally, for Engagement Metrics, GROOVE Enhanced Embeddings score 0.82, outperforming BERT (0.77) and GloVe (0.74), highlighting its high effectiveness in capturing engagement-related features.

Table 7. Feature extraction for GRAFN dataset

Feature	Word2Vec Embeddings	GloVe Embeddings	BERT Embeddings	GROOVE Enhanced Embeddings	Effectiveness
Political Keywords	0.76	0.79	0.83	0.88	High
Sentiment Score	0.73	0.75	0.79	0.84	High
Source URL	0.68	0.71	0.74	0.78	Medium
Text Length	0.70	0.73	0.76	0.80	Medium
Engagement Metrics	0.71	0.74	0.77	0.82	High

Table 8 presents the results of feature extraction using GROOVE for the PubHealth Dataset, comparing the effectiveness of Word2Vec, GloVe, BERT, and GROOVE Enhanced Embeddings across five key features: Medical Terms, Sentiment Score, Source URL, Text Length, and Health Labels.

For Medical Terms, GROOVE Enhanced Embeddings achieve the highest score of 0.85, outperforming BERT (0.80) and GloVe (0.77), demonstrating its high effectiveness in capturing relevant medical terminology. Similarly, Sentiment Score is most effectively extracted with GROOVE, which scores 0.83, surpassing BERT (0.78) and GloVe (0.74), highlighting its strong performance in sentiment analysis.

For Source URL, GROOVE Enhanced Embeddings score 0.76, a noticeable improvement over BERT (0.72) and GloVe (0.70), indicating medium effectiveness in handling URL-related information. The extraction of Text Length also sees GROOVE leading with a score of 0.78, ahead of BERT (0.75) and GloVe (0.73), reflecting medium effectiveness in this area as well.

Finally, for Health Labels, GROOVE again outperforms the other methods with a score of 0.82, surpassing BERT (0.78) and GloVe (0.75), demonstrating high effectiveness in extracting health-related labels from the dataset.

Table 8. Feature extraction for PubHealth dataset

Feature	Word2Vec Embeddings	GloVe Embeddings	BERT Embeddings	GROOVE Enhanced Embeddings	Effectiveness
Medical Terms	0.75	0.77	0.80	0.85	High
Sentiment Score	0.71	0.74	0.78	0.83	High
Source URL	0.68	0.70	0.72	0.76	Medium
Text Length	0.70	0.73	0.75	0.78	Medium
Health Labels	0.72	0.75	0.78	0.82	High

Table 9 presents the results of feature selection using the Relief Algorithm for the Q-Prop Dataset, showing the assigned weights for five key features: Sentiment Score, Source URL, Text Length, Engagement Metrics, and Author Information.

The Sentiment Score receives the highest weight of 0.86, indicating that it is the most influential feature in the dataset according to the Relief Algorithm. This suggests that sentiment plays a crucial role in the analysis. Following closely is Engagement Metrics with a weight of 0.84, highlighting its importance in understanding user interaction or engagement with the content.

Source URL also has a significant weight of 0.80, underlining the relevance of the source of the information in the dataset. Text Length is assigned a weight of 0.78, indicating its moderate influence in the feature selection process. Lastly, Author Information receives the lowest weight of 0.76, still indicating its relative importance but somewhat less influential than the other features.

Table 9. Feature selection for Q-prop dataset

Feature	Relief Algorithm Weight
Sentiment Score	0.86
Source URL	0.80
Text Length	0.78
Engagement Metrics	0.84
Author Information	0.76

Table 10 displays the results of feature selection using the Relief Algorithm for the ISOT Dataset, highlighting the weights assigned to five key features: Sentiment Score, Topic Tags, Language Detection, Text Length, and Engagement Metrics.

The Sentiment Score is assigned to the highest weight of 0.86, indicating its strong importance in the dataset and suggesting that sentiment analysis plays a crucial role in understanding the data. Topic Tags follow closely with a weight of

0.80, highlighting its significance in categorizing and understanding the content's subject matter. Language Detection receives a weight of 0.81, signifying its moderate yet essential role in identifying the language of the content.

Text Length has a weight of 0.79, implying its relevance in shaping the dataset's overall structure, while Engagement Metrics is assigned the lowest weight of 0.75, still showing a notable influence, though less significant compared to the other features.

Table 10. Feature selection for ISOT dataset

Feature	Relief Algorithm Weight
Sentiment Score	0.86
Topic Tags	0.80
Language Detection	0.81
Text Length	0.79
Engagement Metrics	0.75

Table 11 presents the performance metrics of the XLNet classifier across four different datasets: Q-Prop, ISOT, GRAFN, and PubHealth. The table provides key classification performance indicators, including Accuracy, Precision, Recall, and F1-Score.

For the Q-Prop dataset, the XLNet model achieved an impressive Accuracy of 92.3%, with Precision at 91.5%, Recall at 93.0%, and an F1-Score of 92.2%, demonstrating strong performance across all metrics. The ISOT dataset saw slightly lower results, with an Accuracy of 88.7%, Precision of 87.8%, Recall of 89.5%, and an F1-Score of 88.6%, reflecting a solid but less optimal performance compared to Q-Prop.

For the GRAFN dataset, XLNet performed similarly to Q-Prop, attaining a 90.1%Accuracy, 89.2%Precision, 91.0%Recall, and a 90.1%F1-Score, which signifies strong performance in political content classification. The PubHealth dataset had the lowest performance among the four, with Accuracy at 85.4%, Precision of 84.0%, Recall of 86.2%, and an F1-Score of 85.1%, though still demonstrating good results in the public health domain.

Table 11. Performance of the XLNet classifier on the datasets

Dataset	Accuracy	Precision	Recall	F1-Score
Q-Prop	92.3%	91.5%	93.0%	92.2%
ISOT	88.7%	87.8%	89.5%	88.6%
GRAFN	90.1%	89.2%	91.0%	90.1%
PubHealth	85.4%	84.0%	86.2%	85.1%

IMPLICATIONS OF THE METHODOLOGY

1. **Improved Feature Representations:**

The GROOVE-based embeddings ensure that subtle linguistic and semantic nuances in the datasets are captured effectively. This has practical implications for misinformation detection, as deceptive content often relies on minor variations in language use. Future research could explore extending GROOVE to include multimodal data (e.g., images and videos) for enhanced cross-media misinformation detection.

2. **Efficiency Gains with Relief:**

By focusing on the most relevant features, the Relief algorithm reduces computational overhead, making the approach scalable for real-time applications. However, this could be further extended by exploring hybrid feature selection techniques combining Relief with other heuristic methods for domain-specific optimizations.

3. **XLNet's Contextual Strengths:**

XLNet's permutation-based modeling provides robust contextual understanding, enabling effective handling of complex datasets. Future work could investigate fine-tuning XLNet for multilingual or low-resource language datasets, addressing the global challenge of misinformation in diverse linguistic settings.

4. **Domain-Specific Applications:**

The evaluation on datasets from news, politics, and public health domains demonstrates the model's adaptability. Expanding the dataset scope to include user-generated content, such as social media posts, could broaden its practical utility.

FUTURE RESEARCH DIRECTIONS

1. **Integrating Multimodal Data:**

While the current study focuses on textual data, incorporating multimodal datasets (e.g., text, images, and videos) could enhance misinformation detection capabilities. Future research could leverage GROOVE's robust vectorization for image-text fusion tasks.

2. **Expanding Domain-Specific Models:**

The methodology shows promise in detecting misinformation in specific domains. Developing domain-adaptive models tailored to areas like healthcare, education, or climate change could yield more targeted solutions.

3. **Addressing Bias in Datasets:**

The datasets used may carry inherent biases that could influence model predictions. Future studies should emphasize dataset diversity and bias mitigation techniques to ensure fairness and generalizability.

4. **Real-Time Implementation:**

Extending the methodology to support real-time misinformation detection is a crucial next step. Research into lightweight model deployment, such as through edge computing or federated learning, could enable real-time, scalable solutions.

5. **Explainability in Misinformation Detection:**

Incorporating explainability techniques to elucidate model predictions could improve trust and transparency in applications, particularly in sensitive domains like public health.

CONCLUSION

This study highlights the potential of integrating advanced NLP techniques, such as XLNet and the Relief algorithm, for tackling misinformation across various domains. By leveraging permutation-based language modeling, XLNet provides robust document representations, capturing nuanced patterns and contextual relationships essential for accurate classification. The use of the Relief algorithm ensures the selection of the most relevant features, reducing noise and improving model performance. The proposed methodology was successfully applied to datasets from diverse domains, demonstrating its effectiveness in classifying content, distinguishing between fake and legitimate information, and identifying domain-specific misinformation. These results underscore the importance of combining advanced feature selection techniques with cutting-edge NLP models to address the growing challenges of misinformation in a scalable and efficient manner. Future work can explore the adaptation of this approach to multilingual and cross-domain applications to further extend its impact.

REFERENCES

Afchar, D., Nozick, V., Yamagishi, J., & Echizen, I. (2018). MesoNet: A Compact Facial Video Forgery Detection Network. *Proceedings of the 2018 IEEE International Workshop on Information Forensics and Security (WIFS)*. DOI: 10.1109/WIFS.2018.8630761

Ahmed, H., Traore, I., & Saad, S. (2018). Detecting opinion spams and fake news using text classification. *Security and Privacy*, 1(1), e9. DOI: 10.1002/spy2.9

Barrón-Cedeño, A., Da San Martino, G., Jaradat, I., & Nakov, P. (2019). Proppy: Organizing the news based on their propagandistic content. *Information Processing & Management*, 56(5), 1849–1864. DOI: 10.1016/j.ipm.2019.03.005

Bazmi, P., Asadpour, M., & Shakery, A. (2023). Multi-view co-attention network for fake news detection by modeling topic-specific user and news source credibility. *Information Processing & Management*, 60(1), 103146. DOI: 10.1016/j.ipm.2022.103146

Blakley, G. R., Meadows, C., & Purdy, G. B. (1986). Fingerprinting Long Forgiving Messages. In Williams, H. C. (Ed.), *Advances in Cryptology—CRYPTO '85 Proceedings* (pp. 180–189). Springer. DOI: 10.1007/3-540-39799-X_15

Bogonikolos, N., Fragoudis, D., & Likothanassis, S. (1999). "ARCHIMIDES": An intelligent agent for adaptive-personalized navigation within a WEB server. Proceedings of the 32nd Annual Hawaii International Conference on Systems Sciences, 9.

Boneh, D., & Shaw, J. (1998). Collusion-Secure Fingerprinting for Digital Data. *IEEE Transactions on Information Theory*, 44(5), 1897–1905. DOI: 10.1109/18.705568

Bradford, C., & Marshall, I. (1999). A bandwidth friendly search engine. *Proceedings of the IEEE International Conference on Multimedia Computing and Systems*, 720–724. DOI: 10.1109/MMCS.1999.778573

Braşoveanu, A. M. P., & Andonie, R. (2019). Semantic Fake News Detection: A Machine Learning Perspective. *Proceedings of the Advances in Computational Intelligence*, 656–667. DOI: 10.1007/978-3-030-20521-8_54

Chen, X., Zhou, F., Trajcevski, G., & Bonsangue, M. (2022). Multi-view learning with distinguishable feature fusion for rumor detection. *Knowledge-Based Systems*, 240, 108085. DOI: 10.1016/j.knosys.2021.108085

Diouf, R., Sarr, E. N., Sall, O., Birregah, B., Bousso, M., & Mbaye, S. N. (2019). Web Scraping: State-of-the-Art and Areas of Application. Proceedings of the 2019 IEEE International Conference on Big Data (Big Data), 6040–6042.

Dolhansky, B., Howes, R., Pflaum, B., Baram, N., & Ferrer, C. C. (2019). The Deepfake Detection Challenge (DFDC) Preview Dataset. arXiv:1910.08854.

Goldani, M. H., Safabakhsh, R., & Momtazi, S. (2021). Convolutional neural network with margin loss for fake news detection. *Information Processing & Management*, 58(1), 102418. DOI: 10.1016/j.ipm.2020.102418

Guo, L., Rohde, J. A., & Wu, H. D. (2020). Who is responsible for Twitter's echo chamber problem? Evidence from 2016 U.S. election networks. *Information Communication and Society*, 23, 234–251. DOI: 10.1080/1369118X.2018.1499793

Huh, M., Liu, A., Owens, A., & Efros, A. A. (2018). Fighting Fake News: Image Splice Detection via Learned Self-Consistency. *Proceedings of the Computer Vision–ECCV 2018*, 106–124. DOI: 10.1007/978-3-030-01252-6_7

Jing, J., Wu, H., Sun, J., Fang, X., & Zhang, H. (2023). Multimodal fake news detection via progressive fusion networks. *Information Processing & Management*, 60(1), 103120. DOI: 10.1016/j.ipm.2022.103120

Khan, J. Y., Khondaker, M. T. I., Afroz, S., Uddin, G., & Iqbal, A. (2021). A benchmark study of machine learning models for online fake news detection. *Machine Learning with Applications*, 4, 100032. DOI: 10.1016/j.mlwa.2021.100032

Korshunov, P., & Marcel, S. (2018). DeepFakes: A New Threat to Face Recognition? Assessment and Detection. arXiv:1812.08685.

Korus, P., & Memon, N. (2019). Content Authentication for Neural Imaging Pipelines: End-To-End Optimization of Photo Provenance in Complex Distribution Channels. *Proceedings of the 2019 IEEE/CVF Conference on Computer Vision and Pattern Recognition (CVPR)*, 8613–8621. DOI: 10.1109/CVPR.2019.00882

Kotonya, N., & Toni, F. (2020). Explainable Automated Fact-Checking for Public Health Claims. Proceedings of the 2020 Conference on Empirical Methods in Natural Language Processing (EMNLP), 7740–7754. DOI: 10.18653/v1/2020.emnlp-main.623

Li, S., Li, W., Luvembe, A. M., & Tong, W. (2023). Graph Contrastive Learning With Feature Augmentation for Rumor Detection. *IEEE Transactions on Computational Social Systems*, 1–10.

Li, Y., Chang, M. C., & Lyu, S. (2018). In Ictu Oculi: Exposing AI Created Fake Videos by Detecting Eye Blinking. *Proceedings of the 2018 IEEE International Workshop on Information Forensics and Security (WIFS)*. DOI: 10.1109/WIFS.2018.8630787

Li, Y., Jiang, B., Shu, K., & Liu, H. (2020). MM-COVID: A Multilingual and Multimodal Data Repository for Combating COVID-19 Disinformation. arXiv:2011.04088.

Luvembe, A., Li, W., Li, S., Liu, F., & Xu, G. (2023). Dual emotion based fake news detection: A deep attention-weight update approach. *Information Processing & Management*, 60(4), 103354. DOI: 10.1016/j.ipm.2023.103354

Megías, D. (2020). Data Hiding: New Opportunities for Security and Privacy? *Proceedings of the European Interdisciplinary Cybersecurity Conference (EICC 2020)*, 1–6. DOI: 10.1145/3424954.3425511

Megías, D., Kuribayashi, M., Rosales, A., Cabaj, K., & Mazurczyk, W. (2022). Architecture of a fake news detection system combining digital watermarking, signal processing, and machine learning. *Journal of Wireless Mobile Networks, Ubiquitous Computing and Dependable Applications*, 13, 33–55.

Meyers, M., Weiss, G., & Spanakis, G. (2020). Fake News Detection on Twitter Using Propagation Structures. *Proceedings of the Disinformation in Open Online Media*, 138–158. DOI: 10.1007/978-3-030-61841-4_10

Mridha, M. F., Keya, A. J., Hamid, M. A., Monowar, M. M., & Rahman, M. S. (2021). A Comprehensive Review on Fake News Detection With Deep Learning. *IEEE Access : Practical Innovations, Open Solutions*, 9, 156151–156170. DOI: 10.1109/ACCESS.2021.3129329

Parikh, S. B., & Atrey, P. K. (2018). Media-Rich Fake News Detection: A Survey. *Proceedings of the 2018 IEEE Conference on Multimedia Information Processing and Retrieval (MIPR)*, 436–441. DOI: 10.1109/MIPR.2018.00093

Pérez-Rosas, V., Kleinberg, B., Lefevre, A., & Mihalcea, R. (2018). Automatic Detection of Fake News. *Proceedings of the 27th International Conference on Computational Linguistics*, 3391–3401.

Reis, J. C. S., Correia, A., Murai, F., Veloso, A., & Benevenuto, F. (2019). Supervised Learning for Fake News Detection. *IEEE Intelligent Systems*, 34(2), 76–81. DOI: 10.1109/MIS.2019.2899143

Shu, K., Wang, S., & Liu, H. (2017). Exploiting Tri-Relationship for Fake News Detection. arXiv:1712.07709.

Sunstein, C. R. (2001). *Echo Chambers: Bush V. Gore, Impeachment, and Beyond.* Princeton Digital Books.

Tolosana, R., Rodriguez, R. V., Fierrez, J., Morales, A., & Garcia, J. O. (2020). Deepfakes and beyond: A Survey of face manipulation and fake detection. *Information Fusion*, 64, 131–148. DOI: 10.1016/j.inffus.2020.06.014

Wang, R., Juefei-Xu, F., Luo, M., Liu, Y., & Wang, L. (2020). FakeTagger: Robust Safeguards against DeepFake Dissemination via Provenance Tracking. *Proceedings of the 29th ACM International Conference on Multimedia, Virtual Event.*

Yang, X., Zhang, H., He, X., Bian, J., & Wu, Y. (2020). Extracting Family History of Patients from Clinical Narratives: Using Deep Learning Models (Preprint). *JMIR Med. Inform.*, *8*, e22982.

Zhang, Q., Guo, Z., Zhu, Y., Vijayakumar, P., Castiglione, A., & Gupta, B. B. (2023). A Deep Learning-based Fast Fake News Detection Model for Cyber-Physical Social Services. *Pattern Recognition Letters*, 168, 31–38. DOI: 10.1016/j.patrec.2023.02.026

Zhou, X., & Zafarani, R. (2019). Fake News Detection: An Interdisciplinary Research. *Proceedings of the Companion Proceedings of The 2019 World Wide Web Conference, WWW '19*, 1292. DOI: 10.1145/3308560.3316476

Chapter 11
Balancing Innovation and Privacy:
Understanding AI in the Digital World

P. Selvakumar
https://orcid.org/0000-0002-3650-4548
Department of Science and Humanities, Nehru Institute of Technology, India

P. Sudheer
https://orcid.org/0009-0005-1912-6636
CVR College of Engineering, India

Nandini Kannan
https://orcid.org/0009-0000-8068-1747
HKBK College of Engineering, India

ABSTRACT

As we delve into the transformative landscape of artificial intelligence (AI), we encounter a critical juncture where innovation meets the pressing need for digital privacy. Various sectors, including healthcare, finance, and education, offer unprecedented efficiencies and capabilities. The relationship between AI and digital privacy is multifaceted. On the other hand, the same capabilities that enable enhanced security can also be exploited to infringe upon individual privacy. However, enforcement remains a challenge, especially in the face of rapidly changing technologies and the global nature of data flows. This includes prioritizing fairness, accountability, and transparency, particularly when handling personal data. Organizations are encouraged to adopt principles such as data minimization—collecting only the information necessary for a specific purpose—and to implement privacy questions

DOI: 10.4018/979-8-3693-9015-3.ch011

about the implications for marginalized communities.

INTRODUCTION TO AI AND DIGITAL PRIVACY: THE INTERSECTION OF INNOVATION AND RISK

As we delve into the transformative landscape of artificial intelligence (AI), we encounter a critical juncture where innovation meets the pressing need for digital privacy. various sectors, including healthcare, finance, and education, offering unprecedented efficiencies and capabilities. However .The relationship between AI and digital privacy is multifaceted. On the other hand, the same capabilities that enable enhanced security can also be exploited to infringe upon individual privacy. However, enforcement remains a challenge, especially in the face of rapidly changing technologies and the global nature of data flows. Companies often find themselves. Moreover, the role of ethical This includes prioritizing fairness, accountability, and transparency, particularly when handling personal data. Organizations are encouraged to adopt principles such as data minimization—collecting only the information necessary for a specific purpose—and to implement privacy questions about the implications for marginalized communities. Discriminatory practices can be exacerbated by AI systems that rely on biased data, leading to unequal treatment in critical areas like employment, law enforcement, and access to services. In addition to ethical considerations. Public perception of AI and privacy is another critical factor influencing the trajectory of these technologies. As awareness of data privacy issues grows, consumers are becoming more discerning about how their information is used. Companies that prioritize transparency and demonstrate a commitment to protecting consumer data are likely to gain a competitive advantage in the marketplace. Conversely, those that neglect privacy considerations risk eroding public trust and facing backlash from consumers and regulators alike. This evolving landscape underscores it is crucial for stakeholders—governments, organizations, and individuals—to collaborate in developing robust frameworks that prioritize ethical considerations and protect personal privacy. This requires not only adherence to existing regulations but also a forward-thinking approach that embraces technological innovation while addressing the ethical and societal implications of AI.

advancements in technology but also a paradigm shift in how we understand and implement AI in various domains. The story begins in the mid-20th century with the conceptual groundwork systems, where explicit programming dictated the decision-making processes of machines. As computational power increased in the late 20th century, particularly with the advent of more sophisticated hardware and the rise of the internet, machine learning began to flourish. The availability of vast amounts of data transformed how algorithms were trained and validated. Researchers started to explore more complex models, such as support vector machines and ensemble methods, which significantly improved the accuracy of predictions. This era saw machine learning being applied in diverse fields, from finance to healthcare, as organizations recognized its potential to derive insights from data. The breakthrough came with the development of convolutional neural networks (CNNs), which excelled in image recognition tasks, achieving unprecedented accuracy in benchmarks like the ImageNet competition. The success of deep learning can be attributed to several factors.

First, the availability of large labeled datasets, such as those used in image and text recognition, provided the necessary training material for neural networks to learn complex features. Second, advancements in graphics processing units (GPUs) enabled faster computation, making it feasible to train deeper and more complex models. and, more recently (Alsmadi, D., et al.,2018), transformers, deep learning has revolutionized the way machines understand and generate human language. Models like OpenAI's GPT and Google's BERT have demonstrated remarkable capabilities in tasks ranging from translation to sentiment analysis, showcasing power of deep learning in handling linguistic complexities., and transparency have gained prominence (Mahadev Madgule, et al.,2023). Deep learning models, while powerful, are often seen as “black boxes,” making it challenging to interpret their decision-making processes. This opacity can lead to unintended consequences, particularly in sensitive areas such as criminal justice and hiring, where biased training data can result in discriminatory outcomes. Moreover, the proliferation of AI technologies has prompted discussions around data privacy and security. With deep learning models requiring extensive datasets, often sourced from user-generated content, the potential for privacy breaches and misuse of personal information becomes a significant concern. Regulatory frameworks, such as the General Data (Appel, G., et al.,2020) Protection Regulation (GDPR), have emerged to address these. Looking ahead, the future of AI will likely see further integration Reinforcement learning, on the other hand, focuses on training agents to make decisions based on feedback from their environment, opening new avenues for applications in robotics and autonomous systems. Increases in data availability, and breakthroughs in hardware, culminating in the development of models that can tackle a wide array of tasks with remarkable accuracy. principles of fairness, transparency, and respect for privacy. The evolution of AI is not just a technical endeavor; it is a profound transformation that holds the promise of reshaping industries and improving lives around the globe.

UNDERSTANDING DIGITAL PRIVACY: CONCEPTS, LAWS, AND REGULATIONS

control their personal information and how it is collected, used, and shared by organizations and governments. This concept encompasses various aspects, including data protection, online behavior tracking, and the ethical use of technology.(Sugumaran K. M, D.,et al.,2024) As digital interactions become ubiquitous, understanding the principles The foundational concept of digital privacy can be traced to the broader notion of privacy itself, which is traditionally viewed as the right to keep personal matters confidential and free from intrusion. In the digital realm, privacy takes on new dimensions, encompassing the data we provide through online activities, the metadata generated by our interactions, and the implications of surveillance technologies. The rise of the internet, social media, and mobile applications has significantly increased the volume of personal data available, prompting both legal and ethical considerations regarding its management. reflects growing concerns over consumer privacy and has set a precedent for other states considering similar legislation. This patchwork of laws presents challenges for organizations operating across state lines, requiring them to navigate (Apple., et al.,2021) a complex regulatory environment. Proliferation of data analytics, artificial intelligence, and machine learning has made it possible to extract insights from vast datasets, often at the expense of individual privacy. Organizations increasingly rely on tracking mechanisms, such as cookies and pixels, to monitor user behavior online. While these technologies can enhance user experience and inform business decisions, they also raise significant privacy concerns. The debate over user consent and transparency is central to discussions about responsible data practices, as many users.

Moreover, of the data collection practices and the implications of sharing their personal information. However, many users are presented with lengthy privacy policies that are often difficult to understand, leading to a lack of meaningful consent. Efforts to simplify these policies and enhance transparency are underway, with initiatives aiming to provide clearer information about data practices and user rights. The ethical considerations surrounding digital privacy extend beyond compliance with laws and regulations. with consumers. Internationally, digital privacy is also shaped by cross-border data flows and the challenges they pose. With the globalization of data, personal information often crosses international borders, complicating the enforcement of privacy laws. On the need for robust mechanisms to safeguard personal information in an interconnected world, highlighting the ongoing tension between privacy rights and economic interests. and the need for clear regulations to govern their use. As societies grapple with these challenges, there is a growing call for a balanced approach that respects individual privacy while addressing legitimate security (Sugumaran K. M, D., et al.,2024) concerns. essential for individuals to be (Bennett, C. J. et al.,2018) proactive in protecting their personal information. This includes being aware of data collection practices, utilizing privacy settings on online platforms, and advocating for greater transparency and accountability from organizations. .In conclusion, understanding digital privacy requires an appreciation of the complex interplay between concepts, laws, and regulations. will shape the future of technology and society, emphasizing the importance of balancing innovation with the fundamental rights of individuals.

DATA COLLECTION AND AI: THE PRIVACY IMPLICATIONS OF BIG DATA

At the heart of the issue is the scale and scope of data collection. Organizations often collect data with minimal transparency, relying on complex user agreements that many individuals do not fully understand (Vijayakumar G, et al., 2024). This lack of clarity can lead to a false sense of consent among users, who may unknowingly relinquish control over their personal information. For example, when users agree to terms and conditions on digital platforms, they may inadvertently consent to extensive data tracking, including their browsing habits, purchasing behaviors, and even biometric data. Such practices raise ethical influencing everything from targeted advertising to loan approvals. While these applications can improve efficiency and personalization, they also risk reinforcing biases inherent in the data (BMW et al.,2021), potentially leading to discriminatory outcomes. For instance, if a model is trained on biased historical data, it may perpetuate those biases, adversely affecting marginalized groups. Thus, the intertwining of AI and data collection not only raises questions of privacy but also of fairness and accountability. Long-term repercussions for individuals affected. These regulations reflect a growing recognition of is increasingly apparent, as disparate laws can create loopholes that undermine privacy protections. the context of AI, the challenge of ensuring privacy becomes even more pronounced (Paramasivam Selvakumar, et al.,2024). AI privacy risks. Organizations should adopt strategies that prioritize ethical data collection practices, such as anonymization and aggregation, to protect individual identities while still benefiting from data insights. Furthermore, as organizations integrate AI into their operations, the ethical implications of algorithmic decision-making must be considered. Transparency in AI processes is essential for building trust with consumers. Organizations are encouraged to adopt explainable AI (XAI) frameworks, which strive to make AI decision-making (Bornschein, R., et al.,2020) The societal implications of data collection (Ramakrishnan T., et al.,2022) and AI extend beyond individual privacy concerns. As organizations may not reflect the diverse perspectives of all communities, leading to skewed representations and decisions that overlook marginalized voices. This highlights the need for inclusive data practices and diverse input in the development of AI systems to ensure that they serve the interests of all individuals. it also poses serious privacy risks that cannot be ignored. Organizations must navigate the ethical landscape of data collection, prioritize transparency and accountability, and adhere to regulatory requirements to protect individual privacy. As technology continues to evolve, fostering a culture of ethical data practices will be essential emphasizing the need for a balanced approach that respects personal privacy while embracing the potential of innovation.

AI-DRIVEN DATA ANALYSIS: BALANCING INSIGHTS AND INTRUSION

AI-driven data analysis has become a cornerstone of decision-making across various sectors, offering organizations unprecedented insights into consumer behavior, operational efficiency, and market trends. However, s of vast amounts of personal data. This delicate balance between harnessing data for valuable At the heart of AI-driven data analysis is the ability to process and interpret large datasets with remarkable speed and accuracy (Cisco et al.,2020). For instance, in marketing, AI tools analyze consumer interactions and preferences to optimize advertising strategies and personalize user experiences. In healthcare, data analysis powered by AI can lead to early disease detection. financial details, and behavioral data. This extensive data collection poses risks of intrusion into individuals' private lives, leading to a growing apprehension among consumers about how their information is being used. Many users may not be fully aware of the extent of data tracking and the implications of sharing their personal information, resulting in a disconnect between consent and understanding. The challenge lies in ensuring that data collection practices are transparent, fair, and respectful of individuals' privacy rights. The implications of intrusive data practices extend beyond individual concerns; they also impact organizational credibility and consumer trust. Organizations that prioritize aggressive data collection without adequate transparency risk alienating their customers. As consumers become more discerning about their data, those organizations that embrace ethical data practices and prioritize user consent are likely to foster stronger relationships and gain a competitive edge in the market. In response to these challenges, regulatory frameworks have begun to take shape globally.

Legislation like These regulations represent a significant shift toward prioritizing consumer privacy, yet compliance remains a complex issue for many organizations, particularly those operating in multiple jurisdictions with varying legal requirements. where only the information necessary for a specific purpose is collected. By focusing on relevant data and anonymizing personal information, organizations can mitigate privacy risks while still gaining valuable insights. Moreover, organizations should establish clear data governance frameworks that outline policies for data use, storage, and sharing, ensuring accountability and transparency in their data practices. which aims to make AI decision-making processes more interpretable and accessible. By providing clarity on how data informs. AI-generated insights, organizations can enhance trust and mitigate concerns about the potential misuse of technology. Consumer education also plays a crucial role in striking the right balance between insights and intrusion. As individuals become more informed about data privacy issues, they can make better decisions regarding their personal information. Organizations can facilitate this process by offering clear, concise information about their data collection practices, user rights, and how individuals Looking ahead, the landscape of AI-driven data analysis will continue to evolve, necessitating ongoing dialogue about the ethical and privacy implications of these technologies. As organizations harness the power of AI to gain insights, they must remain vigilant in their commitment to protecting individual privacy rights (Cox, K. et al.,2017). By prioritizing ethical data practices, investing in transparency, and fostering consumer awareness, organizations can successfully navigate the complexities of data collection and analysis while building trust and credibility in an increasingly data-driven world. implementing transparent governance maintaining this balance will be crucial for fostering a digital environment that values both insights and the protection of personal information.

THE ROLE OF AI IN DATA PROTECTION: ENCRYPTION, ANONYMIZATION, AND ACCESS CONTROL

These methodologies not only bolster data security but also facilitate compliance with regulatory frameworks, helping organizations navigate the intricate landscape of data protection. Encryption serves as one of the foundational pillars of data security, transforming sensitive information into unreadable encryption processes through advanced algorithms and machine learning techniques. Traditional encryption methods, while effective, can be vulnerable to increasingly sophisticated cyber threats. AI-driven encryption solutions can adapt to emerging threats by continuously learning from patterns in attack behaviors. learning models on breaches to predict potential vulnerabilities, allowing organizations to preemptively adjust their encryption protocols. This proactive approach not only enhances the robustness of encryption but also minimizes the risks associated with data breaches.AI technologies facilitate effective anonymization techniques that maintain the utility of data while protecting privacy. For instance, AI algorithms can intelligently identify and mask personally identifiable information (PII) within datasets, ensuring that the data can be used for analysis without compromising individual privacy. This is particularly valuable in fields such as healthcare and research, where data must be analyzed to derive insights while adhering to strict privacy regulations. By employing AI-driven anonymization Access control is another vital component of data protection, governing who can access sensitive information and under what circumstances.

AI enhances access control mechanisms through intelligent user authentication and behavior analysis. Traditional access control systems often rely on static credentials, such as passwords, which can be easily compromised. In contrast, (de Oliveira Santini, F., et al..,2020), This dynamic approach to access control not only strengthens security but also enhances the user experience by reducing friction associated with traditional authentication methods.. AI can automate compliance processes by continuously monitoring data usage and ensuring that organizations adhere to established protocols. For instance, AI systems can track data access and modifications in real-time, providing an auditable trail that simplifies compliance reporting. Additionally, AI can assist in managing consent preferences by analyzing user interactions and ensuring that data is processed only with the appropriate permissions. The reliance on AI technologies can introduce new vulnerabilities, particularly if algorithms are not properly secured. For instance, adversarial attacks can manipulate AI models, leading to incorrect data processing or compromised security measures. Organizations must invest in robust AI governance frameworks to ensure that these systems are resilient against such threats and operate transparently. This includes implementing rigorous testing protocols, regular audits, and ongoing training to keep AI models updated and effective. Transparency. As AI systems make decisions regarding data access and protection, (Deloitte et al.,2020). By fostering transparency in AI systems, organizations can build trust with their customers and ensure that data protection measures are not only effective but also ethically sound. Additionally, the balance between data protection and data usability is a critical consideration. While anonymization and encryption are essential for safeguarding personal information, they can also limit the potential for data-driven insights. Organizations must carefully assess the trade-offs between security and usability, ensuring that data remains accessible for legitimate business purposes without compromising privacy. In the context of increasing regulatory scrutiny and public awareness regarding data privacy, organizations must prioritize the implementation of AI-driven data protection strategies. By leveraging AI for encryption, anonymization, and access control, organizations can not only enhance their security posture This proactive approach can lead to improved customer trust and loyalty, ultimately contributing to long-term business success and access control strategies that are essential for safeguarding sensitive information in a data-driven world. While the integration of AI technologies presents opportunities for enhanced security and compliance, it also necessitates careful consideration of ethical implications, accountability, and the balance between data protection and usability.

AI-POWERED SURVEILLANCE: FACIAL RECOGNITION, TRACKING, AND PROFILING

surveillance technologies have transformed how governments, organizations, and individuals monitor behavior and gather data. AI-powered surveillance systems leverage advanced techniques, such as facial recognition, tracking, and profiling, to enhance security and operational efficiency. Facial recognition technology is one of the most prominent applications of AI in surveillance. (Hung, H., et al.,2009) By analyzing facial features and matching them against vast databases, this technology can identify individuals in real-time, enabling law enforcement and security agencies to track persons of interest. The potential benefits are significant: facial recognition can aid in locating missing persons, apprehending criminals, and preventing terrorism. However, the deployment of this technology is not without controversy. Critics argue that facial recognition can lead to wrongful identifications, particularly for marginalized communities, The lack of transparency in how facial recognition systems operate and how data is stored further complicates matters, as individuals have little recourse to challenge incorrect or harmful data about them. In addition to facial recognition, AI-powered tracking technologies play a crucial role in surveillance ecosystems.

These systems can monitor an individual's movements through various means, including GPS tracking, mobile phone data, and social media activity. While tracking can enhance safety—such as locating a lost child or monitoring the movements of individuals under protective custody—consent. The ability to track individuals in real-time can lead to invasive monitoring, where personal freedoms are compromised in the name of security. As with facial recognition, the potential for abuse is significant, particularly when tracking data is used for purposes beyond its original intent, such as targeting individuals for political reasons or social profiling. Profiling, a process that involves analyzing collected data to create detailed profiles of individuals or groups, is another area where AI's impact is deeply felt. Organizations can leverage profiling to identify trends and behaviors, which can be useful in marketing, law enforcement, and public policy. However, the use of AI for profiling often relies on algorithms that may inadvertently reflect societal biases, leading to discriminatory practices. For instance, the implications of AI-powered surveillance extend beyond individual privacy concerns; they also pose significant societal challenges. The normalization of surveillance can lead to a culture of mistrust, where individuals feel that their actions are constantly scrutinized. This environment can discourage civic engagement and stifle dissent, as people may fear repercussions for expressing their views or participating in protests. The use of surveillance technologies in public spaces, often justified by the need for security, raises fundamental questions about the rights of individuals in democratic societies. As governments and organizations increasingly adopt AI-driven surveillance, regulatory frameworks are struggling to keep pace. In many jurisdictions, there is a lack of comprehensive legislation governing the use of facial recognition and other surveillance technologies. (Graef, I., et al.,2020) This regulatory gap creates an environment where technologies can be deployed without adequate oversight, leading to potential abuses and violations of civil liberties and provide individuals with the ability to opt out of surveillance measures where feasible. Moreover, regular audits of AI systems can help ensure that they operate fairly and do not perpetuate biases. Engaging with communities to understand their concerns and perspectives is essential for building trust and ensuring that surveillance measures are implemented in a manner that respects individual rights. can expose sensitive information, leading to identity theft or misuse. Therefore, robust data protection measures must be integrated into AI surveillance systems to safeguard individuals' information and ensure that it is used responsibly. The potential for AI to enhance surveillance capabilities is matched by society must grapple with the implications of pervasive surveillance on individual freedoms, privacy, and democracy. A careful evaluation of the trade-offs between security and civil liberties is crucial in navigating this complex landscape. In conclusion, AI-powered surveillance technologies, including facial recognition, tracking, and profiling, present both opportunities and challenges. security and operational efficiency, they also raise significant ethical and privacy concerns. The balance between leveraging AI for public safety and protecting individual rights is a delicate one that requires careful consideration and robust regulatory frameworks. By prioritizing transparency, accountability ongoing dialogue and reflection on these issues will be vital in shaping a future where technology serves the public good without compromising individual freedoms.

household chores and controlling smart appliances to providing instant information and entertainment. However, alongside these benefits, there are significant privacy risks that warrant careful consideration. The dual nature of virtual assistants and smart homes necessitates a nuanced understanding of how to maximize their advantages while minimizing potential threats to personal privacy. enable users to control various smart devices, access information, and even make purchases hands-free. The convenience offered by these technologies is undeniable (Ioannou, A., et al.,2020); for example, users can adjust their home lighting, set thermostats, and play music with simple verbal instructions. This level of integration into daily life enhances the overall quality of living, particularly for those with mobility challenges or busy lifestyles. Additionally, virtual assistants can learn user preferences over time, further personalizing the experience and improving efficiency. Despite these advantages, the deployment of virtual assistants raises serious privacy concerns. At the core of these concerns is the constant data collection inherent to their functionality. Virtual assistants must listen for activation commands, which means they are perpetually While manufacturers assert that recordings are only stored after activation, many users are unaware of the extent of data collection that occurs. The potential for inadvertent recordings—instances where conversations are captured unintentionally—can lead to significant breaches of privacy. Furthermore, these recordings may be stored in the cloud and analyzed to improve AI performance, creating However, the aggregation of data from these devices can provide a comprehensive picture of a person's daily life, habits, and routines. can be exposed, leading to serious repercussions. Another significant privacy risk associated with virtual assistants and smart homes is the potential for unauthorized access. Many devices are. for example, a hacked security camera could provide real-time surveillance of a home, compromising personal safety.

Therefore, users must be vigilant about securing their smart home networks and regularly updating device firmware to protect against such threats. Regulatory frameworks addressing the privacy risks of virtual assistants and smart homes are still evolving. In response to growing concerns, some jurisdictions have begun implementing regulations that require greater transparency from companies regarding data collection practices. consent, granting individuals rights over their personal data. However, there is still a notable gap in comprehensive regulations specifically targeting smart home technologies, leaving consumers largely unprotected from potential privacy infringements. To navigate the privacy landscape associated investing in security measures is crucial for protecting smart home networks. Implementing strong, unique passwords for devices and routers, using two-factor authentication when available, and regularly updating firmware can enhance the security of smart home systems. Users should also be cautious when connecting new devices to their network, ensuring that they understand the security implications of each device before integration. The benefits of virtual assistants and smart homes, such as increased convenience, energy efficiency, and improved security, must be weighed against the inherent privacy risks. While these technologies offer significant advantages, users must remain vigilant and informed about the potential implications for their personal information. . As consumers increasingly rely on AI-powered devices, it is essential to strike a balance between embracing innovation and safeguarding personal privacy. Through informed decision-making, proactive security measures, and an understanding of regulatory developments, individuals can navigate the complexities of virtual assistants and smart homes while protecting their most sensitive information. The ongoing dialogue surrounding privacy in the context of these technologies will play a crucial role in shaping a future where convenience and security coexist harmoniously.

AI-DRIVEN HEALTHCARE: BALANCING PERSONALIZED MEDICINE AND DATA PRIVACY

AI models trained on vast datasets of medical images can assist radiologists in diagnosing conditions such as cancer with remarkable accuracy, often outperforming traditional diagnostic methods. Similarly(Jones, M. R., et al.,2008), AI can analyze genomic data to identify mutations that may inform targeted therapies, thus personalizing treatment plans based on individual genetic profiles. This shift toward personalized medicine promises not only to enhance patient care but also to streamline healthcare resources by reducing trial-and-error approaches that require access to comprehensive datasets. High-profile incidents of data breaches in healthcare have underscored the vulnerabilities associated with storing vast amounts of sensitive information electronically. Such breaches not only compromise patient evolve to ensure that patients are not only aware of their rights but also understand the complexities of data sharing in AI applications. Many individuals may not fully grasp the extent to which their data is utilized for research and AI model training, which complicates their ability to make informed decisions about participation. Yet the rapid pace of technological innovation often outstrips existing regulations (Kaaniche, N., et al. 2020). By anonymizing data used for AI training and analysis, organizations can minimize the risk of re-identification while still deriving valuable insights. Additionally, the use of federated learning—where AI models are trained across decentralized data sources without directly accessing sensitive patient information—represents an innovative approach that can enhance privacy while enabling effective data analysis. Moreover, fostering a culture of transparency and trust is crucial in addressing privacy concerns. Healthcare organizations should engage patients in conversations about data usage, providing clear explanations of how their information will contribute to AI research and personalized treatments. The intersection of AI and personalized medicine also necessitates a focus on ethical AI essential for equitable healthcare delivery. Bias in AI systems can arise from skewed training data, of AI-driven healthcare effectively. This balanced approach will not only enhance patient trust but also lay the groundwork for a future where AI technologies are harnessed responsibly, ultimately improving health outcomes while safeguarding the privacy of individuals. Patient care through personalized medicine. By utilizing vast datasets to inform treatment decisions, the healthcare sector can successfully navigate the delicate balance between leveraging the benefits of AI and ensuring the protection of sensitive patient information. As we look to the future, it is crucial that the dialogue surrounding

GLOBAL PRIVACY REGULATIONS: GDPR, CCPA, AND BEYOND

In an increasingly interconnected digital world, privacy regulations have become. The emergence of various privacy frameworks, (Liu, Y., et al.,2017) conversation about data protection. This has led to a ripple effect, compelling businesses worldwide to comply with its stringent In contrast, the CCPA, enacted in 2018 and effective from January 2020, focuses primarily on enhancing consumer rights in California. While it shares some principles with the GDPR, such on consumer rights reflects a growing trend in the United States toward increased transparency and control over personal data. However, critics argue that it lacks the enforceability and scope of the GDPR, leaving significant gaps in protections. The differences between GDPR and CCPA highlight the challenges of harmonizing privacy regulations globally. While both frameworks aim to protect personal data, they operate within distinct legal and cultural contexts., where businesses often prioritize innovation and economic growth. This divergence complicates compliance for multinational corporations, which must navigate varying legal landscapes while striving to maintain consistent data protection practices. Beyond the GDPR and CCPA, a growing number of jurisdictions are adopting their own privacy regulations, reflecting local priorities and societal values. For instance, (PIPEDA) governs private sector data practices, while several provinces are considering or have enacted their own privacy laws. In Asia, countries like Japan and South Korea have made strides in enhancing data protection, often aligning their regulations with international standards to facilitate cross-border data flows. Privacy regulations continue to evolve, the call for a more unified framework is growing. Organizations increasingly face compliance challenges due to the fragmented nature of privacy laws, which can lead to confusion and inefficiencies. The lack of a consistent global standard complicates the ability of companies to implement cohesive data protection strategies, particularly in industries where data is frequently shared across borders. In response, some stakeholders advocate for international agreements that establish baseline privacy standards, akin to the efforts seen in areas such as trade and environmental policy. The discussion around privacy regulation is also evolving in light of emerging technologies, including, as they often rely on vast amounts of personal data for functionality. Regulators are increasingly tasked with addressing the implications of these advancements, balancing innovation with the protection of individual rights. (Lam, C. K., et al.,2017) Moreover, the rise of data breaches and high-profile incidents of misuse has heightened public awareness and demand for stronger privacy protections. approaches, prompting lawmakers to consider more robust protections and greater enforcement mechanisms. As public sentiment continues to evolve, businesses must adapt to meet growing expectations for transparency and accountability in their data practices. In conclusion, global privacy regulations, exemplified by the GDPR, CCPA, and other emerging frameworks, represent a critical response to the challenges posed by the digital age. in privacy standards. As technology continues to advance, regulators will need to remain vigilant in adapting their approaches to safeguard privacy while fostering innovation. comprehensive and effective privacy framework that addresses the needs of all parties in an increasingly interconnected world.

AI-SPECIFIC REGULATIONS: EMERGING STANDARDS AND GUIDELINES

The emergence of standards and guidelines aimed at regulating AI reflects a growing recognition of the importance of responsible AI development and deployment, ensuring that these powerful tools are used ethically and transparently. One of the most notable developments in AI regulation is This groundbreaking legislation aims to establish a comprehensive regulatory framework for AI within the EU, categorizing AI applications based on risk levels—unacceptable, high, and low risk. Unacceptable risk applications, such as social scoring by governments or biometric surveillance in public spaces, are banned outright. High-risk AI systems, which include those used in critical areas such as healthcare and transportation, must adhere operation. By imposing these requirements, the EU aims to promote trust in AI technologies while protecting fundamental rights and freedoms. In addition to the EU's initiatives, various national governments and international organizations are developing their own frameworks and guidelines for AI regulation. For instance, the United States has taken a more decentralized approach, with several federal agencies proposing principles for AI governance. These guidelines encourage stakeholders to prioritize the ethical development of AI while fostering innovation and economic growth. However, the lack of a cohesive national strategy poses challenges for consistency and effectiveness in AI governance across states and sectors. Beyond government initiatives (Zwick, D., et al.,2004), various industry groups and non-governmental organizations are also contributing promoting transparency, accountability, and privacy. Such industry-led efforts complement governmental regulations by providing additional layers of guidance and best practices for organizations working with AI. As AI systems increasingly operate autonomously, establishing accountability for their outcomes becomes complex (Munoz, J. A., et al.,2020). Regulations are beginning to require organizations to designate responsible parties for AI systems, ensuring that there is a mechanism for addressing potential harms caused by AI decisions.

This accountability framework is vital for maintaining public trust in AI technologies and ensuring that organizations take responsibility for their actions. Moreover, international cooperation is essential in addressing the global nature of AI technology. AI systems often operate across borders, raising challenges related to jurisdiction and enforcement. Collaborative efforts among countries can help harmonize regulations and promote best practices, facilitating the responsible development of AI on a global scale.(Wu, L., et al.,2021) Organizations such as the OECD have initiated discussions on AI principles, advocating for international collaboration to promote responsible AI governance. While engaging with stakeholders, including technologists, ethicists, and the public, is essential for creating effective regulations that reflect diverse perspectives and priorities. In conclusion, the emergence of AI-specific regulations and guidelines marks a critical step and international organizations work to establish standards for ethical AI, a balanced approach is necessary—one that fosters innovation while safeguarding fundamental rights and public trust. The complexities of AI regulation require ongoing dialogue, collaboration, and adaptation to address the evolving landscape of technology and its societal implications. By prioritizing ethical considerations, transparency, and accountability, the regulatory frameworks being established today can pave the way for a future where AI enhances human potential without compromising individual rights or societal values (Nandan, R., 2019).

CORPORATE GOVERNANCE AND AI: ETHICS, ACCOUNTABILITY, AND TRANSPARENCY

The integration of artificial intelligence (AI) into corporate governance has transformed how organizations operate, make decisions, and engage with stakeholders., which encompasses the systems and processes that direct and control companies, must adapt to ensure that AI is deployed responsibly and in alignment with organizational values..Establishing clear lines of accountability is crucial to ensure that stakeholders can seek redress for any negative outcomes associated with AI. Organizations should consider appointing designated AI ethics officers or establishing independent review boards to oversee AI deployments (Privacy International 2019), ensuring that there is accountability at multiple levels. Transparency in AI systems is vital for fostering trust among stakeholders, including employees, customers, and investors. Stakeholders are increasingly demanding clarity. Organizations must prioritize transparency by providing accessible explanations of their AI processes and the rationale behind automated decisions. This can include implementing explainable AI (XAI) techniques that allow users to understand the underlying mechanisms of AI algorithms. By demystifying AI technologies, organizations can enhance trust and confidence among stakeholders, reducing apprehensions about the potential misuse (Xu, H., et al.,2018).

DESIGNING AI SYSTEMS WITH PRIVACY IN MIND: PRIVACY BY DESIGN

This framework is essential for ensuring that personal data is protected, and that individuals' rights are respected in an era where data-driven technologies dominate various sectors, from healthcare and finance to social media and autonomous systems. Privacy by Design comprises seven foundational principles that guide organizations in developing AI systems that prioritize user privacy. The first principle, proactive not reactive, emphasizes the need for organizations to anticipate and address privacy risks before they manifest. This involves conducting thorough risk assessments during the design phase to identify potential vulnerabilities related to data collection, processing, and storage. (Rodger, C. 2019) By adopting a proactive stance, organizations can implement measures to mitigate these risks from the outset, fostering a culture of privacy awareness that permeates the development process. The second principle, By default, users should be presented with options that prioritize their privacy, such as opting out of implementing strong access controls, and ensuring that data processing adheres to ethical standards. For instance, AI systems designed for healthcare applications should include mechanisms to de-identify patient data, thus minimizing the risk of re-identification and protecting sensitive health information. The principle of full functionality recognizes that privacy and utility should not be mutually exclusive. Organizations can design AI systems that deliver valuable services while simultaneously protecting user privacy. For example, can innovate responsibly, delivering services that meet user needs while respecting their privacy rights. End-to-end security This includes using encryption to secure data in transit and at rest, implementing intrusion detection systems, and regularly auditing access logs. By ensuring comprehensive security measures, organizations can safeguard against data breaches and unauthorized access, reinforcing users' confidence in the protection of their information. Use and share personal data. Providing users with easily accessible information about data practices enables them to make informed decisions about their privacy. Transparency also includes offering users' insights into how AI algorithms function and how decisions are made, especially in high-stakes contexts like hiring or (Wong, S. K., et al.,2019).

This commitment to transparency fosters accountability and empowers users to understand their rights regarding personal data. including end-users, in discussions about privacy implications and expectations. This participatory approach allows organizations to better understand user concerns and incorporate their feedback into AI system design. By respecting user privacy and valuing their input, organizations can foster a sense of ownership and trust, ultimately leading to more successful AI deployments demonstrate their commitment to ethical data practices, thereby gaining a competitive advantage in the marketplace. Privacy-centric culture that values ethical considerations alongside business goals. Additionally, technical challenges may arise when integrating privacy features into AI systems.(Roth, E., et al.,2019) For instance, and development to explore innovative solutions that enable privacy-preserving data analysis, such as differential privacy and federated learning.(Wu, C. 2020) These techniques allow organizations to In conclusion, designing AI systems with privacy in mind through the framework of the development process, organizations can create AI technologies that respect individual rights and foster user trust. The principles of Privacy by Design—proactive measures, default privacy settings, embedded protections, functional utility, security, transparency, and user respect—provide a comprehensive roadmap for organizations seeking to navigate the complexities of AI while prioritizing privacy. As regulations evolve and public awareness of privacy issues increases, adopting a proactive approach to privacy will not only ensure compliance but also enhance the ethical deployment of AI technologies. Ultimately, organizations that prioritize

AI-POWERED PRIVACY SOLUTIONS: HOMOMORPHIC ENCRYPTION AND SECURE MULTI-PARTY COMPUTATION

Homomorphic encryption mitigates these risks by allowing data scientists to build and validate models on encrypted datasets. This is particularly advantageous in collaborative environments where multiple organizations need to share insights without revealing their sensitive data. For example, pharmaceutical companies could collaborate on drug discovery using encrypted patient data, accelerating research while safeguarding individual privacy. making it resource-intensive compared to traditional methods. Researchers are actively working to improve the efficiency of homomorphic encryption schemes, but practical applications often require a balance between performance and security. Innovations such as partially homomorphic encryption and optimized algorithms are helping to address these challenges, making the technology more accessible for real-world applications. which relies on encrypting data before processing, MPC allows participants (Wamba, S. F., et al.,2020) to collaborate on computations without sharing their sensitive information. Each party holds a piece of the input, and through cryptographic protocols, they can derive results without revealing their individual contributions. This capability is particularly valuable in scenarios (Salminen, A., et al.,2021) where data cannot be centralized due to privacy regulations or competitive concerns. One practical application of MPC is in collaborative analytics. For instance, organizations in the financial sector can use MPC to perform risk assessments without revealing sensitive financial data to each other. By conducting calculations jointly while ensuring that individual data points remain private, organizations can gain insights that inform decision-making without compromising confidentiality. Similarly, in the healthcare sector, research institutions can collaborate on public health studies while preserving the privacy of patient data, leading to more robust findings without the risk of data exposure.MPC also regulations.

As organizations face increasing scrutiny regarding data privacy, the ability. By enabling data owners to retain control over their information while still participating in collaborative analytics, MPC fosters an environment of trust and compliance. Both privacy-preserving technologies in the age of AI. As organizations seek to harness the power of data while protecting individual rights, these cryptographic methods provide essential tools for achieving that balance. The combination of advanced AI techniques and privacy-enhancing technologies creates opportunities for innovative Moreover, the integration of AI with these privacy solutions enhances their effectiveness. AI algorithms can help identify patterns in encrypted data, enabling organizations to draw insights without compromising privacy. This synergy between AI and privacy technologies not only amplifies the potential of data-driven decision-making but also reinforces the commitment to ethical data use. Despite their potential, widespread adoption of homomorphic encryption and MPC remains a challenge. Factors such as implementation complexity, interoperability, and the need for specialized expertise can hinder their integration into existing systems. Organizations must invest in training and resources to effectively utilize these technologies, which can be a barrier for smaller enterprises or those with limited technical capabilities. (Schmidt, R., et al.,2018) Furthermore, as the landscape of data privacy evolves. The continued evolution of these privacy-preserving techniques, coupled with advancements in AI, promises to unlock new opportunities for responsible data usage across various sectors. As organizations navigate the complexities of data privacy, adopting these innovative solutions will

NAVIGATING THE FUTURE OF AI AND DIGITAL PRIVACY - CHALLENGES, OPPORTUNITIES, AND STRATEGIES

reshaping daily life. However, this progress brings significant challenges concerning digital privacy, necessitating a nuanced approach that balances technological benefits with the need for robust privacy protections. (Tsai, J. Y., et al. (2011). privacy implications is essential for stakeholders across sectors, from government regulators to private organizations and individual users., often requiring sensitive personal information to function effectively. This reliance raises critical concerns about data security, potential misuse, and the erosion of privacy. High-profile data breaches and scandals have amplified public scrutiny regarding how organizations collect, store, and utilize personal data. Consequently, stakeholders must grapple with the ethical implications of data handling, particularly in an age where individuals increasingly demand greater control over their information. Moreover, the issue of Such biases not only violate principles of fairness but also raise significant privacy concerns, as marginalized groups may find themselves subjected to heightened scrutiny or adverse outcomes based on biased algorithmic decisions. Addressing this challenge requires a commitment to diverse data sourcing and rigorous testing of AI systems for bias, fostering inclusivity in both development and deployment. In addition to these challenges, the evolving regulatory landscape surrounding market, appealing to privacy-conscious consumers who prioritize ethical data practices. Strategically navigating the future of AI and digital privacy involves embracing technological innovations that enhance privacy protections. Solutions. By investing in these advanced privacy-preserving techniques, organizations can mitigate risks associated with data breaches and unauthorized access, ultimately fostering greater trust among users. too must the understanding of privacy implications among stakeholders.

Organizations should invest in training programs for employees to ensure they are equipped to navigate the complexities of data privacy in an AI-driven environment. Furthermore, raising public awareness about digital privacy rights and the implications of Collaboration across sectors is essential for creating a cohesive approach to digital privacy in the age of AI knowledge sharing, foster innovation, and establish frameworks for ethical AI use that address privacy concerns. This multi-stakeholder approach can also help shape public policy, ensuring that regulations keep pace with technological advancements while safeguarding individual rights. Moreover, leveraging AI itself can enhance digital privacy efforts. AI technologies can be employed to monitor and detect potential privacy violations, enabling organizations to respond proactively to emerging threats. (Voigt, P., et al.,2017) For example, AI-driven analytics can help identify anomalous data access patterns, triggering alerts and investigations before significant breaches occur. Additionally, AI can support the development of privacy-enhancing technologies by optimizing algorithms for data anonymization and encryption, ensuring that privacy remains a core consideration in AI development. Looking forward, it is essential to establish a culture of privacy within organizations that prioritize ethical considerations alongside business objectives. This culture should extend to every level of the organization, from leadership to frontline employees. Organizations must recognize that prioritizing digital companies can create an environment where ethical data use is championed and valued. The future of AI and digital privacy is fraught with challenges, yet it also presents numerous opportunities for innovation and improvement. proactively address privacy concerns through strategic investments, stakeholder engagement, and ethical practices will be better positioned to navigate this complex terrain. The intersection of AI and digital privacy offers a unique opportunity to redefine how data is used and shared, fostering an environment (van Slyke, C., et al.,2020) where technological advancement goes hand in hand with respect for individual rights. Investing in advanced privacy technologies, and fostering a culture of ethical data use, organizations can build a more secure and trustworthy digital environment. Collaboration among stakeholders, ongoing education, and a commitment to transparency will be crucial in shaping a future where AI serves as a powerful tool for progress without compromising the privacy and rights of individuals. As we move forward, the imperative to safeguard digital privacy will remain a defining characteristic of successful.

CONCLUSION

As we stand at the crossroads of rapid technological advancement and heightened privacy concerns, the imperative to balance innovation and privacy in the digital world has never been more pressing. Artificial intelligence (AI) holds immense potential to transform industries, enhance efficiencies, and deliver personalized experiences that were once thought to be unattainable. However, this transformative power is accompanied by significant responsibilities, organizations must navigate this terrain with a strategic mindset, recognizing that trust is a cornerstone of successful AI deployment. As consumers become more aware of their data rights and the potential implications of AI systems, they increasingly demand transparency, accountability, and ethical practices from organizations. To achieve this balance, a multi-faceted approach is essential. Organizations must prioritize the integration of privacy by design principles throughout the AI development lifecycle. By embedding privacy considerations into the core of their technologies, businesses can ensure that they build systems that respect user data from the outset. . of AI while minimizing the risks associated with sensitive data processing. These innovations enable data analysis without compromising individual privacy, thereby fostering a culture of ethical data use. Organizations that embrace these technologies can differentiate themselves in a crowded marketplace, attracting privacy-conscious consumers and gaining a competitive edge. Education and stakeholder engagement are also critical components of achieving a harmonious balance between innovation and privacy and advocacy groups creates an environment of collaboration and trust. By soliciting feedback and involving stakeholders in decision-making processes, organizations can develop AI solutions that not only meet business objectives but also align with societal values. Rather than viewing regulations as burdensome, organizations should see them as an opportunity to enhance their privacy practices and build consumer confidence. By demonstrating compliance and commitment to ethical data handling, businesses can strengthen their reputation and position themselves as leaders in the responsible use of AI. In addition, it is vital for organizations to remain agile and responsive to the evolving landscape of digital privacy. As new technologies emerge and societal norms shift, the understanding of what constitutes acceptable data use will continue to evolve. Ultimately, the journey toward balancing innovation and privacy is ongoing and requires continuous effort and commitment from all stakeholders. By embracing a holistic approach that prioritizes privacy, invests in advanced technologies, and fosters stakeholder engagement, organizations can navigate this complex landscape effectively.

REFERENCES

Alsmadi, D., & Prybutok, V. (2018). Sharing and storage behavior via cloud computing: Security and privacy in research and practice. *Computers in Human Behavior*, 85, 218–226. DOI: 10.1016/j.chb.2018.04.003

Appel, G., Grewal, L., Hadi, R., & Stephen, A. T. (2020). The future of social media in marketing. *Journal of the Academy of Marketing Science*, 48(1), 79–95. DOI: 10.1007/s11747-019-00695-1 PMID: 32431463

Apple. (2021). Apple Customer Privacy Policy. Apple. https://www.apple.com/legal/privacy/

Bennett, C. J. (2018). The European general data protection regulation: An instrument for the globalization of privacy standards? *Information Polity*, 23(2), 239–246. DOI: 10.3233/IP-180002

BMW. (2021). BMW Group Data Ecosystem. BMW. https://www.bmwgroup.com/en/innovation/technologies-and-mobility/bmw-group-data-ecosystem.html

Bornschein, R., Schmidt, L., & Maier, E. (2020). The effect of consumers' perceived power and risk in digital information privacy: The example of cookie notices. *Journal of Public Policy & Marketing*, 39(2), 135–154. DOI: 10.1177/0743915620902143

Cisco. (2020). Protecting data privacy to maintain digital trust: The importance of protecting data privacy during the pandemic and beyond. Cisco. https://www.cisco.com/c/dam/en_us/about/doing_business/trust-center/docs/cybersecurity-series-2020-cps.pdf

Cox, K. (2017). Gambling services use big data to target recovering gamblers, low-income families. Consumerist. https://consumerist.com/2017/08/31/gambling-services-use-big-data-to-target-recovering-gamblers-low-income-families/

de Oliveira Santini, F., Ladeira, W. J., Pinto, D. C., Herter, M. M., Sampaio, C. H., & Babin, B. (2020). Customer engagement in social media: A framework and meta-analysis. *Journal of the Academy of Marketing Science*, 48(6), 1211–1228. DOI: 10.1007/s11747-020-00731-5

Deloitte. (2020). Data valuation: Understanding the value of your data assets. Deloitte. https://www2.deloitte.com/content/dam/Deloitte/global/Documents/Finance/Valuation-Data-Digital.pdf

Graef, I., & van den Boom, J. (2020). Spill-overs in data governance: Uncovering the uneasy relationship between the GDPR's right to data portability and EU sector-specific data access regimes. *Journal of European Consumer and Market Law*, 9(1).

Hung, H., & Wong, Y. H. (2009). Information transparency and digital privacy protection: Are they mutually exclusive in the provision of e-services? *Journal of Services Marketing*, 23(3), 154–164. DOI: 10.1108/08876040910955161

Ioannou, A., Tussyadiah, I., & Lu, Y. (2020). Privacy concerns and disclosure of biometric and behavioral data for travel. *International Journal of Information Management*, 54, 102122. DOI: 10.1016/j.ijinfomgt.2020.102122

Johnson, G. A., Shriver, S. K., & Goldberg, S. G. (2020). Privacy and market concentration: intended and unintended consequences of the GDPR. United States Federal Trade Commission. https://www.ftc.gov/system/files/documents/public_events/1548288/privacycon-2020-garrett_johnson.pdf

Jones, M. R., & Karsten, H. (2008). Giddens's structuration theory and information systems research. *Management Information Systems Quarterly*, 32(1), 127–157. DOI: 10.2307/25148831

Kaaniche, N., Laurent, M., & Belguith, S. (2020). Privacy enhancing technologies for solving the privacy-personalization paradox: Taxonomy and survey. *Journal of Network and Computer Applications*, 171, 102807. DOI: 10.1016/j.jnca.2020.102807

Lam, C. K., Lee, Y. K., & Chan, A. (2017). Big data privacy and security challenges: A review. *International Journal of Information Management*, 37(2), 89–94.

Liu, Y., & Chen, L. (2017). Digital marketing: The effects of online privacy on customer experience. *Marketing Intelligence & Planning*, 35(3), 442–455.

Mahadev Madgule, N. (2023). Mechanical properties and microstructure of activated TIG welded similar joints of Inconel alloys by desirability approaches. *Materials Today: Proceedings*, 77, 528–533. DOI: 10.1016/j.matpr.2022.12.250

Munoz, J. A., & Orozco, P. (2020). Big data and the right to privacy: A case study of the GDPR. *Journal of Law and Policy for the Information Society*, 16(1), 37–63.

Nandan, R., & Kaur, G. (2019). Privacy concerns of consumers in online shopping: A review of literature and future research agenda. *Journal of Retailing and Consumer Services*, 50, 57–65.

Privacy International. (2019). Data privacy: The importance of consumer awareness and privacy literacy, viewed 20/05/2021, from https://privacyinternational.org/report/3257/data-privacy-importance-consumer-awareness-and-privacy-literacy

Rodger, C. (2019). The GDPR: Implications for marketing communications. *Journal of Communication Management (London)*, 23(1), 7–14.

Roth, E., & Reiner, G. (2019). Toward a systematic understanding of privacy: A model of privacy-related behavior and its antecedents. *Computers in Human Behavior*, 100, 159–169.

Salminen, A., & Ahlgren, P. (2021). Digital marketing strategies in a post-pandemic world: What consumers want. *Journal of Digital & Social Media Marketing*, 9(1), 21–30.

Schmidt, R., & Möhring, K. (2018). The value of personal data: The impact of the GDPR on the marketing and advertising industry. *Journal of Digital Marketing*, 8(1), 1–22.

Sugumaran, K. M. D., Pandiyarajan V., Y. B S, Selvakumar P., & M. S. (2024). Analysis of Electromyography Signals for Control of Mechanical Prosthesis using Machine Learning Techniques. 2024 2nd International Conference on Intelligent Data Communication Technologies and Internet of Things (IDCIoT), 1059-1067. DOI: 10.1109/IDCIoT59759.2024.10467707

Tsai, J. Y., Egelman, S., & Cranor, L. F. (2011). The effect of online privacy information on purchasing behavior: An exploratory study. *International Journal of Human-Computer Studies*, 69(5), 392–404.

van Slyke, C., & Ilie, V. (2020). Organizational response to privacy regulations: A compliance perspective. *Journal of Business Ethics*, 162(2), 315–330.

Voigt, P., & Von dem Bussche, A. (2017). *The EU General Data Protection Regulation (GDPR): A practical guide*. Springer. DOI: 10.1007/978-3-319-57959-7

Wamba, S. F., & Akter, S. (2020). The role of big data analytics in addressing privacy and data protection challenges in the health care sector. *Health Information Science and Systems*, 8(1), 1–15. PMID: 31867102

Wong, S. K., & Cheng, H. K. (2019). Managing privacy in the age of big data: A review of privacy concerns, frameworks, and practices. *International Journal of Information Management*, 47, 101–114.

Wu, C. (2020). Privacy-aware personalized marketing in social networks: Challenges and future directions. *Journal of Interactive Marketing*, 52, 42–56.

Wu, L., & Zhang, D. (2021). Research on privacy protection in cloud computing environments: A survey. *Future Generation Computer Systems*, 117, 328–342.

Xu, H., & Teo, H. H. (2018). Examining the effects of privacy and personalization on user engagement in social media marketing. *International Journal of Information Management*, 38(1), 27–36.

Zwick, D., & Dholakia, N. (2004). Whose identity is it anyway? Consumer agency in the age of database marketing. *Journal of Macromarketing*, 24(1), 31–43. DOI: 10.1177/0276146704263920

Chapter 12
Balancing Educational Benefits With Privacy Concerns in Social Network-Based Learning

Amelie Madeline
https://orcid.org/0009-0005-4642-900X
Université de Limoges, France

ABSTRACT

With changed dynamics in the delivery of education in this generation, it can be affirmatively deduced that social networks will play a growing role. New technologies including artificial intelligence, blockchain, and IoT are possibilities for improving the learning process. But this progress brings in new privacy issues and that is why constant monitoring and constant change is the key here. This chapter strives to give a detailed analysis of the relationship between the educational advantages and privacy issues in social network-based learning. Thus, it tries to provide the reader with knowledge of its advantages and limitations as well as hints on how to avoid the pitfall in this rather sophisticated area. Finally, the goal is to create an educational environment that will enable innovation and preservation of privacy of students and educators in the modern era.

1. INTRODUCTION

Social networks have revolutionized the face of modern education. The practice of education is not only within walls or other physical learning spaces but is reverberating in virtual communities that cross geographical and cultural boundaries

DOI: 10.4018/979-8-3693-9015-3.ch012

(Troussas et al., 2020). Learning through social networks with the help of platforms like Facebook, LinkedIn, Twitter, Edmodo, and even systems tailor-made for the academic environment represents a sea change in pedagogy (Ahmed et al., 2019). Yet with this extreme shift comes duality: while these advantages are enormous, the potential risks, especially those regarding privacy, require far greater scrutiny.

Social media is an effective means in the development of connectivity and collaboration in education. Instead of static webs, such structures provide an interactive network where learners, teachers, and even parents can meet for much-needed resources and discussions to give better value to learning (Azorín & Hernández, 2024). For example, Edmodo and Google Classroom provide a teacher with the opportunity to set assignments, leave feedback, and track the flow of students in real-time. Professional networks like LinkedIn Learning also empower a student with an opportunity to make contact with industry leaders, explore possible career paths, and use resources that can be aligned with professional goals.

This shift from learning to social network-based learning can be regarded as enormously speeded up through technological and global needs for digitalization, particularly after the COVID-19 pandemic (Muftah, 2024). The sudden change over to online learning in this period highlighted the role of digital tools, and how very important it is for the continuation of learning through social networks. From virtual classrooms to support groups among peers, all these form part of the educational landscape nowadays.

Among the significant advantages that social networks may afford in education is the potential for fostering collaboration and participation. Students, who were once silent recipients of information, become active participants in a much greater learning community. Learning through peers about peer-to-peer learning, from which questions can be asked, insights shared, and even the derivation of knowledge from one another, can also be done using these networks. Such multimedia tools allow for the creation of very interactive content, which might foster understanding but also play into the differing learning styles and opt for achievement (Whitworth et al., 2012).

Social networks democratize access to education. It makes it easy for students in remote or underdeveloped places to connect to educators and peers to whom they would otherwise not have access (Parhamnia, 2024). For this reason, inclusiveness will be crucial to their role in increasing equity in education, whereby students from all walks of life are given a chance to acquire knowledge and skills. Even more important is the manner in which data analytics personalizes education. On social networking sites and platforms, there are vast amounts of data collected on user behavior, preferences, and performance (Zeshan et al., 2020). If this information is utilized correctly, then it will provide insights that guide educators in direct instruction to the very needs of the learner, thereby improving the learner's learning outcomes.

Such benefits, however, have come with serious privacy challenges. Features that have made social networks so attractive-data collection, connectivity, and engagement by users-expose users to risks (Ahmad & Whitworth, 2012). Educational data, being considered sensitive, includes not only academic records but personal information, behavioral patterns, and even biometric data in some cases (Hamid et al., 2019). The potential misuse of such data, whether hacking, surveillance, or commercial exploitation, poses a very serious threat against the student's and educator's privacy.

Collecting data in education raises very significant ethical concerns. Furthermore, most social networks make money primarily by monetizing data with business models. However, how much the data of the users of these users are exploited for purposes other than learning, like targeted advertising or predictive profiling, is not known. For minors, such as students, this has medium- and long-term impacts on children's autonomy and trustworthiness in digital systems (Levy et al., 2018).

This lack of transparency in data handling further exacerbates these problems. Users are mostly not informed of what is being collected and who is collecting this, how such data is being put to use, and to whom access extends (Muftah, 2024). This lack of transparency reduces trust and creates a significant hurdle for the adoption of social networks in education (Whitworth & Ahmad, 2013a). This tension between education and privacy emphasizes the importance of striking a balance in implementing these social networking tools in educational spheres. From one perspective, educators and institutions need to promote innovation and student participation by allowing the use of these portals. From another perspective, they are charged with protecting the personal privacy and safety of their students (Kim, Pak & Cho, 2021).

This balance is achieved on a multifaceted platform. Technical means include, but are not limited to data anonymization, encryption, and secure authentication. That setup reduces the risk on one hand but adds accountability due to legal and policy frameworks regulating data practices while providing safeguards on users' rights. Ethical considerations must remain top priorities in the development and implementation of learning platforms through social networks.

It cannot be a single body alone that responds to the privacy challenges of social network-based learning. Collaboration among the stakeholders will be required. Advocacy from educators shall be achieved through educating students to ensure good literacy, especially in the use of digital tools; developers and platform providers, as well as policymakers, will play their respective roles towards data protection and innovation. Parents and students are important stakeholders in this type of debate. Understanding their rights and the risks involved in using social networks would arm them with better decision-making capacities for them to be accountable in holding institutions responsible.

2. EDUCATIONAL BENEFITS OF SOCIAL NETWORK-BASED LEARNING

The incorporation of social networking sites in teaching-learning process has paved way to revolutionary change in teaching-learning process. These platforms have incorporated the class and the online environment, the learning is not strictly bound to school and classroom (Mejbri et al., 2022). In this section, the author disseminates several features of SNA in education, including cooperation, peers' communication, integration, and analytics for customized learning environments.

2.1 Enhancing Collaborative Learning

Collaboration is a core attribute of modern education. Social networks provide perfect conditions to promote this attribute since they can make students and instructors interact with no geographically or institutionally-based barriers (Whitworth & Ahmad, 2013b). Features such as chat forums, shared workspaces, and virtual classrooms can be used to propagate ideas for assignments, projects, and group activities. Other examples include Microsoft Teams and Slack for schools. In these channels, students can co-edit papers, collaborate on shared media resources, and also consider ideas in an imaginary virtual setting that at some point reproduces reality as it would during group work. This interaction not only determines better performance in the learning process but also develops important soft skills, such as teamwork and communication (Peris et al., 2020). Shared learning and social connecting cross boundaries of specific classrooms. The international exchange of such students for course work on personal or professional need through resources like LinkedIn Learning or Coursera allows for the collaboration of diverse students across backgrounds. These changes create cultural awareness and support and better prepare students to enter a global, interconnected world (Sarfraz et al., 2024).

2.2 Peer-to-Peer Interaction and Mentorship

Peer learning is one of the most important aspects of learning, and social networks are great at achieving more contacts. By these social networks, a student community that may develop meaningful discussion and get help from others and share knowledge can be easily brought together (Ahmad et al., 2019). Most of the time, informal experiences draw up the best and most productive experiences from classroom-like settings. For instance, Facebook groups about a topic or course become question-and-answer forum, resource sharing, and idea sharing. Moreover, platforms like Reddit support their communities in AskPhysics or LearnProgramming, enabling students to connect with the rest of their peers and in their subject area with experts.

These interactions increase not only understanding but further deepen a sense of belonging amongst students. Social networking also facilitates leadership through connection of students with influential experts in their respective fields. Through LinkedIn, students can be connected to several professionals, alumni, and faculty, seeking to understand opportunities related to careers and academics. This is particularly necessary for students in small or remote settings where students cannot have face-to-face instruction (Peris et al., 2020).

2.3 Inclusive Education End

With hardly any other strengths of learning facilitated by social networks being that it can give opportunities to foster integration. Those who for one reason or the other cannot access conventional education setups are always locked out of traditional learning paradigms. This is where the reach and availability of social networks offer an opportunity to close these gaps. Students with limitations to mobility can acquire skills that they would otherwise not be able to learn because of their limitations via social networks (Sweet et al., 2020). For instance, students in rural areas who are worried because they don't reach their quality educational material to hand can attend online classes or take tutorials on Google Classroom or Edmodo and many more. In the same manner, students with disabilities such as learning disability have some features that involve captioned videos, text to speak, adjustment in interface or skin all aid learning for such students. Besides providing physical accessibility, social networks are equally good in providing representation and voice. These mediums afford the student a chance to voice their views, disclose their experiences as well as interact on the same level. This is especially relevant for minorities that may often be overlooked and disregard in school as institutions.

2.4 Leveraging Analytics for Personalized Learning

One of the most effective features of social networks is their capacity to accumulate and evaluate big amounts of data. When applied appropriately the aforementioned data is quite useful in understanding the behavior, preferences and performance of the students to serve the individual purpose of shaping their future (Imran & Ahmad, 2022). This personification helps to improve learning through expounding a student's needs that is likely to be on his / her learning type and pace. For instance, learning management systems such as moodle, canvas, has features that monitor the level of engagement of the students. These tools can include patterns like, for example, students having difficulties with certain topics more often or decreasing participation. This information can be valuable for educators, as well as for those who directly work with the child, so that they can capitalize on it and, for example, orient a child to the proper specialists who could help him or her defeat the given difficulties.

Web applications that include elements of social networks and use AI technologies for analysis create the next level of personalization – adaptive learning platforms (). Other systems mentioned, such as DreamBox and Smart Sparrow, self-adapt the level of difficulty and the content of lessons according to a student test. It is ideal for guaranteeing differential differentiation that each student is given challenging tasks but not get overburdened to enhance a constructive process of effective learning (Khan et al., 2022). Social networks also enable the students to assume responsibility for the coursework on their own. These open-source platforms also help the students by giving them the most appropriate analysis of their achievements, thus helping make short- term and long-term goals. On this basis, this self-regulation stimulates various problem-solving aspects including time management, self-evaluation and responsibility.

2.5 Encouraging Lifelong Learning

Due to social networks the practice of education does not stop at the end of a particular course, implying the continuity of education. There is a vast array of accessible courses, certifications and resources available with learners of different ages pinning their interest on LinkedIn Learning, Coursera and Khan Academy. These platforms allow people to gain new knowledge in a certain field, develop own subject interest and always be up-to-date. This is because SNA learning is informal and provides a platform for learners to pursue their curiosity on the network. Interest groups are available to students, and students can join webinars and share a lot of user content from sites like YouTube and Instagram. Fortunately, this form of learning is also informal and adds to the earlier formal education of students by enriching their experiences, as well as helping to develop interest in studies (Eynon & Malmberg, 2021). To the professionals, social networks pose the chance to constant learning and improvement of their practice. This way they can get in touch with industry professional bodies, engage in lessons delivered in virtual classrooms, and exchange best practices with other practitioners, which can help them to meet the competency challenges that often arise in a more dynamic economic environment.

2.6 Fostering Engagement Through Gamification

Another educational advantage of social networks is the usage of game elements in context other than games – use of gamification. A number of the platforms incorporate elements of gamification including the use of score boards, badges and incentives to address the users. These features appeal to self-competitive and self-motivated aspects of people which make learning a lot more fun and fruitful (Ahmad et al., 2022). For example, Duolingo – a social linguistic learning online platform that incorporates social networking elements with a games aspects. Students get certain points for the lessons they have completed, can warm up the rivals and compare results of the lessons on the leaderboards, and get achievements on their way. In addition to making learning fun, these features make it possible for students to participate in learning consistently. Moreover, applying game elements could be effective in solving the problems, which obstruct learners, for instance, low motivation and lack of engagement, both of which are characteristic for traditional learning environments. Breaking information into fun and appropriate pieces assists social networks in keeping students engaged as they work towards attaining the intended goals (Oliveira et al., 2023).

2.7 Addressing the Limitations of Traditional Education

Lastly, factors involved in social network-based learning minimize many of the challenges associated with conventional learning institutions. Due to large groups, few teachers and constrained curriculums, individual time and deviation from set patterns is given less importance. The above challenges are averted in social networks since they offer flexible and adaptable solutions for the various demands. For instance, a teacher who is in charge of many students in a class can mobilize the social networks platform to form other subgroups for class discussions and set individual assignments and track each student's progress. In the same manner, those students who may likely encounter schedule clashes can always get enrolled and participate in recorded lectures, protract consummatory discussion and accomplish assignments flexibly. Social network-based learning has numerous advantages related to collaborative, equal, individualized, and lifelong learning. These platforms have shifted paradigms with the scope of education to provide learners with the conditions of the contemporary world inter-connectively. As the subsequent sections will describe, social networks have important benefits that again come with important privacy concerns that need to be overcome to effectively implement social networks in education while maintaining the highest ethical standards (Ozer & Perc, 2020).

3. PRIVACY CONCERNS IN SOCIAL NETWORK-BASED LEARNING

While social media-based learning offers many educational benefits, it also comes with a myriad of privacy issues needing immediate action. After all, the very basis of the concept of a social network relies on communication, data sharing, and user engagement-issues that pose critical risks in compromising students, teachers, and organizations' privacy (Muhammad & Ahmad, 2021). This section explores the main privacy issues related to social media studies, focusing on the types of data collected, potential risks of misuse, and issues related to data governance.

3.1 The Scope of Data Collection in Educational Preferences

Such educational sites, which base themselves on social media, collect information for personalized and engaging experiences. For example, it mainly collects academic information that includes grades, assignments, and attendance, but these data sources go further than the traditional metrics. Contemporary machines collect behavioral data by means of sentiment analysis, which includes log-in times, activity patterns, frequency of activities, and emotional response. The thing is that sensitive personal data, as collected by the assembly of demographic, geographic, and in some cases, biometric data, is very discomforting (Jain, Sahoo & Kaubiyal, 2021). For instance, an e-learning platform might use facial recognition to proctor tests or to see what's going on in a virtual classroom. This enhances performance but puts users at risk for privacy if the data is not kept in a proper place. Moreover, many platforms also have a way to analyse what is happening across devices and platforms. It uses cookies, trackers, and metadata analysis to create user profiles for reasons that are not necessarily education-related (Ahmad et al., 2020a). What appear to be harmless systems might actually inadvertently create vulnerabilities, which can be exploited for malicious or even commercially beneficial purposes.

3.2 Risks of Data Misuse

The problem of misuse of data in the form of online learning has serious consequences for all stakeholders. Some of the urgent issues faced include unauthorized access, data breaches, and misuse of the user's data. The consequences of these threats can include harming an individual or damaging the reputation of a company.

3.2.1 Cybersecurity Threats

Academic websites have become one of the favored means for cyber hackers seeking to gain access to confidential information. Major universities and online learning websites experienced such breaches in 2022, where students and professors' identities were leaked to the public. Not only does this violation threaten personal and private information but also erodes trust in the very websites and institutions that are entrusted with keeping this information (Samreen et al., 2020a). Besides direct damage to the target by a data breach, it can be used for identity theft, phishing attacks, and defamation. The students and the teaching faculties are not often likely to know about these risks and are exposed to such threats.

3.2.2 Tracking and Profiling

In school, social media enables the monitoring and profiling of students. The data gathered from the time spent online-including browsing history, patterns of interaction, and test scores-can be utilized to create models that predict and place students into targeted groups. In many ways, these examples are well-intentioned to humanize but have the potential to perpetuate the discriminatory practices of limiting opportunities for certain groups based on biases or inadequacies. For instance, analytics tools that may suggest which "at-risk" students need to be identified may unwittingly discriminate against some, thus affecting attitudes and performance. Profiling tends to have enormous effects on higher education, employment prospects, and general public opinion.

3.2.3 Commercial Use

Most commercial social networking sites rely on making money from users through advertisements and joint ventures with third parties. This is particularly problematic within the education sector. Here, ethical issues arise regarding the selling of student data. A commercial website may gather data about educational sites to push advertisements of products, services, and political campaigns to students without their consent (Ahmad et al., 2017). For instance, a student visiting an English language learning website is likely to be targeted with ads related to language teaching service or test preparation materials. Although highly relevant to their current needs, targeted advertising could blur the line over educational support and commercial exploitation. It ensures that the educational experience is compromised in terms of integrity.

3.3 Ethical Considerations in Data Collection and Sharing

The ethical implications of data collection and sharing on educational social networks are considerable. It all relates to the issue of compromise. Those involved, the children, usually do not understand the implications of the information shared (Samreen et al., 2020b). Even when permission is given, in-depth analysis is usually found buried in long and complicated promises. Another fair challenge concerns the issue of ownership information. Here, most schools and providers in charge of user data mean that students and teachers have limited freedom concerning access, correction, or deletion of their information. This freedom deficiency impacts both concepts of information sovereignty and self-empowerment. The moral considerations apply as well. An isolated resort to data-driven algorithmic capabilities to provide personal learning may exacerbate existing disparities. In this process, underrepresented groups will tend to be deprived in education with undesirable reversal outcomes.

3.4 Effect on Student Privacy

The risks concerning internet-based learning on social networks have profoundly significant impacts on students. These risks not only threaten to breach the data of students but also influence the health and performance in academic studies of the students, which further affects school credentials (Jain, Sahoo & Kaubiyal, 2021).

3.4.1 Psychological Impacts

Increased scrutiny because of being monitored increases anxiety and self-care among students. This "drug effect" depresses creativity, critical thinking, and accuracy. This becomes a failure in accomplishing the objective or academic goal.

3.4.2 Loss of Trust

Privacy breaches, in addition, and generally non-transparent practices on data distort trust levels towards educational platforms and institutions. Students may shy away from using digital devices fearing the misuse of some of the information. Such skepticism could negatively affect the full utilization of the new technologies that will, in turn, help reduce the potential of new technologies in better learning results.

3.4.3 Long term effects

Critical discussion can haunt the digital footprint of a student on social media. Forum comments or assignment submissions in a course can often inadvertently come up and have a carry-over effect. For example, controversial remarks that were made during class discussion appear as the reason against admission to university and career.

3.5 Challenges to Educators and Institutions

While educators and institutions face the social media challenges regarding concerns around learning, they have to ensure that they can innovate in new means of teaching with the burden of having student data under their responsibility that requires hard work and cautious consideration (Klapproth et al., 2020).

3.5.1 Lack of Knowledge Training

Many instructors are not technically and professionally competent to appreciate the potential consequences of using social media sites in educational contexts. As knowledge gaps can lead to releasing confidential information, such as posting children's records on secure platforms or failing to properly configure privacy settings, teaching obligations are, inter alia, as follows.

3.5.2 Academic Responsibilities

Institutions have enormous responsibilities over the safeguarding of students' data. Nonetheless, they lack many resources and competencies to achieve more advanced privacy protections. Such factors include financial constraints, outdated infrastructure, and dependency on third-party vendors, which compound these challenges and leave companies vulnerable to data breaches and compliance failures.

3.5.3 Compliance

Another challenge for agencies involves navigating the complex web of data protection laws and regulations. Compliance with frameworks such as GDPR in European Union or the FERPA in the United States requires effort and expertise, especially for organizations dealing with multiple jurisdictions.

Finally, social media learning poses very important issues to do with privacy associated with it. Dilemmas relating to legal challenges and ethical situations arise from risks of data collection and misuse. The environment is rich in complexities; whether individually or collectively they have to be considered and dealt with. It will be realized in the next section that addressing these challenges involves a combination of legal frameworks, technical solutions, and ethical guidelines on behalf of the privacy and security of all stakeholders.

4. LEGAL AND ETHICAL FRAMEWORKS FOR SAFEGUARDING PRIVACY IN SOCIAL NETWORK-BASED LEARNING

As the use of social network-based learning intensifies, there is need to provide sound legal and ethical policies so as to minimize the potential threats to the privacy of users while pursuing the noble course of educating society through those platforms (Ahmad, Whitworth & Bertino, 2022). Current legal requirements, ethical principles, and guidelines aimed at preserving students, educator, and institutional privacy are presented here. It also discusses some of the shortcomings found in current thinking, as well as the growing need for new models that take into account some emerging issues in contemporary digital learning environments.

4.1 Legal Frameworks for Data Privacy in Education

More general data protection laws can be said to comprise the very legal regulation of data protection that applies to SSDL, though where such regulation intersects with education there are specific rules to be considered. Many of the pertinent legal frameworks lie at the core of privacy protection:

4.1.1 General Data Protection Regulation (GDPR)

The data protection law on the European Union is recognized as one of the most extensive laws in the globe today, with the 2018 Regulation. It strictly holds entities responsible for processing personal data, which incorporates educational institutions and social network platforms. Some of the key principles of the GDPR[1] are:

- Obtain Consent with Transparency: This requires explicit consent from users for the collection of their data and clearly informing them of how their data will be utilized.
- Data Minimization: Collected data should be limited to only that needed for specific purposes, thus reducing the scope for misuse.
- Right to Access and Rectification: There is a right to access their personal data and ask for correction. It also contains the right to erasure or "right to be forgotten."

For learning platforms that operate within or provide services to citizens within the EU, compliance with the GDPR is legally required. However, issues are presented when international platforms, not subject to the GDPR, do not meet its high standards.

4.1.2 Family Educational Rights and Privacy Act (FERPA)

FERPA[2] provides privacy protections specifically under the auspices of educational records in the United States. It affords students and parents access and control over educational data as maintained by institutions, but it does not apply to third-party platforms, such as social networks, in which data may be used in the context of education, thereby exposing vulnerabilities in the protection of student privacy.

FERPA also mandates that institutions seek consent before disclosing personally identifiable information, except in certain enumerated exemptions, such as emergencies and auditing. Although this is a positive development, this provision only narrowly impacts the issue of contemporary practices in data gathering.

4.1.3 Children's Online Privacy Protection Act (COPPA)

COPPA[3] focuses on protecting the online privacy of children under 13 in the United States. It mandates parental consent for data collection by online services and requires platforms to provide clear privacy policies. COPPA is very relevant in the primary and middle school environments because social networks are being increasingly integrated into the curriculum. However, enforcement challenges and compliance loopholes have limited its effectiveness.

4.1.4 Other Regional and National Frameworks

All nations worldwide have enacted data privacy legislation but differ significantly in how it is applied within the education context. The Canadian Personal Information Protection and Electronic Documents Act lists principles that apply to data privacy as relevant to educational institutions. Often, these frameworks address more general data governance issues but are not detailed enough to ensure that learning that is based on social networking is properly protected.

4.2 Ethical Standards in Privacy Management

Data protection provides a legal basis, but ethical standards are an essential basis for the proper uses of social networks in education. Ethics is more than compliance and addresses the moral imperatives of educators, institutions, and service providers toward respecting and protecting the privacy of users (Ahmad et al., 2012).

4.2.1 Informed Consent as Moral Imperative

Though the laws like GDPR require consent, ethical reasons make it meaningful and intelligible. Schools have to induct their students as well as their parents with regards to what it is to share information with other people for minors. Making consent forms simple, transparencies and accessible information will build great trust and responsibility.

4.2.2 Equity and Inclusion

Marginalization and bias are some of the risks against which the ethical frameworks for social network-based learning must guard. Such algorithms that analyze student information must be audited for fairness in prevention against profiling or exclusion across a particular group. Therefore, ethical practice needs to be aligned with accessibility to ensure that all the students who can make use of these platforms do so irrespective of barriers occasioned by their socioeconomic status or physical environment.

4.2.3 Respect for Autonomy

Data belonging and which is being processed by students and educators are theirs, and they should be in control over access to, modifications on and deletion of their respective data. This autonomy principle forms the foundation for ethical management of data, where users are entrusted to make choices about their privacy.

4.2.4 Accountability and Transparency

The education institution and platform provider are expected to be transparent in their data practice and are accountable to the protection of user information. Ethical responsibility is extended to responding to privacy breaches, handling user concerns, and continually improving measures for data protection.

4.3 Challenges in Implementing Legal and Ethical Protections

Despite the legal and ethical framework, significant challenges are apparent that may hinder its effective implementation within a social network-based learning environment.

4.3.1 Ambiguities in Jurisdiction and Enforcement

Global social networks often involve operation across several jurisdictions, which create conflicts between regional data protection laws. For instance, a network serving EU and US students must navigate the stringent requirements of the GDPR with that of the much lax provisions set forth by FERPA. Inevitably, such differences create enforcement problems and lack privacy coverage.

4.3.2 Emergence in Technological Advancement

The evolution of social networking and e-learning technologies overtakes the development of legal frameworks and ethics behind them. New trends like AI, bio tracking, and augmented reality raise new privacy concerns that cannot be fulfilled by existing laws.

4.3.3 Resource Constraints

Many educational institutions lack the financial and technical resources to implement robust data protection measures. Smaller schools, in particular, may struggle to comply with complex regulations, leaving them vulnerable to breaches and non-compliance penalties.

4.3.4. User Awareness and Education

Transparency and privacy protections are only as good as the users who are supposed to know them. Students, educators, and even administrators are not sufficiently educated on rights and responsibilities imposed by data protection laws. Such a knowledge gap exacerbates vulnerability and undermines the effectiveness of existing frameworks.

4.4 Emerging Best Practices for Privacy Protection

These challenges have led educational institutions and platform providers to adopt innovative approaches for better protection of privacy in social network-based learning.

4.4.1 Privacy by Design

Privacy by design" means that data protection is built into the architecture of platforms right at the outset. Such features may include, inter alia, end-to-end encryption, the collection of minimal data only, and authentications against misuse for users. Advanced encryption protocols on the side of platforms such as Zoom can greatly limit the potential risks regarding privacy.

4.4.2 Regular Audits and Impact Assessments

DPIAs are a wonderful technique of identifying possible privacy risks and dealing with those risks. Schools are to do compliance checks on practices they undertake for processing personal data with reference to legislation's compliance and Ethics. Third-party audits by independent and impartial professionals could also bring still more objectivity and responsibility to a process.

4.4.3 collaborative governance models.

This is to mean that an alliance of governments, educators, the providers of the platforms, and civil society organizations will emerge at the frontline to establish the privacy frameworks. The Global Privacy Assembly and UNESCO's guidelines regarding the use of AI in education are perfect to serve as dialogue and policies.

4.4.4 User-Centric Approaches

Also, growing into the role of new trends in protecting personal data, there is an approach to equip users with tools that would let them control their data. Flexible privacy settings, activity overviews and data usage descriptions help learners and teachers better manage their online presence.

4.4.5 Constant Evolution:

Due to the fluidity of social network-based learning new legal and ethical issues have to keep emerging. Where possible, decision makers need to be informed of growing technological changes to modify laws and policies to reflect the risks (Hamid et al., 2020). In the same way, institutions educating students and platform providers of services need to continue improvements of their data practices and set privacy as priceless.

Legal and ethical consideration are core elements in privacy protection in social network-based learning. However, the nature of the domain and the development of practices require using regulation as a part of ethical principles and good practice., as mentioned in the following section, the mere utilization of technology itself, and concepts such as privacy-preserving technologies become a potential path for balancing educational values against privacy issues.

5. TECHNICAL APPROACHES TO BALANCING PRIVACY AND EDUCATIONAL NEEDS

Striking the privacy need with the educational value that can be gained from learning through social networks requires technical solutions. Whereas legal and ethical frameworks give general direction, technical solutions will offer the specific ways by which user data can be shielded, and privacy preserved, without compromising the functionality of these sites. It has provided information about some significant technical methods that would align educational requirements with privacy concerns. Some of them include the following:

5.1 Data Encryption: The First Line of Defense

Encryption is a core method of protecting data in digital environments, including social network-based learning platforms. It involves coding readable data into an encoded format, so sensitive information is accessible only by intended parties (Zeshan et al., 2024). Two primary types of encryptions are employed in educational contexts: end-to-end encryption and transport-layer encryption

5.1.1 End-to-End Encryption

End-end encryption (E2EE) comes with the guarantee that the data will be encrypted on a sender's device and decrypted only by the recipient's device. The relative easiness of intercepting data during transmission for E2EE makes it so beneficial to secure students' and educators' communications. For instance, Zoom has adopted E2EE as part of the measure of securing virtual classrooms, and Microsoft Teams has also introduced this technology.

5.1.2 Transport-Layer Encryption

TLS protocols guard data that is in transit between users and servers, and they have, moreover, offered an additional layer of security against cyberattacks. TLS encryption is essential for protecting login credentials, assignment submissions, and other sensitive engagements on learning platforms. Whereas encryption proves fairly effective, the implementation itself introduces trade-offs based on increased computational overhead and potentially even a delay in data processing. Thus, the optimization of educational platforms' encryption protocols is needed to strike a balance between safety and experience.

5.1.3 Privacy Preserving Algorithms and Federated Learning

Some contemporary education platforms use algorithms that are used to analyze the data of their users, generate insights, and give personalized learning experiences. In this case, these algorithms require access to vast datasets, raising numerous privacy issues. Algorithms have been developed to preserve privacy by taking control of the way data is treated, thus reducing exposure.

- Homomorphic Encryption

Homomorphic encryption evaluates computations over encrypted data, without having to decrypt it. This technology enables learning environments to analyze student performance and engagement patterns and the effects of learning in a manner that infers no inference of critical data. For example, using homomorphic encryption, a learning environment might adopt student recommendations without having to access the underlying data; this diminishes privacy risks while still providing the benefits of data-driven education.

- Federated Learning

Federated learning is decentralized machine learning. In other words, it allows for processing data mostly on end-user devices rather than concentrating the data on a server. It would be the solution to offer the possibility of training algorithms on different datasets keeping, in this way, user privacy and anonymity. For instance, a language learning app could refresh the recommendation model based on user interaction without transferring raw data to a central repository. Federated learning is very helpful in educational settings, specifically when concerning data ownership and sovereignty. This ensures that the data stays local, supports the ethical principles of autonomy, and has done away with the potential of data breaches.

5.2 Anonymization Techniques

Anonymization is the removal or obscuring of personally identifiable information from datasets, in such a way that data cannot be traced back to people. This is very much applied in educational research and analytics with a view toward appropriate compliance with privacy regulations (Majeed & Lee, 2020).

5.2.1 K-Anonymity

K-anonymity ensures that individually identifiable data records cannot be distinguished from at least other data records in a dataset. For example, in a dataset of student grades, k-anonymity may ensure individual anonymity by dividing data into general categories. That is how k-anonymity enables research to understand trends without breaching sensitive information.

5.2.2 Differential Privacy

Differential privacy adds controlled noise to datasets to obfuscate individual contributions but preserve aggregate patterns. In this way, it provides a very effective approach for large-scale analytics, such as measuring learning outcomes across an institution. For example, differential privacy protects user data in services such as Google and Apple.

5.2.3 Tokenization

Tokenization replaces sensitive data elements with unique IDs or tokens; hence, minimizing the chances of exposure during processing. For instance, one may tokenize a student's ID if the data were being shared with third party vendors; this means that the original information is kept safe.

5.3 Access Controls and Role-Based Permissions

Access control mechanisms dictate who can see or modify data in a platform. Using permissions attached to user role can ensure that sensitive information is only available to the appropriate staff (Ahmad & Whitworth, 2011).

5.3.1 Multi-Factor Authentication (MFA)

MFA improves security because the users must authenticate themselves through multiple channels such as passwords, biometric, and one-time code before entering the system. This technique is especially useful when securing administrative accounts with access to sensitive student data.

5.3.2 Role-Based Access Control (RBAC)

RBAC bases the authorization on predefined roles- it could be "student," "teacher," or "administrator." For instance, students may only view their grades, while teachers may view the grades of all their students. This fine-grained control will then minimize unauthorized access.

5.4 Secure Data Sharing and Interoperability

Social network-based learning requires, in most cases, data sharing both across platforms and between institutions and third-party services. Protecting privacy will require, therefore, secure data-sharing protocols and standards for interoperability.

5.4.1 Blockchain Technology

Blockchain offers a decentralized, tamper-proof framework for data sharing. Recording transactions in an immutable ledger, blockchain ensures that data exchange is not only transparent but also secure (Ahmed et al., 2024). On blockchain systems, the storing and sharing of educational credentials like transcripts and certificates are highly secure.

5.4.2 APIs and Privacy Preserving Data Exchange

Application Programming Interfaces (APIs) allow for the interoperability of systems with strict controls on privacy. Platforms may implement privacy-preserving APIs to ensure that sensitive information is cleansed from transactions and data-sharing policies are governed, thereby abiding by legal and ethical requirements.

5.5 Usability and User Education

Technical solutions need to be accompanied by user-friendly interfaces and educational initiatives to be maximally effective, so that students and teachers learn how to identify privacy risks, adjust parameters, and develop good usage habits.

5.5.1 Privacy Dashboards

Privacy dashboards will allow users to view their data and settings in one place, thus allowing them to manage permissions, see activity logs, and update their preferences. Features such as this are available on sites like Facebook and Google to increase user control.

5.5.2 Training and Awareness Programs

Regular workshops and tutorials on digital privacy should be conducted by institutions, instilling a sense of importance in secure practices. Topics may include identifying phishing attempts, managing passwords, and data-sharing agreements.

Although promising avenues are presented by technical approaches regarding balancing privacy and educational needs, their implementation is not free from challenges, such as high cost, problem of scalability, and complexity in trying to integrate advanced technologies into systems that already exist. To overcome such barriers, all stakeholders' cooperation, R & D and the recognition of privacy as a scarce resource are essential.

Privacy measures and solutions associated with the making of technical structures of SNaBL refer to vital concepts of safety and effectiveness of learners' interactions within an online environment associated with social networks independently of their learning types. In all these areas, which include encryption and federated learning, anonymization, and access controls, it is beyond doubt that solutions in all these areas would be fundamental to constructing the safety of user data. However, prospects and requirements or possibly organizations cultivation of awareness concerning privacy to its stakeholders will decide more particularly if such solutions can actually be implemented or not. We'll see the ethical considerations and problems regarding these solutions emerge as we move to the next section, which delineates the details of the attempt to enact technology according to the best human values.

6. CHALLENGES AND ETHICAL DILEMMAS IN SOCIAL NETWORK-BASED LEARNING

Social networks' inclusion in education becomes a major issue and an ethical issue. It is such a scenario which arises due to a number of interactions between some privacy problems, educational objectives and general tendencies in development of societal aspects connected with application of digital tools. As connecting platforms have enabled interaction and cooperation into undreamed-of levels, they increase distinct risks whatever is connected with oversight, inequality, data monetization and diminished trust (Bilal et al., 2024). These issues are discussed fully in this section as well as the backgrounds and possible courses of remedy.

6.1 Surveillance in Digital Learning Environments

The most prevalent paradigm in the area of learning within social networks is, without a doubt, the paradigm of surveillance. Due to various critiques, the social networking and learning system strategies for acquiring, processing, and using the information defines the concept of "surveillance culture". This problem includes blatant institutional spying up to spying by third parties that go unnoticed (Beetham et al., 2022).

6.1.1 Institutional Surveillance

Educational institutions are continually using such data-driven tools to track student performance, engagement, and behavior. Most LMSs and social platforms embed features that track activity, monitor attendance, and show analytics dashboards. These tools are valuable in that they provide a good deal of insights but are also causes of overreach and the misuse of data. For example, where monitoring student interaction on social media would blur the line that separates academic oversight from invasion into privacy.

6.1.2 Commercial surveillance

User data is monetized by social networks and third-party providers by means of targeted advertising and profiling. Thus, questions arise about the legitimacy of commodifying student data. A student might unwittingly contribute to datasets used for profit-generating purposes, such as targeted advertising or market research, using a collaborative learning platform. If such practices are not transparent, they exacerbate the concern because users do not know how their data is being exploited.

6.1.3 Psychological Effects of Surveillance

The knowledge of constant surveillance creates the psychological burden of the "chilling effect" where students and teachers modify their actions to avoid penalty or scrutiny. Such a situation affects the authenticity of relationships and inhibits innovation, teamwork, and freedom of expression-all characteristics that are fundamental to learning.

6.2 Data Inequality and Digital Divide

The uptake of social network-based learning also raises questions about data inequality and the digital divide. These problems take place in several dimensions such as unequal access to technology, disparities in terms of the skill to use data, and the existence of systemic biases (Acilar & Sæbø, 2023).

6.2.1 Unequal Access to Technology

Not all learners have equal access to devices, internet connectivity, and digital resources to support social network-based learning. Existing inequalities in education will thus be widened digitally. For instance, students without stable internet can only imagine doing online discussions and access material to read about or collaborate on a project.

6.2.2 Data Literacy Inequities

Even when there are opportunities to access technology, students lack data literacy in areas that may hinder them from efficiently using learning platforms based on social networks. Among the privacy risks the affected students had due to their poor digital skills include unintended sharing of sensitive information and not detecting phishing. It will be prudent that initiatives trying to bridge the gap are focused on enhancing the strength of digital competencies and culture in their application.

6.2.3 Algorithmic Bias and Systemic Inequities

Algorithms governing the use of social networks and learning platforms inevitably reflect and entrench existing biases. Recommendation systems, for instance, may skew to favor one demographic or learning style over others-until only the in-group is left with access. Predictive analytics used to predict the performance of a student can be used to support stereotypes until certain groups are being unfairly treated or learning to lowered expectations (Fatima et al., 2023).

6.3 Innovation vs. Regulation: Tension End

In social network-based learning, the key challenge would be to balance innovation with regulation. Technological progress for education does promise a lot but often goes far ahead of corresponding legal and ethical provisions.

6.3.1 Rapid Technological Advancements

The pace of innovation within the social networks and related technologies substantially outpaces policymakers' ability to regulate quickly and effectively. Newer trends, such as the use of AI, ARs, and biometric tracking, increase new channels of privacy risks that laws do not touch. For example, analyzing facial expressions pertaining to the extent of student engagement in classes using AI platforms raises questions of the type of consent involved, accuracy, and misuse of very sensitive biometric data.

6.3.2 Conflicting Authorities

Social networks operate in multiple jurisdictions distributed across the world, with their data protection law and cultural norms in each location. That makes for a situation prone to conflict and lack of consistency in regulating privacy. For example, the stringent requirements in the GDPR in Europe may confront a more lenient FERPA in the United States. This leads to confusion in enforcing laws in place, leaving gaps in protecting students and educators.

6.3.3 Innovation vs. Privacy

Educational institutions and technology providers are facing a fundamental trade-off. High-quality data-driven insights into learning can produce very strong outcomes for those students, but doing so would have to compromise user privacy; gathering all the necessary data can be impossible without consent and adequate data security. Balancing innovation with respect for privacy is a challenge in and of itself.

6.4 Ethical Dilemmas in Data Use

Ethical dilemmas in social network-based learning frequently result from competing priorities of interest among the various stakeholders, such as learners, instructors, institutions, and service providers (Mir, 2024). This dilemma manifests the challenge of different priorities conformed to shared ethical principles.

6.4.1 Informed Consent and Autonomy

Meaningful consent from users is the foundation of ethical data use, but privacy policies of social networks often are so complex that no one can understand the consent documents. Students, especially young students, cannot make effective decisions regarding their data sharing due to a lack of complete understanding of the subject matter. The interests of students must be taken care of, while, on the other hand, their right to self-determination has to be recognized.

6.4.2 Balancing Surveillance with Trust

While monitoring tools increase accountability and safety, in almost all cases they undermine trust between students and educators. For instance, using proctoring software to monitor online examinations is hotly debated for the ethical vigilance of such intrusive surveillance. Blending both technical and human factors for the delicate balancing act between maintaining academic integrity and the privacy of students is very delicate.

6.4.3 Data Ownership and Control

The concern of ownership and control over student data becomes a highly contentious ethical debate. Social networks and educational platforms continually claim ownership over the data of the user, which effectively restricts students from accessing, modifying, or deleting information about them. This creates exploitative scenarios where users may be monetarily charged for something but without their genuine knowledge or consent. Ethical frameworks really need to think about sovereignty over data so that users hold meaningful control over their digital identities.

6.5 Long Term Effects on Privacy and Learning

Long-term effects of the dangers and dilemmas surrounding learning through social networks would come to define future privacy and learning. This entrenchment requires holistic attention to technological innovation, legal protection, and ethical considerations.

6.5.1 Digital Citizenship

As social networks become more integrated in education, it is no longer a choice but an imperative for students to develop a sense of digital citizenship-the ability to operate responsibly in digital environments and to recognize, once alerted to the implications of their own online actions for privacy, security, and ethics.

6.5.2 Building Trust and Transparency

Trust is the bedrock for effective education systems. Educational institutions and learning venues must be transparent about their use of data: how data are gathered, used, and safeguarded. Building trust requires strict adherence to the law and also living by ethical principles.

6.5.3 Changing Privacy Norms

In the light of changing technology and society, it is no doubt that the principle of privacy also has to change. Fixed conceptions about privacy as a right are never sustainable in dynamic and context-dependent terms (Zeshan et al., 2019). For example, it presents the situation of privacy of learners in a social network-based learning: individual autonomy balanced against collective benefits in terms of bettering the learning results for example, and access in an equitable manner.

Current challenges and ethical dilemmas with regard to social network-based learning underscore complexity in balancing a potential educational benefit over the privacy of these relations. Including from surveillance to data inequality and innovation regulation, it is all to be coped with by strategic and collaborative solutions. Stakeholders need to treat privacy as a fundamental value while embracing digital transformation in education, fostering environments where students are empowered, rights are respected, and there is an impulsion for ethical action. Thus, in a proactive approach to solving these problems, we will have a future where social networks reinforce learning while ensuring the privacy and dignity of the users.

7. STRATEGIES FOR MITIGATING PRIVACY RISKS IN SOCIAL NETWORK-BASED LEARNING

Because social networks are gradually incorporating into educational environments, protecting the privacy of users is absolutely critical for building a safe and trustworthy educational environment. Measures for minimizing these risks have to be comprehensively technical, legal, institutional, and educational (Quach et al., 2022). This section looks at these strategies in more detail particularly from the perspective of their usability and their ability to build a system that is as effective in its delivery of educational value as it is in its protection of privacy rights.

7.1 Designing Privacy-Centric Social Networks

The general and first approach to managing privacy risks is privacy by design, which should be applied to the creation of social network platforms. The thing is to consider privacy as an inherent part of the platform's architecture and design instead of just paying more or less attention to this question.

- Privacy by default ensures that users' data is protected without requiring manual configuration of settings. For instance, default configurations of the social network learning platforms restrict who has access to post the data; it is limited to teachers and other learners in the class instead of enhancing it to allow every one of this large networks. Such restrictions minimize chances of official exposing data that is not meant for recipients at that level.
- Platforms should adopt data minimization principles, collecting only the information necessary to provide educational services. For instance, other than demanding a complete set of demographic information to users, the platforms can ask just for a name and an email address. Minimization minimizes the amount of data that is regarded sensitive; therefore, the chance of a breach is greatly reduced.
- Code creation should be done inconclusively making use of security solutions, encryption, and IDSs to increase the security of user's information. This approach ensures that privacy considerations are integral to the architecture and functionality of platforms, rather than being added as an afterthought.
- Developers must prioritize secure coding practices, encryption, and intrusion detection systems to protect user data. This encompasses the creation of protective measures against the general weaknesses like cross site scripting (XSS) and SQL injection. The use of security assessment and penetration testing is the best practice since platforms need regular security update checkups.

7.2 Enhancing User Awareness and Control

Enabling the users to take control of their data is key especially in preventing Foreign Preprocessing and in enhancing Data Ownership. Methods of user awareness and control involve communication, interface, and education.

- Privacy policies should be understandable to the average Joe and should not be written in the legal language. Transparency refers not only to the declaration of data collection and using practices, but also the explanation of these practices' effects on users. For example, a given policy can clearly indicate whether or not data is passed to third-party advertising agencies or whether it is used for computational profiling.

- There should be a general policy to make platforms' menus and panels considerably intuitive to facilitate users' data privacy management. There are other functionalities that should be easily accessible, these include options to switch on or off data sharing, obtain the personal data and even delete Amara account. While Google and Facebook are examples of systems where such messaging dashboards have been implemented, we have to consider extreme care when implementing such systems in an educational environment due to the navbar issue, the messaging dashboard must be kept simple and only those messages relevant to the learning environment.
- School going children and university students in particular should be taught on the knowledge of digital privacy. Every learner and teacher must grasp fundamental concepts of internet privacy, such as detecting fraud, setting security preferences, and assessing site credibility. That is why they not only help to reduce risks but also promote proper actions among students as digital citizens as well.

7.3 Institutional Policies and Governance

I agreed with Jackson's argument that institutions have a critical role in setting up the benchmarks of privacy protection measures. What's more, by signing strong policies and corporate governance they can build a sound environment which respects users and reduces threats.

- Institutions should follow policies including the legal guidelines of Data Protection Act, GDPR and policies of COPPA in order to maintain an effective policy for the protection of data. These policies should include how to obtain the data, where, with whom, and how to store it, and how to dispose of it. For instance, a university might set retention intervals by which data from students should be taken down to avoid data breaches.
- Legal, technical, academic specialists should create organizational governance committees to oversee the data utilization. They can assess the extent of compliance of the identified SLEs in terms of the relevant social network-based learning platforms in the institutions and weigh various risks in order to make recommendations for enhancement.
- Institutions are particularly required to be ready in case of information security breaches, this implies that they should be able to put mechanisms for handling the incidents in place. It's important that these protocols cover issues such as how to detect that a breach has occurred, how to inform the parties

involved and how to minimize impact. Staff practice and training make them ready and slow the effects of actual scenarios.

7.4 Leveraging Legal Frameworks

Legal requirements form an important pillar in enhancing privacy in social network-based learning. The one way of tackling the risks is by strictly adhering to current law while fighting for modification of current laws where necessary.

- It means that the educational platforms and institutions providing services have to adhere to the existing legislation on the protection of user personal data. For instance:
- GDPR: Charges highly demanding conditions to data processing, concerning the consent and the reporting of a breach within the European Union.
- FERPA: Surgeons the privacy of student education records within the USA.
- COPPA: Intends and controls the data collected from individuals under the age of 13 through the online consent of their parents or guardians.

Following these regulations is useful because it minimizes risks while at the same time establishing trust from the users.

- Where such privacy laws are disconnected or ineffective, stakeholders must call for new laws that effectively deal with issues within SNBL. For example, new laws could require that training data be made public, prohibit the sale of rights to educational data and, at the same time, enhance compliance on cross border data transfers.
- The institutional practices should engage the third-party platform providers in contract agreements to regulate practices being offered to the customers. Such contracts may contain requirements on data encryption; restrictions with regard to data transfer; and obligations to indemnify in case of violation of such provisions.

7.5 Technological Innovations for Privacy Protection

New technology provides better ways of overcoming the challenges of privacy concerns while enhancing the operation social net based learning. Some of these technologies include anonymization, use of block chain, and use of privacy preserving machine learning.

- Anonymization strips out the PII of the patient, whereas pseudonymization replaces PII with a pseudo identity. These techniques provide means of considering user data for insights while still respecting user's right to privacy. For example, the data containing a number of students could be in fact pseudonymized and serve to examine their learning activities without revealing individual identities.
- Blockchain technology forms a decentralized and secure system for records and interactions associated with education. However, applying blockchain can eliminate potentially negative consequences of centralized databases by providing safe and open data sharing. For instance, credentials such as academic records and achievements could go on a blockchain; anyone with permission can access and reveal this information.
- Instead, federated learning carries out the computation on user devices, saving raw data from being sent back to central points. In this way, it is possible to enhance the algorithms as well as the specific users' experience at the same time as sustaining users' privacy. For example, a language learning application can enhance its suggestions on content interaction without violating the privacy of the users' messages.

7.6 Fostering a Privacy-Conscious Culture

Designing the right culture is the right way to involve all the involved users, students, teachers, administration and policy makers. This cultural change is about ensconcing privacy as a procedural principle governing process in education and in the design of the platform.

- Decision making concerning privacy and data use, the various stakeholders need to be more fully engaged. For example, institutions can design meetings in which students and instructors may express their opinions about potential changes in augmenting features or policies on platforms. This is basically important so as to make sure that privacy solutions meet the needs of the people within society.
- Educationists and technologists should take the lead in demanding and defending privacy as a basic civil liberty. This encompasses practicing such features themselves e.g., by being open about their practices and policies, and promoting the right standards in addition to protecting the users than commerce. Responsible leadership helps people develop confidence, and they in return embrace the right things to do.
- Privacy threats and opportunities allow for or are in sync with the changes in technology. It's therefore important for institutions and platforms to always

revisit their policies, technologies and practice and ensure that they are in harmony to eradicate new difficulties. It is a preventive approach whereby privacy measures are put in place to make sure they are effective despite the change.

Managing privacy insecurity in SNA-based learning therefore needs a computerized solution which incorporates technological advancement, legal measures, institutional policies, and user enablement. Through the development of privacy protecting platforms, increasing the awareness of users, promoting legal and privacy regulations and establishing privacy culture, there is every likelihood that the stakeholders would establish environment that would foster education and also protect user rights. As education enters a new era of use of social networks in learning, the strategies propounded here are a guide on how educators and learners can trust the process, have their privacy protected, and use the social networks in an equitable and ethical manner.

8. CONCLUSION

The introduction of social media in education represents a revolutionary change in the way knowledge is shared, knowledge is developed, and collaboration is fostered. These programs present new opportunities for self-directed learning, global communication, and accountability in ways never offered to students or teachers before. But these new possibilities come with critical challenges, like those associated with measuring learning outcomes against the needs and expectations of each individual. It is this combination of opportunities and risks that defines the ongoing debate over online education.

The grounds for this caution are data privacy concerns. Social media is changing fast into using data in an aim of improving the use experience, making things more efficient and turning most sources of revenue. Some of the educative data can be used to track progress and spur action while the costs of a data-driven approach include compromised privacy, diminished trust, and ethical issues around ownership and control. Students would become workers within complex networks of collection and processing of information that would continue running even in pursuit of jobs or income, about which they were unaware.

These issues are not only practical, but also social and legal ones. Improving inequalities, biases of algorithms, and unequal access to resources have resulted in aggravated conflicts over pre-existing inequalities and proven that advancement in technology is not enough to provide assurance of justice or equality. Regulations are lagging behind in the changes even faster than the latter, which hinders and hampers more the search for solutions, placing many institutions and water users without good guidance or reference.

Despite all odds, hope remains as bright as ever. More and more important stakeholders in education, technology, and policy realize the importance of developing responsibly and sustainably. The risks are manageable despite the huge benefits that can be accrued by these networks if the design incorporates privacy, uses new technologies such as blockchain and aggregators, and is strictly regulated. A culture of self-awareness and literacy will also stand to help students and teachers benefit from these spaces appropriately while making responsible choices.

The future of relationships is collaboration. Developers, educators, policymakers, and students have to collaborate to create standards and practice that guarantee the dignity, trust, and integrity of humans. This is going to require leadership very much, frank transparency, and a commitment to innovation in protecting privacy as new technology evolves. Only then can there be a learning environment in which social media "facilitates" rather than "resources.".

Very simply, the road ahead is not smooth and even one. A developing challenge is ongoing in the attempt to balance educational outcomes and concerns over privacy regarding education for the digital age through careful attention to adaptations that demand true consensus regarding education for the digital age. By dealing with all of these issues simultaneously, we can ensure that the transformative power of social media promotes education while protecting the rights and well-being of all involved.

REFERENCES

Acilar, A., & Sæbø, Ø. (2023). Towards understanding the gender digital divide: A systematic literature review. *Global Knowledge, Memory and Communication*, 72(3), 233–249. DOI: 10.1108/GKMC-09-2021-0147

Ahmad, A., Alzahrani, A. S., Ahmed, N., & Ahsan, T. (2020a). A delegation model for SDN-driven federated cloud. *Alexandria Engineering Journal*, 59(5), 3653–3663. DOI: 10.1016/j.aej.2020.06.018

Ahmad, A., & Whitworth, B. (2011, December). Access control taxonomy for social networks. In 2011 7th International Conference on Information Assurance and Security (IAS) (pp. 256-261). IEEE. DOI: 10.1109/ISIAS.2011.6122829

Ahmad, A., & Whitworth, B. (2012, January). Ethical Issues in Online Social Networks. *2012 International Conference on Networks and Information (ICNI 2012).*

Ahmad, A., Whitworth, B., & Bertino, E. (2022). A framework for the application of socio-technical design methodology. *Ethics and Information Technology*, 24(4), 46. DOI: 10.1007/s10676-022-09651-0

Ahmad, A., Whitworth, B., & Janczewski, L. (2012, June). More choices, more control: Extending access control by meta-rights reallocation. In 2012 IEEE 11th International Conference on Trust, Security and Privacy in Computing and Communications (pp. 1113-1118). IEEE.

Ahmad, A., Whitworth, B., Zeshan, F., Bertino, E., & Friedman, R. (2017). Extending social networks with delegation. *Computers & Security*, 70, 546–564. DOI: 10.1016/j.cose.2017.07.010

Ahmad, A., Whitworth, B., Zeshan, F., Janczewski, L., Ali, M., Chaudary, M. H., & Friedman, R. (2019). A relation-aware multiparty access control. *Journal of Intelligent & Fuzzy Systems*, 37(1), 227–239. DOI: 10.3233/JIFS-179080

Ahmad, A., Zeshan, F., Hamid, M., Marriam, R., & Samreen, A. (2022). Application of Gamification in Modern Education. In *Handbook of Research on Promoting Economic and Social Development Through Serious Games* (pp. 60–75). IGI Global. DOI: 10.4018/978-1-7998-9732-3.ch004

Ahmed, M., Ahmad, A., Zeshan, F., & Turab, H. (2024). Blockchain Basics: A Deep Dive Into the Blocks, Chains, and Consensus. In Decentralizing the Online Experience With Web3 Technologies (pp. 57-89). IGI Global.

Ahmed, S., Javaid, S., Niazi, M. F., Alam, A., Ahmad, A., Baig, M. A., Khan, H. K., & Ahmed, T. (2019). A qualitative analysis of context-aware ubiquitous learning environments using Bluetooth beacons. *Technology, Pedagogy and Education*, 28(1), 53–71. DOI: 10.1080/1475939X.2018.1557737

Azorín, C., & Hernández, E. (2024). Leading professional networks in education: Developing connected autonomy across the territory? *School Leadership & Management*, 44(3), 251–270. DOI: 10.1080/13632434.2023.2284354

Beetham, H., Collier, A., Czerniewicz, L., Lamb, B., Lin, Y., Ross, J., & Wilson, A. (2022). Surveillance practices, risks and responses in the post pandemic university. *Digital Culture & Education*, 14(1), 16–37.

Bilal, A., Mirza, H. T., Hussain, I., & Ahmad, A. (2024). Investigating Influence of Google-Play Application Titles on Success. *Big Data Research*, 36, 100443. DOI: 10.1016/j.bdr.2024.100443

Eynon, R., & Malmberg, L. E. (2021). Lifelong learning and the Internet: Who benefits most from learning online? *British Journal of Educational Technology*, 52(2), 569–583. DOI: 10.1111/bjet.13041

Fatima, R., Zeshan, F., Ahmad, A., Hamid, M., Filali, I., Alhussan, A. A., & Abdallah, H. A. (2023). Requirement Change Prediction Model for Small Software Systems. *Computers*, 12(8), 164. DOI: 10.3390/computers12080164

Hamid, M., Ahmad, A., & Aimeur, E. (2019). Factors contributing in failures of software projects. *International Journal of Computer Science and Network Security*, 19(5), 62–77.

Hamid, M., Zeshan, F., Ahmad, A., Malik, S., Saleem, M., Tabassum, N., & Qasim, M. (2022). Analysis of software success through structural equation modeling. *Intelligent Automation & Soft Computing*, 31(3), 1689–1701. DOI: 10.32604/iasc.2022.020898

Hamid, M., Zeshan, F., Ahmad, A., Munawar, S., Aimeur, E., Ahmed, S., Abu Elsoud, M., & Yousif, M. (2020). An intelligent decision support system for effective handling of IT projects. *Journal of Intelligent & Fuzzy Systems*, 38(3), 2635–2647. DOI: 10.3233/JIFS-179550

Imran, M., & Ahmad, A. (2023). Enhancing data quality to mine credible patterns. *Journal of Information Science*, 49(2), 544–564. DOI: 10.1177/01655515211013693

Jain, A. K., Sahoo, S. R., & Kaubiyal, J. (2021). Online social networks security and privacy: Comprehensive review and analysis. *Complex & Intelligent Systems*, 7(5), 2157–2177. DOI: 10.1007/s40747-021-00409-7

Khan, M. S., Ahmad, A., & Humayoun, M. (2022). Building an Effective Automated Assessment System for C/C++ Introductory Programming Courses in ODL Environment. arXiv preprint arXiv:2205.11915.

Kim, J., Pak, S., & Cho, Y. H. (2021). The role of teachers' social networks in ICT-based instruction. *The Asia-Pacific Education Researcher*, 1–10.

Klapproth, F., Federkeil, L., Heinschke, F., & Jungmann, T. (2020). Teachers' Experiences of Stress and Their Coping Strategies during COVID-19 Induced Distance Teaching. *Journal of Pedagogical Research*, 4(4), 444–452. DOI: 10.33902/JPR.2020062805

Levy, B., Ebrahim, R., Chang, J., Multani, H., Sowers, M., Voigt, G., ... Team, S. (2018). Downsides of Digital Technology: How Social Media Influences Human Behavior and Impacts Democracy.

Majeed, A., & Lee, S. (2020). Anonymization techniques for privacy preserving data publishing: A comprehensive survey. *IEEE Access : Practical Innovations, Open Solutions*, 9, 8512–8545. DOI: 10.1109/ACCESS.2020.3045700

Mejbri, R., Mihoub, A., Cheikhrouhou, O., Essalmi, F., Krichen, M., Abid, M., & Hamam, H. (2022, May). Assessment of students performance and E-learning experience using online social networks. In 2022 2nd international conference of smart systems and emerging technologies (SMARTTECH) (pp. 26-31). IEEE.

Mir, A. A. (2024). Transparency in AI Supply Chains: Addressing Ethical Dilemmas in Data Collection and Usage. MZ Journal of Artificial Intelligence, 1(2).

Muftah, M. (2024). Impact of social media on learning English language during the COVID-19 pandemic. *PSU Research Review*, 8(1), 211–226. DOI: 10.1108/PRR-10-2021-0060

Muhammad, T., & Ahmad, A. (2021). A joint sharing approach for online privacy preservation. *World Wide Web (Bussum)*, 24(3), 895–924. DOI: 10.1007/s11280-021-00876-5

Oliveira, W., Hamari, J., Shi, L., Toda, A. M., Rodrigues, L., Palomino, P. T., & Isotani, S. (2023). Tailored gamification in education: A literature review and future agenda. *Education and Information Technologies*, 28(1), 373–406. DOI: 10.1007/s10639-022-11122-4

Ozer, M., & Perc, M. (2020). Dreams and realities of school tracking and vocational education. *Palgrave Communications*, 6(1), 1–7. DOI: 10.1057/s41599-020-0409-4

Parhamnia, F. (2024). Social networks in Iranian academic libraries: Complementary or antagonistic tools? *Library Hi Tech*, 42(5), 1385–1405. DOI: 10.1108/LHT-09-2022-0453

Peris, M., de la Barrera, U., Schoeps, K., & Montoya-Castilla, I. (2020). Psychological risk factors that predict social networking and internet addiction in adolescents. *International Journal of Environmental Research and Public Health*, 17(12), 4598. DOI: 10.3390/ijerph17124598 PMID: 32604834

Quach, S., Thaichon, P., Martin, K. D., Weaven, S., & Palmatier, R. W. (2022). Digital technologies: Tensions in privacy and data. *Journal of the Academy of Marketing Science*, 50(6), 1299–1323. DOI: 10.1007/s11747-022-00845-y PMID: 35281634

Samreen, A., Ahmad, A., & Zeshan, F. (2020a, February). Searching for truth in the post-truth age. In 2020 3rd international conference on advancements in computational sciences (ICACS) (pp. 1-5). IEEE. DOI: 10.1109/ICACS47775.2020.9055948

Samreen, A., Ahmad, A., Zeshan, F., Ahmad, F., Ahmed, S., & Khan, Z. A. (2020b). A collaborative method for protecting teens against online predators over social networks: A behavioral analysis. *IEEE Access : Practical Innovations, Open Solutions*, 8, 174375–174393. DOI: 10.1109/ACCESS.2020.3007141

Sarfraz, A., Ahmad, A., Zeshan, F., & Mirza, H. T. (2024). Synews: A synergy-based rumor verification system. *Social Network Analysis and Mining*, 14(1), 57. DOI: 10.1007/s13278-024-01214-z

Sweet, K. S., LeBlanc, J. K., Stough, L. M., & Sweany, N. W. (2020). Community building and knowledge sharing by individuals with disabilities using social media. *Journal of Computer Assisted Learning*, 36(1), 1–11. DOI: 10.1111/jcal.12377

Troussas, C., Krouska, A., Alepis, E., & Virvou, M. (2020). Intelligent and adaptive tutoring through a social network for higher education. *New Review of Hypermedia and Multimedia*, 26(3-4), 138–167. DOI: 10.1080/13614568.2021.1908436

Whitworth, B., & Ahmad, A. (2013a). Polite Computing. In *The Social Design of Technical Systems: Building technologies for communities* (pp. 77–105). The Interaction Design Foundation.

Whitworth, B., & Ahmad, A. (2013b). The evolution of computing. In *The Encyclopedia of human-computer interaction* (2nd ed.). Interaction Design Foundation. Retrieved from https://www.interaction-design.org/literature/book/the-encyclopedia-of-human-computerinteraction-2nd-ed/socio-technical-system-design

Whitworth, B., Janczewski, L., & Ahmad, A. (2012, July). A Logic of Creation in Online Social Networks. In *2012 World Congress in Computer Science, Computer Engineering and Applied Computing (WORLDCOMP 2012)*, Las Vegas, Nevada, USA.

Zeshan, F., Ahmad, A., Abdel-Aty, A. H., Algarni, F., Mahmoud, E. E., & Ahmad, A. (2020). A hybrid semantic knowledge integration and sharing approach for distributed smart environments. *Sensors (Basel)*, 20(20), 5918. DOI: 10.3390/s20205918 PMID: 33092118

Zeshan, F., dar, Z., Ahmad, A., & Malik, T. (2024). A fuzzy ontology-based context-aware encryption approach in IoT through device and information classification. *The Journal of Supercomputing*, 80(16), 23311–23356. DOI: 10.1007/s11227-024-06317-0

Zeshan, F., Mohamad, R., Ahmad, M. N., Othman, M. B., Elhag, A. A. M., Hussain, S. A., & Babar, I. (2019). Context-Aware ontology and web services discovery for distributed embedded real-time systems. *Malaysian Journal of Computer Science*, 32(3), 186–208. DOI: 10.22452/mjcs.vol32no3.2

ENDNOTES

1. https://gdpr-info.eu/
2. https://studentprivacy.ed.gov/ferpa
3. https://www.ftc.gov/legal-library/browse/rules/childrens-online-privacy-protection-rule-coppa

Chapter 13
Balancing Innovation and Privacy in the Age of Artificial Intelligence

Tunde Toyese Oyedokun
https://orcid.org/0000-0001-5306-038X
Thomas Adewumi University, Nigeria

ABSTRACT

The rapid growth of artificial intelligence (AI) presents significant opportunities for innovation but also raises substantial privacy challenges. This chapter explores the intricate relationship between AI advancement and privacy, advocating for a balanced approach that protects individual rights while fostering technological progress. It discusses AI's transformative potential in operational efficiency, personalization, and predictive analytics, alongside concerns related to data dependency, security risks, and algorithmic bias. The chapter reviews existing regulatory frameworks like the GDPR and emphasizes ethical guidelines focused on transparency and accountability. It proposes strategies such as privacy-preserving technologies and synthetic data to reconcile innovation with privacy. Finally, the chapter highlights the need for evolving privacy laws and public engagement to ensure AI serves the public good without compromising individual rights.

INTRODUCTION

Recent developments in artificial intelligence (AI) have had a profound impact on a number of industries, most notably finance, healthcare, and transportation. AI is transforming personalized medicine in the healthcare industry by enabling customized treatment regimens based on patient data, improving therapeutic approaches, and

DOI: 10.4018/979-8-3693-9015-3.ch013

increasing diagnostic accuracy. AI-powered technologies, for example, can evaluate medical images with precision on par with or better than human specialists, resulting in early disease detection and better patient outcomes. Additionally, predictive analytics powered by AI allows for early diagnosis and risk stratification of chronic diseases, significantly improving survival rates. Operational efficiency is another key benefit, as AI automates routine tasks, improves patient flow, and optimizes resource allocation, examples include AI chatbots for symptom assessment and virtual health assistants that monitor patients remotely (Bajwa, Munir, Nori & Williams, 2021).

In transportation, particularly with autonomous vehicles, AI is reshaping service delivery. Companies are piloting autonomous delivery systems to transport medications and healthcare services, thereby increasing accessibility for patients in remote areas (Marmaglio, Consolati, Amici & Tiboni, 2023). The potential for autonomous ambulances is also being explored, which could allow medical staff to focus more on patient care rather than driving. However, while the benefits of AI are substantial, they come with significant risks. Since AI systems need enormous volumes of data to operate effectively there is a greater chance of data breaches and misuse due to the intensive collecting and processing of personal data. Additionally, ethical considerations, such as accountability for mistakes made by AI systems or improper handling of personal data, must be carefully considered before implementing AI in delicate fields like healthcare (Farhud & Zokael, 2021). Existing legal frameworks cannot keep up with the rapid rate of AI development, which emphasizes the need for new regulations that guarantee the ethical and safe application of these technologies while upholding individual rights. While AI continues to unlock remarkable efficiencies across various industries, it is imperative to navigate the accompanying ethical dilemmas and privacy concerns with diligence; ongoing dialogue among stakeholders will be essential to harness its potential responsibly.

This chapter explores the intricate relationship between AI-driven innovation and privacy concerns, recognizing both the advantages and challenges of integrating AI across various domains. As AI technologies advance, they bring transformative benefits such as enhanced efficiency and improved decision-making capabilities, yet they also pose significant risks to personal privacy. The necessity for a balanced approach is paramount—one that not only embraces the potential of AI but also establishes strong protections for individual privacy rights. Real-world cases illustrate the ethical dilemmas faced by organizations as they navigate this landscape. For instance, while AI can optimize healthcare delivery through personalized treatment plans, it simultaneously raises questions about data security and patient consent. Regulatory developments, such as the European Union's proposals to limit AI surveillance technologies, highlight the growing recognition of these privacy issues and the urgent need for comprehensive governance frameworks. To achieve a responsible and ethically informed adoption of AI, actionable strategies must be identified. These include implementing robust data governance policies, enhancing transparency in AI decision-making processes, and prioritizing user consent mechanisms. This chapter aims to facilitate an equilibrium where technological progress does not compromise individual rights by proposing frameworks and guidelines that inform policy, industry standards, and organizational practices. Ultimately, fostering a culture of responsible AI use will ensure that innovation aligns with ethical considerations, promoting trust and accountability in the age of artificial intelligence.

THE PROMISE OF AI INNOVATION

The transformative potential of artificial intelligence (AI) has generated significant excitement across various sectors, including healthcare, finance, retail, and logistics. As AI continues to evolve, it presents unprecedented opportunities for enhancing operational efficiency, personalizing customer experiences, and leveraging predictive analytics for informed decision-making. For instance, in operational efficiency, AI automates routine tasks and optimizes workflows, allowing businesses to streamline processes and reduce human error. Companies like JPMorgan have utilized AI to drastically cut down on time-consuming tasks; their COiN platform can process thousands of contracts in seconds, saving approximately 360,000 hours of legal review time annually (Galeon, 2017). This automation not only boosts productivity but also enables employees to focus on more strategic initiatives. In terms of personalization, AI enhances customer experiences by analyzing vast amounts of data to tailor services and recommendations. Retailers can utilize AI-driven insights to understand consumer preferences better and adjust their offerings, accordingly, leading to improved customer satisfaction and loyalty (Bhuiyan, 2024). Predictive analytics further empowers organizations by enabling them to forecast trends and anticipate market demands. For example, AI can analyze historical sales data to optimize inventory management, ensuring that stock levels align with consumer demand while minimizing excess inventory.

However, the surge in AI-driven innovation raises critical questions about data dependency and the ethical management of privacy. AI system training requires a large amount of personal data, which raises concerns about data security and human privacy rights. Organizations that depend on AI systems that use vast datasets must deal with the ethical issues of permission and transparency as well as the challenges of data governance (Díaz-Rodríguez, Del Ser, Coeckelbergh, López de Prado, Herrera-Viedma, & Herrera, 2023). Finding a balance between the enormous advantages of AI and the need to preserve public confidence and secure personal data is the difficult part. Even though artificial intelligence (AI) has enormous potential to improve productivity, customization, and predictive capacities in a variety of industries, issues with data usage and privacy management must be addressed. A responsible approach that prioritizes ethical standards will be crucial as organizations continue to integrate AI into their operations, ensuring that technological advancements do not compromise individual rights or societal norms.

Artificial intelligence (AI) is significantly redefining the efficiency landscape across various industries by automating routine tasks, optimizing processes, and minimizing human error. In manufacturing, AI-driven automation facilitates the continuous operation of production lines, thereby reducing downtime and maximizing output. Robotics and AI-enabled systems excel at managing complex, repetitive tasks with remarkable speed and precision, allowing companies to scale operations effectively (Elahi, Afolaranmi, Martinez Lastra & Perez-Garcia, 2023). In addition to significantly reducing costs, this change boosts productivity and frees up human resources to work on more strategic and innovative projects. Artificial Intelligence (AI) solutions in logistics and supply chain management simplify processes by enhancing inventory control, demand forecasting, and route optimization. For instance, companies leverage AI to analyze extensive datasets that include weather conditions, traffic patterns, and customer demand to optimize delivery schedules and enhance fuel efficiency. This capability is particularly crucial in the e-commerce sector, where consumers increasingly expect fast, reliable, and cost-effective delivery services (Joel, Oyewole, Odunaya & Soyombo, 2024).

Additionally, AI-powered predictive maintenance solutions can anticipate equipment problems before they happen, thereby lowering repair costs and downtime in sectors like manufacturing, transportation, and energy. The financial services sector also reaps considerable benefits from AI's impact on efficiency. Algorithms are capable of executing high-frequency trading, detecting fraud, and managing compliance with speed and accuracy that far surpasses human capabilities. Financial institutions, by automating these critical yet time-consuming tasks can operate more effectively while enhancing customer trust and reallocating resources toward innovation (Siddiqui, 2024). Similarly, in the public sector, AI streamlines administrative processes, such as processing applications or sorting public records, freeing government workers to concentrate on more complex responsibilities that directly engage citizens. The integration of AI across these sectors not only drives operational efficiency but also fosters an environment where organizations can adapt swiftly to changing market demands while maintaining high standards of quality and service. As industries continue to embrace AI technologies, the potential for enhanced productivity and innovation remains vast.

AI has enabled a shift towards hyper-personalization, where companies leverage data and algorithms to create tailored experiences for individual customers. In the digital age, consumers expect products, services, and recommendations that align closely with their unique preferences and behaviors. In order to provide tailored services, targeted advertisements, and recommendations, artificial intelligence (AI) analyzes large datasets, such as browsing history, purchase trends, and social media interactions. Retail and e-commerce have harnessed AI to transform the customer shopping experience. AI-driven systems predict which products customers are likely to purchase and recommend them accordingly by analyzing consumer data in real-time (Raji, Olodo, Oke, Addy, Ofodile & Oyewole, 2024). For instance, Amazon's recommendation engine and Netflix's content suggestions are fueled by sophisticated AI algorithms that learn from each user's behavior (Pandita, 2024). This level of personalization drives customer satisfaction, increases engagement, and enhances loyalty, as consumers feel understood and valued by the companies they interact with.

In the healthcare sector, AI personalization has unlocked new possibilities in patient care and treatment. AI is being used, for instance, in precision medicine to examine lifestyle data, medical history, and genetic information in order to customize treatment regimens for each patient. According to Johnson, Wei, Weeraratne, Frisse, Misulis, Rhee, Zhao, and Snowdon (2021), the goal of this individualized approach to healthcare is to enhance results by guaranteeing that patients receive the best treatment for their particular illnesses. Personalization is further enhanced by wearable technology, such as fitness trackers and smartwatches, which continuously monitor health parameters and offer insights for preventive treatment, empowering users to make wellness-related decisions. For individualized client experiences, the banking and financial sector also uses AI. Digital banking apps employ artificial intelligence (AI) to track user spending patterns, suggest savings strategies, and provide financial guidance based on personal financial objectives (Pattnaik, Ray & Raman, 2024). Financial institutions may increase customer satisfaction and forge closer bonds with their customers by anticipating and understanding their demands. However, as personalization becomes more pervasive, the ethical considerations of data collection and usage come into play, raising questions about how much personal information can and should be used to shape these experiences.

Predictive analytics, which makes use of both historical and current data to forecast results and support data-driven decision-making, is one of the most exciting uses of artificial intelligence (AI). In the healthcare industry, this technology is especially revolutionary because it helps with illness breakout prediction, treatment plan customization, and improving diagnostic precision. To determine a patient's likelihood of getting a certain ailment, AI models examine complicated patient data, such as imaging, genetic information, and medical records. Healthcare professionals can take early action thanks to their predictive capabilities, which may stop the progression of the disease and improve patient outcomes overall (Khalifa & Albadawy, 2024). AI helps radiologists in the field of medical imaging by seeing patterns that point to illness. Compared to conventional techniques, machine learning algorithms are more accurate in identifying early indicators of diseases like cancer or heart disease, frequently identifying problems that the human eye could miss (Pinto-Coelho, 2023). Predictive analytics is essential for operational management in healthcare settings in addition to diagnosis. AI-driven demand forecasting enables hospitals to optimize staffing levels, deploy efficient resources, and shorten wait times.

The impact of AI-powered predictive analytics extends beyond healthcare into various other sectors. In agriculture, for instance, AI analyzes data from soil sensors, weather forecasts, and satellite imagery to predict crop yields and inform planting schedules. Retailers use predictive analytics to anticipate demand and optimize inventory management, thereby minimizing stockouts and reducing overstock situations. The integration of AI in predictive analytics not only improves operational efficiency but also empowers organizations across sectors to make informed decisions based on thorough data analysis. Similarly, in finance, predictive models help manage risks, identify market trends, and personalize investment strategies for clients. This helps farmers make informed decisions regarding irrigation, pest control, and fertilization, ultimately leading to higher yields and a reduced environmental footprint (Kumar, Sharma, Kedam, Patel, Kate & Rathnayake, 2024; Badmus, Rajput, Arogundade & Williams, 2024). As industries continue to harness these capabilities, the potential for improved outcomes, whether in patient care or resource management, remains vast.

The transformative potential of artificial intelligence (AI) has sparked significant advancements across industries, offering real-world applications that enhance efficiency, personalization, and decision-making. In healthcare, AI has revolutionized patient care by enabling early disease detection through advanced imaging analysis and predictive analytics. In this case, AI-driven systems analyze patient data to customize treatment plans, improving outcomes and operational efficiency. Virtual health assistance and chatbots also facilitate remote monitoring, streamlining healthcare delivery. Similarly, in finance, AI optimizes operations by automating processes like fraud detection and compliance management. Platforms such as JPMorgan's COiN exemplify this by drastically reducing the time required for legal reviews, saving thousands of hours annually (Mearian, 2019). Retailers have embraced AI to deliver hyper-personalized shopping experiences, using algorithms to analyze consumer behavior and recommend products tailored to individual preferences. This approach not only increases customer satisfaction but also drives loyalty and sales. Case studies further illustrate the profound impact of AI innovation. For instance, Amazon's recommendation engine uses sophisticated algorithms to predict consumer needs, enhancing user engagement and boosting revenue (Hardesty, 2019). In manufacturing, predictive maintenance systems powered by AI anticipate equipment failures before they occur, reducing downtime and repair costs. Another notable example is the use of AI in logistics, where companies optimize delivery routes based on real-time data like weather conditions and traffic patterns. This capability is crucial for e-commerce businesses striving to meet consumer expectations for fast and reliable deliveries. In agriculture, AI analyzes soil data and weather forecasts to optimize planting schedules, improving crop yields while minimizing environmental impact. To ensure the promise of AI innovation aligns with ethical standards and societal needs, actionable insights are essential. Organizations must implement robust data governance frameworks to manage the ethical collection and usage of personal data responsibly. Enhancing transparency in AI decision-making processes is another critical step; stakeholders should understand how algorithms function and their implications for privacy and fairness. Prioritizing user consent mechanisms is equally important to empower individuals in controlling their data. Continuous dialogue among stakeholders, including regulators, developers, and users, is necessary to address emerging challenges and foster trust in AI systems.

One of the primary challenges associated with AI innovation is its dependency on large datasets. To deliver insights and drive decisions, AI systems require vast quantities of information often containing personal and sensitive data (Broekhuizen, Dekker, de Faria, Firk, Nguyen & Sofka, 2023). For instance, in the healthcare sector, predictive analytics relies on patient data to provide accurate forecasts and recommendations. Similarly, personalized services in retail and finance depend on extensive consumer data to refine recommendations and tailor experiences. However, there are privacy and data security risks associated with this reliance on data. Concerns around data collection, storage, and sharing are brought up by the requirement for large datasets. Businesses that handle a lot of data are susceptible to misuse, illegal access, and breaches, all of which can jeopardize the privacy of individuals. Additionally, biases in past data may be reinforced by AI algorithms, which could result in unfair treatment of particular persons or groups. Systemic imbalances could be reinforced, for instance, if a banking sector algorithm learns from biased lending practices and keeps suggesting higher interest rates or rejecting loans based on socioeconomic position or race.

To address these issues, policymakers and organizations are increasingly focusing on data governance, transparency, and accountability. Ethical AI practices encourage companies to limit data collection to what is necessary, implement strong encryption measures, and establish clear data ownership rights for users. Technologies that improve privacy, such federated learning and differential privacy, present intriguing answers by enabling AI to learn from data without jeopardizing personal privacy. For example, federated learning enables AI models to train on decentralized data sources without moving sensitive information to a central place, while differential privacy allows businesses to examine aggregate data while maintaining individual anonymity. As AI develops, it's critical to strike a balance between using data to spur innovation and safeguarding personal privacy. In order to achieve this balance, strong legal frameworks and moral principles that uphold individual rights and encourage responsible innovation will be necessary in addition to technological advancements. In the age of AI, data dependency is both a powerful enabler of progress and a critical area of concern, underscoring the need for responsible data stewardship to build public trust and ensure sustainable growth (Díaz-Rodríguez, Del Ser, Coeckelbergh, López de Prado, Herrera-Viedma, & Herrera, 2023).

PRIVACY CONCERNS IN ARTIFICIAL INTELLIGENCE (AI) DEVELOPMENT

As artificial intelligence (AI) continues to permeate diverse sectors, the protection of individual privacy has emerged as one of the most pressing issues in AI development. AI systems thrive on data, often gathering and processing vast quantities of personal and sensitive information to produce insights, enhance efficiencies, and drive decision-making. However, this dependence on data introduces several privacy concerns that are not easily addressed without regulatory, ethical, and technological considerations (Osasona, Amoo, Atadoga, Abrahams, Farayola & Ayinla, 2024). Key areas of concern include data collection practices, data security risks, and algorithmic bias, all of which have far-reaching ethical, legal, and societal implications. Data collection is the backbone of AI functionality, as the algorithms that power AI systems rely on extensive datasets to learn, make predictions, and deliver personalized services (Belenguer, 2022). However, the methods by which this data is collected, as well as the lack of transparency around its use, have significant privacy implications. One of the primary concerns surrounding data collection is obtaining genuine consent from users. While many platforms and applications require users to agree to terms and conditions before they can access services, these agreements are often complex and challenging for the average user to fully understand. Consequently, many people may consent to data collection without a full comprehension of what data is being collected, how it will be used, or who will have access to it (Andreotta, Kirkham & Rizzi, 2022).

Data ownership is another critical issue. While users generate data through their interactions with various digital platforms, ownership of this data is often assumed by the companies collecting it. This creates an imbalance in control, as users typically have limited rights over how their data is stored, shared, or even sold (Hummel, Braun & Dabrock, 2021). The lack of robust data ownership rights also limits users' ability to request deletion of their data, which could otherwise help reduce privacy risks. Public awareness regarding data collection practices is similarly lacking. Many individuals are unaware of the extent to which their data is used in AI systems, or the potential for their data to be combined with other information to create detailed profiles. This lack of transparency contributes to public mistrust in AI and raises ethical questions about the fairness of data practices (Sanchez, Brenman & Ye, 2024). To address these concerns, data collection processes must become more transparent, with clear disclosures that empower users to make informed decisions about their data. Furthermore, efforts to educate the public on data privacy and ownership can encourage more responsible data-sharing behaviors and foster a culture of transparency that holds organizations accountable.

AI systems are highly reliant on the availability of data, and with this dependency comes an increased risk of data breaches and security vulnerabilities. Data security risks in AI systems stem from the fact that they often process large volumes of sensitive data, making them attractive targets for cybercriminals. Moreover, the complex nature of AI algorithms and their reliance on cloud storage solutions and interconnected systems can introduce multiple points of vulnerability. A breach of these systems can have far-reaching consequences, exposing personal information, trade secrets, and critical business data to unauthorized entities (Kaur, Gabrijelčič & Klobučar, 2023). Machine learning models are particularly susceptible to certain types of cyberattacks. One type, known as adversarial attacks, involves inputting subtle, carefully crafted data to deceive or manipulate AI algorithms (Aloraini, Javed, Rana & Burnap, 2022). For instance, in image recognition systems, small alterations to an image may lead the algorithm to misidentify it, which can have serious security implications (Luo, 2024). For example, in autonomous driving technology, an adversarial attack on a vehicle's object-recognition system could lead to accidents if stop signs or other critical signals are misinterpreted (Giannaros, Karras, Theodorakopoulos, Karras, Kranias, Schizas, Kalogeratos & Tsolis, 2023). Another major risk is data leakage, where sensitive data can be inferred from the outputs of AI models. Even in cases where data is anonymized, advances in re-identification techniques have shown that it is possible to uncover individual identities from anonymized datasets by cross-referencing them with other information (Mühlhoff, 2023). This raises concerns about the effectiveness of traditional anonymization practices in protecting privacy.

Organizations creating AI systems must implement strict cybersecurity procedures to overcome these vulnerabilities. To protect sensitive data, this entails putting strong access controls, secure data storage, and encryption mechanisms into practice. To reduce the privacy issues connected with AI models, methods such as differential privacy, which involves processing data in a way that preserves individual privacy while maintaining the accuracy of aggregate analyses are also being investigated (Villegas-Ch & García-Ortiz, 2023). Another interesting strategy is federated learning, which eliminates the need to consolidate sensitive data in one potentially insecure location by allowing AI models to be trained on decentralized data sources (Mohammadi, Balador, Sinaei & Flammini, 2024). However, data security remains an ongoing challenge, and as AI systems evolve, too, too must the measures taken to protect them.

In the development of AI, one of the most troubling ethical and legal concerns is algorithmic bias. The data that is utilized to train AI systems can contain historical biases, societal injustices, or systemic discrimination, which is often the source of bias in these systems. Learning from biased datasets might cause AI algorithms to reinforce and even magnify existing biases, producing results that unfairly disfavor particular persons or groups (Chen, 2023). Particularly in areas like criminal justice, employment, financing, and healthcare, biased AI systems have serious ramifications. For instance, in the field of criminal justice, algorithms for predictive policing that are trained on past crime data may exacerbate preexisting prejudices by unfairly singling out particular neighborhoods or demographic groups (Hung & Yen, 2023). In hiring, AI-driven systems have been shown to favor certain applicants based on gender or race, due to historical biases embedded in the training data. Similarly, in lending, biased AI algorithms can result in discriminatory loan approval practices, furthering financial exclusion for underrepresented groups (Belenguer, 2022).

The ethical implications of algorithmic bias are profound, as they challenge fundamental principles of fairness, justice, and equality. When AI systems produce biased outcomes, they can lead to discriminatory practices that are not only unethical but also potentially illegal. Several nations' regulatory agencies are starting to address these problems by creating frameworks and norms for the moral application of AI. For example, the General Data Protection Regulation (GDPR) of the European Union enforces data protection principles that demand that companies show their AI systems are transparent, accountable, and equitable (Wu, Huang & Gong, 2020). The EU's proposed Artificial Intelligence Act also seeks to impose stringent guidelines, including prohibitions on discriminatory results, on “high-risk” AI applications. Algorithmic bias has the potential to cause legal action and liability problems for corporations, especially when biased AI systems have a negative impact on protected classes. When using AI in delicate fields, businesses need to carefully consider the possibility of bias in their systems and take precautions against it. Strategies to address algorithmic bias include using more diverse and representative datasets, testing algorithms for disparate impact, and implementing fairness-aware machine learning techniques that actively counter bias in model outputs (Sartor, 2020).

Another important measure is enhancing transparency in AI systems. Explainability where AI decisions can be easily interpreted and understood by humans is critical in reducing bias and building trust. Organizations can better detect and address biases in the system by providing transparency into how AI systems make decisions (Balasubramaniam, Kauppinen, Rannisto, Hiekkanen & Kujala, 2023). However, ensuring explainability is challenging, especially in complex AI models like deep neural networks. Therefore, ongoing research into interpretability methods, such as model-agnostic techniques, is crucial for developing AI systems that can both protect privacy and uphold ethical standards (Markus, Kors & Rijnbeek, 2021). The promise of AI innovation comes with considerable privacy challenges that developers, policymakers, and organizations must address. Data collection practices require transparency, proper consent, and clear ownership rights to empower users and foster trust. Data security risks necessitate robust cybersecurity measures and privacy-preserving techniques to safeguard sensitive information in AI systems (Farayola, Olurunfemi & Shoetan, 2024). Finally, addressing algorithmic bias is essential to prevent unethical and potentially illegal outcomes, with a focus on fairness, transparency, and accountability. As AI continues to grow in influence, balancing innovation with privacy protection will be crucial to building systems that respect individual rights and promote equitable, trustworthy outcomes. Society can work towards a future where AI enhances our lives without compromising our privacy by developing ethical AI frameworks, implementing strong data governance practices, and promoting public awareness of privacy issues.

The integration of artificial intelligence (AI) into various industries has revolutionized many aspects of our daily lives, from healthcare and finance to transportation and entertainment. However, as AI systems become increasingly reliant on vast amounts of personal data, privacy concerns have emerged as a significant challenge. AI technologies, by nature, require access to sensitive information to function effectively, but this raises questions about how that data is collected, used, stored, and protected. As AI continues to advance, addressing these privacy concerns is critical for both legal compliance and maintaining user trust. In the healthcare industry, AI is being used to improve patient outcomes by enabling more accurate diagnoses, personalized treatment plans, and predictive analytics. AI-driven systems, such as those used in medical imaging or personalized care, rely on vast amounts of patient data, including personal health records, genetic information, and medical histories. This creates significant privacy concerns. In this case, unauthorized access to or misuse of sensitive health data could lead to identity theft or discrimination. To address these issues, healthcare organizations can implement robust encryption methods, access control mechanisms, and adopt techniques like federated learning. This latter approach ensures that patient data remains decentralized and local to the healthcare provider, improving privacy while still allowing AI systems to learn and improve.

In the realm of autonomous vehicles, AI is used to process data from sensors, GPS systems, and cameras, allowing self-driving cars to make real-time decisions. However, this also raises privacy issues related to the collection of location data, driving habits, and even passengers' personal preferences (Garikapati & Shetiya, 2024). The potential for tracking individuals' movements without their consent or predicting behaviors through personal data poses significant risks. To mitigate these concerns, car manufacturers and AI developers can anonymize sensitive data during processing, ensuring that location information is not linked back to individuals. Additionally, users should be given clear consent options about what data is being collected and how it will be used (Mulder & Vellinga, 2021). Social media platforms also make extensive use of AI to personalize user experiences, recommending content and advertisements based on individual preferences and behavior. While this enhances user engagement, it also raises privacy concerns regarding data exploitation. Many users are unaware of the extent to which their data is being collected, and AI systems often infer personal information that could lead to violations of user privacy. To address these concerns, social media companies can incorporate privacy-by-design principles, ensuring that data is anonymized and only the minimal amount of data required for specific tasks is collected (Rupp & Grafenstein, 2024). Furthermore, users should be given control over what data is shared and be provided with clear consent processes. In the financial sector, AI is transforming areas like fraud detection, risk assessment, and personalized financial advising. On analyzing vast amounts of transactional data, AI systems can predict and prevent fraud or offer tailored financial advice. However, this also means that sensitive financial information is processed and stored, making it vulnerable to potential breaches. To minimize privacy risks, financial institutions can implement encryption techniques such as homomorphic encryption, which allows data to be processed in an encrypted form. Additionally, financial institutions should have strict data retention policies and ensure that personal financial data is anonymized when it is no longer needed (Olaiya, Adesoga, Adebayo, Sotomi, Adigun & Ezeliora, 2024).

The privacy risks associated with AI development are not just hypothetical; they have been highlighted in several high-profile cases. One notable example is the Cambridge Analytica scandal, where Facebook allowed a third-party company to access personal data from millions of users without their consent (Rehman, 2019). This data was then used to influence political opinions and behaviors through targeted advertisements. The scandal raised widespread concerns about the misuse of personal data and the lack of transparency regarding how AI systems operate. In response, businesses have learned the importance of clear and transparent consent mechanisms, as well as the need to educate users on how their data is being used. Social media platforms should adopt more stringent governance over data sharing, ensuring that users can easily understand and control their data. Another case that highlights privacy concerns in AI development occurred when Google's DeepMind collaborated with the UK's National Health Service (NHS) to develop AI tools for detecting kidney disease. DeepMind gained access to over a million NHS patients' health records, raising concerns about whether patients had given explicit consent for their data to be used in this way (BBC, 2021). This case underscores the need for transparency in data-sharing agreements, particularly when sensitive health data is involved. Moving forward, organizations can ensure that any data-sharing agreements are accompanied by clear consent protocols, allowing individuals to control the use of their personal health information. Similarly, the use of AI-driven facial recognition technology, such as Amazon's Rekognition, has raised significant privacy concerns. Law enforcement agencies have used Rekognition for surveillance purposes, tracking individuals in public spaces without their knowledge or consent (Harwell, 2019). This use of AI for mass surveillance, coupled with the risk of biased algorithms, has prompted debates over the ethical and legal implications of such technologies. To address these concerns, organizations should adopt clear regulatory frameworks that govern the use of facial recognition, ensuring that individuals' privacy rights are respected. Additionally, AI systems should undergo regular fairness audits to detect and mitigate any biases that could lead to discriminatory practices.

Organizations must put privacy first from the beginning in order to reduce the privacy issues related to AI development. Adopting "privacy by design," which entails including privacy safeguards into the architecture and design of AI systems, is one important tactic. This strategy involves the use of privacy-preserving strategies like differential privacy, which anonymizes data so that statistical studies are unable to identify specific persons. Data reduction, which involves simply gathering the information required for a given purpose and making sure it is kept for as long as necessary, is another crucial tactic. AI developers should also create explicit data governance frameworks that guarantee data encryption during storage and transfer and restrict access to sensitive information. Furthermore, transparency and user consent mechanisms are essential for fostering trust and compliance. Users must be informed about what data is being collected and how it will be used, and they should have the ability to opt out of certain data collection practices if they choose. Companies should also ensure that individuals can access and delete their personal data when requested. Regular privacy audits and risk assessments are also crucial for identifying potential vulnerabilities in AI systems and ensuring compliance with privacy regulations such as the General Data Protection Regulation (GDPR) in Europe or the California Consumer Privacy Act (CCPA) in the United States. Finally, the development of AI systems must be accompanied by ongoing education and training for developers, stakeholders, and users. Developers should be made aware of the ethical implications of AI and its potential to infringe on privacy.

REGULATORY FRAMEWORKS AND ETHICAL CONSIDERATIONS

Regulations and ethical standards are essential as artificial intelligence (AI) technology become increasingly pervasive in daily life. Efficient regulation guarantees that AI systems function in a manner that upholds individual liberties, advances equity, and cultivates public confidence. AI has enormous creative potential, but it also presents moral dilemmas that, if ignored, may result in prejudices, privacy violations, and problems with accountability. Addressing these concerns requires a robust regulatory framework alongside clear ethical guidelines to ensure responsible AI development. Additionally, interdisciplinary collaboration plays a vital role in shaping these regulations, as diverse stakeholders bring valuable perspectives on the societal, economic, and ethical impacts of AI. This section explores existing regulations such as the General Data Protection Regulation (GDPR), essential ethical guidelines for AI, and the importance of interdisciplinary collaboration in developing a responsible AI landscape.

One of the most extensive privacy laws in the world and a pillar of AI-related legislation is the General Data Protection Regulation (GDPR), which was passed by the European Union in 2018. GDPR was created to safeguard people's personal information while granting citizens authority over the collection, storage, and use of such information. The GDPR's stringent data handling regulations, which are applicable to any entity processing the data of EU people, regardless of the organization's location, make it relevant to AI. AI systems that depend on extensive data processing are directly impacted by some of the fundamental GDPR principles, including data reduction, purpose limitation, and the right to be forgotten. According to these guidelines, people should have the ability to request the deletion of their personal data, data usage should be clear and detailed, and data collection should be restricted to what is required. GDPR has established a high bar for data protection by enforcing these standards, which companies creating AI systems must adhere to in order to avoid legal ramifications. The necessity for data protection impact assessments (DPIAs) for high-risk data processing activities, like those involving sensitive data or extensive monitoring, is another significant component of GDPR (Sartor, 2020). Because they force enterprises to analyze the possible privacy concerns connected to AI applications, gauge their effects on people, and take action to reduce these risks, DPIAs are essential to the advancement of AI. Additionally, GDPR's accountability principle requires companies to demonstrate compliance with data protection standards, fostering a culture of responsibility within organizations that develop and deploy AI.

In addition to GDPR, a number of additional laws have an impact on global AI development. Similar rights to those guaranteed by the GDPR are granted to Californians under the California Consumer Privacy Act (CCPA), which went into force in 2020. These rights include the ability to access, remove, and refuse to sell personal data. The CCPA highlights the increased awareness and legal action surrounding data privacy in AI, even though it is less strict than the GDPR in some areas (Baik, 2020). The GDPR's focus on informed consent, data minimization, and user rights is closely mirrored in China's Personal Information Protection Law (PIPL), which was passed in 2021 and requires businesses to manage personal data responsibly (Creemers, 2022). With increasing AI adoption, more jurisdictions are following suit, developing privacy regulations that align with these principles to ensure that AI technologies respect individual privacy and data protection standards.

In order to control AI applications according to their degree of risk to people and society, the European Union has also suggested the Artificial Intelligence Act. According to Novelli, Casolari, Rotolo, Taddeo, and Floridi (2024), the act divides AI applications into four risk categories: unacceptable, high, limited, and minimal risk. High-risk applications, like biometric surveillance and AI systems related to employment, are subject to the strongest regulations. This risk-based strategy takes into account the differing effects of various AI applications and is a proactive measure to shield people from dangerous AI applications while enabling less regulated, lower-risk apps to thrive. Ethical principles offer a moral basis for the creation and application of AI technology in addition to legal frameworks. Ethical guidelines concentrate on the larger duties of developers, organizations, and legislators to guarantee that AI promotes society and reduces harm, whilst rules provide legal obligations. In order to direct responsible AI development and promote public confidence in new technologies, three fundamental ethical principles, transparency, accountability, and fairness—are necessary.

In order to foster understanding and trust, transparency in AI is essential. For AI systems to be transparent, end users and stakeholders must be able to comprehend, access, and explain them. This is especially crucial in intricate AI applications like machine learning models, where choices could have a significant influence on people's lives in fields like law enforcement, healthcare, and finance. Users should be able to comprehend the reasoning behind an AI system's decisions by receiving clear and meaningful explanations of those judgments. In order for users and stakeholders to make educated decisions about interacting with AI systems, transparency also entails open information regarding the limitations and potential biases of these systems. Accountability makes businesses and people answerable for the effects of their AI systems. (Balasubramaniam, 2023). According to this principle, AI developers and implementers must accept responsibility for the results produced by their algorithms and make sure that there is a system in place to address and correct biases or errors. Accountability is particularly crucial in situations like job applications, court trials, or medical diagnosis when AI judgments could have a big impact. Organizations must put in place protections like monitoring systems, auditing procedures, and feedback loops to guarantee that AI models operate as planned in order to attain accountability (Busuioc, 2021). The significance of ethical responsibility in AI development is further reinforced by clear accountability frameworks, which make it easier for those who might be negatively impacted by AI systems to pursue legal action.

Fairness is a foundational ethical principle that seeks to ensure that AI systems do not discriminate or reinforce biases against particular groups or individuals. Fairness in AI development involves addressing biases in data, algorithms, and outcomes to prevent discriminatory practices. AI developers must be vigilant in identifying and mitigating biases that may arise from skewed training datasets or historical inequalities reflected in the data. Fairness also encompasses inclusivity, ensuring that AI applications consider the needs and experiences of diverse populations. For example, in facial recognition systems, fairness demands that the system works accurately across different demographic groups, avoiding disparities that may disproportionately affect marginalized communities. Ensuring fairness in AI contributes to more equitable outcomes and prevents the perpetuation of societal biases through automated systems. Together, transparency, accountability, and fairness form a robust ethical foundation for responsible AI. Organizations and developers that adhere to these principles demonstrate a commitment to social responsibility, building trust and credibility with their stakeholders (Ferrara, 2024). While these principles are not enforceable laws, they are essential in fostering ethical AI practices and can guide organizations in achieving compliance with emerging regulations.

Interdisciplinary collaboration is essential in creating a regulatory environment that can effectively address the multifaceted challenges of AI development. The rapid evolution of AI technology demands input from a wide range of stakeholders, including technologists, ethicists, legal experts, industry representatives, policymakers, and the general public. Each group brings unique perspectives, helping to ensure that AI regulations are comprehensive, adaptable, and reflective of societal values. One key benefit of interdisciplinary collaboration is that it enables policymakers to understand the technical complexities of AI, which is critical for developing regulations that are both practical and effective (Al-kfairy, Mustafa, Kshetri, Insiew & Alfandi, 2024). For example, AI developers can inform policymakers about the technical limitations of AI systems, allowing regulations to be crafted in ways that are technologically feasible and do not inadvertently stifle innovation. Ethicists and social scientists can provide insights into the societal and ethical impacts of AI, ensuring that regulations consider issues such as fairness, privacy, and inclusivity. This collaboration can help create balanced regulations that protect individual rights while enabling innovation.

Industry stakeholders also play a vital role in regulatory development, as they can provide practical insights into how AI is deployed across different sectors. Their input helps regulators understand the potential economic and operational impacts of AI regulations, ensuring that policies are realistic and align with industry practices. However, industry influence must be balanced to prevent regulatory capture, where the regulations primarily serve corporate interests rather than public welfare. Engaging with consumer advocacy groups and civil society organizations can counterbalance industry influence and help ensure that regulations prioritize the public good. Public engagement is equally important in shaping ethical and responsible AI practices. Engaging with the public in discussions about AI regulation fosters transparency and builds trust, enabling individuals to voice their concerns and preferences about how AI is used in their lives. This public input can guide regulators to focus on issues that matter most to citizens, such as privacy, accountability, and discrimination, while also providing valuable insights into societal expectations around AI (Machado, H., Silva, S. & Neiva, 2023). Involving diverse voices in the regulatory process not only enhances the legitimacy of AI regulations but also helps ensure that AI is developed in ways that align with broader societal values.

Addressing the global nature of AI technology also requires interdisciplinary cooperation. International collaboration is essential to developing standardized standards that promote uniformity and compliance globally, since AI systems are frequently implemented across national boundaries. In order to minimize conflict for multinational corporations and guarantee that AI systems adhere to uniform ethical standards across jurisdictions, cooperative initiatives like the Global Partnership on AI (GPAI) and the Organization for Economic Co-operation and Development's (OECD) principles on AI encourage countries to harmonize their regulatory approaches (Cancela-Outeda, 2024). To guarantee that these technologies are used responsibly and ethically, legislative frameworks and ethical standards for AI must be developed. Regulations such as GDPR provide critical safeguards for data privacy and set standards for data handling in AI systems, while the principles of transparency, accountability, and fairness serve as ethical cornerstones for AI development. However, developing effective regulations requires input from diverse stakeholders, as AI's impact extends beyond technology into societal, ethical, and legal realms. Society can create a regulatory environment that balances innovation with the protection of individual rights, ensuring that AI serves as a positive force for all. As AI continues to evolve, regulatory and ethical frameworks will need to adapt accordingly, guided by an ongoing commitment to transparency, accountability, and fairness.

STRATEGIES FOR BALANCING INNOVATION AND PRIVACY

Maintaining public support for technical developments and building trust in the era of artificial intelligence (AI) depend on striking a balance between innovation and privacy. The data-driven nature of AI systems, which depend on enormous volumes of private and sensitive data to increase accuracy and performance, frequently raises privacy concerns. It is now crucial to implement solutions that preserve privacy while fostering innovation as AI systems grow increasingly integrated into daily life. A number of strategies are being developed to deal with these issues, such as the use of synthetic data, privacy-preserving technology, and transparent AI systems that prioritize informed permission and explainability. When combined, these tactics provide a means of utilizing AI's promise while preserving people's right to privacy.

Privacy-preserving technologies are essential tools for minimizing privacy risks in AI development. These techniques allow organizations to leverage large datasets for AI training and decision-making without directly exposing sensitive information (Feretzakis, Papaspyridis, Gkoulalas-Divanis & Verykios, 2024). Two widely adopted methods in this domain are differential privacy and federated learning. Differential Privacy is a mathematical technique designed to protect individual data points within a dataset while still enabling accurate, aggregate analysis. In differential privacy, random "noise" is added to the data, which obscures individual data points but preserves overall patterns within the dataset. Differential privacy limits the risk of re-identifying individuals even when the dataset is accessed or analyzed by external parties by ensuring that no single data point can be identified with confidence. Differential privacy has been successfully implemented by organizations like Apple and the U.S. Census Bureau, allowing them to collect and analyze data while minimizing privacy risks. For instance, Apple uses differential privacy in its data collection from iPhone users, enabling them to gather insights on user behavior without directly compromising individual privacy. The U.S. Census Bureau also uses differential privacy to protect individuals' data while sharing valuable demographic information with policymakers, researchers, and the public (Tang, Korolova, Bai, Wang & Wang, 2017). Differential privacy is particularly valuable in high-risk sectors like healthcare, where AI models can provide critical insights without directly exposing sensitive patient data. Healthcare providers can aggregate and analyze data from large patient groups to improve treatment outcomes, monitor disease trends, and conduct research without violating patient confidentiality by leveraging differential privacy. However, implementing differential privacy can present challenges, as adding noise to the data may impact model accuracy. Developers must carefully calibrate the level of noise added to the data, balancing privacy with the need for accurate insights.

Federated Learning is another promising privacy-preserving technology that allows AI models to learn from data across multiple devices or sources without centralized data storage. In federated learning, an AI model is initially trained on a central server using a sample dataset. The model is then distributed to various devices or nodes (e.g., mobile phones, computers), where it continues learning using local data (Yurdem, Kuzlu, Gullu, Catak, & Tabassum, 2024). After each local training session, only the model updates, not the raw data are sent back to the central server. These updates are then aggregated to improve the model, creating a system that benefits from decentralized data without requiring direct access to the raw data itself.

Federated learning has significant implications for privacy, as it enables organizations to build robust AI models without collecting large amounts of centralized data. This technique is particularly beneficial in industries like finance, where personal information is highly sensitive (Hu, Gong, Zhang, Seng, Xia & Jiang, 2024). For example, financial institutions can use federated learning to build fraud detection models by training on transaction data stored locally at different branches or on users' devices. This decentralized approach not only protects individual privacy but also mitigates the risks associated with large-scale data breaches, as the data remains distributed across multiple sources (Mohammadi, Balador, Sinaei & Flammini, 2024). However, federated learning poses challenges related to communication efficiency and the need for reliable aggregation mechanisms, especially when dealing with large-scale or heterogeneous datasets. Despite these challenges, federated learning is a promising approach to advancing AI while respecting user privacy.

Synthetic data is another innovative solution for balancing privacy and innovation in AI development. Without actually having any personal information, synthetic data is data that has been intentionally created to replicate the characteristics and statistical trends of real-world data. This approach allows AI models to be trained on realistic datasets while reducing privacy risks, as synthetic data eliminates the need for sensitive or identifiable information. One of the primary benefits of synthetic data is its potential to expand the scope of AI training while ensuring privacy. Organizations, by using synthetic data, can simulate diverse scenarios, increase the size and variety of their training datasets, and mitigate biases that may be present in real-world data (Pezoulas, Zaridis, Mylona, Androutsos, Apostolidis, Tachos & Fotiadis, 2024). In industries such as healthcare, synthetic data can be generated to model patient information, enabling researchers to develop algorithms that identify trends, predict diagnoses, and recommend treatments without accessing actual patient records. This approach not only enhances privacy but also enables researchers to overcome data access restrictions, accelerating AI innovation in fields where data availability is often limited due to confidentiality concerns (Gonzales, Guruswamy & Smith, 2023). Another significant benefit of synthetic data is that it allows organizations to test AI algorithms under varied conditions. Developers can test their models for accuracy and reliability in diverse environments, by generating synthetic data that represents different demographics, scenarios, or conditions, leading to more robust and inclusive AI systems. Synthetic data is used, for instance, in the autonomous driving sector to model infrequent but crucial occurrences that may be underrepresented in real-world statistics, including pedestrian crossings or unfavorable weather.

Although synthetic data has many benefits, it also has drawbacks. For example, creating high-quality synthetic data requires sophisticated methods like generative adversarial networks (GANs) and variational autoencoders (VAEs), which can be computationally demanding and difficult to implement (Goyal & Mahmoud, 2024). Additionally, the accuracy of AI models trained on synthetic data is dependent on how well the synthetic data mimics real-world patterns; if synthetic data misses significant aspects of real data, models trained on it may perform poorly in real-world situations. Another concern is the potential for data leakage, where synthetic data inadvertently reflects characteristics of the real dataset it was derived from, raising privacy concerns despite the synthetic nature of the data (Hao, Han, Jiang, Li & Wu, 2024). However, as AI develops, methods for creating synthetic data will probably become more complex, allowing the creation of privacy-conscious AI systems in a variety of industries. Synthetic data has enormous potential for AI training, particularly when paired with privacy-preserving technologies like federated learning and differential privacy.

Transparency is a cornerstone of responsible AI development, as it fosters public trust, enhances user understanding, and facilitates informed decision-making. In order to help users and stakeholders comprehend how AI models work and make decisions, transparent AI systems are made to offer concise justifications for their procedures, choices, and data utilization. Transparency is crucial for fostering confidence and guaranteeing ethical AI deployment in a time when AI affects important facets of daily life, such as financial transactions and medical diagnosis (Balasubramaniam, Kauppinen, Hiekkanen, Kujala, 2022). Informed consent and explainability are two essential elements of transparency. The ability of AI systems to give human-understandable justifications for their choices and results is known as explainability. By assisting users in comprehending the elements that influence an AI system's decision-making, explainable AI (XAI) techniques enable users to evaluate the precision, equity, and dependability of outcomes produced by AI. This is especially crucial in high-stakes fields where AI choices can have major repercussions, such as healthcare, banking, and criminal justice (Ali, 2023). An explainable AI system, for example, can assist medical professionals in understanding the rationale behind a specific diagnosis or recommended course of treatment, allowing them to make better judgments and enhance patient outcomes. In order to detect and lessen biases in AI systems, explainability is also essential. To make sure AI systems treat all users equally, developers can examine the variables affecting model outputs, identify biases, and implement remedial measures. To improve AI explainability, techniques like feature attribution, which identifies the elements that most influenced a model's decision and model-agnostic approaches like SHAP (Shapley Additive Explanations) and LIME (Local Interpretable Model-agnostic Explanations) are frequently employed (Yang et al., 2023).

Another crucial component of transparency is informed consent, which guarantees that consumers understand and consent to the ways in which their data is gathered, processed, and used. More than simply getting a user's approval, informed consent necessitates transparent communication that enables users to comprehend the potential hazards, the goal of data gathering, and the ramifications of sharing data. By providing users with opportunities to opt in or out of data collection, making sure they understand how their data contributes to AI functionality, and explicitly defining data usage regulations, AI systems can obtain informed consent (Andreotta, Kirkham & Rizzi, 2022). To help consumers make educated decisions about their data-sharing options, social media sites and mobile applications, for instance, can put in place clear consent procedures that explain how AI systems utilize data to target ads or personalize content. Giving consumers control over their data is another aspect of developing transparent AI systems. These could include tools that let consumers choose the kinds of data that are gathered, adjust their privacy settings, and find out how their data affects AI decision-making (Cheong, 2024). By showcasing their dedication to ethical and responsible AI practices, organizations can not only meet regulatory obligations but also gain the trust of users. A complex strategy that includes the use of synthetic data, privacy-preserving technology, and transparent AI systems is needed to balance innovation and privacy in AI research. Differential privacy and federated learning are two examples of privacy-preserving strategies that enable businesses to leverage data without jeopardizing individual privacy, making them vital resources for industries handling sensitive data (Saha, Hota, Chattopadhyay, Nag & Nandi, 2024). Synthetic data further enhances privacy protection by enabling the training of AI models on artificial datasets, although this approach requires careful management to ensure data quality and relevance. Transparent AI systems build trust through explainability and informed consent, empowering users to make informed decisions and fostering accountability.

FUTURE DIRECTIONS IN AI REGULATION

Effective regulation is becoming more and more necessary as artificial intelligence (AI) grows more widespread. Despite being fundamental, current legal frameworks are changing to handle the intricate security, privacy, and ethical issues that come with AI technologies. Future AI regulations must be flexible and dynamic in order to keep up with the rapid pace of technical development and the wide range of industries that use AI. Global comparisons of regulatory systems, public trust strategies to improve openness and engagement, and changing regulatory landscapes that address new privacy challenges are important areas for future growth. A future

AI regulatory framework that fosters innovation and protects the public interest will be shaped by these factors taken together.

Large volumes of data are used by AI technology, which presents significant ethical and privacy issues with relation to data acquisition, use, and sharing. AI will probably cause major changes to privacy laws as it develops further, moving toward stricter regulations and more aggressive enforcement tactics. One of the anticipated changes in privacy regulation is an increased focus on data minimization principles, which mandate that organizations collect only the data necessary to achieve a specific purpose. Data minimization is critical in reducing the exposure of personal information, as it limits the amount of data available for potential misuse, breaches, or unauthorized access (Sartor, 2020). Another emerging trend is the emphasis on "purpose limitation" in data usage. This principle requires that data collected for one purpose should not be used for another without additional consent. AI systems, which often re-purpose data to improve predictive accuracy or user profiling, will face tighter restrictions on data repurposing, forcing developers to be more transparent about how data will be used throughout the system's lifecycle (Faisal, 2023). Regulatory bodies may introduce requirements for organizations to document data flow within AI systems, making it easier to audit compliance with purpose limitations and assess potential risks to privacy.

Moreover, the concept of "data ownership" is becoming increasingly relevant as AI systems expand into domains like healthcare, finance, and education. Emerging privacy laws may give individuals more control over their data, allowing them to access, correct, or delete their information from AI systems. Countries worldwide are exploring ways to strengthen data ownership rights, following the model set by regulations such as the General Data Protection Regulation (GDPR) in Europe. Future regulations may also include provisions that give users the "right to be forgotten," allowing them to request that their data be deleted from an AI system, particularly in cases where their data no longer serves a valid purpose (Zaeem & Barber, 2020). This would represent a significant shift from traditional data privacy practices, requiring organizations to build AI systems that can accommodate such requests without affecting system integrity. Additionally, regulators are likely to introduce more detailed transparency requirements, obligating companies to disclose not only how data is used but also how AI algorithms make decisions. As AI applications in sensitive areas like criminal justice, healthcare, and finance grow, there is a push for AI systems to be "explainable," meaning that organizations must be able to articulate the basis of AI-driven decisions. These transparency requirements could help individuals understand how AI models impact their lives and offer recourse in cases of errors or biases (Sartor, 2020). Future laws may also require organizations to conduct impact assessments, evaluating the social and ethical implications of their AI systems before deployment.

The European Union (EU) has been a leader in data privacy regulation, setting high standards through its GDPR and its recent proposal for the Artificial Intelligence Act (AIA), a comprehensive framework focused on AI oversight (Panait, Ljubenkov & Alic, 2021). In contrast, the United States has adopted a more sector-specific and innovation-friendly approach, with federal agencies like the Federal Trade Commission (FTC) issuing AI guidance but not adopting a single, overarching AI regulation (The World Bak, 2024). The European Union's Artificial Intelligence Act is a risk-based framework that classifies AI applications according to their potential to harm people or society. High-risk applications, like those used in biometric identification, medical devices, and law enforcement, would be subject to strict requirements, such as transparency obligations, strict data quality standards, and regular audits. The EU's model sets a precedent for protecting against AI misuse while promoting ethical standards, though some argue that its strict regulations could stifle innovation. The EU also emphasizes "algorithmic accountability," which requires organizations to disclose the reasoning behind their AI algorithms and guarantee that AI systems function impartially and fairly. This principle is in line with the EU's larger commitment to individual rights, forcing developers to adopt fairness, transparency, and accountability in AI design. The EU's regulatory approach highlights its desire to position itself as a global leader in ethical AI, prioritizing public welfare over rapid technological advancement (European Parliament, 2024). The GDPR has already influenced privacy laws globally, and the AIA may similarly set a new standard for AI governance that other countries look to emulate or adapt.

The United States (US) has taken a more market-driven approach to AI regulation, focusing on innovation and economic competitiveness. In the US, there is no single federal AI law, but sector-specific regulations cover specific applications in finance, healthcare, and transportation. For example, the Health Insurance Portability and Accountability Act (HIPAA) regulates data privacy in healthcare, while the Fair Credit Reporting Act (FCRA) governs data use in credit reporting and finance. The US approach allows for flexibility, giving organizations leeway to innovate, though it has been criticized for insufficient oversight of AI systems' ethical and social implications (McNicholas & Faircloth, 2024). Recognizing the need for stronger AI governance, the US has recently taken steps to develop AI principles through the National Institute of Standards and Technology (NIST). The NIST framework outlines a voluntary approach to AI risk management, recommending principles such as transparency, fairness, and robustness (NIST, 2023). This approach allows companies to self-regulate and adopt best practices, fostering innovation while promoting ethical guidelines. However, without a mandatory AI law, critics argue that self-regulation may not be sufficient to address issues like algorithmic bias, discrimination, and privacy infringement.

Other Regions, such as China, Japan, and Canada, are also developing their own AI regulatory frameworks, each reflecting unique priorities. China's approach emphasizes government control and national security, mandating that companies disclose their AI algorithms and submitting them to government oversight (Roberts, Cowls, Morley, Taddeo, Wang & Floridi, 2021). Japan, on the other hand, focuses on AI ethics and responsible innovation, adopting guidelines that encourage businesses to uphold transparency and fairness while respecting privacy rights (Wright, 2023). Canada has introduced the Artificial Intelligence and Data Act (AIDA), proposing a risk-based framework similar to the EU's, aiming to regulate AI applications that could pose a significant risk to individuals and society (Chatterjee, 2023). The differences in global AI regulation approaches highlight the challenges of creating a unified regulatory framework. As AI systems are often developed and deployed across borders, international collaboration and harmonization will become increasingly important. A standardized global framework could foster consistency in AI governance and reduce compliance burdens for companies operating in multiple regions, although achieving consensus may be challenging given the varying priorities and cultural differences between regions.

The effective adoption and integration of AI technologies depends on public confidence. A growing number of people are worried about privacy, bias, and transparency as AI systems become more prevalent in daily life. Organizations and regulators must actively interact with the public to build trust by encouraging openness, responsibility, and inclusive involvement in AI decision-making. Strategies for enhancing public trust include implementing transparent AI practices, ensuring ethical oversight, and creating channels for public feedback. Transparency in AI practices involves clear communication about how AI systems function, the type of data they use, and the purposes for which they are deployed. Providing accessible information about AI processes allows individuals to understand how decisions are made, especially in areas with significant personal impact, like healthcare, finance, and criminal justice (Balasubramaniam, Kauppinen, Rannisto, Hiekkanen, & Kujala, 2023). Companies can demystify AI systems, empowering users to make informed decisions and increasing their confidence in AI applications by offering explanations in layman's terms. Transparency also includes implementing explainable AI (XAI) methods, which enable AI systems to provide interpretable insights, thereby helping to address concerns related to opaque or "black box" algorithms.

Ethical oversight is another essential component for building public trust. Organizations can guarantee that AI systems comply with moral standards and the interests of the public by establishing ethical review boards or committees. Diverse stakeholders, including ethicists, legal professionals, technological experts, and public representatives, are frequently included on these boards. The development of AI systems can be supervised by ethical review boards, which can help guarantee that the systems reduce hazards to people and are in line with social values. For example, many companies have adopted AI ethics boards to oversee facial recognition technologies, balancing the benefits of these technologies with their potential impact on privacy and individual rights. Public engagement is also vital for building trust (de Laat, 2021). Regulators and organizations can invite public participation in AI policy-making and development processes by conducting surveys, holding public consultations, and creating forums where individuals can voice their concerns. Engaging the public in discussions about AI applications and regulations can increase public awareness and generate valuable insights on societal expectations. For instance, the EU's consultations on AI ethics involved extensive public input, reflecting a commitment to inclusivity in policy-making (Díaz-Rodríguez, Del Ser, Coeckelbergh, López de Prado, Herrera-Viedma & Herrera, 2023). Governments and companies can make AI systems more responsive to societal needs, by creating platforms for public feedback, which enhances trust and fosters greater acceptance.

Incorporating education and awareness initiatives is another way to build public confidence in AI. As AI technologies become more complex, there is a growing need to educate the public on AI's benefits, limitations, and potential risks. Educational initiatives can be implemented through online courses, public webinars, and partnerships with educational institutions, helping individuals better understand how AI impacts their lives. Organizations can address misconceptions, reduce fear, and empower individuals to engage constructively with AI by increasing AI literacy (Almusaed, Almssad, Yitmen & Homod, 2023). Future directions in AI regulation will require a balanced, dynamic approach that protects individual rights while fostering technological innovation. Evolving regulatory landscapes will need to adapt to new privacy challenges, placing a greater emphasis on transparency, data minimization, and ethical accountability. As global regulatory approaches diverge, international cooperation and harmonization will be crucial for creating a consistent and effective AI governance framework that supports cross-border operations. Public trust is a cornerstone of successful AI adoption, and organizations must implement transparent practices, ethical oversight, and inclusive engagement strategies to build confidence in AI technologies. As regulatory frameworks evolve, they must consider public input, prioritize education, and emphasize the ethical use of AI to ensure a future where AI serves the public good. Society can create an AI regulatory landscape that promotes innovation while protecting privacy, ensuring that AI remains a trustworthy and beneficial force for all.

CONCLUSION

Balancing innovation with privacy concerns in AI development is a challenging yet essential goal as we move toward a more data-driven society. This chapter has explored the promise of AI in enhancing efficiency, personalization, and predictive power across sectors while highlighting the substantial privacy risks that accompany these advancements. Key privacy issues, such as data collection practices, data security vulnerabilities, and algorithmic bias, underscore the urgent need for robust regulatory frameworks and ethical guidelines that uphold transparency, accountability, and fairness. Emerging strategies, like privacy-preserving technologies, synthetic data, and transparent AI systems, offer pathways for achieving this balance, allowing innovation to thrive without compromising individual rights. The active participation of a wide range of stakeholders, including legislators, business executives, developers, and the general public, is essential to the future of AI legislation. A coordinated approach can guarantee that AI systems meet privacy requirements internationally and are in line with societal values when legislative landscapes change on a global scale. Building public trust will require ethical oversight, accessible AI education, and channels for public feedback, making AI development more inclusive and responsive to societal needs. This chapter calls on all stakeholders to adopt and promote ethical practices in AI development, prioritizing human-centric values while leveraging AI's transformative potential. Stakeholders can foster a future where AI serves both innovation and the public good by championing transparency, protecting individual rights, and engaging in interdisciplinary collaboration.

REFERENCES

Al-kfairy, M., Mustafa, D., Kshetri, N., Insiew, M., & Alfandi, O. (2024). Ethical Challenges and Solutions of Generative AI: An Interdisciplinary Perspective. *Informatics (MDPI)*, 11(3), 58. DOI: 10.3390/informatics11030058

Ali, S., Abuhmed, T., El-Sappagh, S., Muhammad, K., Alonso-Moral, J. M., Confalonieri, R., Guidotti, R., Del Ser, J., Díaz-Rodríguez, N., & Herrera, F. (2023). Explainable Artificial Intelligence (XAI): What we know and what is left to attain Trustworthy Artificial Intelligence. *Information Fusion*, 99, 101805. DOI: 10.1016/j.inffus.2023.101805

Almusaed, A., Almssad, A., Yitmen, I., & Homod, R. Z. (2023). Enhancing Student Engagement: Harnessing "AIED"'s Power in Hybrid Education—A Review Analysis. *Education Sciences*, 13(7), 632. DOI: 10.3390/educsci13070632

Aloraini, F., Javed, A., Rana, O., & Burnap, P. (2022). Adversarial machine learning in IoT from an insider point of view. *Journal of Information Security and Applications*, 70, 103341. DOI: 10.1016/j.jisa.2022.103341

Andreotta, A. J., Kirkham, N., & Rizzi, M. (2022). AI, big data, and the future of consent. *AI & Society*, 37(4), 1715–1728. DOI: 10.1007/s00146-021-01262-5 PMID: 34483498

Badmus, O., Rajput, S. A., Arogundade, J. B., & Williams, M. (2024). AI-driven business analytics and decision making. *World Journal of Advanced Research and Reviews*, 24(1), 616–633. DOI: 10.30574/wjarr.2024.24.1.3093

Baik, J. S. (2020). Data privacy against innovation or against discrimination?: The case of the California Consumer Privacy Act (CCPA). *Telematics and Informatics*, 52, 101431. DOI: 10.1016/j.tele.2020.101431

Bajwa, J., Munir, U., Nori, A., & Williams, B. (2021). Artificial intelligence in healthcare: Transforming the practice of medicine. *Future Healthcare Journal*, 8(2), e188–e194. DOI: 10.7861/fhj.2021-0095 PMID: 34286183

Balasubramaniam, N., Kauppinen, M., Hiekkanen, K., & Kujala, S. (2022). Transparency and Explainability of AI Systems: Ethical Guidelines in Practice. In Gervasi, V., & Vogelsang, A. (Eds.), Lecture Notes in Computer Science: Vol. 13216. *Requirements Engineering: Foundation for Software Quality. REFSQ 2022*. Springer. DOI: 10.1007/978-3-030-98464-9_1

Balasubramaniam, N., Kauppinen, M., Rannisto, A., Hiekkanen, K., & Kujala, S. (2023). Transparency and explainability of AI systems: From ethical guidelines to requirements. *Information and Software Technology*, 159, 107197. DOI: 10.1016/j.infsof.2023.107197

BBC. (2021, October 1). *DeepMind faces legal action over NHS data use.* https://www.bbc.com/news/technology-58761324

Belenguer, L. (2022). AI bias: Exploring discriminatory algorithmic decision-making models and the application of possible machine-centric solutions adapted from the pharmaceutical industry. *AI and Ethics*, 2(4), 771–787. DOI: 10.1007/s43681-022-00138-8 PMID: 35194591

Bhuiyan, M. S. (2024). The Role of AI-Enhanced Personalization in Customer Experiences. *Journal of Computer Science and Technology Studies*, 6(1), 162–169. DOI: 10.32996/jcsts.2024.6.1.17

Broekhuizen, T., Dekker, H., de Faria, P., Firk, S., Nguyen, D. K., & Sofka, W. (2023). AI for managing open innovation: Opportunities, challenges, and a research agenda. *Journal of Business Research*, 167, 114196. DOI: 10.1016/j.jbusres.2023.114196

Busuioc, M. (2021). Accountable Artificial Intelligence: Holding Algorithms to Account. *Public Administration Review*, 81(5), 825–836. DOI: 10.1111/puar.13293 PMID: 34690372

Cancela-Outeda, C. (2024). The EU's AI act: A framework for collaborative governance. *Internet of Things : Engineering Cyber Physical Human Systems*, 27, 101291. DOI: 10.1016/j.iot.2024.101291

Chatterjee, S. (2023, June 7). *Requirements for 'High-Risk' AI Applications: Comparing AI Regulations in the EU, US, and Canada.* https://www.holisticai.com/blog/requirements-for-high-risk-ai-applications-overview-of-regulations

Chen, Z. (2023). Ethics and discrimination in artificial intelligence-enabled recruitment practices. *Humanities & Social Sciences Communications*, 10(1), 567. DOI: 10.1057/s41599-023-02079-x

Cheong, B. C. (2024). Transparency and accountability in AI systems: Safeguarding wellbeing in the age of algorithmic decision-making. *Frontiers in Human Dynamics*, 6, 1421273. DOI: 10.3389/fhumd.2024.1421273

Creemers, R. (2022). China's emerging data protection framework. *Journal of Cybersecurity*, 8(1), tyac011. Advance online publication. DOI: 10.1093/cybsec/tyac011 de Laat, P. (2021). Companies Committed to Responsible AI: From Principles towards Implementation and Regulation? *Philosophy & Technology*, 34(4), 1135–1193. DOI: 10.1007/s13347-021-00474-3 PMID: 34631392

Díaz-Rodríguez, N., Del Ser, J., Coeckelbergh, M., López de Prado, M., Herrera-Viedma, E., & Herrera, F. (2023). Connecting the dots in trustworthy Artificial Intelligence: From AI principles, ethics, and key requirements to responsible AI systems and regulation. *Information Fusion*, 99, 101896. DOI: 10.1016/j.inffus.2023.101896

Elahi, M., Afolaranmi, S. O., Martinez Lastra, J. L., & Perez-Garcia, J. A. (2023). A comprehensive literature review of the applications of AI techniques through the lifecycle of industrial equipment. *Discover Artificial Intelligence*, 3(1), 43. DOI: 10.1007/s44163-023-00089-x

European Parliament. (2024, June 8). EU AI Act: first regulation on artificial intelligence. https://www.europarl.europa.eu/topics/en/article/20230601STO93804/eu-ai-act-first-regulation-on-artificial-intelligence

Faisal, K. (2023). Applying the Purpose Limitation Principle in Smart-City Data-Processing Practices: A European Data Protection Law Perspective. *Communication Law and Policy*, 28(1), 67–97. DOI: 10.1080/10811680.2023.2180266

Farayola, O. A., Olurunfemi, O. L., & Shoetan, P. O. (2024). Data privacy and security in it: A review of techniques and challenges. *Computer Science & IT Research Journal*, 5(3), 606-615. https://www.fepbl.com/index.php/csitrj/article/view/909/1192

Farhud, D. D., & Zokaei, S. (2021). Ethical Issues of Artificial Intelligence in Medicine and Healthcare. *Iranian Journal of Public Health*, 50(11), i–v. DOI: 10.18502/ijph.v50i11.7600 PMID: 35223619

Feretzakis, G., Papaspyridis, K., Gkoulalas-Divanis, A., & Verykios, V. S. (2024). Privacy-Preserving Techniques in Generative AI and Large Language Models: A Narrative Review. *Information (Basel)*, 15(11), 697. DOI: 10.3390/info15110697

Ferrara, E. (2024). Fairness and Bias in Artificial Intelligence: A Brief Survey of Sources, Impacts, and Mitigation Strategies. *Sci*, 6(1), 3. DOI: 10.3390/sci6010003

Galeon, D. (2017, August 3). *An AI Completed 360,000 Hours of Finance Work in Just Seconds Pack it up, folks. The machines will take it from here*. Futurism. https://futurism.com/an-ai-completed-360000-hours-of-finance-work-in-just-seconds

Garikapati, D., & Shetiya, S. S. (2024). Autonomous Vehicles: Evolution of Artificial Intelligence and the Current Industry Landscape. *Big Data and Cognitive Computing*, 8(4), 42. DOI: 10.3390/bdcc8040042

Giannaros, A., Karras, A., Theodorakopoulos, L., Karras, C., Kranias, P., Schizas, N., Kalogeratos, G., & Tsolis, D. (2023). Autonomous Vehicles: Sophisticated Attacks, Safety Issues, Challenges, Open Topics, Blockchain, and Future Directions. *Journal of Cybersecurity and Privacy*, 3(3), 493–543. DOI: 10.3390/jcp3030025

Gonzales, A., Guruswamy, G., & Smith, S. R. (2023). Synthetic data in health care: A narrative review. *PLOS Digital Health*, 2(1), e0000082. DOI: 10.1371/journal.pdig.0000082 PMID: 36812604

Goyal, M., & Mahmoud, Q. H. (2024). A Systematic Review of Synthetic Data Generation Techniques Using Generative AI. *Electronics (Basel)*, 13(17), 3509. DOI: 10.3390/electronics13173509

Hao, S., Han, W., Jiang, T., Li, Y., & Wu, H. (2024). Synthetic Data in AI: Challenges, Applications, and Ethical Implications. https://arxiv.org/pdf/2401.01629v1

Hardesty, L. (2019, November 22). *The history of Amazon's recommendation algorithm: Collaborative filtering and beyond*. https://www.amazon.science/the-history-of-amazons-recommendation-algorithm

Harwell, D. (2019, April 30). *Oregon became a testing ground for Amazon's facial-recognition policing. But what if Rekognition gets it wrong?*https://www.washingtonpost.com/technology/2019/04/30/amazons-facial-recognition-technology-is-supercharging-local-police/

Hu, K., Gong, S., Zhang, Q., Seng, C., Xia, M., & Jiang, S. (2024). An overview of implementing security and privacy in federated learning. *Artificial Intelligence Review*, 57(8), 204. DOI: 10.1007/s10462-024-10846-8

Hummel, P., Braun, M., & Dabrock, P. (2021). Own Data? Ethical Reflections on Data Ownership. *Philosophy & Technology*, 34(3), 545–572. DOI: 10.1007/s13347-020-00404-9

Hung, T. W., & Yen, C. P. (2023). Predictive policing and algorithmic fairness. *Synthese*, 201(6), 206. DOI: 10.1007/s11229-023-04189-0

Joel, O. S., Oyewole, A. T., Odunaya, O. G., & Soyombo, O. T. (2024). Leveraging Artificial Intelligence for enhanced supply chain optimization: A comprehensive review of current practices and future potentials. *International Journal of Management & Entrepreneurship Research*, 6(3), 707–721. DOI: 10.51594/ijmer.v6i3.882

Johnson, K. B., Wei, W. Q., Weeraratne, D., Frisse, M. E., Misulis, K., Rhee, K., Zhao, J., & Snowdon, J. L. (2021). Precision Medicine, AI, and the Future of Personalized Health Care. *Clinical and Translational Science*, 14(1), 86–93. DOI: 10.1111/cts.12884 PMID: 32961010

Kaur, R., Gabrijelčič, D., & Klobučar, T. (2023). Artificial intelligence for cybersecurity: Literature review and future research directions. *Information Fusion*, 97, 101804. DOI: 10.1016/j.inffus.2023.101804

Khalifa, M., & Albadawy, M. (2024). Artificial Intelligence for Clinical Prediction: Exploring Key Domains and Essential Functions. *Computer Methods and Programs in Biomedicine Update*, 5, 100148. DOI: 10.1016/j.cmpbup.2024.100148

Kumar, V., Sharma, K. V., Kedam, N., Patel, A., Kate, T. R., & Rathnayake, U. (2024). A comprehensive review on smart and sustainable agriculture using IoT technologies. *Smart Agricultural Technology*, 8, 100487. DOI: 10.1016/j.atech.2024.100487

Luo, Z. (2024). The Application and Development of Image Recognition Technology in the Field of Computer Vision. *Highlights in Science. Engineering and Technology*, 85, 909–914. DOI: 10.54097/g63vgv77

Machado, H., Silva, S., & Neiva, L. (2023). Publics' views on ethical challenges of Artificial Intelligence: A scoping review. *AI and Ethics*. Advance online publication. DOI: 10.1007/s43681-023-00387-1

Markus, A. F., Kors, J. A., & Rijnbeek, P. R. (2021). The role of explainability in creating trustworthy artificial intelligence for health care: A comprehensive survey of the terminology, design choices, and evaluation strategies. *Journal of Biomedical Informatics*, 113, 103655. DOI: 10.1016/j.jbi.2020.103655 PMID: 33309898

Marmaglio, P., Consolati, D., Amici, C., & Tiboni, M. (2023). Autonomous Vehicles for Healthcare Applications: A Review on Mobile Robotic Systems and Drones in Hospital and Clinical Environments. *Electronics (Basel)*, 12(23), 4791. DOI: 10.3390/electronics12234791

McNicholas, E. R., & Faircloth, F. E. (2024, November 6). Cybersecurity Laws and Regulations USA 2025. https://iclg.com/practice-areas/cybersecurity-laws-and-regulations/usa

Mearian, L. (2019, February 14). *J.P. Morgan to launch a U.S. dollar-backed cryptocurrency*. https://web.archive.org/web/20190223020410/https://www.computerworld.com/article/3340373/blockchain/jp-morgan-to-launch-a-us-dollar-backed-cryptocurrency.html

Mohammadi, S., Balador, A., Sinaei, S., & Flammini, F. (2024). Balancing privacy and performance in federated learning: A systematic literature review on methods and metrics. *Journal of Parallel and Distributed Computing*, 192, 104918. DOI: 10.1016/j.jpdc.2024.104918

Mühlhoff, R. (2023). Predictive privacy: Collective data protection in the context of artificial intelligence and big data. *Big Data & Society*, 10(1). Advance online publication. DOI: 10.1177/20539517231166886

Mulder, T., & Vellinga, N. E. (2021). Exploring data protection challenges of automated driving. *Computer Law & Security Report*, 40, 105530. DOI: 10.1016/j.clsr.2021.105530

NIST. (2023). *Artificial Intelligence Risk Management. Framework (AI RMF 1.0)*. USA: Department of Commerce. https://nvlpubs.nist.gov/nistpubs/ai/nist.ai.100-1.pdf

Olaiya, O. P., Adesoga, T. O., Adebayo, A. A., Sotomi, M., Adigun, O. A., & Ezeliora, P. M. (2024). Encryption techniques for financial data security in fintech applications. *International Journal of Science and Research Archive*, 12(1), 2942–2949. DOI: 10.30574/ijsra.2024.12.1.1210

Osasona, F., Amoo, O. O., Atadoga, A., Abrahams, T. O., Farayola, O. A., & Ayinla, B. S. (2024). Reviewing the ethical implications of AI in decision making processes. *International Journal of Management & Entrepreneurship Research*, 6(2), 322–335. DOI: 10.51594/ijmer.v6i2.773

Panait, C., Ljubenkov, D., & Alic, D. (2021). Striking the balance between innovation and regulation in AI - is Europe leading the way or lagging behind? *Europuls Policy Journal*, 1(1), 27-45. https://www.researchgate.net/publication/357992486_Striking_the_balance_between_innovation_and_regulation_in_AI_-_is_Europe_leading_the_way_or_lagging_behind

Pandita, R. (2024, July 14). *How Netflix & Amazon Use AI to do Better Customer Segmentation*. California: Global Headquarters. https://www.teqfocus.com/blog/how-netflix-amazon-use-ai-to-do-better-customer-segmentation/

Pattnaik, D., Ray, S., & Raman, R. (2024). Applications of artificial intelligence and machine learning in the financial services industry: A bibliometric review. *Heliyon*, 10(1), e23492. DOI: 10.1016/j.heliyon.2023.e23492 PMID: 38187262

Pezoulas, V. C., Zaridis, D. I., Mylona, E., Androutsos, C., Apostolidis, K., Tachos, N. S., & Fotiadis, D. I. (2024). Synthetic data generation methods in healthcare: A review on open-source tools and methods. *Computational and Structural Biotechnology Journal*, 23, 2892–2910. DOI: 10.1016/j.csbj.2024.07.005 PMID: 39108677

Pinto-Coelho, L. (2023). How Artificial Intelligence Is Shaping Medical Imaging Technology: A Survey of Innovations and Applications. *Bioengineering (Basel, Switzerland)*, 10(12), 1435. DOI: 10.3390/bioengineering10121435 PMID: 38136026

Raji, M.A., Olodo, H.B., Oke, T.T., Addy, W.A., Ofodile, O.C. & Oyewole, A.T. (2024). E-commerce and consumer behavior: A review of AI-powered personalization and market trends. *GSC Advanced Research and Reviews*, 18(3), 66–77. DOI: 10.30574/gscarr.2024.18.3.0090

Rehman, I. (2019). Facebook-Cambridge Analytica data harvesting: What you need to know. *Library Philosophy and Practice (e-journal)*. 2497. https://digitalcommons.unl.edu/libphilprac/2497

Roberts, H., Cowls, J., Morley, J., Taddeo, M., Wang, V., & Floridi, L. (2021). The Chinese approach to Artificial Intelligence: An analysis of policy, ethics, and regulation. *AI & Society*, 36(1), 59–77. DOI: 10.1007/s00146-020-00992-2

Rupp, V., & Grafenstein, M. (2024). Clarifying "personal data" and the role of anonymisation in data protection law: Including and excluding data from the scope of the GDPR (more clearly) through refining the concept of data protection. *Computer Law & Security Report*, 52, 105932. DOI: 10.1016/j.clsr.2023.105932

Saha, S., Hota, A., Chattopadhyay, A. K., Nag, A., & Nandi, S. (2024). A multi-faceted survey on privacy preservation of federated learning: Progress, challenges, and opportunities. *Artificial Intelligence Review*, 57(7), 184. DOI: 10.1007/s10462-024-10766-7

Sanchez, T. W., Brenman, M., & Ye, X. (2024). The Ethical Concerns of Artificial Intelligence in Urban Planning. *Journal of the American Planning Association*, 1–14. DOI: 10.1080/01944363.2024.2355305

Sartor, G. (2020). *The impact of the General Data Protection Regulation (GDPR) on Artificial Intelligence*. European Parliament. https://www.europarl.europa.eu/RegData/etudes/STUD/2020/641530/EPRS_STU(2020)641530_EN.pdf

Novelli, C., Casolari, F., Rotolo, Taddeo, M & Floridi, L. 2024. AI Risk Assessment:Scenario-Based, A. (2024, May). Proportional Methodology for the AI Act. *Digital Society : Ethics, Socio-Legal and Governance of Digital Technology*, 3(1), 13. DOI: 10.1007/s44206-024-00095-1

Siddiqui, R. (2024). *The impact of artificial intelligence on the financial sector*. Unpublished thesis submitted to the Brac Business School, Brac University. https://dspace.bracu.ac.bd/xmlui/bitstream/handle/10361/24160/21364083_MBA.pdf?sequence=1&isAllowed=y

Tang, J., Korolova, A., Bai, X., Wang, X., & Wang, X. (2017). Privacy Loss in Apple's Implementation of Differential Privacy on MacOS 10.12. *Cryptography and Security*. /arXiv.1709.02753DOI: 10.48550

The World Bank. (2024, May 8). Transformative technologies (AI) challenges and principles of regulation. https://digitalregulation.org/3004297-2/

Villegas-Ch, W., & García-Ortiz, J. (2023). Toward a Comprehensive Framework for Ensuring Security and Privacy in Artificial Intelligence. *Electronics (Basel)*, 12(18), 3786. DOI: 10.3390/electronics12183786

Wright, J. (2023). The Development of AI Ethics in Japan: Ethics-washing Society 5.0? *East Asian Science, Technology and Society*, 18(2), 117–134. DOI: 10.1080/18752160.2023.2275987

Wu, W., Huang, T., & Gong, K. (2020). Ethical Principles and Governance Technology Development of AI in China. *Engineering (Beijing)*, 6(3), 302–309. DOI: 10.1016/j.eng.2019.12.015

Yang, W., Wei, Y., Wei, H., Chen, Y., Huang, G., Li, X., Li, R., Yao, N., Wang, X., Gu, X., Amin, M. B., & Kang, B. (2023). Survey on Explainable AI: From Approaches, Limitations and Applications Aspects. *Hum-Centric Intelligence System*, 3(3), 161–188. DOI: 10.1007/s44230-023-00038-y

Yurdem, B., Kuzlu, M., Gullu, M. K., Catak, F. O., & Tabassum, M. (2024). Federated learning: Overview, strategies, applications, tools and future directions. *Heliyon*, 10(19), e38137. DOI: 10.1016/j.heliyon.2024.e38137 PMID: 39391509

Zaeem, R. N., & Barber, K. S. (2020). The Effect of the GDPR on Privacy Policies: Recent Progress and Future Promise. *ACM Transactions on Management Information Systems*, 12(1), 2. DOI: 10.1145/3389685

Chapter 14
Navigating the Future of Education in Critical Thinking and AI in Digital Citizenship

Jared M. Valenzuela
https://orcid.org/0009-0007-6509-0755
University of Nottingham, Ningbo, China

ABSTRACT

Despite the benefits of AI in teaching and learning, issues in assessing critical thinking have gradually emerged and shifted the discussions on whether AI should be integrated into the assessment due to problems related to it. This chapter addresses the ethical gap in assessing writing by offering an analysis of AI's role and proposing suggestions to fully integrate AI into assessment to prepare students as digital citizens. It also explores the implications of AI in critical thinking in writing assessments, focusing on issues such as plagiarism, AI-detection bypass, and accuracy of content. It examines how digital citizens in educational institutions prepare for more robust AI integration in writing assessments and curricula, exploring AI affordances and constraints that may be used to improve current educational policy in assessment. This chapter explores how digital citizens can maintain academic integrity through an ethical framework, contributing to a more informed approach to digital citizenship.

DOI: 10.4018/979-8-3693-9015-3.ch014

INTRODUCTION

Artificial intelligence (AI) 's impact has shaken educational institutions' foundations by storm, creating a temporary division in its role in education worldwide. However, its recent use has substantially influenced educational institutions among educators and students. In particular, AI has been leveraged to improve student learning, for instance, by providing human-machine conversations through chatbots that permit students to engage dialogically (Kim et al., 2021; Vasquez-Cano et al.,2021). Educators have used AI in teaching through automatic marking in assessment, which provides fast and accurate outcomes (Fu et al.,2020; Kumar & Boulanger,2020). For most university undergraduate students, the most accessible type of AI is Generative AI (GenAi), which is broadly defined as a technological tool that takes advantage of deep learning models that produce words and images that resemble those created by humans (Michel-Villarreal et al.,2023). Due to its advanced generative skills, many students and educators develop their learning and teaching to heights that have never happened before. One example study by Rafida *et al.* (2024) is that of twenty EFL students from Indonesia and Taiwan who were introduced an AI-assisted system in their academic writing. According to the report, 80% responded positively to utilizing AI in their writing, and the majority notes that they use AI to enhance their grammar skills, including formulating sentences and rephrasing words.

As artificial intelligence continues to revolutionize the landscape of academic writing, one question lingers in the air: can AI truly uphold the values of originality, creativity, and intellectual integrity? While AI promises unprecedented efficiency and convenience, it also introduces unsettling possibilities, challenging long-held conceptions of what academic work should be. The tension between innovation and tradition grows, and the answer may determine the future of education itself. Will this technological leap be embraced or will it compromise the principles that underpin academic excellence?

Despite the overwhelming potential for innovations and improvements, concerns about accuracy, plagiarism, misinformation, misrepresentation and reliability have gradually emerged in academic discussions. Chatterjee and Dethlefs (2023) urged GenAI developers and academic researchers to elevate their engagement with it to ensure integrity and uphold ethics against the malicious use of artificial intelligence. Due to this mounting uneasiness, some school districts in the US have banned GenAI entirely (Park,2023). Even UNESCO (2023) found the potential harm to human development and appealed for action to ensure AI is regulated in schools. These concerns are warranted because the bedrock of education is now, perhaps, questioned for its relevance; also, degrees are now challenged as essential educational outcomes are being reevaluated to determine whether they capture the training of critical thinking and problem-solving in education.

One noteworthy example of AI's misleading information comes from the investigation done by Dashti *et al.* (2023) where they aimed to examine the accuracy of the responses from ChatGPT. They asked ChatGPT to identify an article abstract using keywords. They found out that of 75 articles produced by ChatGPT, none of these were accessible and available. The DOI links recommended were entirely unconnected and non-existent. These results are misleading, and emphasise the need for human intervention to ensure the veracity of the outputs.

Furthermore, one construct amid the GenAI revolution that has received cautious skepticism among educators and researchers is critical thinking. The concern stems from whether the current end-of-term essay stands relevant to assessing critical thinking. Given the benefits of GenAI mentioned above, educators are wary as some students have apparently shown increasing dependence on and outsourcing their writing from GenAI (Stokel-Walker,2022), resulting in questioning whether graduates have developed the critical thinking skills to become effective globalized learners in the 21st century. Furthermore, the validity of assessing critical thinking in essays are questioned. Zhai (2022) urged educational policymakers to overhaul assessment practices and formats that conform to the corresponding changes in education. This move ensures that assessment accurately measures learners' critical thinking skills amidst AI assistance in essays.

This paper takes a closer look at the effects of GenAI on assessing critical thinking in higher education academic writing. After discussing the impact of GenAI on the assessment of critical thinking, including issues and potential effects, it will discuss some approaches to addressing AI challenges. Finally, this paper will conclude by presenting a suggestion and implications that might contribute to understanding the necessity of AI integration in the curriculum.

EVOLVING MINDS: THE JOURNEY OF CRITICAL THINKING FROM ANCIENT PHILOSOPHY TO DIGITAL AGE

This section delves into the evolution of the notion of critical thinking from the 1980s to the current scene. It endeavours to explain how critical thinking was perceived from different perspectives, and how it shifted depending on the current focus of each time in light of in search for scholarly and widely accepted definitions, demand from stakeholders (employers), developing graduates,and technological development in Artificial intelligence and challenges in higher education.

The notion of critical thinking (CT) has come to several alterations in many years as scholars have seemingly disagreed in defining the construct that would cover the depth and scope. In the 1980s, Mcpeck's defined critical thinking as involving *reflective skepticism* when engaging in an activity. Some scholars offered Bloom's taxonomy as a definition of critical thinking, particularly evaluation, synthesis, and analysis, as mentioned by Ennis (1981 cited in Ennis, 1993). Other scholars, such as Paul (1987), emphasize dialogical thinking in critical thinking. While all seem to have arguably explained their points, Ennis (1987), in particular, seems to disagree and has strived to argue that Mcpeck's definition is negative and explained the necessity to go beyond levels of skepticism. Also, his argument against Bloom's taxonomy was striking, and marked this definition as problematic as the levels in Bloom's taxonomy are not hierarchical but should be interrelated. Ennis's (1987) definition of critical thinking lies in the realm of reasonable reflection, which involves a list of abilities and dispositions. A definition he thought could capture the essence of critical thinking.

As the field progressed into the 1990s, new perspectives emerged. Facione (1998) explained critical thinking as purposeful and self-regulatory judgment. Even this definition seems to underscore an earlier interpretation of critical thinking by Paul (1991) that emphasizes disciplined and self-directed thinking. Looking back at these two decades of academic debates about critical thinking and despite the different perspectives these scholars emphasized, many of them agreed that CT can be defined as the ability to regulate their own thinking. Building on the developments of the 1990s, the 2000s saw different traction in the field of critical thinking coming from national governments and employers arguing the importance of assisting people in *thinking well and for themselves*, resulting in defining it as 'good thinking and thinking well' ((Pithers & Soden, 2000, p. 237). The same researchers added that this 'good thinking' implies a quest to interrogate knowledge through self-directed search. Also, emphasis on critical thinking in the workplace gained traction from employers who sought graduates who demonstrate critical, analytical, and reflective thought and can contribute to their organizations (Harvey et al., 1997, cited in Pithers and Soden, 2000). As a result, some agencies in the UK, New Zealand, and the USA strived to incorporate critical thinking as one of the 'key skills' in developing graduates with generic abilities. In particular, the European Higher Education Area (2012) emphasizes critical thinking as crucial in developing training programs for student-centered learning outcomes, as mentioned in the Bologna Process Implementation Report.

Despite this burgeoning call for critical thinking to be included in the curriculum, there is scant evidence that it is taught systematically at the undergraduate level (Coil et al., 2010). See (2016) found that undergraduate modules in the first year among UK universities failed to instruct students in argumentation, an aspect of critical thinking, resulting in educational policymakers being encouraged to re-evaluate how students are assessed. This emphasis on argumentation as a closely related construct of critical thinking evolved to a definition that was embraced and espoused by some researchers such as El Soufi and See (2019). They argue that students who can question their own practices and argue commonly accepted theories through critical thinking may become employees in a company who can make independent yet logical decisions, especially in complex situations (Shaw et al., 2019). Also, this emphasis on argumentation is closely related to Shaw et al.'s (2019) research, which adopted the HEIghten Critical Thinking in assessing university students, proved to be a sound assessment tool focusing on two subdimensions: Analytical and Synthetic. The former analyzes arguments and evaluates evidence, while the latter involves understanding implications and formulating their own arguments. These two subdimensions of critical thinking were designed to represent the core processing elements of cognition. These overlapping sub-concepts of critical thinking are now being adapted to assess college students' critical thinking to equip them with the essential skills required to succeed in the real world and ensure that universities instruct and embed critical thinking into their curricula.

However, as soon as artificial intelligence entered academia, these developments in critical thinking have pivoted in focus. Discussions on critical thinking temporarily shifted from the construct definition towards the extent to which critical thinking is applied in education in light of recent GenAI developments. Walczak and Wojciech Cellary (2023) raised the issue of possible erosion of critical thinking skills as concerns about students' overreliance on GenAI may lead to reduced effort in cultivating critical thinking. In contrast, another study conducted by Xie and Wang (2023) on the impact of AI on students' cognitive functions strongly rejects the hypothesis that AI technologies decrease the general cognitive abilities of college students. These two contending perspectives at the opposite ends of a continuum suggest the push and pull dynamics of AI's impact on critical thinking in higher education. This disparity of beliefs concerning AI also exists between teachers and students. Duah and McGivern (2024) reported students' enthusiastic engagement with GenAI while reporting that educators are more sceptical and quite pessimistic about Gen AI roles in higher education. All of these divergent opinions seemingly show that there remains much to explore regarding the role of AI in critical thinking in education.

Amid ongoing debates about the sustainability of artificial intelligence in education, questions persist regarding how human intelligence and AI technology interplay in improving learning outcomes. The role of AI in enhancing learning should not replace what is innate among humans – our own intelligence. Human intelligence should leverage the availability of this type of technology to amplify human's cognitive abilities to focus on the most pressing tasks over mundane activities that can now be executed flawlessly within the given timeframe such as providing students feedback, grading routine assessments and attendance tracking. With this in mind, efforts on magnifying human intelligence supplemented and complemented by AI technology should be considered as a top priority considering how artificial intelligence advancements are exceptionally progressing at a rapid pace. The future of artificial intelligence and education will depend greatly in the collective efforts of the current educators and innovators to equip the digital learners as well as digital citizens both of the current age and the near future.

In addition, Kenedy (2024) examined four challenges of critical thinking in higher education that can potentially assist teachers and researchers in understanding the underlying causes of lack of critical thinking in post-secondary education:

1. Students are not trained to think critically despite the large volumes of information they have to process. Post-secondary education appears to concentrate on quantity over quality.
2. Students are exposed to mass media (tweets, TikTok, blogs, YouTube shorts) that cultivate shallow thinking for entertainment and triviality rather than critical thinking and analytical thinking.
3. Academics' difference of opinion regarding the role of AI in education and critical thinking.
4. Students often stop developing critical thinking after university.

These challenges have compounded as Artificial intelligence entered academia raising the issue of how to foster critical thinking in the present generation.

ISSUES IN ASSESSING CRITICALITY IN THE AI AGE

This section examines how criticality is assessed in the context of AI. Over the years, critical thinking in the field of education is usually assessed through a written examination, or oral production exams such as reporting, dialogues, and group discussions. However, its relevance (particularly with written examinations) has received mixed reactions particularly with the advent of technological revolution in

AI, from many practitioners and scholars in academia. Thus, this section will strive to highlight the issues many academicians face in higher education.

Assessment in the age of artificial intelligence poses a challenge for educators due to two main factors: plagiarism detection bypass and generation of false and inaccurate content. Lo (2023) highlights these concerns, suggesting that institutions should reassess their policies on AI use to uphold academic integrity. This underscores the complexity of assessing critical thinking in students' essays, a skill that is becoming increasingly difficult to evaluate in the age of AI.

One major issue is the ability of GenAI to bypass plagiarism detection tools. According to Rudolph et al. (2023), GenAI can threaten academic essays as an assessment method due to plagiarism detection bypass. GenAI's ability to generate passable essay prose that could avoid triggering AI detection tools is a vital factor why some educators deem essays as an assessment obsolete. Lo (2023) also cautions that this GenAI ability undermines the purpose of assessment and contributes to inequitable student evaluation. The essence of honing criticality to prepare students for future fieldwork through assessment is potentially weakened and undervalued as some students with access to GenAi can generate essays almost effortlessly.

Tools like Turnitin, with advanced AI detection technology, which upholds academic integrity and transparency to foster creativity, originality, and critical thinking, are currently struggling to detect AI-generated content with complete accuracy, leading to false positives. Ventayen (2023) evaluated GenAI by asking it to generate essays based on published works and later checked this for Turnitin's originality. However, Turnitin found a low similarity report. A similar study was done by Khalil and Er (2023) on GenAI, which showed that 40 out of 50 essays written by Chatgpt revealed high originality. These reductions in high originality index scores may be due to using a specialized prompt on GenAI which Rudolph et al. (2023) found that some GenAI users provide a prompt that asks Chatgpt, a famous GenAI, to act as a plagiarism checker to modify the generated text to remain undetected under plagiarism checks to produce a low originality index score. These false positive detections raise issues concerning Turnitin's reliability in upholding academic integrity. This similar attack on academic honesty in higher education is a longstanding issue and recognized phenomenon. An evidence-based review study conducted by Kampa et al. (2024) on an exploration of reasons for committing academic dishonesty shows that one of the four most important perceived causes for academic cheating is the easy accessibility of electronic resources. This outcome underscores earlier research by Sprajc et al. (2017), which reveals that besides accessibility to materials, the ease of copying is also largely responsible for plagiarism in higher education. They could potentially be attributed to the considerable number of internet materials and access to GenAI. In light of the fact that GenAI and internet materials are now easily accessible via modern technologies, essay-based assessment of critical thinking encompassing reflective thinking, disciplined reasoning, evaluation of ideas, and argumentation is now under intense scrutiny. Likewise, given that others are casting doubts on Turnitin as a reliable safeguard against plagiarism and a tool for ensuring critical thinking, it raises concerns about the current assessment integrity measures and the urgent need for alternative methods to prevent erosion of critical thinking where students might rely on shortcuts rather than developing genuine critical thinking skills.

Another impediment to assessment posed by GenAI is content inaccuracy. Lim et al. (2023) infer that GenAI's restriction to non-current data may lead to knowledge deficiencies and false information. They further argued that if Google's massive information were leveraged to address these deficiencies, it would further escalate the problems, such as amplifying existing misinformation, because most data on Google lack thorough curation and verification. Consequently, making assessment challenging to evaluate students' original thought processes as GenAI's generated misinformation may obscure students' reasoning. This was evident in a study done by Terwiesch (2023), who captured how a GenAI surprisingly erred, which could potentially be substantial in considerable scale, in simple grade 6-level Math calculations in one of the final exam questions in the Wharton MBA Program – Operations Management class which is a foundation course about analyzing and improving people's work. This prompts Terwiesch (2023) to argue that students need to develop a foundational understanding of the basics and solid critical thinking to address more complex issues encountered in real-world scenarios.

Moreover, this concern resonates with findings from other researchers, as reflected in a study conducted by Sallam (2023), which revealed that from 60 curated published researches, 51.6% recorded significant risks associated with using ChatGPT, in healthcare education, research, and practice. The reported risks primarily included the dissemination of inaccurate information, the presence of restricted or incomplete knowledge, and the potential for spreading misinformation.

Furthermore, the problem is compounded when AI relies on biased data sources, which further complicates its reliability in assessing content. Perhaps this stems from the information content on which a GenAI (such as Chatgpt) is trained. The information generated is usually from developed countries that may yield research outcomes that can sometimes not be relevant in other parts of the world (Mbakwe et al., 2023). Baidoo-Anu and Owusu (2023) further explain that the biases may also emanate from a dataset of a certain demographic where the GenAI model is programmed, particularly for essays written by students from that location. The issue arises when GenAI cannot determine nuance and context and when students are not trained to critically examine and identify potential biases. As a result, students write essays that are skewed in objectivity and relevance. Thus, Pavlik (2023) raised a critical point in developing a skill in today's age among students: the need for critical monitoring of AI-generated content.

This underscores that content inaccuracy poses a significant challenge, particularly in evaluating critical thinking in essays, which often relies on assessing and engaging with information, data analysis, and developing original ideas. Some GenAI-generated misinformation can blur the lines between a student's independent thought process and AI-produced essays, which are often made with a seemingly decent outcome but faulty upon stringent examination, leading to students' compromised understanding of a subject matter. This occurs when students do not engage in reflective skepticism and analytical rigor in assessing AI-generated information for quality and reliability.

ADDRESSING AI-RELATED ISSUES IN ASSESSMENT

This area of the chapter will outline how most academic institutions respond to the issues raised in the earlier section. It is understandable that many schools had reacted negatively given the fact that AI is a new innovation and its impact is encompassing particularly in the field of teaching and learning as well as in assessment. It will outline the two most common approaches adopted by these institutions: Resticting AI-Use and Integrating AI-Use.

Having explored the complexities of assessing critical thinking in the AI context, it becomes essential how these challenges can be tackled. Addressing AI-related issues in assessment has also divided educators on whether to restrict AI or integrate AI. The panic caused by GenAI has caused some institutions to ban the use of AI rapidly and argue that it would cause more harm than good. Others have argued that AI integration is inevitable and can be harnessed as a transformative tool for teaching and assessment. This section will highlight two different perspectives on addressing AI issues.

Restricting AI use Approach

"AIgiarism" or AI-assisted plagiarism is now becoming a serious offense and constitutes academic misconduct. Critics argue that students who submit essays entirely written by GenAI must be held liable. They think that while the availability of genAI is within reach, plagiarism issues will not be reduced. An alternative method is to completely ban AI use in schools. Yan (2023) found that students in experiential learning sessions on genAI use in writing expressed their disbelief in Chatgpt as a shortcut for writing and claimed strict limitations and punishment on its use. Similarly, Malik et al. (2023) reported that their respondents voiced concerns about the impact of AI on creativity, critical thinking, and human control. Their data revealed that 75% of the 245 participants refrained from using AI in their academic writing because they feared it would constrain the development of critical thinking skills. This suggests that some students are alarmed at how GenAI is manipulated to cheat, disadvantaging others and potentially leading to educational inequality. In addition to the clamor of some students, even some institutions are grappling with AI use. New York Public Schools, the largest US school district, recently banned using GenAI due to limitations in students' critical thinking, which is essential for academic success (Kelly, 2023). The Department of Education in New South Wales and Queensland, Australia, use a firewall due to the mounting concerns regarding cheating in assessments (Cassidy, 2023). A survey done by EdWeek Research Center in 2023 showed that approximately 27% of educators reported their districts prohibit students in the use of GenAI (Klein,2024). The issue extends beyond individual institutions, with some countries implementing bans on GenAI technology, like Italy, the first Western country to ban related privacy concerns (McCallum,2023). While new reforms have been implemented since and are now accessible, this indicates that some countries face significant challenges in adapting their policies in response to the growing influence of AI.

However, while there are some merits as to why some schools want to ban AI completely, other scholars believe that banning AI is a flawed approach. Popenici et al. (2023) argue that educational institutions reacting to banning AI lack serious intellectual efforts, as banning AI is akin to prohibiting the internet, Microsoft, or Google. This may show that restriction of AI usage in schools can potentially disadvantaged future job seekers where navigating AI technology and literacy is valued in the job market.

One possible counterargument to AI restriction is the Streisand Effect. Jansen and Martin (2015) explain that the Streisand effect is a situation where efforts to suppress information actually lead to increased interest and demand for that information, far more than if no action had been taken. This suggests that any attempts to censor the use of AI may lead to unintended consequences of heightening students' interest and awareness towards AI use, resulting in students being undeterred to use. Rasul et al. (2023) argue the importance of promoting academic freedom and preventing academic misconduct, stressing that GenAI use is increasingly interwoven into students' lives academically, personally, and professionally. Consequently, this will produce a well-educated AI user who can critically evaluate the limitations and biases of AI.

Furthermore, the concern that AI restriction may lead to psychological reactance is equally important. Brehm (1989 cited in Lim et al., 2023) notes that psychological reactance results in a situation when restrictive practices can often drive motivation, as many people are spurred to act when faced with prohibitions or limitations. Unlike the Streisand effect, psychological reactance touches on the motivation of people who are driven toward freedom restoration. Lim et al. (2023) argue that this is important as some private school students still have access to AI while other public schools have banned the technology, leading to a clear educational divide that may result in psychological reactance. Instead of more favorable outcomes, students may consciously hide AI use, leading to resentment and defiance.

While the debate around AI restriction raises concerns like the Streisand effect and psychological reactance, its implications extend to language testing. Its restriction could lead to covert AI usage, complicating how students could have been educated in proper AI use and thus complicating the genuine evaluation of critical thinking skills in essays, which may not fully reflect their actual abilities. Students may feel compelled to deceive about their use of AI and strictly comply with AI policy to avoid detection rather than meaningfully engage in assignment tasks.

Integrating AI use Approach

Lim et al. (2023) note that educational institutions could end the conflicting effect of AI restriction by embracing and leveraging it within curriculums. Leveraging AI entails understanding the common assessment work where AI can be leveraged. Miller's (2024) study, which highlighted AI's impact on 12 assessment works in higher education, highlighted two that are directly relevant to this essay: Academic Integrity Challenges and Erosion of Learning and Critical Thinking Skills.

Academic Integrity

According to Miller (2024), challenges in Academic Integrity can be addressed by developing comprehensive ethical frameworks to uphold academic honesty. This is essential, as Cotton et al. (2023) conclude that for universities to maximize GenAI technology, developing policies for AI use while providing training for students and faculty safeguards the integrity and quality of educational programs, including assessment. Similarly, Garcia (2023) demonstrates the necessity of creating guidelines that standardize AI tool adoption to ensure fairness, accountability, and transparency. Echoing these concerns, Malik et al (2023) reported that participants raised reservations about AI's ethical implications in academic writing. Their data demonstrates that 69% of the respondents avoid using AI in academic writing due to possible issue of plagiarism.

Given that GenAI is used to generate text for essay submission, one ethical concern is the ownership of the content. Lund et al. (2023) raise a similar concern, questioning who holds the rights to AI-produced texts as it can potentially question the impact of traditional practices in academia. Hancock et al. (2020) suggest the need to disclose the type of AI involvement and the contexts in which it was used.

This will encourage transparency and accountability while fostering academic integrity. Furthermore, Bashar et al. (2024) highlight the need to create criteria for scholarly attribution and the collaborative nature of AI-assisted work in citation in academic papers, as AI is a significant research and complementary tool to bolster learning and critical thinking. Monash University (2023) published guidelines for responsible and ethical use of AI technology in assessments, including writing in-text citations and reference lists as an exemplar of AI integration in Ethical Policy. Bashar et al.(2024) further argue that passive acknowledgment of AI integration is insufficient and, hence, necessitates establishing a more robust active ethical stewardship concerning nature, parameters of authorship, and originality in AI-generated content. Through this comprehensive scheme, academics can ensure a harmonious relationship between technological advancement and ethical standards in assessment without the need for blanket banning of AI.

Erosion of Learning and Critical Thinking Skills

Due to plagiarism, traditional assessments are slowly being considered failures to capture students' genuine thought processes. Abdelaal et al. (2019) suggest reducing opportunities for cheating in traditional assessments like essays through curriculum enhancement that improves task designs in assessment. Further, they argued that tasks similar to review articles and literature analysis are more likely to be outsourced from GenAI; instead, curriculum developers should focus on tasks like interviews and customized assignments. Similarly, Cotton et al. (2023) propose a critical thinking-centered approach where assessments are redesigned to ensure students demonstrate critical thinking on tasks. They further elaborated that tasks that involve knowledge and skill application, like group discussions and presentations, can potentially diminish the likelihood of students' reliance on GenAI. In particular, they advocate using inquiry-based assessments where students formulate their research questions and defend their arguments. However, while all these may foster critical thinking, one counterargument with these approaches is that they diminish the critical role of AI in developers' task designs and students' task accomplishment. Curriculum developers can leverage AI by designing AI-enhanced learning experience tasks and supporting students by utilizing AI-assisted tools for research and assignments. This fosters the promotion of AI integration skills while honing critical thinking rather than merely focusing on minimizing AI use. Rather, it should be a conduit for task design and assessment support. The refined approach by Bashar et al. (2024) is a hybrid between AI integration and ethical standards in developing pedagogical tasks without compromising critical thinking development, which also acknowledges the ongoing evolution of AI technology. For instance, Rasul et al. (2023) advocate innovative assessment with AI integration in task design by asking

AI to generate essay prompts and drafts where students are invited to critique and evaluate these drafts while exploiting AI chatbots through individualized feedback by adaptive asking and seeking information resulting to a more robust knowledge construction of the task. Through similar activities such as this, the cultivation of AI literacy with a focus on process evaluation rather than outcome evaluation while preventing misconduct and promoting freedom enhances students' employability in the rapidly changing job market (Rasul et al., 2023). Employable graduates are those who can navigate effectively in increasingly AI-prevalent workplaces and understand the social implications, limitations, strengths, and ethical ramifications of AI usage. According to Rasul et al. (2023), universities could maximize this opportunity to integrate GenAI into the curriculum by developing AI literacy among students.

Despite the amount of work that has to be done in the pedagogical preparation of AI-assisted tasks and ensuring students are equally supported with AI-supporting tools, I would argue that this approach is a leap towards cultivating AI-literate students who are capable of exploiting advanced technologies that can be beneficial in real-world situations outside academic, particularly in the workplace. AI integration in assessment and the curriculum within the bounds of ethical regulations in academic integrity fosters inclusiveness, enhances critical thinking, and ensures accountability and transparency, all needed to be globally competitive in today's fast-changing job market.

THE ROLE OF AI IN DEVELOPING CRITICAL THINKING SKILLS

The current section of the chapter focuses on amplifying the development of critical thinking skills in education through the application of AI technologies. It will show the crucial balance of Artificial intelligence and Human intelligence in enhancing critical thinking. It will briefly cover the 7e Learning Model including each of its phases with description and method of use.

The promotion of Artificial Intelligence in human lives should not be at the expense of human intelligence (HI). Although the gap between AI and HI is growing and increasingly blurred, people should find ways to leverage AI to push for HI development. One of the many ways to do so is to emphasize critical thinking. Spector and Ma (2019) highlight using AI to improve critical thinking and human intelligence in an intelligent learning environment through personalized learning experiences. However, they argue that most efforts are situated in laboratory environments where a normal learner typically has no access. Hence, they believe that priority should be given to the development of HI with the support of AI for children. Nassar (2019) notes that both critical thinking and AI should foster a system that, instead of AI taking over humans, AI can act as a tool in enhancing decision-making and critical thinking so humans can perform tasks more effectively. Darwin *et al.* (2023) explain that while AI has its limitations, developing critical thinking skills can be further developed with the robust capitalization of AI on human intelligence. A study they conducted showed that participants emphasized the importance of a balanced approach to critical thinking and artificial intelligence. This shows the careful consideration of AI's drawbacks while leveraging AI's strengths in improving critical thinking. Thus, there is a need for a solid awareness of the many ways AI can complement or supplement human intelligence while using AI ethically.

Baskoro *et al.* (2023) acknowledge that the current generation (Gen Z) can adopt artificial intelligence in their everyday life but encounter obstacles in honing a 21st-century skill in critical thinking. Thus, they proposed a learning cycle model adopting the 7E (Elicit, Engage, Explore, Explain, Elaborate, Evaluate and Extend) learning cycle with peeragogy learning approach with AI applications as a tool. Peeragogy refers to a collaborative approach to learning where peers teach and learn from each other in a cooperative environment using AI tools. It combines peer-to-peer interaction with pedagogical methods.The 7E learning model is appropriate for improving critical thinking skills because as Rahman and Chavhan (2022, as cited in Baskoro *et al.,*2023) explain:

7E learning model

1. Help to understand deeply;
2. Makes efficient learning;
3. Transfer of learning
4. Motivation to learn
5. Develop thinking skills
6. Develop communication and social skills
7. Basis for developing instructional materials

The 7E model can be refined into two categories: front-end and back-end learning process. The front-end process focuses on exploring the idea and generation of knowledge while the back end focuses on evaluation as well as verification of information. Also, the front end focuses on engage, explore, explain and elaboration. These stages are learner-facing. The back-end process, on the other hand, focuses on evaluation and extension. Baskoro *et al.* (2023) explained that in the traditional learning approach, the back-end process which is the verification and confirmation of information can be obtained from physical books, references and lecturers. However, in today's age, students can leverage AI use to help them both in the front-end and back-end process of learning. In the peeragogy learning approach, students can use AI tools to understand the topic and discuss it with peers. The instructor's role is to facilitate and provide feedback. After students' discussion, they can use

AI to further explore the topic or elaborate on the topic and use AI to validate the summary of their discussions. This is one example of how learners can maximize AI use to improve learning dynamics in the classroom.

The 7E learning cycle and the peeragogy approach with AI are examples of maximizing the use of AI without undermining human intelligence. The argument is that both AI and HI can function collectively in honing the students' learning process. Through this synergistic effect, students may able to independently navigate learning of advanced and complex concepts while also able to validate their findings through the use of AI. The capacity to critically evaluate the outputs of artificial intelligence exemplifies a key aspect of critical thinking. As digital citizens navigate the new field of learning through AI use, it is vital that students hone this ability to evaluate and critically question the veracity of AI results.

BRIDGING THE ETHICAL GAP: ETHICAL FRAMEWORK FOR ARTIFICIAL INTELLIGENCE IN ACADEMIC WRITING

At the core of this chapter is the ethical use of artificial intelligence. While the issue of critical thinking in writing provides a backdrop, it can be argued that the central claim lies in the engagement and stimulation of discussion which will hopefully trigger initiatives in preparing digital citizens for ethical use of AI in writing. This is of prime importance because it safeguards the integrity of scholarly work and because it behoves educators to spearhead ventures and practices that adhere to ethical standards. Given the rapid advancements in artificial intelligence, how can academic institutions balance the convenience of AI-generated content with the need to preserve academic integrity and foster critical thinking? Developing a clear framework with AI tools will be essential in safeguarding academic standards.

A recently devised ethical framework for using Large Language Models (LLM) which is a subset of Artificial Intelligence that is trained to generate text-related tasks such as GPT-4, has been co-created by researchers from some of the leading institutions in the world such as the University of Oxford, the University of Cambridge and the National University of Singapore. This new framework aims to establish clear ethical guidelines that respect on one side: originality, authorship, and transparency and on the other side: acknowledge the incredible capabilities of artificial intelligence when leveraged correctly. Porsdam Mann *et al.* (2024) proposed three criteria (see below) for the responsible use of LLM. The criteria are:

1. Human vetting and guaranteeing
2. Substantial Human Contribution
3. Acknowledgement and Transparency

These criteria allow digital citizens to reflect and ensure that while they are in the process of finalizing their manuscripts, the guidelines will stand as a system of checks and balances. The straightforward guidelines enhance clarity and manage the interplay relationship between LLM and human intelligence.

The first criterion (Human vetting and guaranteeing) aims to ensure that authors have reviewed and fact-checked all LLM-assisted work. Porsdam Mann *et al.* (2024) explain that this technology can generate a wide range of texts, but they are not foolproof and thus human intervention through examination of these generated texts is warranted as authors should bear full responsibility for the academic context they publish. This involves curating the data and re-examining the generated texts for accuracy and relevance. Such need for examination was already evident in one case study involving 245 undergraduate students in Indonesia (Malik *et al.,* 2023) where approximately 70% emphasised the need for integration of AI with human writers and highlighted the importance of human authors to adapt and expand AI-generated results.

The second is the Substantial Human criterion, which pertains to the heavy involvement of the authors in producing an academic output. Porsdam Mann *et al.* (2024) note that the use of LLM should not change what constitutes contribution because even when authors use LLM, they have to use new forms of cognitive abilities such as as generating effective prompts for LLM and curating data output. In order to meet this criterion, authors must not merely copy LLM-generated texts with minimal editing and must show that the work is a result of originality and substantial contribution to expanding knowledge in academia.

The third emphasizes the acknowledgement and transparency of the use of Artificial Intelligence. Authors should disclose how and when they have used and leveraged AI in the development of their work but should also be entirely dependent on field-specific standards (Porsdam Mann *et al.*,2024). This encourages a move towards facilitating AI adoption and minimizing any fears and prejudice about the use of LLMs in academic writing. They have added a template for LLM disclosure and acknowledgement. Please see below:

> *This standardized statement serves to testify to the authors' adherence to the three essential criteria for the ethical use of LLMs in academic writing described in this manuscript. It should be included in the manuscript at submission (see the Acknowledgements section for this paper below), and adapted as relevant to each field of research, as well as to each type of research or output within a given field: "Any use of generative AI in this manuscript adheres to ethical guidelines for use and acknowledgement of generative AI in academic research. Each author has made a substantial contribution to the work, which has been thoroughly vetted for accuracy and assumes responsibility for the integrity of*

their contributions. [Optional, as needed to allow reproducibility, judgements of credibility: additional details on LLM use and impact]"

The promotion and adherence to the above criteria increase ethical awareness among digital citizens in higher education in academic writing. For writers and students, in particular, engaging in any scholarly work whether for formative or summative assessment and publications, the criteria will serve as a signpost to vet the accuracy of LLM texts and ensure that a substantial contribution from the authors is presented and evident while also maintaining transparency regarding the use of AI.

CULTIVATING DIGITAL CITIZENSHIP AND DEVELOPING DIGITAL CITIZENS

In this world increasingly driven by technology and artificial intelligence, in particular, how can the next generation of digital citizens be ensured of not only technological proficiency but also ethical and critical awareness in academic writing? This challenge calls for the integration of digital literacy education including knowledge of digital citizenship that emphasizes both responsible technology use and critical thinking skills.

Ribble & Bailey (2007) defined *digital citizenship* as standards for appropriate and responsible conduct in the use of technology. The responsible use of artificial intelligence technology to fulfil their academic obligations and functions at an optimum level should not only be adapted but likewise should be cultivated to produce educated and AI-aware digital citizens. This proposal was exemplified by the International Society for Technology in Education (ISTE) (2016) which published guidelines for preparing students to flourish in a growing technological-educational landscape. It includes understanding the crucial role of digital footprints, digital identity management, inclusivity awareness, responsible interactions online, and acknowledging safeguards for well-being and digital privacy. Such knowledge of digital citizenship and the use of artificial intelligence may bridge the gap of blurring lines of ethical use of technology in higher education. The ISTE has promoted practical ways for using the standards in classrooms that other practitioners in education can mimic and apply in their own personal contexts. Furthermore, the notion of digital citizenship encompasses digital literacy which can be defined as the ability to read and write, and engage with different communities online (Buchholz *et al.,*2020). Consequently, becoming a digital citizen requires acquiring digital literacy. In relation to the impact of critical thinking in higher education, digital citizens should be digitally literate in a manner where students are aware of the technical aspects of technology and the ethical considerations pertaining to AI use involved in interacting with academic communities and digital citizens online.

With this, given that such an important obligation in cultivating students, teachers' role in this process has now emerged again at the forefront. Thus, necessitates well-informed teachers' digital and AI literacy through professional development. It would be unreasonable to place such a herculean task for developing digital citizenship and literacy on teachers if they have not been adequately informed and trained to fulfil this role in the first place. Also, the amount of literature that discusses developing teachers in Artificial intelligence is scant which demonstrates an evident flaw in the priorities of teacher development. It can be argued that to prepare students for digital citizenship in the future, one has to start building the blocks in fundamentally developing teachers' current knowledge of digital literacies including AI and the norms of digital citizenship. Training of professional development among teachers should reflect on the seven categories of teacher knowledge based on Shulman (1986) – see below. The foundation knowledge among current teachers should be secured in order to dispense the duty of producing digitally literate and civilized students. Hence, this knowledge should adhere to teachers' identity and enhance teachers in the following types of knowledge:

1. Content knowledge
2. Pedagogical knowledge
3. Pedagogical content knowledge
4. Curricular knowledge
5. Knowledge of learners and their characteristics
6. Knowledge of educational contexts
7. Knowledge of Educational Purposes and values

Once teachers are properly informed and trained, it can be contended that the process of educating students will naturally ensue. The cycle of this educational process should begin with the educators so they can dispense their duty competitively. The importance of their role can be considered as the subtle yet crucial missing link towards a robust approach to enhancing students' digital literacy and digital citizenship. One example that can provide a basis for developing teachers' AI literacy in the future is the case study done by Zhao *et al.* (2022) among 1013 samples from teachers in Jiangsu, China. The teachers were from different educational stages: primary education, secondary education and higher education. The study recommends that the government plays a vital role in cultivating AI literacy among teachers and suggests:

1. An online platform that will allow teachers to learn anytime and anywhere;
2. Weekly assignments that offer self-directed practice;
3. Courses provide the freedom to select study schedules;

4. Implementation of training programs that adopt new AI technologies;
5. Robust teacher assessment for the training;
6. Increase teacher awareness that AI can be leveraged to assist in teaching.

Institutional stakeholders should also advocate and lead the promotion of teachers' literacy on these aspects through:

1. Developing policies that prioritize teacher education on digital and AI literacy and digital citizenship;
2. Encourage dialogues in enhancing current teacher professional development;
3. Invest in technological and methodological approaches;
4. Promote actively to elevate discussions on teacher development;
5. Conduct evaluative schemes to appraise and improve teacher training;
6. Support scholars in research-related scholarly work about teachers' digital literacy, AI literacy and Digital Citizenship;
7. Lead initiatives that consider teacher development a norm through increasing awareness among other stakeholders such as community leaders, policy developers and funders.

The compounding effect of these actions could solidify teachers' morale and empower them that their role is pivotal in the overall scene of future education through developing present students towards digital citizenship and Digital and AI literacy.

Using the ISTE guidelines and the proposed framework for ethical use in academic writing, the development of a more informed digital citizen with the indispensable assistance of digital and AI literate educators will become more apparent than ever. It is crucial that this process is ensured to produce digital citizens who can successfully navigate the future of education despite the uncertainty of technological innovations which can impact the educational landscape in higher education. The ethical use of LLMs and the notable contribution of human intelligence will display new cognitive critical thinking skills such as evaluating the quality of LLM-produced texts, synthesis of information from multiple AI-generated outputs, and addressing ambiguity and bias while all maintaining originality in thoughts and output. It is profound to recognize that the advent of new technologies such as LLMs will result in a new set of mental abilities particularly in critical thinking. This transition demonstrates that the notion of critical thinking is not simply just to read and write within a social context, it evolves and devolves to accommodate the perpetually dynamic nature of technology. As technology progresses so as the encompassing nature of critical thinking in academic writing and thus it is assumed that citizens are digitally and AI literate and aware of the standards of digital citizenship.

CONCLUSION

Given the focus of critical thinking in reflective scepticism, argumentation, higher-order thinking skills, self-regulatory judgment, and emphasis on synthesis and analysis, deliberate attention has to be devoted to ensuring critical thinking is exemplified in students' works primarily in the age of GenAI where essays can be generated in a matter of seconds. In an attempt to assess students ' AI-generated work, educators have investigated and confronted two predominant issues in essays: AI detector bypass and the generation of false and biased content. To address these issues, scholars have explored the utility of both the restrictive AI use approach and the integrative AI use approach.

The restrictive AI use approach opens more challenges associated with GenAI, including covert AI usage, defiance, resentment, undeterred by policy, and exclusion. These are likely due to Streisand effect and psychological reactance's influence on motivation and behavior. Students are more likely to focus on compliance with AI policy rather than engaging meaningfully with the task. Insisting on AI restriction approach may likely produce students who may not be fully capable of navigating an AI-immersed environment in the future workplace, thus exposing the weakness and insufficiency of current traditional assessment.

On the other hand, the integrative AI approach fosters balancing AI technology and ethical policy in academic integrity and does not blanketly ban AI use. It highlights the collaborative work of AI usage and scholarly contribution in written work with appropriate attribution to the extent and content of AI use. The integrative AI approach does not merely advocate the minimal use of AI but the full exploitation of AI for both pedagogical purposes in task design and AI assessment support for the learners, leading to a shift of focus from outcome evaluation to process evaluation.

However, while the integrative AI approach is the desired step towards cultivating AI literate students, much has to be discussed about the uniformity of AI policies across institutions in a country and worldwide, including journal publications. One potential suggestion to address the varied ethical policies in different universities is considering the establishment of a committee dedicated to AI ethics and use whose sole purpose is streamlining ethical guidelines and promoting AI literacy awareness and collaboration. Such a body could leverage AI to promote critical thinking, transparency, and accountability by coordinating best-shared practices. Doing so would consolidate the collective effort of different universities worldwide to safeguard academic integrity while assuring freedom and inclusivity.

This chapter has aimed to discuss the dwindling focus on critical thinking in higher education due to students' over-reliance on artificial intelligence. It discussed some issues in criticality in assessment and also approaches to addressing AI-related issues in assessment. It has explored some methods adopted by institutions around the world such as restricting AI use and integrating AI use. It has also shown one example using the 7E learning approach and the peeragogy when implementing AI to develop critical thinking. However, the success of any initiatives in developing critical thinking in the age of AI involves the collective effort of the major stakeholders such as the institutions, policymakers, teachers and students. It is through this that future citizens will value the importance of assessment when they see that current leaders, teachers and the rest of the academic community are in unison in safeguarding critical thinking in higher education.

It has delved into the importance of digital citizenship and digital and AI literacy for both teachers and students. To bridge the ethical gap, a proposed framework was also included alongside the ISTE guidelines. To help students achieve this, teachers have to be trained and thus the discussion of teachers' AI literacy in professional development holds the same significance. To navigate the future of education in critical thinking and AI in higher education, both teachers and students have to be both digital citizens and AI literate. By doing so, they will prepare a better path for future citizens, particularly in higher education.

With the developments in artificial intelligence and its impact on education, it is only imperative that the direction that most stakeholders should adopt is towards prioritizing digital citizenship and literacy both for teachers and students. If educators are trained to produce learners that embody the principles of digital citizenship and AI literate informed thinkers, arguably, the future of education could be secured and they will be able to navigate the rapid technological developments and their potential impact on critical thinking in higher education.

REFERENCES

Abdelaal, E., Mills, J., & Walpita Gamage, S. (2019) Artifcial intelligence is a tool for cheating academic integrity. *Proceedings of the AAEE 2019 annual conference*. https://www.researchgate.net/publication/339375213_Artificial_Intelligence_Is_a_Tool_for_Cheating_Academic_Integrity

Baidoo-Anu, D., & Owusu Ansah, L. (2023). Education in the Era of Generative Artificial Intelligence (AI): Understanding the Potential Benefits of ChatGPT in Promoting Teaching and Learning. *Journal of AI*, 7(1), 52–62. DOI: 10.61969/jai.1337500

Bashar, H. S., Shuaibu, M. A., & Abubakar, M. H. (2024). Balancing AI and academic integrity: What are the positions of academic publishers and universities? *AI & Society*. Advance online publication. DOI: 10.1007/s00146-024-01946-8

Baskoro, G., Mariza, I., & Sutapa, I. N. (2023). Innovation to Improve Critical Thinking Skills in the Generation Z using Peeragogy as a Learning Approach and Artificial Intelligence (AI) as a Tool. *Deleted Journal*, 25(2), 121–130. DOI: 10.9744/jti.25.2.121-130

Buchholz, B. A., DeHard, J., & Moorman, G. (2020). Digital citizenship during a global pandemic: Moving beyond digital literacy. *Journal of Adolescent & Adult Literacy*, 64(1), 11–17. DOI: 10.1002/jaal.1076 PMID: 32834710

Cassidy, C. (2023). Queensland public schools to join NSW in banning students from ChatGPT. *The Guardian*. https://www.theguardian.com/australia-news/2023/jan/23/queensland-public-schools-to-join-nsw-in-banning-students-from-chatgpt

Chatterjee, J., & Dethlefs, N. (2023). This new conversational AI model can be your friend, philosopher, and guide ... and even your worst enemy. *Patterns (New York, N.Y.)*, 4(1), 100676. DOI: 10.1016/j.patter.2022.100676 PMID: 36699746

Coil, D., Wenderoth, M. P., Cunningham, M., & Dirks, C. (2010). Teaching the Process of Science: Faculty Perceptions and an Effective Methodology. *CBE Life Sciences Education*, 9(4), 524–535. DOI: 10.1187/cbe.10-01-0005 PMID: 21123699

Cotton, D. R. E., Cotton, P. A., & Shipway, J. R. (2023). Chatting and cheating: Ensuring academic integrity in the era of ChatGPT. *Innovations in Education and Teaching International*, 61(2), 228–239. DOI: 10.1080/14703297.2023.2190148

Darwin, N., Rusdin, D., Mukminatien, N., Suryati, N., Laksmi, E. D., & Marzuki, . (2023). 'Critical thinking in the AI era: An exploration of EFL students' perceptions, benefits, and limitations,'. *Cogent Education*, 11(1), 2290342. Advance online publication. DOI: 10.1080/2331186X.2023.2290342

Dashti, M., Londono, J., Ghasemi, S., & Moghaddasi, N. (2023). How much can we rely on artificial intelligence chatbots such as the ChatGPT software program to assist with scientific writing? *The Journal of Prosthetic Dentistry*. Advance online publication. DOI: 10.1016/j.prosdent.2023.05.023 PMID: 37438164

Duah, J. E., & McGivern, P. (2024). How generative artificial intelligence has blurred notions of authorial identity and academic norms in higher education, necessitating clear university usage policies. *Campus-Wide Information Systems*, 41(2), 180–193. Advance online publication. DOI: 10.1108/IJILT-11-2023-0213

El Soufi, N., & See, B. H. (2019). Does explicit teaching of critical thinking improve critical thinking skills of English language learners in higher education? A critical review of causal evidence. *Studies in Educational Evaluation*, 60(60), 140–162. DOI: 10.1016/j.stueduc.2018.12.006

Ennis, R. H. (1993). Critical Thinking Assessment. *Theory into Practice*, 32(3), 179–186. DOI: 10.1080/00405849309543594

Facione, P. (1998). *Critical Thinking: What it is and Why it counts*. California Academic Press.

Fu, S., Gu, H., & Yang, B. (2020). The affordances of AI-enabled automatic scoring applications on learners' continuous learning intention: An empirical study in China. *British Journal of Educational Technology*, 51(5), 1674–1692. DOI: 10.1111/bjet.12995

Garcia, M. B. (2023). Using AI Tools in Writing Peer Review Reports: Should Academic Journals Embrace the Use of ChatGPT? *Annals of Biomedical Engineering*. Advance online publication. DOI: 10.1007/s10439-023-03299-7 PMID: 37368125

Hancock, J., Naaman, M., & Levy, K. (2020). AI-Mediated Communication: Definition, Research Agenda, and Ethical Considerations. *Journal of Computer-Mediated Communication*, 25(1), 89–100. DOI: 10.1093/jcmc/zmz022

International Society for Technology in Education (ISTE). (2016). ISTE standards for students. Retrieved from http://www.iste.org/standards/for-students#startstandards

Jansen, S. C., & Martin, B. (2015). The Streisand Effect and Censorship Backfire. ResearchGate; University of Southern California, Annenberg School for Communication & Journalism. https://www.researchgate.net/publication/273947761_The_Streisand_Effect_and_Censorship_Backfire

Kampa, R. K., Padhan, D. K., Karna, N., & Gouda, J. (2024). Identifying the factors influencing plagiarism in higher education: An evidence-based review of the literature. *Accountability in Research*, 1–16. DOI: 10.1080/08989621.2024.2335342 PMID: 38290700

Kelly, J. K. (2023). *New York City public schools ban access to AI tool that could help students cheat.* CNN. https://edition.cnn.com/2023/01/05/tech/chatgpt-nyc-school-ban/index.html

Kenedy, R. A. (2024). The Challenges of Critical Thinking in the Era of Artificial Intelligence. *European Journal of Multidisciplinary Studies*, 9(1), 19–33. DOI: 10.26417/hfdngd20

Khalil, M., & Er, E. (2023). *Will ChatGPT Get You Caught? Rethinking of Plagiarism Detection.* DOI: 10.1007/978-3-031-34411-4_32

Kim, H.-S., Kim, N. Y., & Cha, Y. (2021). Is It Beneficial to Use AI Chatbots to Improve Learners' Speaking Performance? *The Journal of AsiaTEFL*, 18(1), 161–178. DOI: 10.18823/asiatefl.2021.18.1.10.161

Klein, A. (2024). Does Your District Ban ChatGPT? Here's What Educators Told Us. Education Week. https://www.edweek.org/technology/does-your-district-ban-chatgpt-heres-what-educators-told-us/2024/02

Kumar, V., & Boulanger, D. (2020). Explainable Automated Essay Scoring: Deep Learning Really Has Pedagogical Value. *Frontiers in Education*, 5, 572367. Advance online publication. DOI: 10.3389/feduc.2020.572367

Lim, W. M., Gunasekara, A., Pallant, J. L., Pallant, J. I., & Pechenkina, E. (2023). Generative AI and the future of education: Ragnarök or reformation? a Paradoxical Perspective from Management Educators. *International Journal of Management Education*, 21(2), 100790. DOI: 10.1016/j.ijme.2023.100790

Lo, C. K. (2023). What Is the Impact of ChatGPT on Education? A Rapid Review of the Literature. *Education Sciences*, 13(4), 410. DOI: 10.3390/educsci13040410

Lund, B. D., Wang, T., Mannuru, N. R., Nie, B., Shimray, S., & Wang, Z. (2023). ChatGPT and a new academic reality: Artificial Intelligence-written research papers and the ethics of the large language models in scholarly publishing. *Journal of the Association for Information Science and Technology*, 74(5), 570–581. Advance online publication. DOI: 10.1002/asi.24750

Malik, A. R., Pratiwi, Y., Andajani, K., Numertayasa, I. W., Suharti, S., Darwis, A., & Marzuki, . (2023). Exploring Artificial Intelligence in Academic Essay: Higher Education Student's Perspective. *International Journal of Educational Research Open*, 5, 100296. Advance online publication. DOI: 10.1016/j.ijedro.2023.100296

Mbakwe, A. B., Lourentzou, I., Celi, L. A., Mechanic, O. J., & Dagan, A. (2023). ChatGPT passing USMLE shines a spotlight on the flaws of medical education. *PLOS Digital Health*, 2(2), e0000205. DOI: 10.1371/journal.pdig.0000205 PMID: 36812618

McCallum, S. (2023, March 31). ChatGPT banned in Italy over privacy concerns. *BBC News*. https://www.bbc.com/news/technology-65139406

Michel-Villarreal, R., Vilalta-Perdomo, E., Salinas-Navarro, D. E., Thierry-Aguilera, R., & Gerardou, F. S. (2023). Challenges and Opportunities of Generative AI for Higher Education as Explained by ChatGPT. *Education Sciences*, 13(9), 1–18. DOI: 10.3390/educsci13090856

Miller, W. (2024). Adapting to AI: Reimagining the Role of Assessment Professionals. Intersection: A journal at the intersection of assessment and learning, Early View. https://aalhe.scholasticahq.com/article/121439.pdf

Nassar, S. (2019). Future Aspects of Critical Thinking and AI.*Proceedings of WR-FASE International Conference*.

Park, S. (2023). *School districts blocking ChatGPT amid fears of cheating, educators weigh in on AI*. FOXBusiness. https://www.foxbusiness.com/technology/school-districts-blocking-chatgpt-amid-fears-of-cheating-educators-weigh-in-on-ai

Paul, R. (1991). Critical Thinking: What Every Person Needs To Survive in a Changing World. *NASSP Bulletin*, 75(533), 120–122. DOI: 10.1177/019263659107553325

Paul, R. W. (1987). Dialogical thinking: Critical thought essential to the acquisition of rational knowledge and passions. In Baron, J. B., & Sternberg, R. J. (Eds.), *Teaching thinking skills: Theory and practice* (pp. 127–148). W H Freeman/Times Books/ Henry Holt & Co.

Pavlik, J. V. (2023). Collaborating With ChatGPT: Considering the Implications of Generative Artificial Intelligence for Journalism and Media Education. *Journalism & Mass Communication Educator*, 78(1), 84–93. DOI: 10.1177/10776958221149577

Pithers, R. T., & Soden, R. (2000). Critical thinking in education: A review. *Educational Research*, 42(3), 237–249. DOI: 10.1080/001318800440579

Popenici, S., Rudolph, J., Tan, S., & Tan, S. (2023). A critical perspective on generative AI and learning futures. An interview with Stefan Popenici. *Journal of Applied Learning and Teaching*, 6(2). Advance online publication. DOI: 10.37074/jalt.2023.6.2.5

Porsdam Mann, S., Vazirani, A. A., Aboy, M. R., Earp, B. D., Minssen, T., Cohen, I. G., & Savulescu, J. (2024). Guidelines for ethical use and acknowledgement of large language models in academic writing. *Nature Machine Intelligence*, 6(11), 1272–1274. DOI: 10.1038/s42256-024-00922-7

Rafida, T., Suwandi, S., & Ananda, R. (2024). EFL Students' Perception in Indonesia and Taiwan on Using Artificial Intelligence to Enhance Writing Skills. *Jurnal Ilmiah Peuradeun*, 12(3), 987–987. DOI: 10.26811/peuradeun.v12i3.1520

Rahman, N. M. S., & Chavhan, N. D. R. (2022). 7E model: An effective instructional approach for teaching learning. *EPRA International Journal of Multidisciplinary Research (IJMR),* 339–345. DOI: 10.36713/epra9431

Rasul, T. (2023). The role of ChatGPT in higher education: Benefits, challenges, and future research directions. *Journal of Applied Learning & Teaching*, 6(1). Advance online publication. DOI: 10.37074/jalt.2023.6.1.29

Ribble, M., & Bailey, G. D. (2007). *Digital citizenship in schools.* International Society of Technology in Education.

Rudolph, J., Tan, S., & Tan, S. (2023). ChatGPT: Bullshit spewer or the end of traditional assessments in higher education? *Journal of Applied Learning & Teaching*, 6(1), 342–363. DOI: 10.37074/jalt.2023.6.1.9

Sallam, M. (2023). The Utility of ChatGPT as an Example of Large Language Models in Healthcare Education, Research and Practice: Systematic Review on the Future Perspectives and Potential Limitations. *MedRxiv*. https://doi.org/DOI: 10.1101/2023.02.19.23286155

See, B. (2016). An Investigation into the Teaching and Learning of Argumentation in First Year Undergraduate Courses: A Pilot Study. *British Journal of Education, Society &Behavioral Sciences (Basel, Switzerland)*, 18(4), 1–25. DOI: 10.9734/BJESBS/2016/29659

Shaw, A., Liu, O. L., Gu, L., Kardonova, E., Chirikov, I., Li, G., Hu, S., Yu, N., Ma, L., Guo, F., Su, Q., Shi, J., Shi, H., & Loyalka, P. (2019). Thinking critically about critical thinking: Validating the Russian HEIghten® critical thinking assessment. *Studies in Higher Education*, 45(9), 1933–1948. DOI: 10.1080/03075079.2019.1672640

Shin, D., & Park, Y. J. (2019). Role of fairness, accountability, and transparency in algorithmic affordance. *Computers in Human Behavior*, 98, 277–284. DOI: 10.1016/j.chb.2019.04.019

Shulman, L. S. (1986). Those Who Understand: Knowledge Growth in Teaching. *Educational Researcher*, 15(2), 4–14. DOI: 10.3102/0013189X015002004

Spector, J. M., & Ma, S. (2019). Inquiry and critical thinking skills for the next generation: From artificial intelligence back to human intelligence. *Smart Learning Environments*, 6(1), 8. Advance online publication. DOI: 10.1186/s40561-019-0088-z

Šprajc, P., Urh, M., Jerebc, J., Trivan, D., & Jereb, E. (2017). Reasons for Plagiarism in Higher Education. *Organizacija*, 50(1), 33–45. DOI: 10.1515/orga-2017-0002

Stokel-Walker, C. (2022). AI bot ChatGPT writes smart essays — Should academics worry? *Nature*. Advance online publication. DOI: 10.1038/d41586-022-04397-7 PMID: 36494443

Terwiesch, C. (2023). *Would Chat GPT3 Get a Wharton MBA? A Prediction Based on Its Performance in the Operations Management Course*. https://mackinstitute.wharton.upenn.edu/wp-content/uploads/2023/01/Christian-Terwiesch-Chat-GTP.pdf

The European Higher Education Area. (2012). Bologna process implementation report. Retrieved from http://www.ehea.info/media.ehea.info/file/2012_Bucharest/79/5.Bologna_Process_Implementation_Report_607795.pdf

UNESCO. (2023). *UNESCO calls for regulations on AI use in school*News.un.org. https://news.un.org/en/story/2023/09/1140477

University, M. (2023) .*Acknowledging the use of generative artificial intelligence*. Student Academic Success. https://www.monash.edu/student-academic-success/build-digital-capabilities/create-online/acknowledging-the-use-of-generative-artificial-intelligence

Ventayen, R. J. M. (2023). OpenAI ChatGPT-Generated Results: Similarity Index of Artificial Intelligence-Based Contents. In Soft Computing for Security Applications. ICSCS 2023. Advances in Intelligent Systems and Computing, vol 1449. Springer. DOI: 10.1007/978-981-99-3608-3_15

Walczak, K., & Wojciech, C. (2023). Challenges for higher education in the era of widespread access to generative AI. *The Poznań University of Economics Review, 9*(2). DOI: 10.18559/ebr.2023.2.743

Xie, X., & Wang, T. (2023). Artificial Intelligence: A help or threat to contemporary education. Should students be forced to think and do their tasks independently? *Education and Information Technologies*. Advance online publication. DOI: 10.1007/s10639-023-11947-7

Yan, D. (2023). Impact of ChatGPT on learners in a L2 writing practicum: An exploratory investigation. *Education and Information Technologies*, 28(11), 13943–13967. Advance online publication. DOI: 10.1007/s10639-023-11742-4

Zhai, X. (2022). ChatGPT User Experience: Implications for Education. SSRN *Electronic Journal*. DOI: 10.2139/ssrn.4312418

Zhao, L., Wu, X., & Luo, H. (2022). Developing AI literacy for primary and middle school teachers in China: Based on a structural equation modeling analysis. *Sustainability (Basel)*, 14(21), 14549. DOI: 10.3390/su142114549

Chapter 15
Preparing Citizens for the Future of Digital Literacy and AI:
With a Focus on Indonesian EFL Teachers

Bachtiar Bachtiar
https://orcid.org/0000-0002-5653-1252
Universitas Terbuka, Indonesia

ABSTRACT

Artificial intelligence (AI) is revolutionizing education worldwide, demanding a redefinition of digital literacy to prepare students for an AI-dominated era. This chapter explores these dynamics with a focus on Indonesian English as a Foreign Language (EFL) teachers, who face unique challenges in bridging advanced AI technologies with culturally grounded pedagogy. Beyond technical skills, digital literacy now requires educators to evaluate AI outputs critically, address ethical considerations such as data privacy and algorithmic bias, and integrate technology in ways that uphold accessibility and equity. In Indonesia, where disparities in digital infrastructure and teacher readiness are prevalent, EFL educators navigate complex decisions about deploying adaptive learning tools and automated assessments while ensuring inclusive and meaningful learning experiences. By combining global perspectives with localized strategies, this chapter presents actionable insights to empower educators to harness AI's potential while maintaining the humanistic essence of teaching.

DOI: 10.4018/979-8-3693-9015-3.ch015

INTRODUCTION

The 21st century has ushered in a rapid technological evolution, with AI emerging as a pivotal driver of this transformation. AI has permeated nearly every facet of human life, including industrial automation, healthcare, transportation, and education. Among these domains, its impact is perhaps most profoundly felt in classrooms, where technology is reshaping not only how students learn but also how educators teach and engage with their learners (Guo & Yu, 2023; Maisaiah, 2024). As AI continues to advance, the educational landscape must confront a critical challenge to redefine the concept of digital literacy to equip individuals with the skills and understanding necessary to thrive in an era shaped by transformative technologies (Taufikin et al., 2024).

Digital literacy, once understood as the basic ability to operate computers and navigate the internet, has evolved into a far more complex construct. The age of AI encompasses technical skills, such as understanding machine learning algorithms and data analysis, as well as the ability to critically assess and responsibly manage sophisticated technologies that increasingly influence daily decision-making (Karroum & Elshaiekh, 2023). This evolution is particularly significant for EFL education, where the adoption of AI tools must not compromise the humanistic and context-driven principles that underpin effective teaching and learning (Alam et al., 2022).

In the context of Indonesia, the intersection of AI and EFL education presents unique challenges and opportunities. As a nation characterized by cultural diversity and unequal access to technology, Indonesia's educational system must navigate significant hurdles, including disparities in digital infrastructure and the varying readiness of teachers to integrate advanced tools into their classrooms (Bezzina & Dingli, 2024; Yeter et al., 2024). English, as a global lingua franca, has long been a vital component of Indonesia's curriculum. However, the rise of AI-powered tools, ranging from language learning apps and automated assessment systems to virtual teaching assistants, places unprecedented demands on Indonesian EFL teachers. They are tasked with integrating these cutting-edge technologies into their pedagogical practices while ensuring that learning remains accessible, equitable, and relevant to all students, regardless of their geographic or socio-economic background (Chisom et al., 2024).

This chapter delves deeply into how AI can be effectively integrated into EFL education in Indonesia and how a robust understanding of digital literacy can equip students for an increasingly digitalized world. Importantly, digital literacy in the AI era transcends technical competencies, requiring educators and students alike to grapple with ethical considerations, such as privacy, data security, and the potential biases embedded in AI algorithms. These issues underscore the need for Indonesian EFL teachers to cultivate not only a critical understanding of AI but also a forward-looking approach to preparing students to become digitally literate global citizens capable of navigating the complexities of a rapidly advancing technological landscape.

By addressing the specific needs and constraints of EFL educators in Indonesia, this chapter offers a framework for navigating the complex interplay between AI, digital literacy, and pedagogy. Drawing comparisons with other countries, such as Vietnam and the Philippines, it highlights best practices and contextual adaptations. Ultimately, it aspires to contribute to the broader discourse on preparing future citizens to thrive in an AI-driven world.

UNDERSTANDING DIGITAL LITERACY IN THE CONTEXT OF AI FOR EFL TEACHERS

In the rapidly evolving digital era, literacy transcends basic technical proficiency, encompassing a nuanced understanding of complex technologies, algorithms, and their ethical implications, particularly within educational contexts such as EFL instruction. For EFL teachers, this transformation presents both significant opportunities and formidable challenges as they adapt their pedagogical practices to integrate advanced technologies. With the advent of AI, the landscape of teaching and learning has been irrevocably altered. Educators are now required not only to harness AI for personalized learning but also to critically engage with its ethical dimensions, such as data privacy, algorithmic bias, and equitable access. This shift demands a profound rethinking of digital literacy, one that includes operational skills, the ability to analyze algorithms, and leveraging data to enhance language learning. Consequently, the next generation of EFL educators must navigate these complexities, equipping students to thrive in a technologically advanced and interconnected world.

The Evolution of Digital Literacy: From Basic Skills to AI Proficiency

Digital literacy has undergone a significant transformation, evolving from foundational technical skills to the multifaceted competencies required in an era increasingly dominated by AI. Initially, digital literacy referred to basic abilities such as using personal computers, navigating the internet, and operating office software. Over time, as technological advancements became more sophisticated, the scope of digital literacy has expanded to encompass understanding algorithms, machine learning, data analysis, and the ethical considerations that arise from technology use (Yuan et al., 2024).

For EFL teachers, this evolution is particularly transformative. Traditional classroom settings once employed digital tools primarily as supplementary aids to enhance existing teaching methods. However, the integration of AI has fundamentally redefined these practices. Educators are now expected to facilitate language acquisition while guiding students in critically engaging with AI-driven tools, such as adaptive learning platforms and automated assessment systems. Adaptive learning platforms, for instance, analyze student performance to identify strengths and weaknesses, tailoring instruction to individual needs. Similarly, AI-powered speech recognition tools provide immediate feedback on pronunciation, enabling students to practice autonomously and build confidence.

Despite these advancements, the shift toward AI in education presents challenges. Teachers must remain vigilant about the limitations of AI, including risks such as dehumanizing the learning experience and fostering overreliance on automated systems. The role of EFL educators extends beyond technological facilitation to preserving the humanistic and relational elements of teaching. By maintaining this balance, educators can ensure that AI enriches, rather than replaces, the cultural and interpersonal dimensions of pedagogy.

Equally critical are the ethical and social implications of digital literacy in the AI era. Teachers must address issues such as data privacy, algorithmic bias, and disparities in access to AI resources. For example, while urban students may benefit from cutting-edge technologies, rural students often face infrastructural challenges that exacerbate educational inequities. Addressing these challenges requires a holistic approach to digital literacy, one that integrates technical expertise with ethical awareness and a commitment to inclusivity.

Global Comparisons: Lessons From Vietnam and the Philippines

While Indonesia faces unique challenges in integrating AI into education, neighbouring countries like Vietnam and the Philippines offer valuable lessons through their innovative approaches to similar challenges. Vietnam, for example, has addressed rural connectivity issues by implementing mobile-based AI tools, ensuring broader access to technology-driven resources even in remote areas (Nguyen et al., 2022). Meanwhile, the Philippines has focused on comprehensive teacher training programs, equipping educators with the technical and pedagogical skills needed for effective AI adoption. These diverse strategies highlight the potential for tailored interventions to overcome educational disparities in different contexts.

The Philippines' deployment of AI tools in under-resourced schools underscores the critical role of private-sector partnerships in bridging infrastructural gaps. These collaborations have facilitated access to affordable devices and digital resources, enabling educators to implement AI-driven solutions even in the most challenging contexts (Santiago et al., 2023). Similarly, Vietnam's focus on localized teacher training emphasizes the importance of professional development tailored to specific cultural and regional needs. By aligning teacher training with the demands of their unique educational environments, Vietnam has successfully integrated AI technologies while maintaining pedagogical relevance (Quy et al., 2023). Together, these strategies demonstrate how context-sensitive solutions can effectively address educational inequities.

These examples offer valuable insights for Indonesia. By adopting Vietnam's strategies for mobile-based AI deployment and the Philippines' emphasis on teacher training, Indonesian policymakers and educators can design targeted interventions to address regional disparities. Such initiatives would position AI as a tool for inclusivity and innovation, ensuring that students across diverse contexts can benefit from its transformative potential.

In summary, advancing digital literacy in the era of AI requires a nuanced approach that balances opportunities with challenges. For EFL teachers, this involves mastering technical proficiencies, addressing ethical considerations, and fostering inclusive practices. By drawing on global examples and prioritizing ethical and pedagogical balance, educators can empower students to navigate a technologically advanced world with confidence. Ultimately, this approach ensures that AI-driven digital literacy becomes a foundation for equitable and innovative education in the 21st century.

CHALLENGES FACING INDONESIAN EFL TEACHERS IN THE AGE OF AI

The integration of AI into EFL education in Indonesia presents significant opportunities alongside considerable challenges. These challenges are shaped by the country's diverse socio-economic landscape, unequal access to technology, and varied levels of teacher readiness. Addressing these issues requires a comprehensive, context-sensitive approach to ensure that AI becomes a tool for equitable and transformative education rather than exacerbating existing disparities.

The Digital Divide: Urban-Rural Disparities

One of the most pressing challenges is the digital divide between urban and rural areas. While urban schools often benefit from advanced infrastructure, high-speed internet, and access to AI-driven educational tools, many rural schools face significant barriers such as limited connectivity, outdated equipment, and financial constraints. This divide perpetuates educational inequities, hindering AI adoption and its potential to enhance learning outcomes.

For instance, schools in Jakarta and Surabaya have successfully implemented AI platforms that support personalized language learning. In contrast, schools in remote provinces like Papua and Sulawesi struggle to access even basic digital tools. This disparity highlights the urgent need for targeted interventions. Government initiatives must prioritize nationwide infrastructure development, including broadband expansion and mobile-based solutions tailored for rural settings. Additionally, public-private partnerships can play a pivotal role in providing affordable devices, subsidized internet access, and offline-capable AI tools. By addressing these infrastructural gaps, stakeholders can create a more inclusive educational ecosystem.

Bridging the Technical Competency Gap

Another critical challenge is the gap in technical competencies among EFL teachers. Many educators, particularly those with decades of experience, lack the training and confidence needed to integrate AI into their teaching practices. This issue is compounded by the rapid pace of technological advancement, which can leave teachers feeling overwhelmed and unprepared. Without comprehensive professional development, teachers may use AI superficially, limiting its transformative potential in the classroom.

Effective training programs must address these gaps by focusing on three key areas. First, teachers should develop technical proficiency to operate AI tools effectively, analyze student data, and troubleshoot common technological issues. Second, ethical literacy should be emphasized to raise awareness about data privacy, algorithmic bias, and responsible AI usage. Third, pedagogical innovation must be fostered to help teachers balance AI-driven insights with human-centered teaching approaches. Evidence from the Philippines demonstrates the transformative potential of such initiatives. Workshops on AI integration have significantly improved teacher confidence and student engagement, underscoring the value of continuous learning opportunities for educators.

Cultural and Pedagogical Challenges

Cultural and pedagogical norms in Indonesia add complexity to AI integration. Traditional teaching methods, which emphasize rote memorization and teacher-centered instruction, often conflict with the collaborative and student-centered approaches enabled by AI. Additionally, resistance from parents and community members, who may perceive AI as a threat to traditional educational values, further complicates adoption efforts.

Overcoming these challenges requires a paradigm shift that positions AI as a complementary tool rather than a replacement for traditional methods. Schools can foster this shift through community engagement programs that educate stakeholders about the benefits of AI while addressing concerns about cultural preservation. Integrating AI tools into existing pedagogical frameworks while maintaining the humanistic elements of education can also help bridge this gap. For example, AI can be used to automate administrative tasks, freeing teachers to focus on creative and interpersonal aspects of teaching. Such blended approaches ensure that technology enhances, rather than replaces, the core principles of education.

Lessons from Regional Initiatives

Regional case studies provide valuable insights into overcoming these challenges. A pilot program in West Java introduced AI-powered language learning tools in secondary schools, achieving notable improvements in student performance and engagement. The program's success was attributed to a holistic approach that included teacher training, community involvement, and infrastructure upgrades. This comprehensive strategy ensured that all stakeholders were prepared and aligned in their efforts.

In contrast, a similar initiative in rural Kalimantan faced setbacks due to inadequate internet access and limited teacher participation. These contrasting outcomes underscore the importance of addressing foundational barriers before implementing advanced technologies. For programs in rural areas, ensuring basic infrastructure and fostering teacher buy-in are critical prerequisites for success.

Building a Future-Ready Educational Ecosystem

Despite these challenges, Indonesian EFL teachers have the potential to lead the way in AI integration, provided they receive adequate support and resources. Several key strategies can help build a future-ready educational ecosystem. First, incentivizing teacher participation in digital literacy workshops and AI training programs through financial and professional rewards can drive engagement. Second, fostering collaboration among educators, technologists, and policymakers can lead to innovative, context-appropriate solutions. Third, embedding AI literacy into teacher training curricula will ensure long-term readiness and capacity building. Finally, cultivating a culture of experimentation and creativity in schools will empower teachers to explore new ways of integrating AI into their classrooms.

By addressing these challenges and capitalizing on emerging opportunities, Indonesia can harness AI to transform its EFL education landscape. This requires a commitment to equity, inclusivity, and innovation, ensuring that all teachers and students are equipped to thrive in an increasingly digital world.

THE ROLE OF AI IN TRANSFORMING EFL EDUCATIONAL PRACTICES

The transformative impact of AI on EFL education is undeniably profound, reshaping both pedagogical approaches and the role of educators. As AI technologies continue to evolve, they offer unprecedented opportunities for enhancing language acquisition through more personalized, efficient, and adaptive learning experiences. This section explores the multifaceted ways in which AI is revolutionizing EFL practices, focusing on its potential to cater to the diverse needs of learners and optimize teaching methodologies. Through the lens of AI-driven tools and platforms, we will examine how the educational landscape is being redefined, offering a glimpse into the future of language instruction where human and machine intelligence synergize to foster more effective learning environments.

AI as a Personalized Learning Tool

The integration of AI into EFL education has revolutionized traditional teaching paradigms, introducing unprecedented opportunities for personalization. AI has the capability to tailor learning experiences to individual students' needs, fostering higher engagement and improving educational outcomes. Unlike conventional methods that often apply a uniform approach to teaching, AI-powered tools analyze student performance, adapt content delivery, and provide real-time feedback, offering a more responsive and effective learning process.

AI technologies such as adaptive learning platforms and virtual assistants are powerful tools in this transformation. Platforms like Twee, Duolingo and Rosetta Stone utilize sophisticated algorithms to assess a student's proficiency level and adjust learning materials accordingly. These systems dynamically calibrate the difficulty of exercises based on a learner's progress, ensuring challenges remain appropriately scaled to their abilities. Similarly, AI-powered virtual assistants, such as

ChatGPT or Grammarly, enable students to practice conversational English or refine their writing through instant, context-aware feedback. These interactions not only improve linguistic skills but also build students' confidence in their language use.

A significant advancement in the use of AI for personalization is found in speech recognition technology. Tools such as Google Speech-to-Text and ELSA Speak analyze pronunciation with precision, offering corrective feedback to help students achieve fluency and accuracy (Al-Shallakh, 2024). These applications are invaluable in regions where access to native speakers is limited, bridging the gap between classroom learning and practical language application. By simulating interactions with native-like accuracy, AI creates an environment where learners can practice and refine their skills effectively (Tolba et al., 2024).

The benefits of personalized learning through AI are extensive, particularly in addressing the diverse needs of students in EFL classrooms. Advanced learners benefit from AI tools that introduce complex linguistic structures and idiomatic expressions, keeping them engaged and challenged. On the other hand, students who struggle with language acquisition can access scaffolded support, with complex tasks broken into smaller, more manageable steps. This flexibility makes AI a highly inclusive solution, catering to learners with varying levels of proficiency, cognitive abilities, and learning styles.

AI-driven personalization is especially transformative in under-resourced areas, where access to qualified EFL teachers and modern educational resources is often limited. In many rural or economically disadvantaged regions, students lack the infrastructure to receive high-quality education. AI tools address these disparities by delivering standardized, high-quality instruction that is accessible anytime and anywhere (Gatenby, 2023). Mobile-based AI platforms, for instance, allow students in remote areas to engage in interactive learning activities even without formal classroom setups. Such tools require minimal infrastructure, often relying only on basic smartphones and internet access, making them a cost-effective and scalable solution for underserved communities.

Despite these advantages, the widespread adoption of AI in personalized learning raises significant concerns about the potential dehumanization of education. Language learning is fundamentally a social and cultural activity, deeply rooted in human interaction. Over-reliance on AI tools risks reducing education to a transactional process, where students engage more with algorithms than with peers or educators (Vinothkumar & Karunamurthy, 2023). This shift could undermine the relational and empathetic dimensions of teaching, which are critical for fostering motivation, creativity, and socio-emotional development.

Striking a balance between technology-driven personalization and the humanistic aspect of teaching is essential. AI should be seen as a complement to, rather than a replacement for, the teacher's role. While AI excels at automating repetitive tasks and generating data-driven insights, it cannot replicate the nuanced, empathetic, and culturally aware contributions of human educators. Teachers play an irreplaceable role in fostering motivation, building rapport, and addressing the unique socio-emotional needs of their students. For example, a teacher's ability to encourage a hesitant student to participate or to adapt instruction based on the mood and dynamics of a classroom remains beyond the capabilities of AI.

To maximize the potential of AI while preserving these humanistic elements, educators must thoughtfully integrate technology into their practices. Teachers can use AI-generated insights to pinpoint areas where students are struggling and then design collaborative or project-based activities to address these gaps. Such approaches not only leverage the strengths of AI but also foster meaningful human interactions, ensuring that the learning process remains holistic. By maintaining their role as facilitators of rich, interactive educational experiences, educators ensure that the benefits of AI are harnessed without compromising the essential relational aspects of teaching.

Redefining the Role of EFL Teachers in the AI Era

The integration of AI into EFL education has fundamentally reshaped the traditional roles of teachers, demanding a reevaluation of their responsibilities and approaches. Educators, once primarily seen as dispensers of knowledge, now find their roles shifting towards mentorship, facilitation, and the integration of technology within the learning process (Idham et al., 2024). This transformation is driven by AI's capacity to automate routine tasks, such as grading, attendance tracking, and lesson planning, which allows teachers to dedicate more time to higher-order educational activities that foster critical thinking, creativity, and deep learning.

In classrooms where AI tools are implemented, teachers are no longer required to spend hours manually correcting grammar errors or managing administrative tasks. Instead, they can focus on facilitating meaningful discussions about language usage, cultural contexts, and communication strategies. For instance, an AI system might provide students with immediate feedback on their written work, identifying grammatical errors and suggesting improvements. While the technology efficiently handles such tasks, the teacher's role shifts to helping students interpret this feedback within broader language-learning goals, ensuring it aligns with contextual and cultural nuances.

This transformation also places teachers at the forefront of ethical guidance in the use of AI. In an era where technology increasingly mediates educational experiences, teachers have a responsibility to educate students about responsible AI use. This includes fostering awareness about potential biases embedded in algorithms, teaching students to critically evaluate AI-generated content, and emphasizing the importance of protecting personal data. By addressing these ethical dimensions, teachers prepare students not only for academic success but also for the broader societal implications of AI, equipping them to navigate an increasingly digital and interconnected world.

Adapting to this dual role as educators and technology integrators requires deliberate strategies and a mindset shift among EFL teachers. Continuous professional development is essential in equipping teachers with both the technical skills to operate AI tools and the pedagogical expertise to integrate them effectively (Chiu et al., 2023). Training programs should go beyond basic technical instruction, focusing on the creative and critical use of AI in enhancing educational outcomes. For example, workshops and online courses can introduce teachers to the latest advancements in AI-powered learning platforms while providing opportunities to practice designing lesson plans that incorporate these tools.

Collaboration among educators also plays a critical role in facilitating this transition. Professional learning communities, both local and global, offer valuable platforms for teachers to exchange ideas, discuss case studies, and collectively address challenges. Through such collaborative networks, teachers can share insights into how AI tools can be adapted to meet diverse classroom needs, develop innovative strategies for implementation, and learn from each other's experiences. This spirit of collective problem-solving fosters a culture of innovation and resilience, empowering teachers to embrace the possibilities of AI with confidence.

Encouraging innovation and experimentation is another crucial element of this transformation. Teachers should be supported in exploring creative ways to integrate AI into their teaching practices, whether through gamified learning experiences, virtual reality simulations, or collaborative projects that leverage AI tools. For instance, an educator might use an AI-powered platform to create an interactive language-learning game that engages students while reinforcing vocabulary and grammar. Such initiatives not only enhance student motivation but also position teachers as active contributors to the evolving landscape of AI-enabled education.

While the opportunities presented by AI are significant, the transition also poses psychological and professional challenges for many educators. Teachers may experience anxiety or resistance when confronted with rapidly changing technologies, fearing that their roles may become obsolete or questioning their ability to adapt. This is particularly true for veteran educators who may lack familiarity with digital tools or feel overwhelmed by the steep learning curve associated with AI. Without adequate support, such concerns can lead to frustration, disengagement, or reluctance to adopt new technologies.

Institutional support is critical in addressing these challenges. Schools and education policymakers must prioritize providing resources, mentoring programs, and ongoing training to build teachers' confidence and competence. This support should extend beyond technical training to include psychological encouragement, fostering a culture that values teachers' efforts and acknowledges their struggles during this period of transition (Zheng et al., 2024). Recognizing and celebrating successes, even small ones, can help alleviate feelings of isolation or inadequacy and motivate educators to continue exploring the potential of AI.

Another challenge lies in balancing the technological and human elements of teaching. While AI can streamline many aspects of education, it cannot replace the empathy, intuition, and relational skills that teachers bring to the classroom. Maintaining this balance requires intentional decision-making about when and how to deploy AI tools. Teachers must critically evaluate whether a task is better suited to technology or to human intervention, ensuring that their professional identity as educators remains central to the learning process. For example, while an AI system might efficiently assess students' written work, a teacher's personal feedback can provide deeper insights into the student's thought processes, offering encouragement and guidance that technology cannot replicate.

The integration of AI into EFL education has opened new pathways for personalized learning and transformative teaching practices. As teachers navigate this evolving landscape, their ability to embrace technology while preserving the humanistic core of education will determine the success of AI in enhancing learning outcomes. By fostering ethical awareness, encouraging collaboration, and addressing psychological and professional challenges, educators can harness the potential of AI to create a balanced and inclusive educational environment. This process requires strategic training, institutional support, and a commitment to innovation, ensuring that EFL teachers remain at the heart of an educational system that values both technological advancement and human connection.

ETHICAL CONSIDERATIONS IN AI AND DIGITAL LITERACY EDUCATION FOR EFL TEACHERS

As AI integration into EFL education accelerates, addressing the ethical implications of its deployment is critical to ensuring effective and equitable learning environments. These considerations extend beyond technical issues to include privacy, fairness, and inclusivity, which have far-reaching implications for the success and equity of AI-driven education. EFL educators must not only leverage AI tools to enhance language acquisition but also critically evaluate their ethical ramifications. This section examines key ethical challenges, focusing on privacy and data governance, algorithmic bias, and the shared responsibilities of educators and policymakers in fostering equitable and effective learning ecosystems.

Privacy and Data Governance

Privacy and data governance are fundamental to the ethical use of AI in EFL education. To provide personalized learning experiences, AI tools collect extensive data, including performance metrics, engagement patterns, and even audio recordings. While such data enhances the precision and adaptability of AI systems, it also introduces significant risks, such as data breaches, unauthorized access, and misuse of sensitive information. These challenges are especially critical in educational contexts, where students, particularly younger learners, are among the most vulnerable.

In Indonesia, the lack of comprehensive data protection regulations exacerbates these concerns. Unlike the European Union, which enforces stringent privacy measures through the General Data Protection Regulation (GDPR), Indonesia lacks robust frameworks to safeguard personal data in educational settings. This regulatory gap undermines public trust in AI technologies, potentially deterring their adoption by educators, students, and parents (Williams, 2023; Zhou, 2024).

Educators' Role in Ensuring Data Governance

Educators play a critical role in addressing privacy concerns and promoting ethical data governance within educational settings. To build trust and transparency, they must clearly communicate how data is collected, stored, and used, ensuring that students and their families understand the purposes behind data collection and the measures implemented to protect their privacy. By providing this information, educators empower families to make informed decisions regarding the use of AI tools in learning environments. Transparent communication fosters confidence in the ethical use of AI, making it an integral part of effective teaching practices.

In addition to transparency, educators should implement stringent data protection measures to safeguard sensitive student information. This includes anonymizing data to prevent identification, limiting collection to metrics essential for learning, and regularly reviewing the privacy policies of AI tools to ensure they adhere to ethical standards. Beyond classroom practices, educators must also advocate for institutional policies that align with international best practices in data governance. By supporting robust frameworks at the school or district level, educators contribute to a secure and trustworthy AI ecosystem that upholds the rights and safety of all learners.

Policymakers' Responsibility

Policymakers play a vital role in establishing robust data governance standards to ensure the ethical use of AI in education. Adapting global frameworks such as the GDPR to fit Indonesia's unique educational context is essential for creating a secure and trustworthy environment for AI integration. These localized standards should prioritize comprehensive privacy protections tailored to address the specific challenges faced by schools and learners. By doing so, policymakers can create a regulatory framework that balances innovation with the safeguarding of sensitive data.

To further strengthen data governance, policymakers must mandate secure practices such as encryption, data minimization, and secure storage protocols to reduce the risk of breaches. Collaboration with AI developers is equally important to embed privacy-by-design principles into educational tools, ensuring that data protection measures are integrated from the outset. By prioritizing privacy and working closely with developers and educators, policymakers can rebuild public trust in AI technologies and encourage their responsible adoption in classrooms. This trust is a cornerstone for the successful and ethical integration of AI in education, promoting equitable learning opportunities for all students.

Algorithmic Bias and Its Impact on Learning Outcomes

Algorithmic bias is a significant challenge in the application of AI for EFL education. AI systems rely on large datasets for training, and the quality and diversity of these datasets play a crucial role in determining their accuracy and fairness. When biases are embedded in the training data, the outcomes can disproportionately disadvantage students from underrepresented linguistic and cultural backgrounds, exacerbating existing educational inequities (Mekheimer, 2023). Speech recognition technologies, for example, often struggle to accurately interpret non-native accents, penalizing students for their regional or cultural identities rather than their linguistic proficiency. Similarly, automated writing assessment tools may favour Western grammatical structures and rhetorical styles, marginalizing non-Western expressions and perspectives. These biases compromise the quality of feedback, negatively impacting students' confidence and motivation.

The consequences of algorithmic bias extend beyond individual learning experiences. Persistent exposure to biased systems reinforces systemic inequalities, particularly for students in rural or marginalized communities, who may receive lower-quality feedback. This limitation restricts their access to equitable learning opportunities and perpetuates disparities in educational outcomes. Addressing algorithmic bias requires a comprehensive, multi-stakeholder approach. Educators must critically evaluate AI-generated feedback to identify and mitigate patterns of bias, while fostering students' digital literacy to help them engage critically with AI tools. Developers must diversify datasets to reflect linguistic and cultural variety, ensuring inclusivity in AI functionalities. Policymakers, on the other hand, should implement rigorous standards for algorithmic fairness and conduct regular audits to rectify biases before they negatively affect students' learning experiences. Through these collective efforts, algorithmic bias can be mitigated, paving the way for a more equitable application of AI in education.

Empowering Teachers Through Professional Development

Professional development programs are critical for empowering educators to navigate and address algorithmic bias effectively in their teaching practices. These programs should begin by helping teachers understand how algorithmic bias arises in AI systems, emphasizing its connection to the quality and diversity of training data. By fostering this foundational knowledge, educators can become more aware of the subtle ways biases manifest in AI-generated outputs, enabling them to identify and address these issues proactively in the classroom.

In addition to raising awareness, professional development initiatives should equip educators with practical strategies for mitigating bias in classroom applications of AI. For example, teachers can be trained to critically evaluate AI-generated feedback, ensuring that it aligns with the diverse linguistic and cultural contexts of their students. They can also learn to integrate supplementary tools and techniques to counterbalance biases, such as providing personalized feedback or adapting instructional methods to accommodate students from underrepresented groups. These strategies not only enhance the inclusivity of AI tools but also support the broader goal of equitable education.

Lastly, professional development programs should promote equitable teaching practices that responsibly leverage AI tools to maximize their benefits while minimizing potential harm. By encouraging collaboration among educators, developers, and policymakers, these initiatives can create a shared understanding of ethical AI use in education. Workshops and training sessions that prioritize inclusivity, fairness, and transparency will ensure that educators are well-prepared to foster a learning environment where all students, regardless of their backgrounds, can thrive. Through these efforts, professional development becomes a powerful means of addressing algorithmic bias and promoting ethical AI integration in education.

Fostering Ethical and Inclusive Learning Ecosystems

Addressing the ethical challenges of AI integration in EFL education is not only a moral imperative but also a strategic necessity for optimizing its transformative potential. Prioritizing privacy, data governance, and algorithmic fairness ensures that AI tools foster an inclusive, trustworthy, and responsive learning environment. Collaborative efforts between educators, policymakers, and developers are key to creating an AI ecosystem that supports diverse student needs and promotes equity in education.

By equipping teachers with the knowledge and skills to navigate these ethical complexities, the EFL classroom can become a space where all learners thrive, irrespective of their linguistic or cultural backgrounds. Through thoughtful interventions and collective commitment, AI has the potential to transform education into a more equitable and effective domain for future generations.

EFL TEACHERS' PRACTICES AND PERCEPTIONS OF AI INTEGRATION

The integration of AI into EFL classrooms has sparked a profound shift in pedagogical practices, offering both opportunities and challenges for educators. As the educational landscape evolves, EFL teachers' practices and perceptions of AI have become critical in understanding how these technologies are shaping language instruction. This section explores the diverse responses of EFL teachers to AI integration, examining the positive and negative perceptions that influence their adoption of AI tools. By critically analyzing these perspectives, we can better understand the complex interplay between innovation and tradition in language teaching, highlighting the potential of AI to enhance educational outcomes while addressing concerns related to its ethical and practical implications.

Positive Perceptions of AI in EFL Classrooms

The integration of AI into EFL classrooms has been widely lauded for its potential to enhance teaching efficiency, foster personalized learning, and address diverse student needs. Many EFL teachers perceive AI as a transformative force that simplifies instructional tasks, provides data-driven insights, and improves student engagement. Teachers who have embraced AI in their practices frequently highlight its ability to alleviate administrative burdens, such as grading and attendance tracking, allowing them to focus on more meaningful instructional activities. For example, AI tools can automate repetitive tasks, freeing teachers to design interactive lessons and mentor students more effectively, which ultimately leads to enriched educational experiences.

AI's role in personalizing learning experiences is particularly noteworthy. Through adaptive learning platforms, students receive content tailored to their proficiency levels and learning paces. For instance, tools like Duolingo and Grammarly use sophisticated algorithms to analyze a student's strengths and weaknesses, delivering exercises that match their individual needs. These systems dynamically adjust the difficulty of lessons, ensuring students are neither overwhelmed nor under-challenged.

Teachers report that such tools enable them to provide differentiated instruction without overwhelming workloads. Furthermore, these platforms facilitate self-paced learning, empowering students to take greater ownership of their educational journeys. This autonomy not only enhances motivation but also fosters lifelong learning habits that are crucial in an increasingly digital and interconnected world.

Success stories from Indonesian EFL teachers illustrate the profound impact of AI integration. In urban schools where technological infrastructure is more robust, educators have effectively utilized AI tools to support diverse classroom needs. One such example is the implementation of speech recognition software in secondary schools in Jakarta, where students practiced pronunciation using AI-driven feedback systems (Hasan et al., 2020). Teachers observed significant improvements in students' speaking skills and noted increased confidence in their verbal communication. Similarly, educators in Surabaya have leveraged AI-powered assessment tools to automate essay grading, providing students with immediate and constructive feedback (Rahman & Rahmawati, 2021). These initiatives underscore the potential of AI to enhance both teaching and learning experiences. However, the success of these cases was also influenced by external factors, such as teacher training programs and institutional support, emphasizing the importance of a comprehensive approach to AI adoption.

Beyond urban areas, AI's scalability offers promising opportunities for addressing educational disparities in rural regions. Mobile-based AI platforms, which require minimal infrastructure, have been adopted in remote areas of Indonesia, enabling students to access quality language education despite geographical barriers. Teachers in these settings have expressed optimism about AI's ability to bridge the digital divide, citing its potential to democratize education. For instance, in rural Sumatra, students using AI-powered language apps have demonstrated marked improvements in vocabulary acquisition, showcasing the accessibility and adaptability of such tools. While challenges persist, such as inconsistent internet connectivity and limited teacher training, these success stories demonstrate the scalability of AI-based practices when supported by targeted interventions, including infrastructural investments and localized professional development programs.

Despite these advantages, the successful adoption of AI in Indonesian EFL classrooms often depends on the readiness and willingness of educators to embrace new technologies. Teachers who perceive AI as a complementary tool rather than a replacement for traditional methods tend to achieve better outcomes. By viewing AI as an enabler of innovative pedagogy, they are more likely to integrate it into their practices in ways that enhance, rather than disrupt, the learning experience. For example, rather than relying solely on AI for feedback, teachers can combine AI-generated insights with their own contextualized input, creating a more balanced and effective learning environment.

The adoption of AI in EFL classrooms has also been recognized for its capacity to foster inclusivity and cater to diverse learner profiles. Students with learning disabilities, for example, can benefit significantly from AI tools that provide customized support tailored to their unique challenges. For instance, text-to-speech and speech-to-text applications enable students with dyslexia or other language-processing disorders to engage with materials in ways that suit their strengths. Similarly, AI-powered tools that offer visual aids or gamified learning modules can motivate students who may struggle with traditional, text-heavy approaches. Teachers have noted that these tools not only improve accessibility but also create a more equitable learning environment, allowing all students to participate fully and confidently in the language acquisition process. This inclusivity is particularly vital in fostering a sense of belonging among students, which has been shown to correlate with higher academic achievement and overall well-being.

Furthermore, AI's ability to analyze large datasets in real-time offers teachers unprecedented insights into classroom dynamics and individual student progress. By identifying patterns in students' learning behaviors, AI systems can highlight areas where intervention is needed, enabling educators to provide targeted support. For example, if an AI tool detects a recurring issue with verb conjugation among a subset of students, the teacher can design a focused lesson to address this gap. Such data-driven decision-making not only improves learning outcomes but also enhances teachers' ability to reflect on and refine their instructional strategies. This integration of AI into formative assessment processes empowers teachers to make evidence-based adjustments to their practices, ensuring that every student's learning journey is as effective and personalized as possible.

In addition to enhancing assessments, AI has proven valuable in supporting collaborative learning. Tools like AI-powered discussion platforms and virtual collaborative workspaces enable students to work together on language projects, fostering peer interaction and communication. Teachers have reported that these tools encourage active participation, particularly among shy or hesitant students who might otherwise be reluctant to engage in traditional classroom discussions (Yoon & Lee, 2023). By facilitating such interactions, AI strengthens not only language skills but also essential soft skills like teamwork and problem-solving.

Finally, the versatility of AI enables teachers to address emerging challenges and adapt to evolving educational needs. For instance, during the COVID-19 pandemic, AI-powered platforms played a pivotal role in maintaining continuity in EFL instruction through virtual learning environments. Teachers leveraged AI to track student progress, deliver engaging content, and maintain regular communication despite the physical constraints of remote learning. This adaptability highlights the resilience and relevance of AI in navigating complex and unpredictable educational landscapes.

Negative Perceptions and Concerns About AI

The adoption of AI in EFL education, while promising, has been met with considerable skepticism and resistance from many educators. This resistance is driven by concerns regarding the cultural, professional, and practical ramifications of integrating AI into teaching practices. These apprehensions, rooted in both personal and systemic factors, underscore the complexity of incorporating technology into education. It is essential to address these concerns comprehensively to ensure AI's effective integration into the EFL classroom.

A primary concern among EFL educators is the potential erosion of the humanistic element in teaching. Language learning is intrinsically social and cultural, fostering interpersonal interactions that promote empathy, communication, and cultural exchange (Nassaji & Tian, 2022). Teachers worry that excessive reliance on AI tools may transform the classroom into a transactional environment dominated by algorithms, reducing opportunities for authentic human connection. For instance, while AI can provide immediate feedback on grammar and pronunciation, it lacks the ability to grasp cultural and emotional nuances that are essential for meaningful communication. This limitation raises questions about whether AI can fully replicate the holistic learning experiences that human educators facilitate, particularly in fostering students' interpersonal skills and cultural awareness.

In addition to cultural concerns, the technical challenges associated with AI integration often hinder its adoption, particularly in resource-constrained contexts. Many educators, especially those in rural or underserved areas, feel overwhelmed by the technical demands of AI tools, which require a steep learning curve. Teachers may lack the technical skills and confidence needed to navigate these tools effectively, leading to frustration and reluctance to adopt AI. Furthermore, inadequate infrastructure, such as unreliable internet connectivity and outdated devices, exacerbates these challenges. In such contexts, teachers often find themselves unable to fully capitalize on AI's potential, exacerbating the gap between technologically advantaged and disadvantaged educational institutions.

Professional scepticism also plays a significant role in shaping teachers' perceptions of AI. Many educators view AI as a potential threat to their professional autonomy and job security, particularly as AI tools automate tasks that have traditionally been part of their role. This fear is particularly prevalent among veteran teachers who have built their careers on traditional pedagogical methods. For these educators, AI's ability to provide immediate feedback or streamline administrative tasks may seem to encroach upon their expertise, leading to resistance. Without adequate support and reassurance, these educators may perceive AI as a disruptive force, rather than an opportunity for innovation and professional growth.

Another critical concern lies in the ethical dilemmas posed by AI systems that monitor and assess students' performance and behavior. Teachers worry about the implications of surveillance-driven AI, which tracks students' activities without clear ethical boundaries. While these systems aim to provide actionable insights, they can inadvertently create a climate of constant surveillance, discouraging students from taking risks in their language use for fear of penalization. Moreover, educators question the ethicality of AI algorithms that may perpetuate biases or make decisions based on incomplete or contextually irrelevant data, potentially undermining student progress and reinforcing inequalities.

Long-term dependence on AI tools for core instructional and decision-making processes is another pressing issue. While AI offers the potential for efficiency and enhancement, over-reliance on these systems could undermine essential teaching skills such as creative problem-solving, personalized mentorship, and the ability to adapt to classroom challenges. Educators fear that as AI systems assume greater responsibility in teaching, their professional expertise and judgment may be undervalued or ignored. This dependency on AI could reduce education to a mechanistic process focused on efficiency rather than fostering meaningful student-teacher relationships and promoting deeper learning.

To mitigate these concerns, a multifaceted approach is necessary, focusing on targeted support, professional development, and community engagement. Teachers must receive comprehensive training that not only builds technical competence but also emphasizes how AI can enhance (rather than replace) their role. Professional development programs should highlight how AI tools can automate routine tasks such as grading, allowing teachers to devote more time to higher-order instructional activities, including fostering critical thinking, creativity, and cultural awareness. This approach can help educators see AI as a tool to complement their work rather than a threat to their professional identity.

Equally important is the engagement of the broader educational community, including parents, administrators, and local stakeholders, in discussions about AI integration. Open forums and informational sessions can help demystify AI, addressing misconceptions and clarifying its ethical implications. By fostering a collaborative environment, schools can build trust and create a shared vision for responsible and equitable AI adoption. This collaborative approach not only alleviates cultural scepticism but also ensures that AI adoption aligns with the community's values and needs, ensuring a more inclusive and ethically grounded integration.

Finally, AI tool design and implementation must incorporate the perspectives of educators to ensure their relevance and effectiveness. Teachers' insights into classroom dynamics, cultural contexts, and student needs are crucial for creating AI systems that are user-friendly, pedagogically sound, and culturally sensitive. Collaborative efforts between AI developers, educators, and policymakers can lead to the creation of AI systems that serve as effective extensions of the teacher's role rather than substitutes. For example, involving educators in developing speech recognition tools can lead to systems that accommodate diverse accents and linguistic nuances, enhancing their usefulness for EFL learners. Such inclusive design ensures that AI tools align with the specific needs of EFL classrooms while reinforcing the teacher's central role in the learning process.

Strategies for Effective AI Integration in EFL Teaching

A structured, thoughtful, and human-centred approach is essential to maximize the potential of AI in EFL education. Effective integration must prioritize collaboration, critical thinking, and ethical engagement, ensuring that AI enhances rather than disrupts the pedagogical core of teaching. This deliberate strategy not only optimizes AI's transformative possibilities but also safeguards the humanistic values vital to effective education. By thoughtfully merging technological innovation with traditional teaching principles, educators can create a harmonious blend that empowers both students and teachers.

One of the most effective ways to integrate AI into EFL teaching is through project-based learning. Educators can foster dynamic and immersive learning environments by designing real-world, collaborative projects that utilize AI tools. For instance, students can use AI-powered translation software to create bilingual magazines or cross-cultural digital presentations. These projects provide meaningful contexts for students to practice language skills while also encouraging teamwork and creativity (Yoon & Lee, 2023). Such activities deepen cultural understanding and inspire students to engage with the material critically, transforming AI into a supportive tool that enriches the learning experience rather than overshadowing traditional teaching methods.

In addition to enhancing collaboration, AI can play a pivotal role in developing students' critical thinking and analytical skills. Tools such as AI-assisted writing platforms and virtual debate systems challenge students to evaluate, refine, and articulate their ideas more effectively. For example, students might generate initial arguments with AI tools and refine their reasoning through peer discussions and teacher-guided revisions. This iterative process fosters critical engagement with AI-generated content, teaching students to assess its validity while integrating their insights. Such practices strengthen their linguistic and cognitive skills and prepare them for the complexities of communication and decision-making in a digital and AI-driven world.

The role of teachers in AI integration extends beyond classroom application to active participation in the design and refinement of AI tools. Educators are uniquely positioned to shape AI technologies with their deep understanding of student needs, classroom dynamics, and cultural contexts. Collaborations between teachers and developers can result in AI tools that are culturally sensitive, pedagogically aligned, and inclusive, such as speech recognition systems designed for diverse accents or writing evaluation tools that respect non-Western rhetorical traditions. Institutional partnerships among educators, policymakers, and AI developers are crucial to fostering innovation while addressing ethical and practical challenges, ensuring that AI remains a meaningful and adaptable resource.

For successful integration, it is vital to invest in infrastructure and professional development. Reliable internet connectivity, modern devices, and intuitive platforms are foundational to ensuring that AI tools are accessible and functional across diverse educational contexts. At the same time, professional development programs must equip teachers with not only technical skills but also strategies to balance AI's capabilities with human-centered pedagogical practices. These programs should emphasize creativity, ethical considerations, and adaptability, complemented by ongoing technical support and peer networks. This dual focus on infrastructure and teacher capacity ensures that AI adoption is both sustainable and effective.

Reflective practices are equally critical in evaluating the impact of AI on teaching and learning. Teachers can assess AI tools through journals, student feedback, and peer discussions to determine their effectiveness in achieving pedagogical goals. Such reflections foster a culture of continuous improvement and ensure that AI remains aligned with educational objectives. Furthermore, fostering a sense of digital agency among students is essential. Activities that encourage students to personalize their learning experiences with AI, such as curating vocabulary lists or designing multimedia projects, empower them to take ownership of their education. This approach not only enhances their linguistic proficiency but also builds their confidence in navigating AI-powered resources.

Incorporating ethical literacy into AI integration is a crucial step toward a more holistic approach. Educators can guide students in exploring issues such as data privacy, algorithmic bias, and the cultural implications of AI tools. For instance, discussions about how translation software handles idiomatic expressions across languages can illuminate the cultural nuances and challenges of AI. These conversations deepen students' understanding of AI's societal impact and encourage them to engage with technology responsibly and thoughtfully. This integration of ethical considerations ensures that students develop a balanced perspective, combining technological fluency with moral and cultural awareness.

The integration of AI in EFL education must balance technological innovation with the preservation of the relational and cultural dimensions of teaching. Educators can harness AI as a catalyst for inclusive and effective learning by prioritizing collaboration, critical engagement, and ethical responsibility. This approach ensures that AI enriches rather than diminishes the interpersonal and cultural depth that defines quality education. With thoughtful implementation, continuous reflection, and a commitment to human-centered values, AI can transform EFL classrooms into dynamic spaces where both teachers and students thrive in a rapidly evolving educational landscape.

POLICY RECOMMENDATIONS FOR AI LITERACY AND DIGITAL EDUCATION IN EFL CONTEXT

The integration of AI into EFL education presents a paradigm shift in teaching and learning methodologies. As AI technologies continue to evolve, they offer profound opportunities for personalized learning, improved instructional strategies, and enhanced student engagement, while simultaneously raising complex ethical and infrastructural challenges. This section explores critical policy recommendations that aim to address these dual concerns, focusing on establishing robust ethical frameworks, fostering professional development for educators, and ensuring equitable access to AI-driven tools in diverse educational settings. By examining the implications of AI literacy and digital education, we provide actionable guidelines to ensure that AI integration in EFL contexts is both effective and ethically responsible, contributing to the advancement of global educational standards.

Ethical Guidelines for AI Usage in Education

As AI becomes an integral part of education systems worldwide, establishing robust ethical guidelines is paramount to safeguard all stakeholders' rights, privacy, and dignity. AI systems hold immense potential to revolutionize education through personalized learning, efficient assessment, and accessibility enhancements. However, these benefits come with significant ethical concerns, particularly regarding data privacy, bias, accountability, and inclusivity. Without well-defined ethical frameworks, the deployment of AI in education risks exacerbating existing inequalities, marginalizing vulnerable populations, and undermining trust in technology (Holmes et al., 2022).

At the core of ethical AI integration is the need for comprehensive data governance. AI systems often rely on vast datasets to deliver personalized learning experiences and monitor student progress. These datasets frequently include sensitive information such as student demographics, behavioural patterns, and academic performance. The absence of robust safeguards can result in data breaches, unauthorized access, or misuse of personal information, posing risks to both students and educators. Ethical guidelines must mandate the principles of data minimization, ensuring that only essential information is collected and that it is anonymized and securely stored. Additionally, these guidelines should emphasize transparency, requiring institutions to inform students and parents about how data is collected, stored, and used. Drawing from models such as the General Data Protection Regulation (GDPR), policymakers can adapt these principles to local contexts to ensure their relevance and effectiveness (Wachter, 2018).

Transparency extends beyond data collection to the functioning of AI algorithms. Many AI systems operate as opaque "black boxes," producing outputs without revealing their underlying logic. This lack of algorithmic transparency can lead to mistrust among educators and students, as well as the uncritical acceptance of potentially flawed AI-generated recommendations. Ethical guidelines should require developers to disclose the design principles, limitations, and biases inherent in their AI systems (Bogina et al., 2022). For example, in speech recognition tools, teachers must understand whether the training datasets represent diverse accents and linguistic patterns to ensure fairness. By fostering algorithmic transparency, educators are empowered to critically evaluate AI outputs and make informed decisions about their integration into teaching practices.

Fairness and inclusivity are additional pillars of ethical AI implementation in education. AI tools must be designed to accommodate the diverse linguistic, cultural, and socioeconomic backgrounds of learners (Evurulobi et al., 2024). This is especially critical in global EFL classrooms, where students often represent a wide array of cultural and linguistic identities. Developers must prioritize diverse training datasets that reflect this spectrum, ensuring that AI systems do not inadvertently privilege one group over another. For instance, incorporating various accents, dialects, and cultural contexts into the development of language learning applications can significantly improve their accessibility and accuracy for non-native speakers. Policymakers can enforce these inclusivity standards through regular audits, certifications, and accountability mechanisms, ensuring that AI technologies promote equity rather than reinforce existing disparities.

These general ethical concerns become even more nuanced when narrowed to the EFL context. Language learning involves not only acquiring linguistic skills but also understanding cultural nuances, interpersonal communication, and emotional expression. While AI can provide valuable tools for grammar correction, pronunciation practice, and adaptive content delivery, it cannot fully replicate the relational and cultural aspects of language teaching. Ethical guidelines for AI in EFL education must account for these limitations, emphasizing the complementary role of technology rather than its replacement of human teachers (T. Lim et al., 2023). For example, AI tools that evaluate written essays should provide recommendations for improvement while allowing teachers to offer personalized feedback that considers the student's cultural background and intent.

In Indonesian classrooms, the ethical integration of AI in EFL teaching faces additional challenges and opportunities due to the country's cultural diversity, varied technological infrastructure, and socioeconomic disparities. Indonesia is home to hundreds of languages and dialects, creating a unique linguistic landscape for English language education. AI tools deployed in this context must be sensitive to the multilingual realities of Indonesian students. Developers should include local languages in training datasets to ensure that speech recognition systems and language learning platforms accurately interpret and respond to students' needs. Additionally, cultural norms and values should inform the design of AI systems to ensure that their application aligns with the expectations of Indonesian teachers, students, and parents.

Infrastructure and accessibility are critical considerations for ethical AI integration in Indonesia. Many rural schools lack the technological resources needed to implement AI-based tools, such as reliable internet connectivity and modern devices. Without addressing these disparities, AI risks becoming a tool that benefits only urban, well-resourced schools while excluding students in underserved areas. Ethical guidelines should emphasize the need for equitable access to AI technologies, supported by targeted government initiatives to bridge the digital divide. For example, mobile-based AI platforms that require minimal infrastructure can be prioritized for deployment in rural areas, ensuring that students across Indonesia can benefit from technological advancements.

In addition to infrastructure, teacher training is a key element of ethical AI usage in Indonesian EFL classrooms. Many educators in Indonesia, particularly in rural areas, lack the technical skills and confidence needed to integrate AI tools effectively. Ethical guidelines must address this gap by mandating comprehensive professional development programs that equip teachers with both technical and pedagogical knowledge. These programs should include training on ethical issues, such as data privacy, algorithmic bias, and the limitations of AI, to empower teachers to make informed decisions about their use of technology. For instance, teachers can be trained to recognize potential biases in AI-generated assessments and to provide culturally responsive feedback that complements the technology's outputs.

To ensure accountability, schools and educational institutions in Indonesia should establish ethics committees to oversee the deployment and monitoring of AI tools. These committees can include representatives from diverse stakeholder groups, such as teachers, parents, students, and technologists, to ensure that all perspectives are considered. The committees can evaluate the alignment of AI tools with ethical guidelines, assess their impact on learning outcomes, and address concerns raised by educators and students. This collaborative approach fosters trust and ensures that AI integration is guided by the shared values of fairness, inclusivity, and cultural sensitivity.

Professional development must also emphasize the importance of balancing technology with humanistic teaching practices. While AI can enhance efficiency and provide valuable insights, it should not overshadow the role of teachers as mentors, facilitators, and cultural guides. Teachers in Indonesian EFL classrooms must be encouraged to use AI as a tool to support their pedagogical goals rather than as a replacement for their expertise. For example, AI can handle routine tasks such as grading and attendance tracking, allowing teachers to focus on fostering meaningful interactions, addressing individual student needs, and cultivating a supportive learning environment.

Finally, ongoing evaluation and refinement of ethical guidelines are essential to ensure their continued relevance and effectiveness. As AI technologies evolve, so too must the frameworks that govern their use. Policymakers, educators, and developers should engage in regular dialogues to review the impact of AI tools on Indonesian EFL education, identify emerging challenges, and update ethical guidelines accordingly. By adopting a proactive and iterative approach, stakeholders can ensure that AI integration remains aligned with the principles of transparency, equity, and cultural sensitivity.

Infrastructure and Professional Training for EFL Teachers

The successful integration of AI in EFL education requires robust infrastructure and comprehensive professional training programs for teachers. As AI tools continue to redefine pedagogical practices, it is critical to equip educators with the necessary skills and resources to adapt to this transformation effectively. Professional training for teachers is not merely an operational requirement; it is a foundational strategy for empowering educators to harness the full potential of AI in a manner that enhances learning outcomes while preserving the humanistic aspects of education.

Globally, there is a growing recognition of the need to prioritize professional development for teachers to navigate the complexities of AI integration. AI technologies are evolving rapidly, and their successful implementation in classrooms demands that educators acquire a blend of technical, pedagogical, and ethical competencies. This involves understanding the functionalities and limitations of AI tools, critically assessing their outputs, and adapting them to diverse classroom contexts. A well-structured professional training program can bridge the knowledge gap, fostering confidence and competence among teachers. For example, training workshops can introduce educators to AI-assisted grading systems, adaptive learning platforms, and speech recognition tools, helping them understand how these technologies can complement their teaching strategies.

When narrowing this focus to the application of AI in EFL teaching, the importance of tailored professional development becomes even more pronounced. Language learning is a dynamic process that involves not only linguistic proficiency but also cultural understanding and interpersonal communication. AI tools can enhance this process by providing personalized feedback, enabling self-paced learning, and automating repetitive tasks. However, their effective use requires teachers to adapt these tools thoughtfully to the unique needs of EFL learners. For instance, educators must learn how to interpret AI-generated data on student performance and use it to design targeted interventions. Professional training programs should include scenario-based exercises where teachers practice integrating AI tools into lesson plans, analyzing their impact on student engagement and progress.

For Indonesian EFL teachers, the need for professional training in AI usage is underscored by the country's diverse linguistic and cultural landscape. Indonesia's multilingual environment presents unique challenges and opportunities for AI in language education. Teachers must be equipped to navigate these complexities, using AI tools to address the varying levels of English proficiency among students while respecting their cultural identities. Training programs should include modules on leveraging AI to support multilingual classrooms, such as using translation tools to bridge linguistic gaps or employing speech recognition systems that account for regional accents. These programs can also focus on enhancing teachers' ability to balance AI-driven insights with their own professional judgment, ensuring that technology complements rather than dictates pedagogical decisions.

Infrastructure development is another critical component of successful AI integration, particularly in the Indonesian context. Many rural and underserved schools in Indonesia face significant technological constraints, including limited access to high-speed internet, outdated devices, and unreliable power supplies. These infrastructural gaps hinder the adoption of AI tools, creating disparities in educational opportunities between urban and rural areas. Governments and educational institutions must prioritize investments in digital infrastructure to ensure that all teachers and students have equitable access to technology. Mobile-based AI platforms designed to function on low-bandwidth networks can be a practical solution for remote areas. Additionally, public-private partnerships can play a pivotal role in bridging the infrastructure gap, with technology companies providing affordable devices and connectivity solutions for underserved schools (Mustopa et al., 2024).

In tandem with infrastructure improvements, mentorship, and peer learning initiatives can enhance the effectiveness of professional training programs. Experienced teachers who have successfully integrated AI into their classrooms can serve as mentors, offering practical insights and guidance to their peers. These mentorship programs can foster a sense of collaboration and shared learning, enabling teachers to exchange ideas, discuss challenges, and co-develop innovative strategies for using

AI tools. For example, regional workshops and online forums can facilitate knowledge sharing among EFL teachers, creating a supportive community of practice that drives continuous professional growth.

Another dimension of professional training involves addressing the ethical considerations associated with AI usage in education. Teachers must be equipped to navigate issues such as data privacy, algorithmic bias, and the ethical implications of AI-assisted assessments. Training programs should include discussions on these topics, helping educators develop a critical understanding of the potential risks and limitations of AI tools. For instance, teachers can be trained to identify biases in AI-generated feedback, such as speech recognition systems that may struggle with non-native accents. By fostering this ethical awareness, professional development programs can empower teachers to use AI responsibly and advocate for its fair and inclusive application in EFL classrooms.

For Indonesian EFL teachers, training programs must also account for the unique socioeconomic realities of their students. Many learners in Indonesia, particularly those in rural and low-income areas, face barriers to accessing digital resources. Teachers need strategies to ensure that AI tools are implemented in a way that does not exclude these students. Professional training should include practical solutions for promoting inclusivity, such as designing lesson plans that incorporate offline AI tools or using collaborative activities to engage students with limited access to individual devices. By addressing these challenges, professional development can enable teachers to create equitable and inclusive learning environments that leverage AI to benefit all students.

To ensure the sustainability of these efforts, long-term funding mechanisms and policies must be established to support infrastructure and professional training initiatives. Governments can provide grants for schools to upgrade their technology, subsidies for teacher training programs, and incentives for technology companies to collaborate with educational institutions. These investments should be accompanied by mechanisms for monitoring and evaluating the impact of AI integration on teaching and learning outcomes. For example, regular assessments can track how professional training programs influence teachers' confidence in using AI tools and their ability to enhance student engagement and achievement.

Finally, professional training programs should foster a forward-looking mindset among teachers, encouraging them to view AI as an opportunity for innovation and creativity in the classroom. By emphasizing the potential of AI to enhance rather than replace their roles, training initiatives can inspire teachers to experiment with new pedagogical approaches and adapt to the evolving educational landscape. For example, teachers can explore using AI to create gamified learning experiences, develop interactive language exercises, or analyze trends in student performance to inform their instructional strategies. This proactive approach ensures that teachers remain active agents of change, shaping the integration of AI in ways that align with their pedagogical values and the n,eeds of their students.

Fostering International Collaboration in AI and Education Standards

The integration of AI into EFL education presents both opportunities and challenges that transcend national borders. Addressing these requires a collaborative approach that harnesses the collective knowledge, resources, and expertise of the global education community. International collaboration provides a powerful mechanism for advancing AI's role in education by facilitating the exchange of best practices, fostering innovation, and establishing shared standards. Through such efforts, countries can ensure that AI serves as a tool for equitable and effective education while addressing the unique needs of diverse linguistic and cultural contexts.

One of the most significant advantages of international collaboration lies in its ability to pool resources and expertise to tackle common challenges. Many countries face similar issues in integrating AI into their education systems, such as infrastructure limitations, ethical concerns, and teacher readiness. By working together, nations can leverage collective problem-solving to identify effective strategies and scalable solutions. For example, partnerships between developed and developing countries can enable the transfer of technology and knowledge, reducing the digital divide and promoting equitable access to AI tools. This collaborative approach not only accelerates progress but also fosters a sense of global responsibility for improving education.

To further enhance the impact of international collaboration, establishing regional consortia can provide a focused platform for addressing the unique challenges of specific areas. In Southeast Asia, for example, a regional consortium dedicated to AI and education could serve as a hub for knowledge exchange, joint research, and capacity building (Lim et al., 2021). Member countries could collaborate on the development of training materials tailored to the linguistic and cultural diversity of the region, ensuring that AI tools are contextually relevant and effective. Additionally, the consortium could organize regional workshops, conferences, and online forums, fostering a sense of collective responsibility for advancing educational outcomes. Such a consortium would not only strengthen regional ties but also position Southeast Asia as a leader in AI-driven education innovation (Hassan et al., 2023).

Encouraging knowledge exchange through international conferences and joint initiatives is another vital strategy for fostering collaboration. Events like the International Conference on AI in Education provide opportunities for educators, researchers, and policymakers to share insights, showcase innovative practices, and build networks (Wang & Zhang, 2020). These conferences serve as a platform for highlighting success stories, discussing challenges, and exploring new ideas. For example, a presentation on the use of AI-powered speech recognition tools in rural Indonesian classrooms could inspire similar initiatives in other countries facing similar challenges. Joint initiatives, such as collaborative research projects or teacher exchange programs, further strengthen these connections by creating pathways for sustained engagement and mutual learning.

Teacher exchange programs, in particular, hold immense potential for enhancing international collaboration in AI and education. By enabling educators to observe and participate in AI integration practices in diverse settings, these programs enrich their perspectives and teaching strategies. For instance, an Indonesian EFL teacher participating in an exchange program in Japan could learn about the use of AI for personalized learning in urban classrooms, while sharing insights on addressing linguistic diversity in rural contexts. These exchanges foster cross-cultural understanding and professional growth, equipping teachers with the skills and knowledge needed to navigate the complexities of AI integration.

An essential component of fostering international collaboration is the establishment of shared standards for AI use in education. These standards should address key aspects such as data privacy, algorithmic transparency, and inclusivity, ensuring that AI tools uphold ethical principles and promote equity. By working together, countries can develop guidelines that reflect the values and priorities of the global education community while allowing for regional adaptations. For example, a global standard might mandate the inclusion of diverse linguistic and cultural datasets in AI development, while regional consortia ensure that these datasets reflect the specific needs of their communities. Establishing shared standards not only enhances the quality and consistency of AI tools but also builds trust among educators, students, and parents.

Monitoring and evaluation are critical to the success of collaborative efforts. To maximize the impact of joint initiatives, it is essential to establish mechanisms for tracking progress and assessing outcomes. Collaborative projects should include clear objectives, measurable indicators, and regular assessments to ensure that they achieve their intended goals. For instance, a regional consortium could analyze the adoption of AI tools across member countries, examining their impact on student performance, teacher satisfaction, and equity in education. These evaluations provide valuable feedback for refining strategies, scaling successful practices, and addressing emerging challenges.

In the context of Indonesia, fostering international collaboration can have profound implications for EFL education. As a country with diverse linguistic and cultural landscapes, Indonesia stands to benefit significantly from global partnerships that offer tailored solutions to its unique challenges. Collaborations with countries that have advanced AI integration in education can provide valuable insights and resources for addressing issues such as infrastructure limitations, teacher training, and linguistic diversity. For example, partnerships with nations like Singapore or South Korea could facilitate knowledge exchange on using AI for multilingual classrooms, while collaborations with international organizations could support infrastructure development in rural areas.

Finally, fostering international collaboration is not only about addressing current challenges but also about preparing for the future of education. As AI technologies continue to evolve, so too will their implications for teaching and learning. By working together, countries can anticipate these changes and develop proactive strategies to ensure that AI remains a force for good in education. This requires a commitment to ongoing dialogue, research, and innovation, as well as a shared vision for the role of AI in shaping the future of learning.

CONCLUSION

The integration of AI into EFL education presents transformative opportunities and significant challenges, particularly in a diverse and rapidly evolving context like Indonesia. AI technologies hold immense potential to personalize learning experiences, automate repetitive tasks, and increase accessibility for students across varying socio-economic backgrounds. However, the successful implementation of AI in EFL education hinges on addressing key barriers such as disparities in digital infrastructure, ethical concerns related to data privacy and algorithmic bias, and the varying levels of technological readiness among educators. To navigate these complexities effectively, a holistic, inclusive, and ethically guided approach to AI integration is essential.

Addressing the digital divide must be a priority to ensure equitable access to AI-enhanced education. Significant investments are required to expand digital infrastructure, particularly in under-resourced and rural regions, where limited connectivity and inadequate resources often hinder progress. This includes providing affordable devices and developing offline-capable AI tools tailored to the specific needs of diverse learners. Such efforts are vital to bridging gaps in accessibility and fostering equal opportunities for all students, regardless of their geographic location or socio-economic status. Without such interventions, the transformative potential of AI in education will remain unrealized for many.

Equally important is the role of educators, whose preparedness and confidence determine the success of AI integration. Comprehensive teacher training programs that focus on technical proficiency, ethical awareness, and pedagogical adaptation are critical for equipping educators with the skills needed to harness AI effectively. By fostering teachers' ability to navigate AI tools responsibly and creatively, these programs ensure that AI complements and enhances their role rather than undermines it. Furthermore, establishing robust ethical frameworks to govern the use of AI in education, addressing data protection, algorithmic bias, and transparency, will build trust among stakeholders and safeguard students' rights.

Looking ahead, Indonesia must strive to create an education system that balances technological innovation with human-centered teaching. While AI offers powerful tools to transform the learning experience, the human elements of education (creativity, critical thinking, and socio-emotional development) remain irreplaceable. Teachers play a central role in fostering these qualities and must continue to serve as the cornerstone of education. Through sustained investment, global collaboration, and adherence to ethical practices, Indonesia can harness the power of AI to build inclusive, innovative, and student-centered learning environments that prepare learners not only for academic success but also for meaningful participation as global citizens in an increasingly digital world.

REFERENCES

Al-Shallakh, M. A. I. (2024). Embedding Artificial Intelligent Applications in Higher Educational Institutions to Improve Students' Pronunciation Performance. *Theory and Practice in Language Studies*, 14(6), 1897–1906. DOI: 10.17507/tpls.1406.31

Alam, A., Hasan, M., & Raza, M. M. (2022). *Impact of Artificial Intelligence (AI) on Education: Changing Paradigms and Approaches*. Towards Excellence. DOI: 10.37867/TE140127

Bezzina, S., & Dingli, A. (2024). The Transformative Potential of Artificial Intelligence for Education. *Proceedings of the International Conference on Networked Learning, 14*(3), 34–47. DOI: 10.54337/nlc.v14i1.8077

Bogina, V., Hartman, A., Kuflik, T., & Shulner-Tal, A. (2022). Educating Software and AI Stakeholders About Algorithmic Fairness, Accountability, Transparency and Ethics. *International Journal of Artificial Intelligence in Education*, 32(3), 808–833. DOI: 10.1007/s40593-021-00248-0

Chisom, O. N., Unachukwu, C. C., & Osawaru, B. (2024). Review of AI in Education: Transforming Learning Environments in Africa. *International Journal of Applied Research in Social Sciences*, 5(10), 637–654. DOI: 10.51594/ijarss.v5i10.725

Chiu, T. K. F., Xia, Q., Zhou, X., Chai, C. S., & Cheng, M. (2023). Systematic Literature Review on Opportunities, Challenges, and Future Research Recommendations of Artificial Intelligence in Education. *Computers and Education: Artificial Intelligence*, 4(2), 84–98. DOI: 10.1016/j.caeai.2022.100118

Evurulobi, C. I., Dagunduro, A. O., & Ajuwon, O. A. (2024). Language Learning Technologies: A Review of Trends in the USA and Globally. *World Journal of Advanced Research and Reviews*, 23(3), 2697–2707. DOI: 10.30574/wjarr.2024.23.3.2851

Gatenby, A. B. (2023). The Development of Artificial Intelligence in Computing Education. In *Inclusive Computing Education in the Secondary School* (pp. 624–639). Routledge. DOI: 10.4324/9781003193685-3

Guo, Y., & Yu, H. (2023). Exploration of Education Transformation and Teacher Literacy in the Age of Artificial Intelligence. *2023 5th International Workshop on Artificial Intelligence and Education (WAIE)*, 38–42. DOI: 10.1109/WAIE60568.2023.00014

Hasan, M. M., Hossain, M. A., & Hossain, S. M. (2020). Impact of speech recognition technology in English pronunciation training: A case study in Indonesia. *International Journal of Educational Development*, 16(3), 95–110.

Hassan, R., Lee, S., & Chong, A. (2023). AI-driven Educational Initiatives in Southeast Asia: Addressing Cultural and Linguistic Diversity through Regional Collaboration. *International Journal of Artificial Intelligence in Education*, 34(4), 238–257.

Holmes, W., Porayska-Pomsta, K., Holstein, K., Sutherland, E., Baker, T., Shum, S. B., Santos, O. C., Rodrigo, M. T., Cukurova, M., Bittencourt, I. I., & Koedinger, K. R. (2022). Ethics of AI in Education: Towards a Community-Wide Framework. *International Journal of Artificial Intelligence in Education*, 32(3), 504–526. DOI: 10.1007/s40593-021-00239-1

Idham, A. Z., Rauf, W., & Rajab, A. (2024). Navigating the Transformative Impact of Artificial Intelligence on English Language Teaching: Exploring Challenges and Opportunities. *Jurnal Edukasi Saintifik*, 4(1), 8–14. Advance online publication. DOI: 10.56185/jes.v4i1.620

Karroum, S. Y. A., & Elshaiekh, N. E. M. (2023). Digital Transformation in Education: Discovering the Barriers that Prevent Teachers from Adopting Emerging Technologies. *2023 24th International Arab Conference on Information Technology (ACIT)*, 1–5. DOI: 10.1109/ACIT58888.2023.10453908

Lim, Tan, K., & Yap, H. (2021). Enhancing Regional AI Consortia to Promote Educational Innovation in Southeast Asia. *Journal of Educational Technology Development and Exchange*, 17(2), 115–132.

Lim, T., Gottipati, S., & Cheong, M. (2023). Ethical Considerations for Artificial Intelligence in Educational Assessments. In *Creative AI Tools and Ethical Implications in Teaching and Learning* (pp. 32–79). DOI: 10.4018/979-8-3693-0205-7.ch003

Maisaiah, N. (2024). The Part of Artificial Intelligence in Education. *International Journal of Scientific Research in Engineering and Management*, 08(02), 1–13. DOI: 10.55041/IJSREM28680

Mustopa, M., Nasikhin, N., Chamami, R., Nihayah, H., Habibullah, M. R., & Manshur, A. (2024). Challenges in Artificial Intelligence Development in Higher Education in China, India, and Indonesia: International Students' Perspectives. *International Journal of Learning. Teaching and Educational Research*, 23(2), 354–373. DOI: 10.26803/ijlter.23.2.17

Nassaji, H., & Tian, J. (2022). Humanism and second language teaching: The power of empathy in fostering language acquisition. *Language and Intercultural Communication*, 22(5), 522–536.

Nguyen, G., Nguyen, N., & Giang, N. T. H. (2022). Situation and Proposals for Implementing Artificial Intelligence-based Instructional Technology in Vietnamese Secondary Schools. [IJET]. *International Journal of Emerging Technologies in Learning*, 17(18), 53–75. DOI: 10.3991/ijet.v17i18.31503

Quy, V. K., Thanh, B. T., Chehri, A., Linh, D. M., & Tuan, D. A. (2023). AI and Digital Transformation in Higher Education: Vision and Approach of a Specific University in Vietnam. *Sustainability (Basel)*, 15(14), 1093–1107. DOI: 10.3390/su151411093

Rahman, A., & Rahmawati, M. (2021). AI-driven Feedback Systems for Essay Grading in EFL Classrooms: A Case from Surabaya. *Journal of Language and Linguistic Studies*, 17(4), 1189–1203.

Santiago, C. S., Embang, S. I., Acanto, R. B., Ambojia, K. W. P., Aperocho, M. D. B., Balilo, B. B., Cahapin, E. L., Conlu, M. T. N., Lausa, S. M., Laput, E. Y., Malabag, B. A., Paderes, J. J., & Romasanta, J. K. N. (2023). Utilization of Writing Assistance Tools in Research in Selected Higher Learning Institutions in the Philippines: A Text Mining Analysis. *International Journal of Learning. Teaching and Educational Research*, 22(11), 259–284. DOI: 10.26803/ijlter.22.11.14

Taufikin, M. S. I., Supa'at, Azifah, N., Nikmah, F., Kuanr, J., & Parminder. (2024). The Impact of AI on Teacher Roles and Pedagogy in the 21st Century Classroom. *2024 International Conference on Knowledge Engineering and Communication Systems (ICKECS)*, 1–5. DOI: 10.1109/ICKECS61492.2024.10617236

Tolba, R. M., Elarif, T., Taha, Z., & Hammady, R. (2024). Interactive Augmented Reality System for Learning Phonetics Using Artificial Intelligence. *IEEE Access : Practical Innovations, Open Solutions*, 12(4), 1219–1231. DOI: 10.1109/ACCESS.2024.3406494

Vinothkumar, J., & Karunamurthy, A. (2023). Recent Advancements in Artificial Intelligence Technology: Trends and Implications. *Quing: International Journal of Multidisciplinary Scientific Research and Development*, 2(1), 1–11. Advance online publication. DOI: 10.54368/qijmsrd.2.1.0003

Wang, Q. L. X., & Zhang, F. (2020). Impact of teacher exchange programs and joint research initiatives in AI education: Evidence from Southeast Asia. *Journal of Collaborative Education and Research*, 15(3), 98–112.

Yeter, I. H., Yang, W., & Sturgess, J. B. (2024). Global initiatives and challenges in integrating artificial intelligence literacy in elementary education: Mapping policies and empirical literature. *Future in Educational Research*, 8(2), 132–145. DOI: 10.1002/fer3.59

Yoon, S. Y., & Lee, J. (2023). Exploring AI-Powered Collaborative Platforms in Language Learning: Impacts on Interaction and Student Engagement. *Journal of Educational Technology & Society*, 26(3), 45–60.

Yuan, C. W., Tsai, H. S., & Chen, Y.-T. (2024). Charting Competence: A Holistic Scale for Measuring Proficiency in Artificial Intelligence Literacy. *Journal of Educational Computing Research*, 62(7), 1675–1704. DOI: 10.1177/07356331241261206

Zheng, R., Xu, H., Wang, M., & Lu, J. (2024). The Impact of Artificial General Intelligence-Assisted Project-Based Learning on Students' Higher Order Thinking and Self-Efficacy. *IEEE Transactions on Learning Technologies*, 17(3), 2207–2214. DOI: 10.1109/TLT.2024.3488086

Chapter 16
Exploring Experts' Positionings Towards AI

Emilia Rodrigues Araujo
https://orcid.org/0000-0003-3600-3310
Universidade do Minho, Portugal

Paula Urze
Nova University of Lisbon, Portugal

ABSTRACT

This chapter delves into the perceptions of artificial intelligence (AI) experts on the societal implications, governance, and ethical responsibilities associated with AI. Drawing on qualitative research, including interviews with six AI experts, the study investigates three key questions: experts' perceptions of AI's societal impacts, their visions for an AI-governed society, and their views on their responsibilities in addressing AI's consequences. The findings suggest that AI experts emphasize the importance of balancing innovation with education and regulation to ensure AI's responsible development and application, leaving out important questions to analyze further, such as their role in AI political governance, and the interest of wide public participation in the process of AI creation.

INTRODUCTION

Today, innovation in science and technology takes place in extraordinarily complex contexts. Scientists activities cover a wide range of areas and relate to both the economy and politics. The reality is far from the ideal advocated by Weber (1972), or Merton (1942), about the lack of interest and detachment of the world from the work of scientists and a predominant characteristic of mode one presented by Gib-

DOI: 10.4018/979-8-3693-9015-3.ch016

bons (2013).In fact, scientists are deeply immersed in controversies around science and technology, involving issues of economic and political nature (Latour, 1979; Callon, 1981, 1987; Collins & Evans, 2007; Jasanoff, 2015). Their work enacts the "mode 3" science, which is characterized by the intricacy of relations between them, governments, companies, the media, and the environment (Gibbons, 2013; Carayannis & Campbell, 2009).Issues related to the ethical and social implications of artificial intelligence (hereafter referred to as AI) should be analyzed in this context, particularly if the aim is to understand how scientists define and perceive what role they play in this dynamic. In fact, scientists who influence and shape the debate on the social and cultural values of AI cut across various fields, especially academia, and business. Therefore, their views on AI also tend to be diverse and sometimes contradictory. While some scientists consider AI to hold unparalleled promise for humanity, others point to real consequences for people and democratic systems. As it is undeniable that AI is radically transforming society and imposing new benchmarks, it becomes particularly important to understand more and better who these scientists are and what are their perceptions on the social implications of AI. This analysis is particularly relevant in the context where the media is a major player in shaping public representations of science, as well as the type of information and knowledge that people in general have about AI. Therefore, this chapter investigates the scientists' perspectives and looks to explore these issues by investigating their positions in relation to the social implications of their field. Specifically, it analyzes how their views contribute to broader discussions on AI governance and responsible innovation. Based on six interviews with leading AI experts, the article considers three main themes: i) perceptions of the societal impacts of AI; ii) visions for an AI-governed society; and iii) policy responsibilities.

The chapter is organized into four main sections. The first section describes the theoretical framework. The second section describes the method and then presents the findings. The chapter concludes by discussing the broader implications of the findings for AI governance and responsible innovation.

THEORY

Collins and Evans deconstruct and analyze the concept of expertise as the knowledge or competence needed to act or judge appropriately in specific contexts, concluding that it goes far beyond technical or formal knowledge and is intrinsically linked to social recognition and political legitimacy (Collins & Evans, 2007). The authors propose three distinctions, which are relevant to a better understanding of the current controversies about AI and the role that non-scientists play in its construction: contributory expertise, interactional expertise and noetic or experiential expertise. The first refers to the technical and in-depth knowledge of a specific area, acquired by scientists and other professionals who contribute to the development of the scientific and technological field. Interactional expertise, according to Collins, consists of the ability to interact with contributing experts without producing technical knowledge in the field. This category includes, for example, science journalists, who have sufficient knowledge to mediate debates or communicate complex concepts to the public. Collins argues that interactional expertise is particularly significant in the contexts of public policy and ethical debates, where decisions depend not only on technical knowledge, but also on the ability to interpret and communicate this knowledge to wider audiences. This does not mean that everyone should be treated as an expert, but rather that science should recognize the value of different forms of experience and knowledge. Finally, noetic expertise, in a more literal translation of the work, includes tacit, intuitive, or experiential knowledge of actors who are not formal experts, but accumulate practical skills in a specific context over time. Although not everyone owns contributory expertise, Collins argues that distinct types of expertise can coexist and are valued differently depending on the context. However, the idea that "we are all experts" can in fact be problematic when used to delegitimize scientific expertise, as these dynamics contribute to what Collins (2021) describes as "epistemic populism", where all opinions - regardless of scientific validity - are treated as equally authoritative. This complicates informed decision-making, especially when it comes to critical issues such as the social implications of AI, as they are increasingly embedded in many controversies around its benefits and pitfalls. There are authors saying that AI does not make life easier or safer for everyone (Sloane & Moss, 2019). Other state that "Instead, AI can exacerbate inequality, perpetuate discrimination, and inflict harm based on race, gender, and social class (Noble, 2018, cited in Lindgren & Holmström, 2020). Bostrom (2014) envisions a dystopian scenario where "superintelligence" surpasses human capabilities, raising deep ethical and existential concerns. Other studies emphasize futuristic narratives, exploring a spectrum of possibilities that AI enables, raising deep ethical and existential concerns. Houser and Raymond (2021, cited in Sartori and Theodorou, 2022) discuss the 'global AI race' as nations compete to develop the ultimate algorithms that allow them to antecipate. On the other hand, optimistic perspectives highlight the potential of AI to address significant human and societal challenges through superintelligent systems. In *The Sciences of the Artificial* (1969), Herbert Simon raised the question: 'Natural science is knowledge about natural objects and phenomena: "We ask whether there cannot also be an 'artificial' science - knowledge about artificial objects and phenomena" (Rahawan et al., 2019). In line with Simon's vision, researchers have advocated an interdisciplinary domain to study 'intelligent machines' not just as engineering artifacts, but as social phenomena. Despite this warning about the social dimension of technology, a still deterministic view of AI persists. Recent studies emphasize the importance of promoting open debates on AI policies that reflect diverse perspectives, values, and interests (Ulnicane & Erkkilä, 2023) deconstructing that determinism, sometimes confused with neutrality of (socio)technic objects termed as "tools". In *Artifictional Intelligence* (2021), Harry Collins advocates keeping a balance between the use of technology and the principles of democracy. The author warns against excessive dependence on machines that cannot fully understand the complexities of human social dynamics and emphasizes the need for diverse knowledge in the responsible development of AI. As the introduction states, scientists are essential in shaping scientific controversies and play a key role in deconstructing the complexities of science and technological innovations, contributing to respond to that responsibility. However, scientists face tensions that are growing as science becomes increasingly embedded in society, the economy, and politics. The conceptions around the 'mode 2' and 'mode 3' of science (Carayannis & Campbell, 2009) highlight the complexity of the practices and discourses in which science and technology are developed, and also show the ambivalences and dissonances that characterize scientific performances, for at least two important reasons: i) AI scientists (developers) are spread across different fields, orienting their work towards different purposes - from public universities to private companies, holding different and possibly conflicting views on the social implications of AI; ii) public debates are deeply shaped by different types of expertise, each trying to impose their voice and influence the way people think about and react to AI.

In this chapter, we will analyze the views of scientists working in public universities and understand which themes they consider central, as well as the issues they consider less relevant to the problematization of AI in terms of its relationship with the transformation of society.

METHOD

This chapter is influenced by the authors' position as sociologists and academics, and is structured on the basis of interpretative methodological assumptions, guided by the interest in understanding the meanings attributed by scientists to the social implications of AI and to account for the complexity of the "expertise" (Collins,2007) that intersects today in the analysis of these controversies. In this sense, as well as including participant observation by the authors who interact with scientists on a daily basis, the chapter focuses on the analysis of interviews conducted with scientists who develop AI, seeking to ascertain the implicit meanings of their discourses and the complexity of the meanings constructed by the participants about the processes of innovation in AI, its actors and effects. In the context of this search for the dimension of experience and the subjectivities constructed and unveiled by the answers to our questions, the study follows some of the basic principles of grounded theory, especially in the context of Charmaz's approach (2006, 2012) which favors the reading of contexts and discourses and which takes as its starting point the researcher's own interaction with the phenomenon under study, as the author states "Researchers construct their respective products from the fabric of interactions, both witnessed and lived." (2006, p.178). (2006, p.178).

Sampling

In the context of the assumptions of qualitative methodology and the inductive approach of grounded theory, the study followed the theoretical sampling procedure, seeking to explore more specifically how AI scientists with positions in academia and science position themselves in the face of the list of implications with which AI is increasingly associated. In this sense, the sample included nationally and internationally recognized scientists who have very prominent characteristics: they work in universities where they are professors in computer engineering or departments of electrical and computer engineering; they hold leadership positions in leading research centers, perform project coordination functions, interact directly with decision-making bodies and supervise cutting-edge research projects on fundamental and applied research in AI. In addition to their research, these academics play a vital role in shaping the future of AI in Portugal. They supervise PhDs in the field and collaborate with research networks that contribute to the development of AI policies at national, European, and international levels. This institutional position allows them to have a global view of the dynamics of the creation and development of AI and the ongoing debates on various AI issues, including those related to the social impacts of AI, as well as the effects of its development and expansion on the private sector.

Interview Script

The social implications of AI are vast. The guide we present in the appendix is more extensive, as it encompasses other issues that we will explore in other publications. In this chapter, we try to find out which ones scientists identify, how they understand them and what challenges they impose, particularly in terms of the governance of society and the role expected of scientists, and what the relationship is between what they say and the institutional position they occupy, particularly as professors in universities, as presented below:

Data Analysis

We used Charmaz's (2006) grounded theory framework to analyze the interviews using thematic analysis. Charmaz says: 'Most qualitative researchers code for topics and themes. Grounded theorists code for actions and meanings and do so in gerunds as much as possible' (Charmaz, 2012, p.5). In this sense, the interviews were transcribed and then analyzed, first in an open-ended way, allowing the identification of the main categories that were then aggregated based on the concepts mobilized for this analysis, in particular: i) implications of AI on the economy and time; role of social media in the expansion of AI; need for regulation of AI; importance of AI education; demystifying and critical role of scientists; freedom and autonomy of scientists in the face of political decisions.

Ethical Requirements

The study was conducted in compliance with ethical guidelines. Participants were contacted using the publicly available addresses listed on the websites of their respective institutions. The aims of the project were clearly presented to them. Each participant received a consent form to ensure their informed agreement to take part. All information was analyzed anonymously to keep confidentiality. During the project, the authors organized meetings and conducted interviews during which the findings were discussed.

Limitations

The study is currently being expanded to include a larger sample, covering more Portuguese AI scientists as well as scientists from international institutions. However, despite the depth of the information collected and the targeted nature of the sample - including experts with coordinating roles in the development of Portuguese AI processes - the data is not generalizable and is incomplete on the views of scientists working exclusively in the business sector.

FINDINGS

AI professionals' perceptions of the social implications of AI

Saving Time, Productivity, And Efficiency

The first theme that stands out in the content analysis of the interviews refers to the association between AI and the benefits it brings in terms of time savings. Participants talk about the positive effects that AI has on society, better forecasting, and therefore greater efficiency. This is because AI can save what they call "less skilled" time, free people up for more meaningful tasks and, most importantly, increase the level of foresight. Therefore, the participants emphasize the role of AI in improving routine tasks and speeding up complex calculations, comparing it to historical advances such as the use of calculators by construction engineers. An example that illustrates this idea is transcribed below, in which the participant details how AI "saves" time.

" We can automate many tasks to increase efficiency and save time. Before the invention of electronic calculating machines, civil engineers performed bridge calculations manually, a time-consuming process. Today, engineers enter data into machines that perform these calculations." (P2)

The possibility of accurately predicting and anticipating futures is one of the strongest ideas in the voices of the participants who illustrate how, in fact, companies use AI to anticipate the products they are promoting and make them meet people's needs and expectations, from the moment they capture their attention until they are consumed.

"Capturing a person's attention, knowing their preferences, their tastes, what they do, and then selling them what are called "futures", futures in the language of economics. I know that this person is going to buy a car in the next six months, so this is extremely valuable information. [...] Company X is a huge platform that knows its customers well and can delight me with books that I will like. (P5)

Participants highlighted the possibility of predicting human behavior as a value. From consumer-related examples to crime-related examples, AI is perceived as a powerful tool for prediction and anticipation. Scientists interviewed spoke of AI's potential to name epidemics faster than institutions or to see patterns in medical shopping sites to discover the prevalence of certain diseases, by geographical area. As one participant said:

"An increase in google searches for [name of medicine] in a specific region indicates an increase in certain health behaviors or concerns." (P5)

For some participants, this ability to predict and expect is fundamental to the dynamics of the modern economy (which they call the economy of the future).

" The available data is significantly limited; however, this scarcity produces efficiency gains. Consequently, these gains arise from our ability to predict future behavior. By predicting potential buyers of specific items, we can target our offers directly at these individuals, rather than surveying the entire area." (P1)

Anticipation

Most of the time, the effects are analyzed in terms of how AI helps with prediction, anticipation, and work relief, all of which have to do with how it changes and speeds up economic transactions. Generative AI, on the other hand, is seen as having the potential to grow and be used in many social areas. However, the advance of AI and the growing dependence on technological systems are highlighted as sources of uncertainty and risk. In the following excerpt, the participant states that one of the biggest risks of AI is the lack of knowledge about its purposes and explains how users may not know the consequences of their actions:

> *" So, without paying too much attention to it and starting to use it without much thought, we run into these problems of "small autonomous weapons", which is an issue directly related to this: if I can't understand why the system is making its decisions, when it decides to kill people, that's a bit worrying... Adapting these systems raises a number of ethical questions. There are also added ethical issues, such as those presented by autonomous vehicles. Curiously, autonomous cars seem to have dropped off the radar... At one point, we thought autonomous cars could be revolutionary, but then we stopped hearing about them altogether. Other issues are related to work because, for the time being, there is the question - although this happens in all revolutions... (...) I do not know if we'll see what happened in previous revolutions, where new jobs emerged to make up for the lost ones. I am not sure this time will be any different. Some professions will disappear, others will appear, but I am not sure that so many will appear this time. If they do not, some job restructuring will be necessary... On the other hand, it's possible that we won't need so much work in the future." (P4)*

Data Protection and Regulation

Most participants (three) highlighted privacy as a critical ethical issue in AI research. They believe that it is necessary to regulate the expansion of AI, particularly about the ease with which large companies collect data from people without their knowledge. Assuming that AI operates between the conventions of a black box and a gray box, they demonstrate what the explanatory procedures could be to ensure that people have the possibility of knowing in advance what can be done with their data and how the intelligent systems embedded in the procedures and the machines handle with information to arrive at certain results. Two participants agree that AI incorporates processes which, if not used based on socially just algorithms, can crystallize prejudices, and legitimize pre-existing social inequalities. In this sense, they advocate the need for greater firmness on the part of regulatory bodies.

AI Experts' Perspectives on AI And Society

Data protection, regulation, and loss of race

But this focus on data protection and the need for regulation is in itself ambivalent and controversial, as some of the scientists who defend the need to strengthen it also point to the dilemmas it entails when the subject turns to the AI economy and the global "race" for the most attractive innovations with the capacity to enter the market. The fear of being left behind in the race is a key point in their speeches.

Determinism and the general need for adaptation and education

As noted above, experts see AI as an inevitable development, indicative of a view based on technological determinism: AI is a job-transforming engine, to which society and politics will have to adapt and for which they will have to consider corrective measures.

Concerns about the harmful effects of AI are linked to what scientists call a general lack of "social and individual literacy" about AI. One participant state that:

" That is, we first need to be aware of what these tools are, that they exist and that they strongly influence our existence on various levels. After that, we can talk about what I think this influence can be, but the role that each of us plays is very much what we have as citizens. It is important to be aware of the existence of these tools, to understand their function as fully as possible and to try to influence political and regulatory authorities within the framework of our representative democracy - where the power to regulate is located - to ensure that the use of these tools is in line with accepted community values and ethical standards." (P4)

Two participants (3, 5) emphasize the impact of AI on cognitive and everyday practices, often resulting in harmful bias or false perceptions of accuracy. A critical point raised is what they consider to be the general lack of public awareness about AI operations, particularly about how social media algorithms work to create new realities. Participants speak of misunderstandings or misrepresentations about the capabilities of AI and how this can lead to further difficulties in terms of social discrimination. Consequently, the experts emphasize the imperative of "informing" and "educating" the public about AI - especially AI that is used in everyday acts of daily life:

" The economic lifeblood of the Internet is advertising - on social media, google, and other platforms. Advertising and recommendation systems form the basis of this model. For example, we can describe X (big global company) as a massive recommendation platform that has a deep understanding of its customers.

It uses this knowledge to captivate me with suggestions of books I am likely to like. Many people don't realize that social media users are targeted by an algorithm to keep them using the site as much as possible for the benefit of the social network owner." (P5)

Information gaps and (huge) lack of knowledge and the role of scientists

The participant below explicitly says that he feels the need to contribute to the demystification of AI amongst the population, especially about the unknown potential that AI can have. Proposing that AI is a "tool", the participants in the study state that it is necessary for people to have a critical perspective on how they use AI, so as not to impoverish themselves, but to gain more skills.

"By using ChatGPT to get ahead, people think they are smart, but it is destroying their brains. Eventually, they will become irrelevant. Not only that, but given the potential of these tools, which is truly incredible, their impact is no longer just a technological development that can affect one or two professions. Suddenly, it could affect humanity in a much more global way. And that is why, for me, I have several roles in all of this, right? My research and teaching area in this field, but I feel that my most significant role right now is to demystify these AI tools so that people realize that they are limited. I would almost use the term "preaching", but I warn against using it too loosely because of the potential negative impact it can have on society. And we have not even started talking about redistribution of wealth, unemployment, etc. That's another dimension."

Trust and dependence

Similarly, the social implications of AI appear from expert discussions, particularly in relation to its potential influence on human cognition. One expert articulated a concern about AI supplanting essential cognitive functions. He says that while people are aware of the positive effects of AI and its potential to open new opportunities, they are also genuinely concerned that widespread misinformation about AI's capabilities will cause people to rely and depend excessively on these technologies. This over-dependence puts critical thinking and cognitive skills at risk, making individuals susceptible to manipulation by both AI systems and their operators. In addition, the lack of effective regulation worsens the problem of disinformation due to widespread ignorance about AI.

" In the tool design phase, let us face it: today, most AI-based tools need data. Right. Not all of them, but a large amount of what is currently in the media needs data. And so it's important that the community, the people whose data will be

used to develop these tools, are aware of the value of their data and what can be done with it to ensure that they only provide, or make available, their data consciously, knowing its potential use. But on the other hand, even at this stage of building the tools, through their political participation, they ensure that their political representatives and political actors implement adequate regulation to ensure that these tools are developed according to ethical principles and everything else. In the same way that we do not tolerate the pharmaceutical industry not being regulated, we do not accept the car industry not being regulated. Only a certain ignorance on the part of society today about what AI is, and its potential effect allows this industry to continue to operate, or until recently, largely unregulated." (P3)

Regulation: the overlapping of specialists

Participants who talk about a regulatory environment emphasize the "delays in appropriate legislative action". They say this makes it harder for people and governments to make good decisions because they do not have enough information. This worsens the spread of misinformation and creates major problems for the ethical and responsible use of AI. In this regard, participants say that public misunderstanding and confusion often fuel disinformation about AI. One expert says that people's dispute and anthropomorphizing of AI (when they mistakenly think that statistical text processing is the same thing as real intelligence) leads to unrealistic expectations and fears due to this misinformation:

"This prevents individuals and governments from making informed decisions, delaying the regulation and deliberate use of AI."

In this context, "education" becomes an ethical obligation to deal with disinformation. Participants emphasize the need to inform the public about the authentic characteristics of AI to ensure its responsible use. Expert 4 states that:

"This issue is different from control, right? It occurs when we're not voluntarily giving up control; instead, we're tricked into believing we have authority when, in reality, we don't - an occurrence that may have always been somewhat true." (P4)

In addition, the participants warn against relying too much on AI tools without fully understanding their limitations. They emphasize that a lack of technical knowledge and critical thinking can lead to AI-driven decisions that do not involve human judgment, highlighting the need for a more informed public and a more cautious approach to integrating AI. The emphasis on education and the misuse of AI link to scientists' views on data privacy and the ease with which data can be obtained for unintended purposes. In their view, AI often relies on substantial amounts of data to function, raising significant concerns about privacy and how companies collect, store or use data.

The participants also express concern about the potential for deception in widely used AI tools and warn that AI tools such as ChatGPT can create illusions of intelligence and accuracy that mislead users, which can lead to misunderstandings about the true capabilities and limitations of AI, as well as a greater over-reliance on these technologies:

" Some companies that are currently leading this AI revolution for commercial reasons are often interested in misinformation. Often, these products do not have the necessary features or capabilities. And that creates a very complicated situation here because, on the one hand, we have tools that do things that until recently we didn't dream a tool could do, which are difficult to explain, even from a technical point of view." (P4)

Researchers focused on understanding how AI is used today, pointing out how important it is to use AI in the right way to avoid manipulation and reduce the risks for people and companies that come from the unethical use of AI and for strictly economic purposes, but which allow discrimination against people:

" And then, because these are decisions that can affect people, for example, if they block my credit card, it is annoying and unpleasant; these decisions should not disproportionately affect different population groups, for example. One thing that sometimes happens is that older people are more vulnerable to certain types of fraud. On the other hand, this also happens more often because they are older; their transactions are seen as potentially problematic. This is seen as unfair; it is bad treatment of a different population segment. This can be formulated and formalized mathematically, and systems can be developed that are more robust or more immune to this kind of unfairness. Researchers can study this area from a technical perspective. It incorporates ethical considerations and offers a range of technical tools for application. (P5)

The opinions of the participants interviewed are strongly rooted in the idea of the need to adjust and adapt society:

"Society must adapt by building infrastructure and enacting legislation, similar to the approach taken with cars," highlighting the need for society to adapt to AI by developing proper structures and regulations. Experts argue that social media, once perceived as positive, is now a problem. AI could follow a similar trajectory. This idea is that, as AI becomes more common, it could cause problems that were not anticipated because "artificial intelligence is a tool designed for engineers to implement, then utilized by individuals, significantly impacting society."(P4)

In this view, engineers are essential to ensuring that AI is developed on an ethical basis, so they emphasize that the public, whose data will be used in the development of AI, must be aware of the value of their information and the impact that data donation can have on their lives. Against this backdrop, experts see the role of scientists as essential in ensuring that the disruptive potential of AI is carefully managed, although they agree that decisions about governance should be made by political figures, not by them.

"It has a huge impact on society in many different ways. However, deciding how these impacts are managed, cared for, and dealt with is a technical problem; it has technical aspects, but it is also a political problem - one of political economy, decision-making and the way society is organized. What kind of society do we want? This is a political problem, and politicians need to be aware of this and have proposals on the table. The European Commission, which previously dealt with privacy and GDPR, is now dealing with AI law. But there is a problem: the development of AI is going extremely fast, and the legislative process is much slower. Now, for example, they have been caught in the middle; when ChatGPT was launched, they were on to something else that did not consider this kind of technology. That is why I consistently say that those who shape the structure of society are not the creators of technology. They have some responsibility and need to inform the decision-makers." (P5)

However, experts recognize that scientists play a technical role, but should collaborate with stakeholders, including policymakers and psychologists, such as:

"The precise parameters of this are self-evident; common sense prevails. Our professional training makes us familiar with specific case studies and more observant of such issues. This is akin to the process of consuming news: you cultivate a critical perspective, engage with news pertinent to these issues and can find discrepancies. However, the leap to self-legislation is illogical." (P2)

One of the main challenges we find in scientists' speeches is, in fact, the fear of the expansion of AI in the private sector and the way it can be used in an unregulated way, leading to very diverse social implications, firstly because it becomes possible to endow any technical device with this ability to capture and process data.

"A system makes decisions based on observations with a defined objective." Any system that a human can observe and consider exhibiting intelligent behavior covers a broad spectrum. This ranges from a basic device like a thermostat on an iron, which operates intelligently, albeit rudimentarily, by deciding to turn the temperature on or off, to the algorithms that power social media platforms." (P5)

Participating are aware of the social divides that AI can create, by transforming society and creating new hierarchies of professions that become checked and highly vulnerable, given the centrality of activities that have the power to concentrate data. In general, they agree on the need for regulatory standards, but also tend to remain distant from preventing or solving emerging social problems, i.e. what to do with the time that is freed up by the use of AI in society and how it will be possible to distribute the work that tends to disappear and make the most of the abundant time that we are beginning to have in society, but which is not paid for.

"Moreover, work plays a role in this inequality. If we are not careful - this has probably happened during other technological revolutions - we could create a huge gap between those who remain in dying professions and can't adapt and others. Compare the AI computer scientist, who is in high demand and well paid, with the lawyer who becomes obsolete. This gap exists between individuals, organizations, and nations - those with access to these tools and those without. These tools are extremely powerful and, if we're not careful, they can create an inequality gap, leading to obvious social problems." (P2)

The general focus of experts' voices

Participant 4 says that engineers are responsible for the initial design and implementation of the instrument. Afterwards, users must employ technology, and society must adjust to its presence:

"If we look at artificial intelligence dispassionately, simply as a tool that is developed by engineers, and that, like any tool, serves to solve problems, serves to act on the world, on any problem. That is, the hammer also serves to drive nails and acts on the world. If we look dispassionately at what an artificial intelligence tool is, whatever that is. So, the role of each of the stakeholders must be looked at according to what this tool is and what it is for. It is up to the engineers to first design and implement this tool. And then it is up to the users to use that tool, and it is up to society to adapt to the existence of that tool. This is true for any tool, it is true for a car, engineers construct a car that is suitable to travel from one place to another" (P4).

We can set up two distinct types of discourse, considering the interviews: those that focus on ethical and privacy issues and those that emphasize the elements of collaboration between governments and organizations to make people more aware of the demands of AI, as follows:

Focus on ethical issues (1 and 4): These participants emphasize privacy concerns and an interest in providing AI with the ability to prove explanations and ensure transparency. Criticism of the influence of networks on people's lives and the possibility of being swallowed up by AI is key.

Focus on collaboration and governance (2, 3 and 5). These participants tend to highlight the need for government entities to collaborate with AI professionals and develop proper methodologies to support and deepen digital literacy. They are not clear about the type of professionals to be included, nor about how people should be involved, but they are open and insist on interdisciplinary collaboration, including social sciences and humanities.

DISCUSSION

This chapter aimed to explore the perspectives of scientists involved in AI research and innovation, highlighting the main dimensions of their discourses on the social implications of AI and the conditions shaping the evolution of a future society structured around AI. The findings point to a prevailing view of AI as a transformative and disruptive force, the full implications of which remain undefined and unknown. According to the scientists themselves, addressing these challenges requires informed policy decisions that they see as primarily the responsibility of politicians. Interviews show that the relationship between science, society and politics is inherently complex, particularly due to its entanglement with the economy in contemporary contexts. While scientists emphasize the potential of AI, they are also aware of the latent pitfalls. Some portray almost dystopian visions of how AI could harm society, destroying humanity and culture. Most of them refer to the almost inevitable loss and transformation of jobs, the emergence of abundant and/or precarious free time, and the reconfiguration of global power through new ruling elites controlling what people need, do, and buy. Based on Collins' perspectives on science, expertise and populism, this chapter has been aligned with the idea that AI experts play a key role in reflecting on the social and political implications of AI, since they assume themselves to be stakeholders in the phenomenon. Luís and Rodríguez (2020, p. 261) state that, "There is no future in the development of AI without a civic and democratic character (...) democratic action must result from participatory efforts and be guided by ethical principles rooted in the context of the new technological scenario." Indeed, different perspectives are essential for a comprehensive approach to AI, especially considering it as a socio-technical system. However, AI experts do not entirely agree with the idea of feeling responsible for the cultural future presented by AI and how AI will promote democratic impoverishment or inequalities. Nevertheless, their voices highlight some fundamental points about the ambiguities that permeate the development of AI. Their discourses on AI are a mixture of enthusiasm and reticence, not due to the technology itself, but to the cultural and educational backgrounds that they consider low and inadequate for dealing with AI. In this sense, Hermínio Martins' discussions on technological maximalism and cautious approaches to technological futures seem particularly relevant to the ongoing debate on AI and expert engagement. In fact, Martins (2006) warns against the uncritical acceptance of technology, emphasizing the importance of assessing its implications within the framework of democratic values and discussing the type of society that is intended in the future.

SOLUTIONS AND RECOMMENDATIONS

AI scientists interviewed for this survey acknowledge their position: while they do not see themselves as responsible for addressing the wider societal implications of AI (such as job displacement) or making policy decisions, they do feel an indirect obligation to engage with policy. However, rather than adopting a participatory model from the outset - one that involves citizens in the design and creation of AI - scientists emphasize the need to develop AI within ethical and legal frameworks and educate people on how to use AI in ways that avoid or mitigate the potential risks that come with AI. The exploration of AI needs a broad understanding of the perspectives presented by AI academics, as these insights help elucidate current trends and the growing role of AI in various aspects of human life. Participants highlight the substantial potential of AI in social contexts, particularly in relation to its predictive capabilities, advanced data processing methodologies and its ability to recreate new realities. For example, in all sectors, AI tools have fundamentally transformed work processes, accelerating individual and organizational performance across the board. It is therefore essential to recognize that the applicability of AI extends to multiple spheres, significantly reshaping interpersonal relationships, governance structures and international relations and dependencies. Participants believe that setting up ethical and legal frameworks focused on protecting data privacy is a crucial step, given the rapid evolution of AI technology and its broad market applications. Analysis supports the view that individuals must understand how to manage and use data responsibly to mitigate exposure to potential risks. However, the deep integration of AI into public and private organizational structures amplifies the complexity of these issues and reduces the level of participation and reflection on the implications of AI, so that individuals often struggle to discern proper actions on their data and interactions with AI systems. This shift in perceptions of risk and uncertainty underscores the importance of directly involving individuals in shaping AI systems. Although scientists don't claim this and are quite critical about the implications of AI for transforming values and especially for instilling democratic illiteracy, in fact, AI is currently mainly a top-down initiative - something that is created and then integrated into social processes in which different professionals intervene to create new functionalities. Examples from the education, health and other labor areas show how socio-technical imaginaries often predict the transformative influence of AI, while confronting predicted repercussions, including data governance, authoritarianism, administrative rationalism, and the potential displacement of human labor by technological advances. These imaginaries embody narratives that are both optimistic and dystopian, as knowledge about AI is continuously spread across many different categories of experts who hold diverse knowledge, although it may be in conflict and may emerge and have different relevance to the public depending on the profile of the communicative platform they use. In our view, AI scientists, particularly those working in academia, have added challenges to face because they need to confront processes of legitimization and establishment of truth regimes that find many ways to feed into the offer that AI can provide. This engagement is fundamental to understanding AI as an inherently social phenomenon, rather than a mere technological artifact.

FUTURE RESEARCH

The interviews we have conducted so far demonstrate the ambiguity that lies within the position of scientists regarding AI. The scientists interviewed are very focused on issues related to AI literacy, the need for education for the use of AI and the importance of increasing legal scrutiny, in particular on companies. Today, there are several lines of analysis that are opening up for AI research, given the importance that AI has on time management, the emergence of new professions and new lifestyles. In practice, we are witnessing an increasingly critical discourse on the part of scientists about AI, as they consider that people in general are in a situation of knowledge deficit that allows them to have a critical view and a cautious practice in relation to AI. But this critical dimension of the debate is very much grounded in the idea that technology is unescapable and that people will have to try to adjust to AI and live with its challenges, but also with its challenges. In other words, scientists today are furnished to "demystify" AI, demonstrate the behind-the-scenes economics that powers AI, and invest in AI that is more transparent, from the user's point of view. Scientists political stance demonstrates their concern with AI. However, we still know little about their intentions regarding the way they think about power of influence in the field, or about the effects that their speeches may have on the AI scientific community, in general in the country and beyond. We also know little about how they interact with and negotiate the social implications of technology, either as professionals or as partners in collaborative projects that instigate the use of AI. It would be of enormous importance to address in more depth how the network of meanings about AI is established, how the controversies are fed and who participates in these controversies. At this point, it would be important to pay special attention to scientists, seeking to map and understand the differences and semblances between their positions, depending on whether they are academic scientists (more linked to academia), or practical scientists (working directly in companies). The race to AI is very broad slowing down more and more sectors of society. Companies today suffer the rebound of AI, precisely because the predictive capacity it offers also represents a drawback for them, since there is great volatility in information, speeches and buying behavior, hence AI is highly sought after by companies, precisely in order to face this variation in demand. It is not possible to establish standards for action on AI research and implementation, but it is legitimate to think about the combination of interests between researchers from different disciplinary areas and develop cross-cutting projects that include contributions aimed at both the creation phase of AI and monitoring and implementation. These projects would involve direct contact with people in order to identify and understand the uses of technology, but also with organizations and entities that could promote involvement projects with a participatory dimension. Other prospective projects, using the Delphi technique and other scenario creation methods, would also help in the construction of visions of the future of AI that can positively influence its development. An area of necessary development is the area of teaching and learning, especially in higher education, where it is necessary to increase transversal training with the potential for curricular change and where the knowledge of the various areas is understood and valued equally, enhancing the perception and deconstruction of AI as a socio-technical element that imposes structural dilemmas on society.

FINAL CONSIDERATIONS

Although participants are aware of the ethical issues that can arise from not knowing how the same AI can be used in different situations, they are not good at naming the effects of AI because they see it as a normal part of change that will require adjustments through new job restructuring or even changes in how work is valued. The attachment to the promises of AI is clear when the participant assumes that AI can simply end the need to work; however, he/she does not advance how the absence of work will compensate for the absence of money. Rudin says: "There has been a recent surge of interest in developing methods for 'explainable AI', where models are created to explain how a first 'black box' machine learning model arrives at a particular decision. It can be argued that efforts should be directed towards building inherently interpretable models in the first place, particularly where they are applied to applications that directly affect human lives, such as in healthcare and criminal justice" (Rudin, 2019, wp). Based on qualitative interviews with six prominent AI researchers, it sheds light on their perceptions, responsibilities, and proposed strategies for aligning technological advances with social values. The findings reveal a double consciousness among AI experts: while they recognize the transformative potential of AI, they also emphasize the need for regulation, education, and interdisciplinary collaboration to mitigate its risks and unintended consequences. A recurring theme in the interviews is the gap between technological innovation and the broader social and ethical frameworks needed to guide its development. AI experts highlight the critical importance of fostering public literacy, promoting transparency in AI systems and encouraging participatory approaches to governance. They also express concerns about the concentration of power within corporations and the potential misuse of AI technologies, warning against over-reliance on opaque systems that can worsen social inequalities and erode democratic values. Despite this awareness, AI experts recognize significant challenges in tackling these issues. They highlight the slow pace of regulatory processes, limited public understanding of the implications of AI and the complex and global nature of technological governance. While emphasizing the importance of their role in shaping ethical AI practices, they also point to the shared responsibility of policymakers, social scientists, and citizens in creating a more inclusive and fair technological future.

In conclusion AI scientists highlight their awareness of both the vast potential and the concerns and perverse effects of AI. While they emphasize that they cannot take responsibility for decision taking, they stress that their expertise and knowledge must be integral to the ongoing dialogue around AI regulation, in which policymakers must actively engage. These scientists recognize the need for public education and regulation to ensure that AI is used responsibly, with benefits that extend to society at large. While they understand that the ethical use of AI depends not only on their input, but also on the active debates to address risks and ensure transparency in the development and implementation of AI, they do not present a clear path to promote social engagement and participation in discussions during the creation and design phases of AI. On the other hand, they express some concerns about the wide range of data that AI companies can collect and the potential misuse of such data for purposes that are neither democratic nor respectful of human rights and principles of justice. These uses, they argue, are often not in line with the aims of the so-called "industry of the future", which promises significant advances through AI applications. Despite the openness to discuss the issues, the two main structuring elements are unclear in the view of AI experts: in) the paths to interdisciplinarity and ii) the acceptability within the AI scientific community of social engagement throughout the AI design process.

REFERENCES

Bostrom, N. (2016). *Superintelligence: Paths, dangers, strategies*. Oxford University Press.

Callon, M. (1981). Towards a sociology of technological controversies. *Fundamenta Scientiae*, 2, 381–399.

Callon, M. (1987). Society information: The examination of technology as a tool for sociological analysis. In Bijker, W., Hughes, T., & Pinch, T. (Eds.), *The social construction of technical systems: New directions in the sociology and history of technology* (pp. 83–106). MIT Press.

Carayannis, E. G., & Campbell, D. F. J. (2009). 'Mode 3' and the 'Quadruple Helix': Advancing a 21st century fractal innovation system. *International Journal of Technology Management*, 46(3-4), 201–230. https://doi.org/10.1504/IJTM.2009.023374

Charmaz, K. (2012). The power and potential of grounded theory. Medical Sociology Online, 6 (2), 3. http://www.

Collins, H. (1990). *Artificial Experts: Social Knowledge and Intelligent Machines*. MIT Press.

Collins, H. (2013). Refining the tacit. *Philosophy of Science*, 17(3). https://journals.openedition.org/philosophiascientiae/895

Collins, H. (2020). *Artificial Intelligence: Opposing the Subjugation of Humanity to Computers*. Polity Press.

Collins, H., & Evans, R. (2007). *Rethinking expertise*. University of Chicago Press.

Deng, A. (2018). Smart contracts and blockchains: catalysts for collusion? *SSRN*. https://doi.org/10.2139/ssrn.3187010

Dignum, V. (2023). Responsible artificial intelligence: recommendations and lessons learned. In Eke, D. O., Wakunuma, K., & Akintoye, S. (Eds.), *Responsible AI in Africa: social-and-cultural-studies-of-robots-and-AI* (pp. 195–214). Palgrave Macmillan., https://doi.org/10.1007/978-3-031-08215-3_9

Epstein, S. (1996). *Impure Science: AIDS, Activism, and the Politics of Knowledge*. University of California Press.

Gibbons, M. (2013). Mode 1, Mode 2, and innovation. In Carayannis, E. G. (Ed.), *Encyclopedia of creativity, invention, innovation, and entrepreneurship*. Springer., https://doi.org/10.1007/978-1-4614-3858-8_451

Jasanoff, S. (2015). Imperfect futures: Science, technology, and the imaginations of modernity. In Jasanoff, S., & Kim, S. H. (Eds.), *Dreamscapes of modernity: Sociotechnical imaginaries and the fabrication of power* (pp. 1–33). University of Chicago Press., https://doi.org/10.7208/chicago/9780226276663.003.0001

Latour, B., & Woolgar, S. (1979). Laboratory life: The social construction of scientific facts. *Sage (Atlanta, Ga.).*

Lindgren, S., & Holmström, J. (2020). A social science perspective on artificial intelligence: Building blocks for a research agenda. *Journal of Digital Social Research*, 2(3), 1–15. https://doi.org/10.33621/jdsr.v2i3.65

Lindgren, S., & Holmström, J. (2020). A social science perspective on artificial intelligence: Building blocks for a research agenda. *Journal of Digital Social Research*, 2(3), 1–15. DOI: 10.33621/jdsr.v2i3.65

Marshall, W., Tang, M., & Durham, S. A. (2012). Integration of science, technology, and society (STS) courses into the engineering curriculum. *ASEE Annual Conference and Exposition, Conference Proceedings.*

Martins, H. (2006). Dilemmas of the technological republic. *Analise Social*, 41(181), 959–979.

Merton, R. K. (1942/1973). The Normative Structure of Science. In *The Sociology of Science: Theoretical and Empirical Investigations*. University of Chicago Press.

Rahwan, I., Cebrian, M., & Obradovich, N. (2019). Machine behaviour. *Nature*, 568, 477–486. DOI: 10.1038/s41586-019-1138-y

Ren, D. (2021). Reflections and perspectives on artificial intelligence: From philosophical and physical points of view. *Cultura e Scuola*, 4(3), 109–111. https://doi.org/10.1177/20966083211056988

Rudin, C. (2019). Stop explaining black-box machines learning models for high-risk decisions and use interpretable models instead. *Nature Machine Intelligence*, 1(5), 206–215. DOI: 10.1038/s42256-019-0048-x

Sartori, L., & Theodorou, A. (2022). A socio-technical view on the future of AI: Narratives, inequalities, and human control. *Ethics and Information Technology*, 24(4), 1–4. https://doi.org/10.1007/s10676-022-09624-3

Sartori, L., & Theodorou, A. (n.d.). A sociotechnical perspective for the future of AI: Narratives, inequalities, and human control.

Shanmugam, A. (2020). 'Artificial intelligence' - A 'futuristic vision'. *International Journal of Advance Research, Ideas, and Innovations in Technology*, 6, 48–50.

Simon, H. A. (1969). *Sciences of the artificial.* MIT Press.

Simon, H. A. (1969). *The sciences of artificial.* MIT Press.

Trzesicki, K. (2020). The concept of artificial intelligence. *Studia Humana*, 9, 37–65.

Urze, P., & Araújo, E. (2024). O admirável mundo novo da IA. In *Estudos sociais da ciência e tecnologia: Olhares e perspetivas*. Tinta da China.

Weber, M. (1972). *A ciência como vocação*. Cultrix.

ADDITIONAL READING

Akbar, A., & Rsur, R. (2021). Community engagement in engineering: A necessity. *Proceedings of the Conference on Engineering Ethics and Social Responsibility*, 4–5.

Ansari, W. (2023). *The ethical implications of artificial intelligence on human society*. Social Science Research Network.

Collins, H., & Evans, R. (2007). *Rethinking Expertise*. University of Chicago Press., DOI: 10.7208/chicago/9780226113623.001.000

Collins, H. M. (1985). *Changing order: replication and induction in scientific practice*. University of Chicago Press.

Collins, H. M., & Evans, R. (2002). The third wave of science studies: Studies of expertise and experience. *Social Studies of Science*, 33(2), 235–296.

Etzkowitz, H., & Leydesdorff, L. (1997). *Universities and the Global Knowledge Economy: A Triple Helix of University-Industry-Government Relations*. Pinter Publishers.

Etzkowitz, H., & Leydesdorff, L. (Eds.). (2000). The dynamics of innovation: From national systems and "mode 2" to a triple helix of university-industry-government relations. *Research Policy*, 29(2), 109–123.

Fekete, A. (2019). Social vulnerability (re-)assessment in context to natural hazards: Review of the usefulness of the spatial indicator approach and investigations of validation demands. *International Journal of Disaster Risk Science*, 10, 220–232. DOI: 10.1007/s13753-019-0213-1

Felt, U. (2009). *Knowing and living in academic research: Convergence and heterogeneity in research cultures in the European context*. Institute of Sociology of the Academy of Sciences of the Czech Republic.

Felt, U. (2016). Science and its publics: Reflexively making sense of the mutual relationships. In Felt, U., Fouché, R., Miller, C. A., & Smith-Doerr, L. (Eds.), *The handbook of science and technology studies* (4th ed., pp. 135–162). MIT Press.

Felt, U., & Fochler, M. (2010). Machines for making publics: Inscribe and describe publics in public engagement. *Minerva*, 48(3), 219–238.

Felt, U., Fouché, R., Miller, C., & Smith-Doerr, L. (Eds.). (2017). *The Handbook of Science and Technology Studies*. MIT.

Ferrand, N., Hassenforder, E., & Girard, S. (2024). Engineering participation: Preparing and designing a participatory process. In *Transformative participation for socio-ecological sustainability*. QUAE.

Fisher, E., & Fortmann, L. (Eds.). (2018). *The moral economy of science*. Routledge.

Haraway, D. (1988). Situated knowledge: The question of science in feminism and the privilege of the partial perspective. *Feminist Studies*, 14(3), 575–599.

Harsh, N., Niles, J., & Tamburi, R. (2017). Preparing engineers for community engagement: A framework for inclusive practices. *International Journal of Engineering Education*, 33(6), 1776–1785.

Jasanoff, S. (2010). States of Knowledge: The Coproduction of Science and Social Order. International Library of Sociology. London, Routledge.

Jasanoff, S., & Kim, S.-H. (Eds.). (2015). *Dreamscapes of modernity: sociotechnical imaginaries and the construction of power*. University of Chicago Press.

Joyce, K., & Cruz, T. M. (2024). A sociology of artificial intelligence: Inequalities, power, and data justice. *Socius: Sociological Research for a Dynamic World*, 10. Advance online publication. https://doi.org/10.1177/23780231241275393

Karlsen, J., Græe, K., & Massaoud, M. (2008). Building trust in project-stakeholder relationships. *Baltic Journal of Management*, 3, 7–22. DOI: 10.1108/17465260810844239

Kelty, C. M. (2008). *Two Bits: The cultural significance of free software*. Duke University Press.

Knorr-Cetina, K., & Reichmann, W. (Eds.). (2016). *Epistemic cultures: how the sciences produce knowledge*. Harvard University Press.

Law, T., & McCall, L. (2024). Artificial intelligence policymaking: An agenda for sociological research. *Socius: Sociological Research for a Dynamic World*, 10. Advance online publication. https://doi.org/10.1177/23780231241261596

Shen, B. (1975). Scientific literacy and public understanding of science. *American Scientist*, 63(3), 265–268.

Tiwari, R. (2023). Ethical and societal implications of AI and machine learning. International Journal of Scientific Research in Engineering and Management.

Turner, S. (2001). What's wrong with experts? *Social Studies of Science*, 31(1), 123–149. https://www.jstor.org/stable/285821

Turner, S. P. (2014). *The politics of expertise*. Routledge.

Warr, M. A., & Rather, M. S. (2024). Sociological analysis of artificial intelligence, benefits, concerns, and its future implications. *International Journal of Indian Psychology*, 12(3), 178. https://doi.

KEY TERMS AND DEFINITIONS

Ethical AI: an approach to developing AI that considers the needs of society, transparency, and fairness in accessing and using AI.

Interdisciplinary collaboration: collaboration between experts from different fields of study for an in-depth understanding of the implications of AI in all spheres of society.

Technological determinism: a deep-rooted assumption that technology is the main driving force of society, and society needs to adjust and adapt to its developments. This understanding partially supports the idea that technology is always capable of proposing a new solution to any problem that is caused by technology itself.

Responsible innovation: innovation developed within ethical guidelines and cultural values, ensuring that no harm comes to people. The European Commission has launched updated frameworks for AI.

Data privacy: The rights and measures that protect personal data from being stored or used in datasets. There are different national legal frameworks on these topics. Important decisions are needed about the effects of information on people's lives in the future. Important diagnostics are needed to find out how public and private organizations work on these topics and ensure data protection.

Public AI literacy: Practices designed to inform people and engage them in critical thinking and the use of AI. They should be discussed and debated in a way that motivates people to create solutions and commit to change.

AI Time: Patterns of time use, and management brought about by the use and development of AI.

Social engagement in AI: any form of engagement in which stakeholders engage in critically discussing, evaluating, and visualizing the use of AI in social processes.

AI co-creation: A bottom-up approach to AI development, where all stakeholders, including people of different ages, genders, and races, are heard about solutions to be implemented and methods to be followed. Various methods can be used to involve people in the discussion of AI and its future scenarios. Interdisciplinarity is crucial at this stage.

Explainable Artificial Intelligence (XAI): methods used in the development of AI guaranteeing transparency and fairness in the uses of AI.

Chapter 17
Ethical Considerations in the Use of AI and Big Data in Corporate Decision-Making

Gaurab Kumar Sharma
https://orcid.org/0000-0001-9343-071X
Swami Vivekanand Subharti University, India

Ekta Tyagi
https://orcid.org/0009-0008-6022-6876
Swami Vivekanand Subharti University, India

Amrita Chaudhary
https://orcid.org/0009-0004-7345-1977
Swami Vivekanand Subharti University, India

ABSTRACT

In an era where artificial intelligence and big data have become integral to corporate management, the ethical challenges associated with their deployment cannot be overlooked. As businesses increasingly rely on AI-driven insights and vast data streams for decision-making, the potential for misuse, bias, and violations of privacy grows. This chapter explores into the ethical considerations that corporations must address to harness AI and big data responsibly. It explores the implications of these technologies on corporate decision-making, highlighting the risks of algorithmic bias, data exploitation, and transparency issues. Through a comprehensive analysis, the chapter proposes a framework for ethical AI and big data utilization, emphasizing the need for corporate governance structures that prioritize ethical

DOI: 10.4018/979-8-3693-9015-3.ch017

practices, data integrity, and accountability. The chapter aims to provide business leaders, managers, and policymakers with actionable insights to balance innovation with ethical responsibility.

1. INTRODUCTION

1.1 The Rise of AI and Big Data in Corporate Management

The rise of Artificial Intelligence (AI) and Big Data has revolutionized corporate management, altering the landscape of business decision-making. These technologies have ushered in a new era where data-driven insights and automation guide strategic decisions, enhance operational efficiency, and foster innovation. As a result, organizations are increasingly relying on AI and Big Data to navigate complex markets, streamline their operations, and offer personalized services to their customers. This transformation is not just a technological shift but a fundamental change in how businesses operate, make decisions, and interact with customers and stakeholders.

AI refers to the simulation of human intelligence processes by machines, particularly systems that learn, reason, and self-correct (Russell & Norvig, 2016). It encompasses a broad range of technologies, including machine learning, natural language processing, and robotics, which enable machines to analyze vast amounts of data, identify patterns, and make predictions with minimal human intervention. Big Data, on the other hand, refers to the enormous volume, variety, and velocity of data generated daily by businesses, social media platforms, sensors, and other digital tools (Mayer-Schönberger & Cukier, 2013). The combination of AI and Big Data offers a potent toolset for companies to gain deeper insights into customer behavior, market trends, and operational efficiencies, leading to more informed and faster decision-making.

In modern corporate management, these technologies are no longer just buzzwords but integral elements of business strategy. AI and Big Data are transforming how companies compete, innovate, and create value. For example, AI-driven tools like predictive analytics help businesses anticipate customer demands, optimize supply chains, and tailor products to individual preferences (Davenport & Ronanki, 2018). Big Data analytics enables organizations to analyze historical data to forecast future trends, uncover hidden patterns, and improve decision-making processes (Chen, Chiang, & Storey, 2012). Together, AI and Big Data provide businesses with a comprehensive view of their environment, enabling them to adapt quickly and stay competitive in a fast-evolving market.

The impact of AI and Big Data extends across various sectors, each benefiting from these technologies in unique ways. In finance, AI algorithms are used to detect fraudulent transactions, automate trading, and assess credit risk (Arner, Barberis, & Buckley, 2016). In healthcare, Big Data analytics help in the development of personalized medicine, improving patient outcomes through predictive models that analyze medical records, genetic information, and environmental factors (Raghupathi & Raghupathi, 2014). Similarly, in the retail industry, AI-powered recommendation engines analyze consumer preferences and purchasing behavior to drive personalized marketing and product suggestions (Gentsch, 2018). These examples highlight the transformative potential of AI and Big Data across industries, demonstrating their role as catalysts for innovation, efficiency, and competitive advantage.

Moreover, these technologies have significant implications for corporate governance, decision-making structures, and organizational culture. The adoption of AI and Big Data often necessitates a shift in how companies think about data privacy, ethics, and decision-making transparency. As organizations increasingly rely on algorithms to make decisions, they must also grapple with issues such as algorithmic bias, data privacy, and accountability (O'Neil, 2016). Therefore, it is crucial for businesses to not only adopt AI and Big Data technologies but also develop ethical frameworks to guide their use. Ensuring that AI and Big Data are deployed responsibly is essential to maintaining public trust and fostering long-term sustainability in a digitally driven business environment.

The transformative potential of AI and Big Data also introduces new challenges and opportunities for managers and leaders. As organizations adopt these technologies, they must address the changing roles of employees, the need for new skill sets, and the evolution of leadership in the digital age (Westerman, Bonnet, & Ferraris, 2014). AI and Big Data are not just tools for enhancing operational efficiency but also have the potential to reshape organizational structures, leadership approaches, and decision-making processes. The rise of AI-driven automation and analytics tools presents both opportunities for businesses to gain a competitive edge and challenges in terms of workforce transformation and talent management.

1.2 The Importance of Ethical Considerations

The integration of Artificial Intelligence (AI) and Big Data into corporate decision-making processes has undeniably transformed the way businesses operate. However, as organizations increasingly rely on these technologies, there is a growing need for ethical considerations in their application. AI and Big Data offer unprecedented opportunities for efficiency, innovation, and competitive advantage, but they also raise significant ethical dilemmas that must be addressed to ensure responsible use. The need for ethics in the age of AI and Big Data is critical not only for protecting stakeholders but also for fostering trust and long-term sustainability in business operations.

The Need for Ethics in the Age of AI and Big Data

AI and Big Data have the potential to dramatically reshape industries by automating decision-making, personalizing services, and optimizing operations (Davenport & Ronanki, 2018). These technologies are capable of processing vast amounts of data and generating insights that would be impossible for humans to achieve on their own. However, as businesses increasingly rely on AI and Big Data to make critical decisions, ethical challenges arise regarding how data is collected, used, and interpreted.

One of the main concerns is the issue of algorithmic bias. AI systems are often trained on historical data, which may contain inherent biases based on race, gender, socioeconomic status, or other factors (O'Neil, 2016). If these biases are not identified and addressed, AI systems can perpetuate and even amplify existing inequalities, leading to discriminatory outcomes in areas such as hiring, lending, or law enforcement. Ethical considerations, therefore, require that AI systems be designed and implemented with fairness and equity in mind to prevent harm to marginalized groups.

Additionally, data privacy is another critical ethical issue. The vast amounts of data generated and processed by businesses today often include sensitive personal information, such as health records, financial data, and consumer behavior. The collection and use of this data without proper consent or oversight can violate individuals' privacy rights and erode public trust in organizations (Zeng, 2017). As such, ethical principles in the handling of Big Data must prioritize the protection of personal privacy and ensure transparency in how data is gathered, stored, and used.

The rapid development of AI and Big Data also raises questions about accountability. When decisions are made by algorithms rather than humans, it becomes unclear who is responsible for the outcomes, particularly if those decisions lead to negative consequences. Establishing clear accountability structures is essential to ensure that organizations can be held responsible for the actions of their AI systems (Dastin, 2018). Without accountability, there is a risk that businesses may ignore or overlook the consequences of unethical AI practices, potentially causing harm to consumers and society.

Key Ethical Dilemmas and Why They Matter for Businesses

Several key ethical dilemmas arise from the use of AI and Big Data in business practices, each of which has significant implications for organizations. These dilemmas not only affect the reputation and trustworthiness of businesses but also pose legal and financial risks.

1. **Algorithmic Bias and Discrimination**: As mentioned earlier, one of the most pressing ethical concerns in AI is the potential for bias in algorithms. AI systems often learn from historical data, and if this data reflects biased patterns, the algorithms will replicate these biases in their decision-making processes. For instance, AI algorithms used in hiring processes may favor certain demographic groups over others, perpetuating discrimination. This can lead to legal challenges, reputational damage, and reduced customer trust. Businesses must take proactive steps to ensure that their AI systems are fair and equitable, by regularly auditing algorithms for bias and using diverse datasets during the training process (O'Neil, 2016).
2. **Data Privacy and Security**: The vast quantities of personal data collected by organizations present significant risks in terms of privacy breaches and unauthorized access. In the absence of clear ethical guidelines, companies may misuse data, whether intentionally or unintentionally, putting consumers' sensitive information at risk. High-profile data breaches have led to increased regulatory scrutiny, with laws such as the General Data Protection Regulation (GDPR) in Europe imposing strict requirements on data collection and processing (Zeng, 2017). Ethical considerations in the collection, storage, and sharing of data are not only essential for protecting individuals' privacy but also for maintaining compliance with legal standards.
3. **Lack of Transparency in AI Decision-Making**: AI systems often operate as "black boxes," making decisions based on complex algorithms that are difficult to understand or explain. This lack of transparency raises ethical concerns regarding the fairness and accountability of AI-driven decisions. For example, in the case of AI systems used for credit scoring, it may be unclear how decisions are made, leading to confusion or distrust among consumers who are affected by these decisions. Ethical principles demand that businesses ensure their AI systems are explainable and that stakeholders, including consumers, are provided with clear explanations of how decisions are made (Dastin, 2018).
4. **Job Displacement and Workforce Impact**: The rise of AI and automation also brings forth ethical concerns related to workforce displacement. As AI technologies take over more tasks traditionally performed by humans, there is a growing concern about the future of work and the ethical implications

of replacing human labor with machines. While AI and automation can lead to significant cost savings and efficiencies, businesses must consider their responsibility to retrain and reskill employees who may be displaced by these technologies. Ethical considerations require that companies invest in workforce development programs to ensure that employees can transition to new roles in the evolving digital economy (Brynjolfsson & McAfee, 2014).

Key ethical dilemmas such as algorithmic bias, data privacy, accountability, and workforce impact must be addressed to ensure that these technologies are used responsibly and transparently. Failure to do so can result in legal, financial, and reputational risks that may undermine the trust and sustainability of organizations in the long term.

1.3 Chapter Objectives and Scope

Explanation of the Chapter's Purpose and What It Aims to Achieve

The purpose of this chapter is to explore the ethical considerations surrounding the use of Artificial Intelligence (AI) and Big Data in corporate decision-making. As these technologies continue to transform businesses across industries, there is an increasing need to address the ethical challenges they present. This chapter aims to provide a comprehensive understanding of the ethical dilemmas that arise from AI and Big Data adoption, particularly in the context of corporate governance, transparency, fairness, and accountability.

AI and Big Data offer tremendous potential to improve operational efficiency, foster innovation, and create competitive advantages (Davenport & Ronanki, 2018). However, their application raises concerns related to privacy, bias, fairness, and transparency. Businesses are increasingly using AI to make critical decisions, from hiring and promotions to loan approvals and customer targeting (O'Neil, 2016). While these technologies can enhance decision-making, they also raise significant ethical questions. For instance, the use of biased data in AI algorithms can perpetuate discrimination and unfair treatment (Dastin, 2018). Similarly, the collection and analysis of vast amounts of personal data can infringe on privacy rights if not handled responsibly (Zeng, 2017).

This chapter aims to provide readers with a framework for understanding these ethical issues and the tools to address them. It will discuss the key ethical principles that should guide the use of AI and Big Data, such as fairness, accountability, transparency, and privacy. Furthermore, it will explore best practices for implementing these technologies in a way that minimizes harm and ensures ethical outcomes. Ultimately, the goal of the chapter is to equip corporate leaders, managers, and other stakeholders with the knowledge and strategies needed to integrate AI and Big Data ethically into their business operations.

2. ETHICAL CONCERNS IN AI AND BIG DATA

2.1 Algorithmic Bias

Definition and Examples of Algorithmic Bias

Algorithmic bias refers to systematic and unfair discrimination that arises in algorithms and machine learning models. This bias occurs when an algorithm produces results that are prejudiced or skewed due to the data it is trained on or the design of the algorithm itself. Algorithms are not inherently biased, but their outputs can reflect existing inequalities or assumptions embedded in the data they process. Machine learning algorithms rely on historical data to make predictions or decisions. If the data is unbalanced or reflects societal biases, the algorithm will likely reinforce those biases, making them part of automated decision-making processes (O'Neil, 2016).

One common example of algorithmic bias can be found in facial recognition technology. These systems, often used by law enforcement and other security entities, have been shown to misidentify individuals from minority racial groups at significantly higher rates than white individuals (Buolamwini & Gebru, 2018). A study by Joy Buolamwini and Timnit Gebru revealed that commercial facial recognition systems performed poorly on darker-skinned individuals, particularly women. This occurs because these systems are often trained on datasets with a disproportionate number of lighter-skinned faces, which results in inaccurate identification for individuals with darker skin tones. Such biases in facial recognition technology can have serious implications, including wrongful arrests or biased surveillance targeting.

Another example of algorithmic bias is found in hiring algorithms used by companies to screen job applications. In 2018, Amazon scrapped an AI system it had developed to help with recruitment because it demonstrated bias against female candidates. The system was trained on resumes submitted to Amazon over a 10-year period, and because the data reflected a male-dominated industry, the algorithm learned to favor resumes submitted by men, disadvantaging women applicants (Dastin, 2018). This bias, which was not intentional, reflected the historical data of the tech industry rather than an inherent flaw in the algorithm's design. Despite the potential of AI to streamline recruitment processes, it underscores how historical biases in data can perpetuate inequality.

Impact of Bias on Decision-Making and Corporate Outcomes

Algorithmic bias poses significant risks to decision-making and corporate outcomes. One of the most profound effects is the reinforcement of existing inequalities. When biased algorithms are used to make decisions in hiring, lending, healthcare, or law enforcement, they perpetuate discriminatory patterns that may have existed in society for years. This not only exacerbates inequality but also undermines the principles of fairness and justice that organizations are expected to uphold. If an AI system discriminates against a particular demographic group, it could lead to missed opportunities for talented individuals from that group, resulting in a less diverse and inclusive workforce (O'Neil, 2016).

For example, in the case of lending, algorithms used by banks and financial institutions to assess creditworthiness may disproportionately disadvantage certain racial or socioeconomic groups. If these algorithms are trained on historical data that reflects biased lending practices (e.g., fewer loans being issued to minority communities), the algorithm will likely replicate these biases, making it harder for individuals from those communities to obtain loans, regardless of their actual financial situation (Binns, 2018). Such bias not only harms individual consumers but can also damage the reputation of the company, leading to legal consequences, regulatory scrutiny, and loss of customer trust.

Algorithmic bias can also compromise the quality and accuracy of decisions, leading to poor business outcomes. In cases where AI systems are used to predict customer behavior or optimize supply chain management, biased algorithms may generate inaccurate predictions. For example, if an AI system is trained on biased data that over-represents certain customer segments while under-representing others, the company may fail to recognize the needs of underrepresented groups, leading to ineffective marketing strategies or inventory management (Barocas, Hardt, & Narayanan, 2019). This can result in missed opportunities and wasted resources as the company makes decisions based on skewed or incomplete data.

Furthermore, the legal and reputational risks associated with algorithmic bias can significantly affect corporate outcomes. As awareness of algorithmic bias increases, companies that deploy biased systems may face legal challenges and public backlash. In the case of Amazon's recruitment tool, for instance, the company faced criticism for developing a system that discriminated against women, which not only posed legal risks but also negatively impacted its reputation as a fair employer. Similarly, in the financial services industry, organizations that use biased lending algorithms may be subject to regulatory fines and lawsuits, particularly if the discrimination is found to violate anti-discrimination laws such as the Equal Credit Opportunity Act (ECOA) in the U.S.

In addition to legal risks, algorithmic bias can erode customer trust. Consumers are increasingly concerned about how their personal data is being used, and if they perceive that an organization's AI systems are making biased decisions, they may take their business elsewhere. A study by Edelman (2020) found that consumers are more likely to trust companies that demonstrate a commitment to fairness and transparency, and that a lack of transparency around how AI systems make decisions can lead to negative perceptions of the brand. For businesses that rely on customer loyalty, algorithmic bias represents not only a legal and ethical challenge but also a significant risk to their bottom line.

To address these risks, companies must implement strategies to identify, mitigate, and monitor algorithmic bias. One effective approach is to ensure diverse and representative data sets are used to train AI systems, reducing the likelihood that the algorithm will learn from biased data. Additionally, regular bias audits and transparency reports can help organizations assess the fairness of their AI systems and make necessary adjustments. By embedding ethical considerations into the design, implementation, and monitoring of AI and Big Data systems, organizations can reduce the risk of bias and ensure that their decision-making processes are more equitable, accurate, and trustworthy.

2.2 Data Privacy and Consent

Data privacy and consent have become critical issues in the age of Artificial Intelligence (AI) and Big Data. With the proliferation of data-driven technologies, organizations now have unprecedented access to personal and sensitive information. However, this access comes with significant ethical and legal responsibilities. Issues surrounding data collection, consent, and usage, as well as the implications of data breaches and unauthorized use, have far-reaching consequences for individuals, businesses, and society at large.

Issues Surrounding Data Collection, Consent, and Usage

Data collection lies at the heart of Big Data and AI applications. Organizations gather vast amounts of data from various sources, including social media platforms, mobile applications, and Internet of Things (IoT) devices. While this data is invaluable for decision-making, targeted marketing, and personalized services, the process of data collection often raises ethical concerns. One key issue is the lack of informed consent. Many users are unaware of the extent to which their data is being collected, how it will be used, or who will have access to it (Zeng, 2017). Terms of service agreements are often lengthy and written in complex legal language, making it difficult for users to fully understand the implications of agreeing to them.

Another critical concern is the potential for misuse of collected data. In some cases, organizations may use data for purposes beyond what was originally agreed upon, such as selling user data to third parties or employing it for invasive advertising techniques. For example, the Facebook-Cambridge Analytica scandal revealed how user data could be exploited for political purposes without explicit consent, sparking a global debate on data ethics and regulation (Isaak & Hanna, 2018). Such incidents highlight the need for stricter guidelines on how data is collected and used.

The issue of data usage also involves the ethical treatment of sensitive information, such as health records, financial data, and location tracking. Mismanagement of such data can lead to discriminatory practices, financial fraud, and even personal harm. As AI systems increasingly rely on personal data to generate insights, businesses must ensure that their data usage practices align with ethical standards and legal frameworks, such as the General Data Protection Regulation (GDPR) in the European Union, which emphasizes transparency, accountability, and the right to privacy (Voigt & Von dem Bussche, 2017).

Implications of Data Breaches and Unauthorized Use

The implications of data breaches and unauthorized use of data are profound and multifaceted, affecting individuals, organizations, and society. At the individual level, data breaches can expose sensitive personal information, such as social security numbers, credit card details, and medical records. This can lead to identity theft, financial loss, and emotional distress for affected individuals. For example, the Equifax data breach in 2017 exposed the personal information of over 147 million people, causing widespread panic and significant financial consequences for those impacted (Mills, 2018).

For organizations, data breaches can result in severe reputational damage, legal penalties, and financial losses. Businesses found to have inadequate security measures in place may face fines under regulations like the GDPR or the California Consumer Privacy Act (CCPA). Moreover, public trust in the organization may be eroded, leading to a decline in customer loyalty and market share. Research indicates that consumers are more likely to disengage from companies that fail to protect their data, underscoring the importance of robust data privacy measures (Edelman, 2020).

Unauthorized use of data also poses significant risks. When organizations or malicious actors exploit data without proper authorization, the consequences can range from targeted harassment and discrimination to large-scale manipulation of public opinion. The misuse of data in political campaigns, as seen in the aforementioned Cambridge Analytica case, illustrates how unauthorized data use can undermine democratic processes and erode public trust in institutions (Isaak & Hanna, 2018). These risks emphasize the importance of accountability and oversight in the handling of personal data.

The Path Forward

To address the ethical concerns surrounding data privacy and consent, organizations must adopt transparent and accountable data practices. Key measures include implementing clear and concise privacy policies, obtaining informed consent from users, and ensuring that data collection practices comply with relevant regulations. Additionally, businesses should invest in robust cybersecurity measures to prevent data breaches and unauthorized access. Encryption, regular security audits, and employee training on data privacy are essential components of a comprehensive data protection strategy (Voigt & Von dem Bussche, 2017).

Organizations should also consider adopting ethical frameworks that prioritize user rights and societal well-being. For example, the principle of "privacy by design" emphasizes incorporating privacy protections into the development of technologies and processes from the outset, rather than treating them as an afterthought. By proactively addressing data privacy concerns, businesses can build trust with their customers and stakeholders while mitigating legal and reputational risks.

2.3 Transparency and Explainability

Transparency and explainability are essential principles in the ethical deployment of Artificial Intelligence (AI) and Big Data in corporate decision-making. As organizations increasingly rely on these technologies to streamline operations and enhance decision-making, the opacity of AI algorithms poses significant challenges. Ensuring that AI systems are transparent and explainable is vital for maintaining trust, fairness, and accountability. However, achieving transparency and explainability is not without its hurdles, as complex algorithms and proprietary technologies often make it difficult to clarify how AI systems arrive at their decisions.

The Need for Transparency in AI Decision-Making Processes

Transparency in AI decision-making refers to the ability of stakeholders to understand how an AI system processes data and arrives at a particular outcome. This principle is foundational to building trust among consumers, employees, and regulators. Without transparency, organizations risk eroding trust and facing reputational damage, particularly if their AI systems produce biased or harmful outcomes (Burrell, 2016).

In corporate decision-making, transparency ensures that AI systems are not perceived as "black boxes" — opaque systems that generate outputs without revealing their internal processes. For instance, when AI is used in hiring, credit scoring, or medical diagnosis, stakeholders need to understand the rationale behind decisions to ensure fairness and accountability. Transparency is particularly critical in high-stakes domains, where AI-driven decisions can significantly impact people's lives, such as loan approvals, legal judgments, or healthcare recommendations (Doshi-Velez & Kim, 2017).

Transparency also plays a role in regulatory compliance. As governments and regulatory bodies introduce policies to govern AI, such as the European Union's General Data Protection Regulation (GDPR) and the proposed AI Act, organizations are increasingly required to demonstrate the fairness and accountability of their AI systems (Voigt & Von dem Bussche, 2017). A lack of transparency can lead to legal challenges, financial penalties, and public backlash, emphasizing the importance of ensuring that AI systems are open to scrutiny.

Moreover, transparency fosters organizational accountability by allowing internal and external stakeholders to audit AI systems. When organizations are transparent about their AI practices, they can identify and address potential biases, inaccuracies, or ethical risks before they lead to significant consequences. Transparency also empowers stakeholders to question and challenge AI-driven decisions, creating a culture of ethical oversight and continuous improvement (Pasquale, 2015).

Challenges in Explaining AI-Driven Decisions to Stakeholders

While the importance of transparency and explainability is widely recognized, achieving these principles in practice presents significant challenges. One primary challenge is the inherent complexity of modern AI systems. Many AI algorithms, particularly those based on machine learning and deep learning, are highly intricate and involve layers of computations that are difficult for even experts to interpret. This opacity, often referred to as the "black box problem," limits the ability of organizations to explain how AI systems arrive at their decisions (Burrell, 2016).

For example, neural networks, a common type of machine learning model, use multiple layers of interconnected nodes to process data and generate predictions. While these systems can achieve remarkable accuracy, their decision-making processes are often too complex for humans to follow. This creates a dilemma for organizations that need to provide stakeholders with clear explanations of AI-driven outcomes, particularly in industries like finance and healthcare where decisions must be transparent and defensible (Rudin, 2019).

Another challenge is balancing explainability with performance. Simplifying AI systems to make them more explainable can sometimes reduce their accuracy and effectiveness. For instance, linear regression models are highly explainable but may not perform as well as more complex models like gradient-boosted trees or neural networks. Organizations must navigate this trade-off to ensure that their AI systems are both effective and understandable to stakeholders (Doshi-Velez & Kim, 2017).

Proprietary technologies and intellectual property concerns further complicate transparency. Many AI systems are developed by third-party vendors who may be unwilling to disclose the inner workings of their algorithms due to competitive reasons. This lack of access to underlying models can prevent organizations from fully understanding or explaining the systems they deploy, creating ethical and legal risks (Pasquale, 2015).

Cultural and organizational barriers also play a role in limiting transparency. In some cases, employees or decision-makers may lack the technical expertise needed to interpret AI systems, leading to over-reliance on automated outputs without understanding their implications. Additionally, organizational resistance to change or fear of exposing flaws in AI systems can hinder efforts to increase transparency (Burrell, 2016).

The Path Forward

To address these challenges, organizations must adopt strategies that prioritize transparency and explainability in AI systems. One approach is to develop and deploy interpretable models, such as decision trees or rule-based systems, which are easier to understand and explain. For complex models, techniques like Local Interpretable Model-Agnostic Explanations (LIME) or SHapley Additive exPlanations (SHAP) can provide insights into how specific inputs influence AI predictions, enabling stakeholders to gain a better understanding of the decision-making process (Ribeiro, Singh, & Guestrin, 2016).

Organizations should also implement policies that require regular audits of AI systems to identify potential biases and ensure compliance with ethical and legal standards. Transparent communication with stakeholders, including customers, employees, and regulators, is essential for building trust and accountability. Providing detailed documentation of AI systems, including their limitations and potential biases, can help stakeholders make informed decisions about their use.

Finally, fostering a culture of transparency within organizations is critical. This involves training employees on AI ethics and explainability, encouraging open discussions about AI practices, and involving diverse perspectives in the development and deployment of AI systems. By prioritizing transparency and explainability, organizations can ensure that their AI systems are fair, accountable, and aligned with societal values.

2.4 Data Ownership and Rights

The era of Artificial Intelligence (AI) and Big Data has introduced complex questions around data ownership and control. As organizations increasingly rely on data-driven technologies to enhance decision-making, personalize services, and drive innovation, understanding who owns and controls the data has become a critical ethical and legal issue. Additionally, the monetization and sharing of data raise significant ethical concerns that must be addressed to ensure fairness, accountability, and trust.

Questions Around Data Ownership and Control

Data ownership refers to the legal rights and ethical responsibilities associated with collecting, storing, and utilizing data. Determining ownership is often complex due to the diverse sources from which data is generated, including individuals, businesses, and automated systems. For example, data collected by IoT devices, such as smart home systems or wearable health trackers, often involves multiple stakeholders, including the users of the devices, the manufacturers, and third-party service providers. Each stakeholder may have competing claims to ownership, leading to ambiguities in how the data can be used or shared (Kitchin, 2014).

Moreover, individuals whose actions generate data, such as customers making online purchases or employees using workplace systems, often have little control over how their data is handled. Despite being the primary source of data, users typically relinquish their rights to data ownership through terms of service agreements, often without fully understanding the implications (Zuboff, 2019). This lack of clarity raises ethical concerns about consent, privacy, and the potential misuse of personal information.

Organizations also face challenges in maintaining control over the data they collect. Data breaches and cyber attacks can expose sensitive corporate or customer data, leading to legal liabilities and reputational damage. Additionally, as regulations like the General Data Protection Regulation (GDPR) in the European Union and the California Consumer Privacy Act (CCPA) impose stricter requirements on data governance, businesses must navigate the legal complexities of data ownership and ensure compliance (Voigt & Von dem Bussche, 2017).

Ethical Considerations in Data Monetization and Sharing

Data has become a valuable asset, often referred to as the "new oil" due to its potential for generating significant revenue. Companies monetize data by selling it to third parties, using it for targeted advertising, or integrating it into analytics to gain competitive insights. However, the commercialization of data raises ethical concerns, particularly when it involves personal information.

One ethical challenge is ensuring that individuals whose data is monetized are adequately informed and compensated. Many users are unaware that their data is being sold or shared, and even when informed, they may have little recourse to opt out. For instance, social media platforms often use personal data to create targeted advertisements, generating substantial profits without sharing the benefits with the users who provide the data (Isaak & Hanna, 2018). This lack of reciprocity challenges notions of fairness and equitable value exchange.

Another critical concern is the sharing of data across organizations and industries. While data sharing can foster innovation and collaboration, it also increases the risk of misuse or unintended consequences. For example, health data shared between pharmaceutical companies and insurers could lead to discriminatory practices, such as denying coverage based on genetic predispositions or pre-existing conditions (Floridi, 2019). To address these risks, organizations must adopt robust data-sharing agreements that prioritize transparency, accountability, and the ethical use of shared information.

The Path Forward

To navigate the complexities of data ownership and rights, organizations must implement clear policies that define ownership and establish protocols for data usage and sharing. Regulatory frameworks like GDPR provide valuable guidance by emphasizing principles of data minimization, purpose limitation, and user consent. Additionally, organizations should adopt ethical frameworks that prioritize user rights, such as the concept of data sovereignty, which empowers individuals to retain control over their personal information (Zuboff, 2019).

By addressing questions of data ownership and the ethical implications of data monetization and sharing, businesses can build trust, foster accountability, and contribute to a more equitable digital ecosystem.

3. FACIAL RECOGNITION TECHNOLOGY

Facial Recognition Technology (FRT) has emerged as one of the most transformative applications of Artificial Intelligence (AI). It is widely deployed in various domains, including law enforcement, retail, healthcare, and personal authentication. Despite its potential to enhance security and convenience, FRT also raises significant ethical concerns related to privacy, bias, and regulation. A close examination of these issues through real-world case studies underscores the importance of robust governance and ethical oversight.

Case Study: Ethical Implications of FRT in Law Enforcement

The use of FRT by law enforcement agencies has sparked considerable debate. A prominent example is its deployment by the London Metropolitan Police, which adopted live facial recognition systems for public surveillance. While the technology was intended to identify suspects and enhance public safety, it was criticized for its inaccuracies and potential to infringe on individual rights (Barrett, 2020).

Studies have shown that FRT systems often exhibit racial and gender biases, with higher error rates for women and people of color compared to white men. Research by Buolamwini and Gebru (2018) revealed that commercial FRT systems misclassified darker-skinned women at rates up to 34.7%, compared to error rates below 1% for lighter-skinned men. These biases, rooted in the lack of diversity in training datasets, can lead to wrongful identifications and exacerbate systemic discrimination.

For example, the wrongful arrest of Robert Williams, an African American man in Detroit, based on a misidentification by FRT, illustrates the real-world consequences of these biases. Williams' case highlighted the flaws in relying on FRT for law enforcement decisions and the need for accountability and oversight to prevent similar incidents (Garvie, 2019).

Analysis of Privacy, Bias, and Regulatory Concerns

1. **Privacy Concerns** One of the most significant ethical challenges of FRT is its impact on privacy. Unlike other biometric systems, facial data can be captured without an individual's knowledge or consent, often through public cameras or social media images. This capability enables mass surveillance, raising concerns about the erosion of anonymity in public spaces. Countries like China have utilized FRT for extensive surveillance, sparking fears of state overreach and abuse of power (Floridi, 2019).

Furthermore, the storage of facial data poses cybersecurity risks. Data breaches involving facial recognition databases could lead to identity theft, fraud, and other malicious activities. The lack of stringent data protection measures exacerbates these vulnerabilities, making it crucial for organizations to prioritize cybersecurity in FRT implementations.

2. **Bias and Discrimination** The biases inherent in FRT algorithms reflect broader societal inequities. As seen in the cases of Williams and the London Metropolitan Police, biased algorithms can disproportionately impact marginalized communities, leading to unjust outcomes. These biases undermine the credibility and fairness of FRT, raising questions about its suitability for applications like policing and hiring (Buolamwini & Gebru, 2018).

Efforts to address bias include using more diverse datasets and conducting regular audits of FRT systems. However, these measures alone may not eliminate bias entirely, highlighting the need for transparency and accountability in the design and deployment of FRT technologies (Garvie, 2019).

3. **Regulatory Concerns** The rapid adoption of FRT has outpaced the development of comprehensive regulatory frameworks. In many jurisdictions, there are no clear guidelines governing the use of FRT, leaving room for misuse. For example, private companies may deploy FRT for profit-driven purposes without adequately addressing privacy or ethical considerations (Floridi, 2019).

In response to these challenges, some cities, such as San Francisco, have banned the use of FRT by government agencies, citing concerns over privacy and discrimination. Additionally, the European Union has proposed stringent regulations for AI technologies, including FRT, under the AI Act. These efforts underscore the importance of establishing legal frameworks to ensure responsible use and protect individual rights (Barrett, 2020).

The Path Forward

Addressing the ethical challenges of FRT requires a multi-faceted approach:

1. **Transparent Governance**: Governments and organizations must establish clear policies for the use of FRT, including requirements for obtaining consent and conducting bias audits.

2. **Diverse Data and Bias Mitigation**: Developers should ensure that datasets are representative and inclusive, and algorithms should undergo regular testing to identify and mitigate biases.
3. **Strong Privacy Protections**: Comprehensive data protection measures, such as encryption and access controls, are essential to safeguard facial data.
4. **Regulatory Oversight**: Governments should develop and enforce robust legal frameworks to govern FRT, ensuring accountability and ethical use.
5. **Public Engagement**: Engaging stakeholders, including civil society organizations and affected communities, can help build trust and ensure that FRT applications align with societal values.

3.1 Predictive Analytics in Hiring

Predictive analytics in hiring has revolutionized recruitment processes by enabling organizations to identify the most suitable candidates efficiently. By leveraging Artificial Intelligence (AI) and machine learning algorithms, predictive analytics can assess resumes, analyze interview responses, and evaluate behavioral patterns to predict job performance. However, despite its efficiency, the use of predictive analytics in hiring raises significant ethical concerns regarding bias, fairness, and diversity.

Examination of AI in Recruitment and Its Potential Biases

AI-driven recruitment tools rely heavily on historical data to predict the suitability of candidates. These systems are trained on resumes, performance metrics, and other datasets to identify patterns and characteristics associated with successful employees. While this approach can optimize hiring processes, it is prone to perpetuating existing biases present in the training data (O'Neil, 2016).

For example, Amazon's AI recruitment tool, which was designed to evaluate resumes, demonstrated gender bias. The system, trained on data from the tech industry—a predominantly male-dominated field—downgraded resumes that included terms like "women's chess club captain" or education from women's colleges. This occurred because the AI interpreted male-dominated resumes as a baseline for success (Dastin, 2018). This example illustrates how biased data can lead to discriminatory outcomes, disadvantaging underrepresented groups and reinforcing systemic inequities.

Another source of bias in predictive analytics is algorithmic design. If algorithms prioritize certain traits or skills based on historical data, they may inadvertently exclude candidates from diverse backgrounds who possess unconventional but equally valuable qualifications. For instance, a system trained to prioritize technical skills might overlook candidates with strong interpersonal abilities, leading to a homogenized workforce that lacks diverse perspectives (Barocas, Hardt, & Narayanan, 2019).

Discussion on Fairness and Diversity in Hiring Practices

The integration of predictive analytics into hiring processes presents both challenges and opportunities for promoting fairness and diversity. On one hand, AI has the potential to eliminate human biases, such as those based on race, gender, or age, by focusing solely on objective data. On the other hand, if not carefully designed, AI systems can perpetuate or even amplify existing biases.

Fairness in Hiring Fairness in recruitment requires that all candidates have an equal opportunity to succeed, regardless of their background. To achieve this, organizations must address both data-related and algorithmic biases. One approach is to use anonymized resumes, removing information such as names and educational institutions that could trigger biases, whether human or algorithmic.

Regular audits of AI systems are also crucial for identifying and mitigating bias. These audits should evaluate the performance of algorithms across different demographic groups to ensure equitable treatment. For example, by analyzing the acceptance rates of candidates from diverse racial or gender backgrounds, companies can identify potential disparities and adjust their models accordingly (Raghavan et al., 2020).

Diversity in Hiring Diversity in hiring is not only an ethical imperative but also a business advantage. Research shows that diverse teams are more innovative, better at problem-solving, and more representative of a global customer base (Hunt et al., 2018). Predictive analytics can contribute to diversity by identifying candidates from underrepresented groups who may have been overlooked in traditional hiring processes.

However, fostering diversity requires a deliberate effort to counteract biases embedded in training data. For example, organizations can supplement their datasets with information from diverse sources, ensuring that the AI system is exposed to a broad range of experiences and qualifications. Additionally, designing algorithms to prioritize diversity metrics can help balance the representation of different demographic groups.

Ethical Considerations and Best Practices

To ensure that predictive analytics in hiring aligns with ethical principles, organizations must adopt best practices that promote fairness, transparency, and accountability:

1. **Bias Mitigation**: Implement strategies to identify and eliminate biases in training data and algorithmic design.
2. **Transparency**: Provide candidates with clear explanations of how AI systems evaluate applications and make decisions. This builds trust and ensures accountability.
3. **Regulatory Compliance**: Adhere to anti-discrimination laws, such as the Equal Employment Opportunity Commission (EEOC) guidelines, to avoid legal and ethical pitfalls.
4. **Continuous Monitoring**: Regularly evaluate AI systems for unintended biases or discrepancies in outcomes and adjust models as needed.

3.2 Data-Driven Marketing

Data-driven marketing leverages Big Data and advanced analytics to deliver personalized and targeted campaigns to consumers. By analyzing consumer behavior, preferences, and demographics, organizations can create marketing strategies that are more effective and relevant. However, the use of personal data for marketing purposes raises significant ethical concerns, particularly around privacy and consent. Balancing consumer privacy with the business benefits of data-driven marketing is crucial for maintaining trust and ensuring responsible practices.

Ethical Issues in Personalized Marketing Using Big Data

Personalized marketing offers businesses the ability to create tailored experiences for consumers, enhancing engagement and driving sales. However, the collection and use of personal data to enable these practices often occur without full transparency, leading to ethical dilemmas.

One key issue is the lack of informed consent. Many consumers are unaware of the extent to which their data is collected, stored, and analyzed for marketing purposes. For example, websites and mobile applications often use cookies and tracking technologies to gather detailed information about user behavior. While these practices are disclosed in privacy policies, the language is frequently too complex for the average consumer to understand, making it difficult for individuals to give truly informed consent (Isaak & Hanna, 2018).

Another concern is the potential for intrusive targeting. Algorithms that analyze consumer data can predict preferences with remarkable accuracy, sometimes crossing the line into perceived invasiveness. For instance, the case of Target identifying a teenager's pregnancy based on her purchasing patterns—before she had disclosed it to her family—highlighted the unintended consequences of hyper-personalized marketing (Hill, 2012). Such incidents can lead to consumer discomfort and distrust, raising questions about the ethical boundaries of data use.

Discrimination and bias are also ethical challenges in data-driven marketing. Algorithms trained on historical data may inadvertently perpetuate biases, leading to unfair treatment of certain demographic groups. For example, targeted advertising for credit or employment opportunities may exclude individuals based on race, gender, or socioeconomic status, exacerbating inequality and violating anti-discrimination laws (Barocas et al., 2019).

Balancing Consumer Privacy and Business Benefits

Businesses benefit significantly from data-driven marketing through improved customer acquisition, retention, and revenue generation. However, these advantages must be weighed against the ethical imperative to protect consumer privacy.

Transparency and Consent: To achieve this balance, organizations must prioritize transparency in their data collection and usage practices. Clear and concise privacy policies, along with user-friendly opt-in mechanisms, can empower consumers to make informed choices about sharing their data. For instance, companies like Apple have implemented app tracking transparency features that require explicit user consent before collecting data, setting a standard for ethical practices (Apple, 2021).

Data Minimization and Purpose Limitation: Another strategy is to adopt principles of data minimization and purpose limitation, as outlined in regulations like the General Data Protection Regulation (GDPR). Collecting only the data necessary for specific marketing objectives reduces the risk of misuse and aligns with ethical data handling practices (Voigt & Von dem Bussche, 2017).

Algorithm Accountability: Ensuring fairness in data-driven marketing also requires accountability in algorithm design and deployment. Regular audits of algorithms can identify and mitigate biases, ensuring that marketing campaigns do not exclude or disadvantage certain groups. Techniques like adversarial testing and fairness-aware machine learning can further enhance the ethical integrity of predictive models (Raji et al., 2020).

Consumer-Centric Marketing Adopting a consumer-centric approach can help businesses strike the right balance between personalization and privacy. This involves actively listening to consumer preferences, respecting their boundaries, and allowing them to control the level of personalization they receive. For example, offering consumers the ability to adjust their data-sharing settings or providing them with tailored recommendations without intrusive tracking fosters trust and loyalty.

4. DEVELOPING AN ETHICAL FRAMEWORK FOR AI AND BIG DATA

4.1 Principles of Fairness

Fairness is one of the most critical ethical principles when developing AI systems, especially those that leverage Big Data. AI has the potential to significantly enhance decision-making and automate complex processes, but it also carries the risk of perpetuating or exacerbating existing biases and inequalities. Therefore, ensuring that AI systems are fair is essential to preventing discrimination and ensuring equitable outcomes for all users. This section outlines guidelines for designing and implementing fair AI systems and strategies to address discrimination and inequality in AI outcomes.

Guidelines for Designing and Implementing Fair AI Systems

To design fair AI systems, organizations must incorporate fairness from the very beginning of the AI development lifecycle. Here are key guidelines for achieving fairness in AI systems:

1. **Diverse and Representative Data**: Fair AI systems begin with diverse and representative data. The data used to train AI models must reflect the diversity of the population the system will serve. When training datasets are not representative, AI models may develop biases that disproportionately favor certain groups. For example, facial recognition systems trained primarily on images of white individuals may struggle to identify people of color, leading to inaccuracies and unfair treatment. Ensuring that datasets include a broad range of demographics—such as race, gender, age, and socio-economic status—helps mitigate such biases (Buolamwini & Gebru, 2018).
2. **Bias Detection and Mitigation**: Regular bias detection and mitigation are essential throughout the development and deployment of AI systems. Organizations should perform thorough audits of the data used to train AI models and the algorithms that process the data. These audits can identify unintentional biases, such as gender or racial biases, and take corrective measures to minimize them. Techniques such as fairness-aware machine learning algorithms, adversarial testing, and counterfactual fairness can be used to assess and reduce biases in AI models (Barocas et al., 2019).
3. **Transparent Algorithms and Accountability**: For AI systems to be fair, they must operate transparently. This means that stakeholders should be able to understand how decisions are made by the system. Transparency is not only

about providing explanations of individual decisions but also about explaining the broader decision-making process and the underlying models. It is crucial to ensure accountability in case of unfair or discriminatory outcomes. Organizations should develop clear procedures for handling grievances and correcting errors, such as wrongful decisions made by AI systems (Dastin, 2018).

4. **Inclusive and Collaborative Design Process**: Fairness in AI requires an inclusive and collaborative approach to system design. Organizations should involve diverse teams of data scientists, ethicists, domain experts, and members of the affected communities in the AI development process. This diverse input helps identify potential issues early on and ensures that the AI system addresses the needs of all users. Consulting with external stakeholders, including advocacy groups and policymakers, can also help identify broader societal concerns related to fairness and inclusion (O'Neil, 2016).

Addressing Discrimination and Inequality in AI Outcomes

AI systems, if not carefully designed and monitored, can lead to discriminatory outcomes that exacerbate existing inequalities. Addressing these issues requires specific actions and strategies that focus on both technical and social dimensions of fairness:

1. **Equitable Treatment and Opportunity**: AI systems should be designed to treat all individuals equitably, ensuring that no group is unfairly disadvantaged or privileged. For example, predictive hiring algorithms should not favor applicants from a particular gender or racial group but should evaluate all candidates based on relevant qualifications and competencies. In applications such as loan approval or criminal justice sentencing, AI systems must not use proxies for protected characteristics (e.g., using zip code as a proxy for race) that could lead to unfair outcomes (Binns, 2018). One approach to achieving equitable treatment is to ensure that the criteria used in AI decision-making are directly relevant to the task at hand, rather than relying on indirect indicators that could lead to discrimination.
2. **Disparate Impact Analysis**: AI systems should undergo disparate impact analysis to evaluate whether their decisions have disproportionate effects on specific groups. For example, in the case of credit scoring, AI models must be assessed to ensure that they do not unfairly disadvantage certain demographic groups based on historical patterns of inequality in credit access. When a system produces disproportionate impacts on one group, adjustments must be made to ensure that the AI system does not replicate or reinforce historical discrimination. Tools such as fairness constraints and regularization methods can be

incorporated into the model to prevent disparate impacts while maintaining the system's performance (Barocas et al., 2019).

3. **Continuous Monitoring and Adaptation**: Fairness is not a one-time goal; it is an ongoing process that requires continuous monitoring and adaptation of AI systems. Once an AI system is deployed, it is important to regularly monitor its performance to ensure that it remains fair over time. This includes collecting data on the outcomes produced by the system and analyzing them for any signs of bias or inequity. Continuous feedback loops can help identify issues and allow for quick corrections to prevent discriminatory outcomes. This iterative approach ensures that AI systems remain aligned with ethical standards throughout their lifecycle (Raji et al., 2020).
4. **Public Policy and Legal Compliance**: Ensuring fairness in AI also involves adhering to public policies and legal frameworks that protect individuals from discrimination. Laws such as the Equal Employment Opportunity Commission (EEOC) regulations in the United States and the General Data Protection Regulation (GDPR) in Europe set standards for non-discrimination, fairness, and transparency. AI systems must be designed to comply with these regulations, ensuring that they do not violate individuals' rights to fair treatment. Moreover, AI systems should be developed with an understanding of the broader societal implications, ensuring that they contribute to creating an equitable society rather than exacerbating existing inequalities (Voigt & Von dem Bussche, 2017).

4.3 Data Integrity and Privacy Protection

As organizations increasingly rely on Big Data and AI to drive decision-making, ensuring data integrity and protecting privacy are paramount to maintaining trust, legal compliance, and operational effectiveness. Data integrity involves ensuring the accuracy, consistency, and reliability of data throughout its lifecycle, while privacy protection focuses on safeguarding personal data from unauthorized access, misuse, or breaches. This section explores best practices for data governance and privacy protection and provides frameworks for maintaining data accuracy and reliability.

Best Practices for Data Governance and Privacy Protection

1. **Implementing Clear Data Governance Policies**: Data governance refers to the policies, processes, and standards that ensure data is managed effectively and used responsibly across an organization. To protect data integrity and privacy, organizations must develop and enforce clear data governance policies. These policies should address key aspects such as data access, usage, storage, sharing, and retention. For example, access controls should be implemented to restrict

data access based on the principle of least privilege, ensuring that only authorized personnel can view or modify sensitive information (Khatri & Brown, 2010).

Furthermore, data governance policies should define roles and responsibilities for data stewardship, ensuring accountability and clarity regarding data management practices. Data stewards or data governance teams should be responsible for ensuring that data is accurate, consistent, and compliant with applicable laws, such as the General Data Protection Regulation (GDPR) or the California Consumer Privacy Act (CCPA).

2. **Data Encryption and Secure Storage**: Encryption is one of the most effective ways to protect data from unauthorized access. Both in transit (while being transmitted over networks) and at rest (when stored in databases or on servers), sensitive data should be encrypted to prevent breaches and protect user privacy. Strong encryption standards, such as AES (Advanced Encryption Standard) with 256-bit keys, should be used for both personal and organizational data. Additionally, organizations should implement secure storage solutions, such as on-premises servers with high-level security or cloud storage providers that meet regulatory standards for data protection (Voigt & Von dem Bussche, 2017).
3. **Regular Data Audits and Monitoring**: Regular data audits are essential for identifying and rectifying issues related to data integrity and privacy. These audits involve reviewing data usage practices, verifying data accuracy, and ensuring that the organization's data management practices comply with privacy regulations. Monitoring systems should be in place to track any unauthorized access or data anomalies that may signal potential breaches or inaccuracies. Implementing automated tools that continuously monitor data activity and generate reports on compliance with governance standards can help detect and address issues proactively (Hosein, 2018).
4. **User Consent and Transparency**: An essential component of privacy protection is ensuring that data is collected and used only with informed consent from individuals. Organizations should provide clear and easily understandable privacy policies that explain how data will be collected, used, and shared. Consent mechanisms should be designed to allow users to opt-in or opt-out of data collection practices, particularly in cases where sensitive personal data is involved. Transparent data practices build trust and allow individuals to make informed decisions about sharing their data (Zeng, 2017).
5. **Data Anonymization and Deletion**: Anonymization is the process of removing personally identifiable information (PII) from datasets to prevent identification of individuals. By anonymizing data, organizations can reduce the risks associated with data breaches and ensure compliance with privacy regulations.

Additionally, organizations should implement strict data retention policies, ensuring that data is only kept as long as necessary for business purposes. Once the data is no longer required, it should be securely deleted to minimize the risk of unauthorized access or misuse (Cavoukian, 2012).

Frameworks for Maintaining Data Accuracy and Reliability

Maintaining data accuracy and reliability is essential for decision-making processes that rely on AI and Big Data. Inaccurate or unreliable data can lead to faulty conclusions, which may have serious consequences for businesses and individuals. To maintain data integrity, organizations should adopt frameworks that promote accuracy and reliability at every stage of the data lifecycle.

1. **Data Quality Management Framework**: A robust data quality management framework helps organizations ensure that the data they use is accurate, complete, and consistent. This framework should include processes for:
    - **Data Validation**: Ensuring that data entered into the system is accurate, complete, and within acceptable ranges.
    - **Data Cleaning**: Regularly identifying and correcting or removing inaccurate, incomplete, or duplicate data.
    - **Data Enrichment**: Augmenting datasets with additional data points or external sources to improve accuracy and contextual understanding.

Establishing data quality metrics—such as completeness, consistency, timeliness, and accuracy—can help organizations assess and improve their data over time. These metrics should be continuously monitored, and corrective actions should be implemented when data quality issues are identified (Redman, 2016).

2. **Data Provenance and Lineage Tracking**: Data provenance refers to the documentation of the origins and transformations of data throughout its lifecycle. By tracking data lineage, organizations can trace the journey of data from its source to its final use, ensuring that it remains accurate and reliable at every stage. This practice helps identify errors and discrepancies in the data flow, making it easier to locate and correct mistakes. It also supports transparency, as stakeholders can trace how data was used and transformed to arrive at specific decisions (Khatri & Brown, 2010).
3. **Automated Data Integrity Checks**: To maintain data accuracy, organizations can implement automated data integrity checks. These systems continuously evaluate the integrity of the data, flagging any inconsistencies or errors in real-time. Automated tools can identify issues such as missing values, duplicate entries,

or conflicts between data sources. By automating these checks, organizations can quickly detect and address data quality issues before they affect business operations or decision-making processes (Bertot et al., 2018).

4. **Cross-Validation and Verification**: Cross-validation and verification involve comparing data from multiple sources or systems to ensure consistency and reliability. For example, if an organization gathers customer data from both online surveys and social media platforms, cross-referencing these data points can help verify accuracy and highlight any discrepancies. By integrating data from multiple channels and sources, organizations can improve the reliability and robustness of their data, ensuring more accurate predictions and better business outcomes.

Data integrity and privacy protection are critical to the ethical use of AI and Big Data. By implementing best practices for data governance, encryption, and transparency, organizations can protect sensitive information and maintain trust with their stakeholders. Moreover, adopting frameworks for maintaining data accuracy and reliability, such as data quality management and provenance tracking, ensures that data remains dependable throughout its lifecycle. As AI and Big Data continue to shape business operations, it is essential that organizations prioritize data integrity and privacy to create responsible, ethical, and sustainable practices.

4.4 Ethical Audits and Monitoring

Ethical audits and continuous monitoring are integral to ensuring that AI and Big Data systems remain aligned with ethical standards and organizational goals. As AI becomes increasingly embedded in decision-making processes, the need for systematic reviews and real-time oversight grows. Regular ethical audits not only help identify risks related to fairness, transparency, and privacy but also facilitate the development of responsible AI practices that align with societal values. This section explores the importance of ethical audits and introduces tools and techniques for ongoing monitoring of AI and Big Data systems.

Importance of Regular Ethical Audits

1. **Identifying and Mitigating Risks**: Regular ethical audits are essential for identifying and mitigating risks associated with the deployment of AI and Big Data systems. AI systems, particularly those using machine learning, are continuously evolving as they process more data. However, without regular audits, organizations may fail to recognize potential biases or unethical outcomes until they manifest in significant ways, such as discriminatory decision-making or

privacy violations. Ethical audits can uncover issues that are not immediately apparent, providing organizations with the opportunity to address them proactively (Raji et al., 2020).

2. **Ensuring Alignment with Ethical Standards**: Ethical audits provide a structured framework for evaluating whether AI and Big Data systems comply with ethical principles such as fairness, transparency, accountability, and privacy. These audits help ensure that the technology's deployment aligns with the organization's values and any relevant legal or regulatory frameworks. For example, organizations must assess whether their AI systems adhere to anti-discrimination laws or the General Data Protection Regulation (GDPR), which mandates strict data protection and privacy measures. Regular audits help organizations identify deviations from ethical standards and make necessary adjustments (Barocas et al., 2019).
3. **Building Trust and Accountability**: Performing ethical audits not only ensures that AI systems operate ethically but also fosters trust and accountability with stakeholders. When organizations publicly disclose the findings of their audits, it demonstrates their commitment to ethical practices and transparency. This can strengthen relationships with consumers, regulators, and other stakeholders by providing reassurance that the AI systems used are fair, safe, and reliable. Furthermore, establishing an audit trail makes it easier for organizations to demonstrate accountability in case an AI system produces biased or harmful outcomes (Doshi-Velez & Kim, 2017).
4. **Continuous Improvement and Adaptation**: AI systems are dynamic and may evolve over time as they process more data or are fine-tuned for better performance. Therefore, a one-time audit is insufficient to ensure ongoing ethical compliance. Ethical audits should be part of a continuous improvement cycle, where organizations review and adapt their AI systems regularly to align with changing societal expectations, legal requirements, and ethical standards. This iterative approach allows organizations to keep their systems updated, improving their effectiveness while minimizing potential harms (Raji et al., 2020).

Tools and Techniques for Ongoing Monitoring of AI and Big Data Systems

1. **Bias Detection Tools**: One of the primary ethical concerns in AI and Big Data systems is bias, which can lead to unfair outcomes. Several tools and techniques are available to monitor and detect bias in AI systems continuously. For example, fairness-aware machine learning algorithms can help assess whether the AI model disproportionately impacts certain demographic groups (Barocas et al., 2019). Tools like IBM's AI Fairness 360 Toolkit and Fairness Indicators

from Google can help organizations evaluate model fairness by running tests for disparate impact across different groups. These tools provide metrics such as demographic parity or equal opportunity to assess whether the model's predictions are equitable.

2. **Explainability and Transparency Tools**: In addition to bias detection, monitoring the explainability and transparency of AI models is crucial. Tools like LIME (Local Interpretable Model-Agnostic Explanations) and SHAP (SHapley Additive exPlanations) allow for the interpretation of complex models by showing how individual features contribute to the model's predictions. Regularly using these tools helps ensure that AI systems remain interpretable and that the decisions they make can be explained to stakeholders in a clear and understandable way (Ribeiro, Singh, & Guestrin, 2016). By continuously using these explainability tools, organizations can monitor AI systems for transparency and accountability, ensuring that the systems remain aligned with ethical guidelines and regulatory expectations.
3. **Real-Time Monitoring Dashboards**: Real-time monitoring dashboards are an effective tool for tracking the ongoing performance of AI and Big Data systems. These dashboards provide live metrics on system behavior, including data usage, model accuracy, and decision outcomes. By monitoring these metrics in real-time, organizations can quickly identify any deviations from ethical standards or system performance issues. For example, if an AI system's predictions begin to favor one demographic group disproportionately, real-time monitoring can detect this bias early, allowing corrective measures to be implemented promptly (Gana & Raji, 2020).
4. **Automated Auditing Systems**: Automated auditing tools can help organizations continuously track data usage, model predictions, and fairness. These tools run in the background, auditing AI systems for compliance with ethical standards and regulatory requirements. For instance, DataRobot offers automated machine learning models that can be regularly audited for fairness and compliance. Automated systems can monitor for errors, track compliance with data protection regulations, and ensure the integrity of the models. By using these tools, organizations can reduce the cost and time associated with manual audits while maintaining continuous oversight of their AI systems.
5. **Compliance and Reporting Tools**: To maintain regulatory compliance, especially in industries with stringent privacy and security requirements, organizations can use tools designed to track adherence to laws such as GDPR and CCPA. These tools can automatically generate reports on data processing activities, consent management, and breach detection. Tools like OneTrust and TrustArc provide platforms that help businesses track their data handling practices, assess privacy risks, and report on compliance with legal frameworks. Regular use of

these tools ensures that AI systems meet legal standards and continue to protect user privacy (Voigt & Von dem Bussche, 2017).

Ethical audits and ongoing monitoring are fundamental to ensuring that AI and Big Data systems are used responsibly and align with ethical standards. By implementing regular audits, using bias detection tools, and fostering transparency and accountability, organizations can detect and correct any unethical outcomes before they cause harm. Furthermore, automated auditing systems and real-time monitoring tools enable continuous oversight of AI systems, ensuring that they remain compliant with legal requirements and meet ethical guidelines. By prioritizing ethical audits and monitoring, organizations can build more reliable, fair, and transparent AI systems that benefit both their business operations and society as a whole.

5. CORPORATE GOVERNANCE AND ETHICAL LEADERSHIP

5.1 The Role of Corporate Governance in Ethical AI

As Artificial Intelligence (AI) and Big Data become increasingly integral to corporate operations, the role of corporate governance in ensuring their ethical use has never been more crucial. Corporate governance refers to the systems, processes, and policies that control and direct a company's operations, ensuring accountability, transparency, and fairness. When it comes to the deployment of AI and Big Data, governance structures play a pivotal role in mitigating risks, ensuring compliance with ethical standards, and aligning the company's strategic objectives with broader societal values. This section explores how corporate governance can influence the ethical use of AI and Big Data and how ethics can be effectively integrated into corporate decision-making structures.

How Corporate Governance Can Influence the Ethical Use of AI and Big Data

1. **Establishing Ethical Standards and Frameworks**: Corporate governance is responsible for establishing and maintaining ethical standards that guide the use of AI and Big Data. By setting clear policies and principles for AI development and data usage, corporate governance ensures that these technologies are deployed responsibly. This includes ensuring that AI systems do not perpetuate bias or discrimination, safeguarding consumer privacy, and ensuring transparency in decision-making processes. For example, many organizations now have formalized policies to prevent the use of biased algorithms, with gov-

ernance bodies overseeing the development and deployment of these systems. These policies often align with external regulations, such as the General Data Protection Regulation (GDPR) in Europe, and aim to ensure that AI applications are used fairly and transparently (Voigt & Von dem Bussche, 2017).

2. **Monitoring and Risk Management**: Corporate governance structures play a critical role in monitoring AI and Big Data systems to ensure they operate within ethical boundaries. Board members and executives are responsible for assessing the potential risks of using these technologies, including privacy breaches, algorithmic biases, and reputational damage. Effective governance structures ensure that AI systems are regularly audited for compliance with ethical guidelines, allowing for timely identification and mitigation of risks. This monitoring extends to ensuring that data collection and usage are in line with both legal standards and ethical expectations. By taking a proactive role in risk management, governance structures can prevent unethical practices and guide organizations toward more sustainable AI applications (Raji et al., 2020).
3. **Ensuring Accountability and Oversight**: Corporate governance is responsible for ensuring that organizations remain accountable for the outcomes generated by their AI systems. When AI systems make decisions that affect individuals—such as determining eligibility for loans, hiring decisions, or medical diagnoses—it is essential that businesses take accountability for any negative or biased outcomes. Governance bodies should establish clear lines of responsibility within the organization, defining who is responsible for ensuring the ethical deployment of AI and Big Data technologies. This may include the formation of ethics committees or the appointment of an AI ethics officer to oversee the design, implementation, and monitoring of these systems (Pasquale, 2015). Furthermore, it is important that stakeholders, including consumers and regulators, have access to information about how AI systems work and are empowered to challenge any unethical decisions made by AI.

Integration of Ethics into Corporate Decision-Making Structures

1. **Ethics Committees and Advisory Boards**: To integrate ethics into corporate decision-making, organizations can establish dedicated ethics committees or advisory boards focused on AI and Big Data. These bodies are responsible for overseeing the ethical implications of AI projects and ensuring that AI systems align with the company's values and ethical standards. These committees can include a diverse group of stakeholders, such as ethicists, legal experts, data scientists, and representatives from marginalized communities. By involving a wide range of perspectives, these committees ensure that ethical considerations

are integrated into all stages of AI development, from initial conception to deployment and beyond.

Ethics committees can also act as an advisory body for the executive leadership team, providing guidance on controversial or high-risk AI projects. For instance, when deciding whether to implement an AI system for hiring or loan approval, these committees can assess the potential for discrimination or bias, advising the company on how to mitigate these risks while ensuring fairness and transparency (Binns, 2018).

2. **Incorporating Ethics into Strategic Decision-Making**: Ethical considerations must be embedded in the corporate decision-making process at all levels of the organization. Corporate governance should ensure that ethics are not an afterthought but a core aspect of the decision-making framework. This involves integrating ethical goals into business strategies and objectives, ensuring that every decision related to AI and Big Data aligns with the organization's values. For example, companies can set up decision-making criteria that include ethical metrics alongside traditional business performance metrics. These criteria could assess how AI systems impact privacy, fairness, transparency, and social good.

In practice, this means that AI projects would be reviewed through an ethical lens during the strategy formulation stage. Companies can implement frameworks such as *Ethics by Design* to ensure that ethical considerations are incorporated from the outset of AI development, rather than being introduced as a compliance step later in the process. This proactive approach prevents potential ethical issues from emerging once systems are deployed (Floridi, 2019).

3. **Training and Development**: For ethical AI and Big Data practices to thrive within an organization, employees across various departments must be trained in ethical decision-making. Governance bodies should mandate regular ethics training for data scientists, engineers, managers, and other relevant staff, ensuring they are aware of the ethical issues surrounding AI deployment. Training should cover topics such as fairness, bias mitigation, data privacy, and transparency, as well as how to implement these principles into their work. This ensures that ethical behavior becomes embedded in the corporate culture and informs day-to-day operations, fostering a culture of ethical responsibility within the organization (O'Neil, 2016).
4. **Corporate Social Responsibility (CSR) and AI Ethics**: Corporate governance should also include AI ethics as a key part of the organization's Corporate Social Responsibility (CSR) efforts. By promoting responsible AI, companies not only

comply with ethical standards but also align their strategies with broader social values, enhancing their reputation and fostering public trust. Public-facing policies related to data privacy, environmental sustainability, and social equity can reflect the company's commitment to ethical AI. Additionally, organizations should be transparent about how their AI technologies are contributing to social good, such as improving healthcare, education, or accessibility for underserved communities (Brynjolfsson & McAfee, 2014).

Corporate governance plays a crucial role in the ethical deployment of AI and Big Data systems. By establishing clear ethical standards, fostering accountability, and integrating ethics into strategic decision-making, organizations can ensure that AI systems are deployed responsibly. This process involves the creation of ethics committees, comprehensive training, and continuous monitoring to ensure that AI technologies align with organizational values and meet societal expectations. Ethical governance in AI not only mitigates risk but also contributes to sustainable, socially responsible innovation, fostering trust with consumers, employees, and other stakeholders.

5.2 Establishing Ethics Committees and Advisory Boards

As AI and Big Data become integral to corporate operations, establishing ethics committees and advisory boards is essential for ensuring that these technologies are deployed responsibly and in line with ethical standards. Ethics committees and advisory boards play a crucial role in guiding decision-making processes, providing oversight, and ensuring that organizations align their technological advancements with societal values. This section explores the formation and role of ethics committees in corporations and provides case examples of successful ethics oversight models.

The Formation and Role of Ethics Committees in Corporations

1. **Purpose and Structure of Ethics Committees**: An ethics committee is a group within a corporation that is specifically tasked with overseeing the ethical implications of business activities, particularly the use of AI and Big Data. The committee's role is to ensure that the organization adheres to ethical standards and regulations, addresses ethical dilemmas, and provides guidance on the responsible use of technology. The formation of an ethics committee typically involves selecting individuals with diverse expertise and backgrounds, including ethicists, legal experts, data scientists, and other stakeholders relevant to the company's operations. The committee should also represent a range of perspectives to ensure that decisions are well-rounded and consider the interests

of different demographic groups, including marginalized communities. In addition to technical experts, ethics committees often include members of senior management to ensure that ethical considerations are integrated into corporate strategy and decision-making processes. The committee's structure can vary depending on the size and nature of the organization. In large corporations, ethics committees may consist of several sub-committees or task forces that focus on specific issues, such as AI fairness, data privacy, or sustainability. In smaller organizations, a single ethics board may oversee all aspects of AI ethics and governance. Regardless of size, ethics committees are typically charged with providing recommendations, conducting audits, and ensuring transparency in the organization's use of AI and Big Data (Pasquale, 2015).

2. **Functions and Responsibilities**: The primary responsibility of an ethics committee is to assess the ethical implications of AI and Big Data technologies. Key functions of the committee include:
    - **Policy Development**: Ethics committees are responsible for developing ethical guidelines and policies that govern the use of AI and Big Data. These policies should cover areas such as data privacy, algorithmic fairness, transparency, and accountability.
    - **Risk Assessment**: The committee must assess the risks associated with deploying AI systems, such as the potential for bias, discrimination, or privacy violations. This includes conducting regular audits to evaluate whether AI systems are functioning as intended and whether they comply with ethical standards.
    - **Stakeholder Engagement**: Ethics committees often engage with external stakeholders, including customers, regulators, and advocacy groups, to ensure that the organization's AI systems align with public interests and societal values. This external input can help identify potential issues that the internal team may not have considered.
    - **Advisory Role**: The committee acts as an advisory body to senior management, providing guidance on ethical concerns and recommending strategies to address ethical challenges. The committee should ensure that AI systems are developed and deployed with ethical principles at the forefront (O'Neil, 2016).

Case Examples of Successful Ethics Oversight Models

1. **Google's AI Ethics Board**: Google's AI Ethics Board is one example of an ethics committee designed to provide oversight for AI systems. The board was formed to ensure that Google's AI technologies adhere to ethical standards and reflect the company's commitment to responsible innovation. The committee

is composed of external experts in AI, ethics, and human rights, who provide guidance on issues related to privacy, fairness, and transparency.

In 2019, Google disbanded its initial AI Ethics Board after backlash related to the inclusion of controversial members. This incident highlights the importance of selecting the right mix of members for ethics boards to ensure credibility and inclusivity. Despite this, Google reestablished its commitment to AI ethics by creating new frameworks and oversight mechanisms to address concerns about bias and inequality in its AI systems. This case underscores the importance of diverse perspectives in AI ethics oversight and the need for committees to be adaptive in responding to challenges (O'Neil, 2016).

2. **IBM's AI Ethics Board**: IBM's AI Ethics Board is another prominent example of effective oversight. The company has been at the forefront of AI ethics, emphasizing the need for transparency, fairness, and accountability in its AI technologies. The AI Ethics Board at IBM plays a critical role in overseeing the company's AI initiatives, particularly in areas such as algorithmic bias, privacy, and data governance. IBM's board is composed of internal and external experts, including ethicists, legal advisors, and industry professionals, who provide continuous feedback and conduct regular audits of IBM's AI systems. IBM also developed the *AI Fairness 360* toolkit, which is designed to help organizations detect and mitigate bias in AI models. This toolkit reflects the company's commitment to ensuring that AI systems are ethically sound and inclusive. The work of IBM's AI Ethics Board serves as a model for other organizations seeking to integrate ethical oversight into their AI development processes (Dastin, 2018).
3. **Microsoft's AI and Ethics in Engineering and Research (AETHER) Committee**

Microsoft's AETHER Committee is another successful model of ethical oversight. The committee provides guidance on the ethical challenges associated with AI technologies, ensuring that Microsoft's AI products align with the company's values of inclusivity, privacy, and fairness. The AETHER Committee is tasked with evaluating the ethical implications of AI and data-driven products across various stages of development and deployment. A key feature of Microsoft's ethics board is its integration with the company's research and engineering teams. By including technical experts in the ethical oversight process, Microsoft ensures that ethical concerns are addressed alongside technical challenges. Additionally, the AETHER Committee works closely with external organizations, including advocacy groups and regulators, to align its AI practices with societal norms and expectations (Brynjolfsson & McAfee, 2014).

Establishing ethics committees and advisory boards is essential for organizations seeking to implement AI and Big Data responsibly. These committees play a vital role in guiding decision-making, monitoring AI system performance, and ensuring that technologies align with ethical standards. Case examples from Google, IBM, and Microsoft illustrate the importance of diverse perspectives and continuous feedback in maintaining responsible AI practices. By forming robust ethics committees and integrating them into their corporate governance structures, organizations can foster trust, promote fairness, and ensure that AI and Big Data systems contribute positively to society.

5.3 Regulatory Compliance and Self-Regulation

As Artificial Intelligence (AI) and Big Data continue to shape business practices across industries, the need for clear regulatory frameworks and responsible self-regulation has become increasingly urgent. Governments around the world are implementing and evolving regulations to address the ethical, privacy, and security risks posed by these technologies. At the same time, many organizations are adopting self-regulatory practices to demonstrate their commitment to ethical standards and to stay ahead of regulatory changes. This section provides an overview of the current regulations governing AI and Big Data, as well as the advantages and challenges of self-regulation in corporate contexts.

Overview of Current Regulations Governing AI and Big Data

1. **The General Data Protection Regulation (GDPR)**: The General Data Protection Regulation (GDPR) is one of the most comprehensive data protection regulations globally, with far-reaching implications for businesses that handle personal data. Introduced by the European Union (EU) in 2018, GDPR aims to strengthen data privacy rights for individuals and regulate the use of personal data across member states. It requires organizations to ensure transparency in their data processing practices, obtain informed consent from data subjects, and provide individuals with greater control over their personal data (Voigt & Von dem Bussche, 2017). In the context of AI and Big Data, GDPR plays a crucial role in limiting how personal data is collected and used. For instance, it restricts the use of automated decision-making, including profiling, unless specific conditions are met. Companies that rely on AI-driven models for decision-making must ensure that their processes are transparent, explainable, and aligned with the rights of individuals under GDPR. Failure to comply with these regulations can result in significant fines, making GDPR a critical consideration for companies using Big Data and AI technologies (Zeng, 2017).

2. **The California Consumer Privacy Act (CCPA)**: The CCPA, which took effect in 2020, provides consumers in California with greater control over their personal data. It grants individuals the right to know what data is being collected about them, the right to request deletion of their data, and the right to opt out of the sale of their data. The CCPA is similar to the GDPR in its emphasis on transparency and consumer rights but is tailored to the specific legal and regulatory landscape in the United States. For companies operating in California or dealing with Californian consumers, compliance with the CCPA is essential. Organizations must ensure that they provide clear privacy policies and allow consumers to exercise their rights under the law. AI systems that process personal data must be designed to respect these rights and ensure that data collection and usage practices are transparent and fair (Morrison, 2020).
3. **AI Act (EU)**: The European Union is also in the process of developing the AI Act, a regulatory framework that aims to create a legal framework for the development, deployment, and use of AI in Europe. The AI Act classifies AI applications based on their risk level, with higher-risk applications, such as those in healthcare, transportation, and law enforcement, subject to more stringent requirements. These include ensuring transparency, providing explanations for AI decisions, and implementing robust safeguards to prevent harm. The AI Act aims to create a balance between fostering innovation and ensuring that AI systems are safe, ethical, and aligned with EU values, including privacy, fairness, and non-discrimination (European Commission, 2021).
4. **Other International Regulations**: In addition to GDPR and the AI Act, various countries have started to develop their own AI and Big Data regulations. For instance, the United States has proposed the Algorithmic Accountability Act, which seeks to require companies to audit and disclose information about the algorithms they use, particularly in areas like hiring, lending, and policing. Similarly, China has introduced the "Civil Code" which includes provisions on data protection and privacy, although its approach to regulation is seen as more state-centric compared to the EU's approach (Zeng, 2017).

These international regulatory efforts highlight the growing global focus on ensuring that AI and Big Data are used in ways that protect individual rights, ensure fairness, and promote accountability.

Advantages and Challenges of Self-Regulation in Corporate Contexts

1. **Advantages of Self-Regulation**

- **Proactive Risk Management**: One of the key advantages of self-regulation is that it allows organizations to proactively manage risks associated with AI and Big Data technologies. By developing internal policies and practices, companies can address potential ethical concerns, such as bias, privacy violations, and transparency issues, before they lead to regulatory penalties or reputational damage. Self-regulation enables companies to set high standards for their technologies and foster public trust by demonstrating a commitment to ethical principles (Brynjolfsson & McAfee, 2014).
- **Flexibility and Innovation**: Self-regulation offers more flexibility than government-imposed regulations, which may be slower to adapt to new technological developments. Companies that implement self-regulation can adjust their policies and practices in response to emerging ethical challenges or changes in public opinion. This flexibility encourages innovation while maintaining ethical oversight, allowing organizations to stay ahead of regulatory requirements and better align with evolving societal expectations (Brynjolfsson & McAfee, 2014).
- **Enhanced Reputation**: Companies that implement self-regulation demonstrate leadership in ethical practices, which can enhance their reputation among customers, investors, and regulators. By establishing themselves as responsible stewards of AI and Big Data, companies can differentiate themselves from competitors and attract consumers who prioritize ethical business practices. Self-regulation can also be a key factor in attracting investment from socially conscious investors who value sustainability and ethical governance (Pasquale, 2015).

2. **Challenges of Self-Regulation**
    - **Lack of Standardization**: One of the major challenges of self-regulation is the lack of standardization across industries and regions. Without a universally accepted framework for ethical AI and Big Data, companies may struggle to develop policies that align with broader industry norms or legal requirements. This inconsistency can create confusion and increase the risk of non-compliance with emerging regulations. Additionally, without a clear set of guidelines, companies may unintentionally overlook critical ethical issues (Pasquale, 2015).
    - **Potential for Inadequate Oversight**: Self-regulation relies on the goodwill and commitment of the organization to adhere to ethical practices. However, there is a risk that self-regulation may be superficial or insufficient, particularly if companies prioritize business objectives over ethical concerns. Without external oversight or accountability, companies may cut corners to save costs or expedite processes, which could re-

sult in unethical outcomes. Third-party audits and independent reviews are essential to ensure that self-regulation is meaningful and effective (Raji et al., 2020).

- **Resource Constraints**: Implementing effective self-regulation requires resources, expertise, and dedicated personnel, which can be a challenge for smaller organizations or those with limited budgets. Establishing comprehensive data governance policies, conducting regular audits, and investing in training and technology for ethical compliance can be costly. For companies that lack the necessary resources, self-regulation may be less effective or inconsistent (Raji et al., 2020).

Regulatory compliance and self-regulation play complementary roles in ensuring that AI and Big Data technologies are deployed ethically and responsibly. While regulatory frameworks like GDPR and the AI Act provide legal structures for governing the use of these technologies, self-regulation allows companies to proactively address emerging ethical challenges, foster innovation, and build consumer trust. However, self-regulation must be implemented carefully, with clear policies, external oversight, and sufficient resources to ensure that companies live up to their ethical commitments. By balancing regulatory compliance with effective self-regulation, organizations can navigate the complexities of AI and Big Data responsibly, ensuring that these technologies benefit society while minimizing risks.

5.4 Stakeholder Engagement and Ethical Communication

As organizations increasingly adopt AI and Big Data technologies, transparent communication with stakeholders and building trust through ethical practices have become essential for responsible AI deployment. Stakeholders—including customers, employees, investors, regulators, and the broader public—expect organizations to use these technologies ethically, ensuring that their deployment does not harm individual rights or societal values. Transparent communication helps ensure that stakeholders understand how AI and Big Data systems work, how their data is used, and how ethical considerations are incorporated into decision-making processes. This section explores approaches to transparent communication with stakeholders and the importance of building trust through ethical practices.

Approaches to Transparent Communication With Stakeholders

1. **Clear and Accessible Information**: One of the key components of transparent communication is providing clear, accurate, and accessible information about how AI and Big Data technologies are being used. Organizations should make

information available to stakeholders about how AI models function, what data they use, and the potential impacts of their decisions. This includes explaining the rationale behind AI-driven decisions in a way that is understandable to both technical and non-technical audiences. Transparency can be achieved through clear privacy policies, user-friendly terms of service, and detailed explanations of how AI systems make decisions (Doshi-Velez & Kim, 2017). For example, if an organization uses AI for hiring decisions, it should communicate to job applicants how their data is being used, what factors are considered in the decision-making process, and how the system has been designed to ensure fairness and minimize bias. This transparency builds confidence that the AI system is being used responsibly and that applicants' data is protected.

2. **Proactive Disclosure of Data Collection Practices**: Proactively disclosing data collection practices is another important aspect of transparent communication. Organizations should explain what data they are collecting, how it will be used, and who will have access to it. This can be done through privacy notices, consent forms, and other communications that inform stakeholders about their rights regarding data sharing and usage. For example, companies like Facebook and Google have introduced clearer, more accessible privacy policies to address concerns about how user data is collected and used for targeted advertising (Isaak & Hanna, 2018). By giving users control over their data and the ability to opt in or out of certain data collection practices, companies foster greater transparency and trust.
3. **Regular Reporting and Updates**: Organizations should engage in regular reporting to stakeholders about how AI and Big Data systems are functioning, particularly when these systems impact individuals' lives. For instance, companies should provide updates on the performance of AI systems, how they are aligned with ethical standards, and any adjustments made to address emerging ethical issues. Regular communication on these topics allows stakeholders to stay informed and ensures accountability. Public-facing reports and impact assessments, especially when AI systems affect vulnerable groups, can help demonstrate that ethical considerations are consistently monitored and addressed (O'Neil, 2016).
4. Engagement with External Auditors and Third-Party Reviews: Transparency can be further enhanced by engaging external auditors and third-party reviewers to assess AI systems. Third-party assessments of algorithmic fairness, data privacy, and transparency allow for unbiased evaluations that can be shared with stakeholders. These assessments provide an independent verification of the organization's practices and help build trust with both external and internal stakeholders. Organizations like IBM and Google have conducted third-party audits of their AI models to ensure they adhere to ethical standards, ensuring

credibility and reducing the potential for conflict of interest (Brynjolfsson & McAfee, 2014).

Importance of Building Trust Through Ethical Practices

1. **Trust as a Foundation for Long-Term Relationships**: Trust is a critical factor in maintaining long-term relationships with stakeholders. For organizations utilizing AI and Big Data, establishing and maintaining trust hinges on ethical practices. Stakeholders are more likely to engage with companies that they trust to handle their data responsibly and make decisions that are fair and transparent. AI and Big Data technologies have the potential to significantly impact individuals' lives, so the ethical use of these technologies is essential to earning the trust of stakeholders (Floridi, 2019). For example, businesses that adopt fair AI practices, such as addressing algorithmic biases and ensuring data privacy, are more likely to foster trust with customers and employees. Trust can lead to increased loyalty, better brand reputation, and a more positive public perception, which ultimately benefits the organization in terms of growth and sustainability.
2. **Ethical Communication Builds Public Confidence**: Building trust through ethical practices also involves maintaining a commitment to responsible communication. Public confidence in AI systems can be bolstered when organizations openly acknowledge the limitations of their technologies and take steps to address any issues that arise. Ethical communication means being honest about the potential risks and challenges of AI, not only the benefits. For instance, if an AI system is found to be biased or making flawed decisions, companies must communicate these findings transparently and outline the corrective measures they are taking (Pasquale, 2015). When organizations are transparent about their commitment to correcting issues and improving AI systems, it demonstrates accountability and fosters public trust. This proactive and responsible communication helps to establish the organization as a leader in ethical AI practices and strengthens its reputation in the marketplace.
3. **Engaging with Diverse Stakeholders**: It is important to recognize that different stakeholder groups may have varying concerns about AI and Big Data. For example, consumers may be concerned about privacy, while employees may worry about job displacement due to automation. Engaging with diverse stakeholders and actively listening to their concerns allows organizations to address potential ethical issues early and ensure that their AI systems serve the best interests of all groups. Diversity in stakeholder engagement fosters inclusivity and ensures that the benefits of AI and Big Data technologies are equitably distributed. Additionally, organizations should collaborate with exter-

nal advocacy groups, regulators, and civil society organizations to ensure their AI practices align with societal values and ethical norms. Engaging with these groups helps organizations stay informed about broader societal concerns and make necessary adjustments to their systems (O'Neil, 2016).

4. **Demonstrating Accountability**: Ethical practices not only involve transparent communication but also demonstrating accountability. By taking responsibility for the outcomes of AI and Big Data systems, organizations show their commitment to ethical practices. This includes not only ensuring that AI systems are fair, transparent, and non-discriminatory but also addressing any negative outcomes promptly and effectively. Demonstrating accountability reassures stakeholders that the organization is committed to minimizing harm and making decisions that benefit society (Raji et al., 2020).

Transparent communication with stakeholders and building trust through ethical practices are fundamental to the responsible use of AI and Big Data. By providing clear information about data usage, ensuring transparency in decision-making processes, and engaging with stakeholders regularly, organizations can foster greater trust and accountability. Ethical practices, such as addressing bias, ensuring privacy protection, and being transparent about AI system limitations, play a crucial role in building long-term relationships with consumers, employees, and other stakeholders. As AI and Big Data continue to shape industries, organizations that prioritize ethical communication and transparency will be better positioned to navigate the complexities of these technologies and ensure their responsible use.

6. RECOMMENDATIONS FOR ETHICAL CORPORATE PRACTICES

6.1 Guidelines for Ethical AI and Big Data Use

As AI and Big Data technologies continue to transform industries, it is critical for organizations to adopt ethical strategies for their development and deployment. Ethical AI and Big Data practices not only promote fairness and transparency but also help businesses minimize risks, comply with regulations, and build trust with stakeholders. To ensure that AI and Big Data are used responsibly, companies should follow a set of practical guidelines that address core ethical considerations, such as fairness, privacy, accountability, and transparency. This section outlines practical steps for companies to implement ethical AI and Big Data strategies.

1. Establish Clear Ethical Policies and Frameworks

The first step in implementing ethical AI and Big Data strategies is to establish clear policies and ethical frameworks. These policies should define the organization's commitment to ethical practices in data collection, AI development, and decision-making. Ethical frameworks should include:

- **Data Privacy and Protection**: Clearly articulate the company's stance on data privacy, ensuring that all data collection and usage practices comply with regulations such as GDPR or CCPA. Companies should also establish protocols for obtaining informed consent, ensuring individuals understand how their data will be used and giving them control over their personal information.
- **Bias and Fairness**: Create policies that address bias in AI algorithms and promote fairness in data usage. Ensure that AI systems are regularly tested for bias and that corrective actions are taken if biases are detected. Policies should promote the use of diverse and representative datasets to avoid reinforcing existing inequalities.
- **Transparency**: Ensure that AI systems and Big Data practices are transparent, providing clear explanations of how decisions are made, particularly in high-impact areas like hiring, lending, or healthcare.

2. Promote Diversity and Inclusivity in AI Development

To mitigate biases and ensure fairness in AI systems, organizations should prioritize diversity and inclusivity throughout the AI development lifecycle. This includes:

- **Diverse Teams**: Build teams with diverse backgrounds and perspectives to ensure that AI systems are designed to address the needs of all groups. Diverse teams are more likely to identify and mitigate biases that could affect underrepresented communities. This includes hiring data scientists, ethicists, and domain experts from diverse demographic backgrounds.
- **Inclusive Design**: Ensure that AI models and algorithms are designed to be inclusive of all groups, considering factors such as race, gender, age, and socio-economic status. AI development should aim to eliminate unintended discrimination and ensure equitable outcomes for everyone, regardless of their background.

3. Implement Robust Data Governance and Security Measures

Data governance and security are foundational to ethical AI and Big Data practices. Companies must implement robust data governance frameworks to ensure data is accurate, secure, and used responsibly. Key steps include:

- **Data Quality Control**: Establish protocols for ensuring the quality, accuracy, and consistency of data used to train AI systems. Data cleaning and validation procedures should be regularly conducted to eliminate errors or inconsistencies that could lead to biased or inaccurate outcomes.
- **Data Security and Encryption**: Implement strong data security measures to protect against data breaches and unauthorized access. Sensitive personal data should be encrypted both during storage and in transit. Regular security audits and monitoring systems should be in place to detect and prevent security vulnerabilities.
- **Data Retention and Deletion Policies**: Define data retention policies that specify how long data will be retained and when it will be deleted. Data should only be kept for as long as necessary for legitimate business purposes, and users should have the right to request data deletion where applicable.

4. Ensure Transparency and Explainability of AI Systems

One of the key ethical concerns in AI is the opacity of decision-making processes. To address this, organizations should prioritize the transparency and explainability of AI systems:

- **Explainable AI (XAI)**: Adopt explainable AI models that can provide clear and understandable reasons for the decisions they make. XAI tools, such as Local Interpretable Model-Agnostic Explanations (LIME) and SHAP (SHapley Additive Explanations), can be used to explain AI decisions to stakeholders in non-technical terms (Ribeiro, Singh, & Guestrin, 2016).
- **Clear Documentation and Reporting**: Maintain clear documentation about how AI systems are developed, including information about the data used, the algorithms deployed, and the intended outcomes. Regular reports on AI performance and ethical compliance should be shared with stakeholders to demonstrate transparency.
- **User Consent and Control**: Provide users with control over their data and AI-driven interactions. Offer clear options for individuals to opt-in or opt-out of data collection and AI systems that affect them. Transparency in data

usage and algorithmic decisions will empower users and increase trust in AI technologies.

5. Establish Ethical Oversight and Accountability Structures

Ethical oversight is essential for ensuring that AI and Big Data systems are deployed in a responsible and accountable manner. Companies should establish clear accountability structures to ensure that ethical practices are maintained throughout the lifecycle of AI systems. This includes:

- **Ethics Committees and Advisory Boards**: Create internal ethics committees or advisory boards that can assess AI systems for ethical concerns and provide guidance on decision-making. These committees should include diverse stakeholders, including ethicists, legal advisors, data scientists, and community representatives. They should regularly review AI systems to ensure they align with ethical standards and societal values.
- **Algorithmic Audits**: Conduct regular algorithmic audits to identify and address issues related to fairness, bias, and transparency. Independent audits can provide an unbiased assessment of AI systems and help identify areas for improvement. These audits should be incorporated into the company's continuous monitoring strategy.
- **Accountability for Outcomes**: Establish mechanisms for holding organizations accountable for the outcomes generated by AI systems. This includes defining responsibility for negative outcomes, such as biased decisions or privacy violations, and implementing corrective actions when necessary.

6.2 Foster a Culture of Ethical Awareness and Education

Building an ethical culture within the organization is critical to ensuring that AI and Big Data practices are aligned with societal values. Companies should:

- **Ethics Training and Education**: Provide regular training for employees on ethical AI practices, data privacy, and the potential societal impact of AI technologies. This training should be mandatory for all employees involved in AI development and deployment and should emphasize the importance of fairness, transparency, and accountability.
- **Encourage Ethical Innovation**: Foster an organizational culture that encourages ethical innovation. Encourage employees to identify potential ethical challenges in AI and Big Data systems and propose solutions. Providing

a safe space for ethical concerns and promoting open discussions can help organizations stay ahead of emerging issues and implement best practices.

Implementing ethical AI and Big Data strategies is essential for ensuring that these technologies are deployed responsibly and for the benefit of society. By following practical steps such as establishing clear ethical policies, promoting diversity in AI development, ensuring robust data governance, prioritizing transparency, and fostering ethical oversight, organizations can create AI systems that are fair, transparent, and accountable. Ethical practices in AI and Big Data not only build trust with stakeholders but also ensure long-term success and sustainability for businesses in an increasingly data-driven world.

6.3 Best Practices for Managing Ethical Risks

AI and Big Data technologies bring immense opportunities for businesses and societies, but they also introduce significant ethical risks. These risks—ranging from data privacy violations and algorithmic biases to lack of transparency and accountability—can undermine public trust and lead to legal and reputational damage. Therefore, it is critical for organizations to identify and mitigate these risks proactively. This section outlines best practices for managing ethical risks associated with AI and Big Data, focusing on risk identification, mitigation strategies, and the implementation of responsible practices.

1. Identifying Ethical Risks in AI and Big Data

To effectively manage ethical risks, organizations first need to identify the key risks associated with AI and Big Data technologies. Some common ethical risks include:

- **Bias and Discrimination**: One of the most significant ethical risks in AI systems is bias, which can lead to discriminatory outcomes. Bias may arise from unrepresentative training data, algorithmic design flaws, or historical inequalities embedded in the data. For example, AI models used in recruitment may unintentionally favor male candidates over female candidates due to biased training data.
- **Privacy Violations**: The collection and use of personal data by AI and Big Data systems can lead to privacy breaches. Unauthorized data collection, misuse of sensitive information, and lack of transparency in data processing practices can undermine individuals' privacy rights.

- **Lack of Transparency and Explainability**: Many AI systems, particularly those based on machine learning and deep learning, are often regarded as "black boxes" because they are difficult to interpret and explain. Lack of transparency can lead to mistrust, especially when AI systems are used for critical decisions in areas like healthcare, finance, or law enforcement.
- **Security Risks**: AI and Big Data systems are vulnerable to cyberattacks and data breaches. Mismanagement of data security, such as inadequate encryption or access control mechanisms, can expose sensitive information and harm individuals.
- **Accountability and Liability**: When AI systems make decisions, it can be unclear who is responsible if things go wrong. The lack of clear accountability mechanisms raises ethical questions about who should be held liable for AI-driven errors or harmful outcomes.

2. Mitigating Ethical Risks in AI and Big Data

Once ethical risks are identified, organizations can implement strategies to mitigate these risks and ensure that AI and Big Data systems are developed and used responsibly.

1. **Bias Mitigation and Fairness** To mitigate bias and ensure fairness in AI systems, organizations should:
    - **Ensure Diverse Data Sets**: One of the most effective ways to reduce bias is to ensure that training datasets are diverse and representative of the population the AI system will serve. AI systems should be trained on datasets that include various demographic groups, including race, gender, age, socio-economic status, and geographic location. This helps prevent biased outcomes that disadvantage specific groups.
    - **Regular Bias Audits and Testing**: Organizations should conduct regular audits of AI models to assess whether they produce biased results. These audits should evaluate the fairness of decision-making processes, particularly in areas like hiring, lending, and criminal justice. Tools such as fairness-aware machine learning algorithms can help identify and correct biases in AI models (Barocas et al., 2019).
    - **Implement Fairness Constraints**: AI models should be designed with fairness constraints to ensure that they do not favor one group over another. This can involve developing algorithms that optimize for fairness metrics, such as demographic parity or equal opportunity, alongside traditional performance metrics (Raji et al., 2020).

2. **Data Privacy and Protection**: To mitigate the risk of privacy violations, organizations should:
    - **Adhere to Privacy Regulations**: Organizations must comply with privacy regulations like the GDPR and CCPA, which set guidelines for the collection, processing, and sharing of personal data. These regulations require organizations to obtain informed consent from individuals, minimize data collection to what is necessary, and ensure the security of collected data.
    - **Implement Privacy-By-Design**: Privacy should be integrated into AI and Big Data systems from the outset. This involves incorporating privacy protections at every stage of data collection and processing, including data anonymization, encryption, and access controls. Privacy-by-design practices help minimize the risk of privacy breaches and ensure that user data is handled ethically (Cavoukian, 2012).
    - **User Control and Transparency**: Give users control over their data and allow them to easily access, update, or delete their personal information. Additionally, organizations should clearly communicate how data is collected and used, giving individuals the opportunity to opt out if they do not want their data to be used.
3. **Ensuring Transparency and Explainability** To address the risks of opacity and build trust with stakeholders, organizations should:
    - **Adopt Explainable AI (XAI)**: Organizations should use explainable AI models that can provide clear, understandable reasons for decisions. XAI methods, such as SHAP (SHapley Additive exPlanations) and LIME (Local Interpretable Model-Agnostic Explanations), allow organizations to interpret and explain AI model decisions in a way that is understandable to non-technical stakeholders (Ribeiro, Singh, & Guestrin, 2016). This transparency builds trust with users, particularly in high-stakes applications like healthcare or hiring.
    - **Document AI Decision-Making Processes**: Organizations should maintain clear documentation on how AI systems make decisions, including the data used, the algorithms applied, and the factors influencing the decisions. This documentation should be accessible to stakeholders and reviewed regularly to ensure ongoing transparency.
4. **Strengthening Security Measures**: To mitigate security risks and protect data from cyberattacks, organizations should:
    - **Implement Robust Cybersecurity Protocols**: Protect AI and Big Data systems with strong cybersecurity measures, including data encryption, firewalls, and secure access controls. Regular security audits and pen-

etration testing should be conducted to identify vulnerabilities and address them before they can be exploited.
- **Data Anonymization and Minimization**: Minimize the amount of personally identifiable information (PII) collected and stored by anonymizing data wherever possible. This reduces the risk of exposing sensitive data in the event of a breach.

5. **Establishing Accountability and Oversight**: To address accountability concerns, organizations should:
   - **Create Ethical Oversight Bodies**: Establish internal ethics committees or advisory boards to oversee the ethical use of AI and Big Data. These bodies should review AI systems for potential ethical issues, including bias, transparency, and accountability, and provide guidance on addressing these concerns.
   - **Clearly Define Liability**: Organizations should define clear lines of responsibility and accountability for AI-driven decisions. This includes establishing protocols for handling errors or harms caused by AI systems and ensuring that affected individuals have access to recourse.
6. **Ongoing Monitoring and Auditing**: To ensure that AI systems continue to operate ethically over time, organizations should:
   - **Implement Continuous Monitoring Systems**: Set up automated systems to continuously monitor AI models for performance issues, biases, or unintended consequences. Real-time monitoring allows organizations to quickly identify and address ethical risks as they arise.
   - **Conduct Regular Audits**: Regularly audit AI systems for compliance with ethical standards, fairness, and transparency. Audits should include internal reviews as well as third-party evaluations to ensure impartial assessments of AI practices.

Managing ethical risks associated with AI and Big Data requires a proactive approach that includes identifying potential risks, implementing strategies to mitigate them, and ensuring ongoing monitoring and oversight. By following best practices such as ensuring data diversity, conducting regular audits, adopting privacy-by-design principles, and fostering transparency, organizations can mitigate the ethical risks of AI and Big Data systems. Proactively addressing these risks will not only help organizations comply with legal requirements but also build trust with stakeholders, ensuring that AI and Big Data technologies are used responsibly and ethically.

6.4. Creating a Culture of Ethical Responsibility

Creating a culture of ethical responsibility is essential for ensuring that AI and Big Data technologies are used in a way that aligns with an organization's values and societal expectations. Ethical behavior must be ingrained at all levels of the organization, from executives to employees, and must be supported by effective training, leadership, and clear policies. By fostering an ethical culture, organizations can not only mitigate the risks associated with AI and Big Data but also build trust with stakeholders, improve decision-making processes, and enhance long-term organizational success. This section explores strategies for encouraging ethical behavior across the organization and the importance of training and development programs focused on ethics.

1. Encouraging Ethical Behavior Across All Levels of the Organization

To create a culture of ethical responsibility, it is critical that ethical behavior is promoted at every level of the organization. From top leadership to entry-level employees, everyone in the organization must understand the importance of ethics in AI and Big Data and be held accountable for their actions. The following approaches can help encourage ethical behavior throughout the organization:

1. **Leadership Commitment to Ethics**: The tone for ethical behavior in an organization is set by its leaders. Senior management and board members must demonstrate a clear commitment to ethical principles by prioritizing ethics in their decision-making and publicly supporting ethical AI and Big Data practices. Leaders should set an example by being transparent, accountable, and responsible for the decisions they make, particularly those that involve AI and data usage. When leadership consistently models ethical behavior, it sends a strong message throughout the organization that ethics are a core value (Brynjolfsson & McAfee, 2014). Furthermore, ethical leadership involves making strategic decisions that prioritize long-term sustainability over short-term gains. For example, executives can support investments in ethical AI, such as ensuring that AI systems are free from bias or adopting privacy-by-design principles in data usage, even if these choices are more resource-intensive in the short run. Ethical leadership fosters an organizational culture where employees feel empowered to act ethically and where ethical practices are integrated into every aspect of business operations.

2. **Clear Ethical Policies and Expectations**: For ethical behavior to be encouraged, there must be clear and well-communicated policies that define the organization's stance on AI ethics and data responsibility. These policies should set out specific guidelines and expectations for how employees are expected to handle ethical issues related to AI and Big Data. For example, organizations should have a code of ethics that includes specific provisions on issues like fairness, data privacy, transparency, and accountability. Employees should understand how to recognize ethical dilemmas and know who to turn to for guidance. These policies should also address how ethical violations will be handled, ensuring that there are clear consequences for unethical behavior. This creates a system of accountability where individuals are held responsible for their actions and are motivated to act in alignment with the organization's ethical standards (O'Neil, 2016).
3. **Encouraging Ethical Decision-Making at All Levels**: Ethical behavior should not be limited to senior leadership; it must be encouraged at all levels of the organization. Employees should be empowered to make ethical decisions in their day-to-day work, with the understanding that their actions have consequences for both the organization and society at large. Providing employees with the tools, resources, and support they need to make ethical decisions is essential. For example, employees working with AI models or Big Data should have access to decision-making frameworks that help them assess the ethical implications of their actions. Organizations can also create platforms for employees to raise ethical concerns or report violations of ethical guidelines, ensuring that individuals feel safe and supported when confronting difficult situations (Raji et al., 2020). A well-structured whistleblower program can encourage employees to report unethical practices without fear of retaliation, further promoting a culture of accountability.

2. Training and Development Programs Focused on Ethics

Training and development programs are crucial for building an organization-wide understanding of ethics in AI and Big Data. These programs ensure that all employees, from technical teams to non-technical staff, have the knowledge and skills needed to navigate the ethical complexities of these technologies. The following strategies can help organizations develop effective ethics training programs:

1. **Comprehensive Ethics Training for All Employees**: Ethics training should be comprehensive and tailored to different roles within the organization. While technical staff, such as data scientists and AI engineers, need training on algorithmic fairness, data privacy, and bias mitigation, other employees, such as

business leaders and marketers, need training on how to handle data ethically and ensure that AI applications align with organizational values.

Ethics training should cover key topics, such as:

- **AI Bias and Fairness**: Understanding how bias can creep into AI systems and how to mitigate it.
- **Privacy Protection**: How to comply with data protection laws (e.g., GDPR) and protect consumer privacy.
- **Transparency and Accountability**: How to ensure that AI decisions are explainable and that organizations are accountable for the outcomes of their AI systems.

By providing targeted training, organizations can ensure that employees understand their role in maintaining ethical standards and how to apply ethical principles to their work.

2. **Scenario-Based Training and Ethical Dilemmas**: To help employees understand the practical implications of ethical decision-making, organizations should incorporate scenario-based training that simulates real-world ethical dilemmas in AI and Big Data contexts. These scenarios can involve situations such as detecting and addressing bias in AI systems, ensuring that customer data is used ethically in marketing campaigns, or making decisions about AI's impact on employee job security. By engaging employees in these scenarios, organizations can help them develop the critical thinking skills needed to navigate ethical challenges and make informed, responsible decisions. Additionally, these exercises can foster discussions about the complexities of ethical decision-making and encourage a deeper understanding of the consequences of AI and Big Data practices (Zeng, 2017).
3. **Continuous Learning and Ethical Awareness**: Ethical training should not be a one-time event; it should be an ongoing process that is integrated into the organization's culture. Regular workshops, seminars, and training sessions on emerging ethical issues in AI and Big Data can help keep employees up to date on new ethical challenges and regulatory changes. By promoting continuous learning, organizations ensure that ethical awareness remains a priority and that employees are always prepared to address new ethical dilemmas as they arise.
4. **Incorporating Ethics into Leadership Development**

Leaders play a key role in shaping organizational culture, so it is essential that ethics training is also integrated into leadership development programs. Managers and executives should receive specialized training on ethical decision-making, the societal impacts of AI, and how to foster an ethical culture within their teams. This ensures that ethical behavior is supported at all levels of leadership, creating a top-down approach to ethics in the organization.

3. Recognizing and Rewarding Ethical Behavior

In addition to training and clear policies, organizations should recognize and reward ethical behavior. Recognizing employees who demonstrate a commitment to ethical practices not only reinforces the importance of ethics but also incentivizes others to follow suit. Ethical behavior can be rewarded through recognition programs, bonuses, or career advancement opportunities. By publicly acknowledging those who prioritize ethics, organizations create positive reinforcement that encourages a culture of responsibility and integrity.

7. CONCLUSION

7.1 Summary of Key Insights

As Artificial Intelligence (AI) and Big Data continue to revolutionize industries and societies, the ethical challenges they pose cannot be overlooked. From biased algorithms and privacy violations to the lack of transparency and accountability, these technologies raise significant concerns that demand proactive and responsible management. This section recaps the key ethical challenges explored throughout this discussion and the proposed solutions for mitigating these issues, ensuring that AI and Big Data are developed and used in a way that aligns with societal values, legal requirements, and organizational goals.

Key Ethical Challenges

1. **Bias and Discrimination in AI Systems**:One of the most pressing ethical challenges in AI and Big Data is bias, which can manifest in various forms, including racial, gender, and socioeconomic biases. AI systems trained on unrepresentative or flawed datasets can perpetuate and even exacerbate existing inequalities, leading to unfair outcomes, such as biased hiring decisions, discriminatory lending practices, or unequal access to services.

2. **Privacy and Data Protection**: With the vast amount of personal data collected by AI and Big Data systems, ensuring privacy is a critical concern. Organizations must navigate the ethical implications of data collection, use, and sharing, ensuring that individuals' personal information is protected and they have control over how their data is used. Privacy violations can lead to significant trust issues, legal liabilities, and reputational damage.
3. **Lack of Transparency and Explainability**: Many AI systems, particularly those using machine learning techniques, are often considered "black boxes" due to their complexity and lack of interpretability. This lack of transparency raises concerns about accountability, especially when AI systems make decisions that directly affect individuals' lives, such as in healthcare, finance, and law enforcement. Without clear explanations of how decisions are made, stakeholders may feel powerless and distrustful of these technologies.
4. **Accountability and Responsibility**: AI and Big Data systems often operate autonomously, raising questions about who is accountable when things go wrong. Whether it's an AI model making an unfair decision or a data breach compromising sensitive information, organizations must establish clear accountability mechanisms to ensure that they are responsible for the outcomes of their systems.

Proposed Solutions:

1. **Ensuring Fairness and Mitigating Bias**: To address the risk of bias, organizations should focus on creating diverse and representative datasets for training AI systems. Regular audits and testing for fairness should be conducted to identify and correct any biases. Furthermore, fairness constraints should be implemented in AI algorithms to ensure that systems do not disproportionately benefit or harm specific groups.
2. **Strengthening Data Privacy and Protection**: Companies must adopt privacy-by-design principles, ensuring that data protection is integrated into AI and Big Data systems from the outset. This includes implementing strong encryption, ensuring compliance with privacy regulations like GDPR and CCPA, and providing users with clear, understandable information about how their data is collected and used. Organizations should also give individuals control over their data, allowing them to opt-in or opt-out of data collection and sharing.
3. **Promoting Transparency and Explainability**: To enhance transparency, organizations should prioritize explainable AI (XAI) that allows stakeholders to understand how decisions are made. This can involve using interpretable models, providing clear documentation of the decision-making processes, and making algorithms and data sources more accessible to both technical and non-

technical audiences. Ensuring that AI systems are explainable helps build trust and accountability.

4. **Establishing Accountability and Ethical Oversight**: Organizations should implement robust governance structures, including ethics committees and advisory boards, to oversee AI and Big Data projects and ensure that they align with ethical principles. Regular audits, both internal and external, should be conducted to assess compliance with ethical standards. Clear accountability mechanisms must be established so that organizations are held responsible for the outcomes of their AI systems, particularly when they impact individuals' rights and well-being.
5. **Creating a Culture of Ethical Responsibility**: For ethical practices to be truly effective, they must be embedded into the culture of the organization. This involves training employees at all levels on the ethical implications of AI and Big Data, encouraging ethical behavior, and recognizing and rewarding those who demonstrate a commitment to ethical practices. Ethical leadership from senior management is crucial in setting the tone for the organization and ensuring that ethical principles are prioritized in decision-making processes.

While AI and Big Data offer significant benefits and opportunities, they also present complex ethical challenges that must be carefully managed. By addressing issues such as bias, privacy, transparency, and accountability, organizations can build AI systems that are fair, transparent, and aligned with societal values. Implementing practical solutions, such as bias mitigation strategies, privacy-by-design practices, explainable AI models, and strong ethical governance, will help mitigate these challenges and ensure the responsible use of AI and Big Data. As AI and Big Data technologies continue to evolve, maintaining a culture of ethical responsibility will be essential for fostering trust, ensuring compliance, and promoting long-term sustainability.

7.2 The Future of Ethical AI and Big Data in Corporate Management

As AI and Big Data technologies continue to evolve and reshape industries, the future of their ethical management will be shaped by advancements in both the technology itself and the frameworks designed to govern its use. Ethical considerations in AI and Big Data are becoming increasingly vital as their integration into corporate management deepens. As businesses harness these technologies for competitive advantage, they must adapt to emerging ethical challenges while embracing new opportunities to promote responsible innovation. This section explores the evolving landscape of ethical AI and Big Data, highlighting future trends and the key areas that will define ethical practices in corporate management.

1. Increasing Regulatory Scrutiny and Global Standards

As AI and Big Data technologies become more pervasive, the regulatory landscape is expected to become more stringent. Governments and regulatory bodies are recognizing the need to create comprehensive frameworks to govern these technologies and ensure that they are used responsibly. The European Union's General Data Protection Regulation (GDPR) and the proposed AI Act are early examples of efforts to create regulatory structures that address privacy, fairness, and accountability in AI systems.

In the future, we can expect a convergence of global standards and regulations that address ethical concerns in AI and Big Data. As AI's global reach grows, international collaboration between regulatory bodies will become essential to create unified ethical guidelines that protect individuals' rights and promote fairness across borders. These global standards will likely focus on ensuring transparency in AI decision-making, addressing data privacy risks, and preventing algorithmic biases, with companies being held accountable for ensuring their systems comply with these regulations.

The introduction of more robust legal frameworks will drive companies to be more proactive in aligning their AI and Big Data practices with ethical standards. Organizations will need to invest in compliance mechanisms, including continuous audits and reporting systems, to adhere to evolving regulatory demands. These legal frameworks will provide clarity and consistency in ethical AI practices and will encourage organizations to integrate ethics into their business strategies.

2. The Role of Explainable AI and Ethical Decision-Making

One of the most promising trends in the future of ethical AI is the growing emphasis on explainable AI (XAI). As AI systems become more complex, the need for transparency in AI decision-making processes will be even more critical. Explainable AI aims to create models that are not only accurate but also interpretable, allowing humans to understand and explain the reasoning behind AI decisions. This is especially important in sectors like healthcare, finance, and criminal justice, where AI-driven decisions have significant consequences for individuals' lives.

The demand for XAI will likely increase as consumers, regulators, and organizations push for greater accountability and transparency. By making AI systems more interpretable, companies can ensure that their AI applications are not only ethical but also trustworthy. This trend will influence how businesses design AI systems, with a greater focus on providing explanations for every decision made by AI models. The future will see a more significant integration of ethical decision-making frameworks within AI models, ensuring that AI systems are aligned with organizational values and societal expectations.

In parallel, the concept of ethical decision-making in AI is expected to mature. As companies develop AI systems capable of making decisions autonomously, organizations will need to ensure that these systems reflect human ethical principles. This will include embedding values such as fairness, justice, and inclusivity directly into AI algorithms, allowing these systems to make ethical choices in complex scenarios. For example, AI-driven decision-making in hiring or loan approvals will need to be designed to mitigate bias and promote fairness, ensuring that AI systems do not perpetuate historical inequalities.

3. Ethical AI as a Competitive Advantage

In the future, ethical AI and Big Data will not only be a legal and social responsibility but also a strategic differentiator. As consumers and employees become more conscientious about the ethical practices of the companies they engage with, businesses that prioritize ethical AI and data use will gain a competitive advantage. Ethical considerations in AI will likely become a core part of corporate social responsibility (CSR) and a key factor in building long-term brand loyalty.

Companies that implement ethical AI strategies—such as reducing bias, protecting privacy, ensuring transparency, and maintaining accountability—will differentiate themselves in the marketplace. As AI continues to shape business operations, ethical considerations will increasingly influence customer choices and employee engagement. Organizations that can demonstrate their commitment to responsible AI practices will attract ethically-minded consumers and talent, building trust and loyalty.

Moreover, the integration of ethical AI practices into corporate strategy will help businesses avoid costly ethical violations, regulatory fines, and reputational damage. Ethical AI will evolve from being a "nice-to-have" to a competitive necessity, as consumers and employees demand more accountability from companies using AI technologies.

4. Advances in Autonomous and Adaptive AI Systems

As AI technology advances, the future will likely see the development of more autonomous and adaptive AI systems capable of learning and evolving without human intervention. These systems will be able to self-improve and adapt to new data, making decisions that may be more efficient or optimized than human decision-making.

However, with these advancements come new ethical challenges. Ensuring that autonomous AI systems remain aligned with ethical principles will be a top priority. Companies will need to develop methods to ensure that adaptive AI continues to make ethical decisions over time, even as it learns from new data. This may involve the creation of self-regulating mechanisms within AI systems that can detect and address ethical issues as they arise. Continuous monitoring and auditing of adaptive AI will be essential to ensure that these systems remain aligned with the company's values and do not produce unintended harmful outcomes.

Additionally, adaptive AI will likely be more sensitive to context and better able to balance conflicting ethical principles. For example, AI systems may need to balance privacy concerns with the need for data-driven insights or fairness with efficiency. The future of AI will involve sophisticated mechanisms to make such trade-offs transparently and ethically.

5. Increased Collaboration between AI Developers and Ethical Experts

The growing complexity and societal impact of AI and Big Data will necessitate greater collaboration between technical AI developers and ethical experts. In the future, we can expect to see interdisciplinary teams composed of data scientists, ethicists, legal experts, and social scientists working together to ensure that AI systems are developed with ethical considerations at the forefront. Ethical experts will play a crucial role in helping AI developers understand the broader social implications of their systems and guide them in making decisions that promote fairness, justice, and respect for human rights.

This collaboration will be essential in addressing ethical dilemmas in AI, such as ensuring that AI models do not discriminate against certain demographic groups or that they respect privacy while enabling innovation. Interdisciplinary approaches will help ensure that ethical principles are not only embedded into the design process but also that they evolve with the technology, adapting to new ethical challenges as AI and Big Data systems continue to evolve.

7.3 Final Thoughts on Balancing Innovation with Ethics

As AI and Big Data continue to drive transformative innovations across industries, the challenge for organizations lies not just in harnessing the potential of these technologies, but in ensuring that they are used ethically and responsibly. The rapid pace of technological advancement often outpaces the development of regulations and frameworks that ensure ethical practices, which creates a significant risk of ethical lapses, unintended harm, and public distrust. In this environment, ethical leadership becomes paramount. This section emphasizes the importance of ethical leadership in balancing innovation with ethics in the digital age and reflects on the need for leaders to navigate these complexities with responsibility, foresight, and accountability.

1. The Role of Ethical Leadership in the Digital Age

Ethical leadership is a critical element in balancing innovation with ethics in today's data-driven world. As AI and Big Data technologies have the power to reshape industries, they also have the potential to create societal and ethical dilemmas. In this context, leaders who prioritize ethical decision-making and integrity play a pivotal role in shaping the ethical direction of their organizations and the broader impact of their innovations. Ethical leadership is about leading with principles that promote fairness, accountability, transparency, and respect for human rights.

Leaders must understand the ethical implications of the technologies their organizations develop and deploy. They must demonstrate a commitment to social responsibility by ensuring that AI and Big Data are used to benefit all stakeholders, rather than exacerbating inequality or harming vulnerable groups. Ethical leadership involves guiding an organization through complex moral choices, considering both the short-term and long-term consequences of technological decisions. It also includes making decisions that are not only legally compliant but are also morally justifiable in the eyes of the broader public.

Ethical leadership also requires transparency in communication. As organizations develop AI-driven systems, leaders must be transparent about the potential risks and limitations of these technologies, as well as their efforts to mitigate those risks. Open communication fosters trust with stakeholders, such as customers, employees, and regulators, and ensures that the organization remains accountable for the impact of its innovations.

2. Creating a Culture of Responsibility and Trust

The importance of ethical leadership goes beyond individual decisions; it influences the organizational culture. Leaders must foster a culture where ethical considerations are integrated into every aspect of AI and Big Data development. This includes building a workplace environment where employees feel empowered to make ethical decisions and where ethical considerations are prioritized alongside technical or business objectives.

One of the most effective ways to establish an ethical culture is through continuous education and training, as discussed earlier. Organizations should invest in programs that help employees understand the ethical implications of AI and Big Data, providing them with the tools to make decisions that align with both corporate values and societal norms. Ethical leadership ensures that the entire organization operates with the same ethical standards and remains vigilant about the potential risks of their AI systems.

Furthermore, ethical leaders should create mechanisms that encourage employees at all levels to raise ethical concerns. Open channels for reporting ethical violations, bias, or unfair practices must be established, supported by clear policies and protections for whistleblowers. By doing so, leaders create an environment where ethical challenges can be addressed promptly, ensuring that problems do not escalate into larger, more damaging issues.

3. Innovation with Integrity: The Balance

Balancing innovation with ethics requires an approach that does not sacrifice one for the other. Innovation should not come at the cost of ethical values such as fairness, transparency, and accountability. Ethical leadership means recognizing that innovation and ethics are not mutually exclusive but can, and should, coexist.

While AI and Big Data offer vast potential for driving business growth, improving customer experiences, and optimizing operations, they must be developed and deployed with careful consideration of their societal impact. Ethical leaders recognize that their organization's success is not solely measured by technological advancements or market share, but by how responsibly they leverage these innovations. Companies that prioritize ethical AI practices are more likely to sustain long-term success, as they foster customer trust and loyalty, which are vital for continued growth.

Leaders must also ensure that AI and Big Data technologies serve the greater good. For example, AI applications in healthcare should be designed to enhance patient care and improve outcomes, not to exclude vulnerable populations or perpetuate inequalities. In financial services, AI systems should help to democratize access to credit, not reinforce discriminatory lending practices. By adopting ethical innovation, leaders can ensure that technological advancements are used to create value for society as a whole, rather than just for the profit of a few.

4. The Path Forward: Leading with Purpose

Looking forward, the role of ethical leadership in the digital age will only become more critical. As AI and Big Data continue to evolve, the ethical challenges will multiply, requiring leaders to adopt a proactive stance in managing these risks. Ethical leadership is about leading with purpose, integrating ethics into the organization's core values, and ensuring that technological progress benefits society.

Ethical leaders must stay ahead of emerging issues, including the rise of autonomous systems, the growing use of predictive analytics in hiring and criminal justice, and the ongoing debate about privacy in the age of surveillance capitalism. To do this, leaders will need to engage in ongoing education about emerging ethical challenges, collaborate with policymakers to shape regulations, and actively involve a wide range of stakeholders in the decision-making process.

Furthermore, ethical leadership means demonstrating humility and openness to feedback. No system is perfect, and AI models are not immune to errors, biases, or unintended consequences. Leaders must be willing to admit when things go wrong, take responsibility, and take corrective action. This accountability will build public trust and show that organizations are committed to improving not only their technological capabilities but also their ethical standards.

REFERENCES

Apple. (2021). App tracking transparency: User privacy and data use. Retrieved from https://www.apple.com/privacy/features/

Arner, D. W., Barberis, J. N., & Buckley, R. P. (2016). FinTech, regTech, and the reconceptualization of financial regulation. *Northwestern Journal of International Law & Business*, 37(3), 371–411. DOI: 10.2139/ssrn.2847505

Barocas, S., Hardt, M., & Narayanan, A. (2019). *Fairness and machine learning: Limitations and opportunities*. https://fairmlbook.org/

Bertot, J. C., Jaeger, P. T., & Grimes, J. M. (2018). *The intersection of public policy and technology: Data privacy, ethics, and governance*. Springer.

Binns, R. (2018). Fairness in machine learning: Lessons from political philosophy. *Proceedings of the 2018 CHI Conference on Human Factors in Computing Systems*, 1-15. DOI: 10.1145/3173574.3174125

Brynjolfsson, E., & McAfee, A. (2014). *The second machine age: Work, progress, and prosperity in a time of brilliant technologies*. W. W. Norton & Company.

Buolamwini, J., & Gebru, T. (2018). Gender shades: Intersectional accuracy disparities in commercial gender classification. *Proceedings of the 1st Conference on Fairness, Accountability, and Transparency*, 77-91. DOI: 10.1145/3287560.3287593

Burrell, J. (2016). How the machine 'thinks': Understanding opacity in machine learning algorithms. *Big Data & Society*, 3(1), 1–12. DOI: 10.1177/2053951715622512

Cavoukian, A. (2012). *Privacy by design: The 7 foundational principles*. Information and Privacy Commissioner of Ontario. Retrieved from https://www.ipc.on.ca/privacy/privacy-by-design/

Chen, H., Chiang, R. H. L., & Storey, V. C. (2012). Business intelligence and analytics: From big data to big impact. *Management Information Systems Quarterly*, 36(4), 1165–1188. DOI: 10.2307/41703503

Dastin, J. (2018, October 10). Amazon scraps secret AI recruitment tool that showed bias against women. *Reuters*. https://www.reuters.com/article/us-amazon-com-jobs-automation-idUSKCN1MK08G

Davenport, T. H., & Ronanki, R. (2018). Artificial intelligence for the real world. *Harvard Business Review*, 96(1), 108–116. https://hbr.org/2018/01/artificial-intelligence-for-the-real-world

Doshi-Velez, F., & Kim, B. (2017). Towards a rigorous science of interpretable machine learning. *arXiv preprint arXiv:1702.08608*. /arXiv.1702.08608DOI: 10.48550

Edelman. (2020). *Edelman Trust Barometer Special Report: Brands and the Coronavirus*. Retrieved from https://www.edelman.com/trust/2020-trust-barometer-special-report-brands-and-coronavirus

European Commission. (2021). *Proposal for a regulation laying down harmonized rules on artificial intelligence (Artificial Intelligence Act)*. Retrieved from https://ec.europa.eu/digital-strategy

Floridi, L. (2019). *Ethics of data and analytics: Concepts, practices, and challenges*. Springer.

Gana, A., & Raji, I. D. (2020). Real-time monitoring of algorithmic decision-making. *Proceedings of the 2020 Conference on Fairness, Accountability, and Transparency*. DOI: 10.1145/3351095.3372875

Garvie, C. (2019). *The perpetual lineup: Unregulated police face recognition in America*. Georgetown Law Center on Privacy & Technology. Retrieved from https://www.perpetuallineup.org/

Gentsch, P. (2018). *AI in marketing, sales and service: Digital transformation in the age of artificial intelligence*. Springer.

Hill, K. (2012, February 16). How Target figured out a teen girl was pregnant before her father did. *Forbes*. Retrieved from https://www.forbes.com

Hosein, G. (2018). *The role of data governance in protecting privacy*. Springer.

Hunt, V., Yee, L., Prince, S., & Dixon-Fyle, S. (2018). Delivering through diversity. *McKinsey & Company*. Retrieved from https://www.mckinsey.com/featured-insights/gender-equality/delivering-through-diversity

Isaak, J., & Hanna, M. J. (2018). User data privacy: Facebook, Cambridge Analytica, and privacy protection. *Computer*, 51(8), 56–59. DOI: 10.1109/MC.2018.3191268

Khatri, V., & Brown, C. V. (2010). Designing data governance. *Communications of the ACM*, 53(1), 148–152. DOI: 10.1145/1629175.1629210

Kitchin, R. (2014). *The data revolution: Big data, open data, data infrastructures and their consequences*. SAGE Publications.

Mayer-Schönberger, V., & Cukier, K. (2013). *Big data: A revolution that will transform how we live, work, and think*. Eamon Dolan/Houghton Mifflin Harcourt.

Mills, E. (2018). The Equifax breach: One year later. *CNET*. Retrieved from https://www.cnet.com/news/the-equifax-breach-one-year-later/

Morrison, M. (2020). The California Consumer Privacy Act (CCPA): A practical guide. *Journal of Privacy and Data Protection*, 12(4), 5–19.

O'Neil, C. (2016). *Weapons of math destruction: How big data increases inequality and threatens democracy*. Crown Publishing Group.

Pasquale, F. (2015). *The black box society: The secret algorithms that control money and information*. Harvard University Press. DOI: 10.4159/harvard.9780674736061

Raghavan, M., Barocas, S., Kleinberg, J., & Levy, K. (2020). Mitigating bias in algorithmic hiring: Evaluating claims and practices. *Proceedings of the 2020 Conference on Fairness, Accountability, and Transparency*, 469–481. DOI: 10.1145/3351095.3372828

Raghupathi, W., & Raghupathi, V. (2014). Big data analytics in healthcare: Promise and potential. *Health Information Science and Systems*, 2(1), 3. DOI: 10.1186/2047-2501-2-3 PMID: 25825667

Raji, I. D., Mitchell, M., & Smith, B. (2020). Closing the AI accountability gap: Defining an end-to-end framework for internal algorithmic auditing. *Proceedings of the 2020 Conference on Fairness, Accountability, and Transparency*, 33-44. DOI: 10.1145/3351095.3372873

Redman, T. C. (2016). *Data driven: Creating a data culture*. Harvard Business Review Press.

Ribeiro, M. T., Singh, S., & Guestrin, C. (2016). "Why should I trust you?" Explaining the predictions of any classifier. *Proceedings of the 22nd ACM SIGKDD International Conference on Knowledge Discovery and Data Mining*, 1135-1144. DOI: 10.1145/2939672.2939778

Rudin, C. (2019). Stop explaining black box machine learning models for high stakes decisions and use interpretable models instead. *Nature Machine Intelligence*, 1(5), 206–215. DOI: 10.1038/s42256-019-0048-x PMID: 35603010

Russell, S., & Norvig, P. (2016). *Artificial intelligence: A modern approach* (3rd ed.). Pearson Education.

Voigt, P., & Von dem Bussche, A. (2017). *The EU General Data Protection Regulation (GDPR): A practical guide*. Springer International Publishing. DOI: 10.1007/978-3-319-57959-7

Westerman, G., Bonnet, D., & Ferraris, P. (2014). The digital advantage: How digital leaders outperform their peers in every industry. *MIT Sloan Management Review*, 55(2), 1–25.

Zeng, D. Z. (2017). Big data privacy and ethical challenges. *Journal of Digital Information Management*, 15(4), 248–255. DOI: 10.1109/JDIM.2017.8351116

Chapter 18
Data Cooperatives to Strengthen Digital Citizenship:
Opportunities and Risks

Silvio Andrae
https://orcid.org/0000-0002-8586-7812
Independent Researcher, Germany

ABSTRACT

This chapter explores the concept of data cooperatives as an innovative organizational form in the modern data economy. Data cooperatives enable citizens to collectively manage, control, and use their data to achieve collective benefits. The chapter highlights the definition and principles of data cooperatives, their central functions, and the necessary technical and organizational infrastructure for their implementation. It shows how data cooperatives can help strengthen digital citizenship, promote innovation, and enable a fairer distribution of the benefits of data use. The challenges and limitations of this model are also discussed. The practical implementation of data cooperatives in various areas is illustrated based on practical examples. The chapter argues that data cooperatives represent a promising model for reducing the power asymmetries in the current data economy and for shaping a fairer, more transparent, and more democratic digital future, thereby instilling a sense of security and trust in the audience.

DOI: 10.4018/979-8-3693-9015-3.ch018

1. INTRODUCTION

Over the last decade, discussion about how to handle data and digital technologies has evolved. The rapid development of technologies such as artificial intelligence, big data, and automation has led to the collection and analysis of data becoming one of the most valuable resources in the digital economy. It is accompanied by increasing concern about compliance with ethical standards and security when using these technologies. As a result, the use of digital technologies is increasing interest. In response, 'digital citizenship' has become synonymous with the responsible use of digital technologies. Specifically, it is about the right to access information, privacy, and freedom of expression in digital space. These rights are matched by the responsibility to behave ethically and responsibly in the digital space, e.g., by respecting others and protecting personal data. Digital citizenship, in this context, refers to the rights and responsibilities of individuals in the digital space, including the right to access information, privacy, and freedom of expression, and the responsibility to behave ethically and responsibly, such as by respecting others and protecting personal data. These rights and responsibilities are complemented by active participation in shaping the digital society, e.g., by helping to design digital services and participating in digital debates.

The increasing concentration of power and influence among a few major—mainly global technology companies—makes it more difficult for citizens to use their rights and duties and participate appropriately. Platforms such as Google, Amazon, or Meta dominate the market and have access to immense amounts of data collected from user behavior, social interactions, and other sources. This concentration of power entails risks. Citizens and smaller organizations often do not influence how their data is collected or used. Many users are also unaware of how their data is processed or monetized. Finally, data misuse and surveillance can endanger individual freedoms.

The current data economy raises the question of how to create fairer access to data and more responsible use of it. New approaches like data cooperatives are becoming increasingly important in this context. They represent a promising alternative for reclaiming sovereignty over personal data and strengthening digital self-determination. The concept of a data cooperative is based on the principles of collective ownership, democratic governance, and fair data practices. Within co-operation, citizens pool their data, which is then managed, protected, and used for negotiations with companies and institutions in the interests of the members. This empowers citizens, offering them a hopeful alternative in the digital society (Bühler et al., 2023; Kapoor et al., 2024; Ruijer, 2021; Fink, 2024).

The functions of data cooperative essentially include

1. secure storage and protection against unauthorized access,

2. information about how data is used and the ability to control its use, and finally,
3. negotiation with companies and institutions about data use for the benefit of members.

The importance of such initiatives lies in the fact that they offer members transparency, control, and privacy while at the same time enabling them to benefit collectively from the use of data. A data cooperative can provide information about how and for what purposes data is collected, how companies use the data, and ensure that members' interests are protected. This model strengthens digital self-determination and gives citizens control over their digital identities (Robles-Carrillo, 2024). At the same time, it creates new opportunities for collective innovation and social justice in the data economy, inspiring a new wave of progress and fairness.

Data cooperatives have far-reaching implications for various sectors, including institutional politics, education, health, and economics. Data cooperatives are playing an increasingly important role in the political landscape, particularly in data protection, regulation, and the democratization of data. The concept of 'democratization of data' refers to the process of making data more accessible and usable by a wider range of people and organizations. This is particularly significant in the context of data cooperatives, as it can lead to a more equitable distribution of data resources. The policy implications of data cooperatives may inspire lawmakers to develop new privacy laws and regulations that protect not only the interests of large corporations but also the rights of individuals and communities that collectively manage their data. The idea of data cooperatives could encourage the creation of institutions that further strengthen these principles and advance the policy agenda around data privacy and sovereignty.

Imagine a future where data cooperatives revolutionize the education landscape, transforming how educational data is collected, used, and shared. Instead of large technology companies dominating the collection and management of data about students and teachers, schools and educational institutions could jointly manage data cooperatively. This shift would enable greater control and understanding of the use of educational data and protect students' data protection and privacy. One practical example is the possibility of combining educational data in a data cooperative to develop personalized learning strategies that better meet the individual needs of learners. Integrating data on teaching methods and learning materials can also lead to data-based improvements in educational processes, offering a hopeful and optimistic vision for the future of education.

In healthcare, the data cooperative model offers the opportunity to collaboratively manage large amounts of health data to accelerate research, drug development, and healthcare progress. Imagine the inspiration and motivation that comes from the potential of data from different hospitals, healthcare providers, and research institutions being combined in a data cooperative to develop more precise and personalized treatment options. Maintaining patient privacy is of the utmost importance here, which targeted data protection measures within the cooperatives can ensure.

In the business context, data cooperatives have the potential to change the way companies access and use data significantly. Instead of companies accessing private data sources or buying large pools of data from third-party providers, they could invest in data cooperatives and access collective, collaboratively managed data. This shift would not only strengthen competition in the market but also give smaller companies better access to valuable data previously reserved for large corporations, encouraging and offering a hopeful vision for the future of business. One example of the economic benefits of data cooperatives is in the agricultural sector, where farmers can share their data to optimize agricultural practices, increase yields, and develop sustainable practices. Access to better data can help farmers make informed decisions, resulting in higher yields and less waste (Andrae, 2025).

Although data cooperatives are promising, a number of challenges need to be considered in their implementation. These challenges concern the technical infrastructure, i.e., the secure storage and management of large amounts of data requires advanced technical solutions that are difficult for many communities to access. Furthermore, the legal framework is only sometimes compatible with the organizational form of a data cooperative. Finally, there are often financial and organizational challenges.

This paper analyzes the opportunities and challenges of data cooperatives in the context of digital society. Methodically, the chapter is based on a literature review and evaluation. Recent scientific publications, specialist books, and reports on data cooperatives and related concepts such as digital citizenship and data sovereignty were evaluated. In addition, case studies of successful data cooperatives were examined to gain practical insights into implementation and challenges. The insights gained were systematically analyzed and placed in the broader context of the current data economy and digital rights debates. The aim is to show how this model can help to strengthen digital citizenship by enabling transparency, privacy, and collective decision-making, engaging the audience in the cause of digital rights.

The paper is structured into the following sections: Section 2 presents the background and context of the current data economy in more detail, including the technical conditions such as the rapid development of technologies like artificial intelligence, big data, and automation, the economic conditions such as the increasing value of data in the digital economy, and the social conditions such as the increasing concern about compliance with ethical standards and security when using these technologies. Section 3 introduces the concept of data cooperatives, highlighting the principles, functions, and technical foundations. Section 4 examines the opportunities and potential of data cooperatives, including their role in strengthening digital self-determination and promoting innovation. Section 5 is dedicated to the challenges that arise in practical implementation, including technical, legal, and organizational hurdles. Section 6 presents practical examples that contrast the theoretical considerations with real-world applications. Finally, Section 7 summarizes the findings and provides an outlook on possible developments.

2. BACKGROUND AND CONTEXT

The data economy has undergone a profound transformation in recent decades. Technological advances such as artificial intelligence, big data, and automation have made data one of the central drivers of the modern economy. At the same time, problems such as the concentration of power, a lack of data sovereignty, and the unequal distribution of resources are raising fundamental questions about justice, democracy, and digital self-determination (Schaake, 2024).

The data economy originated in the early days of computerization when data was initially used primarily for internal business purposes. With digitalization in the 1990s and the advent of the internet, a new era began in which data was increasingly seen as a strategic resource. Companies like Google and Amazon established business models based entirely on collecting and analyzing user data. A decisive turning point was the transition from static databases to dynamic, cloud-based systems that enable real-time processing. With the introduction of platform economies in the 2000s, data collection was centralized and monetized. Users became data suppliers, while companies like Meta (formerly Facebook) and Google made massive profits from exploiting this data.

Despite these developments, data access has not been democratized. Data has remained primarily in the hands of large companies, which gained almost monopolistic control over data streams through their market power. An unequal distribution of data resources characterizes the data economy. A few companies, often called 'data monopolies,' dominate the market and control access to the most valuable data. At the same time, there is a worrying gap between the Global North and South. While industrialized countries benefit from technological advances and the data economy, many countries in the Global South lack the necessary infrastructure and resources to participate adequately in this development, reinforcing existing global inequalities.

A further problem is the need for more transparency. For most users, how their data is collected and used remains to be seen. It leads to a significant power imbalance, with individuals and minor players needing more influence over data use. This concentration of data and power in the hands of a few companies poses serious threats to democracy and competition. It hinders innovative players and smaller companies, which find it difficult to compete against the market power of the data giants. Furthermore, the interests of the general public are often neglected in favor of maximization of private profit. Introducing concepts such as data cooperatives could be one way of regaining data sovereignty and strengthening digital citizenship.

3. THE CONCEPT OF DATA COOPERATIVES

At its core, a data cooperative is an organizational form in which members collectively manage, control, and use their data to achieve significant collective benefits. In contrast to traditional data management models, in which individual actors or companies have control over the data, a data cooperative is based on the principles of community ownership, democratic co-determination, and the promise of substantial collective benefit (Parra-Moyano, 2024). This chapter highlights the definition and principles of data cooperatives, their central functions, the infrastructure necessary for their implementation, and a comparison with other data use models, underscoring the potential for significant collective benefits.

3.1 Definition and Principles

A data cooperative is a collaborative organization in which multiple stakeholders—individuals, communities, organizations, or businesses—democratically pool their data and make joint decisions about its collection, storage, and use. This model ensures that the cooperative members retain control over their data and that the decisions are made according to the community's shared goals and values. Therefore, a data cooperative combines digital citizenship and collaborative management with a cooperative organizing principle (Bühler et al., 2023; Girish & Avery, 2022).

The International Cooperative Alliance (ICA) proposes seven core principles shared by the cooperative movement worldwide (Cheney et al., 2023):

1. voluntary membership,
2. democratic control by the members,
3. the economic participation of members,
4. autonomy and independence,
5. education, training and information,
6. cooperation between cooperatives, and
7. concern for the community.

Data cooperatives can have different objectives. Some focus on the commercial exploitation of data, with the proceeds used collectively, while others concentrate on the protection and sustainable use of community data. A key advantage of this model is that it balances the power asymmetries that often favor large companies or state institutions in the conventional data economy. Rather than centralizing power over the data, a cooperative distribution control ensures that the communities from which the data originates share in the decisions and potential profits. The members jointly own the data and retain control over its use. Unlike centralized platforms, the data does not belong to a single institution but to all cooperative members equally. Decisions about data use are made collectively. Each member has one vote, regardless of how much data they have contributed. This model promotes equality and protects against the concentration of power within the cooperative, while also delivering significant community benefits (Bühler et al., 2023; Fink, 2024).

Once governed in a cooperative, the data can be used, governed, and shared for many purposes. To date, the largest and most successful data cooperatives are health data cooperatives, where individuals upload and share health data while maintaining precise control over their data (Section 6.1). So, instead of giving consent at the point of data collection and letting the data disappear into databases that ordinary users cannot access, dealer management systems allow users to change access permissions at any time and to understand which groups and for what purpose their data is being used. Individuals are, therefore, joining data cooperatives to gain more power and control over data sharing, but also for data altruism—the possibility to use personal data collectively and consensually for altruistic purposes such as pharmaceutical research (Bietti et al., 2021). Some cooperatives may be structured and require little member involvement, while others may require significant involvement in individual data management and control (Hardjono & Pentland, 2019; Micheli et al., 2020).

Furthermore, data cooperatives are often based on transparent governance structures. They give members insight into how their data is used and managed. Data cooperatives are committed to using ethical and transparent methods when collecting, storing, and further processing data. The data is used in the members' best interests and with data protection in mind (Bühler et al., 2023; Fink, 2024).

3.2 Functions

Data cooperatives perform several important tasks and functions that cover the entire data life cycle—from collection and management to analysis and use and finally to knowledge creation and sharing. These processes enable members to control and use data effectively. They ensure that decision-making is collective and transparent, reflecting the democratic nature of data cooperatives and the inclusion of all members in the process.

The first essential task of a data cooperative is to organize and coordinate data collection and management. When collecting and managing data, it is important to ensure that the data is collected from members in a way that meets the cooperative's ethical standards and respects the members' individual and collective rights. In practice, this means that members decide which data is essential for the cooperative, who has access to the data collection, and how the data collection is organized. Particular emphasis is placed on protecting data sovereignty, which Abbas et al. (2024) define as protection, participation, and provision (the three Ps). This emphasis on data sovereignty ensures that members feel secure and in control of their data. The concept is not necessarily congruent with digital citizenship (Section 4.1). Protection emphasizes fundamental rights such as data ownership, participation ensures a clear division of tasks, and provision encompasses control, security, and compliance mechanisms to ensure that fundamental rights are respected during and after data sharing.

When personal data is shared, privacy becomes a crucial aspect of protection, leading to challenges regarding ownership between data providers and data subjects, compliance requirements, and the enforcement of controls. The concept presented by Abbas et al. (2024) provides the basis for a comprehensive and coherent theory development on data sovereignty as a complex, multi-layered construct. It could be effectively tested in data cooperatives that provide a safe environment for data sharing. Data cooperatives often develop specific guidelines to ensure that data collection is aligned with the needs and values of the community. For example, a collaborative governance model that ensures integrity and data protection can oversee digital tools and platforms for data collection (Fink, 2024).

The second important function of data cooperatives is data analysis and the responsible use of the collected data. Once the data is collected and stored securely, the analysis process gains valuable information and insights. Cooperatives play a crucial role in this process, ensuring that the analysis processes are aligned with the interests of the community and respecting the values of its members.

Another important aspect of data use is its potential economic, political, or scientific exploitation. Data cooperatives offer a way to distribute the economic benefits of data use pretty. It could be achieved by making data available for research or commercial projects, with the cooperative guarantee that the community receives a fair share of the profits. At the same time, it is necessary to ensure that sensitive information remains protected and is only used in line with shared values (Fink, 2024).

As a central hub for building and sharing knowledge within the community, data cooperatives empower all members by providing access to expertise and skills. This aspect is crucial as data and digital technologies often require expertise that is not equally accessible to all. By acting as a platform for exchanging knowledge and skills, cooperatives ensure that all members can participate in decision-making processes, thus fostering a sense of empowerment and inspiration (Fink, 2024). One example is training members in data management, protection, and analysis. By offering educational programs and technical training, cooperatives enable their members better to understand the technical and legal aspects of data management. Building technical knowledge is crucial to upholding digital citizenship.

Data cooperatives play a multifaceted role that goes beyond mere data storage. They are responsible for the fair collection, management, and analysis of data, as well as for building the knowledge and skills of the community. Calzada (2021) shows how data is shared via peer-to-peer (p2p) repositories in citizen-centered smart cities and how data sovereignty is claimed as a digital right for communities/citizens. Data cooperatives, especially when developed in collaboration with municipalities, play an important role in this technopolitical dimension. The functions described strengthen the digital self-determination of members and, at the same time, promote the responsible use of data in the public and private sectors, thereby fostering a sense of digital citizenship and responsibility among the audience.

3.3 Technical and Organizational Infrastructure

Another critical aspect of administration is the storage of the collected data. Data cooperatives play a central role in this by creating secure infrastructures that enable members to store and access their data with utmost safety. The stringent security measures in data cooperatives, including careful technical and organizational design, provide a reassuring environment for data storage.

The technical infrastructure forms the backbone of a data cooperative and includes several key components. Central to this are secure data platforms, which are typically cloud-based and implement strict encryption and access controls. These platforms ensure that sensitive data is protected from unauthorized access. Complemented by user-friendly data management tools, these platforms enable efficient administration, analysis, and visualization of the collected data, making the data handling process more manageable for all members.

At the organizational level, a central member administration system is essential. This system is not only used to coordinate members but also to organize votes and other cooperative processes. Governance mechanisms that support democratic decision-making processes are also of great importance. Regular general meetings play an important role here. A clear legal framework in the form of a detailed set of statutes is essential for the smooth functioning of the data cooperative. These statutes define the rights and duties of the members as well as the responsibilities of the cooperative, thus creating clarity and security for all parties involved

Combining these technical and organizational aspects enables data cooperatives to function as effective and trustworthy platforms for collaborative data management. They provide a framework in which data can be securely managed, democratically controlled, and used for the benefit of all members. At the same time, they enable scalability so that the model can also be applied to larger communities or across sectors.

3.4 Comparison to Other Models of Data Utilization

Data cooperatives stand out from other data use models, such as data trusts or platform cooperatives, by placing a strong emphasis on collective ownership and democratic decision-making. This approach empowers individuals, giving them a sense of control and independence over their data.

Data trusts, which manage data on behalf of individuals or groups, often lack mechanisms for data providers to have a say. In contrast, data cooperatives ensure full control and transparency, providing a sense of security and empowerment. Data trusts are particularly useful when dealing with sensitive data that requires high control and transparency (Zarkadakis, 2020). Platform cooperatives, while based on similar principles to data cooperatives, focus more on the collaborative organization of labor platforms (e.g., for gig workers) and less on specific data governance.

Despite these differences, data cooperatives, data trusts, decentralized autonomous organizations (DAOs)-which are entities that operate without a central authority and are governed by smart contracts and consensus mechanisms-and data unions-which are associations that represent the collective interests of data workers-have in common that they regard data as a form of collective value and pass the benefits on to their members. These intermediaries work to align the social and economic value of the aggregated data with the normative interests of the individuals described in it (Duncan, 2023).

Data cooperatives present a promising alternative to the current power concentration in the data economy. By integrating collective ownership, democratic governance, and ethical data practices, they can enhance the digital self-determination of citizens and foster a more equitable data economy. Their technical and organizational infrastructure enables sustainable and transparent data management, setting them apart from other data-use models. Data cooperatives are thus a tool for data protection and a crucial building block for democratizing the digital world, ensuring that everyone feels included and valued.

4. OPPORTUNITIES AND POTENTIALS

Data cooperatives offer a promising way to address the challenges of the data economy. They strengthen citizens' rights, promote innovation, and create a fairer distribution of the benefits that result from the use of data. This Section highlights the key opportunities and potential of data cooperatives.

4.1 Strengthening Digital Citizenship

The concept of digital citizenship (DC) is gaining importance in our increasingly digitally networked world. It involves the conscious and responsible use of data and active participation in shaping its use. However, as Chen et al. (2021) argue, there is no consensus among scholars on a standard definition for 'digital citizenship.' From a practical standpoint, one could argue that data cooperatives align with DC, as they empower individuals to reclaim control over their data, which has often been collected and processed anonymously and without the direct influence of those affected. This shift in control has the potential to reshape the digital landscape, offering a more optimistic and forward-thinking future.

Calzada (2023) develops a taxonomy of five emerging regimes of digital citizenship in the EU. These regimes will cause European nation states to resize themselves (Calzada, 2022). In this taxonomy, data cooperatives could be characterized as a 'Metropolitan Citizenship Regime.'

Pandemic times have been a turning point for city-regional transformation and community awakening, offering an opportunity for experimentation with data cooperatives, working towards more responsive systems of care, adequate medical services, and a fairer, more participatory data economy. (Calzada, 2023, p.178)

A central aspect of data cooperatives is the promotion of co-determination and transparency. Such a cooperative's members can make collective decisions about how their data is used. It extends to economic aspects, such as selecting companies that are given access to the data, and ethical questions, such as how discrimination can be avoided through data use. This participatory approach not only raises awareness of the importance and value of personal data but also actively promotes and involves individuals in the concept of digital citizenship.

Furthermore, data cooperatives contribute to the expansion of digital rights. By pooling data and negotiating power, they can effectively help enforce important digital rights such as data protection, access control, and the right to be forgotten. Importantly, this influence goes beyond individual protection and can potentially shape and advance the debate in society on the responsible use of data, making the audience feel engaged and part of a larger movement.

Overall, data cooperatives not only promote the protection of the individual but also strengthen collective awareness of the importance of data in our society. They provide a platform where individuals can actively fulfill their role as digital citizens by collectively making decisions about using their data, thus shaping the digital landscape. This empowerment through collective decision-making significantly promotes and strengthens informed, self-determined, and responsible digital citizenship.

4.2 Promoting Privacy and Transparency

Data cooperatives are a clear and promising alternative in today's data economy, a system where data is a valuable commodity often characterized by a need for more transparency and more precise usage practices. They offer an approach that focuses on both privacy protection and transparency.

A central concern of data cooperatives is protecting their members' privacy. Various measures ensure it. First, the data is stored in secure environments and is only shared with third parties with the express consent of the members. In addition, data cooperatives rely on advanced technologies such as encryption, blockchain, and secure multi-party computation to prevent unauthorized access to the data. This combination of technical and organizational measures creates a high level of data security and protection of personal information.

At the same time, data cooperatives place a high value on transparency. They regularly and comprehensively inform their members about the use of their data, including detailed reports on who has accessed the data and for what purpose it was used. Data cooperatives conduct regular audits and reviews to ensure compliance with the agreed-use terms, which are the specific conditions under which the data can be used as agreed upon by the cooperative and its members. This open communication and continuous monitoring of data usage create an environment of trust between the cooperative and its members.

This transparent approach has far-reaching positive effects. It strengthens members' trust in the cooperative and promotes more responsible data usage in general. Data cooperatives are setting new standards in the data economy by showing that it is possible to handle personal data ethically and transparently. They demonstrate that economic interests and privacy protection do not have to contradict each other but can go hand in hand, providing a sense of security and reassurance to all involved.

Overall, data cooperatives offer a way to empower individuals, allowing them to regain control over their personal data while benefiting from the advantages of the data economy. By focusing on privacy and transparency, they create a model that meets the needs of the individual and the requirements of a modern, data-driven society. They show that ethical, transparent, and user-oriented data use is not only possible but can also benefit all parties involved.

4.3 Democratization of the Data Economy

The current data economy is characterized by a pronounced concentration of power in the hands of a few global players. In this context, data cooperatives offer a promising opportunity to break this power asymmetry and achieve a fairer distribution of influence and control over data.

One key aspect that makes data cooperatives an effective tool for redressing power imbalances is their ability to create collective bargaining power. By pooling their members' data, cooperatives significantly increase their bargaining power vis-à-vis companies and public institutions. For instance, they can negotiate better data privacy policies or fairer compensation for data use. This combined strength enables them to negotiate fairer terms for the use of data. Instead of acting as individuals, often powerless individuals, members of a data cooperative can act as a cohesive unit and thus represent their interests more effectively.

Furthermore, data cooperatives play an important role in promoting local communities. In a world often dominated by global tech giants, they strengthen the position of smaller players, such as local businesses or non-governmental organizations. These would otherwise risk being squeezed out by the dominant platforms. Data cooperatives create networks that promote innovation and collaboration at the local level. They provide a platform where local actors can pool their resources, share experiences, and jointly develop solutions tailored to their needs.

The democratization of the data economy through cooperatives helps to distribute economic power more fairly. It creates a counterweight to dominant players and enables smaller entities to survive and thrive in the digital economy. At the same time, data cooperatives open up new forms of collaboration. They foster an ecosystem where cooperation and mutual support are emphasized rather than a pure competition model. For example, members can share best practices, collaborate on research projects, or even jointly develop new products or services.

Data cooperatives offer a way to make the data economy more inclusive and equitable. They enable individuals and local communities to actively participate in and benefit from the digital economy without giving up their autonomy or control over their data. By promoting transparency, co-determination, and local collaboration, they help create a more balanced and sustainable data use model that meets the needs of a broader society, offering a promising future for data use.

4.4 Benefits

Data cooperatives play a unique role in opening up a wide range of economic opportunities that benefit their members and companies. These innovative structures not only offer the potential for efficiency gains but also promote a sustainable and fair economy, a key concern for many in the digital age.

One of the key advantages of data cooperatives is their role in improving decision-making in companies. By centrally pooling and managing data, these structures can significantly reduce administrative and technical costs, making optimizing resources and exploiting synergies possible. This results in cost reductions for all parties involved and provides companies with access to high-quality, structured data for market analysis, product development, and service improvement.

Furthermore, data cooperatives open up the possibility for innovative business models. For example, they could offer their members attractive incentives by monetizing data. The resulting revenues could be reinvested in collaborative projects, benefiting both individual members and the cooperative. This approach creates a cycle in which the value of the data flows directly back into the community.

In addition, data cooperatives provide a platform for developing personalized services based on ethical standards. Companies could use cooperative data to develop customized offers that meet users' needs while adhering to high ethical standards of data protection and transparency. It opens up new opportunities for companies to create innovative and trustworthy products that stand out from conventional offers.

These approaches offer financial benefits for all parties involved and promote a sustainable and fair economy. Data cooperatives create an ecosystem in which the value of data is distributed fairly and in which ethical considerations play a central role, reassuring all stakeholders. They make it possible to reap the benefits of the data economy without neglecting the rights and interests of individuals.

Overall, data cooperatives demonstrate that economic success and ethical responsibility can go hand in hand. They offer a model that benefits both companies and individuals while contributing to a fairer and more sustainable digital economy. By combining efficiency gains, innovative business models, and ethical principles, data cooperatives are setting new standards for responsible economic activity in the digital age, giving hope for a better future.

4.5 Support for Innovation and Fair Data Distribution

Data cooperatives have the potential to serve as platforms for innovation and social justice by providing a unique approach to data governance and use. These organizations combine promoting innovation with pursuing a more equitable distribution of the benefits arising from data use.

Data cooperatives, in their role as promoters of innovation, are empowering. By providing access to cooperatively managed data, they are accelerating research and development in various fields. In medicine, for instance, large data sets are being used to develop new treatments and gain a better understanding of disease progression. In sustainable urban planning, aggregated data helps to design more efficient transportation systems and optimize energy consumption. Moreover, data cooperatives are leveling the playing field, giving start-ups and smaller companies access to valuable data resources that were once out of reach. This empowerment is paving the way for new business ideas and innovative solutions that can build a broader database.

Another central aspect of data cooperatives is their contribution to the fair distribution of the benefits arising from the use of data. In contrast to traditional models, in which large technology companies often derive the main benefit from data, cooperatives ensure that the benefits flow directly back to the members. It can take the form of financial gains or access to developed applications and services based on the collected data. Focusing on local needs and collective goals ensures that disadvantaged communities can also benefit from the advantages of the data economy and are not left behind.

By promoting innovation and pursuing equity, data cooperatives are creating a sustainable foundation for the further development of the data economy. They are fundamentally changing the way we handle data, strengthening individuals' digital self-determination by giving them more control over their personal data. At the same time, they are promoting privacy and transparency through clear rules and open communication about data use. This emphasis on ethical data handling should reassure the audience about the responsible use of data.

Thanks to their democratic structure, data cooperatives contribute to democratizing the data economy, which means making the benefits and control of data more widely accessible. They distribute the power that comes with control over data more widely and enable smaller players to participate in the data economy. The resulting economic and social benefits benefit not only individual companies but society as a whole.

These characteristics make data cooperatives a central building block for a sustainable and fair digital future. They offer a way to exploit digitalization opportunities, which are the chances for growth and development that arise from the increasing use of digital technologies, without losing sight of ethical principles and social justice. Data cooperatives create an economically prosperous and socially responsible model by driving innovation while ensuring a more equitable distribution of resources and benefits. It gives them a promising approach for shaping a data economy that meets the needs and values of a broad society.

5. CHALLENGES AND RISKS OF DATA COOPERATIVES

While data cooperatives offer enormous potential for democratizing the data economy and, thus, for digital citizenship, their implementation and long-term establishment face significant challenges and risks. As data cooperatives are still in their infancy, there are still unanswered questions regarding the long-term sustainability and security of the data in the event of a cooperative's closure. The governance and usage models must be more attested, underscoring the need for further research into their effectiveness and inclusiveness. Many data cooperatives depend on broad membership or participation in data sharing, and it remains to be seen whether the general public is motivated to share data, for what reasons, and in what contexts (Fink, 2024). This chapter not only analyzes the key challenges but also emphasizes the crucial role of further research in addressing these challenges and shaping the future of data cooperatives.

5.1 Technical Complexity and Security of AI Models

The technical infrastructure of data cooperatives is a significant challenge, necessitating not only high investments but also a continuous commitment to expertise. Data cooperatives rely on advanced technologies that are expensive to acquire and demand ongoing maintenance and customization. This is crucial for the secure and efficient management of their members' data.

A key concern in managing data cooperatives is the significant security risks. Data, especially when it is large and personal, is a desirable target for cyber attackers. A successful attack on a data cooperative could have devastating consequences in terms of immediate data loss or misuse and a loss of trust among members. Such a breach of trust could jeopardize the long-term existence of the cooperative. Data cooperatives must invest in robust security measures to counter these risks. These include advanced encryption technologies, the implementation of multi-factor authentication, and the execution of regular security updates. These measures require significant financial resources and highly qualified personnel who can keep pace with constantly evolving threats.

Another technical challenge lies in the complexity of the AI models based on the cooperatively managed data. These algorithms must be powerful, transparent, fair, and secure. The risk of bias in the models is a serious problem that necessitates continuous review and adjustment. It's crucial to ensure that AI systems do not produce discriminatory or unethical results, making it necessary to monitor and fine-tune the algorithms continuously. This task requires technical expertise and a deep understanding of ethical issues and the societal impact of AI systems.

Overcoming these technical challenges is not only crucial but also promising for the success and credibility of data cooperatives. With sufficient technical expertise and comprehensive safeguards, data cooperatives can effectively protect their members and avoid failing to achieve their goals. Investing in a robust and secure technical infrastructure is, therefore, a technical necessity and an ethical obligation to members and society in general.

Thus, data cooperatives face the challenge of finding a balance between using innovative technologies for data processing and analysis on the one hand and ensuring the highest security and ethical standards on the other. This requires not only significant financial resources but also a commitment to continuous training and adaptation to new technological developments and security threats. Only by overcoming these technical challenges and staying abreast of the latest advancements can data cooperatives realize their full potential as trusted and effective stewards of data and achieve their vision of a more equitable and transparent data economy.

5.2 Technological Requirements and Risks

The use of modern technologies such as blockchain, federated learning, and zero-knowledge proofs not only offers innovative possibilities for designing secure and efficient data cooperatives but also empowers data producers. These technologies can improve transparency, security, and data protection, ensuring that the interests of data producers are safeguarded and they remain in control of their data.

Blockchain, with its immutable and transparent storage of transactions, plays a crucial role in establishing trust among members of a data cooperative (Naz et al., 2019). It can be used to document voting processes, record interactions with stored data, and ensure compliance with data protection rules. The use of smart contracts further enhances this trust, governing the use of data in licensing or profit sharing. The Ocean Protocol is a prime example of how blockchain can be used to operate a secure and decentralized data marketplace, providing reassurance and confidence to data providers.

Federated learning, by enabling the training of machine learning models without passing the underlying data to a central location, plays a significant role in protecting sensitive data (Ding et al., 2024; Zhu et al., 2024). The data remains stored decentrally, making this method suitable for scenarios in which data is distributed geographically, such as in globally operating data cooperatives. OpenMined's tools for secure federated learning further enhance this protection, enabling data cooperatives to conduct machine learning without compromising sensitive data and ensuring the audience feels secure and protected.

Zero-knowledge proof (ZKPs) make it possible to verify a statement without revealing details about the underlying data (Zhu et al., 2024). Members of a data cooperative can prove that they own certain rights or data without explicitly disclosing them. ZKP can verify compliance with rules and data protection standards without disclosing private information. For example, the Open Algorithms Initiative (OPAL), initiated by the Massachusetts Institute of Technology, uses ZKP to enable secure data analysis. The data remains at its point of origin, while only aggregated results are shared.

Modern technologies such as blockchain, federated learning, and ZKP offer decisive advantages for developing secure and efficient data cooperatives. One key aspect is increased security: sensitive data remains protected even when analyzed or used. It minimizes the risk of data breaches and strengthens members' trust in the cooperative. Another advantage is improved transparency. Technologies such as blockchain enable clear traceability of processes and interactions, ensuring that all operations are traceable and compliant. It builds trust among members and increases acceptance of the data cooperative.

In addition, these technologies promote members' self-determination. Members retain full control over their data and can decide for themselves how and under what conditions it is used. This autonomy not only strengthens trust but also supports a fairer distribution of the value created by the use of data.

5.3 Scalability and Financial Sustainability

One of the biggest challenges facing data cooperatives is their scalability and long-term financial viability. These aspects are crucial to their sustainable success and effectiveness in the rapidly developing data economy.

A key problem is the cost-intensive infrastructure required to operate a data cooperative. Building and maintaining a secure data platform requires significant investments in hardware and software. These initial costs are supplemented by ongoing expenses for maintenance, qualified personnel, and legal advice. The sum of these costs can seriously endanger the financial sustainability of the cooperative, especially in the early stages of its development or when it has yet to reach the necessary size to exploit economies of scale.

Another critical challenge is member recruitment and scaling. Data cooperatives depend on a critical mass of members to negotiate effectively and operate economically. However, acquiring new members and integrating their data poses significant organizational challenges. Compelling arguments and clear advantages must persuade individuals or organizations to join. In addition, the technical and organizational infrastructure must be able to keep pace with growth, which requires additional resources.

Another serious problem for many data cooperatives is the need for more sources of income. Many cooperatives need help generating enough income to cover their operating costs. This creates a dilemma: on the one hand, they need to find ways to operate in a financially sustainable manner, but on the other hand, an overemphasis on monetizing data could jeopardize the cooperative's fundamental values and principles. The pressure to make a profit could push the original goals of digital citizenship and member protection into the background. Moreover, it could lead to potential conflicts of interest, data misuse, and erosion of trust among members and the public.

Data cooperatives must develop innovative models that balance scalability and financial sustainability without jeopardizing their members' rights and interests to succeed in the long term. It could include developing new services based on the collected data, such as personalized analytics or data-driven insights, or partnering with research institutions and ethical companies, like universities or non-profit organizations. Strengthening the financial base could also involve securing funding or developing membership models that offer both financial and non-financial benefits.

Overcoming these challenges requires a careful balance between economic necessities and the core principles of the data cooperative. It will take creative solutions and new legal and financial frameworks to support data cooperatives. Your support as stakeholders is crucial in finding this balance. Only if we succeed in finding this balance can data cooperatives realize their full potential as an alternative to the dominant models of the data economy and play an important long-term role in shaping a fair and sustainable digital future.

5.4 Ensuring Data Quality and Interoperability

The quality of the data collected and used, as well as its interoperability, are central factors in the success of data cooperatives. These two aspects play a crucial role in their effectiveness and reach in the modern data economy. Data quality is of fundamental importance for the performance of a data cooperative. Only complete or accurate data can significantly impact the efficiency and credibility of the cooperative. Data quality can lead to better analysis, positively impacting decision-making and the value of data assets for members and potential partners. Robust mechanisms for verifying and continuously improving data quality are essential to address this issue. It may include implementing data validation processes, regular audits, and AI-powered quality assurance tools. It has been observed that the low data quality of a cooperative information system (CIS) often leads cooperative organizations to re-enter data instead of using the data already in the system. Liu et al. (2022) suggest improving data quality not by verifying the data but by controlling the data quality of subsystems. Only by ensuring high data quality can cooperatives guarantee the reliable use of their data assets, which is crucial for the smooth functioning of their operations and the trust of their members and partners.

Equally important is data interoperability. In an increasingly connected digital world, data must be available in formats that different systems and applications can use. It requires the development of and adherence to standardized interfaces and data formats. A lack of interoperability can lead to data cooperatives working in isolation, reducing their bargaining power and relevance. Seamlessly exchanging data between different platforms and actors is crucial to creating added value and expanding the cooperative's influence. It can facilitate collaboration with research institutions, other cooperatives, or ethical companies, thus maximizing the benefits for members.

These challenges make it clear that data cooperatives must be effectively organized internally and consider external networks and technological standards. Successfully addressing these tasks requires a holistic strategy that combines technical expertise, the ability to cooperate, and a deep understanding of the evolving standards of the data economy.

Data cooperatives must, therefore, continuously invest in improving their data quality and developing interoperable systems. This is not just a recommendation, but a necessity in the rapidly evolving data landscape. It can include working with technology experts, participating in standardization initiatives, and developing flexible data architectures. At the same time, they must build networks with other players in the data ecosystem to benefit from synergies and strengthen their position in the data landscape.

By overcoming these challenges, data cooperatives can increase their effectiveness and serve as pioneers for best practices in data governance and usage. This not only strengthens trust in cooperative data models but also cements their role as an important alternative to centralized data monopolies. Ultimately, successfully addressing these challenges can shape a fairer, more transparent, and more efficient data economy that meets the needs of all stakeholders, instilling a sense of hope and optimism in the data landscape.

5.5 Legal and Regulatory Requirements

The significance of transparency requirements in privacy and data protection laws cannot be overstated. These mandates, which play a pivotal role in informing individuals, civil society, and public authorities about the processing of personal data in digital services and products, form the bedrock for enforcing data protection measures. They empower individuals to better protect their data. However, a more uniform interpretation and application of these principles across different jurisdictions is crucial for a comprehensive understanding (Xu et al., 2024).

Existing data protection laws worldwide provide an important framework for supporting the development of data cooperatives. These cooperatives, which are entities owned and controlled by the individuals whose data they hold, play a crucial role in the global data protection system. They act as intermediaries between data subjects and data controllers, ensuring that data protection laws are upheld, and individuals' rights are respected.

- In the European Union, the General Data Protection Regulation (GDPR) has been in place since 2016. It regulates the processing of personal data by private companies and public bodies in Europe.
- The California Consumer Privacy Act (CCPA) in the US was passed in California in 2018 and gives consumers the right to control their data. It requires companies to be transparent and allows consumers to request information about their data, request its deletion, or object to its sale.
- The Lei Geral de Proteção de Dados (LGPD), which came into force in 2020, is the Brazilian equivalent of the GDPR. It aims to protect personal data and sets strict requirements for transparency, purpose limitation, and data minimization.
- The Personal Information Protection Law (PIPL) came into force in 2021 and is China's first comprehensive data protection law. It regulates the collection, processing, and transfer of personal data and imposes strict requirements for companies, especially regarding data exports abroad. The gravity of these requirements cannot be overstated.
- The Digital Personal Data Protection (DPDP) Act was passed in India in 2023. It aims to protect personal data and give citizens rights of control. It includes regulations on consent, data storage, and data sharing.

Complying with these regulations, which require extensive resources and expertise to obtain member consent and transparently document data storage, is a formidable challenge. The technical and organizational measures required for compliance further increase complexity. However, it's crucial to understand that data cooperatives could provide a bridge between citizens and regulators by ensuring compliance with these significant legal requirements.

The Data Governance Act (DGA) (Regulation (EU) 2022/868) creates structures to enable data holders to pool their data through intermediaries, such as data cooperatives. The EU designates six data intermediaries (Micheli, 2023) that can offer their services commercially. However, they should act neutrally concerning the data itself. Therefore, they should enable and facilitate the use of the data by others, e.g., through analysis or linking. At the same time, they should only be 'facilitators' and not be able to see the data, ideally not be able to see it at all. They are not involved in the co-creation of the data or the co-management of data use. It means that both the original and secondary use of data are outside the scope of such data cooperatives. They, therefore, do not—or only to a limited extent—help strengthen the weaker parties in digital environments, as proponents of alternative data management often demand. According to the DGA, data cooperatives do not qualify as data communities in the definition of digital citizenship. From a legal perspective, they are more comparable to data unions.

Furthermore, significant legal uncertainties exist because many legal frameworks are not specifically geared towards data cooperatives. This leads to uncertainties when it comes to founding and operating such organizations. In particular, questions of collective ownership of data and liability often need to be more regulated, which entails additional risks for cooperatives.

Another complicated area concerns international cooperation. When data flows across borders, different national regulations must be considered, further complicating the organization and operation of data cooperatives. This diversity of regulations can lead to significant administrative hurdles and require careful legal planning and advice.

Given the myriad challenges faced by data cooperatives, the need for a clear and comprehensive legal framework is paramount. Such regulations would not only help resolve existing uncertainties but also bolster trust in this form of organization and foster its widespread adoption. Clear and consistent legal guidelines are essential for data cooperatives to fully realize their potential and act as reliable players in the data economy.

5.6 Risks Within the Data Cooperatives

While data cooperatives are being established to reduce the power asymmetry of the current data economy, it's important to remember the potential benefits they could bring. Despite the paradoxical risk of creating new concentrations of power, these cooperatives hold the promise of a more balanced and equitable data economy. This potential problem, if managed effectively, can be averted, preserving the original goals and values of the cooperative idea.

Inequalities may arise within the cooperative that contradict basic democratic principles. Members with greater data volume or financial resources could exert disproportionate influence over decision-making processes. Without proper governance mechanisms, hierarchies could develop that undermine the cooperative's egalitarian approach. It could lead to the interests of a few members being placed above those of the community, which would contradict the basic idea of cooperative solidarity.

Data breaches in data cooperatives can have far-reaching and serious consequences for the individuals concerned. These breaches affect not only the immediate privacy of users but also their rights and security in the digital space. If personal or sensitive data is misused or shared without consent, individuals can be identified and monitored and potentially become victims of identity theft, fraud, or discrimination. The risk of personal data being sold on the black market is also a real threat that undermines trust in digital platforms and can lead to severe financial losses for the individuals concerned. Data breaches have psychological effects (e.g., loss of confidence or stress due to unauthorized data use) and direct economic impact. For example, affected users may suffer harm due to the unauthorized use of their data for fraudulent purposes or in connection with unlawfully obtained credit or transactions.

AI in data cooperatives can maximize the benefits of collected data by providing analysis and recommendations that help members make better decisions or develop new business models. However, it's crucial to be aware of the potential for misuse of this powerful technology. There is a risk, particularly in analyzing personal data and the potential creation of 'weak' or disadvantaged groups through unfair algorithms. This awareness can help us remain cautious and vigilant in our use of AI. It may be necessary to enact specific regulations and laws to govern the use of AI within these collaborative structures. These regulations must ensure that AI algorithms are privacy-compliant, transparent, and explainable to strengthen members' trust in technology. Ensuring fairness and avoiding bias in AI algorithms is a particularly sensitive issue. These biases can arise, for example, from unbalanced data or unfair decision-making processes, which is problematic in an environment that relies on the exchange and use of data.

On a broader level, there is a risk of institutionalized concentration of power. Over time, data cooperatives could develop into centralized institutions susceptible to abuse and lacking transparency. They may lose sight of their original mission and put economic gain before the interests of their members. Such a development would alienate the cooperatives from their roots. It could turn them into organizations that hardly differ in functioning from the large data corporations they intended to replace or complement.

These risks underscore the need to establish and maintain robust democratic structures and transparent decision-making processes within data cooperatives. The assurance of open and transparent decision-making processes, along with mechanisms that ensure an even distribution of power and influence, is essential. Regular reviews of governance structures, open communication channels, and participatory decision-making processes are crucial to maintaining the integrity of data cooperatives and keeping all stakeholders informed.

Ultimately, the successful implementation of the cooperative model in the data sector requires constant awareness of these potential pitfalls and a continuous effort to prioritize the principles of democracy, transparency, and member orientation. It is only through this unwavering commitment that data cooperatives can live up to their claim of offering a real alternative to the existing power structures in the data economy. This should inspire and motivate us to contribute to a fairer and more democratic digital future.

The challenges and risks of data cooperatives are manifold and require well-thought-out solutions. Technological complexity, financial sustainability, legal uncertainties, and internal power structures are some obstacles that must be overcome. Nevertheless, data cooperatives offer a promising opportunity to make the data economy fairer and more sustainable. These challenges can be overcome by building secure and scalable infrastructures, developing standardized processes, and creating clear legal frameworks. For instance, to address the issue of internal power structures, implementing mechanisms for even distribution of power and influence can be beneficial. Strengthening the democratic structures within the cooperatives remains crucial to upholding the basic principles of transparency, fairness, and collective responsibility.

6. PRACTICAL EXAMPLES AND CASE STUDIES

Practical examples and case studies show how data cooperatives work in the real world and the challenges and opportunities associated with their implementation (Girish & Avery, 2022). This chapter examines successful initiatives, identifies lessons from failed projects, and highlights the relevance of data cooperatives for different industries, such as healthcare, energy, agriculture, and construction.

6.1 Successful Data Cooperatives

Some data cooperatives have been successfully established and provide valuable insights into the implementation and impact of this model. Three models are briefly presented below.

A. MIDATA Cooperative

The MIDATA cooperative (https://www.midata.coop/en/home/) in Switzerland is an innovative model for the governance and use of health data. It empowers citizens to securely store their health data while retaining complete control. A key feature of MIDATA is that members can independently decide whether they want to make their data available anonymously for research purposes, giving them a sense of autonomy and control.

MIDATA's success is based on several factors. First, the cooperative has achieved high acceptance among the population through its transparency and intense focus on data protection. It is underscored that MIDATA operates as a non-profit organization and reinvests revenues to improve its platform and services. Second, MIDATA has established successful collaborations with research institutions, contributing to medical innovation advancement.

MIDATA has developed several best practices that can serve as a model for similar initiatives. One of these is the clear communication of the benefits for members. MIDATA emphasizes that participants not only contribute to medical research but can also benefit from app-based services, making them feel valued and important. In addition, MIDATA uses modern technologies for secure data management. All data sets are encrypted, and only account holders can access their data, ensuring their privacy and security.

Another important aspect is MIDATA's regional focus. The model is designed to support the establishment of national or regional MIDATA cooperatives that share the data platform infrastructure. It enables local adaptation on an everyday technological basis. MIDATA is also based on open-source technology. The MIDATA platform is based on open-source software developed at ETH Zurich and Bern University of Applied Sciences (BFH). It promotes transparency and allows others to review and further develop the technology. Overall, the example of MIDATA shows how data cooperatives can operate successfully by putting the interests of citizens first while contributing to the common good.

B. Netherlands Data Union Foundation

The Netherlands Data Union Foundation (https://www.thedataunion.org/) is another noteworthy example of an innovative data cooperative. This initiative aims to give individuals more control over their data while creating new opportunities for fair participation in the data economy. The Data Union Foundation functions as a decentralized platform where users can store, manage, and share their data in a secure and controlled manner. A core principle of the cooperative is the self-determination of its members: they decide independently what data they want to share, with whom, and under what conditions.

The Data Union Foundation's successes include developing innovative technologies for decentralized data management. These make it possible to process and store data locally on users' devices, protecting privacy and increasing efficiency. In addition, the cooperative has successfully established partnerships with companies and research institutions to develop ethical models for data use, providing reassurance and security to its members.

A unique feature of the Data Union Foundation is its focus on collective action. The cooperative enables members to join in 'data unions', which are collective bargaining units formed by users to negotiate better conditions for using their data. This strengthens the position of individual users vis-à-vis large data companies. The Data Union Foundation places a strong emphasis on education and awareness. It offers its members extensive information and training on data protection, digital rights, and how the data economy works. In doing so, it helps to raise general awareness of the value of personal data and the importance of digital self-determination.

Overall, the Data Union Foundation's example shows how data cooperatives can operate successfully by putting individuals' interests first while developing innovative solutions to the challenges of the modern data economy. The cooperative demonstrates that it is possible to seize economic opportunities while respecting users' privacy and autonomy and strengthening members' collective bargaining power.

C. Ag-Data Hub

The Ghanaian hub for digital agricultural data (https://poc.miphost.com/), the 'Ag-Data Hub,' is an ambitious initiative that revolutionizes Ghana's agricultural sector. It provides a centralized national agricultural data platform as the digital backbone for seamless stakeholder information flow. This initiative is not just about overcoming the challenges of fragmented data systems and inefficiencies, but also about empowering stakeholders by involving them in the design and implementation process. It introduces a coherent and interoperable infrastructure that aligns with international best practices in data management, giving stakeholders a sense of influence and involvement.

One of the fundamental aspects of the Ag-Data Hub is its commitment to the FAIR data principles. The aim is to organize and document data so that it is easy for other people and machines to find and use (Wilkinson et al., 2016). The FAIR principles can promote the accessibility and usability of data while strengthening the self-determination of data owners:

- Findability: A cooperative's data, whether user behavior, usage statistics, or aggregated information, can be tagged with metadata that makes it easy for all cooperative members to find and understand the data.
- Accessibility: Access conditions can also be clearly defined and transparently documented in a cooperative. Members could decide who can access the data, how they can access it, and how it is managed, strengthening the sense of community and trust in the cooperative.
- Interoperability: Data cooperatives could use standards and protocols to ensure that data can be seamlessly exchanged between members and cooperatives. In this way, similar data cooperatives could benefit from each other and develop common standards.
- Reusability: By providing clear licenses and documentation for their data, cooperatives enable future use and sharing within and outside the cooperative. It can facilitate commercial use of the data while making the knowledge available for other non-commercial uses.

To this end, the hub provides a full range of tools and infrastructure to facilitate the migration of traditional data formats into standardized, FAIR-compliant formats. These include user-friendly data conversion tools, intuitive metadata management systems, and easy-to-use data documentation platforms. This migration ensures that agricultural data can be easily shared, understood, and used by various stakeholders, from smallholder farmers to agribusinesses and policymakers, making them feel comfortable and at ease with the system.

The Ag Data Hub emphasizes a seamless data flow architecture that enables efficient communication and sharing across the agricultural value chain. This architecture includes secure APIs to bridge data gaps, facilitate information sharing between parties, and support third-party software integration. By using these APIs, developers can create applications that enhance the usability and functionality of the hub's services, ensuring that data is not only stored but also actionable.

These successful examples illustrate that data cooperatives can be a viable alternative to the centralized data economy if they are technically well-implemented and designed with the needs of their members in mind.

6.2 Governance Models

A central basis for successful cooperatives in different industries is the democratic decision-making process. Members should have a say in all relevant issues, especially about the management and use of data. It includes:

- Uniform votes: Each member has one vote, regardless of the amount of data contributed, to prevent an imbalance of power based on the size of the data contributions.
- Regular votes: Decision-making processes should be accompanied by regular votes in which all members can express themselves and exert influence, especially on important strategic and ethical issues.
- Transparency and accountability: The governance structure should ensure complete transparency regarding the decisions and their impact. All members must have access to information at all times in order to make informed decisions. An annual 'statement of accounts' could be introduced to evaluate the cooperative's progress and challenges.

No single person or group of actors within the data cooperative must completely control the decision-making processes. It can be achieved through a combination of vertical and horizontal distribution of power:

- Vertical power distribution: The top decision-making level could consist of a board of directors elected by the general assembly. This board can create specialized teams or committees to address specific areas such as data governance, ethics, and legal compliance.
- Horizontal power distribution: The horizontal structures should be designed so that members at all levels have equal rights and can regularly communicate their concerns. Regular meetings and forums for exchanging ideas and discussing decisions could be established.

Data cooperatives must not allow themselves to be overly influenced by external stakeholders, such as large companies or private investors. To this end, governance models such as 'independent supervisory boards' could be introduced to ensure that the cooperative's objectives and the well-being of its members are paramount, providing a sense of security and protection.

Implementing a fair mechanism for conflict resolution and a transparent system of sanctions for violations of cooperative rules is crucial. It guarantees that all members are treated equally, fostering a sense of fairness and equality within the cooperative.

6.3 Lessons Learned From Failed Initiatives

Establishing a data cooperative requires legal, technical, and organizational frameworks to ensure long-term sustainability and fairness. The following measures could serve as a basis (Kapoor et al., 2024):

A. Creation of a Legal Framework

One of the key elements in the establishment of a data cooperative is a clear and legally well-defined establishment process. This process is crucial as it ensures that all members are fully aware of their rights and obligations, thereby promoting transparency and fairness. A 'founding contract' could be used to detail the duties and rights of members.

Contracts within a data cooperative should not only address current issues but also be flexible enough to adapt to future changes in data protection and utilization. They should include explicit provisions on data ownership, liability in the event of data breaches, and the distribution of profits and benefits.

B. Creation of Compliance Checklists and Guidelines

To facilitate the establishment and operation of data cooperatives, standardized checklists, and guidelines could be developed that outline the most important requirements and best practices. These points include:

- Data protection requirements. This checklist should include detailed requirements for compliance with data protection regulations such as the GDPR to ensure that all processes are carried out in a data protection-compliant manner.
- Governance principles. These should include clear recommendations on structure and decision-making and build on proven governance models from other sectors (Section 6.2).
- Technical standards: The guidelines should also include minimum technical requirements for data management and data security protocols to ensure the protection and integrity of the data.

C. Support Through Funding Initiatives

Funding initiatives could be provided at the EU or national level to make data cooperatives accessible to small and medium-sized companies in particular. These initiatives could offer not only financial support but also access to legal, technical, and advisory resources. This comprehensive support is designed to encourage and motivate stakeholders, making the establishment of such cooperatives more feasible and less daunting.

Not all attempts to establish data cooperatives have been successful. However, failed projects can offer valuable lessons that, when learned from, can empower us with the knowledge needed for future initiatives.

One notable example is OpenMined in the United States of America. The project aimed to build a secure data-sharing platform through decentralized data storage. However, it encountered significant technological hurdles, particularly a need for interoperability and high complexity. Two important lessons can be learned from this failure: firstly, user-friendliness is crucial, as complex technologies must be made understandable to laypeople. Secondly, a lack of financial resources can jeopardize operations and thus threaten the sustainability of the project.

Another instructive example is SMart in Europe. This initiative aimed to support freelancers by collectively managing data and resources. However, a lack of governance led to internal conflicts and a loss of trust. The lessons learned from this case underline the importance of transparent and democratic decision-making processes, which ensure that all voices are heard and valued, and the threat that internal power struggles can pose to the cooperative's mission.

From these and other experiences, we can draw general lessons. A clear legal framework is essential to avoid uncertainties when setting up and operating data cooperatives. Furthermore, long-term financing must be secured to prevent scaling problems. These are key factors that should be considered in any future data cooperative initiatives.

These examples illustrate that while building successful data cooperatives is a complex task, it is not an insurmountable one. With careful planning, technical expertise, transparent governance, and a solid financial basis, future initiatives can significantly improve their chances of success and develop more robust models for collaborative data management.

7. CONCLUSION

Data cooperatives, with their transformative potential, represent a promising model for overcoming the challenges of the current data economy and enabling fairer, more democratic data use. This concluding chapter not only summarizes the most important findings but also underscores the revolutionary impact of data cooperatives on the digital future. It provides recommendations for action and formulates open research questions central to this concept's further development, inspiring policymakers, researchers, and practitioners to explore this innovative model.

Digital citizenship and data cooperatives are closely linked. While digital citizenship describes individuals' rights, duties, and competencies in the digital space, data cooperatives provide a concrete framework for exercising these rights and strengthening digital participation. Through active membership in a data cooperative, citizens can expand their digital competencies and develop a deeper understanding of how to handle their data. They gain more control over their data and decide how it is used and shared. It strengthens individual data protection rights and contributes to the democratization of the data economy. Instead of making their data available to large tech companies, they can use it in collaborative self-organization to develop innovative services and products—a form of 'algorithms of resistance' (Bonini & Treré, 2024).

The analysis has made it clear that data cooperatives can play a significant role in strengthening digital self-determination. Several key insights have emerged. One core aspect is the democratic control that data cooperatives enable. Collective ownership and democratic governance structures give members control over their data. It represents a fundamental difference from conventional data usage models, in which individuals often have little influence over how their personal information is used (Miller, 2021).

At the same time, the analysis highlights both the opportunities and risks associated with data cooperatives. On the one hand, they can promote innovation and contribute to greater transparency in data use. On the other hand, they face significant challenges. These include the technical complexity of the required infrastructures, legal uncertainties in a rapidly developing regulatory environment, and the danger that concentrations of power can also develop within the cooperatives.

Finally, the analysis places data cooperatives in the larger context of digital democracy. As part of a broader movement to democratize the digital world, they help to reduce existing power asymmetries and strengthen citizen participation in shaping the digital future. In doing so, they contribute to developing a fairer and more inclusive digital society. Another form of participation is the design of democratic digital services in data-driven ecosystems (Horn & Draude, 2024).

Overall, the analysis shows that data cooperatives are a promising model for addressing the challenges of the modern data economy. They offer a way to realize the benefits of data use while protecting the rights and interests of individuals. Despite the challenges that exist, they have the potential to play an important role in shaping a fairer and more democratic digital future. However, a coordinated effort by various actors is needed to realize this potential fully. Policymakers have a crucial role to play here. The creation of a suitable legal framework is not just important, but urgent, as it can strengthen data cooperatives and increase their legal security. Funding programs and tax incentives can further support the establishment and operation of data cooperatives. In addition, promoting international cooperation is necessary to regulate cross-border data traffic and ensure consistent governance.

The business community can help to spread the concept by integrating data cooperatives into existing business models. Partnerships and joint projects can open up new business opportunities and strengthen competitiveness. At the same time, the development of technical standards is essential to ensure smooth cooperation between data cooperatives and other players.

Society needs to be made aware of the advantages of data cooperatives. Awareness campaigns can help increase acceptance and promote participation in such initiatives. Supporting local initiatives, especially in disadvantaged regions, is particularly important to enable broad social participation.

Despite the potential, numerous questions require in-depth scientific consideration. Technical challenges arise, particularly in developing scalable and secure technical solutions. Technologies such as blockchain, federated learning, and ZKPs promote security, transparency, and self-determination, providing a robust foundation for the future of data cooperatives. Sociological and organizational issues revolve primarily around avoiding power asymmetries within the cooperatives and developing effective governance models that consider all members' interests equally. In addition, legal and political frameworks should be created to integrate data cooperatives into existing legal systems better. The question of appropriate state funding and regulation is of central importance here. Finally, economic aspects such as long-term financial sustainability and the design of cooperation models with private companies are highly relevant. To fully exploit the potential of data cooperatives, intensive interdisciplinary research is needed that takes equal account of technical, social, legal, and economic aspects, emphasizing the need for collaboration and shared responsibility in this endeavor.

In the digital future, data cooperatives could be a tool for promoting digital self-determination and serve as a model for the democratization of other economic and social sectors. They embody the vision of a data-based economy that is not only characterized by efficiency and the pursuit of profit but also by transparency, justice, and collective good.

REFERENCES

Abbas, A. E., van Velzen, T., Ofe, H., van de Kaa, G., Zuiderwijk, A., & de Reuver, M. (2024). Beyond control over data: Conceptualizing data sovereignty from a social contract perspective. *Electronic Markets*, 34(1), 20. DOI: 10.1007/s12525-024-00695-2

Andrae, S. (2025 in press). The use of artificial intelligence in agriculture: Opportunities for data cooperatives and platforms. In Gupta, A., & Tewary, T. (Eds.), *Sustainable and smart farming eco-systems: Changing landscapes in the age of technology*. Emerald.

Bietti, E., Etxeberria, A., Mannan, M., & Wong, J. (2021). Data cooperatives in Europe: A legal and empirical investigation. The New School's Platform Cooperativism Consortium. https://cyber.harvard.edu/sites/default/files/2022-02/Data_Cooperatives_Europe-group2.pdf

Bonini, T., & Treré, E. (2024). *The everyday fight against platform power*. The MIT Press. DOI: 10.7551/mitpress/14329.001.0001

Bühler, M. M., Calzada, I., Cane, I., Jelinek, T., Kapoor, A., Mannan, M., Mehta, S., Mookerje, V., Nübel, K., Pentland, A., Scholz, T., Siddarth, D., Tait, J., Vaitla, B., & Zhu, J. (2023). Unlocking the power of digital commons: Data cooperatives as a pathway for data sovereign, innovative and equitable digital communities. *Digital*, 3(3), 146–171. DOI: 10.3390/digital3030011

Calzada, I. (2021). Data co-operatives through data sovereignty. *Smart Cities*, 4(3), 1158–1172. DOI: 10.3390/smartcities4030062

Calzada, I. (2022). How digital citizenship regimes are rescaling European nation-states. *Space and Polity*, 26(1), 44–52. DOI: 10.1080/13562576.2022.2072197

Calzada, I. (2023). Emerging digital citizenship regimes: Pandemic, algorithmic, liquid, metropolitan, and stateless citizenships. *Citizenship Studies*, 27(2), 160–188. DOI: 10.1080/13621025.2021.2012312

Chen, L. L., Mirpuri, S., Rao, N., & Law, N. (2021). Conceptualization and measurement of digital citizenship across disciplines. *Educational Research Review*, 33, 100379. DOI: 10.1016/j.edurev.2021.100379

Cheney, G., Noyes, M., Do, E., Vieta, M., Azkarraga, J., & Michel, C. (2023). *Cooperatives at work*. Emerald Publishing. DOI: 10.1108/9781838678258

Ding, K., Feng, X., & Yu, H. (2024). To be global or personalized: Generalized federated learning with cooperative adaptation for data heterogeneity. *Knowledge-Based Systems*, 301, 112317. DOI: 10.1016/j.knosys.2024.112317

Duncan, J. (2023). Data protection beyond data rights: Governing data production through collective intermediaries. *Internet Policy Review*, 12(3). Advance online publication. DOI: 10.14763/2023.3.1722

Fink, A. (2024). Data cooperative. *Internet Policy Review*, 13(2). Advance online publication. DOI: 10.14763/2024.2.1752

Girish, S., & Avery, M. (2022). Data cooperative: Enabling meaningful collective negotiation of data rights for communities. http://dx.doi.org/DOI: 10.2139/ssrn.4414473

Hardjono, T., & Pentland, A. (2019). Data cooperatives: Towards a foundation for decentralized personal data management. *arXiv*. /arXiv.1905.08819DOI: 10.48550

Horn, V., & Draude, C. (2024). The ladder of data citizen participation: A sociotechnical lens for designing democratic digital services in the data economy. *Interacting with Computers*, iwae038. Advance online publication. DOI: 10.1093/iwc/iwae038

Kapoor, A., Tait, J., & Vaitl, B. (2024). How to build a data cooperative: A practitioner's handbook. https://data2x.org/wp-content/uploads/2024/06/Data-Cooperative-Handbook.pdf

Liu, Q., Feng, G., Zheng, W., & Tian, J. (2022). Managing data quality of cooperative information systems: Model and algorithm. *Expert Systems with Applications*, 189, 116074. DOI: 10.1016/j.eswa.2021.116074

Micheli, M., Farell, E., Carballa-Smichowski, B., Posada-Sánchez, M., Signorelli, S., & Vespe, M. (2023). Mapping the landscape of data intermediaries: Emerging models for more inclusive data governance. [Report]. Publications Office of the European Union. https://data.europa.eu/doi/10.2760/8943

Miller, K. (2021). Radical proposal: Data cooperatives could give us more power over our data. Stanford University Human-Centered Artificial Intelligence, Oct 20, 2021. https://hai.stanford.edu/news/radical-proposal-data-cooperatives-could-give-us-more-power-over-our-data

Naz, M., Al-zahrani, F. A., Khalid, R., Javaid, N., Qamar, A. M., Afzal, M. K., & Shafiq, M. (2019). A secure data sharing platform using blockchain and interplanetary file system. *Sustainability (Basel)*, 11(24), 705. DOI: 10.3390/su11247054

Parra-Moyano, J. (2024). Data entrepreneurs of the world, unite! How business leaders should react to the emergence of data cooperatives. *The Capco Institute Journal of Financial Transformation, 59*, 20–25. https://www.capco.com/Capco-Institute/Journal-59-innovation-and-control

Robles-Carrillo, M. (2024). Digital identity: An approach to its nature, concept, and functionalities. *International Journal of Law and Information Technology*, 32(1), eaae019. Advance online publication. DOI: 10.1093/ijlit/eaae019

Ruijer, E. (2021). Designing and implementing data collaboratives: A governance perspective. *Government Information Quarterly*, 38(4), 101612. DOI: 10.1016/j.giq.2021.101612

Schaake, M. (2024). *The tech coup: How to save democracy from Silicon Valley*. Princeton University Press.

Wilkinson, M., Dumontier, M., Aalbersberg, I. J., Appleton, G., Axton, M., Baak, A., Blomberg, N., Boiten, J.-W., da Silva Santos, L. B., Bourne, P. E., Bouwman, J., Brookes, A. J., Clark, T., Crosas, M., Dillo, I., Dumon, O., Edmunds, S., Evelo, C. T., Finkers, R., & Mons, B. (2016). The FAIR guiding principles for scientific data management and stewardship. *Scientific Data*, 3(1), 160018. DOI: 10.1038/sdata.2016.18 PMID: 26978244

Xu, M., Jug, Z., & Tamo-Larrieux, T. (2024). A cross-cultural analysis of transparency: The interplay of law, privacy policies, and user perceptions. *International Data Privacy Law*, 14(3), 197–222. DOI: 10.1093/idpl/ipae011

Zarkadakis, G. (2020). 'Data trusts' could be the key to better AI. *Harvard Business Review*. https://hbr.org/2020/11/data-trusts-could-be-the-key-to-better-ai

Zhu, Y., Wu, Y., Luo, Z., Ooi, B. C., & Xiao, X. (2024). Secure and verifiable data collaboration with low-cost zero-knowledge proofs. *Proceedings of the VLDB Endowment International Conference on Very Large Data Bases*, 17(9), 2321–2334. DOI: 10.14778/3665844.3665860

Chapter 19
Educational Leadership and AI in the Post-COVID-19 Era: Ethical Challenges and Opportunities in Catalonia

Maria-Antònia Guardiola
https://orcid.org/0000-0002-5488-6711
Open University of Catalonia, Spain

ABSTRACT

The integration of artificial intelligence (AI) in education has accelerated, especially during the COVID-19 pandemic, as institutions adopted remote and hybrid learning solutions. In Catalonia, a region known for innovation, AI has been applied to personalized learning, grading systems, and virtual teaching assistants. However, this rapid adoption raises ethical concerns, including data privacy, algorithmic bias, and digital inclusion. While AI can enhance personalized education, it risks exacerbating inequalities if technology and data are mismanaged. This chapter examines the ethical challenges of AI in education through the lens of Catalonia's leadership, emphasizing equity and inclusion. By analyzing case studies, it highlights strategies to address privacy, fairness, and ethical AI use, particularly for marginalized groups. The chapter provides insights for global educators and policymakers on balancing innovation with ethical responsibility, advocating for an approach that promotes technological progress while safeguarding equity, fairness, and transparency.

DOI: 10.4018/979-8-3693-9015-3.ch019

1. INTRODUCTION

The COVID-19 pandemic served as a transformative event in the education sector, revealing both the immense potential and inherent limitations of digital technologies. As education systems worldwide transitioned to remote learning, educators, students, and administrators were thrust into an unprecedented reliance on technology. This rapid shift underscored the essential role of digital tools in maintaining educational continuity. Among these technologies, Artificial Intelligence (AI) emerged as a particularly significant driver of educational transformation, offering solutions such as personalized learning, automated grading systems, and adaptive platforms (UNESCO, 2021). However, the accelerated adoption of AI also exposed deep-rooted challenges related to equity, privacy, and digital access, requiring urgent attention from educational leaders.

Catalonia, an autonomous community in northeastern Spain, has long been recognized as a leader in educational innovation. The region's commitment to equity and inclusion is reflected in its proactive stance on integrating digital tools into education, even prior to the pandemic (Bosco et al., 2016). Early initiatives like the eduCAT 1×1 program equipped students and educators with essential technological resources, laying the groundwork for broader AI integration. Yet, the pandemic amplified the scale and scope of AI adoption, highlighting both its potential benefits and its ethical dilemmas. Catalonian educational leaders found themselves navigating the dual responsibility of ensuring the effectiveness of AI systems while upholding ethical principles of fairness and inclusivity. The task was particularly critical for marginalized communities, who remain disproportionately affected by digital inequalities (Alonso et al., 2014).

The transformative potential of AI in education cannot be overstated. Adaptive learning platforms, for instance, offer personalized experiences by dynamically tailoring content to individual student needs, enhancing engagement and learning outcomes. Similarly, AI-powered grading systems provide real-time feedback and reduce administrative workloads for educators, allowing them to focus on strategic instructional tasks. Despite these advantages, Selwyn (2019) reminds us that these technologies are not value-neutral. Instead, they reflect the socio-economic and cultural contexts in which they are developed, raising critical concerns about transparency, accountability, and equity in AI-driven education systems.

Catalonia's experience illustrates how these challenges are further compounded by ethical considerations around data privacy and algorithmic bias. AI systems rely on large datasets, often sourced from student information, to operate effectively. While the General Data Protection Regulation (GDPR) provides a robust legal framework for safeguarding such data, its application to AI in education requires continuous vigilance and adaptation. As the Autoritat Catalana de Protecció de Dades (2022) has highlighted, ensuring compliance with GDPR is necessary but insufficient to fully address the unique risks posed by AI. Algorithmic bias remains another persistent issue, as AI systems trained on incomplete or skewed datasets risk perpetuating or even exacerbating existing inequalities, particularly for underrepresented student populations (Luckin, 2017).

Accessibility remains another pressing concern in the equitable deployment of AI in education. While AI technologies hold the promise of enhancing learning experiences, they also risk exacerbating disparities between urban and rural schools. In Catalonia, the digital divide has been a long-standing challenge, brought into sharp focus during the pandemic. Schools in rural areas often lacked the necessary infrastructure, such as reliable internet connectivity and access to AI-powered tools, leaving their students at a significant disadvantage. UNESCO (2021) has emphasized that "True digital inclusion requires not just access to technology but also the skills and support to use it effectively." Catalonia's leadership has sought to address these gaps through targeted interventions, though challenges persist.

This chapter delves into the ethical challenges and leadership strategies associated with AI integration in Catalonia's education system. It examines key areas, including data privacy, algorithmic bias, and digital inclusion, through case studies and policy analysis. The chapter seeks to provide actionable insights and best practices for educators, policymakers and technologists seeking to implement AI in ways that are both innovative and equitable. It emphasizes the importance of adopting a balanced approach that maximizes AI's potential to transform education while safeguarding core principles of equity, transparency, and fairness.

Furthermore, the chapter argues that Catalonia's leadership in addressing these challenges offers valuable lessons for other regions navigating similar complexities. By focusing on the ethical dimensions of AI implementation and the strategies employed to mitigate its risks, this analysis contributes to the growing body of literature on educational leadership in the digital age. Catalonia's experiences provide a blueprint for how educational systems worldwide can harness the transformative power of AI responsibly, ensuring that technological advancements serve as tools for equity and inclusion rather than sources of division.

2. CATALONIA AS A MICROCOSM FOR GLOBAL TRENDS

Catalonia's educational landscape offers an instructive case study for understanding the broader global implications of Artificial Intelligence (AI) in education. Recognized for its long-standing commitment to educational innovation, the region has leveraged AI not only to enhance learning outcomes but also to address systemic challenges, including the digital divide, socio-economic inequities, and the need for personalized learning solutions. Catalonia's early adoption of AI and digital tools, paired with robust educational policies, positions it as a microcosm reflecting the complexities and possibilities of integrating advanced technology into education systems worldwide.

The region's proactive approach to AI implementation is anchored in its emphasis on equity and inclusivity, principles that remain central to its educational strategies. As UNESCO (2021) aptly observes, "The integration of technology in education is not merely a matter of innovation; it is a commitment to ensuring that every student has the opportunity to succeed, regardless of their background or circumstances." Catalonia embodies this principle through the development of programs and policies that prioritize underserved communities, ensuring the benefits of AI extend across diverse learner demographics.

One of the most defining characteristics of Catalonia's approach is its dual focus on infrastructure development and capacity building among educators. This duality acknowledges that technological advancement must be accompanied by efforts to empower educators to maximize its potential. Luckin (2017) asserts, "AI in education is not just about the tools but about empowering educators to use those tools effectively." Catalonia exemplifies this philosophy by investing in professional development initiatives designed to equip educators with the skills required to integrate AI meaningfully into their classrooms. Peer reviewers emphasized the significance of such measures, noting the global importance of linking technological deployment with teacher readiness to ensure effectiveness.

Moreover, Catalonia's leadership in tackling ethical concerns associated with AI - such as data privacy, algorithmic bias and inclusivity - has set a benchmark for other regions. Through the implementation of policies like the Ethical AI Integration Guidelines (2022), the region demonstrates that technological innovation and ethical responsibility can coexist. As Floridi (2016) highlights, "The governance of AI in education must strike a balance between innovation and the preservation of fundamental ethical values." This framework ensures that Catalonia's AI-driven educational reforms remain aligned with broader societal objectives, underscoring the region's role as a thought leader in ethical AI adoption.

This section explores Catalonia's unique position as a microcosm of global trends in educational AI integration. It examines how the region's innovative policies and practices have not only transformed its own educational landscape but also provided valuable insights for other regions navigating the complexities of AI adoption in education. By analyzing Catalonia's strategies, the discussion aims to illuminate pathways for educational leaders worldwide to harness AI in ways that promote equity, inclusion, and excellence in learning outcomes.

2.1 Historical Context and Evolution of Educational Leadership in Catalonia

Catalonia's leadership in educational innovation has deep historical roots, dating back to its 19th-century commitment to universal literacy. Early 20th-century reforms introduced pedagogical techniques inspired by thinkers such as Montessori and Dewey, emphasizing student-centered learning and equity. According to Alonso et al. (2014), these approaches laid the groundwork for a flexible and progressive education system capable of adapting to societal and technological changes.

In the post-Franco era, Catalonia capitalized on its newfound autonomy to craft education policies that prioritized inclusivity and innovation. The 1985 School Autonomy Act, as noted by Diari d'Educació (Kirchner, 2020), marked a turning point by empowering local leaders to experiment with governance structures and pedagogical approaches, fostering a culture of creativity and responsiveness. This autonomy allowed for bold initiatives in the late 20th century, such as the integration of digital technologies in classrooms.

The introduction of the eduCAT 1×1 program in 2010 exemplifies Catalonia's forward-thinking approach to education. As Floridi (2016) observes, this program represented "a proactive effort to bridge the digital divide and ensure equitable access to technology," equipping over 300,000 students and teachers with devices and fostering digital literacy across diverse socio-economic backgrounds. This initiative also set a foundation for the region's seamless integration of more advanced technologies like Artificial Intelligence in the years that followed.

Catalonia's historical trajectory underscores its progressive stance and commitment to educational equity and technological advancement. As UNESCO (2021) aptly states, "Educational innovation does not occur in isolation; it is the product of a systemic commitment to equity, adaptability, and strategic foresight." These qualities are reflected in the region's current leadership in AI adoption and serve as a model for global educational systems.

2.2 Catalonia's Educational Landscape

Catalonia has consistently led educational innovation in Spain, setting benchmarks that other regions have sought to emulate. The region's integration of digital tools into education predates the COVID-19 pandemic, with significant milestones achieved through forward-thinking initiatives like the eduCAT 1×1 program, launched in 2010. This initiative aimed to mitigate the digital divide by providing every student and educator with a digital device, fostering digital literacy, and enabling equitable access to technology in education (Alonso et al., 2014). By 2020, the program had equipped over 300,000 students with devices and trained more than 60,000 teachers, creating a robust digital ecosystem foundational for subsequent AI adoption.

Building upon this foundation, the Government of Catalonia introduced the eduCAT 2.0 program in 2011, which expanded digital integration through interactive whiteboards and individual laptops for upper primary and secondary students. These initiatives collectively positioned Catalonia as a leader in leveraging technology to drive educational reform, paving the way for the region's adoption of AI-powered tools (Alonso et al., 2014).

In 2024, Catalonia launched the Artificial Intelligence Strategy of Catalonia (Estratègia d'Intel·ligència Artificial de Catalunya), aimed at ensuring the ethical and responsible use of AI across sectors, including education (Government of Catalonia, 2024). The strategy underscores the advancement of digital literacy, personalization of learning experiences, and addressing the diverse needs of students. Its ethical framework is designed to ensure that AI adoption aligns with core values of equity and inclusivity, a principle highlighted by peer reviewers who stressed the need for transparent and adaptable governance in AI policies.

One of the standout contributions of Catalonia's educational reforms is the deployment of adaptive learning systems. These AI-driven tools analyze individual student data to customize content and pacing, delivering highly personalized learning experiences. Adaptive systems have proven particularly beneficial for diverse student populations, including gifted learners and those with specific learning disabilities, facilitating more equitable access to quality education. Reviewers pointed to this as a global best practice, emphasizing its scalability and adaptability to other educational contexts.

However, these advancements are accompanied by ethical challenges. Data privacy, algorithmic bias, and equitable access remain pressing concerns that demand proactive oversight from educational leaders. As Floridi (2016) notes, ethical governance is not a secondary consideration but a central requirement for ensuring that technological innovation does not inadvertently perpetuate existing inequalities. Catalonia's continuous efforts to refine its governance frameworks provide a roadmap for other regions seeking to navigate similar complexities.

2.3 The Impact of COVID-19 on AI Adoption

The COVID-19 pandemic acted as a catalyst for the widespread adoption of AI and digital technologies in education, and Catalonia was no exception. The disruption of traditional schooling necessitated an overnight shift to remote learning, which tested the resilience of education systems globally. Thanks to its pre-existing digital infrastructure, Catalonia was better positioned than many regions to navigate this transition. AI-powered platforms such as Google Classroom, Moodle, and Edmodo were extensively deployed to deliver lessons, monitor progress, and provide personalized feedback, ensuring educational continuity during school closures.

Despite these advantages, the pandemic exposed significant inequities in access to digital tools. According to Idescat (2021), rural areas in Catalonia faced unique challenges, including unreliable internet connectivity and inadequate hardware. Students in urban schools generally had greater access to technology, while those in rural or economically disadvantaged settings struggled to engage with AI-powered tools. Peer reviewers highlighted the importance of Catalonia's targeted interventions, such as partnerships with telecommunication providers and the distribution of additional devices, in addressing these disparities.

The socio-economic divide was another stark challenge exacerbated by the pandemic. Students from low-income families often lacked personal devices or reliable internet access, creating barriers to effective participation in online education. As UNESCO (2021) notes, "The pandemic underscored the urgency of addressing the digital divide by ensuring equitable access to both technology and the skills to use it effectively." Catalonia's leadership in mitigating these disparities - through initiatives such as subsidized broadband and community tech hubs - demonstrates its commitment to minimizing inequities.

While the pandemic revealed vulnerabilities, it also highlighted AI's transformative potential. AI-driven platforms provided real-time analytics, enabling educators to identify learning gaps and tailor interventions more effectively. Yet, this rapid adoption raised ethical questions about how student data was collected, stored, and used. Catalonia's adherence to the General Data Protection Regulation (GDPR), coupled with ongoing audits and stakeholder consultations, illustrates the importance of governance frameworks in safeguarding privacy and ensuring transparency (Autoritat Catalana de Protecció de Dades, 2022).

Catalonia's experience during the pandemic underscores the critical role of proactive leadership in navigating the ethical and practical challenges of AI integration. By investing in infrastructure, fostering digital literacy, and addressing systemic inequities, the region offers valuable lessons for global educators and policymakers striving to leverage AI responsibly.

3. ETHICAL CHALLENGES IN AI INTEGRATION

The integration of Artificial Intelligence (AI) into education systems offers transformative opportunities but also presents significant ethical challenges that must be carefully addressed by educational leaders. These challenges range from concerns about data privacy and algorithmic bias to issues of accessibility and equity, especially in regions where the digital divide remains pronounced. As AI technologies become increasingly embedded in educational practices, they raise critical questions about ensuring their responsible and equitable use.

Catalonia, a leader in educational innovation, provides a valuable lens for examining these challenges. Through proactive measures, the region has sought to balance technological advancement with moral and social responsibility. As UNESCO (2021) highlights, "The ethical deployment of AI in education requires a comprehensive framework that prioritizes fairness, transparency, and inclusivity." Catalonia's experiences underscore the necessity of developing such frameworks to ensure AI enhances learning while safeguarding fundamental values.

Among the most pressing ethical concerns are data privacy and security. AI-powered tools collect vast amounts of personal information, making the safeguarding of student data a top priority. As Floridi (2016) asserts, "Data protection in AI is not just a legal requirement but an ethical imperative, especially when it involves vulnerable populations like students." Catalonia has demonstrated leadership by adhering to stringent data protection regulations such as the General Data Protection Regulation (GDPR).

Algorithmic bias presents another significant challenge, as AI systems often rely on datasets that may inadvertently reinforce existing inequalities. Selwyn (2019) observes, "AI systems are only as unbiased as the data they are trained on, and biased data will inevitably lead to biased outcomes." Catalonia has tackled this issue by auditing its AI systems and ensuring that training datasets reflect the diversity of its student population.

Inclusivity and digital equity also remain critical. AI has the potential to exacerbate the digital divide in underfunded or rural areas where access to technology and connectivity may be limited. Catalonia's targeted efforts, such as providing devices through the eduCAT 1×1 program and investing in teacher training, illustrate the importance of holistic approaches to digital inclusion. As Luckin (2017) emphasizes, "True digital inclusion goes beyond access; it encompasses the skills and resources necessary for meaningful engagement with technology."

This section explores the multifaceted ethical challenges associated with AI integration in education, focusing on Catalonia's strategies to address them. By examining the region's approach, this discussion aims to provide actionable insights for educational leaders worldwide. The lessons drawn from Catalonia highlight the necessity of aligning AI integration with ethical principles, ensuring that these powerful tools foster equity, transparency, and trust in education systems.

3.1 Data Privacy and Security

The reliance of AI on vast amounts of data for learning analytics, predictive assessments, and personalized education makes data privacy and security overarching concerns. Sensitive information such as students' academic performance, behavioral tendencies, and biometric data is often collected, processed, and stored by AI systems. Without robust protections, this data becomes vulnerable to misuse, raising questions about consent, transparency, and trust (Autoritat Catalana de Protecció de Dades, 2022).

Catalonia has adopted stringent measures to safeguard data privacy, adhering to the GDPR's ethical standards. The GDPR mandates that all data collection and processing respect the rights of individuals. As the Autoritat Catalana de Protecció de Dades (APD) asserts, "Educational institutions bear a fundamental ethical obligation to prioritize data protection, which extends beyond legal compliance" (APD, 2022).

During the COVID-19 pandemic, the shift to AI-powered remote learning platforms amplified concerns over data security. Platforms like Google Classroom and Moodle collected vast datasets to monitor student engagement and performance. To address these risks, Catalonia implemented strict protocols for anonymizing data and obtaining informed consent from students and families. Luckin (2017) emphasizes, "Transparency is foundational to building trust in AI systems, and the long-term sustainability of AI in education depends on it."

Catalonia's schools also conducted regular audits to identify vulnerabilities in their AI systems. These audits revealed that while anonymization reduced risks, stronger encryption methods were needed to ensure comprehensive protection against breaches. Floridi (2016) argues that "While data collection is essential for AI's efficacy, it must be conducted within strict ethical boundaries to prevent misuse."

3.2 Algorithmic Bias

Algorithmic bias is a critical ethical challenge that arises when AI systems inadvertently reinforce existing inequities. Since AI algorithms are trained on historical data, they often reflect biases inherent in those datasets, leading to discriminatory outcomes. In education, this can manifest in skewed grading systems, unfair evaluations, or biased recommendations for academic advancement (Selwyn, 2019).

In Catalonia, predictive analytics tools used to assess student performance have been scrutinized for potential bias. Research conducted by the Centre for Innovation for Data Tech and Artificial Intelligence (CIDAI) revealed disparities in how AI systems evaluated students from different socio-economic backgrounds. Wealthier students, whose data included more comprehensive academic records, were disproportionately favored, highlighting the system's tendency to perpetuate inequities (CIDAI, 2021).

To mitigate this, Catalonia implemented regular algorithmic audits. These audits identified sources of bias and informed strategies for retraining AI systems with more diverse datasets. Selwyn (2019) asserts, "AI systems are only as fair as the data they are trained on, and addressing algorithmic bias requires deliberate efforts to diversify inputs."

Additionally, Catalonia developed Ethical AI Guidelines to ensure fairness in algorithmic decision-making. These guidelines emphasize stakeholder involvement, with teachers, students, and parents participating in AI evaluations. UNESCO (2021) advocates for "algorithmic fairness as a cornerstone of ethical AI design, particularly in education, where outcomes have far-reaching implications."

3.3 Digital Inclusion

Digital inclusion is perhaps the most pressing ethical challenge in AI adoption. While AI has the potential to bridge educational gaps through personalized learning, it also risks exacerbating inequalities if access to technology and digital literacy are not addressed. UNESCO (2021) notes, "True digital inclusion requires not only access to devices but also the skills and support necessary to use them effectively."

Catalonia has prioritized digital inclusion through initiatives like the eduCAT 1×1 program, providing devices to all students regardless of socio-economic status (Alonso et al., 2014). However, physical access alone is insufficient. During the pandemic, disparities in internet connectivity underscored the need for comprehensive strategies addressing infrastructure and digital skills. For example, rural schools in Lleida and Tarragona faced significant connectivity challenges, hindering their use of AI-powered platforms effectively (Idescat, 2021).

To bridge the digital divide, Catalonian leaders partnered with telecommunications companies to provide subsidized internet plans and install Wi-Fi hotspots in underserved areas. Teacher training programs were also introduced to enhance educators' ability to integrate AI tools into their teaching. These efforts empowered teachers to maximize the benefits of personalized learning systems.

Expanding digital inclusion globally requires multi-faceted approaches. Governments, educational institutions, and technology developers must collaborate to ensure equitable access to AI tools while addressing the digital literacy gap. Luckin (2017) observes, "Empowering all students with the skills to navigate AI-driven learning environments is essential for ensuring that technology serves as an equalizer rather than a divider."

Catalonia's experience serves as a model for other regions, demonstrating that ethical AI integration requires investments in both technological infrastructure and human capital. This dual approach ensures AI benefits all students equitably while addressing ethical concerns accompanying its adoption.

4. CASE STUDIES IN CATALONIA

Catalonia's strategic approach to integrating Artificial Intelligence (AI) into its education system provides valuable insights into both the opportunities and ethical challenges associated with this transformative technology. As a region historically championing innovation in education, Catalonia has showcased how AI can be effectively leveraged to address critical issues such as infrastructure disparities, algorithmic bias, and data privacy concerns. By addressing these challenges through targeted programs and regional initiatives, Catalonia has positioned itself as a leader in the ethical deployment of AI in education.

A defining characteristic of Catalonia's approach is its commitment to balancing technological innovation with equity and inclusivity. As UNESCO (2021) highlights, "The ethical integration of AI into education systems requires a commitment to inclusivity, transparency, and fairness." Catalonia embodies this principle by ensuring that all students, regardless of socio-economic status or geographic location, have access to AI-powered educational tools.

Catalonia's initiatives include a focus on infrastructure improvement, targeted teacher training, and the development of ethical guidelines to ensure fairness in AI integration. By prioritizing these areas, the region has worked to bridge the digital divide, address algorithmic bias, and safeguard data privacy. These efforts, as Luckin (2017) emphasizes, illustrate the importance of aligning technological advancements with equity and broader societal goals.

This section presents three detailed case studies from Catalonia, demonstrating how the region has tackled infrastructure gaps, algorithmic fairness, and data privacy concerns. These examples underscore the importance of strategic planning, ethical leadership, and collaborative stakeholder engagement in achieving equitable AI integration.

4.1 Rural Schools in Lleida and Tarragona

Rural schools in Catalonia, particularly in Lleida and Tarragona, have long faced challenges in integrating technology into education. Issues such as limited infrastructure, unreliable internet access, and socio-economic disparities disproportionately affect rural communities, perpetuating educational inequities (Idescat,

2021). Historically, these schools struggled to keep pace with urban counterparts in adopting digital education tools.

To address these disparities, Catalonia launched the eduCAT 1×1 program, providing digital devices to students and teachers to bridge the digital divide (Alonso et al., 2014). However, implementing AI technologies in rural areas required more than devices - it demanded robust connectivity and targeted training for educators.

Leadership Strategies

1. **Infrastructure Development**: Catalonia's government collaborated with telecommunications companies to establish reliable broadband networks in underserved areas. Schools in Lleida and Tarragona benefited from these efforts, gaining high-speed internet to support AI-powered learning platforms (Government of Catalonia, 2024).
2. **Educator Empowerment**: Professional development programs trained rural educators in integrating AI tools into their teaching. These sessions covered the use of adaptive learning platforms and strategies for addressing students' unique needs in rural contexts (Luckin, 2017).
3. **Localized AI Solutions**: AI systems were adapted to function effectively in low-bandwidth environments, ensuring accessibility for schools with limited connectivity. These efforts highlighted the importance of localized solutions to promote equitable technology access (UNESCO, 2021).

Outcome

By 2023, rural schools in Lleida and Tarragona reported a 25% increase in student engagement and notable improvements in learning outcomes (Idescat, 2021). Teachers leveraged adaptive learning platforms to address individual student needs, demonstrating the impact of infrastructure investments and educator training in bridging rural-urban educational gaps.

4.2 Algorithmic Audits in Barcelona

Barcelona, Catalonia's largest urban center, has been at the forefront of adopting advanced AI systems in education. However, early implementation revealed significant challenges, particularly concerning algorithmic bias. Predictive analytics tools used to assess student performance and recommend learning pathways disproportionately favored students from affluent neighborhoods, perpetuating socio-economic inequalities (CIDAI, 2021).

Leadership Strategies

1. **Algorithmic Transparency**: Educational leaders engaged stakeholders - teachers, parents, and students - in discussions about AI systems' operations and data utilization, fostering trust and accountability (Selwyn, 2019).
2. **Bias Mitigation**: Algorithmic audits identified disparities in grading and recommendations. Developers retrained AI models using diverse datasets to address bias, reinforcing the need for regular evaluation and adjustment (Floridi, 2016).
3. **Teacher Training**: Teachers were trained to identify and mitigate potential biases in AI outputs, ensuring human oversight complemented algorithmic decision-making (UNESCO, 2021).

Outcome

These interventions reduced grading disparities by 40%, narrowing equity gaps in AI-driven outcomes (CIDAI, 2021). Additionally, stakeholder trust in AI systems improved significantly, demonstrating the importance of regular audits and inclusive governance in ensuring fairness.

4.3 Smart Classrooms in Girona

Girona has embraced the concept of "smart classrooms," integrating technologies like AI-powered virtual assistants and adaptive learning systems to enhance teaching efficiency and personalized learning. However, implementing these innovations raised concerns about data privacy and surveillance (Autoritat Catalana de Protecció de Dades, 2022).

Leadership Strategies

1. **Compliance with GDPR**: Schools adhered strictly to the GDPR, implementing robust data anonymization techniques and obtaining informed consent from students and parents before collecting data (Autoritat Catalana de Protecció de Dades, 2022).
2. **Digital Citizenship Education**: Girona integrated AI ethics into its curriculum, teaching students about data collection, privacy implications, and responsible technology use, fostering ethical awareness (Luckin, 2017).
3. **Transparent Communication**: Workshops informed stakeholders about data usage policies, addressing concerns about surveillance and building trust in AI tools (Floridi, 2016). **Outcome**

By 2024, Girona's smart classrooms achieved widespread adoption of AI technologies, supported by strong data protection policies and ethical education initiatives. Transparency and stakeholder engagement played pivotal roles in building trust. Moreover, AI ethics education prepared students for responsible interaction with these technologies, emphasizing the importance of ethical awareness in education (UNESCO, 2021).

5. COMPARATIVE ANALYSIS WITH GLOBAL REGIONS

Catalonia's AI-driven educational strategies exemplify the region's commitment to equity, inclusivity, and ethical governance in education. These efforts form part of a broader global conversation about the integration of Artificial Intelligence (AI) into learning systems, with regions like Finland, Singapore, and the United States offering alternative models. While similarities can be drawn, Catalonia's emphasis on public policy-driven innovation sets it apart, positioning the region as a benchmark for addressing systemic inequities in education through AI. As UNESCO (2021) asserts, "The ethical deployment of AI in education is essential not only for fostering innovation but also for ensuring that its benefits reach all learners, regardless of socio-economic background."

5.1 Finland: Emphasis on Teacher

Training Finland, often lauded for its world-class education system, has adopted a teacher-centered approach to AI integration. The country recognizes that equipping educators with both technical expertise and ethical awareness is critical for implementing AI tools effectively. This approach mirrors Catalonia's strategy of prioritizing professional development, as reflected in teacher training programs under the eduCAT 1×1 initiative. Finland's emphasis on fostering educators' agency aligns with Luckin's (2017) observation that "teachers play a central role in ensuring that AI complements, rather than replaces, traditional pedagogy." One notable Finnish initiative involves integrating AI training into teacher certification programs, ensuring that new educators are prepared to use AI responsibly from the outset. Additionally, ongoing workshops and professional learning communities allow teachers to share best practices and address challenges collaboratively. Catalonia's similar focus on continuous professional development demonstrates the global consensus that empowered educators are key to successful AI adoption. Peer reviewers have pointed out that this dual focus on technical skill-building and ethical training serves as a replicable model for regions seeking to integrate AI into their education systems responsibly.

5.2 Singapore: Personalized Learning at Scale

Singapore's National AI Strategy offers another compelling parallel to Catalonia's approach, particularly in its focus on leveraging AI for personalized learning. Singapore's AI-enabled classrooms emphasize tailoring lesson plans and assessments to individual student needs through adaptive learning platforms, much like Catalonia's use of similar tools to enhance equity and engagement. As UNESCO (2021) emphasizes, "Personalized learning powered by AI has the potential to bridge learning gaps, ensuring that no student is left behind." However, Singapore's approach differs in its centralized and highly technological implementation, supported by significant government investment. For example, initiatives such as the Smart Nation program have provided schools with cutting-edge AI solutions, including real-time learning analytics and virtual teaching assistants. In contrast, Catalonia's grassroots efforts - such as engaging local stakeholders and prioritizing rural connectivity - highlight a different path to achieving similar outcomes. Selwyn (2019) underscores this distinction, noting, "Technological solutions are most effective when they align with the socio-cultural values of the communities they serve." Catalonia's commitment to participatory governance, involving teachers, parents, and students in decision-making processes, complements Singapore's top-down strategy by fostering trust and adaptability. The comparison illustrates how different governance models can achieve meaningful outcomes while addressing the unique needs of their respective populations.

5.3 The United States: Market-Driven Solutions

In contrast to the public policy-driven frameworks seen in Catalonia and Finland, the United States relies heavily on market-driven AI solutions in education. Companies like TeachFlow.ai and Edmodo have pioneered innovative platforms that streamline administrative tasks, personalize learning, and provide data-driven insights. However, this approach has often prioritized profit-driven objectives over equity, exacerbating disparities in access to AI tools. As Selwyn (2019) critiques, "The commercialization of educational technology risks prioritizing innovation at the expense of inclusivity and fairness." This dynamic is particularly evident in resource-strapped districts, where schools lack the funding to procure advanced AI tools, leaving students in wealthier areas with a significant advantage. Catalonia's public policy initiatives, such as the subsidization of devices under the eduCAT 1×1 program and investments in broadband infrastructure for rural areas, offer a striking contrast. These measures demonstrate how government-led interventions can counterbalance market inequalities, ensuring that AI benefits are distributed more equitably. Moreover, the ethical governance frameworks employed in Catalonia, such as the Ethical AI Integration Guidelines (2022), emphasize transparency and inclusivity, aspects often neglected in the United States' privatized model. As Floridi (2016) highlights, "Ethical frameworks must guide the deployment of AI to ensure that its transformative potential serves societal good rather than exacerbating existing divides."

5.4 Lessons From Global Comparison

The comparative analysis underscores the diverse approaches to AI integration in education, with Catalonia, Finland, Singapore, and the United States each offering valuable insights. While Finland's focus on teacher training and Singapore's emphasis on personalized learning reflect shared priorities, Catalonia's holistic approach - rooted in equity, public policy, and stakeholder engagement - stands out as a replicable model for fostering inclusivity in AI-driven education systems. As Luckin (2017) concludes, "The transformative potential of AI in education lies not only in its technological capabilities but in its alignment with human-centered values and equitable practices." By synthesizing lessons from global leaders, Catalonia demonstrates how AI can be leveraged responsibly to enhance learning outcomes while addressing systemic inequities. This balance of innovation and inclusivity positions Catalonia as a benchmark for educational leaders worldwide striving to navigate the complexities of AI adoption responsibly.

6. OPPORTUNITIES FOR EDUCATIONAL LEADERS

The integration of Artificial Intelligence (AI) into education, while posing ethical and technical challenges, offers transformative opportunities for educational leaders to innovate and address long-standing inequities in learning environments. AI technologies empower leaders to enhance student outcomes, optimize resource allocation, and foster inclusivity by personalizing learning experiences. Catalonia, a region with a history of progressive educational practices, exemplifies how AI can be strategically leveraged to address systemic challenges. As Luckin (2017) notes, "AI's capacity to personalize education and provide data-driven insights has the potential to revolutionize how learning is delivered and accessed." Catalonia's leaders have demonstrated that the ethical deployment of AI is feasible and necessary to build stakeholder trust and ensure equitable technological benefits. AI tools, integrated thoughtfully, have helped identify at-risk students, address resource gaps, and improve educational quality. These efforts align with Selwyn's (2019) assertion that "AI must serve as a tool for empowerment, enabling educators to respond more effectively to the complex needs of their students." AI also provides an unprecedented opportunity to address equity issues. UNESCO (2021) emphasizes that "AI technologies, when implemented responsibly, can bridge educational gaps by offering access to quality learning opportunities for underrepresented and underserved communities." Catalonia's initiatives, such as adaptive learning platforms and professional development programs, illustrate this potential. However, the opportunities presented by AI are not automatic. They require deliberate planning, ethical oversight, and structural equity considerations. As Floridi (2016) asserts, "The ethical deployment of AI in education is not merely a technical challenge but a moral imperative." Catalonia's experience serves as a case study in leveraging AI responsibly and effectively, offering a roadmap for educational leaders worldwide. This section explores how AI presents opportunities for educational leaders, focusing on enhancing decision-making, promoting ethical practices, and preparing students for an AI-driven future.

6.1 Enhancing Decision-Making With AI

AI has been integrated into Catalonia's educational framework to enhance decision-making processes, equipping leaders with data-driven insights to improve teaching and learning outcomes. The regional government's guidelines emphasize equipping educators with tools for AI integration and fostering reflective practices among teaching staff (Govern.cat, 2024). This commitment highlights the need for strategic frameworks that unify AI's application across schools.

Studies on Catalonia's schools indicate that while technological and pedagogical innovations are underway, many lack a cohesive strategy for AI integration (Álvarez et al., 2021). A unified approach is essential for AI to fully realize its potential in decision-making and school management.

Globally, AI has proven instrumental in personalizing education and streamlining administrative tasks. Adaptive learning tools monitor student progress, identify learning gaps, and enable targeted interventions (TeachFlow.ai, 2023). Such systems empower educators to implement informed strategies for student engagement. Luckin (2017) notes, "AI-powered systems enable a more personalized, responsive approach to education, fostering success in diverse learning environments."

In Catalonia, AI tools are used to analyze data on student performance, resource needs, and teaching efficacy, enabling resource optimization and targeted interventions (Govern.cat, 2024). However, researchers emphasize the need for strategic coordination to maximize the technology's impact (Álvarez et al., 2021).

Targeted Interventions

AI-powered predictive analytics have transformed how educators identify and support at-risk students in Catalonia. These systems analyze historical data to predict learning trajectories and suggest tailored interventions. Luckin (2017) emphasizes, "AI-powered systems facilitate responsive education, enabling timely, individualized interventions." Schools in Tarragona, for instance, use predictive models to correlate attendance with academic outcomes, addressing underlying issues early (Govern.cat, 2024).

Resource Allocation

AI technologies also enhance resource allocation, identifying where additional staff, materials, or technological upgrades are needed. During the COVID-19 pandemic, AI tools guided broadband expansions and device distributions, reducing the digital divide. Selwyn (2019) states, "AI's potential lies in enhancing efficiency and equity through intelligent resource management." These initiatives have improved teaching quality and accessibility in underserved areas.

6.2 Promoting Ethical AI Practices

Catalonia has prioritized ethical AI deployment through frameworks emphasizing transparency, fairness, and stakeholder engagement. These efforts mitigate risks like algorithmic bias and data privacy breaches, ensuring equitable access to AI benefits.

Ethical AI Training for Educators

Targeted training equips teachers with the skills to identify and address biases in AI tools. Floridi (2016) asserts, "Educators mediate the impact of AI, making their role central to ethical implementation." Catalonia's professional development programs empower educators to navigate AI's complexities responsibly.

Transparency and Stakeholder Engagement

Schools engage parents, students, and teachers in AI-related decisions, ensuring data privacy and accountability. Forums and workshops foster trust and collaborative oversight. This aligns with UNESCO (2021) guidelines emphasizing transparency as fundamental to ethical AI adoption.

Promoting Digital Citizenship

Catalonia integrates AI ethics into curricula, preparing students for the challenges of an AI-driven world. Discussions on bias, privacy, and societal impacts encourage critical thinking, fostering informed digital citizenship (Luckin, 2017).

6.3 Preparing Students for an AI-Driven World

Catalonia recognizes the importance of preparing students for an AI-driven future through initiatives that combine technical skills and ethical awareness. Programs like CreaTIC equip students with foundational AI knowledge and ethical considerations, fostering responsible engagement with the technology (Government of Catalonia, 2022).

Technical and Ethical Skills

AI education focuses on algorithm functionality, applications, and societal impacts. Project-based learning fosters technical understanding while exploring ethical dilemmas, such as bias and data privacy (Luckin, 2017).

Partnerships With Technology Companies

Collaborations between schools and tech firms provide students with hands-on AI experience and mentorship. UNESCO (2021) highlights, "Public-private collaborations bridge theoretical knowledge with practical applications, fostering readiness for technological advancements." These partnerships ensure students gain relevant skills while understanding AI's ethical dimensions.

7. FUTURE TRENDS IN AI AND EDUCATION

Emerging technologies such as Generative AI, Explainable AI (XAI), and predictive analytics are poised to redefine education in profound ways. These advancements promise to extend the capabilities of current AI applications, enabling more personalized, equitable, and transparent learning environments. As Luckin (2017) notes, "The true potential of AI in education lies in its ability to adapt dynamically to student needs, fostering engagement and understanding."

7.1 Generative AI in Education

Generative AI, capable of creating content such as lesson plans, quizzes, and multimedia materials, represents a game-changer in educational content delivery. By leveraging natural language processing (NLP) and machine learning, Generative AI can produce customized resources tailored to individual student needs and learning preferences. For example, adaptive educational materials could be generated in real-time, ensuring that students receive targeted support in areas where they struggle. This dynamic content creation has the potential to engage learners more deeply and foster better academic outcomes.

Catalonia is well-positioned to incorporate Generative AI into its educational ecosystem. The region's ongoing investment in digital infrastructure and its focus on ethical AI implementation provide a solid foundation for integrating such cutting-edge technologies. However, the deployment of Generative AI also raises ethical concerns, including issues related to intellectual property and content bias. As Selwyn (2019) emphasizes, "AI tools must be critically evaluated to ensure they reinforce, rather than undermine, equity and academic integrity."

7.2 Explainable AI (XAI) and Transparency

Explainable AI (XAI) is another transformative trend that holds significant promise for education. XAI aims to make AI systems more transparent by providing insights into how decisions are made, thus building trust among educators, students, and parents. Transparency is particularly critical in education, where algorithmic decisions - such as grading or personalized recommendations - can have lasting impacts on student outcomes. According to UNESCO (2021), "Transparency is the cornerstone of ethical AI adoption, fostering trust and accountability among stakeholders."

Catalonia's existing frameworks, such as the Ethical AI Integration Guidelines (2022), align closely with the principles of XAI. By incorporating XAI into its AI systems, Catalonia can address concerns about algorithmic bias and ensure that stakeholders understand and trust the decisions made by AI tools. For example, deploying XAI in grading systems could allow teachers to see the criteria used by the algorithm, enabling them to validate or adjust outcomes as needed. As Floridi (2016) asserts, "Explainability is essential for ensuring AI systems operate within ethical and societal boundaries."

7.3 Advanced Predictive Analytics

Predictive analytics, already used in Catalonia to identify at-risk students and optimize resource allocation, is expected to evolve further. Future advancements could enable more nuanced applications, such as predicting students' career trajectories or mental health needs. By analyzing diverse datasets - ranging from academic performance to social-emotional indicators - AI systems could provide educators with actionable insights to support student well-being and long-term success.

Catalonia's emphasis on ethical governance and data protection positions it to leverage these capabilities responsibly. The Autoritat Catalana de Protecció de Dades (2022) has underscored the importance of safeguarding sensitive data, a critical consideration as predictive models become increasingly complex. As Luckin (2017) notes, "The power of predictive analytics lies in its ability to offer personalized interventions, but it must be wielded with care to avoid perpetuating inequalities."

7.4 Preparing for the Future

To fully harness these emerging trends, Catalonia must continue to prioritize ethical governance, professional development, and stakeholder engagement. Teacher training will remain a critical component, as educators must be equipped not only to use these tools but also to understand their implications. Partnerships with technology developers and academic institutions can further accelerate innovation, ensuring that Catalonia remains at the forefront of AI-driven education.

As Selwyn (2019) aptly states, "The future of AI in education depends not just on technological innovation but on the ability of educational systems to align these tools with broader societal values." Catalonia's ongoing commitment to equity, transparency, and inclusivity provides a strong foundation for navigating this rapidly evolving landscape.

8. GLOBAL IMPLICATIONS AND LESSONS LEARNED

Catalonia's innovative approach to integrating Artificial Intelligence (AI) into education serves as a blueprint for educational systems worldwide. By emphasizing ethical considerations, inclusivity, and transparency, the region has demonstrated how AI can be deployed responsibly to enhance learning outcomes while maintaining alignment with broader social and educational values. The strategies adopted in Catalonia provide critical insights into transparency in AI use, ethical implementation, and inclusivity, offering global relevance and applicability.

8.1 Transparency in AI Use

Transparency is a cornerstone of Catalonia's AI strategy, fostering trust among stakeholders and encouraging the responsible use of AI in education. UNESCO (2021) asserts, "Transparency ensures trust, facilitates understanding, and promotes responsible AI adoption." In Catalonia, open communication about AI technologies is central to building confidence and ensuring legitimacy.

For example, during the implementation of AI-powered adaptive learning tools, Catalonia prioritized clear explanations of how these systems function, the data they collect, and how it is processed. Regular community meetings were held to address concerns and provide updates on AI applications. The *Autoritat Catalana de Protecció de Dades* (APD) emphasized the necessity of transparent communication to alleviate public skepticism and build trust in AI systems (APD, 2022).

Global Implication: Educational systems worldwide can replicate Catalonia's success by embedding transparency into their AI strategies. This involves maintaining open communication with stakeholders, adopting explainable AI (XAI) tools, and addressing concerns about data collection and use. According to Luckin (2017), "Transparent AI fosters collaboration and reduces resistance, paving the way for sustainable educational transformation."

8.2 Ethical AI Implementation

Ethical AI integration is central to Catalonia's approach, guided by the understanding that AI technologies have significant implications for equity and fairness in education. The Ethical AI Integration Guidelines (2022) developed by the Catalonian Department of Education underscore principles such as privacy, fairness, and accountability.

Compliance with the General Data Protection Regulation (GDPR) has been a critical focus. Educational institutions in Catalonia anonymize data, secure informed consent from stakeholders, and implement robust data security measures. Floridi (2016) highlights, "Ethical AI systems must protect user data while maximizing societal benefits."

To address algorithmic bias, Catalonia has conducted regular audits and diversified training datasets. These measures ensure fairness in AI systems and mitigate the risk of perpetuating inequities. Selwyn (2019) underscores, "Fairness in AI requires ongoing evaluation and refinement."

Global Implication: Ethical AI frameworks should be a priority for regions adopting AI in education. This includes conducting regular algorithmic audits, designing diverse datasets, and adhering to global data protection standards like

GDPR. Ethical AI is both a technical challenge and a moral imperative for fostering educational equity.

8.3 Inclusivity Through AI

Inclusivity is a defining feature of Catalonia's AI strategy, emphasizing efforts to bridge the digital divide and ensure equal access to AI-powered tools. Initiatives like the eduCAT 1×1 program have provided devices to students across socio-economic backgrounds, while targeted interventions address systemic disparities (Alonso et al., 2014).

Infrastructure improvements in rural areas, such as Lleida and Tarragona, highlight Catalonia's commitment to equity. By collaborating with telecommunication providers, Catalonia has enhanced internet connectivity in underserved regions. Teacher training programs further empower educators to integrate AI tools into diverse learning environments, reducing the urban-rural gap (Idescat, 2021).

Global Implication: Educational leaders globally should focus on infrastructure investment and digital literacy programs to promote inclusivity. Luckin (2017) emphasizes, "AI must bridge, not deepen, educational divides, offering greater opportunities for all."

8.4 Building Global Collaboration for AI in Education

Collaboration has been vital to Catalonia's AI initiatives, both within the region and internationally. Partnerships with organizations, technology firms, and academic institutions have been instrumental in shaping Catalonia's AI strategy. By fostering collaborative approaches, Catalonia has incorporated global best practices while addressing local challenges.

Global Implication: International collaboration is essential for scaling AI in education responsibly. UNESCO (2021) advocates, "Global cooperation enables the sharing of resources, expertise, and ethical frameworks, ensuring AI technologies are developed to benefit humanity."

A Roadmap for the Future

Catalonia's experience provides a roadmap for integrating AI into education systems worldwide. By prioritizing transparency, ethical practices, inclusivity, and collaboration, the region demonstrates how to harness AI's transformative potential while mitigating risks. Luckin (2017) aptly states, "AI's promise lies not only in its technical capabilities but in its ability to enhance human potential when aligned with ethical and social values."

Educational systems can adapt these lessons to navigate the complexities of AI integration. By aligning technological innovation with broader societal and educational goals, policymakers and leaders can ensure that AI serves as a tool for empowerment and equity rather than division or inequality.

9. MEASURING IMPACT AND SUCCESS

Catalonia's ambitious AI initiatives in education require rigorous evaluation to ensure accountability, continuous improvement, and the realization of their intended benefits. Establishing robust metrics is essential not only for assessing the success of these initiatives but also for informing future policy decisions and maintaining stakeholder trust.

9.1 Key Metrics for Evaluation

1. **Learning Outcomes**

The effectiveness of AI tools should be measured by analyzing before-and-after student performance. Metrics such as exam results, skill acquisition rates, and student engagement levels can provide clear indicators of AI's impact on learning outcomes. As Luckin (2017) states, "Data-driven evaluations allow educators to identify what works, paving the way for evidence-based decision-making."

2. **Equity Metrics**

A critical objective of Catalonia's AI strategies is bridging the urban-rural digital divide. Progress should be evaluated through metrics like reductions in disparities in internet connectivity, device availability, and AI adoption rates between urban and rural schools. UNESCO (2021) emphasizes that "Measuring equity is as important as measuring outcomes; both are necessary to ensure inclusive educational systems."

3. **Stakeholder Satisfaction**

Feedback from students, teachers, and parents is vital for understanding the broader impact of AI integration. Surveys and focus groups can assess stakeholder satisfaction, identifying strengths and areas for improvement. As Selwyn (2019) notes, "AI implementation succeeds when it is aligned with the needs and expectations of its users."

4. **Infrastructure Improvements**

The adoption of AI-enabled learning tools and the availability of essential infrastructure, such as reliable internet and smart classrooms, are foundational metrics. Tracking the percentage of schools equipped with these resources will highlight the scalability and accessibility of Catalonia's AI initiatives.

9.2 Continuous Improvement Through Metrics

By establishing these evaluation criteria, Catalonia can ensure that its AI-driven educational strategies remain adaptive and responsive to evolving needs. Metrics provide actionable insights, guiding adjustments to policies and interventions. Moreover, transparent reporting of these outcomes can reinforce Catalonia's position as a global leader in AI-driven education.

As Floridi (2016) emphasizes, "Evaluation is not just a measure of success; it is a tool for shaping the future, ensuring that innovations align with societal values and goals."

10. MEASURING IMPACT AND SUCCESS

Evaluating the effectiveness of Catalonia's AI-driven educational initiatives is crucial for ensuring continuous improvement, accountability, and alignment with ethical and educational goals. The integration of Artificial Intelligence (AI) into education has opened transformative possibilities, but without robust evaluation frameworks, its potential may remain underutilized or misdirected. As the OECD emphasizes in *Education at a Glance 2022*, "regular assessment of learning outcomes and systemic reforms is essential for understanding their impact and driving further innovation" (OECD, 2022). This section proposes key metrics and approaches that Catalonia could adopt to measure the success of its AI initiatives effectively.

10.1 Learning Outcomes

A fundamental measure of success lies in the improvement of learning outcomes. Catalonia must evaluate how AI tools influence students' academic performance through before-and-after analyses of metrics such as test scores, comprehension levels, and subject mastery. AI-driven adaptive learning platforms, widely implemented in Catalonia, offer real-time data on student progress, enabling targeted interventions.

As noted by UNESCO in its *Artificial Intelligence in Education: Guidance for Policymakers*, "Data from adaptive systems must be leveraged not just for personalization but also for assessing overall efficacy in improving learning outcomes" (UNESCO, 2021). For instance, Catalonia could analyze how AI's personalized feedback affects student performance compared to traditional instructional methods, ensuring that AI integration is genuinely enhancing learning.

10.2 Equity Metrics

Equity remains a cornerstone of Catalonia's educational policies, and evaluating its AI initiatives through equity-focused metrics is essential. Metrics should measure reductions in disparities between urban and rural schools, socio-economic groups, and marginalized communities. The European Commission's *Digital Education Action Plan (2021-2027)* highlights the importance of addressing regional and social divides, emphasizing, "Equity in digital education is not just about access to technology; it requires ensuring all learners have equal opportunities to benefit from its application" (European Commission, 2021).

Catalonia's eduCAT 1×1 program, which has provided devices to students across socio-economic backgrounds, already lays a foundation for such assessments. By analyzing participation rates in AI-enabled programs and monitoring resource allocation across diverse demographics, Catalonia can ensure its policies are effectively bridging digital divides.

10.3 Stakeholder Satisfaction

The perspectives of students, teachers, and parents are crucial in evaluating the success and acceptance of AI initiatives. Conducting regular surveys and feedback sessions can provide insights into user satisfaction, challenges faced, and areas needing improvement. As the OECD asserts, "Involving stakeholders in evaluation processes fosters a culture of responsiveness and trust, ensuring that educational reforms align with community needs" (OECD, 2022).

For example, Catalonia could implement focus groups in schools utilizing AI tools, gathering qualitative data to complement quantitative performance metrics. Such feedback mechanisms would also support continuous refinement of AI applications based on real-world classroom experiences.

10.4 Infrastructure and Accessibility

Measuring the extent of infrastructure improvements is vital for understanding the scalability and inclusivity of Catalonia's AI-driven initiatives. Metrics should assess the percentage of schools equipped with AI-enabled learning tools, the quality of internet connectivity, and the availability of necessary hardware and software.

The *Digital Education Action Plan* emphasizes, "Building a high-performing digital ecosystem requires consistent monitoring of infrastructure development and ensuring its alignment with educational goals" (European Commission, 2021). By evaluating these aspects, Catalonia can ensure that its investments in digital infrastructure translate into tangible educational benefits.

10.5 Teacher Training and Professional Development

Teachers play a pivotal role in the success of AI in education. Evaluating the number of educators trained in AI tools, the quality of professional development programs, and ongoing support mechanisms is critical. Floridi (2016) highlights, "Empowering educators with AI literacy is central to ethical and effective deployment of educational technology."

Catalonia's current teacher training programs, which include workshops on integrating AI into curricula, offer a strong starting point. However, detailed assessments of teacher readiness and comfort levels with AI tools can help identify gaps and enhance these programs further.

10.6 Ethical Compliance and Data Privacy

Ethical governance is fundamental to building trust in AI-driven education. Catalonia must evaluate compliance with data protection regulations such as GDPR, the implementation of ethical guidelines, and instances of data breaches or ethical violations. The European Commission underscores that "robust data protection measures are a non-negotiable component of digital education initiatives" (European Commission, 2021).

Regular audits of AI systems, focusing on algorithmic fairness, transparency, and data security, can help Catalonia maintain its leadership in ethical AI deployment. These evaluations should also assess the use of Explainable AI (XAI) to ensure that all algorithmic decisions are transparent and easily interpretable by educators and stakeholders.

10.7 Longitudinal Studies and Global Comparisons

Finally, conducting longitudinal studies to track the impact of AI initiatives over time will provide valuable insights into their sustainability and effectiveness. Comparing Catalonia's metrics with those from global leaders such as Finland and Singapore can also highlight best practices and areas for improvement. Selwyn (2019) notes, "Benchmarking educational reforms against global trends fosters a culture of learning and adaptation, ensuring continuous progress."

10.8 Closing Reflections

The measurement of success in Catalonia's AI-driven educational initiatives is not merely a technical endeavor; it reflects the broader societal commitment to equity, transparency, and ethical responsibility. As Luckin (2017) aptly notes, "The power of AI in education lies not in the technology itself but in the opportunities, it creates for meaningful transformation." Catalonia's focus on robust evaluation metrics - such as learning outcomes, equity indicators, stakeholder satisfaction, and infrastructure improvements - reinforces its role as a global leader in ethical AI deployment.

These metrics do more than assess success; they also provide a roadmap for continuous improvement. Floridi (2016) emphasizes, "Ethical governance of technology demands a cycle of reflection, measurement, and action." Catalonia's emphasis on evidence-based approaches ensures that policies and practices remain adaptive and responsive to emerging challenges. For instance, by prioritizing equity metrics, the region addresses the persistent digital divide between urban and rural areas, underscoring its commitment to inclusivity and fairness (UNESCO, 2021).

Moreover, stakeholder satisfaction surveys from students, teachers, and parents serve as critical tools for maintaining trust and alignment with community needs. As Selwyn (2019) observes, "AI in education cannot succeed in isolation - it thrives when it is co-designed with those it aims to serve." Catalonia's participatory approach to policy development ensures that diverse perspectives are integrated into its AI strategy, creating a model of shared responsibility and accountability.

Ultimately, the evaluation of Catalonia's AI initiatives should not only measure immediate success but also anticipate future challenges and opportunities. As Generative AI and explainable AI (XAI) continue to evolve, Catalonia's leadership in adopting these technologies responsibly will hinge on its ability to refine existing metrics and create new ones that capture the complexities of AI's long-term impact. By doing so, the region sets a precedent for educational systems worldwide, offering actionable insights on how to balance innovation with equity and ethics.

These reflections emphasize that measuring impact is not an end but a continuous journey, aligning with UNESCO's (2021) assertion that "Success in integrating AI into education is defined not by perfection but by the pursuit of progress grounded in ethical responsibility and inclusivity." Catalonia's approach provides a template for how educational leaders globally can harness AI to create equitable and transformative learning environments.

11. CONCLUSION

Catalonia's innovative journey toward integrating Artificial Intelligence (AI) into its educational system provides an exemplary framework for navigating the ethical, practical, and strategic challenges posed by emerging technologies. The region's emphasis on transparency, ethical governance, inclusivity, and collaborative decision-making underscores the transformative potential of AI when aligned with equity-focused policies. Catalonia's experience highlights that technological progress, when guided by clear ethical and societal goals, can serve as a tool for addressing systemic inequities and improving learning outcomes.

Through a combination of forward-thinking policies, stakeholder engagement, and targeted initiatives, Catalonia has shown how AI can bridge educational divides, optimize resource allocation, and enhance personalized learning. These efforts reflect a deeper commitment to fairness, accountability, and human-centered development. As Floridi (2016) aptly emphasizes, "The ethical integration of AI is not just a technical challenge but a societal one, requiring careful consideration of its implications on human values and rights."

The region's focus on bridging the digital divide, empowering educators, and embedding AI ethics into curricula sets it apart as a model for inclusive AI integration. By prioritizing underserved communities and leveraging public policy, Catalonia has demonstrated how AI can serve as an equalizer rather than a divider. UNESCO (2021) underscores this by stating, "Digital inclusion is not simply about access to technology but about fostering the capacity to use it effectively, equitably, and ethically."

Key Lessons for Global Educational Leadership

1. **Transparency and Trust as Foundations**

Catalonia's transparent processes for AI integration - such as public consultations and stakeholder workshops - have fostered trust and minimized resistance. UNESCO (2021) asserts, "Transparency must be the cornerstone of AI integration to ensure trust and collaborative problem-solving." The region's open communication about AI's objectives and limitations offers a replicable model for fostering accountability and public confidence.

Global Implication: Educational systems worldwide must prioritize explainable AI (XAI) tools, maintain clear communication channels, and actively involve communities to ensure trust and widespread adoption.

2. **Ethical Governance of AI**

Catalonia's ethical frameworks, including the Ethical AI Integration Guidelines (2022), prioritize fairness, algorithmic transparency, and data protection. Regular algorithmic audits have uncovered and mitigated biases, demonstrating the importance of proactive oversight. As Selwyn (2019) emphasizes, "Ethical AI governance is not an afterthought but a necessary foundation for technological progress."

Global Implication: Establishing and regularly updating ethical AI frameworks is indispensable for maintaining accountability and ensuring equitable outcomes. Involving diverse stakeholders in these evaluations will further strengthen governance systems.

3. **Digital Inclusion as a Core Objective**

By implementing initiatives like eduCAT 1×1 and improving connectivity in underserved areas, Catalonia has ensured that digital transformation benefits all learners equitably. Luckin (2017) notes, "The real promise of AI lies not in the technology itself but in the human capacity to use it wisely and effectively." Catalonia's investments in infrastructure and teacher training exemplify this principle.

Global Implication: Policymakers must pair investments in technology access with digital literacy programs and capacity-building initiatives to reduce socioeconomic and geographic disparities.

4. **Preparing Students for an AI-Driven World**

Programs such as CreaTIC emphasize technical skills alongside ethical awareness, equipping students to navigate the complexities of an AI-dominated future. This dual focus aligns with Luckin's (2017) assertion that "Preparing students for AI requires a balance of technical literacy and ethical engagement."

Global Implication: Embedding AI education into school curricula and fostering partnerships with technology firms can bridge the gap between theoretical knowledge and practical application, ensuring students are well-prepared for the future.

Final Reflections: Catalonia's Blueprint for AI-Driven Education

Catalonia's experience illustrates that integrating AI into education requires a deliberate balance of innovation and responsibility. By prioritizing equity, inclusivity, and ethical governance, the region has provided a roadmap for other regions aiming to harness AI's transformative potential. As UNESCO (2021) emphasizes, "Transparency and ethical practices are crucial to ensuring that AI technologies benefit all, fostering trust and equity in their deployment."

The region's initiatives demonstrate that ethical AI adoption can address systemic challenges such as the digital divide and algorithmic bias while fostering inclusive educational ecosystems. Ethical governance frameworks, such as Catalonia's AI guidelines, safeguard student data, promote algorithmic fairness, and mitigate risks. As Floridi (2016) highlights, "Ethics must guide technological progress to serve the greater good."

Globally, Catalonia's proactive approach serves as a beacon for leveraging AI to improve learning outcomes while upholding human-centered values. Selwyn (2019) aptly notes, "AI in education can either reinforce inequalities or challenge them - its impact depends on how it is designed and deployed." Catalonia's approach to AI demonstrates the promise of technological advancement lies not only in innovation but also in its ability to create inclusive, equitable, and just educational systems.

By aligning AI integration with societal values and ethical principles, educational leaders worldwide can emulate Catalonia's model, ensuring that AI serves as a tool for empowerment, equity, and opportunity. This balance of technological progress and ethical responsibility is crucial for navigating the complexities of AI-driven education and building a future that benefits all learners.

REFERENCES

Alonso, C., Bosco, A., Corti, F., & Rivera, P. (2014). *Teaching practices mediated by 1×1 environments: A case study in compulsory education in Catalonia.* Profesorado, Revista de Currículum y Formación del Profesorado, 18(3), 99–118. https://revistaseug.ugr.es/index.php/profesorado/article/view/19325

Autoritat Catalana de Protecció de Dades (APD). (2022). *Data protection in education.*https://apdcat.gencat.cat/ca/inici

Bosco, A., Sánchez-Valero, J.-A., & Sancho-Gil, J. M. (2016). Teaching practice and ICT in Catalonia: Consequences of educational policies. *KEDI Journal of Educational Policy*, 13(2), 201–220.

Brynjolfsson, E., & McAfee, A. (2018). *The second machine age: Work, progress, and prosperity in a time of brilliant technologies.* W.W. Norton & Company.

Catalonia Department of Education. (2022). *Ethical AI integration guidelines.* https://educacio.gencat.cat

Catalonia.AI. (2020). *Estratègia d'Intel·ligència Artificial de Catalunya.*https://civicai.cat/wp-content/uploads/2023/10/Estrategia_IA_Catalunya_VFinal_CAT.pdf

Centre for Innovation for Data Tech and Artificial Intelligence (CIDAI). (2021). *Algorithmic audits and bias in education.*https://cidai.eu

Centre for Innovation for Data Tech and Artificial Intelligence (CIDAI). (2022). *Algorithmic fairness in Catalonia: Best practices for ethical AI implementation in schools.*https://cidai.eu

Floridi, L. (2016a). *The ethics of artificial intelligence and education.* Cambridge University Press.

Floridi, L. (2016b). *The fourth revolution: How the infosphere is reshaping human reality.* Oxford University Press.

Government of Catalonia. (2021). *eduCAT 1×1 program review.*

Government of Catalonia. (2022). *CreaTIC: AI education initiatives in Catalonia.* https://govern.cat

Government of Catalonia. (2024). *Educació presenta un recull d'orientacions i recomanacions per incorporar la intel·ligència artificial al sistema educatiu.*https://govern.cat/salapremsa/notes-premsa/580202/educacio-presenta-un-recull-d-orientacions-i-recomanacions-per-incorporar-la-intelligencia-artificial-al-sistema-educatiu

Idescat. (2021). *Catalonia educational statistics.*https://idescat.cat

INE. (2020). *Digital divide in Spain.*https://ine.es

Kirchner, X. (2020, May 14). *eduCAT 1×1, la digitalització a l'escola que es va iniciar fa deu anys*. Diari de l'Educació. https://diarieducacio.cat/blog/2020/05/14/educat-1x1-la-digitalitzacio-a-lescola-que-es-va-iniciar-fa-deu-anys/

Luckin, R., George, K., & Cukurova, M. (2022). *AI for school teachers.* Routledge: EDUCATE Ventures.

Selwyn, N. (2019). *Should robots replace teachers? AI and the future of education.* Polity Press.

Singapore Ministry of Education. (2023). *AI in education: Transforming Singapore's education system with Student Learning Space.*https://www.tech.gov.sg/media/technews/ai-in-education-transforming-singapore-education-system-with-student-learning-space

TeachFlow.ai. (2023). *AI in education: Global success stories unveiled.*https://teachflow.ai/ai-in-education-global-success-stories-unveiled

UNESCO. (2021). *Artificial intelligence and education: Guidance for policymakers.* UNESCO Publishing. https://unesdoc.unesco.org/ark:/48223/pf0000376709

About the Contributors

Mahmoud Hawamdeh is an experienced professional specialising in the fields of digital learning, instructional technology and digital citizenship. He holds a doctoral degree in the field of computer education and instructional technology. Dr. Hawamdeh currently serves as the Director of the Continuing Education Center at Al-Quds Open University in Palestine. He is responsible for the planning and implementation of a variety of projects and lifelong learning initiatives. Previously, he held the position of Director of the Center for Digital Learning at the same institution. He was instrumental in the establishment of the centre and the implementation of the university's digital learning strategies. In addition to his administrative responsibilities, he serves as a full-time faculty member at Al-Quds Open University and a part-time faculty member at the Arab American University of Palestine (AAUP) and Palestine Ahliya University. He teaches courses within the Master's programme at the Faculty of Graduate Studies and is responsible for the supervision of Master's theses. Additionally, Dr. Hawamdeh has coordinated and contributed to numerous projects and grants about education, digital learning, and capacity building. Further details regarding these projects can be accessed via the following link: https://cec.qou.edu/en. Dr. Hawamdeh has contributed to a number of academic articles, books, and book chapters, including, but not limited to, the following articles: Additionally, he has conducted a comparative analysis of students and faculty level of awareness and knowledge of digital citizenship practices in a distance learning environment, as well as a systematic analysis of the effectiveness of using mobile technologies (MT) in teaching and learning foreign languages. Furthermore, he has edited the book Embracing Technological Advancements for Lifelong Learning, published by IGI Global.

* * *

Emília Araújo is a faculty member in the Department of Sociology at the University of Minho, a core researcher at the Communication and Society Research Centre of the same university, and a collaborating researcher at the Research Centre of the University of Lisbon. She has taught courses in Sociology of Work and Organizations for several years and currently lectures on Methodology for Social Sciences, Social Studies of Science and Technology. Throughout her academic career, she has focused on topics such as the Sociology of Time, Culture, and Technology, developing projects that intersect these fields, with particular emphasis on scientific careers and academic mobility. Her interests in studying time and its relationships with society and culture have led to deeper exploration of methodologies for social engagement and co-creation. She has served as Vice President of the Institute of Social Sciences at the University of Minho, as the school's representative on the Doctoral College, and as the director of the Master's and Doctoral programs in Sociology. She currently represents the institute in the ARQUS network.

Alan Bruce is CEO and Director of Universal Learning Systems – an international consultancy firm specializing in research, training and project management. It has offices in Ireland, Barcelona, Helsinki, Sao Paulo, Athens and Chicago. Dr Bruce is a sociologist who studied and taught in universities in Los Angeles, Galway, Amsterdam and Hull. In 2016 he was appointed as Visiting Professor for Global Learning in the National Changhua University of Education in Taiwan. In 2016 he was course author for the Master in Online, Open and Distance Learning for Charles Sturt University, Australia. He is Academic Coordinator for the Conflicts of Interest program validated by Queens University Belfast. A member of the Association for Historical Dialogue and Research in Cyprus, he has lectured in Kosovo, Bosnia, Romania, Cyprus and Northern Ireland on conflict transformation, human rights and innovative learning. In 2018 he was appointed as External Expert for the European Commission in Brussels on migration policy. He was also appointed as Learning Design Expert with Universidad Nacional de Educación (UNAE) in Ecuador.

Amrita Chaudhary serves as an Assistant Professor in the Department of Liberal Arts and Humanities, Faculty of Arts and Social Sciences, at Swami Vivekanand Subharti University, Meerut. With 14 years of enriching teaching experience, she has made significant contributions to academia through her extensive research and publications. She is the proud holder of two copyrights and has authored a book that reflects her scholarly depth. Her research credentials include numerous papers published in UGC CARE-listed and peer-reviewed journals, demonstrating her commitment to advancing knowledge in her field. Additionally, she has contributed 12 insightful book chapters, further showcasing her expertise and dedication to academic excellence.

Nurul Ain Chua Binti Abdullah is a Senior Lecturer at Universiti Malaysia Terengganu (UMT), where she focuses on teaching Mandarin as a foreign language to non-native learners. She is actively involved in research related to Mandarin language acquisition and educational technology in language learning. Dr. Nurul Ain has over 30 years of experience in education and has taught at various levels, from primary to tertiary. She has presented her research at numerous national and international conferences. Her research interests include technology-enhanced language learning, language pedagogy, and differentiated instruction.

Maria-Antònia Guardiola is an experienced educator, researcher, consultant, and evaluator with over two decades of service at the Department of Education of Catalonia. Maria-Antònia has extensive expertise in educational leadership, policy, and innovation, with a strong focus on digital education and AI-driven initiatives. As Director and Consultant at Universal Learning Systems (ULS), a global consultancy specializing in learning development, and Research Director at the Lead Impact Institute, Maria-Antònia collaborates with international organizations to design and implement impactful educational strategies. As an external expert on education for the European Commission and a member of the European Digital Education Hub (EDEH), Maria-Antònia contributes to shaping educational policies and practices across Europe. With over a decade of experience managing international graduate programs for the United Nations Institute for Training and Research (UNITAR) and the Open University of Catalonia (UOC), Maria-Antònia also serves as a Professor at UOC, guiding students in Educational Leadership and Language Learning. A registered Secondary Teacher, Maria-Antònia has coordinated the Key Competences Network, promoting educational excellence. Maria-Antònia's project portfolio spans Africa, Europe, and the United States, with recent involvement in the EU Capacity Building project TEFL-ePAL in Palestine. As Associate Director of the Global Listening Centre and a member of the International Management Association, Maria-Antònia fosters global collaboration and innovation. Currently engaged in AI and Data Science, Maria-Antònia focuses on leadership, education policy, digital education, e-learning, training design, and conflict resolution projects. Passionate about the intersection of education and technology, Maria-Antònia thrives in diverse, innovative partnerships in Barcelona, Dublin, Chicago, New York and beyond.

Rohan Jowallah has worked in education for over twenty years. He has taught at various levels: elementary school, middle school, high school, and university. He currently works as an associate instructional designer at the University of Central

Florida (UCF). Before joining UCF's Instructional Design Team, Rohan was employed as an Academic Program Planner by The University of The West Indies Open Campus. Rohan has presented at several international conferences and has had several peer-reviewed publications. He continues to develop work for publication. He has also been a reviewer of several international journals. Rohan also teaches online as an adjunct lecturer for two universities. Rohan's current research interests are teaching and learning in higher education, with particular emphasis on online learning and teaching, blended learning and inclusive practices in higher education.

Grace Kaletski-Maisel G. joined the Instructional Design team in May 2023. She holds a Master of Science in Information Studies and a Graduate Certificate in Information Architecture from Florida State University, a Master of Arts in Women's Studies from the University of Alabama, and a Bachelor of Arts in English and Political Science from Birmingham-Southern College. She comes to UCF with a background as an academic librarian and worked in libraries for 16 years, specializing in teaching information literacy and research skills at the university level. Her research interests include digital literacy in online learning.

Tunde Toyese Oyedokun is the Acting University Librarian at Thomas Adewumi University, Oko-Irese, Kwara State, Nigeria. He is passionate about integrating emerging technologies into libraries and education, with research interests in AI, Industry 5.0, and digital learning ecosystems. Oyedokun has contributed to academic literature on topics such as AI in small businesses, next-generation libraries, and digital transformation. His ongoing projects include a review of present-day academic libraries and AI applications in solar energy optimization. He is actively involved in fostering inclusive educational communities. Tunde Toyese Oyedokun remains dedicated to advancing library science through technology and innovation.

Selvakumar P. is currently an Associate Professor in the Department of Science and Humanities at Nehru Institute of Technology, Coimbatore, Tamil Nadu, India. Since 2023, he has served as the Department IQAC Coordinator at the institute. Prior to joining Nehru Institute of Technology, he held positions as an Assistant Professor in the Department of Science and Humanities various engineering colleges in Coimbatore, Tamil Nadu, India, spanning from 2011 to 2023. Dr.P. Selvakumar's academic and research interests lie primarily in the field of phytochemistry. He has made significant contributions to his field, with an impressive record that includes 30 journal publications, 12 patents, and 20 conference papers. Additionally, he has organized 5 seminars and conferences, further demonstrating his commitment to academic and scientific exchange. Throughout his career, Dr. P.Selvakumar has been recognized for his dedication and excellence in teaching, having been honored with several awards, including the Best Teacher Awards. He holds a prominent position in the academic community, contributing actively to research.

Gaurab Kumar Sharma is an esteemed Associate Professor in the Faculty of Management and Commerce at Swami Vivekanand Subharti University, Meerut, Uttar Pradesh, India. With a distinguished Ph.D. in Marketing, Dr. Gaurab Kumar Sharma specializes in Marketing and Strategic Management, boasting over 14 years of teaching experience complemented by 2 years in industry. As an approved Ph.D. guide, he has played a pivotal role in shaping the academic journeys of numerous scholars. Dr. Gaurab Kumar Sharma's commitment to academia extends beyond the classroom, as evidenced by his active participation in organizing departmental and university-level workshops, conferences, and events. His contributions to the academic community are further underscored by a plethora of research paper publications in esteemed national and international UGC and Scopus Indexed journals. Additionally, he has presented research papers at various regional and national seminars and conferences. An accomplished mentor, Dr. Gaurab Kumar Sharma has successfully guided over 150 UG and PG research projects, nurturing the next generation of scholars in their pursuit of knowledge. His expertise, dedication, and scholarly contributions make him a valuable asset to the academic community and a respected authority in the fields of Marketing and Strategic Management.

Paula Urze holds a Ph.D. in Economic and Organizational Sociology (School of Economics and Management, ISEG/UL). Since April 2018 she is head of the Department of Applied Social Sciences, Faculty of Sciences and Technology, NOVA University of Lisbon (FCT NOVA), and professor in the same department and researcher at the Interuniversity Centre for the History of Science and Technology (CIUHCT). Her main research areas are: Innovation, Science and Technology, R&D networks and knowledge transfer in multinational corporations (FDI). She is author and co-author of various national and international publications – scientific journals, book editions, and conference proceedings. She has been leading national research projects developed with research institutions and industry (e.g. R&D.COM - Local R&D Competencies in Global Value Chains, (FCT/MCTES), 2005- 2009; e.g. CoRe – Competencies to value creation in R&D networks, IPL, BIT (BRISA, Inovação e Tecnologia), 2012-2014 and has participated in international and national projects and networks - H2020 e.g. InsSciDE – Inventing a shared Science Diplomacy for Europe (2018-2021); e.g. Antropolands - Engineering the Anthropocene: The role of colonial Science, Technology and Medicine on changing of the African landscape, FCT/MCTES, 2016-2019. She has served in scientific societies in the field of economic sociology, sociology of innovation and organizations – e.g., coordinator of the thematic session of Work, Professions and Organizations of the Portuguese Association of Sociology (2014 -). She has systematically participated in reference international conferences on sociology of science and technology and innovation - European Sociological Association (ESA), International Sociological Association (ISA) and European Association for the Study of Science and Technology (EASST). She belongs to the team that was distinguished by the Santander Totta / NOVA University of Lisbon 2011 Scientific Merit Award, dedicated to the area of Social and Human Sciences, with the project entitled Work in Times of Crisis: Factors and Strategies for Insertion. Higher Education Graduates. The H2020 HERACLES project (2016-2019), in which she was involved in the topic of socio-economics risk analysis, was selected as the European Commission Success Story, awarding the high scientific quality of the results and their extensive interdisciplinary work. She is a board member of several scientific societies, and currently serves as a board member to the Portuguese Association of Political Economy (2016 -) and she is the President of the Portuguese Association of Professionals in Industrial Sociology, Sociology of Organizations and Work (2014 -). Currently, she is co-supervising 4 PhD on the subject of science and technology studies and methodological issues and she has been involved in organization and scientific committees of international conferences on her field of work e.g. the ISSOW entitled Work, (In)equalities and Social Relations in the Digital Economy (March, 2020) and also in the organization of panels in international conferences e.g. RC23 Sociology of Science and Technology: Governance in Science and Technology: Research, Innovation and Knowledge, 3rd ISA Forum of Sociology, 2016; Innovation, Science, Technology and the Transformation of Work, Conference Democracy and Participation in the 21st Century, ISA, RC10 – Participation, Organisational Democracy & Self-Management, 2017. Making Science and Diplomacy: Historical and Contemporary Entanglements, EASST, 2018.

Jared Valenzuela is an EAP tutor at the University of Nottingham Ningbo China where he specializes in supporting students in developing their academic English skills in writing and speaking. Before moving to China, he was involved in language teaching and teacher development in Saudi Arabia. With a strong background in higher education, he is an HEA Fellow and a BALEAP Associate Fellow, demonstrating his strong commitment to advancing the field of English for Academic Purposes.

Lee Ann Rawlins Williams, PhD, CRC, CFLE, is a Clinical Assistant Professor in the Education, Health and Behavior Studies Department at the University of North Dakota. She serves as Program Director of Undergraduate Inclusive Rehabilitation Sciences Program (formerly Rehabilitation and Human Services Program). Dr.

Williams has extensive academic experience working with programs focusing on disability and rehabilitation at various universities. In addition, her professional experiences include work in the field of rehabilitation in the areas of blindness and low vision, general rehabilitation counseling, human resource training/development, education and mental health and student services. Dr. Williams has held a variety of leadership positions at the local, state, regional, national, and international levels for professional rehabilitation associations. She has published research in peer-reviewed journals and co-authored two books focusing on case and caseload management.

Tie Xiaoyao, male, born in 1989, is a member of the Communist Party of China, doctoral candidate. He inherits the classic tradition of oil painting and is committed to inheriting and carrying forward the art of oil painting. He has rich teaching experience and solid painting skills. Invited to participate in overseas academic lectures for many times, to explain and demonstrate the methodology of the paper. Many Academic papers and art reviews have been published in journals such as International Journal of Education & Technology and Journal of Academic Research (CUeJAR). Currently, he is an associate professor of the School of Art of Qilu institute of Technology, a member of Xinxiang Artists Association, the second doctoral supervisor of Amity global institute EdD program with TEESSIDE University, and the training program assistant of Shenzhen University.

Goh Ying Soon is a senior lecturer and he currently teaches Mandarin as the third language to non-native learners in MARA University of Technology, Malaysia. He is a member of the International Society for Chinese Language Teaching. He has experiences in teaching Mandarin at primary, secondary and tertiary level for more than 25 years. He has been actively presenting papers in national and international conferences. His research interests are on the use of educational technology in Mandarin teaching and learning, web-based instruction, translation, and etc.

Index

A

B

C

D

E

F

H

I

L

M

N

P

R

T

U

X

www.ingramcontent.com/pod-product-compliance
Lightning Source LLC
LaVergne TN
LVHW080355011026
849161LV00009B/2313
* 9 7 9 8 3 6 9 3 9 0 1 5 3 *